*Dining at
The Homestead*

To Monie Yonkel
1994

many happy meals

David & Jennifer

Dining at The Homestead

Albert Schnarwyler

Eleanor & James Ferguson

Romulo Yanes, Photography Consultant

Virginia Hot Springs, Incorporated

Hot Springs, Virginia 24445

*Copyright © 1989
Albert J. Schnarwyler,
Eleanor E. Ferguson,
James G. Ferguson, Jr.
All rights reserved.
Printed in Japan by
Toppan Printing Company*

*Set in Galliard by
G&S Typesetters
Designed by Richard Hendel*

*We wish to thank
the Vendome Press,
515 Madison Avenue,
New York, New York 10022
for permission to
reproduce the photographs
on pages 4 and 534
from* Châteaux of the Loire
*by Daniel Philippe,
Vendome Press, 1986.*

*Library of Congress Cataloging-
in-Publication Data
Schnarwyler, Albert.
   Dining at the Homestead /
Albert Schnarwyler, Eleanor &
James Ferguson; Romulo Yanes,
photography consultant.—
Hot Springs, Va. : Virginia Hot
Springs, Inc., c1989.
xxii, 585 p. : ill.
(some col.); 31 cm.
Includes bibliographical
references.
ISBN 0-9627650-0-7
   1. Cookery. 2. Homestead
(Hotel: Hot Springs, Va.)
I. Ferguson, Eleanor, 1943–
II. Ferguson, James, 1941–
III. Homestead (Hotel: Hot
Springs, Va.) IV. Title
TX714.S36   1989
641.5—dc20   89-163241 CIP
Published June 1989
Second Printing 1994*

For

Amanda and Eliza

that their generation

may keep the flame

Contents

Acknowledgments xv
From the Chef's Office xv
   Beyond the Kitchen
      Door xv

Note from the Chef xix

Steady at the Helm in Hot
   Springs, Virginia 1
by James and Eleanor Ferguson

SAUCES 49

Stocks 60
Court Bouillon 60
Fish Stock 60
White Chicken Stock 61
Brown Chicken Stock 62
White Veal Stock 63
Brown Stock 63

Thickening Agents 64
Arrowroot and Cornstarch 64
Browned or Roasted Flour 64
Beurre Manié 64
   Roux 65
      White Roux 65
      Blond Roux 65
      Brown Roux 65
Glace de Viande 65
Egg Yolk and Cream Liaison 65
Crème Fraîche 66

Sauces Based on Roux or Stock 66
Sauce Béchamel 66
Sauce Mornay 67
Sauce Velouté de Poisson 68
Sauce Vin Blanc de Poisson 68
Lobster Butter and Cream
   Sauce 69
Sauce Nantua 70
Sauce Américaine 71
Sauce Velouté de Poulet 73
Sauce Suprême 74
Sauce Velouté de Veau 74

Sauce Allemande 75
Demi-glace Brun I 75
Demi-glace Brun II 76
Sauce Madère 76
(Variation) Sauce Marsala 77
Sauce Périgueux 77
Armagnac Sauce with Green
   Peppercorns and Grapes 77
Sauce Marchand de Vins 78
Sauce Vinaigre de Vin
   Alsacienne 79
Sauce Bordelaise 79
Sauce Chasseur 80
Basic Curry Sauce 80

Cold Seasoned Butters and Hot
   Butter Sauces 81
Beurre Maître d'hôtel 81
Beurre Café de Paris 82
Beurre au Citron 83
Gremolada 83
Beurre Noisette 84
Beurre Noir 84
Beurre Blanc 84
Raspberry Vinegar Butter
   Sauce 85
Orange Cream Curry Sauce 86

Herb and Vegetable Sauces 87
Basil Butter Sauce 87
Green Herb Butter Sauce 87
Leek Butter Sauce 88
Asparagus Butter Sauce 89
Tomato Butter Sauce 89
Red Pepper Butter Sauce 90

Liaisons Dangereuses: Egg Yolk
   Sauces 91
Sauce Hollandaise I 91
(Variation) Sauce Hollandaise
   II 92
Sauce Mousseline 92
Sauce Maltaise 93
Sauce Béarnaise 93
Mayonnaise 94
Sauce Chantilly 95

Curry Mayonnaise 95
Mustard Sauce 95
Swedish Mustard Sauce 96
Quick Green Sauce 96
Sauce Tartare 97
(Variation) Sauce
   Remoulade 97
South of the Border
   Mayonnaise 97
Homestead Seafood Sauce 98
"Another" Cold Fish Sauce 98
Green Herb Mayonnaise 99

Fruited Sauces 100
Cumberland Sauce 100
Rhubarb Sauce 101
Homestead Passion Fruit
   Sauce 101
Pear Brandy Sauce 102

*Flavored Vinegars and
   Dressings* 103
Sauce Mignonette 103
Homestead Raspberry
   Vinegar 103
Raspberry Vinegar and Poppy
   Seed Dressing 104
Olive Oil and Lemon Juice
   Dressing 104
Homestead Grille Hot Bacon
   Dressing 105
Homestead Sauce
   Vinaigrette 105
Homestead French
   Dressing 106
Fine Herbs Dressing 107
Roquefort Dressing 107
Buttermilk Dressing 108
Cocktail Sauce 108
(Variation) Homestead Cocktail
   Sauce 109

Soups 111

Cold Soups 116
Gazpacho 116
Homestead Cantaloupe
   Soup 117
Homestead Mango Soup 118
Cucumber Soup 118
Persian Yogurt Soup 119
Senegalese Soup 119

Vichyssoise 120
Homestead Watercress
   Vichyssoise 121
Carrot Vichyssoise 122
Celery Vichyssoise 123
Asparagus Vichyssoise 123
Obroschka 123
Aspic 124
Jellied Madrilene 125

Hot Soups 125
Potage St. Germain 125
Lentil Soup with
   Frankfurters 127
(Variation) Old-fashioned Navy
   Bean Soup 128
Swiss Barley Soup 128
Rossolnik 129
Minestrone alla Milanese 130
Bisque of Vegetables Rosa 131
Soupe à l'Oignon Gratinée 133
Basler Mehlsuppe 134
Russian Onion Soup 135
Borscht à la Russe 136

Hot Cream Soups 137
Zuppa alla Modenese 137
Cream of Watercress Soup 139
Potage Germiny 140
Cream of Asparagus Soup 141
Cream of Celery Soup 142
Cream of Mushroom Soup 143
Mulligatawney 144
Cream of Chicken Soup
   Virginia 145
Bisque of Shrimp 146
Billi Bi 147

Bouillons and Consommés 148
Chicken Bouillon 148
Cantonese Egg Drop Soup 149
Essence de Caille Royale 150
Beef Bouillon 151
Consommé Double 152
Celery Broth 153
Consommé Madrilene 154
English Beef Tea 154

Hors d'Oeuvres and Salads 157

Hot Hors d'Oeuvres 162
Broiled Persian Chicken Kebabs 162
Pirojskis 163
Shiitake Mushrooms with Mustard Sauce 164
Mélange de Champignons au Vol-au-Vents 165
Clams Casino 166
Mussels Provençale 167
Coquilles Saint-Jacques au Beurre Blanc et Essence de Citron 168
Baked Oysters with Crabmeat Gratinée Homestead 169
Crabmeat Remick 170
Homestead Crab Cakes 171

Cold Hors d'Oeuvres 172
Hummus 172
Marinated Mushrooms 173
Marinated Shrimp 174
Canapé Morgon 174
Avocado Southampton 176
Crabmeat Ravigote 176
Gravlax with Dill and Mustard Sauce 177
Pâté Maison 178
Galantine of Capon 179
(Variation) Galantine of Capon Jardinière 181

Salads 182
Salade Tiède d'Epinards 182
Pressed Cucumber Salad 183
Beet Salad 183
Homestead Potato Salad 184
Ambassador Potato Salad 185
Tortellini Salad 186
Fisherman's Salad 187
Islander Salad 188
Winter Salad of Fresh and Dried Fruits 189

Fish and Shellfish 191

Trout 198
Sautéed Mountain Trout Homestead 198
Baked Mountain Trout with Tarragon Stuffing 199
Charcoal Grilled Mountain Trout 200

Shad 202
Baked Shad and Roe in Phyllo Pastry 202
Sautéed Shad and Roe Grenobloise 203

Salmon 204
Escalopes de Saumon Homestead 204
Escalopes de Saumon Lac Léman 206
Suprêmes de Saumon Amoureuse 207
Suprêmes de Saumon avec son Caviar et Sauce Champagne 209
Soufflé de Saumon en Croûte 210
Quenelles de Saumon 211
Coulibiac de Saumon à la Russe 212
Saumon Poché 214
Chaud-Froid Mousse de Sole et Saumon "Tricolor" 216

Sole and Friends 218
Fillets of Sole Amanda 218
Quenelles de Sole 219
Soufflé de Sole Lucernoise 221
Paupiettes of Sole Florentine with Tomato Butter Sauce 222
Paupiettes de Sole Tout-Paris 223
Baked Fillets of Flounder Homestead 225
Suprêmes of Halibut with Sauce Doria 226
Suprêmes of English Turbot with Beurre Blanc and Red Pepper Butter Sauce 227

Pompano 228
Baked Fillets of Pompano with Balsamic Vinegar Butter Sauce 228
Sautéed Fillets of Pompano Moderne 229
Pompano en Papillote 230

Ocean Anglers' Favorites 232
Broiled Fillets of Red Snapper Maître d'hôtel 232
Grilled Swordfish Steak Everglades 233
Suprêmes de Loup de Mer à l'Orange et Poivre Vert 234

Crustaceans: Crab, Shrimp, and Lobster 236
Sautéed Soft-shelled Crabs with Lemon Butter 236
Breaded Fried Soft-shelled Crabs with Fried Parsley 237
Gratinéed Lump Crabmeat Homestead 239
Shrimp Bahía 240
Mixed Seafood Newburg 241
Baked Lobster Thermidor 242
Broiled Maine Lobster 243
Mousse d'Homard Américaine 245

Scallops 246
Marinated Bay Scallops 246
Sautéed Sea Scallops Gremolada with Tomato Butter Sauce 247
Coquilles Saint-Jacques en Papillote au Printemps 248

Mélange Méditerranéen: Pasta, Rices, and Maritime Stews 250
Fettuccine Fruits de Mer 250
Fettuccine Orientale with Shrimp and Scallops 251
Pilaff of Mussels à la Marinière 253
Paella 254
Bouillabaisse 255
Aegean Fisherman's Stew 257

POULTRY AND GAME 259

Poultry 259
Suprêmes de Volaille Kiev 264
Suprêmes de Volaille Normande 266
Suprêmes de Volaille Cordon Bleu 268
Papillons de Poulet avec Sauce Framboise 269
Breast of Chicken Homestead with Essence of Wild Mushroom Sauce 270
Fillets of Chicken Breast Hungarian 272
"Some Like It Not So Hot" Chicken Breast Fillets 273
Homestead Sweet and Sour Lemon Chicken 274
Baked Breast of Chicken Virginia 276
Baked Breast of Chicken with Caraway Sauce 277
(Variation) Baked Breast of Chicken with Anisette Sauce 279
Baked Breast of Chicken Maharajah 279
Baked Breast of Chicken Kaunaoa 281
Baked Breast of Chicken with Tarragon Stuffing 282
Baked Breast of Chicken Ambassador 283
Baked Breast of Chicken Florentine 285
Pollo alla Cacciatora 287
Arroz con Pollo 288
Poulet Mode de Meurice 289
Coq au Vin Mode de Bourgogne 291
Chicken in the Pot Homestead 294
Poulet Rôti à l'Estragon 295
Roast Boned Chicken with Wild Rice and Hazelnut (or Chestnut) Stuffing 296
Foies de Volaille Sautés Chasseur 298
Canard Rôti à la Framboise 298
(Variation) Canard Rôti à l'Orange 300
(Variation) Roast Duckling with Walnut and Pomegranate Sauce 301
Oie Rôtie au Jus Lié 302
Roast Double Breast of Turkey with Ham, Apricot, and Pecan Stuffing 303
(Variation) Roast Double Breast of Turkey with Olive Stuffing 305

Game 306
Roast Stuffed Quail
  Virginia 309
Suprêmes de Faisan au
  Madère 311
(Variation) Suprêmes de Faisan
  au Périgueux 312
(Variation) Suprêmes de Faisan
  avec Sauce Vinaigre de Vin et
  Poivre Vert 312
(Variation) Suprêmes de Faisan
  au Bordelaise 312
Roast Young Pheasant with
  Green Olives and Raspberry
  Vinegar Sauce 313
Hasenpfeffer 314
Southern Fried Rabbit 316
French Venison Stew 318
Medallions of Venison with
  Juniper Cream Sauce 320
Roast Stuffed Tenderloin of
  Venison with Cream Mustard
  Sauce 321

VEAL 325

Medallions of Veal Picante 329
Scaloppine di Vitello al
  Limone 330
Wienerschnitzel 331
(Variation) Scaloppine di Vitello
  Milanese 333
Saltimbocca alla Romana 333
Scaloppine di Vitello al
  Marsala 335
Piccata di Vitello Veronese 336
Rahmschnitzel 338
(Variation) Escalopes de Veau à
  la Russe 340
(Variation) Escalopes de Veau au
  Calvados 340
(Variation) Escalopes de Veau
  aux Morilles 341
Rollatini di Vitello 341
Roulades de Veau au
  Roquefort 343
Escalopes de Veau Cordon
  Bleu 344
Côtes de Veau Pojarski 346
Roast Loin of Veal with
  Tarragon Cream Sauce 347

Rognonnade de Veau 348
Blanquette de Veau à
  l'ancienne 349
Côtes de Veau
  Bourguignonne 351
Ossobuco alla Milanese 353
Foies de Veau Suisse 354
(Variation) Sauté de Foies de
  Veau au Madère 355
Braised Sweetbreads with Sherry
  Favorite 355
(Variation) Braised Sweetbreads
  Catherine de' Medici 357
Sautéed Sweetbreads
  Souvaroff 358
(Variation) Sautéed Sweetbreads
  Cordon Bleu 359
(Variation) Sautéed Sweetbreads
  Gismonda 359

BEEF, LAMB, AND PORK 361

Beef 363
Teriyaki Marinated Short Ribs of
  Beef Homestead 365
Barbecued Short Ribs of Beef
  Homestead 366
Sauerbraten 367
Boeuf à la Bourguignonne 368
Marinated Steaks 370
Tenderloin of Beef
  Stroganoff 372
Tenderloin of Beef Café
  Martin 373
Sauté de Mignonettes de Boeuf à
  la Printanière 374
Roast Three-Pepper Tenderloin
  of Beef with Armagnac
  Sauce 376
(Variation) Roast Black Pepper
  Tenderloin of Beef with
  Armagnac Sauce, Green
  Peppercorns, and Raisins 377
Roast Tenderloin of Beef
  London House with Truffle
  Sauce 378

Lamb 380
Muslin Kababs 383
Shashlik Caucasian 384
(Variation) Shish Kebab 385

Curry of Lamb Madras 385
Scotch Lamb Stew 387
Irish Lamb Stew 388
Roast Leg of Lamb au Jus 389
Carré d'Agneau Persillé 391
(Variation) Carré d'Agneau Diable 393
Broiled Marinated Tenderloin of Lamb with Fresh Mint Cream Sauce 394
Roast Saddle of Lamb with Green Peppercorns and Rosemary 395
Tenderloin of Lamb en Croûte Florentine 397
(Variation) Tenderloin of Lamb en Croûte à l'Estragon 399

Pork 400
Chinese Barbecued Spareribs 402
Piccata of Pork 404
Noisettes de Porc en Sanglier 405
Roast Loin of Pork Stuffed with Apricots 406
(Variation) Roast Loin of Pork Stuffed with Prunes in the Style of Sweden 407
Baked Virginia Smithfield Ham with Homestead Southern Fruit Dressing 407

PASTA, RICE, AND POTATOES 411

Pasta 412
Fettuccine Alfredo 415
Fettuccine Primavera 416
Fettuccine Carbonara 417
Pesto 418
Spätzle 419
(Variation) Spinach Spätzle 420
Homestead Noodle Pudding 420

Rice 421
Steamed Rice 423
Saffron Rice 424
Rice Pilaff 424
(Variation) Riz Valencienne 425
(Variation) Turkish Rice 426
Rice Creole 426
Exotic Fried Rice 426
Risotto 428
(Variation) Risotto alla Milanese 429
(Variation) Risotto con Pomodori 429

Potatoes 430
Whipped Potatoes 433
Baked Stuffed Potatoes 434
Roesti 435
Pommes de Terre Boulangère 435
Swiss Stewed Potatoes 436
(Variation) Hungarian Potatoes 437
Pommes de Terre Duchesse 437
Sweet Potatoes Duchesse 438
Pommes de Terre Macaire 439
Potato Croquettes 440
(Variation) Potato Croquettes with Almonds 440
Pommes de Terre Dauphine 440
Pommes de Terre Parisienne Rissolées 442
(Variation) Pommes de Terre Noisette Rissolées 443

VEGETABLES 445

Asparagus 453
(Variation) Asparagus Parmesan 454

Beans 455
String Beans 455
String Beans Country Style 456
Flageolets Bretonne 456

Brussels Sprouts 457
Braised Red Cabbage 458
Carottes Glacées 459
(Variation) Carottes Vichy 460
Purée of Carrots 460
Hearts of Celery Parmesan 460
Purée of Celery 461

Corn 462
Homestead Corn Pudding 462
Polenta alla Milanese 463
Spoon Bread 464
Gnocchi alla Romana 464

Baked Eggplant Niçoise 466
Belgian Endive 466
Hearts of Fennel Parmesan 467
Gratin of Leeks 468
Navets Glacés 469
Snow Peas 470
Creamed Spinach 470
(Variation) Epinards
   Etouffés 471

Squash 472
Acorn Squash Baked with
   Honey 472
Ratatouille of Zucchini 473
Sautéed Zucchini Oregano 474
Zucchini alla Genovese 474

Tomatoes 475
Fassifern Tomatoes 475
Stewed Tomatoes 476
(Variation) Winter Stewed
   Tomatoes 476
Tomatoes Provençale 477

BREADS 479

Yeast Breads 485
White Bread 486
French Bread 487
Pullman Loaf 488
Brioche Bread 490
Rye Bread 490
Dinner Rolls 491
Overnight Sweet Rolls 492
Brioches 493
Croissants 494
Cinnamon Pecan Ring 497
Danish Pastry 498

Quick Breads 500
Banana Nut Bread 500
Sour Cream Raisin Tea
   Loaf 501
Blueberry Muffins 502
Baking Powder Biscuits 503
Buttermilk Biscuits 504
Corn Bread 504

PASTRY AND DESSERTS 507

Pastry Basics 510
Pie Pastry 511
Pâte à Foncer 512
Pâte Sucrée 512
Pâte Feuilletée 513
Vol-au-Vents 514
Paillettes 515
Crème Anglaise 516
Crème Pâtissière 516
Butter Cream 517
Sauce Sabayon 518
Sugar Syrup 518
Succés 519
Crêpes Sucrées 520
Crêpes Parisienne 521
Crêpes Noisette 521

Cakes 522
Génoise à la Vanille 523
(Variation) Génoise au
   Chocolat 524
Pound Cake 524
Double Apple Sauce Cake 525
Old-fashioned Spice Cake 526
Milk Chocolate Cheesecake 527
Swiss Chocolate Roulade 528
German Chocolate Cake 529
Schwarzwald Kuchen 530
Coconut Cream Cake 532
Bourbon Pecan Cake 533
Gâteau Chambord 534
Gâteau Princess Marie 536
Rum Torte 536
Swiss Kirsch Torte 537

Pies, Tarts, and Cookies 538
Apple Pie 539
Apple Pumpkin Pie 540
Strawberry Tart 541
Plum Tart 542
Honey Cookies 545
Palmiers 546
Macarons à la Vanille 547
(Variation) Macarons au
   Chocolat 548

*Mousses, Soufflés, and a
   Pudding* 548
Mousse à la Framboise 550
Mousse au Chocolat Glacé 550
Soufflé à la Vanille 551
Soufflé au Chocolat 552
Soufflé au Grand Marnier 553
(Variation) Homestead Bourbon
   Soufflé 553
Rice Pudding 554

Ice Creams and Sorbets 554
Vanilla Ice Cream 556
Chocolate Ice Cream 557
Coconut Ice Cream 557
Banana Ice Cream 558
Rum Raisin Ice Cream 559
Rose Ice Cream 560
Caramel Ice Cream 561
Simple Syrup 562
Sorbet à la Framboise 562
Sorbet à l'Ananas 563
Sorbet au Calvados 564
Sorbet au Pamplemousse 565
Sorbet à la Poire 565

Notes on Ingredients and Techniques 568

Batterie de Cuisine 569

Photography Credits 571

Bibliography 572

Index 573

Acknowledgments

From the Chef's Office

To write, edit, translate my mixed-up English and German and Michel Finel's French into proper English, to take thousands of photographs, to travel numerous times to Hot Springs, to coordinate the work between the Homestead management, the book's designer, the photographer, and the kitchen staff here has been a paramount labor. The Fergusons put their heart and soul into this project, reflecting their love of the Homestead and their personal commitment to serious cooking. *Dining at the Homestead* never would have been written without their encouragement, inspiration, and perseverance. This book exists because of their personal belief in me and their honest belief in what the Homestead stands for in its pledge to offer our valued guests a premier resort environment, personal services, and a unique experience.

My special thanks to—

Mr. Daniel Ingalls, Sr., chairman of the board and Mr. Thomas Lennon, president (retired) for their confidence and support of the publication of this book.

Mr. Daniel Ingalls, Jr., president and chief executive officer and Mr. Gordon Rockwell, vice president and general manager for their great help, encouragement and enthusiasm, and for providing the means and freedom to create this book.

All the Homestead management for their dedication to quality in food and service, to achieving excellence above all.

Hans Huebner, a catering manager of excellence, patience, and understanding. Paul Marian, Josef Schelch, Brian Puhle, Michel Finel, Thomas Woodzell, B. G. McElwee and all the members of a truly talented, committed, enthusiastic, loyal staff who make coming to work a pleasure and adventure.

Headwaiters Jerry Adderton, Arthur Bryan, Mario Buffone and their dedicated staff which contributes so much to our guests' satisfaction.

Rich Hendel whose design of this book provides an elegant setting for our words.

Romulo Yanes whose photographs tell a story themselves.

Maxine, my wife, for her patience with me while papers were strewn all over the house, for tasting the recipes, for being an honest and helpful critic.

Amanda, our daughter, whose love of riding gave me hundreds of afternoon hours writing and working at the horse ring!

Our loyal clientele for its appreciation of quality and demand of our best efforts.

Albert Schnarwyler

Beyond the Kitchen Door

In the global sense, this book is an acknowledgment of our appreciation of Albert Schnarwyler, his cuisine, and the Homestead—an appreciation made more specific in the first chapter. We owe a great debt to the chef, not only for his own prodigious labor on this project, but for his efforts on behalf of ours. His ready accessibility and tolerance of our being underfoot, even as hundreds of hungry guests awaited their food, have brought an immediacy to this story which otherwise would be lacking. To the roster of Homestead people he thanked, we would add one who is indispensable to us on the outside—Clifford Nelson, resident manager. At his customary station across from the reception desk, he is a reassuring and vigilant presence. Few guests are aware of his role in keeping the trains running and on time, and an accurate description of his duties would fill a small volume. This volume would still be in progress were it not for all of his assistance to us in threading our literal and figurative way through the maze which is the Homestead.

Our production group begins in Hot Springs with professional photographer Werner Gattinger, who gave us much of his time and ready access to his substantial collection, part of which you will encounter throughout these pages. And if, before reading a single recipe, you devour most of the large photographs opening chapters and illustrating recipes, it will be due to the work of Romulo Yanes, our photography consultant. Among the best food photographers in the land, he has produced masterpieces which many of you have seen every month for years, but never before have so many varied compositions been gathered in one place. Most far-flung of all was Angela Rossbach, of Photo-Planet in Stuttgart, who supervised the finishing of thousands of photographic prints.

Photographs do not compose themselves, and thus Thomas Haymaker of the Jefferson, florist to the Homestead, must have special mention. You will see his handiwork throughout—sometimes a single flower, sometimes an immense display—but always the proper touch of live color that distinguishes the true professional. On several occasions food and flower alike were beautifully set off by furnishings and gracious assistance from Keith H. Knost Fine Gifts.

Words do not correct themselves either, and we are deeply grateful to two individuals who have kept our words as consistent, honest, and accurate as possible. Bill Neal, noted author and professional chef, reviewed the entire manuscript, providing a priceless critique, without which it would have been a much lesser work. Paula Wald, proofreader par excellence, constantly embarrassed us by finding lurking errors and prickly issues which had escaped the scrutiny of four pairs of eyes. There is a technical side to this volume as well, for once these nearly two million characters were entered in and checked by our unfailing Exxon 520 tiger machine, they had to be teleprocessed to G&S Typesetters in Austin, Texas. Once there, Jon Schubkegel and Richard Workman transformed them into typeset galleys, at times having them back in North Carolina within thirty-six hours.

The book you have in your hands is an extraordinarily complex feat of design. To transform the vast cauldron of inchoate alphabet soup the three of us had concocted into handsome typography, and illustrate it with just the right bouquet garni of photographs, demands a finesse akin to that of the medieval manuscript illuminator. How fortunate we were to have Richard Hendel, ably assisted by Laura Dunne, to design and layout every page of this cookbook. Not to mention Rich's obvious and sustaining enthusiasm for the project as the desserts grew more numerous with each revision of the recipe list.

That accounts for our production staff. Now, before getting on to more diffuse intellectual matters, a word is in order for our support staff. To ensure success in your kitchen, these recipes had to be tested in ours. Few cookbook writers are fortunate enough to have access for nearly three years to a panel of judges who were always hungry, almost always appreciative, and occasionally critical of missed results. To Ezra Barbee, Karl Boyd, John Chase, Ray Moore, Jock Morris, Gary Phillips, Tim Price, and Randy Williams, all of whom got in on the ground floor, heartfelt thanks. And then there were those times when we were "cooked out" and in need of sustenance. At such times we were thankful that Louis XV awarded the *cordon bleu* for excellence to Madame du Barry's *cuisinière*. We would award no less to Charles Smith and Davis Blackwell of Amber Alley's Rathskeller for their Blue Ribbon Special. And, for sustenance of the spirit, our dear friend and fellow traveler, Tom Kenan, provided cheerful and constant encouragement through the many incidents by the way.

Ideas are nurtured as well. Three decades ago, under the visual and written tutelage of Raymond Oliver in France and Julia Child in America, vast numbers of us became curious about cuisine and learning to cook well. Classical techniques hitherto considered mysteries were rendered accessible, cooking from scratch with fresh ingredients became de rigueur, and we began to rediscover the truths many of our grandmothers knew.

Among the boat and plane loads of Americans who voyaged to Europe there were those of us who, inspired by the timeless writings and meanderings of Samuel and Narcissa Chamberlain, would strike out on pilgrimages to French gastronomic shrines. For the dedicated among us there was always a sincere welcome, and the ability to appreciate and write about the cuisine of the Homestead comes in part from countless privileged hours spent learning from and talking with such superb chefs as the late Jean Troisgros and his brother Pierre, of Roanne, and Roger Vergé of Mougins. Along with their Michelin three-star colleagues, they have kept the culinary flame of Carême, Escoffier, and Point, just as Albert Schnarwyler and André Soltner have done in America. No matter how they are reinterpreted, classical principles always seem to want to shine through, and setting them down again is one of the reasons for this book.

The other reason is at once anecdotal and almost trivial, except for its clear implications for preserving fine cuisine. The event took place far from Hot Springs, in passage across the North Atlantic on the *QE2*. Late one October evening we were having a wide-ranging discussion with Executive Chef John Bainbridge. The last of the great transatlantic chefs, he was lamenting the increasing difficulty of serving first-class cuisine to such numbers of passengers as the *QE2* carried. There seemed a conspiracy between government restrictions and labor policies which was dooming the cuisine we three had known on the North Atlantic express liners. Economics were playing a part as well, just as they had when staggering oil prices forced the *France* to be withdrawn from transatlantic service in 1974, long before it had reached middle age for an ocean liner.

As we listened to this estimable colleague of Henri Le Huédé, it occurred to us that there *is* a place where contemporary classical cuisine was flourishing, and that the story needed telling. A telephone call to Albert Schnarwyler followed, leading eight years later to the book you have in your hands. Cook from it in good health and when you feel assaulted by the latest culinary fad, put it in perspective by taking this volume off the shelf, finding a comfortable chair, and planning a reassuring menu from Hot Springs for dining at your own homestead.

Eleanor & James Ferguson
Chapel Hill, North Carolina

Note from the Chef

Curiously enough, I first became acquainted with the job description of home cook at the invitation of the United States government. Fresh from apprenticeship at the Kunsthaus Restaurant in my hometown of Lucerne and training at the Montana Hotel School, as well as being a commis de cuisine at the Schwanen Restaurant in Lucerne and at the Hotel Saint Gotthard in Zurich, I came to this country in 1950 and began working as a cook in hotels and restaurants. Somehow, however, Uncle Sam felt that he could not achieve success in Korea without me, so this Swiss, who fantasized about being an army interpreter in Europe, wound up fighting the war in a general's kitchen in North Carolina. Basic training does have a way of sorting your life out for you.

Well, was I in for a surprise. There was no pastry chef when I needed pâte feuilletée or a little gâteau for eight. All of a sudden I was the sauce cook, roast cook, vegetable preparer and cook, dessert chef, baker, and, it goes without saying, pot and dishwasher. And, somewhere in the middle of all that I was the commissary steward, maître d'hôtel, waiter, and busboy. This tour of duty gave me a keen insight into the domestic kitchen. In fact, I would recommend this solo experience to my professional colleagues. Thanks to Escoffier we are able to manage culinary tours de force on a daily basis because our specialists are organized in the most efficient way. However, I will go out on a limb and say that dedicated home cooks probably produce a better all-around cuisine than any one department head could in the same setting.

I must give the general and his family a great deal of credit for taking my goofs and miscalculations so much in stride. After all, history tells us there are alternatives. Napoleon expressed his displeasure with a cook by having him shot, and the general could have shipped me out to Korea. And, looking back, I think I gave him ample cause.

Speaking of retrospective glances, I would like to take this occasion to make a point or two about late twentieth-century American cuisine. For historical roots we will always look to Europe, the Orient, and the Middle East for ingredients and their preparation—this book is witness to that. But this relationship is evolving into one of exchange. Corn and turkeys may have been part of the New World's original contribution to European cuisine, but, thanks to air transportation and enlightened trade policies, America's unequaled fresh bounty has come to play a major role in the global marketplace. Inevitably, this has benefited our field because concern for a better environment in concert with a movement toward a more natural, simple, and healthier kitchen has prompted what might be called an American fresh market cuisine. Occasionally such ready availability entails higher costs, and sad to say, there are those in the profession who will seize on the apparent greater expense of fresh market cooking to justify exorbitant prices for the sake of seeming exclusive. Fortunately, the American system is such that in due time someone with a better ethical sense will open another establishment around the corner.

A far greater concern for me is ensuring and enhancing continuity in the cooking profession. Now that we really are making progress, we must sustain the momentum. American society is finally paying the chef his or her due and increasingly granting the cooking craft the status it has traditionally enjoyed in other cultures. This, in turn, is attracting more young people into the profession. But, to be successful they need an appreciative audience, and here there is still much to be done. Americans are coming to value quality over quantity, but to completely effect this transformation they must become educated in many facets of the culinary art. Knowledge must be broadened and standards elevated, and for this to happen people must learn to discriminate, judge, and appreciate quality in order to recognize and support excellence.

Here I am speaking of management and client alike, and I especially want to doff my toque to the Homestead management for allowing the kitchen departments to be run by culinary experts who are "behind the range" every day filling orders for the guests. I feel the greatest threat to any quality food operation is the throttling of freedom and stifling of creativity by "food managers." Usually generalists with an overall view of food service, but with no specific expertise, these people are placed in charge of recipes, menus, and the highly trained chefs who execute them. However, they bear no direct responsibility for meeting meal deadlines, nor most likely do they have the ability to do so. At best this leads to mediocrity in food service, at worst it leads to low morale, high turnover, and an impasse. Carl Rietz, in *A Guide to the Selection, Combination, and Cooking of Foods*, puts it this way, "it is not possible for a person to qualify as a judge of food who does not know how to prepare it."

And so we come to the reason for *Dining at the Homestead*. These days, any restauranteur who has established some kind of a reputation is inevitably asked, "When are you going to write a cookbook?" Our kitchen is no exception; guests have been asking this for decades. But, as I thought about it, I realized that the important thing was not just to set down a selection of recipes, it was to show how we do things here, and to make it possible to do these same things at home. Any large hotel or ocean liner serves thousands of meals a day, but few serve food which is memorable. I think our cuisine receives favorable notice because we bring the same care to what we do that the serious home cook brings to preparing dinner for six or eight. Obviously our size permits us to purchase some ingredients and serve some dishes which are beyond the reach of all but the most dedicated amateur, but every recipe in this book can be successfully executed at home.

Throughout, I have emphasized doing as much preparation in your own kitchen as possible—just as we do here. Like the artist mixing pigments we must start with the best ingredients in their simplest form to be creative. This is the foundation of our tradition and one key to passing it on. Another lies in following established methods which produce impeccable results, reliably. The artist's works endure whereas ours are appreciated in their consumption, leaving only a memory. Thus the process, from creation to presentation, allows for no compromise if the result is to be *worth* remembering. Regardless of the scale of our kitchens, we are bound together by the desire to prepare and serve the best cuisine to our families and guests. To illustrate my point, let me include a story told by Craig Claiborne about Henri Le Huédé, the chef of the liner *France*. "I once expressed astonishment at the highly maneuverable, productive nature of the kitchen where each day the kitchen's skillets turned out crêpes by the thousands while the ovens baked more than 2,000 *petits pains*, the small, crisp rolls served at each place setting. 'How can you,' I asked 'produce such splendor on such a vast scale?' The gentleman smiled and shrugged. And in his typical, modest fashion answered, 'It is only the work of the cuisinier.' "

The recipes in this volume will give you a complete tour of the Homestead kitchen and the work of the cuisinier. Above all, let me say that you should use them as a guide, not, in Point's words, as a "codex formula." This is not a culinary ten commandments handed down from Warm Springs Mountain, it is an attempt to convey a fair sampling of Homestead preparations set in the background of classical technique and our culinary philosophy. I urge you to experiment with alterations and variations, as we do, but only after you have prepared a recipe all the way through, as it is written, the first time. And, if you get discouraged at what appears to be a miserable failure the first time, remember that I never did get sent to KP in Korea because I tried again the next day.

Before starting our tour I should tell you a few things about the way we constructed the book. Above all we wanted the recipes to be complete and easy to follow, so you will not have to wander all over the book to cook from it. For example, there are some soups which vary on a master theme, but because there may be considerable change in ingredients, you will find the whole set of instructions repeated so you have exactly what you need on the pages in front of you. In fact, only when a variation is a simple alternative, do we not give thorough instructions. At the back of the book you will find the Batterie de Cuisine, which is helpful for setting up a kitchen. Every item needed to prepare these recipes is listed there and all the equipment recommendations are drawn from it. These are intended to help you select recipes according to your own *batterie*, and in most instances you can make appropriate substitutions. If not, we tell you so. Since the cookbook marketplace is increasingly global, metric equivalents (rounded for volume and weight, exact for temperature) have been given. In addition, we have given weights where the metric system would most likely use them instead of volume. To make this book easier to use, cross-references to recipes in this book are capitalized—especially helpful when it comes to compiling menus. Also useful for cross-referencing is the section called Notes on Ingredients and Techniques. Here you will find basic items which are called for too often to be repeated throughout the text. Read it first to familiarize yourself with assumptions we have made about such things as size of eggs and type of butter.

One last thing—wine. We spent a great deal of time discussing the matter of wine suggestions and even the possibility of a chapter on wine. We feel that well-chosen wines are the other half of any carefully composed menu, and we much prefer to serve them to our guests instead of cocktails which dull the palate. The problem one encounters in making suggestions is the change occurring in the wine industry here and abroad. As vintners experiment, traditional names no longer carry the same meaning, thus a suggestion made here might become dated within five years. We certainly have seen this in excellent cookbooks we have on our shelves. So, with very few exceptions, we have entrusted you to your local wine merchant to help with selections, which in itself is an honored tradition.

Well, I am anxious to get started, so to your stations, and I'll see you when we meet Saucier Brian Puhle at the stockpot.

Steady at the Helm in Hot Springs, Virginia

by James and Eleanor Ferguson

But novelty is the universal cry—novelty by hook or by crook! It is an exceedingly common mania among people of inordinate wealth to exact incessantly new or so-called new dishes. Sometimes the demand comes from a host whose luxurious table has exhausted all the resources of the modern cook's repertory, and who, having partaken of every delicacy, and often had too much of good things, anxiously seeks new sensations for his *blasé* palate. Anon, we have a hostess, anxious to outshine friends with whom she has been invited to dine, and whom she afterwards invites to dine with her.

Novelty! It is the prevailing cry; it is imperiously demanded by everyone.

For all that, the number of alimentary substances is comparatively small, the number of their combinations is not infinite, and the amount of raw material placed either by art or by nature at the disposal of a cook does not grow in proportion to the whims of the public. . . .

In reality the planning of these alimentary programmes is among the most difficult problems of our art, and it is in this very matter that perfection is so rarely reached. In the course of more than forty years' experience as a chef, I have been responsible for thousands of menus, some of which have since become classical and have ranked among the finest served in modern times; and I can safely say, that in spite of the familiarity such a period of time ought to give one with the work, the setting-up of a presentable menu is rarely accomplished without lengthy labour and much thought, and for all that the result is not always to my satisfaction. From this it may be seen how slender are the claims of those who, without any knowledge of our art, and quite unaware of the various properties belonging to the substances we use, pretend to arrange a proper menu.

However difficult the elaboration of a menu may be, it is but the first and by no means the only difficulty which results from the rapidity with which meals are served nowadays. The number of dishes set before the diners being considerably reduced, and the dishes themselves having been deprived of all the advantages which their sumptuous decorations formerly lent them, they must recover, by means of perfection and delicacy, sufficient in the way of quality to compensate for their diminished bulk and reduced splendour. They must be faultless in regard to quality; they must be savoury and light. The choice of the raw material, therefore, is a matter demanding vast experience on the part of the chef; for the old French adage which says that "La sauce fait passer le poisson" has long since ceased to be true, and if one do [*sic*] not wish to court disapprobation—often well earned—the fish should not be in the slightest degree inferior to its accompanying sauce.

While on the subject of raw material, I should like, *en passant*, to call attention to a misguided policy which seems to be spreading in private houses and even in some commercial establishments; I refer to the custom which, arising as it doubtless does from a mistaken idea of economy, consists of entrusting the choice of kitchen provisions to people unacquainted with the profession, and who, never having used the goods which they have to buy, are able to judge only very superficially of their quality or real value, and cannot form any estimate of their probable worth after the cooking process.

If economy were verily the result of such a policy none would object to it. But the case is exactly the reverse; for, in the matter of provisions, as in all commercial matters, the cheapest is the dearest in the end. To obtain good results, good material in a sufficient quantity must be used, and, in order to obtain good material, the latter should be selected by the person who is going to use it, and who knows its qualities and properties. Amphitryons who set aside these essential principles may hope in vain to found a reputation for their tables.

—Georges Auguste Escoffier

When first conceived in 1982, *Dining at the Homestead* was seen as a relatively modest collection of approximately 250 recipes from the chef's constantly evolving repertoire. Not an inconsequential volume, mind you, but not a magnum opus either. Rather, something a Homestead guest or fellow culinary traveler might wish to have for a kitchen bookshelf as a vignette of classically based cuisine in a resort setting. But such a volume was not to be. Other than numbering all the current recipes and randomly choosing 250, there is no kitchen "short story"—because there is no Homestead short story. Now in its fourth generation of direct, dedicated, and concerned family ownership, the Homestead eludes simple description. The publicist's usual evocative phrase, "luxury resort," falls far short because the hotel is a community of families bound together by the tradition of dedication to service and hospitality to visitors as well as concern for each other. Gracious abundance, not tawdry opulence, is found here, and for the gastronome, it is a mecca. This collection of recipes, large though it may seem to some, is still a selection. During the three and one-half years required to compile and produce this volume, scores of new preparations enjoyed by multitudes of Homestead guests have begged in vain for inclusion in this book, but a limit must be set. Do not despair, simply go to Hot Springs and see for yourself what's cooking at the Homestead. The basis always remains the same—a classical foundation, mastery of technique, first-class ingredients, and the encouragement of innovation.

The mere term "classical foundation" implies history, tradition, ritual—a whole body of knowledge ripe for exploration. So much of our lives is spent in the preparation and consumption of food that we have a cultural obligation to be informed about its history. Certainly, Brillat-Savarin devoted much talent and energy to his ambitious epic, *La Physiologie du Goût* (1825), and its prominent place in the culinary archives testifies to his enduring importance. Now, more than one hundred and fifty years later, we want to establish a historical context for this cookbook. How much culinary history is "enough"? One thing is certain—"no" history is not enough. Escoffier's 1902 writings sound contemporary, yet the misunderstanding of his cuisine and principles served as a rallying point for many of the fads which have caught the public's eye since the mid-twentieth century. The culinary landscape has been littered with them—"natural," "nouvelle," "*minceur*," "California," "Creole," and others—each with its own dedicated and genuine adherents as well as the inevitable sideshow promoters. But, because so many of these people turned their backs on, or were ignorant of, history, they were in Santayana's words, "doomed to repeat it."

For the purpose of establishing a framework, we have attempted a middle ground between trivia and pedantry. The cognoscenti among you will fill in our necessary omissions and the newly initiated will hopefully be inspired to learn more. The story which follows weaves together several disparate strands,

moving from a historical culinary perspective to an overview of the Homestead food service; the latter is inextricably linked to the former. Culinary history is also linked to your own culinary experience, whether you are preparing Gâteau Chambord or Suprêmes de Volaille Cordon Bleu, deciding between serving at the table or from the kitchen, or whether you are at the Homestead, viewing the carved ice figures and *pièce montée* at special buffets.

Obviously, part of culinary history began with the first accidental barbecue outside a cave, but not even Brillat-Savarin was able to date that for us. Our concern is with what has come to be known variously as grand cuisine, classic cuisine, or, as in the title of Raymond Oliver's compendium, *La Cuisine*. Like Escoffier, we are speaking of the rule of careful technique and principle over excess, ostentation, or whimsy.

You will not be surprised to learn that the geographic locale was France. You may be surprised that the political source was Italian. During the reign of François I, last and most powerful of the Valois kings, the French Renaissance reached its peak. The period following his ascent to the throne in 1515 saw the confluence of the elite of the Italian beaux arts with newly made French fortunes, giving rise to some of the most breathtaking architecture in the Loire Valley—the châteaux at Chenonceau, Azay-le-Rideau, Beauregard, and Chaumont. Among the Italian luminaries François I brought to Blois were Benvenuto Cellini and Leonardo da Vinci, and it is da Vinci who is reputed to have drawn the first plans for Château de Chambord, a structure which would be rivalled only by Versailles. Begun by François I, construction continued under his son Henri II, and was not completed until the reign of Louis XIV.

François I was also a political son of Machiavelli. Knowing that strong alliances are forged by conquest or marriage, he arranged the latter between his son Henri II and Catherine de' Medici. This proved to be a domestic conquest by Catherine, who brought a good deal more with her than fine Florentine saddlebags. (In fact, many attribute the decline of the political power of the Loire Valley following the death of François I in 1547 to her political machinations and the weakness of Henri II.) As Roy Andries de Groot notes, it was the famous marriage that got the French pot simmering:

> At table, France was in no way ahead of England, Germany, or Spain and was far behind the civilized nobility of Florence, Rome, or Venice.
>
> The first gastronomic revolution was brought to France by Catherine de' Medici, daughter of Lorenzo of Florence, when she became engaged to the Duke of Orléans (later, King Henri II). On a visit to her fiancé, she was horrified

by the food and the manners at table. So, in 1533, when she left Florence to become Queen of France, she brought with her sixteen crack Florentine cooks and a whole wagon train of herbs, spices and vegetables, including a green leaf that grew wild on the Florentine hills but had never before been tasted in France —*spinaci*. (This is why, on a French menu, any dish with spinach is still called *à la Florentine*.) Male-chauvinistic Frenchmen dislike admitting that the basic foundation of *La Grande Cuisine* (as well as the prototypes of handmade, silver cutlery) were imported into France by an Italian woman.

The marriage of Catherine and Henri II is generally given the credit for the French debut of grand or classical cuisine, but, to be accurate, it began in Italy. The first printed book on cooking was published in Venice in 1475—written in Latin by Platina (the Vatican librarian, Bartolommeo de Sacchi), *De Honesta Voluptate* was a wide-ranging treatise on food, health, and temperate living. This book, translated into French in 1505, acquainted France with new foods and foodways, among them aspic and the use of pastry.

After Catherine's arrival, the Italian influence continued to spread throughout France as ideas from the royal court were copied in entertainment by lesser nobility, and by the seventeenth century, relative political calm under Henri IV and Louis XIII had further improved culinary prospects for the less privileged. Delicacies such as salmon and mutton and such rare game as partridge and venison, previously reserved to the nobility, were now accessible to Parisian working-class people. The year 1651 is especially noteworthy because it marked the publication of *Le Cuisinier Français* by François Pierre de La Varenne, who figuratively wore the first *toque blanche* (the starched white hat which is the hallmark of the culinary profession). His excellent writings contributed broadly to the field because they treated every aspect of the cooking process—including ovens and utensils. His recipes show his own inventiveness and reflect important changes which were occurring in cuisine—sauces which had been little more than highly spiced blankets of gluten gave way to light creations, in many cases simple vinegar or lemon deglazes of cooking pans. Butter replaced oil in pastries and was joined in sauces by the delicate flavor of mushrooms and truffles. In his early years even La Varenne fell under the Italian spell, for he was in the employ of the Duchesse de Bar, who was related by marriage to Catherine de' Medici (through Marie de' Medici, a younger cousin who had also brought her own Florentine cooks with her when she married Henri IV).

Among La Varenne's specific legacies is Sauce Duxelles, made of mushrooms and shallots, said to have been created while he was in the employ of the Marquis d'Uxelles. But, it is above all the totality of his impact which matters. No Frenchman since Taillevent (Guillaume Tirel) in his *Le Viandier* (1375) had so much influenced French cuisine, and no one would again until Carême and Escoffier in the nineteenth century.

By the mid-seventeenth century, specific developments were emerging which led to the culinary tradition we honor today. It was the time of Louis XIV, whose tainting of the monarchy with extravagance and gluttony created the currents which swept it away in the reign of Louis XVI. But the "Sun King" also directly and indirectly benefited the world of cuisine. Order and method came into royal entertaining, delicacy and finesse appeared in the composition of menus, and the mounds of various kinds of meat formerly heaped on tables in front of guests were replaced by portions actually determined by the number of people to be served. This trend toward simplicity spread beyond the palace walls as the ever more prosperous bourgeoisie began to entertain. The combination of the smaller purse of the middle class with its aspiration to what it saw as the refined life of the nobility was indeed felicitous because it made opulence for its own sake unattainable while also allowing for certain aristocratic refinements to be adopted.

Book titles of the period point to the increasing importance of middle-class cuisine—as early as 1588 and 1597, two cooking books had been published in England, *The Good Hous-wives Treasurie* and *A Booke of Cookerie*. Similarly, in France, Massialot's *Le Cuisinier Roial et Bourgeois* was published in 1691, and Audiger's *La Maison Réglée* appeared in 1692. By the mid-1700s, the impact of publications such as François Marin's *Les Dons de Comus* (1739) and Menon's *La Cuisinière Bourgeoise* (1746) on middle-class cuisine was profound. Marin, for example, provided a sauce section (containing at least 100 recipes) which elevated sauces to an independent status, making them elegant accompaniments to simple dishes rather than masking, binding, or moistening agents. Perhaps the most important outgrowth of the middle class assimilation of aristocratic foodways, however, was the refinement of French regional cooking and the subsequent evolution of bourgeois country cooking—what the late Jean Troisgros of Roanne said "has always been ultimately the best."

Equally important are the beginnings of the restaurant. In 1765, a Parisian soup vendor named Boulanger chanced to hang out a sign above his stall calling his soups "restaurants" (restoratives). But the profession really got its start when Boulanger won a ruling from Parliament allowing him to serve his clients a preparation of sheep feet cooked in a white wine sauce. (Hitherto, only *traiteurs* or eating-house keepers, could serve whole pieces of meat on fixed menus at fixed times.) Always ready to begin a craze, Parisians descended on his stand to taste this new discovery, which even made its way to the table of Louis XV at Versailles.

Another story shows that, even in the Bourbon era, "liberation" was in the air. Chefs were generally held in low esteem, if they were acknowledged at all, but women—other than Eleanor of Aquitaine, Catherine and Marie de' Medici, Diane de Poitiers—who were they? Louis XV found out when, by Madame du Barry's clever subterfuge, he was served a dinner prepared by a woman. When the king asked to meet the chef (presumably so that he might hire "him"), Madame du Barry knew she had scored a victory. So she said, "Right, France, I have you, it wasn't a chef who cooked dinner, it was a woman . . . so for my *cuisinière* I cannot accept less than a *cordon bleu*." Thus, when you see the term *cordon bleu*, it should only be used for women, in honor of the Royal Order of Saint Esprit—thanks to Madame du Barry.

The Revolution of 1789 touched every part of society, but perhaps because even revolutionaries have to eat, the kitchen was left relatively unscathed, and although Napoleon sent Louis XVI to the guillotine, he saw to it that the royal cuisine stayed behind. Other by-products of the Revolution, however, were far-reaching. The democratization of society elevated tablefare for the *citoyen* to a level previously unknown. Broadened land ownership, efficient government structure, and revised hunting laws (which made much more varied fare available) all strengthened the already indissoluble French bond between cooking and the products of the land. But most important for hoteliers and restauranteurs everywhere, France began to "eat out." Overnight, talented chefs who had served the noble houses had to find employment, and what better (or more "democratic") way than to offer one's services to the public? One of Paris's most noted restauranteurs, Beauvilliers, called his establishment the "Restaurant of the Republic—Palace of Equality" as a clearly calculated way to capitalize on the new social order. The ultimate development, however, was the rise of the *chef-patron* who owns his (or her) restaurant; such people are the backbone of good cuisine the world over.

Beginning in the early nineteenth century, two figures would successively come to dominate the field to the present day. True culinary revolutionaries, Marie-Antoine Carême (1784–1833) and Georges Auguste Escoffier (1846–1935), wrought extraor-

dinary changes in both professional and domestic kitchens which will be felt well into the future. Born into a large and extremely poor family, Carême was literally abandoned at the city gate of Paris after a farewell meal with his father in a tavern. Unable to support his family, he sent his eight-year-old son into the world with this exhortation: "Go, little one. In this world there are excellent callings. Leave us to languish; misery is our lot and we must die of misery. This is the time of fine fortunes, it only needs wit to make one, and wit you have." Could it have been other than Providence that one who was to be called the "Cook of kings and King of cooks" happened to knock on the door of a modest cookshop whose owner gave him his first cooking instruction? Carême's brilliant but short career enriched the culinary field in ways both obvious and subtle. His invention of the fanciful and exquisite *pièce montée* brought architecture to cuisine. Such creations are familiar to Homestead guests, who have seen the large Indian brave at the Casino as well as the stunning ice carvings which grace buffets at Thanksgiving, Christmas, Easter, and other special occasions. Spun-sugar fantasies, cornucopiae overflowing with the colorful harvest of fall, and great flower arrangements in the center of serving tables—all of these visual feasts trace their lineage to Carême.

Less visible but more important than Carême's showpieces was his dedication to the lot of his fellow chefs. Those in the cooking profession are indebted to him as the first reformer to call attention to the abysmal conditions in the kitchens of the day. Closing a sketch of the early nineteenth-century chef he noted, "this is the way we spend the best years of our lives. But when duty commands one must obey even when physical strength fails. Our greatest enemy is coal." An avid reader, he was also a prolific author and our culinary libraries have been enriched by his considerable writings. Among his eight books, some rather specialized, is the five-volume *L'Art de la Cuisine Française au 19ième siècle*, an encyclopedic study of eating which ranged from the nature of teeth to a practical and accessible family tree and catalog of sauces still in use today. It is a mark of his stature that this treatise held complete sway over cuisine for more than thirty-five years.

Carême died in poverty, leaving only his writings. But he would have had it no other way. When offered retirement in the château of Baron de Rothschild, in whose employ he was at the time, he replied, "My prayer is not to end my days in a château but in humble lodgings in Paris, and to publish a comprehensive survey of the state of my profession at the present time." And, so it was with the father of *la grande cuisine*—his profession and his art above all else, money and recognition concomitant but

unsought and unimportant aspects of his station—he was a model for the field, indeed for humanity.

One other fundamental "revolution" of this period has changed the way we eat. Although Carême and others favored the elaborate presentations of table service *à la Française*, it was a method of table service with severe practical limitations. Because the meal was set in two halves, food in the first half inevitably became cold and sauces turned solid. Furthermore, since items were not passed, diners ate what was within reach—no doubt prompting spontaneous displays of athletic prowess. During the 1850s, however, service *à la Russe* came into favor. Each course was served from the kitchen, enabling plates with hot, fresh food to be brought to each diner—as is the custom today at any fine hotel or restaurant.

And now Escoffier. The son of the blacksmith in the Alpes-Maritimes village of Villeneuve-Loubet, Escoffier displayed an early interest in art along with a drawing ability. But his father saw no pragmatic role in these pursuits, and, at thirteen, the boy was taken to Nice to work in his uncle's establishment, Le Restaurant Français. In 1865, at age nineteen, Escoffier was hired as a *commis-rôtisseur* at Le Petit Moulin Rouge in Paris, and he was called for military service in the 28th Infantry Regiment. The former experience (under the direction of a brutal chef, Ulysse Rohan) laid the groundwork for his crusade for change in the kitchen and the latter led to important advances in the technique of preserving and storing food for military and expeditionary purposes.

Following service in the Franco-Prussian War, Escoffier returned to Nice in 1872 as Head Chef of the Hotel du Luxembourg. In 1873 he became chef at Le Petit Moulin Rouge, beginning a division of time between Paris and Nice which would continue until he was hired by César Ritz to be chef at Monte Carlo's Grand Hotel during the 1883-84 season—the beginning of a collaboration which would forever change the world of the international traveler. Synonymous with French cuisine and luxurious hospitality, Ritz hotels in Budapest, London, Madrid, Montreal, New York, Paris, Philadelphia, and Pittsburgh; the Grand in Rome; and Savoy and Carlton in London were the flagships of an early twentieth-century worldwide empire. It is said that, being Swiss, Ritz had hotel management in his blood. Every detail of a new hotel—structural, architectural, and decorative—received his scrutiny, just as every detail of kitchen planning and operation was scrutinized and organized by Escoffier. A very significant by-product of the Ritz-Escoffier enterprise was the extension of their expertise into maritime gastronomy. In 1904, Escoffier was engaged by the Hamburg-Amerika Lines to

design the kitchens for an elite transatlantic à la carte food service called the "Ritz-Carlton Restaurants." First, the 43,000-ton *Amerika*, then the 45,000-ton *Kaiserin Auguste Victoria*, and finally, in 1912, the 53,000-ton *Imperator* were fitted out with kitchens planned and supervised by Escoffier.

It is safe to say that no one man has had more influence on the cooking profession, and this is due in part to the times in which he worked. The Revolution may have done away with royalty, but it did not democratize cooking—far from it. By the late nineteenth century, the distinction between *haute cuisine* (professional cooking) and *cuisine bourgeoise* (home cooking) was firmly established. Not that professional chefs were better, they simply prepared food that was more complicated, extravagant, and for the most part very inefficiently produced. Just as Napoleon brought order to governmental function, so Escoffier brought it to the professional kitchen. When he began his career, chefs had already been working at *parties* (kitchen stations), but with no coordination or overlap, so the *poissonnier* (fish chef) might stand idly by as the *rôtisseur* (roast chef) grilled a turbot. And the *poissonnier* would make the dough for the *mousse de brochet en brioche*, not the *pâtissier* (pastry chef).

Escoffier rationalized kitchen production so that several *chefs de partie* were involved in producing dishes at different stages, bringing into being grand cuisine for the public in an elegant setting. When you dine at the Homestead and one of your party orders Allegheny Mountain Trout Sautéed in Sweet Butter, another orders Filet of Beef with Beurre Café de Paris, and another orders Roast Quail with Wild Rice and Hazelnut Stuffing, you should thank Escoffier for making possible the timely arrival of all of these entrées, hot and cooked to order. As Joseph Wechsberg notes, so it was for Le Huédé on the *France*:

> At the salamander Tomates Farcies stood on large trays, ready to be given the final touch. "The principle," said Le Huédé, "is to have everything prepared but very little actually ready to be served. The *tomates* will be finished only when the orders come in. That is, of course, the law in all good kitchens. But we may have to serve a thousand of them, and each will have the fresh taste that's absolutely necessary—and that isn't easy. Here, take a bite of the Potato Croquettes. Good, aren't they? They were fried just a moment ago. There you are. We must always be ready without really having anything ready."

Without Escoffier's Hamburg-Amerika Line galleys as a precedent, the hundreds and hundreds of *tomates* and potato croquettes would have been impossible, let alone *Turbot Sau-*

monée à la Presidente and *Gourmandines de Veau* prepared on command for special passengers in the midst of preparing any of seven or eight entrées for four hundred first-class and fourteen hundred tourist-class passengers. This is his legacy to the professional kitchen.

Escoffier foresaw the changing tastes of the twentieth century. Clearly, he had no patience with novelty for its own sake, but he also sensed and led the movement away from rich cooking. Carême had designated four sauces—*velouté*, *béchamel*, *allemande*, and *espagnole*—as indispensable to classical cuisine. Escoffier disagreed, replacing the latter two with *fumets*—much lighter and more aromatic reductions of the cooking liquids containing fish, vegetables, or meat. He also realized that flour added undesirable properties to sauces, and was looking to the day when they would be thickened with purer substances such as starch or arrowroot. The revision of sauces exemplifies his anticipation (and therefore molding) of the future of the profession through his comprehensive vision. Is it any wonder that *Le Guide Culinaire* (1902), containing five thousand recipes (a book which he modestly described as an "aide-mémoire de cuisine pratique"), can be found on the bookshelf of most professional chefs?

Before leaving Escoffier, let us return to the issue of fads. In the 1960s it was fashionable to describe the "nouvelle cuisine" as an overthrow of the tyranny of his "heavy" cuisine. This was incorrect and those saying it should have known better. Most of the food we prepare today is derived from a centuries-old tradition which has been passed on to us by many people, Escoffier included. He simply did his job too well. So powerful and all-encompassing were his writings that there seemed to be no room for change or experiment—there was Escoffier's way, period. In fact, he did not see it this way (he even wrote about the "inconstant" nature of cuisine), but unfortunately it may have suited a convenient purpose to pay little attention to his philosophical statements. Had good archival research taken the place of promotion, the "nouvelle" would have been seen as the successor it was rather than the revolution it was not. Anthony Blake and Quentin Crewe put it this way:

> The public looked at the modified dishes, liked them, as they were bound to since they were what they needed, and called them *nouvelle cuisine*. Of course they were nothing of the sort. We had been through it all before. Listen to the reverend Jesuit fathers, Brunoy and Bongeant, in 1739: "Modern cuisine, built on the foundations of the old, with less fuss, less equipment and quite as much variety, is simpler, cleaner and perhaps more knowledgable."

> . . . Certainly cuisine develops, but rarely is anything new. Many of the dishes being served today, and hailed as new cuisine, are simply revivals of dishes which suited a moment in history when tastes coincided with ours. It is, as Escoffier observed, a question of fashion.

From the vantage point of the 1980s it is too soon to identify the next "giant" in the field. Certainly the late Fernand Point of Vienne, whose Restaurant de la Pyramide in the early 1930s was one of the first to receive the three-star rating from the *Guide Michelin* stands apart from all figures thus far. Not only did he create extraordinary fare based on classical cuisine, but he alone was responsible for training most of the French *chefs-patron* who achieved their Michelin three-star ratings in the 1960s and 1970s. It remains to be seen if any from this group or their protégés will assume the mantle of great teacher from "Papa" Point.

Albert Schnarwyler and His à la Minute Cuisine

> M. Le Huédé had problems which the late Fernand Point or today Michel Guérard never dreamed about. Le Huédé couldn't send out to the market for more oysters or partridges when he hadn't enough. A sudden storm might wreck his carefully made plans. In fact, his greatest problem was not the complicated special orders of postgraduate gourmets. Rather, it involved trying to guess how many people would order a certain dish on the menu. His first command was, *"Il faut surtout honorer le menu,"* the menu must be honored. It would be bad if he found himself stuck with hundreds of artichokes and other highly perishable things. But it would be worse if he put them on the menu and had not enough of them. Once something was printed there, there was no excuse for running out of it. In a great French restaurant, latecomers accept the fact that something may be sold out. Not in the first-class dining room of the *France* however.
>
> —Joseph Wechsberg

As this book goes to press, it has been almost a decade and a half since the *France* last sailed. Henri Le Huédé retired to Bourg de Batz, in his native Brittany, leaving the faithful with priceless culinary memories from the Salles Chambord and Versailles. Around the world many of the great old hotels have been absorbed by large chains and, by economic necessity, almost all of the new ones have been constructed by these same corporate groups. In some instances, the hotel chains are only one operation of a highly diversified corporation—and you can be sure that "Ritz" on the marquee is no longer a guarantee that the spirit of Escoffier guides the kitchen. The quest for superior cuisine in a vacation setting can be frustrating unless one has access to the excellent small inns and hotel-restaurants found in Europe and increasingly in the United States. But small properties must concentrate their staff and resources on food and lodging, leaving little for other amenities. At the other end of the spectrum, large chain-owned hotels with lush golf courses, vast numbers of tennis courts, and sparkling swimming pools, serve "large chain-owned hotel" cuisine. Not even an army of white-gloved captains serving from silver-plated domed carts and trolleys can disguise the first cousin of "airline" food.

The Homestead stands in proud contradiction of this slide toward mediocrity. A resort in the classical European sense, complete with subterranean hot mineral springs, it is a place to restore the soul, tone the body, and delight the palate. Natural beauty, walking and horse trails, and every conceivable sports facility (including an outdoor swimming pool with a "beach" made of sand from the seashore) abound on this 15,000-acre estate, whose size surpasses even the 13,600-acre park which surrounds the Château de Chambord. But, significant as all of this may be, if that were all, there would be no reason for this book or this introduction. However, there is extraordinary cuisine, an intricate and complicated system of supply, preparation, and service, and behind it all—modestly, almost anonymously behind it all—is a talented executive chef named Albert Schnarwyler. Unlike many culinary showmen here and abroad, he would not write an introduction such as this because he does not admit the importance of his own role. Shy almost to a fault, it is rare even to catch a glimpse of him unless he is making a quick supervisory reconnaissance of the Casino buffet, Grille, or the progress of an important banquet. Jacques Pic, *chef-patron* of three-star (Michelin) Restaurant Pic in Valence, describes himself in words which could be easily applied to Albert Schnarwyler: "I am a man of the kitchen-range because I love it, but also because I am a shy man and do not really like being in the dining room. It is in the kitchen that I can express myself best."

This shyness, however, must not be mistaken for uncertainty or indecisiveness—such attributes could scarcely be the driving force behind the consistently excellent cuisine at the Homestead. Like Pic and most of his noted French three-star confreres, Albert Schnarwyler is firmly rooted in the tradition of classical cuisine. Always interested in innovation, he nevertheless eschews fads because they are just that—fads. When it comes to organization, he is without peer and probably is the best living argu-

ment one is likely to encounter for leaving the computer out of the kitchen. (When the sophisticated reservations system projects a guest count which he somehow distrusts, he relies on his experience for purchasing and menu planning and is usually correct.) Inevitably, his Swiss background emerges in another way as well. Convinced that quality does not have to come at the expense of efficiency, he is ever mindful of not wasting resources, and his elaborate cold buffets are marked by the frugal inventiveness which is so distinctive a part of French cuisine. But, Albert Schnarwyler is not the sum total of this story—he is at once the head of one team and part of another. As with everyone, he finds himself in a unique place and time, and it is the combination of the three which is the focus of this introduction.

Development of the unique place began with a young Indian messenger in the sixteenth century. Delayed by fierce winter weather en route to an urgent coastal tribal council, he fell to the ground in exhaustion. To his amazement, he found himself in a warm mineral spring, which so invigorated him that he recovered sufficient strength to complete his journey, giving rise to the legends promoting the curative power of the valley waters. Since 1766, when Thomas Bullitt constructed a small lodge on the site, a hotel of some description has been located in Hot Springs. Today's building, however, was not begun until the fire of 1901 destroyed the sizable wooden structure. By March 1902 the new main section was completed, followed by the West Wing in 1904 and the East Wing in 1914—all of brick construction. The most ambitious phase of the building campaign took place during 1928–29, which saw the completion of the million-dollar tower section designed by Warren and Wetmore, architects of New York's beaux-arts Grand Central Terminal. Extensively renovated in 1985, the tower is the architectural

symbol of the Homestead. In 1973, the South Wing, with 197 guest rooms and a conference center capable of accommodating 1,100 people in meetings was completed, bringing the maximum capacity of the entire hotel to slightly more than 1,100 guests.

Although Hot Springs has received most of the attention in recent decades, two other thermal springs in the Warm Springs Valley were early resort sites—Warm Springs in the mid-1700s and Healing Springs in the mid-1800s. In fact, Alexander Hamilton, Thomas Jefferson, George Washington, and Robert E. Lee all spent considerable time in Warm Springs. (Lee, Jefferson, and possibly Washington visited the Homestead.) In Healing Springs, two and one-half miles south of Hot Springs, a hotel was built in the mid-nineteenth century and was in existence until the late 1800s, at which time all but the dining hall was torn down. After serving briefly as a young women's finishing school in the early twentieth century, the structure became the Cascades Inn, a charming small hotel with dining facilities and rooms for 100 guests (usually dedicated golfers). In combination with the two Cascades golf courses and Cascades golf club, this property is also owned and operated by Virginia Hot Springs, Incorporated, the owner of the Homestead.

In this book you will encounter references to many ocean liners, including the great French Line steamship *France*. Any hotel accommodating 1,100 guests will have an imposing physical plant, but, somehow, the layout of the Homestead with its long corridors even suggests an imaginary ocean liner curiously beached in the Allegheny Mountains. While not as isolated as a ship at sea, a hotel located in the mountains of Virginia must be self-contained and self-reliant. Even though major supplies arrive twice a week via private refrigerated transport and dairy items arrive daily, almost all of the food is prepared in its entirety in the Homestead's bakery, pastry shop, butcher shop, and kitchens. For the *France* and the Homestead alike it is a matter of preference and necessity. Only if one prepares things does one control their quality. But delivery of supplies is only a process—their selection is the cornerstone upon which the quality of the kitchen rests. Just as Henri Le Huédé would turn away grain-fed chickens from Bresse at dockside if they did not suit him, so Albert Schnarwyler sends back Pennsylvania pheasants if they are not absolutely fresh. And in both cases, a supplier making this mistake might not have a second chance—such was and is the prestige and buying power of the *France* and the Homestead.

To understand the Homestead and its cuisine, one must first know something of its milieu. This resort is of a vanishing genre.

Regardless of size, the impetus for most of these resorts came from fortunes derived from manufacturing and developing real estate or railroad empires. Just as with the sixteenth-century Loire châteaux, this meant personal, not corporate, architectural visions. Architects such as Addison Mizner, Leonard Schultze, and even Frank Lloyd Wright were commissioned to translate these often elaborate fantasies into working reality. For example, Milton Hershey reportedly showed the architect for the Hotel Hershey a postcard from a Mediterranean hotel and said that he wanted "something like that."

Common to all the resorts was a clientele accustomed to spending freely and expecting first-class service in return—at least until 1929. Permanent economic changes beginning in the Great Depression and furthered by World War II have resulted in the closing of some of the hotels and a changed clientele for others. Families which once booked suites for themselves and their retinue for entire seasons have given way to two-career couples who stay for long weekends or traditional holidays. Corporate conventions, often accounting for as much as 85 percent of the annual bookings, have come to be major clients at the larger resorts, creating a dilemma for conscientious management. Satisfying the demands of 250 to 1,000 convention guests without compromising the personal attention and service expected by private guests, typically paying expensive room rates, is a significant challenge. The successful resolution of this dilemma will determine whether a resort continues as such or becomes a "convention hotel" and loses its private clientele altogether.

The surviving resorts are diverse. They range in size from accommodations for 200 to 1,600, in location from mountain valleys to ocean fronts, and in quality of cuisine from the relentless monotony of cycle menus to the inspired use of seasonal variation in fresh markets by talented chefs. The best among them belong to the select group annually receiving the Mobil five-star award for excellence. As of this writing, it is a distinction, comparable in prestige to the Michelin three-star rating in France, shared by fewer than thirty-five restaurants, lodges, and resorts in the United States. Of the four resort hotels in this category, unique circumstances lead the Homestead to stand out, and to understand their impact, the analogy of the ocean liner is helpful. You might ask, why a ship and not a château? Although architecturally stunning, none of these great country estates, not even Château de Chambord with its 440 rooms, was intended to ply hundreds of guests with luxurious amenities and gastronomic wonders. They were showplaces for their owners and display cases for their collections. The great North Atlantic express liners, however, were designed with the comfort and palates of their clientele in mind as they raced from New York to Southampton, Cherbourg, Le Havre, or Bremerhaven.

First, the physical comparisons. As an ocean surrounds a ship, so do the Allegheny Mountains surround the Homestead—magnificent, but isolating settings both. The very location, set in the vast landholding of Virginia Hot Springs, Incorporated, is as priceless and valued a part of visiting the Homestead as a sunrise, a sunset, or a turn on the Promenade Deck. One does not take an ocean voyage or visit the Homestead to stay in close touch with daily concerns—jet aircraft and hotel chains more than adequately meet that need. As the Cunard Line used to say, "getting there is half the fun." However, such distance from daily life impinges on the cuisine of both liner and resort.

In describing the great transatlantic ships the term "floating city" was often invoked to suggest their size and completeness. To reverse an image, "landlocked liner" might be used for the Homestead, so complete is the sense of self-sufficiency. (The powerhouse, in fact, at one time generated electricity for the hotel and surrounding area, recalling the statistic that, in 1935, the *Normandie* was the fourth largest thermal power station in Europe, capable of supplying one-fourth of France's electrical needs.) From the late 1930s on, superliners built by the Compagnie Générale Transatlantique (C.G.T. or French Line) and Cunard—*Normandie*, *Queen Mary*, *Queen Elizabeth*, and *France*—were massive and swift, each carrying a normal complement of three thousand or more first-class, cabin, and tourist passengers and crew across the Atlantic in little more than ninety-six hours. The *QE2*, built in the days of escalating oil prices, was designed to cross in five days and therefore reduce fuel consumption. The Homestead and Cascades Inn, when filled to capacity, house twelve hundred guests, all in first-class accommodations, requiring a staff of nearly one thousand. Life for the Homestead guest is reminiscent more of the elegance of the *Normandie* and comfort of the earlier *Queens* than of the sleek, woodless *QE2*, or, save for the cuisine, even the magnificent *France*, which last crossed the Atlantic under C.G.T. colors in September 1974.

As with these great 1,000-foot-long ships, it is impossible to apprehend the size of the Homestead at first glance. Sweeping down the rather steep drive, one passes a spacious lawn with massive maples and oaks stretching beyond the East Wing to the Magnesia Spring and the upper tennis courts. The observant eye will spot one of the two rushing streams where watercress abounds year-round, and an occasional cavorting muskrat may be caught unawares by an early morning walker. Directly ahead, the Tower and the front of the Main Building fill the view, obscuring the north portion and the West Wing. Depending upon

the season, the alighting guest will be greeted by the clip-clop of horse's hooves or the bracing aroma of hardwood smoke coming from the brightly glowing logs in the two marble-trimmed fireplaces in the Great Hall. Once the guest is under the protection of the imposing porte cochère, a liveried staff composed of a doorman, bellman, and parking valet immediately appears to assist with baggage and automobiles. Having ascended the stairs and crossed the great verandah, the guest passes through one of the wide entrance doors—brass trim polished to mirror reflection. Entering, and looking instinctively for the reception desk, the first-time visitor is immediately struck by the size and grandeur of the Great Hall, whose 211-foot length is arranged by two parallel rows of ten columns into a central aisle and two smaller aisles. One's eye is drawn up the Corinthian columns crowned by intricate capitals which carry the beams and purlins of the elaborate ceiling—the whole unified by a subtle combination of soft cream, yellow, and green. A clerestory complements and enriches this composition with the subdued hues of polychrome windows.

Returning from this visual flight to matters at hand, a turn to the left brings the guest to the front desk. If the housekeeping inspector has certified the room ready for occupancy, keys and any waiting messages are delivered and the journey to the room begins, past the Tower Lounge for those in the East Wing, down the Palm Beach shopping corridor for those in the West Wing—in both instances along hushed corridors whose length awakens memories for those who have been on shipboard. For West Wing guests this impression is made the more vivid by passing the elegant Main Dining Room, which, with its 600-seat capacity, compares in scale to the First Class Dining Rooms on the *Normandie* (700) or *Queen Elizabeth* (850).

Most guests arrive as preparations for afternoon tea are underway in the Great Hall. Just as hot bouillon is a tradition on the North Atlantic, so is the 4:00 P.M. serving of tea, coffee, pastries, and petits fours at the Homestead. Regardless of season and house count, the strains of light classical and popular music played by a formally attired trio announce that all is ready, and black-uniformed waitresses with crisp, white aprons unobtrusively make their way among the seated guests, delivering requested beverages and tempting little morsels. Nothing too elaborate mind you, for an exquisite dinner of as many as six courses is a mere three hours away—which for many is the occasion for coming to the Homestead. The ingathering of other guests finishing their various daily activities also begins at this time, filling the Great Hall with golfers, tennis players, horseback riders, skiers, skaters, hikers, and walkers—depending on

Afternoon Tea in the Great Hall

the season. Some pause for tea, others pass through on the way to their rooms; all are eagerly anticipating the dinner hour.

And now the question whose answer is the raison d'être of this cookbook. Why is the cuisine of the Homestead consistently judged to be among the best in the United States?

The unique place has been defined. The unique moment began with developments in the early 1950s that began to nudge the traditionally excellent cooking of the Homestead in a classical French direction. At this point a very significant trio from the Carlton Hotel in Washington, D.C., became involved. In September of 1952, the Virginia Hot Springs board brought Thomas J. Lennon to be general manager, joined by Clifford H. Nelson as assistant manager in March of 1953. Following his retirement from the Carlton, Chef Armand Fisson was brought in as a culinary consultant for several seasons. From the outset the hallmark of Lennon's management was a concern for excellence in cuisine and service—a focus especially congenial to emerging culinary developments in the 1960s.

An exciting time for cuisine on both sides of the Atlantic, the period beginning in the late 1950s has seen the professional emergence of the students of Fernand Point. *Chefs-patron* in their own right, Bocuse, the Troisgros brothers, Chapel, Outhier, and Bise were on their way to three Michelin stars as were others who did not train with Point—Vergé, the Haeberlins, Guérard, Pic, Thuilier, and Barrier.

In the United States, two Europeans assumed positions which were to become of major culinary importance. In 1961, André Soltner, the young Alsatian, left Paris's Chez Hansi to become chef at New York's famed Lutèce. The following year, a young Swiss, Albert Schnarwyler, left the Sheraton East Ambassador Hotel in New York City to become executive chef at the Homestead. Although their operations differ in scale, they share a humility, a dedication to work, an inventiveness, and a culinary philosophy which has guided both of their establishments to a coveted longevity in possession of Mobil's five stars—as of this writing twenty-six consecutive years for the Homestead and sixteen consecutive years for Lutèce. For almost three decades, these chefs have been responsible for acquainting, reacquainting, and sustaining tens of thousands of people with the best cuisine to be found in America. Both ridicule the notion that "nouvelle" is new (Apicius spoke of "nouvelle cuisine" as early as the first century A.D.) and that chefs are stars. In a March 1986 *Gourmet* interview, André Soltner responded to a question about the wunderkinder, "if they think they've invented anything, let them think so.... But until you give me a major new ingredient—some kind of meat or vegetable unlike anything known on

20

earth—I cannot create anything new, and neither can they. All any of us can do is revise and refine and do little variations of dishes that have existed for two thousand years." Concurring on the value of a classical base, Schnarwyler adds that "cooking, be it in a resort, in a restaurant, or in the home achieves its best results from the 'touch of the cook,' where the freedom to improvise, adjust, experiment, and improve exists."

Shared philosophy aside, how does a resort serving as many as thirty-five hundred meals a day approach the cuisine of what is widely considered the best French restaurant in the United States? Both establishments emphasize kitchen teamwork, but the sheer size of the Homestead places an even greater demand on the staff because its team is responsible for food preparation and service in several locations. Addressing this, Schnarwyler notes, "all of a sudden the cook and chef become a small part in a well run and organized operation, part of the team rather than a star player—and *team* effort it must be to succeed."

Joseph Wechsberg shed light on this question in his excellent discussion with M. Le Huédé concerning the differences between cooking on the *France* and in the Michelin-rated three-star restaurants in his homeland.

> Henri Le Huédé, the *chef des cuisines* aboard the *France*, was pleased when people said his restaurant belonged to the great gastronomic temples of France, but he felt the *France* should not be compared with them. Madame Point's magnificent Pyramide in Vienne rarely serves more than sixty people, and the most prominent disciples of the school of Point—Paul Bocuse, the Troisgros Brothers, Alain Chapel—serve not many more. At the Tour d'Argent in Paris they might serve one hundred and fifty but Claude Terrail admits that may be a strain. Contrarily, the kitchens of the *France* might serve two thousand passengers on an Atlantic crossing, three times a day, as well as eleven hundred crew members. On cruises when the *France* became all first class, in an attempt to establish the semblance of democracy, M. Le Huédé was asked to provide gastronomic miracles in the Chambord and Versailles dining rooms, for fourteen hundred people. The very size of the enterprise was out of proportion, compared to the terrestrial temples of gastronomy, and so was the organization and entire philosophy.
>
> "We had well-known French chefs here," Le Huédé once told me. "They had been successful in great restaurants in France but were completely lost on the *France*, unable to cope with the problems of maritime gastronomy."

Every good kitchen is a masterpiece of organization and teamwork, but the kitchens of the *France* were organized almost like an automobile factory. Various things were done at various stations, and at some point everything was put together. But the food never tasted as though it had come off an assembly line. "The problem is not only size," said M. Le Huédé. "But in spite of size every dish should give the passenger the feeling that it was made especially for him. I dread the cooking in some luxury hotels where everything seems to have the same taste after the third or fourth day. It is said that good hotels in France rarely have outstanding restaurants. Perhaps the combination is too demanding. On the *France*, a great moving luxury hotel, we proved that it can be done."

For most hotels the combination may be too demanding, but since Schnarwyler's arrival in 1962, it has been the order of the day for the Homestead. In some ways this is an even greater accomplishment because, unlike a great liner, the Homestead cannot follow the sun to warmer waters in the winter. It operates every day of the year, through every season, with guest counts of twelve (a possibility on a mid-winter weekday) to eleven hundred. And each season brings spectacular changes in the landscape, as well as important changes in food service locations—the opening or closing of the Grille, Casino, Ski Lodge, Cascades Inn, Cascades Club Restaurant, and Lower Cascades Club.

The first ingredient in this culinary feat is well-managed personnel. A full kitchen complement on the *France* was 180, on the *QE2*, 210, but as Executive Chef John Bainbridge noted, shore leave requirements usually reduced his crew on the *QE2* by about 70. In contrast, the Homestead kitchen staff numbers 85 during high season and peak holiday periods—occasions which often call for augmenting service in the Main Dining Room and Grille with the Commonwealth, Dominion, Georgian, Crystal, Hunt, and Empire Rooms, as well as three separate dining rooms in the Conference Center. Many of these groups will have differing menus, all of which will vary from the menu in the Main Dining Room—a logistical and culinary complexity Henri Le Huédé never had to contemplate. But as with Le Huédé, all of Schnarwyler's diners must have food which tastes as though "it was made especially for him" without tasting "as though it had come off an assembly line"—the essence of his "à la minute cuisine." For him to serve such food to all of these clients requires the teamwork he mentioned, and to assemble such a group is not simply a matter of snapping one's fingers. As

John Bainbridge once told us, "we get superior graduates from the British culinary training schools on the *QE2*, but when they arrive, we have to begin by teaching them that lettuce is torn by hand, not shredded by machine." Practical kitchen training is critical for culinary school graduate and institution alike, as each depends on the other for survival. Thus, Schnarwyler maintains a very active apprenticeship program, with trainees from the United States and abroad. But as an important further step, each year he and his brigade donate their time to preparing, transporting, and serving an elaborate feast (a nine-course banquet in 1988) in the Roanoke area to raise funds for culinary scholarships.

Sensitive management creates staff loyalty. To a man, Le Huédé, Bainbridge, Soltner, and Schnarwyler would minimize their own contributions, and such modesty, in addition to talent and knowledge, is the key to low staff turnover. André Soltner loses less than 10 percent a year, and it is common to hear Schnarwyler's staff say "if it weren't for Chef, I wouldn't be here." This very same sentiment has young would-be *commis* anxiously lining up for months to apprentice with Soltner and his three-star colleagues in France.

Coordination and teamwork undergird the executive direction of the kitchen as well. Any well-run organization has a chief executive who must be concerned with the overview of the operation, formulating its goals, dealing with other department heads and the outside world. To be free to tend to these duties, a trusted and competent first lieutenant must handle other functions including seeing that the menus selected by the chef are correctly executed, supervising day-to-day operations, and counseling employees. Obviously, much depends upon the integrity of this two-person team, and the high quality of Schnarwyler's kitchen is in part due to his long-time assistant, Paul Marian. Beginning as a saucier under Armand Fisson in 1959, Marian has been a sous-chef since 1982, and his steady personality and subtle wit are a ready source of stability in an environment whose peak activity borders on ordered chaos. By 1987, the Homestead's popularity had so increased demands on the kitchen brigade that Josef Schelch was hired as executive sous-chef to assist both Marian and Schnarwyler.

Mention Switzerland, and organization and precision come to mind along with fine chocolate and timepieces. Perhaps there is a Swiss muse somewhere in the friendly clutter in Schnarwyler's office because predictability and accuracy permeate the Homestead food operation, ensuring its extraordinary quality and consistency. Without much thought, one might ask why achieving a predictable environment is difficult. After all, guests *do* make

reservations don't they? Yes and no—and herein lies a major difference between the ocean liner and the restaurant operation. The former has a finite "captive" population, the latter a confirmed number of covers—in the case of Lutèce, usually a month in advance. At the Homestead some large groups are booked five years in advance and many families have spent Thanksgiving and Christmas (including a decorated tree in their room) for three generations. However, let six inches of new snow fall on a Wednesday in January and the projected weekend house count may jump by 600 or 700—3,600 to 4,200 meals. Honoring the menu under these conditions is just as important to Schnarwyler as it was to Le Huédé. Honoring it with a minimum of stress and confusion for the staff is the cornerstone of his management philosophy. He insists that, although the unexpected must be accommodated, the essence of a well-run organization is "no surprises." Quite simply it is the only way to control costs and ensure consistently high quality. And lest one diminish the importance of consistency, the Troisgros brothers had an important observation: "to do a good dish for a month is easy. To do it for twenty years, that is hard."

The Homestead food service system evolved from a concern for the most efficient way to provide guests with the highest quality cuisine available. Again the importance of teamwork, this time at the management level. Without the diligent and sus-

tained effort of Thomas Lennon (who served as president from 1963 until his retirement in 1986), Resident Manager Clifford Nelson, Executive Chef Albert Schnarwyler, and Hans Huebner, director of the Catering Department, this innovative mechanism would not exist. The success of the system these men devised depends upon accurate forecasts by the Catering Department—estimates of bookings which may originate five years in advance and can be revised as late as the day of registration. When the initial booking is made, menus from previous bookings (if any) by the same group are reviewed, preferences noted, and any required changes made. From this point, continuous correspondence flows between the Catering Department and the booking party, with active planning becoming successively more focused at the twelve-, eight-, and six-month reviews, but the first major review of the food requirements comes three months prior to arrival, at the weekly forecast meeting which is held every Tuesday.

At this meeting, forecasts showing projected social and convention guest counts are presented. If, as is frequently the case, several smaller groups have booked the hotel for the same period, decisions allocating personnel and facilities are made. Paramount in these planning sessions is the creation of an atmosphere of special attention for social and convention guest alike. All of the major resort hotels have selection criteria for groups they will accept, but beyond this the Homestead is deeply concerned about protecting its ambience or "bon cadre." Wrinkled linens and stale rolls are just as unacceptable here as they are at Lutèce.

In converting three-month forecasts into working plans, decisions are made about recreation, meeting, and dining facilities. Depending on season and group preference, scheduling of tennis courts, golf courses, ski slopes, trail riding, and skeet shooting has to be integrated with group meetings and food service. For example, the Casino and Cascades Inn have independent kitchens, but they are closed from early November to late April, leaving the Ski Lodge as the only meal service location apart from the hotel during the winter months. And, although it has facilities for cooking hearty fare for hordes of hungry skiers, any complicated meals must be prepared in the main kitchen and transported. Sam Snead's Tavern, a cozy and rustic restaurant managed by the Homestead, is open all year, but does not figure into resource planning because it is available to residents and guests alike.

The next important planning sessions occur at six and two weeks prior to arrival. At the latter, projections made for banquets and the Main Dining Room allow menus to be drawn up

25

which balance social and group guests. (As an example of his penchant for precision, Schnarwyler retains portion tickets from convention groups for two years so that he knows not only what they ate, but also how much—an excellent means of controlling costs.) Equally important, at all of these meetings there is always a review of functions immediately past. Comments from guests and staff alike are discussed to assess performance and quality—all part of the relentless fine-tuning which characterizes the Homestead operation. Forecasts continue to be refined at ten days, three days, the morning of arrival, and finally, even as late as registration. Nelson points out that each department receives daily forecasts for the next three days with an attempted accuracy of 3 percent variance. This in turn enables the department heads to make projections for that day and the day following.

To begin a closer look at the extraordinarily complex food supply and preparation system, it is necessary to step back to the two-week mark. The Homestead offers convention groups an annually revised menu book listing approximately sixty complete meals ranging from breakfasts to eight-course seated banquets. In addition, coffee breaks, picnic luncheons, and special functions such as cocktail buffets are also specified. Discussions between client and the Catering Department result in establishing menus which are available to the Chef's Department anywhere from two months to three weeks before the occasion. To allow for last-minute changes by the client, banquet menus are updated each week for the month preceding the event.

Every Sunday, Schnarwyler reviews the social and convention guest projections for the coming two weeks and outlines his menus for the period, enabling him to make advance personnel, purchasing, and scheduling decisions. For example, of the eight to ten banquets which might be scheduled for an evening, some may have ordered roast pheasant, requiring extra notice for the Butcher Shop to prepare three or four hundred birds. Similarly, if large quantities of roast beef are called for, they must be ordered in sufficient time to age from ten to fourteen days in the Homestead's lockers. Suppliers of imported fresh foods or exotic game must be contacted to ensure the availability of unusual items such as free-range venison or cheese and produce requiring air shipment from abroad. And if guests are having Roast Prime Rib of Shorthorn Beef at a Saturday banquet, he will be sure not to schedule it Friday night as an entrée in the Main Dining Room. Once identified, these special needs are combined with the normal provisioning requirements to produce the first of Commissary Steward B. G. McElwee's "shopping lists" for the week—one on Monday for the Tuesday truck pickup and one on Thursday for the Friday pickup. Sunday's official duties con-

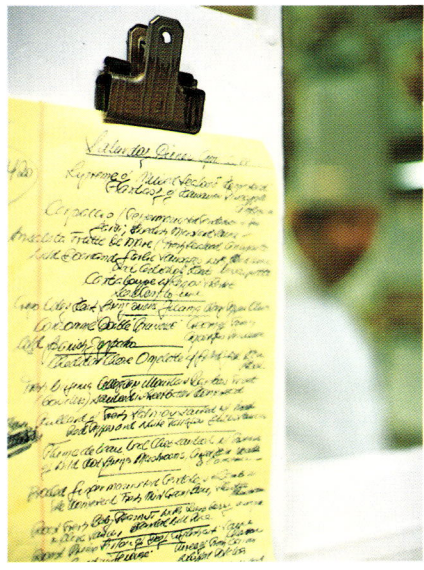

clude with one of Schnarwyler's daily rituals, the composition of the menu for three days hence. Always written out in longhand on yellow legal paper, this simple sheet sets the entire culinary machine in operation—no memoranda, no slick piece of laser printery, just a handwritten menu in the best tradition of M. and Mme Point—one posted outside the Chef's Office and one copy each for the Print Shop and Butcher Shop.

Schnarwyler's culinary philosophy emphasizes his distaste for cycle menus and his insistence on only the freshest and best ingredients. At resorts or hotels where the average length of stay is short or the guests are not as particular about their food, cycle menus may have their place, but the continued repetition of the same dish every so many days does little to promote interest and creativity by the kitchen staff. Schnarwyler is quick to point out that the location of Hot Springs is no obstacle to the procurement of fresh supplies. Twice weekly the Homestead's own refrigerated tractor trailer calls on suppliers in Washington (some have served the hotel since the late 1800s) to collect items transshipped from overseas and New York suppliers as well as those purchased in Washington. When peak times require it, trips are more frequent, and air freight is flown into Roanoke and the hotel's own airport, Ingalls Field.

Like the Troisgros' native Burgundy, Warm Springs Valley has always furnished the kitchen with many of its provisions. At one time, the Homestead owned a complete farm operation which supplied all of its meat, produce, and dairy products. Still today, a few miles away from the hotel, the perennial Homestead favorite, mountain trout, is lifted from rushing streams. Cool mountain summers, when combined with just the right amount of rainfall, produce bumper crops of chanterelles in the woods within walking distance from the hotel—providing a culinary delight for the guests and a profitable pastime for kitchen staff turned pickers in their free time. Nor are local farmers ignored. For generations, vegetables from their gardens have brought the vivid tastes and colors of summer to the plates of Homestead guests. This closeness to the land, already identified as the foundation of the best French regional cooking, is central to Schnarwyler as well for it enables him to provide guests a sense of place by giving them menus drawing on the seasonal variety and bounty of the region.

At no time are Schnarwyler's philosophical concerns more evident than when he plans menus—the real point of departure for the kitchen tour. As he approaches this task, requiring one to two hours, he is conscious of several, often conflicting, considerations. "One must be aware of not just what one would like to see on the menu, but of a balanced variety of items for our

*B. G. McElwee's
Shopping List*

AGING COOLER
Beef (rib roast), 1,800 lbs.

CHEESE COOLER
*American cheese (sliced), 120 lbs.
Bel Paese, 32 lbs.
Brie (2 kg wheels), 6
Cheddar (processed spread), 120 crocks
Cream cheese, 60 lbs.
Gruyère (Tiger 1-oz. packs), 6 boxes
Roquefort, 30 lbs.*

DAIRY COOLER
*Butter (unsalted, individual pats), 600 lbs.
Butter (unsalted, 1-lb. boxes), 1,080 lbs.
Buttermilk, 4 gallons
Cottage cheese, 240 lbs.
Cream (half-and-half), 102 gallons
Cream (sour), 240 lbs.
Cream (heavy), 12 gallons
Eggs (fresh), 21,600
Milk (chocolate, 1/2 pints), 768
Milk (1/2 gallons), 288
Milk (1/2 pints), 3,840
Milk (5-gallon dispensers), 25
Milk, skim (1/2 pints), 576
Yogurt (Yoplait, flavored), 24 cases
Yogurt (5-lb. tubs), 10*

EMPLOYEES' CAFETERIA
*Beans (whole green), 7 cases
Beef (corned brisket), 100 lbs.
Beef (green pepper steaks), 2 cases
Beef (hamburger, 3 patties/lb.), 240 lbs.
Beef (hamburger, 8-oz. patties), 180 lbs.
Beef (5-oz. cubed steak), 7 boxes
Carrots (sliced, cans), 4 cases
Chicken (patties), 180 lbs.
Cod (salted), 20 lbs.
Fruit cocktail (cans), 4 cases
Hamburger buns, 50 dozen
Hot dog buns, 36 dozen
Ice cream (5-oz. cups), 576
Juice (grapefruit, cans), 8 cases
Milk shake base (chocolate, 3-gallon containers), 9
Peaches (sliced, canned), 10 cases
Pork (loins), 6
Sauce (cheese), 4 cases
Sauerkraut (shredded, cans), 3 cases*

FISH COOLER
*Boston scrod, 90 lbs.
Clams (top neck, 250 pieces), 2 bags
Crabmeat (jumbo lump), 60 lbs.
Dover sole, 80 lbs.
Flounder (jumbo), 106 lbs.
Grouper, 46 lbs.
Lobster (tails), 80 lbs.
Pompano, 120 lbs.
Red snapper, 372 lbs.
Salmon (smoked), 270 lbs.
Salmon, 672 lbs.
Scallops (bay), 2 gallons
Scallops (sea), 2 gallons
Sea bass, 200 lbs.
Shrimp (under 15 count), 200 lbs.
Shrimp (18/20 count), 400 lbs.
Swordfish, 132 lbs.
Trout (mountain, 10-oz.), 475
Trout (mountain, 8-oz.), 24
Trout (smoked), 49 lbs.
Whitefish (smoked), 184 lbs.*

FREEZER
*Apples (sliced, 30-lb. cans), 12
Blueberries, 4 cases
Corn (shoepeg), 240 lbs.
Ice cream (Häagen-Dazs), 162 gallons
Juice (lemon), 4 cases
Peas (petite), 12 cases
Potatoes (french fries), 600 lbs.
Sherbet (Häagen-Dazs, lemon, 3-gallon containers), 30
Sherbet (Häagen-Dazs, raspberry, 3-gallon containers), 20*

FRUIT COOLER
*Figs, 2 flats
Grapefruit, 10 cases
Grapes (red flame), 6 flats
Kiwi fruit, 12 cases
Lemons (165 count), 20 cases
Limes, 28 boxes
Melons (cantaloupe), 40 cases
Melons (crenshaw), 60 cases
Oranges (juice, 100/113 count), 60 cases
Oranges (table, 56 count), 8 cases
Papayas, 16 boxes
Peaches (38-lb. boxes), 12
Pears, 2 boxes
Pineapple, 60 boxes
Plums, 6 boxes
Raspberries, 12 flats
Strawberries, 96 flats*

MEAT COOLER
*Beef (boneless chuck), 144 lbs.
Beef (bottom round), 586 lbs.
Beef (chipped), 80 lbs.
Beef (corned bottom round), 136 lbs.
Beef (corned brisket), 600 lbs.
Beef (filets), 648 lbs.
Beef (short ribs), 300 lbs.
Beef (short shin), 676 lbs.
Frankfurters, 220 lbs.
Lamb (legs), 322 lbs.
Lamb (loins), 200 lbs.
Lamb (racks), 466 lbs.
Meatloaf (German), 62 lbs.
Pork (bellies), 88 lbs.
Pork (boneless country ham), 288 lbs.
Pork (Canadian bacon), 58 lbs.
Pork (Genoa salami), 40 lbs.
Pork (knackwurst), 160 lbs.
Pork (link sausage), 400 lbs.
Pork (liverwurst), 20 lbs.
Pork (loose sausage), 276 lbs.
Pork (schinkenwurst), 26 lbs.
Pork (scrapple), 16 lbs.
Pork (smoked loins), 100 lbs.
Pork (smoked Texas wild boar), 20 lbs.
Pork (tenderloins), 80 lbs.
Pork (Virginia bacon, sliced), 700 lbs.
Rabbit, 2 cases
Veal (bones), 480 lbs.
Veal (calf's liver), 80 lbs.
Veal (loins), 700 lbs.
Veal (Swiss schueblig), 40 lbs.
Veal (sweetbreads), 60 lbs.
Veal (weisswurst), 40 lbs.
Venison (Texas wild-range hindquarters), 85 lbs.*

POULTRY COOLER
*Chicken (livers), 30 lbs.
Chicken (2 1/2 lb.), 800 lbs.
Chicken (3 1/2 lb.), 1,200 lbs.
Duck, 471 lbs.
Fettuccine (fresh), 60 lbs.
Partridge, 4 dozen
Pheasant (1 lb.), 120
Pheasant (3 lb.), 72
Quail (boned), 576
Ravioli (fresh tomato), 100 lbs.
Spaghetti (fresh), 60 lbs.
Turkey (smoked), 36 lbs.
Turkey, 2,474 lbs.*

STOREROOM
*Anchovies (flat), 1 case
Bananas, 6 boxes
Beans (dried flageolets), 5 cases
Beans (dried kidney), 4 cases
Beans (pinto), 100 lbs.
Cereal (assorted), 6 cases
Chocolate (Bavarian sweet), 25 lbs.
Chocolate (vanilla glaze), 2 cases
Chocolate (vermicelli), 1 case
Cinnamon (chips), 100 lbs.
Cinnamon (ground), 3 cases
Coconut (flake), 60 lbs.
Coffee (extract), 1 bottle
Coffee (Homestead blend), 750 lbs.
Coffee (Sanka, single packs), 2 cases
Cracker meal, 100 lbs.
Crackers (Doo dads), 6 cases
Crackers (Finn crisp), 10 boxes
Crackers (Goldfish cheese), 5 cases
Crackers (Ritz), 5 cases
Crackers (Ry brot), 10 cases
Fettuccine (dry), 6 cases
Figs (cans), 5 cases
Flour (all-purpose), 2,400 lbs.
Flour (brioche), 65 lbs.
Flour (cake), 250 lbs.
Flour (white rye), 25 lbs.
Flour (whole wheat), 25 lbs.
Foie gras (with truffles), 48 cans
Fondant (white), 3 cases
Food coloring (red), 6 quarts
Grits, 3 cases*

Honey (1-lb. packs), 96
Honey (4-lb. packs), 30
Juice (cranberry, cans), 4 cases
Juice (grape, cans), 6 cases
Macaroni (dry elbow), 6 cases
Malt, 50 lbs.
Morels (imported, dried), 2 lbs.
Nussfix, 55 lbs.
Oil (olive), 24 gallons
Oil (peanut), 80 gallons
Oil (salad), 60 gallons
Olives (plain queen), 10 cases
Olives (stuffed queen), 6 cases
Onions (pearl, cans), 10 cases
Onions (Spanish, fresh), 1,000 lbs.
Oranges (mandarin, cans), 6 cases
Peaches (halves, canned), 10 cases
Peas (split, dried), 100 lbs.
Peppercorns, 2 cases
Peppers (cherry), 4 cases
Pickles (imported sweet gherkins), 5 cases
Potatoes (boiling), 1,500 lbs.
Potatoes (Idaho baking), 20 boxes
Potatoes (new red bliss), 200 lbs.
Preserves (apple butter), 6 cases
Preserves (apricot), 2 cases
Preserves (Bing cherry), 2 cases
Preserves (bitter orange marmalade), 12 cases
Preserves (blackberry), 2 cases
Preserves (blueberry), 2 cases
Preserves (gooseberry), 2 cases
Preserves (raspberry), 8 cases
Preserves (red cherry), 2 cases
Preserves (strawberry), 8 cases
Prunes (cans), 10 cases
Relish (corn), 4 cases
Rice (plain), 600 lbs.
Rice (wild), 23 lbs.
Salt (80-lb. bags), 3
Sardines, 400 cans
Sauce (barbecue), 4 cases
Sauce (Grey poupon mustard), 6 cases
Sauce (Homestead cocktail), 5 cases
Sauce (Homestead heavy duty mayonnaise), 35 cases
Sauce (ketchup, bottles), 6 cases
Sauce (ketchup, single packs), 10 cases
Sauce (Worcestershire), 4 cases
Shortening, 125 lbs.
Snails (cans), 2 cases
Starch (corn), 4 cases
Sugar, 500 lbs.
Syrup (blueberry), 1 case
Syrup (Vermont Grade A Maple), 8 gallons
Tea (individual bags), 1,000
Tomatoes (diced, canned), 20 cases
Topping (butterscotch), 1/2 case
Topping (marshmallow), 1/2 case
Topping (nut), 2 1/2 cases
Topping (walnut), 1 case
Tuna (solid white, cans), 10 cases
Vinegar (cider), 6 cases
Vinegar (red wine), 2 1/2 cases
Yeast, 48 lbs.

VEGETABLE COOLER
Artichokes, 6 cases
Asparagus (jumbo), 60 lbs.
Avocados, 6 double boxes
Beans (green), 180 lbs.
Beets, 2 bushels
Broccoli, 8 crates
Cabbage (red), 100 lbs.
Cabbage, 2 crates
Carrots (50-lb. bags), 6
Cauliflower, 10 cases
Celeriac, 2 cases
Celery, 20 cases
Chicory, 4 cases
Chives, 48 bunches
Corn (baby), 200 pieces
Corn (white), 6 crates
Cucumbers, 4 crates
Dill, 48 bunches
Egg rolls, 1,000
Eggplant, 4 boxes
Endive (Belgian), 60 lbs.
Fennel, 8 cases
Lettuce (Boston), 20 cases
Lettuce (Bibb), 36 cases
Lettuce (iceberg), 20 cases
Lettuce (red leaf), 4 crates
Lettuce (romaine), 14 crates
Mushrooms (enoki), 24 packs
Mushrooms (shiitake), 40 lbs.
Mushrooms (white), 300 lbs.
Parsley, 6 cases
Peas (snow), 40 lbs.
Peppers (green), 8 cases
Peppers (red), 4 boxes
Peppers (yellow), 4 boxes
Potato (jicayma), 80 lbs.
Radicchio, 6 cases
Radishes, 6 cases
Rosemary, 48 bunches
Sauerkraut (5-gallon cans), 4
Scallions, 192 bunches
Shallots, 20 lbs.
Spinach (leaf), 26 boxes
Squash (green), 10 cases
Squash (yellow), 2 cases
Tomatoes (cherry), 8 cases
Tomatoes, 60 boxes
Turnips (with greens), 8 cases
Watercress, 50 cases

The Homestead Kitchen Staff

executive chef	Café Albert supervisor	
	head baker	
	1st assistant	
	2nd assistant	
	head butcher	
	1st assistant	
	2nd assistant	
	3rd assistant	
	pastry chef	
	1st assistant	
	2nd assistant	
	3rd assistant	
	executive sous-chef	Grille cooks breakfast and lunch
		Casino chef
		1st assistant
		2nd assistant
		fry chef
		1st assistant
		2nd assistant
		roast chef
		1st assistant
		sauce chef
		1st assistant
		2nd assistant
		3rd assistant
		vegetable chef
		1st assistant
		2nd assistant
	sous-chef	pot washers
		kitchen cleaners
	Grille chef dinner à la carte	relief chef
	1st assistant	1st relief
	2nd assistant	2nd relief
	Sam Snead's Tavern chef	garde-manger
		1st assistant
		2nd assistant
	Cascades Inn chef Cascades Club Restaurant chef	pantry chef
		1st assistant
		2nd assistant

guests, which the brigade is capable of doing at its best at all times." He adds, "the work load associated with the various menu items must be spread evenly among the different kitchen departments, and above all, the finest and freshest ingredients appropriate to the season must be incorporated." Echoes of Escoffier.

The client is Schnarwyler's paramount concern. Because the Homestead offers a prix fixe menu, he points out, "we get a good feel for trends and preferences because our guests order what appeals to them without being influenced by price." The popularity of every menu item is tracked by the number of orders and, if appropriate, by the clients ordering it. Occasionally this leads to humorous consequences, as it did during a medical meeting in 1985. Early in the week preceding this convention, accounts of a European health study linking diets rich in seafood to lowered incidence of heart disease were widely circulated in the international press. Already preferential consumers of fish, the doctors had picked the Homestead's amply stocked seafood lockers clean by Friday evening. Instinctively, the Chef called on his ability for crisis management and, come Saturday morning, air freight operations at Roanoke's Municipal Airport were literally aswim with Schnarwyler's emergency "fish lift" for the remaining weekend meals. "Il faut surtout honorer le menu."

Just as the Chef brings resourcefulness to honoring the menu, so he brings inventiveness to its creation. On one occasion, the three of us were having a working dinner in our home on a crisp fall evening. The season seemed to call for some of the robust flavors of southwestern France, so we prepared an entrée featuring lightly roasted duck breasts with a wild mushroom sauce in the style of Bordeaux. As usual, the conversation was fast-moving, touching on many subjects, some concerning this book, and some not, but always he came back to the mushroom sauce. Something intrigued him about its rich color and earthy flavor lightly infused with Port. After a casual listing of the ingredients, the conversation drifted on to other things, and we made a mental note to photocopy the rather complicated recipe and forward it to him. Intentions being what they are, it was four or five days before we got this done. But no matter. Back in the Homestead kitchen the afternoon after our dinner, he reconstructed the sauce from memory for his chief saucier, Brian Puhle. After a diagnostic session, the two adapted the recipe for use on the Homestead scale, and by the time our photocopy reached Hot Springs, it had been on the menu long enough to sell four or five hundred orders. (Oh yes, it did make it into the book—you will find it listed as Breast of Chicken Homestead with Essence of Wild Mushroom Sauce.)

Anecdotes such as these reveal two critical aspects of Schnarwyler's approach to cuisine. First, although he designed and implemented an electronic tote board for entrées to keep the brigade and himself apprised of each order as it comes in from the waiters, he sees the computer's role in the kitchen as limited. In the case of the medical convention, an automated data system would have tracked the rise in fish consumption, and no doubt would have connected it with the presence of the doctors. However, few data management systems would have made the necessary causal connection to the newspaper report of the health study. Thus, a food and beverage manager at another hotel, looking only at printouts, might incorrectly infer that a new trend was in the making, whereas this canny Swiss chef knew otherwise.

Respect for inventiveness and innovation based on a classical technical base are hallmarks of this chef extraordinaire—it is the necessary creative tension between the Troisgros' "doing a good dish . . . for twenty years," and Quentin Crewe's observation that "no one chef is the same for two different days." Like Soltner, Schnarwyler has both an institutional rating and professional standing to protect, but it is precisely this exquisite interchange between old and new, theme and variation, that keeps them both at the forefront of the American culinary scene. Ultimately it is a matter of personal style. Both men eschew the "enfant terrible" image cultivated by the wunderkinder. Rather, their view of the chef's role is more akin to the "deus ex machina"—a sufficient and necessary first cause which sets things in motion, but entrusts the motion to talented subordinates—stepping in only when needed and otherwise tending to the overview which keeps the entire operation running smoothly and on time. As with Soltner, it is "a velvet hand in a velvet glove."

Because Schnarwyler's handwritten menus are posted three days in advance they serve as orders and schedules for the whole staff—nothing more is required. Experience tells Head Baker Thomas Woodzell how many croissants, brioches, Pullman loaves, Danish pastries, and baguettes to make, just as it tells him whether to make five hundred or fifteen hundred dinner rolls. Likewise, Executive Pastry Chef Michel Finel knows how many hundreds of sinfully rich Homestead honey cookies, chocolate chip cookies, or "fait à la maison" chocolates will be purchased by hungry patrons of Café Albert. He will not have to be asked to prepare ten Gâteaux Chambord, two hundred Soufflés à la Vanille, fifteen Swiss Kirsch Tortes, or five gallons of Sorbet de Pamplemousse. He knows.

And so it goes with all the members of this extraordinary bri-

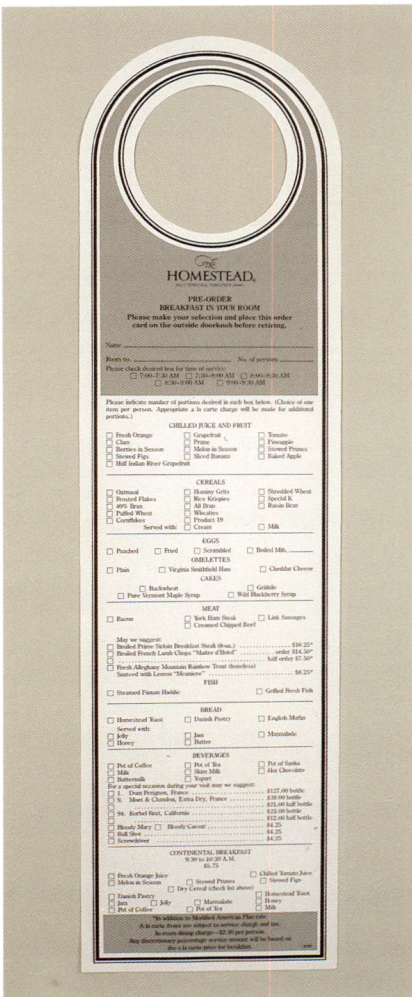

gade. Sous-chef Paul Marian arrives early in the morning, taking charge of breakfast and special function operations, and Chief Saucier Brian Puhle notes the sauce and soup requirements for the day (and next three days in the case of English Beef Tea). Room Service Headwaiter Arthur Bryan collects the breakfast "hangout" orders (left on doorknobs by retiring guests) from the Front Desk, the first step in setting in motion a process whose result is an eagerly anticipated sound familiar to generations of Homestead guests—the soft knock at the door which heralds the arrival of breakfast. The rolling table holds underneath it the portable warming case filled with the previous evening's agonized choice among brioches, croissants, Homestead toast, pastries, buckwheat cakes, pancakes, French toast, omelets, eggs cooked to order, bacon, sausage, York ham steaks, grits, hashed brown potatoes, not to mention à la carte lamb chops, mountain trout, or steaks. All served on linen reserved only to Room Service. Later in the morning, B. G. McElwee automatically integrates the Chef's food orders with replenishment of all dairy items, canned goods, and staples in the vast storeroom, which supplies the Kitchen, Employees' Cafeteria, Grille, Casino, Ski Lodge, Sam Snead's Tavern, Cascades Inn, and Upper and Lower Cascades restaurants.

But the food service is so complex that, as the following "clock" shows, Schnarwyler's kitchen, like Le Huédé's on the *France*, operates twenty-four hours a day—a necessity for such numbers of guests or passengers. For the guest to feel that food was "made especially for him," it must be prepared from scratch on the premises—just as it should be at home. But behind it all is the team—at home, one, two, or more—at the Homestead as many as eighty-five. And for "Chef" it is a team, not just an assemblage of characters. Fernand Point's analogy of an orchestra captures the essence of such an organization, individuals working as a whole, at once soloists and part of an ensemble, others supporting players, all directed by a talented conductor with a vision of the whole production and the knowledge to guide the group to attain it.

What follows is a "snapshot" of a typical day in the life of this atypical resort food operation. Sometimes there is more activity and sometimes less—according to the season. Because it is a twenty-four-hour operation there is no end and no beginning, but perhaps the point is best made by starting the clock when most guests have retired for the evening with visions of buckwheat cakes, maple syrup, and York ham steaks dancing in their heads.

The Homestead Clock

2300

Night bakers Junior Sams, Phillip Stemphlet, and helpers arrive and begin firing the Homestead's two nineteenth-century, brick-lined main ovens. Bakers begin scaling and mixing 7 gallons of Pullman loaf dough. The helpers begin cleaning and greasing all pans and bread molds.

The night cleaner arrives to steam clean the Kitchen and clean the ovens and broilers.

Arthur Bryan and Room Service staff members serving banquets and special parties leave.

The View closes.

2330

Junior Sams and Phillip Stemphlet begin mixing and scaling English muffin dough.

2400

Junior Sams and Phillip Stemphlet begin mixing and scaling sweet dough.

The Grille closes, and cook Malaki Wilson secures the kitchen and leaves. After seeing that all is ready for breakfast setup, Maître d'hôtel Mario Buffone leaves.

Evening room service ends, and the captain and remaining waiters leave.

0030

Baker's helpers begin cutting and making melba toast.

0100

Junior Sams, Phillip Stemphlet, and helpers mold and pan approximately 40 Pullman loaves for toast and sandwiches and finish cutting and making melba toast.

Charlie Bogan's Kenworth Continental diesel rumbles to life and he and his helper set off on their biweekly trip to Washington with the Homestead's 40-foot refrigerated tractor trailer.

Evening gaiety comes to an end as the Homestead Club and Sam Snead's Tavern close.

0130

Junior Sams and Phillip Stemphlet begin making English muffins.

0200

Junior Sams and Phillip Stemphlet take sweet dough and make and pan sweet rolls, cinnamon and pecan buns, and snowflake rolls—approximately 450 pieces in all.

Thomas Woodzell, with the Homestead since 1960 and Head Baker since 1977, arrives and begins mixing doughs for sourdough rye, whole wheat, pumpernickel, and French bread.

0300

Junior Sams, Phillip Stemphlet, and helpers begin mixing doughs for 350 to 450 croissants (or brioches on alternating days), brioche bread, and 480 to 720 pieces of Danish pastry. Firing of the main ovens stops when they have reached 475F.

0400

Bakers roll out croissant and Danish pastry dough in rectangles and roll in chilled butter, rerolling the doughs twice for the first and second turns (*tours*), forming the first 9 layers. Sourdough rye, whole wheat, and pumpernickel breads are scaled and panned.

0430

Bakers make third and fourth turns in croissant and Danish pastry dough, rerolling each time, producing 81 layers, and return dough to refrigerator. Helpers bake cinnamon and pecan rolls.

0500

Bakers and helpers make Pullman loaves, followed by sourdough rye, whole wheat, and pumpernickel. Fifth and sixth turns in croissant and Danish pastry dough are finished, rerolling each time, for a dough of 729 layers. All sweet rolls are baked.

0530

Bakers and helpers make 150 servings each of biscuits and corn bread and begin icing all the sweet rolls. Bakers form Danish pastries, and cut croissant dough into triangles and roll them into crescent shapes.

Head Cook Clovis Lamar arrives at the Employees' Cafeteria and begins preparing hot cereals and breakfast meats.

0600

Bakers bake croissants and Danish pastries. Helpers set up all breakfast items for Dining Room, Grille buffet, Room Service, private functions, coffee breaks, and Café Albert.

Charlie Bogan and his helper stop in Springfield, Virginia, to pick up a load of staples and canned goods.

Counter person arrives in the Employees' Cafeteria and begins setting up the serving line as well as preparing juices, condiments, and pastries.

The Chef's Department brigade, day fry cooks, roast cooks and helper, garde-manger, pantry personnel, and pot washers arrive to staff positions.

Sous-chef Paul Marian arrives and begins breakfast preparations for food service from Main Kitchen, Grille buffet, and special functions.

Pantry staff begins squeezing 12 cases of juice oranges, brewing 60 gallons of Homestead special blend coffee, and preparing pancake batters, fresh fruit, and other juices. All breakfast items are picked up from the bakery and set up and loaves are sliced for toasting.

Roast cooks set up ham steaks, sausage, and bacon for breakfast and begin cooking the required amounts for Room Service and the Grille buffet. All fish items are readied to be broiled, boiled, or poached to order.

Fry cooks prepare hot cereals and creamed chipped beef, sauté apples and hashed brown potatoes, get ready to fix griddle cakes, and work on daily breakfast specials. Eggs are readied for cooking to order as needed.

Room Service busboy arrives and sets up Early Bird coffee service and light continental breakfast in the Sun Room.

Chief Saucier Brian Puhle and assistants start stocks, luncheon soups, sauces, and hot entrées. Hams and shrimp are cooked for cold preparations, and special orders are started for Café Albert, Sam Snead's Tavern, and, depending upon the season, Cascades Inn and Club restaurants, Casino, and Ski Lodge. Consommés, cream soups, and special function soups for dinner are started.

Roast cooks begin roasting turkeys, rib roasts, legs of lamb, and pork roasts needed for sandwiches and hot or cold luncheon buffet items.

Garde-manger staff checks all cold meat refrigerators for leftover items to be sent to the Employees' Cafeteria or returned to the Butcher Shop before preparing orders for Café Albert, Sam Snead's Tavern, Cascades Club Restaurant, Grille breakfast and luncheon buffets, and items needed by other departments. Following this, early requests for box lunches are filled, luncheon salads are prepared, and special orders for private functions are tended to.

Room Service Headwaiter Arthur Bryan arrives, collects "hangout" breakfast room service orders at the Front Desk on his way in, and arranges them in order of requested service.

0630

Thomas Woodzell begins making and scaling approximately 60 large loaves of French bread, 40 to 50 loaves of white bread,

and 36 loaves of sourdough rye bread for dinner in the Grille and retail sale at Café Albert; 10 loaves of brioche bread for Café Albert, the View, and luncheon in the Grille; and 40 to 80 petits pains and 70 to 80 hamburger buns for Sam Snead's Tavern.

Junior Sams, Phillip Stemphlet, and helpers clean up the Bake Shop and equipment.

Breakfast service begins in the Employees' Cafeteria.

Michel Finel, pâtissier at the Homestead since 1978 and Executive Pastry Chef since 1982, arrives and begins work on pastries, tarts, and cakes for luncheon at the Grille, Casino, Café Albert, and Sam Snead's Tavern and dinner at the Cascades Inn.

Room Service operators, captains, waiters, and busboys arrive and Room Service staff begins complimentary Early Bird continental breakfast and coffee service in the Sun Room.

Mario Buffone and staff arrive to ready the Grille for the breakfast buffet.

Head Butcher Walker May and staff arrive and begin filling meat, fish, and poultry orders for Café Albert, Sam Snead's Tavern, and, depending upon the season, the Grille, Casino, Cascades Inn and Club restaurants, and the Ski Lodge. Orders for Main Kitchen luncheon, dinner, and special function menus are filled.

0640

Full breakfast service to rooms begins as Room Service captains give order tickets to waiters for processing. Arthur Bryan and captains review the function sheets for coffee breaks, picnic boxes, and special function breakfasts, luncheons, and banquets.

0645

Paul Marian checks quality of coffee before it is served..

0650

Paul Marian checks Grille buffet breakfast preparations.

0700

Junior Sams, Phillip Stemphlet, and helpers leave.

Charlie Bogan and helper arrive in Washington at their second pickup point for fresh fruit and vegetables.

Breakfast service begins in the Grille.

Commissary Steward B. G. McElwee and Assistant Commissary Steward Richard Byrd arrive in the Storeroom. B. G. McElwee opens the mail for market quotations from New York and Washington.

Dining Room Headwaiter Jerry Adderton and staff arrive, and check to see that all is set up for breakfast service in the Main Dining Room or Commonwealth Room, depending upon the guest count. Assistant Headwaiter Woody Pettus arrives and checks to see that the staff is present and ready for service.

The Casino truck arrives to pick up Butcher Shop and Storeroom orders placed the previous evening and delivers them along with fresh linens for the luncheon buffet.

The Casino staff arrives to work on the buffet luncheon. Sue Puhle begins cutting bread and preparing watercress, spinach, and other green salads. Alice McElwee starts preparing the fern decorations, condiments, butter, and dessert sauces. Before arriving at the Casino, Chef Raymond Cauley checks with the Butcher Shop and Garde-manger for items to be used in the buffet.

The Kitchen brigade begins to eat breakfast at 30-minute intervals.

The Cascades Inn truck picks up breakfast pastry and rolls from the Bake Shop for the Inn.

0715

Paul Marian checks the refrigerators for vegetables and sauces to be sent to the Employees' Cafeteria for luncheon preparations.

0730

Thomas Woodzell mixes the first batch of hard roll dough, forms it into 450 dinner rolls (150 poppy seed, 150 sesame seed, and 150 plain), and sets them to proof.

Executive Sous-chef Josef Schelch arrives, assists Paul Marian if needed, and otherwise sets about planning the day's kitchen schedule.

Director of Catering Hans Huebner arrives.

Breakfast service begins in the Main Dining Room.

Early Bird coffee service and continental breakfast ends in the Sun Room.

Breakfast service begins at the Cascades Inn.

0800

Charlie Bogan arrives at his second Washington stop and takes on additional produce, as well as seafood, meat, game, caviar, smoked salmon, smoked meats, Homestead special blend coffee, and imported chocolate.

Paul Marian checks the Storeroom and coolers to ensure that stock is being properly rotated.

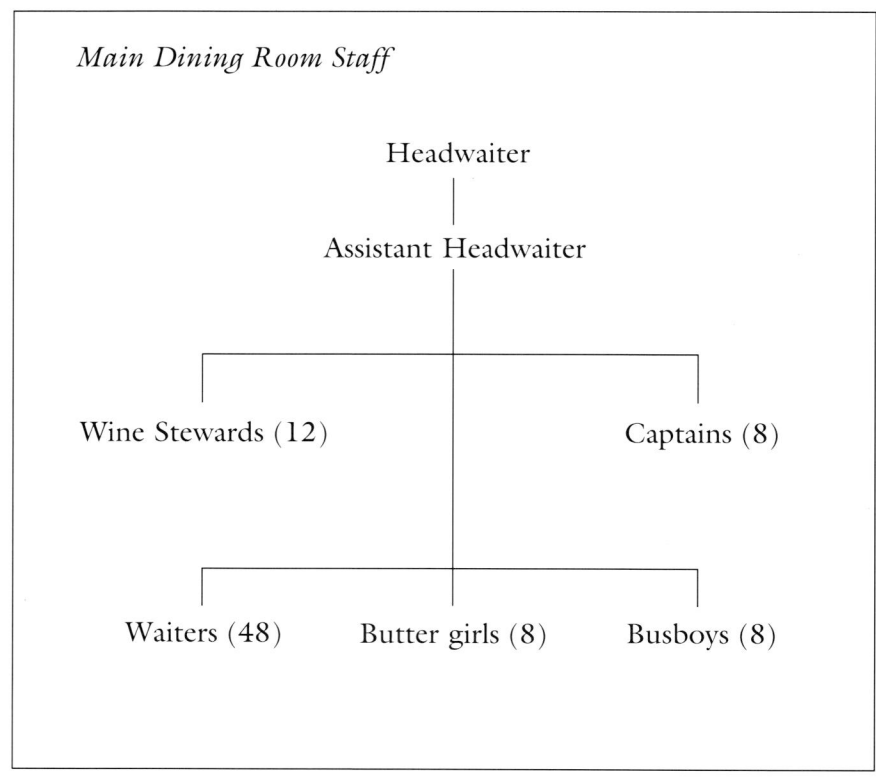

Main Dining Room Staff

The vegetable cooks arrive and begin "mise en place" (preparing vegetables for cooking as well as garnishes) for luncheon, dinner, and special functions.

B. G. McElwee begins to receive telephone produce quotations from Washington and New York.

Hans Huebner collects function sheets from the Front Desk in order to determine the number of banquets and special events for the day and the guest count of each.

Audrey Gutshall arrives and collects the Chef's handwritten menus to be typeset for the printed guest menu.

Thelma Hansford, the Chef's secretary, arrives and begins payroll reports.

Employee Cafeteria Supervisor Jerry Hostetter arrives, checks the daily menu, and prepares Butcher Shop and Storeroom requisitions. After checking food availability from the Butcher Shop and Main Kitchen she writes the menu for the next day.

0815

Chef Albert Schnarwyler arrives, has a cup of coffee, samples any new items the baker might have for him, checks the day's function sheets, and opens his mail.

The Cascades Inn truck arrives to pick up requisitioned provisions from the Main Kitchen, Storeroom, Wine Cellar, and Butcher, Pastry, and Bake shops for delivery to the Inn, Cascades Club Restaurant, and Lower Cascades Club.

0830

Thomas Woodzell mixes his second batch of hard roll dough, forms another 450 dinner rolls, and sets them to proof.

Breakfast service ends and coffee break service begins in the Employees' Cafeteria.

Café Albert Supervisor Kathy McCollum and staff arrive to prepare for light breakfast and retail service.

The Commissary staff delivers supplies to Café Albert.

0900

Thomas Woodzell bakes all the special-order items such as small loaves and hamburger buns for Sam Snead's Tavern. When these are completed, he injects steam at 30 lbs/in^2 (to produce a brittle, golden brown crust) and bakes the first batch of dinner rolls, followed by French bread (baguettes).

B. G. McElwee orders dry goods from Washington, New York, and other areas.

Breakfast ends at the Cascades Inn.

Café Albert opens for breakfast and retail sales.

0930

If the guest count exceeds 650, Thomas Woodzell mixes a third batch of hard roll dough, forms another 450 dinner rolls, and sets them to proof.

Audrey Gutshall lays out the menus and sets them up on the compositor for the Print Shop.

B. G. McElwee and Richard Byrd begin their inventories of: fish, poultry, and meat in the Butcher Shop; individual coolers for vegetables, fruit, dairy products, and cheese; the freezer; and the Storeroom.

Canapé Chef Douglas Bird arrives and begins preparing hot and cold canapés for cocktail parties and receptions.

The Kitchen day cleaning crew arrives and begins cleaning the steam pots, sweeping and mopping floors, and general cleaning.

Breakfast service ends in the Main Dining Room.

Breakfast service ends in the Grille and setup for luncheon begins when the last guest leaves.

Full breakfast service from Room Service ends and continental breakfast begins.

Continental breakfast service begins in the View.

The Casino truck picks up supplies from the Storeroom, Main Kitchen, and Bake, Butcher, and Pastry shops for Sam Snead's Tavern.

0945

At the Casino, the housekeeping staff cleans off the outdoor

tables, wipes dew off the chairs, sets up the umbrellas, and puts cushions in the chairs.

1000

Thomas Woodzell bakes the second batch of dinner rolls and prepares special orders for afternoon tea service in the Great Hall.

Charlie Bogan makes his third Washington call and takes on his first large shipment of freshwater fish and seafood.

Coffee break service is ended in the Employees' Cafeteria.

Michel Finel begins work on pies and tarts for dinner as well as sorbet or ice cream, according to the menu. As time permits, he works on birthday, anniversary, and "VIP" cakes.

Audrey Gutshall delivers menus to the Print Shop for printing a quantity equivalent to 80 percent of the guest count.

Casino Headwaiter Walter Rhett, with the Homestead since 1948, arrives to supervise the preparation of indoor and outdoor luncheon service. Steward Jimmy Carter sets up shaved ice for all the chilled foods in the buffet, followed close behind by Alice McElwee, who begins to lay out the various cold dishes.

Paula Lindsay arrives at the Cascades Club Restaurant to begin luncheon preparations.

Bobby Fry checks luncheon preparations at the Lower Cascades Club.

1015

Part of the Casino wait staff arrives and begins setting up the tables with linens, flatware, glassware, and condiments.

1030

Kitchen brigade has lunch at 30-minute intervals.

B. G. McElwee and Richard Byrd complete the food inventories.

Albert Schnarwyler, Paul Marian, and Patricia Hodge give cooking demonstrations in the Conference Center as time permits.

Room Service ends continental breakfast and begins mid-morning snack service.

Dinner Cook Haflin Clarke arrives in the Employees' Cafeteria, helps with luncheon service, and begins dinner preparations.

Mario Buffone arrives at the Casino.

1045

Evening shift counter person arrives to help with luncheon service in the Employees' Cafeteria.

1100

Charlie Bogan stops in Alexandria, Virginia, and collects his

second shipment of seafood and freshwater fish along with imported cheeses, frozen foods, and canned goods.

Thomas Woodzell bakes the third batch of dinner rolls, any remaining special orders, and leaves.

The split-shift roast cook assistants, fry cooks, and saucier's assistant leave, to return for the evening meal preparations.

B. G. McElwee meets with the chef to make out food orders based on the inventories and the expected business for the next three days.

The Steward's Department collects the printed menus for the day from the Print Shop.

Edward Rhett, with the Homestead since 1952, arrives and begins supervision of preparations for cocktail parties and receptions.

Luncheon service begins in the Employees' Cafeteria.

The Casino truck delivers hot food from the Main Kitchen for the luncheon buffet.

Chef Jay Brinkley and staff arrive at Sam Snead's Tavern to begin luncheon preparations.

1130

Sous-chefs check the Casino, Grille, and Café Albert to ensure that luncheon preparations are complete.

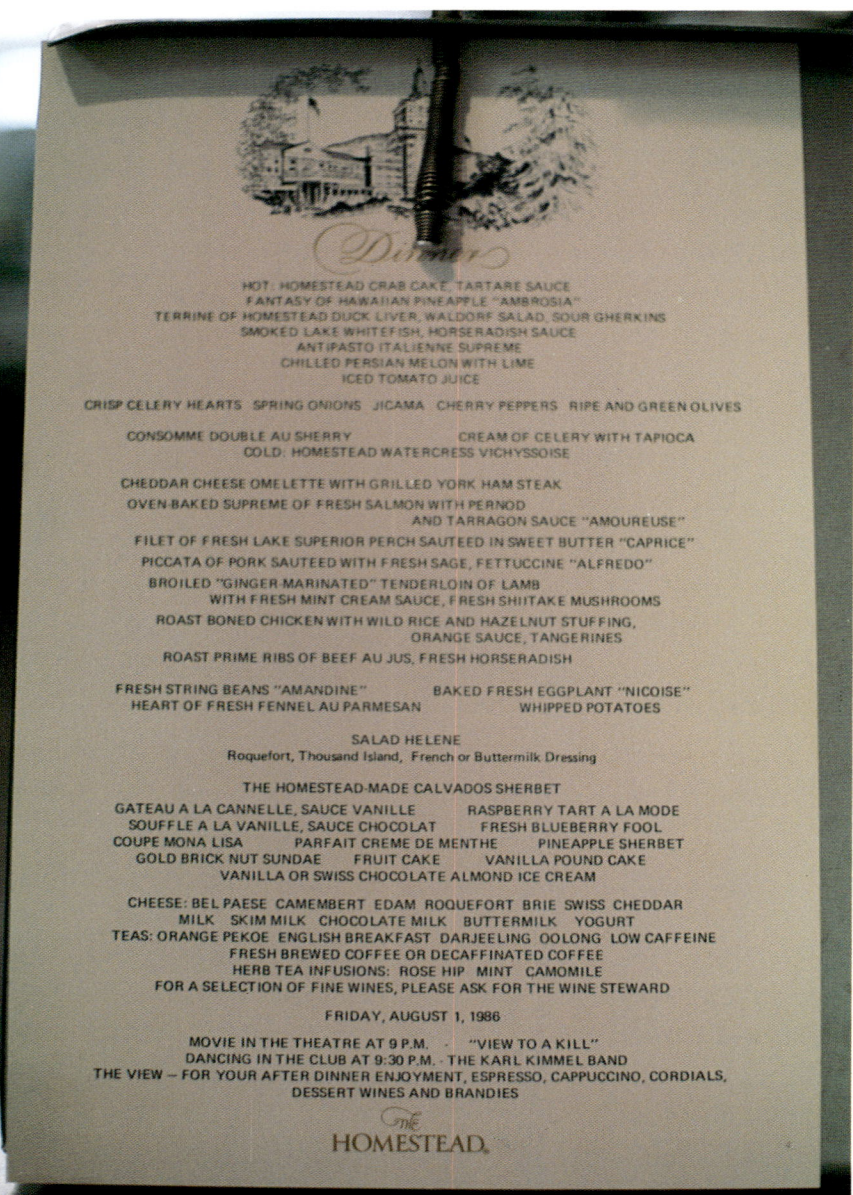

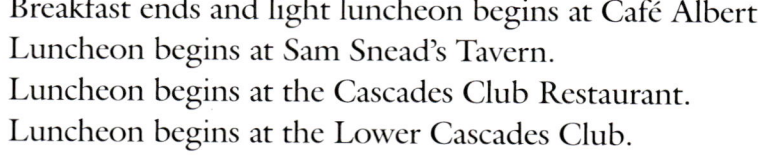

Breakfast ends and light luncheon begins at Café Albert.
Luncheon begins at Sam Snead's Tavern.
Luncheon begins at the Cascades Club Restaurant.
Luncheon begins at the Lower Cascades Club.

1200

Michel Finel finishes the dinner dessert orders and leaves.

B. G. McElwee begins telephoning in food orders for Charlie Bogan's next trip.

In the View, continental breakfast ends and light luncheon service begins.

Mid-morning snack service ends in Room Service and luncheon begins.

Buffet and à la carte luncheon service opens in the Grille.

The luncheon buffet opens at the Casino.

At the Cascades Inn, Chef John Grasso takes inventory and prepares food orders based on his three-day forecast.

1230

Albert Schnarwyler, Paul Marian, and Josef Schelch have lunch together.

Night garde-mangers arrive.

1300

Kitchen brigade night staff, saucier and assistants, and fry cooks arrive. Saucier and assistants roast small items such as pheasants, ducks, and quail to the holding point, begin preparations of private party soups if not already started, work on garnishes, finish complicated sauces such as Nantua and Américaine, and prepare "mise en place" for dinner service. Garde-mangers handle afternoon orders, prepare appetizers for dinner service, and other "mise en place" for special parties. Pantry staff begins preparation of salads, fruit, and salad dressings for dinner service.

Josef Schelch leaves, to return for dinner service.

Split-shift vegetable cooks leave.

Arthur Bryan and Room Service staff who will be serving banquets or special functions in the evening leave.

Luncheon service ends in the Employees' Cafeteria.

John Grasso places the food order for the Cascades Inn with B. G. McElwee.

1330

Coffee break service begins in the Employees' Cafeteria.

1400

Charlie Bogan arrives in Newmarket, Virginia, and takes on more than a ton of fresh poultry.

Clovis Lamar and the morning counter person leave the Employees' Cafeteria and the evening crew continues dinner preparations.

Albert Schnarwyler leaves, to return for dinner service.

Luncheon ends and afternoon snack service begins in Room Service.

Luncheon ends in the Grille, and Chef Jim Wolfe and staff arrive to begin preparations for dinner service.

Jerry Adderton and Woody Pettus leave, to return for dinner service in the Main Dining Room.

1430

Night Chef and Roast Cook Charles Braxton arrives and starts roasting beef or other large roasts for dinner, takes care of afternoon orders, and works on other dinner preparations.

Night pot washers arrive.

Paul Marian, Brian Puhle, and day roast cooks, garde-mangers, pantry staff, and day pot washers leave.

Coffee break service ends in the Employees' Cafeteria.

Buffet luncheon service at the Casino ends, and à la carte sandwich service from the Casino grill begins.

1500

B. G. McElwee ends his food ordering for the day and he and Richard Byrd leave.

Hans Huebner leaves.

At the Cascades Inn, John Grasso and his staff begin meat, vegetable, soup, and sauce preparations for dinner.

1530

Charlie Bogan arrives in Staunton, Virginia, to take on a last load of canned goods and frozen food before heading home. As evening shadows gather in mountain hollows, his powerful Kenworth turbo-diesel tractor warms to the challenge of pulling B. G. McElwee's "shopping cart" up the gentle, but taxing, switchbacks on Route 39 as it winds up Warm Springs Mountain.

Main Dining Room staff begins setting up for tea service in the Great Hall.

Table setup for dinner service in the Main Dining Room begins.

In the Grille, table setup for à la carte dinner begins.

1600

Tea service begins in the Great Hall, accompanied by light classical music played by a trio in formal attire.

The Homestead Club opens.

Luncheon service ends at the Cascades Club Restaurant and, after cleaning up, the wait staff leaves.

Luncheon service ends at the Lower Cascades Club and, after cleaning up, the wait staff leaves.

Mario Buffone and Walter Rhett leave the Casino.

1630

Arthur Bryan and Room Service captains, waiters, and busboys return for evening banquet and special function service.

Cooks at the Cascades Club Restaurant and Lower Cascades Club leave.

1700

The Homestead tractor trailer arrives at the Kitchen loading dock and B. G. McElwee and Richard Byrd return to help the staff and Charlie Bogan unload tons of choice provisions. Produce is checked for weight, quality, and correct invoice

pricing before going to the coolers. Meat, fish, and poultry are weighed before delivery to the Butcher Shop, and the remaining items are taken to the Storeroom.

The night roast cook helper arrives. Fish for the dinner service comes up from the Butcher Shop, and dinner meat and garnish preparations are started. Cooks begin to eat dinner at 30-minute intervals.

Tea service ends in the Great Hall.

Light luncheon service ends and the cocktail menu begins in the View.

Dinner service begins in the Employees' Cafeteria and Jerry Hostetter leaves.

The Casino grill ends à la carte sandwich service and Alice McElwee and Sue Puhle leave.

At Sam Snead's Tavern, luncheon service ends and dinner service begins.

Jerry Adderton and Woody Pettus return to begin supervision of dinner preparations in the Main Dining Room.

Hans Huebner arrives to check on finishing details for cocktail parties, receptions, and banquets.

1730

The Kitchen split-shift roast cook assistant, fry cooks, and assistant saucier return.

Michel Finel and staff arrive, finish pies and tarts for dinner, and begin work on Homestead honey cookies, chocolate chip cookies, fondant-filled chocolates, and chocolate truffles for Café Albert.

Jerry Adderton begins taking reservations for dinner in the Main Dining Room.

At the Casino the outdoor cushions are put away, the umbrellas taken down, and the tables cleaned off.

1800

Albert Schnarwyler and Josef Schelch arrive to supervise dinner service for special banquets and the Main Dining Room. Split-shift vegetable cooks arrive.

Soups, pastry, and breads arrive at the waiters' station from Kitchen departments.

Woody Pettus begins to organize the wait staff for dinner service in the Main Dining Room.

Mario Buffone arrives to supervise dinner service in the Grille.

The Casino closes.

Café Albert closes.

1830

Dinner service ends in the Employees' Cafeteria.

1845

Albert Schnarwyler and Josef Schelch taste all soups and sauces for seasoning and check dinner service preparations.

Woody Pettus has roll call for wait staff, explains the menu, and makes any announcements concerning special events in the Dining Room.

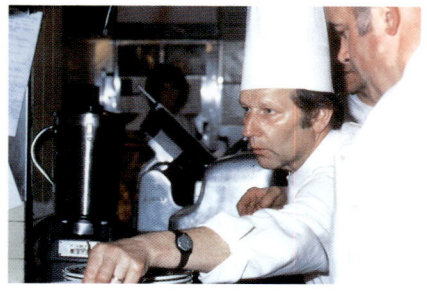

1900

Unloading completed, Charlie Bogan returns the tractor trailer to the parking yard, and B. G. McElwee, Richard Byrd, and staff leave.

The chef and sous-chef have dinner.

The Main Dining Room opens for dinner.

The Grille begins à la carte dinner service.

In Room Service, the afternoon snack menu ends and dinner service begins.

Dinner service begins at the Cascades Inn.

1930

The chef and sous-chef supervise special functions. By this point in the evening, the tally of entrées on the electronic tote board usually gives an accurate forecast of the flow in the Main Dining Room for the whole meal. If one or more entrées is more popular than anticipated, there is ample time to order additional quantities to be prepared and sent up from the Butcher Shop.

The evening crew leaves the Employees' Cafeteria.

2000

Seating for dinner service ends at the Cascades Inn.

2030

In the View the cocktail menu ends and the light pastry menu begins.

Dinner service ends and the late snack menu begins in Room Service.

Seating for dinner service ends in the Main Dining Room.

2130

Albert Schnarwyler and Josef Schelch leave. Night saucier and assistant, vegetable cooks, fry cooks, split-shift roast cook, garde-mangers, and Pantry staff leave. Charles Braxton assumes command of the Kitchen.

Dancing and live music begin in the Homestead Club.

Dinner service ends and snack service begins at Sam Snead's Tavern. Chef Jay Brinkley and his staff secure the kitchen and leave.

2200

Charles Braxton begins to secure the Main Kitchen.

Michel Finel and pastry staff leave.

In the Grille, à la carte dinner service ends, and the supper menu begins.

Setup for breakfast in the Main Dining Room begins. Jerry Adderton leaves.

At the Cascades Inn, John Grasso secures the kitchen, and he and his staff leave.

2230

In the Kitchen, night pot washers and split-shift cleaners leave. Charles Braxton makes a final check and leaves.

Jim Wolfe and his assistant chef leave the Grille.

Woody Pettus leaves.

So there you have it. The preceding pages, concluding with our *tranche de vie culinaire*, have attempted to sketch the lineage, philosophy, and workings of Albert Schnarwyler's cuisine. Yet, this book can only hint at the culinary adventures awaiting you in Hot Springs. It has been years since the Tricolor saw its last sunset over the taffrail of the *France*, but, today, as the sun peeks over Warm Springs Mountain, you will find Doorman Steve Carpenter raising the Stars and Stripes at the Homestead. And, in the restaurants nestled away in "America's favorite mountain resort," a Swiss chef extraordinaire quietly nourishes the tradition of Escoffier, Point, and Le Huédé as he guides us toward the twenty-first century.

Chief Saucier Brian Puhle

Sauces

> It is the sauce which distinguishes a good chef. The *saucier* is a soloist in the orchestra of a great kitchen. . . . Take a *béarnaise* . . . what is it? A yolk of egg, a shallot, some tarragon. But, believe me, it takes years of practice before the result is perfect. Let your eyes wander for a moment and the sauce is unusable.
>
> —Fernand Point

Point's statement is an apt summation of the saucier's art. Perhaps the most complex area of cuisine, sauce making demands keen powers of observation, an exquisite sense of timing, and an understanding of the "chemistry" of ingredients and flavors. This is not to take for granted the importance of excellence in other kitchen areas—we all have grimaced at overcooked beans which gave up the pretense of being green long before we arrived at the table or a grilled filet mignon whose interior was the color and texture of slate. But the saucier's task is made different by the multidimensional nature of sauces—liquid compounds made up of subcompounds and flavorings, all interacting with and changing each other (usually with the application of heat) as time elapses. By contrast, careful cooking of a vegetable or meat usually involves keeping an eye on only two variables—proper heat and elapsed time. Of course, it is possible to become preoccupied with the complexity of a sauce and miss the main point that it must taste good and be an appropriate accompaniment, but for the academic fun of it we have included a brief excerpt from Harold McGee's excellent volume, *On Food and Cooking: The Science and Lore of the Kitchen*. His chapter on sauces has a very thorough treatment of chemistry, and we join the discussion as he is describing the less than straightforward role played by Point's "yolk of egg" in sauce béarnaise.

> Walker's most important contribution was to reintroduce to the debate a factor that had been recognized decades earlier in books on colloids and emulsions: the emulsifying action of the egg yolks and, in particular, of the phospholipid lecithin. He experimented with several different salts, thereby changing the distribution of charge in the sauce, and the results did not support the hypothesis of the elec-

trical double layer. Emulsifiers appear to be a more likely source of stability.

If this is the case, then it seems obvious that the way to lessen the danger of a broken emulsion is to use plenty of egg yolk. Alas it's not that easy. Yolk is about half water, so that adding some extra would dilute the sauce and require both more flavoring and more oil to produce a sauce of the same quality. And we all know that egg yolk contains a goodly amount of cholesterol. It turns out that cholesterol, like lecithin, is an emulsifier. Unlike lecithin, however, it stabilizes a water-in-oil emulsion like sauce béarnaise. As we mentioned above, the properties of an emulsifier depend on its molecular structure. It is a general rule that whichever liquid a particular emulsifier is more soluble or dispersible in, that liquid will constitute the continuous phase of the stable emulsion. The reason for this may be simply a matter of geometry. The more an emulsifying molecule is immersed in the phase outside the droplets, the more it blocks the droplets from each other. If most of the molecule is buried in the droplet, then not much of it is doing the desired work of guarding the droplet surface. Only one small corner of the cholesterol molecule can be ionized and so interact with water molecules; the bulk of it consists of nonpolar hydrocarbon rings. Lecithin, on the other hand, has a larger water-soluble head and so can stabilize oil-in-water systems. Egg yolk, then, contains substances both favorable and unfavorable to the formation of emulsified sauces, and so is not an unqualified help.

Emulsifiers? Phospholipid lecithin? Colloids? Molecular structure? You know, one of the coauthors on this book always has maintained that cooking is applied organic chemistry, and reading the entire eight-page section on béarnaise chemistry from which the above passage was taken can be very convincing. Most cooks are unaware of the molecules and ions that are slamming into each other in their saucepans, which causes no difficulty if they take the time to understand and master the techniques of sauce construction. This is precisely Point's message—sauces are simple if you know what you are doing.

We say construction because most sauces are "built" on a base, hence the reason the French call stocks (the base of many sauces) "fonds," or foundations. As with many things in culinary history, sauces have changed a great deal, but as early as the third or fifth century A.D., Apicius gave instructions for sauces which would be similar to our contemporary condiments. However, the medieval late-winter practice of using spice-laden camouflage to mask the increasingly unappetizing taste of dwindling fall meat supplies is fortunately now a memory. Refrigeration, sanitary meat inspection, and modern curing methods have made possible a ready supply of meat, poultry, fish, and game throughout the developed world. As Escoffier said, it is no longer the case that "la sauce fait passer le poisson."

Aside from the dish and pot washers who are the most important people in the kitchen, if I were allowed only one other person from the brigade, it would be a saucier. (Actually the saucier is even more important than the executive chef, but don't pass that on to Brian Puhle, or he'll want a raise.) Point's musical analogy is apt; a great kitchen is like an orchestra, and the saucier, a soloist. And, like the soloist, whose interpretation of a classic passage can bring the audience to its feet or send it packing for the exits, so can the saucier work magic that will have a line of patrons reaching out into the street or produce mediocrity that will grow cobwebs on the reservations telephone. This is no exaggeration. The quality of a kitchen—at home, the Homestead, or any other establishment—is greatly revealed by its sauces. About now, you are saying to yourself, all well and good, Chef, but I am neither an organic chemist nor a prima donna saucier, so what hope is there for me?

This is one instance where patience is its own reward. If you will take the time to master the fundamentals, you will be well on the way to building up an impressive repertoire of sauces. And, who knows, you may be an undiscovered talent—if so, send me your resumé. No doubt about it, some sauces are tricky, some are time-consuming and complex, but all are rewarding and can be mastered. Part of this mastery does involve learning kitchen chemistry, so you know why egg yolks scramble, sugar caramelizes, or oil and vinegar separate. But in this classroom, experience is the best teacher, and your eyes, mouth, nose, and common sense, the students. In time you will not only make Sauce Béarnaise, but also discover that by keeping a careful eye on the egg yolk mixture as it cooks, you can make thin or thick sauce depending upon its purpose. But, all in due course. First, the drawing board.

We referred earlier to construction because it is useful to think of "building" sauces. Like structures which stand because they are built according to certain architectural principles, successful sauces follow specific procedures. The nave vaults of Beauvais cathedral fell from their magnificent 158-foot height in 1284 because the builders had ignored a basic support principle, and hollandaise will curdle every time if you exceed the capacity of the egg yolks to absorb butter. But the structural analogy applies in a deeper sense. Catherine de' Medici's cooks made substantial revisions in French sauce making, but the establishment of a "system" came after the Revolution of 1789. First, Carême set forth four sauces—béchamel, velouté, espagnole, and allemande—as the base from which all others could be made. In 1902, Escoffier added hollandaise and tomate, revised espagnole and allemande as *fumets*, and derived from this group of five a comprehensive French system of two hundred sauces. In fact, with ill-disguised jealousy, the English would snivel and dismiss these sauces as made necessary only by the inferior quality of French meat, poultry, and fish. With the possible exception of Italy, however, which tends to favor fresh tomato-based sauces, most western European countries have accorded the French classification a place in their cuisine.

Back to structure and also the Homestead. As we have noted, the French system begins with certain foundations as bases. You may want to think of these as being like the footings under your house because they support the structure of the sauce. (Unlike footings, however, they better not have the color or consistency of concrete.) Stocks are made from scraps, trimmings, and bones either used as is or browned for brown stocks. Meat, game, and poultry stocks are simmered with vegetables and herbs at some length—four to five hours or more—to release their flavors and to thicken as gelatin is released and water evaporates. Fish stock is the sole exception to the long simmering rule. About half an hour yields the gelatin—beyond that time the stock will tend to turn bitter. In all instances, the more slowly the stock is brought to a simmer, the clearer it and subsequent sauces will be. When sufficiently reduced, the stocks are run through fine strainers to remove any impurities and then allowed to cool to congeal the fat for easy removal. That is about all we have to say about stocks except for two pointers.

First, water. At the Homestead we are blessed with pure water from our own mountain watershed. If your water is treated with numerous chemicals, we would advise you to use the spring water available at most grocery stores. Because stocks are reduced through simmering, chemicals become concentrated and can add unpleasant flavors to the final sauce. Second, the question of storage. We make stock continuously—some is used in sauces the day it is made and some becomes the basis for further refinements such as demi-glace or consommé—but you are probably wondering what to do with the three and one-half quarts of stock you have left after drawing off the two cups you needed for the recipe. The answer is as close as your freezer. Using plastic containers, put the stock up in one-, two-, or four-cup quantities. When it is frozen, unmold it, put it in heavy plastic wrap, and keep it frozen until needed. This way it will last for months.

But, be sure to label it well—it would be a real shame to pull out fish stock to make a Sauce Suprême for your chicken breasts.

Now that your stocks are made, the question is how to thicken them so they will be able to support the next step of sauce making. Thinking again of construction, one might call this the "framing" stage, in which the network holding the sauce together is constructed. Apicius used pieces of bread and others used raw flour (and some still do) before the properties of cooked flour were understood, but now we have an extraordinary variety of agents from which to choose. The French system guides these decisions, depending upon whether the sauce is to be white or dark. Lighter colored sauces often call for a white or blond roux prepared by cooking butter and flour together whereas dark sauces use demi-glace, a further reduction of the basic stock with aromatic vegetables and bones. In addition to these two classic routes, we have included several others. Arrowroot is tasteless, requires no cooking, and can be added at the last minute to give body and a limpid, deep appearance. Cornstarch, like flour, comes from grain and has to be simmered in the sauce to remove the raw taste. Both arrowroot and cornstarch congeal as they cool, so you should always make sure your plates are warmed and that you use only enough to thicken your sauce—otherwise you will end up with an unintended chaud-froid de quelque chose on your guests' plates and a sure invitation for any of the younger set to make the inevitable and unkind comparison to Jello.

Glace de viande, egg yolk and cream liaison, and crème fraîche are also excellent last minute additions. Glace is prepared by slowly reducing demi-glace without any vegetables. Usually it is at least a two-to-one reduction so one quart will yield two cups. Glace—which also freezes well—is just the thing to have up your sleeve when you have deglazed your sauté pan with wine or wine vinegar and want to drop in a tablespoon of concentrated flavor and color before adding the final enrichment. An egg yolk and cream liaison is the traditional way to produce a satiny finish in a cream soup or sauces such as Allemande or Suprême. A note of caution: add the hot liquid ever so slowly so as not to curdle the yolks. Ah, crème fraîche—the saucier's accomplice—a French kitchen staple. Finally, it has come out of the Mason jar into the American dairy case as a gourmet item. A real workhorse, it eclipses cream for finishing sauces because it does not curdle under high heat, and has about one-half as many calories as butter. These features also make crème fraîche a superb topping for broiling delicacies like chicken breasts and fish fillets because its whey layer protects and bastes at the same time. Equally important, the lightly fermented, slightly nutty taste makes it more interesting than cream in sauces, dressings, and even *tout seul* with fresh raspberries or blueberries. Vive la France!

Before filling out our house of sauces, we would like to go on record about the issue of fat and the "nouvelle cuisine." In the 1960s "fat-bashing" became a fad and it was de rigueur to criticize *la grande cuisine* and to eschew its excesses. We do not advocate stuffing upon stuffing, sauce upon sauce, and fat for its own sake—solely to obscure the taste of what is underneath it all. However, as historians trying to make their own case are wont to do, culinary writers of the 1960s tended to treat the cuisine of earlier periods as if it were always a matter of choice and not necessity. Consider, for example, that only at the beginning of this century did Escoffier have refrigeration at his disposal. Then consider the lack of electricity, reliable gas service or hot and cold running water, not to mention ventilating and air conditioning systems to evacuate smoke and fumes and maintain various zones of the kitchen at proper temperatures for cook and food alike. Nowadays we take fresh ingredients for granted, but Escoffier could not count on refrigerated overnight delivery because there were no refrigerated trucks and railway cars—let alone telephones with which to place the orders. In short, before decrying the "excesses" of our forebears, let us be mindful of their constraints. Would we have done differently?

Back to fat. As with most prolific writers, it is easy to find what one wants in Escoffier, hence his statement, "La Grande Cuisine demands butter, butter, and more butter." Similarly, Point said, "Butter. Give me butter and then more butter." However, in examining their professional activity we find the immediate roots of the "nouvelle cuisine." Escoffier devised and called for sauces using stocks and reductions derived from fish, meat, poultry, and vegetables. His goal was to retain the appeal of classical cuisine while eliminating large quantities of ingredients too rich for daily consumption. Point's genius brought these changes to fruition and inspired students and disciples to further refine them. All of us who started to come into our own professionally in the 1960s were directly or indirectly influenced by Point, but one must realize that any movement has extremists and showmen. I disagree with those who say roux should be out of the dictionary or that we should eliminate butter and cream. To be sure, "gratuitous" fat must be eliminated wherever possible, and I applaud the development of leaner meat and poultry. But I defend the use of two tablespoons of roux in a quart of stock to produce the "velvety" texture for which velouté is named, and, to carry the point to its ridiculous conclusion, when enriched with cream or crème fraîche as in Sauce Suprême, it yields servings with an average of thirty calories each—less than one-third those in a tablespoon of butter. Similarly, the amount of butter in a serving of Sauce Madère is one-sixth to one-quarter of a tablespoon, or sixteen to twenty-five calories. For the sake of comparison this is less than one-third those contained in a three-ounce glass of wine or one-tenth to one-sixth of those in a two-ounce scotch and soda. One must make choices. The defense rests.

Now where were we? Oh yes, the rest of the house of sauces. We have included some graphics to help you visualize the relationships among the sauces in the first section of the chapter. Figure I shows the three simplest groups of light-colored sauces—béchamel, velouté de veau, and velouté de poulet. In each, a roux is combined with either milk or stock to produce the basic sauce, and subsequent enrichments yield, respectively, sauces Mornay, Allemande, and Suprême.

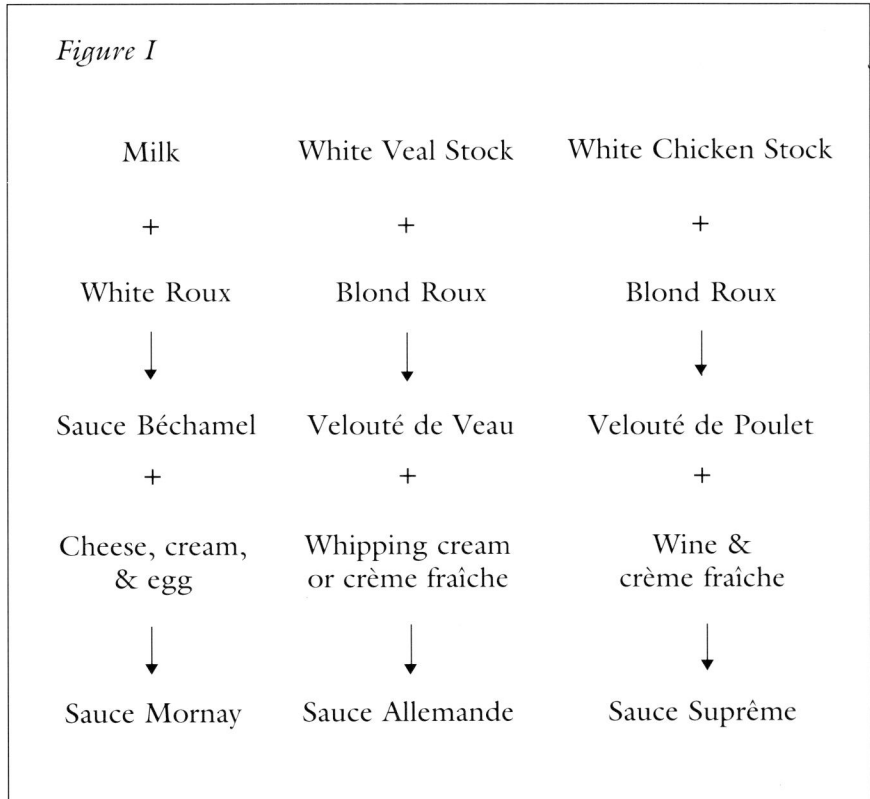

Figure I

Milk	White Veal Stock	White Chicken Stock
+	+	+
White Roux	Blond Roux	Blond Roux
↓	↓	↓
Sauce Béchamel	Velouté de Veau	Velouté de Poulet
+	+	+
Cheese, cream, & egg	Whipping cream or crème fraîche	Wine & crème fraîche
↓	↓	↓
Sauce Mornay	Sauce Allemande	Sauce Suprême

Because the fish sauces are more complicated, they are displayed separately in Figure II. Again, roux and stock combine to yield a velouté, which with simple enrichment becomes Sauce Vin Blanc. Notice, however, the three other sauces which proceed directly from fish stock. Two, Nantua and Américaine, have only the slightest touch of roux, and the Lobster Butter and Cream Sauce receives a small enrichment of cream and butter at the end. All three derive their body from the shrimp or lobster that is simmered in them, so they are slightly akin to the demi-glaces we are about to discuss.

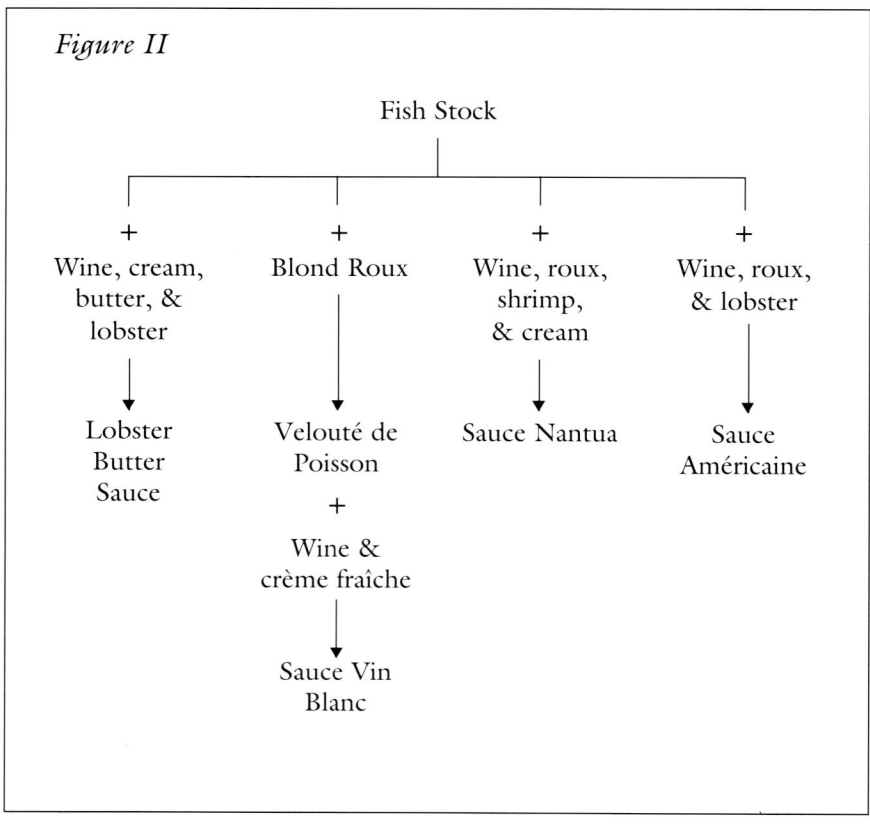

Figure III is devoted to the sauces built upon a brown stock. Traditionally made from beef, veal, or a mixture of the two, brown stock can also be made from lamb or game for recipes such as Curry of Lamb Madras, Scotch Lamb Stew, or Medallions of Venison with Juniper Cream Sauce. Pork does not produce a satisfactory stock. For all but the most delicate veal or pork recipes, a brown stock made from beef and beef bones will suffice.

Demi-glace Brun I, however, should be made with veal bones. Adding Browned or Roasted Flour to the ingredients for Demi-glace I produces Demi-glace Brun II—a variation I prefer for recipes with long braising times. In both instances, simmering brown stock with the bones, wine, vegetables, and tomato paste produces a type of espagnole (minus the mirepoix), which was in Carême's classification. A rich, dark brown sauce, demi-glace is a solid platform on which to construct numerous distinguished elaborations. We have already discussed glace de viande, which you can see is a continued reduction of Demi-glace Brun I. Of the four simple sauces shown, two, Madère and Marchand de Vins, serve in turn as bases for compound sauces Périgueux and Bordelaise, respectively.

Including Basic Curry Sauce, which is made with velouté derived from the basis for the curry, you now have a group of nineteen sauces based on stocks. This collection will see you through all of the fish, poultry, game, and meat recipes in this

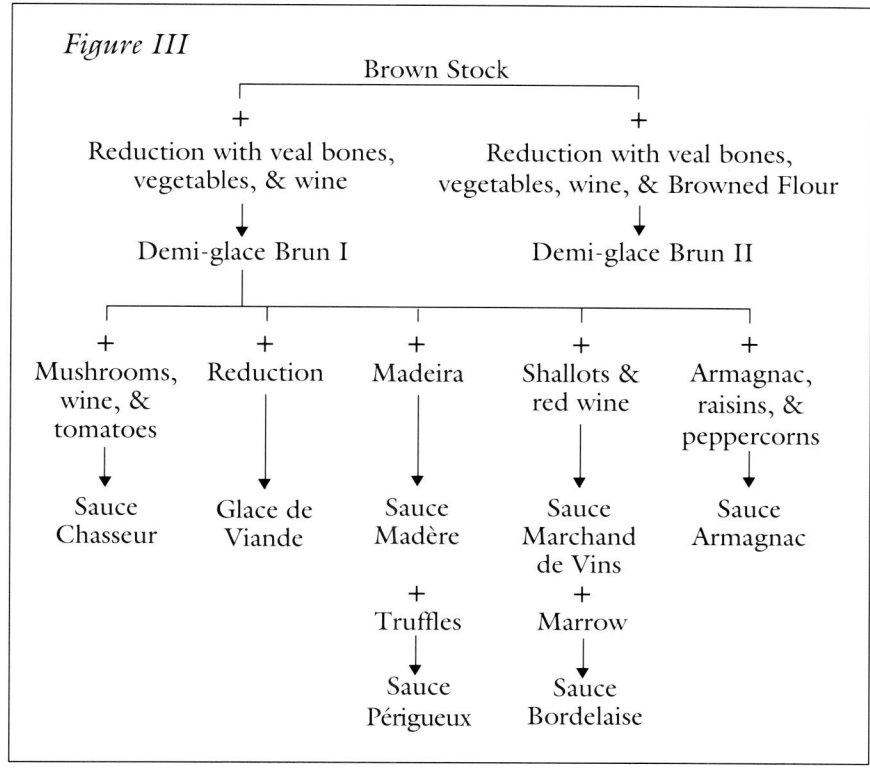

Figure III

book, and should serve as a useful resource as you venture into developing your own variations.

And now, the x-rated section of the chapter—sauces based on inverted cream emulsion and free oleic acid—a.k.a. butter and oil. Seasoned cold butters, hot butter or butter and egg yolk sauce, and mayonnaise occupy an esteemed and historic place in cuisine. However, if they are medically verboten, we urge you to consult the many books available with low-calorie alternatives. Otherwise, used in moderation and paired with the right companion, these preparations will extend your repertoire immeasurably. There is but one rule—use the best unsalted butter you can find.

Six simple recipes comprise the first set—two cold butters and four cooked preparations. Grilled meats and fish often pose a problem at serving time—especially for light meals or occasions when another sauce also appears in the meal. Here we propose two solutions, either the elegant simplicity of the traditional maître d'hôtel, or the more colorful and complex café de Paris. Both can be prepared well in advance—solving yet another problem for the busy "staff."

Also in the "à la minute" category is the quartet of quickly prepared cooked butters. Based on combining lemon juice with butter, they are excellent for sautéed fish, veal, and chicken. Our favorite, Gremolada (de rigueur with ossobuco), is especially colorful and a natural for sautéed scallops.

The nine sauces comprising the next group require a bit more in the way of technique and preparation time, but the only thing to worry about is allowing the finished sauce to overheat and separate. Among the nine you will find a diversity of flavors and colors ranging from the restrained tang of the venerable beurre blanc to raspberry, orange curry, basil, mixed green herbs, and four vegetable bases—leek, asparagus, tomato, and the flash of red bell peppers. These sauces complement an astounding array of dishes—seafood mousses and timbales, poached or broiled fish and poultry, and the ever popular pasta.

Well, exam time has come. Get out the whisks, heavy-bottomed saucepans (double boilers for the faint hearted), and mixing bowls—water-in-oil emulsion day is here. Colloids and phospholipids are going to slug it out in your kitchen, right before your very eyes. Branches of the same family (one hot, one cold) spring from the same basic principle—in both you are trying to hoodwink egg yolks into accepting large quantities of two things they really do not like at all—butter or oil. Gentle persuasion is the key, droplets at first, then a thin stream, followed by increasing amounts until the emulsion is complete. If either one should curdle, don't head for the lifeboats, we have given you a remedy in each instance. One last thought. Although you can use bottled mayonnaise in a pinch in some of the mayonnaise-based variations, never, never, *never* yield to the temptation to use hollandaise-based sauce mixes. Ersatz simply will not do.

The hollandaise group is composed of a basic recipe and four classical variations, three rather simple ones well suited to eggs, light fish dishes, and vegetables, and the slightly more complicated fourth, béarnaise—that great companion to grilled meat. Similarly, the basic mayonnaise recipe is followed by eleven variations, whose applications run the gamut from hot vegetables to cold seafood. Several of them make excellent dips for raw vegetables, and you will delight in the two versions specifically designated for seafood—no more shrimp cocktails with the tired old workhorse made of ketchup and horseradish. The section closes with a green herb mayonnaise that will make your cold poached salmon the talk of the buffet crowd.

The mention of fruited sauces may immediately conjure up visions of turkey and cranberry sauce; however, to show their versatility, we have included four rather different recipes. We serve Cumberland Sauce with our pâté maison, and we have included it here, but I also want you to try the alternative Rhubarb Sauce, which can be served either hot or cold. If you are looking for new sauces for roast chicken, roast duckling, or baked ham, the last two fruited sauces, one with passion fruit and the other, a pear brandy creation of our head saucier, Brian Puhle, are excellent candidates. These especially tasty sauces are ideally suited to low-fat diets.

It may seem to you that we compiled the final section of the chapter by cleaning out the attic because it appears to be a grab bag of miscellany. Au contraire, we have actually tried to provide a small collection of Homestead favorites. The first two are flavored vinegars, one specific to oysters and clams on the half shell and the other a raspberry-based preparation which we call for in two recipes. Incidentally, once you make it, commercial versions will pale in comparison. Just by coincidence, the salad dressings open with a poppyseed and raspberry vinegar recipe. This is followed by an olive oil and lemon juice version of "o and v" which, along with its variations, you may find a refreshing alternative to what you currently make.

Rather different is the hot bacon dressing from the Grille. More tangy and complex than most similar preparations, this is perfect for a fresh spinach salad. Vinaigrette and French dressings follow this one, but we must caution you that they will take more time than you are accustomed to spending on such recipes. But we must also caution you that the rewarding flavor—so rich and complex—is addictive. Two cream-style dressings follow: our version of roquefort and a unique Homestead recipe featuring buttermilk, both of which have a real affinity for watercress. And finally, a maverick. If you must have a ketchup-based seafood sauce, at least try the two popular ones from our cocktail buffet I have included here.

Well, Court Bouillon to Homestead Cocktail Sauce, how far we seem to have come from Point, and yet not really far at all. He said, "Cuisine is not invariable like a Codex formula. But one must guard against tampering with the essential bases." In this chapter you have a sample of the "essential bases" from the culinary archives, and we have also tried to show how one builds on these bases. Now, as with the rest of us, your only limits are your resources and your imagination. Bonne chance et bonnes sauces.

Stocks

Court Bouillon

Court Bouillon is a versatile medium for preparing fish and shellfish, whether served hot or cold. Suitable for poaching large fish such as salmon and bass when they are to be enjoyed hot, it is equally good for cooking shellfish and crabs when they will be offered cold. If the fish or shellfish is being served cold, be sure to let it cool in the bouillon.

Yields 4 quarts

4 quarts (4 L) cold water
1 large or 2 medium onions, sliced
4 shallots, sliced
1/3 bay leaf
1 clove
1 celery stalk, sliced
6 white peppercorns, crushed
1 parsley sprig
A pinch of salt (optional)

Recommended equipment

An 8-quart (8 L) stockpot.

Bring water to a boil and add all ingredients. Reduce heat and simmer for 10 minutes before using.

If using for live lobster, add 1/2 cup (118 ml) white vinegar to broth for a 1 1/2- to 2-pound (675 to 900 g) lobster and simmer for 15 minutes.

A popular French preparation for live trout is "truite au bleu." The fish must be live or still wet and slippery with coat intact and must be handled very gently while killing and cleaning. Only freshly killed trout will turn blue, and the best results I had were with rainbow trout. To cook in the court bouillon, add the white vinegar as for lobster and simmer the trout for 5 to 6 minutes (for a 14- to 16-ounce fish). If serving hot, present fish directly from the broth and sauce them with Beurre Noisette or Beurre au Citron *(see pages 84, 83)*.

Fish Stock

Yields 1 quart

2 1/2 pounds (1125 g) fish bones and trimmings
1 onion, sliced
1 celery stalk, cut coarsely
1/4 bay leaf
1/8 teaspoon thyme
1 parsley sprig
1 tablespoon (15 g) butter
6 crushed peppercorns
1 pinch salt (optional)
4 cups (950 ml) cold water
1 cup (235 ml) dry white wine

Recommended equipment

An 8-quart (8 L) or larger stainless steel stockpot, large fine-mesh sieve.

Rinse fish bones in cold water, drain, and put them into the stockpot. Simmer fish trimmings, vegetables, herbs, and seasoning in butter over low heat for 3 to 4 minutes, stirring occasionally. Add water and wine and bring *slowly* to a light boil. Reduce heat and simmer for 30 minutes, skimming frequently. Remove from heat and strain. Refrigerate or freeze as needed.

❧

Aluminum stockpots *cannot* be used for fish stock because the metal and the ingredients interact to distort the flavor of the stock. If a stainless steel pot is not available, an enamel-lined casserole will serve equally well. Use only bones, trimmings, and heads from white-fleshed fish such as halibut, flounder, snapper, etc. Trimmings from dark-fleshed fish are too oily for use in stocks.

Unlike other stocks, fish stock does not improve by simmering longer than thirty minutes, it merely becomes bitter.

If the stock is to be used in a soup, replace the wine with an additional quart of cold water.

❧ *White Chicken Stock*

Yields 2 quarts

2 leeks (white part only)
2 1/2 to 3 pounds (1125 to 1350 g) chicken parts (necks, wings, backs, gizzards)
1 large or 2 medium onions, sliced
4 celery stalks, sliced in 1-inch (2 1/2 cm) pieces
4 large sprigs parsley
1 clove
1 bay leaf
1/2 teaspoon freshly crushed white or black peppercorns
4 quarts (4 L) cold water

Recommended equipment

An 8-quart (8 L) stockpot with lid, colander, large fine-mesh sieve, large mixing bowl.

Wash the leeks under running cold water, being careful to remove any sand and grit, and slice. Place all ingredients in stockpot. Bring *slowly* to a boil (the slower this process, the clearer the stock—this may take as long as 30 minutes). Reduce heat and simmer slowly, partially covered, for at least 3 hours. At the end of the simmering period, lift chicken and vegetables out of the pot and place them in the colander set over the mixing bowl. Measure out stock and return it to the stockpot for additional simmering if the amount is much greater than 2 quarts. When sufficiently reduced, pour stock through the sieve into the bowl and cool to room temperature. Then cover the bowl with plastic wrap and refrigerate overnight to solidify the fat layer. Skim fat from top and refrigerate or freeze in desired quantities. Refrigerated stock will keep for about two weeks, frozen stock for many months.

❧

Chicken stock may be substituted with no difficulty for white veal stock if necessary. Parts for chicken stock are easy to come by—simply keep a plastic bag of them in the freezer and add them whenever you prepare chicken.

Brown Chicken Stock

Yields 2 quarts

2 1/2 to 3 pounds (1125 to 1350 g) chicken parts (necks, wings, backs, gizzards)
2 teaspoons peanut oil
2 leeks (white part only)
1 large or 2 medium onions, sliced
4 celery stalks, sliced in 1-inch (2 1/2 cm) pieces
2 large sprigs parsley
1 clove
1 bay leaf
1/2 teaspoon freshly crushed white or black peppercorns
4 quarts (4 L) White Chicken Stock *(see page 61)*

Recommended equipment

A 12-inch (30 cm) enameled cast-iron baking dish or lined copper plat à sauter, wooden spatula, slotted spoon, 8-quart (7 1/2 L) stockpot with lid, colander, large fine-mesh sieve, large mixing bowl.

Preheat oven to 350F (177C).

Sauté the chicken parts in hot peanut oil in the baking dish or plat à sauter over medium high heat, stirring occasionally with the wooden spatula, until they are sizzling in the pan. Rinse the leeks under cold running water, slice, add them with the other vegetables and seasonings to the chicken parts, stirring them in, and sauté for a few minutes. Then remove the pan from heat and set it into the oven for the parts to finish browning. Stir them occasionally to avoid any burned spots that will give the stock a bitter taste.

When the parts are brown, remove them from the oven, and lift them with the slotted spoon into the stockpot. Remove all grease from the sauté pan, set it over medium high heat, add 1 cup (235 ml) chicken stock, and bring to a simmer. Deglaze the pan by scraping up all the brown bits while the stock simmers for a few minutes. Then add the sauté pan contents to the stockpot and set the pot over medium heat. Add the remaining chicken stock to the pot, bring slowly to a boil, and reduce heat so that the stock simmers gently, partially covered, for about 2 hours.

When the simmering is finished, lift chicken and vegetables out of the pot and place them in the colander set over the mixing bowl. Measure out stock and return it to the stockpot for additional simmering if the amount is much greater than 2 quarts. When sufficiently reduced, pour stock through the sieve into the bowl and cool to room temperature. Cover bowl with plastic wrap and refrigerate it overnight to solidify the fat layer. Skim fat from top and refrigerate or freeze in desired quantities. Refrigerated stock will keep for about two weeks, frozen stock for many months.

Brown duck or pheasant stock is made using the same procedure. You can supplement the duck or pheasant parts with chicken bones, if needed.

🍂 White Veal Stock

Yields 1 1/2 to 1 3/4 quarts

Follow the procedure for White Chicken Stock *(see page 61)*. Substitute 2 to 2 1/2 pounds (900 to 1125 g) veal bones cut into small pieces and 1 pound (450 g) veal trimmings or veal knuckle for the chicken. Omit the leeks. Simmer the stock for at least 6 hours, skimming the scum from the surface from time to time.

🍂 Brown Stock

Yields approximately 2 quarts

10 pounds (4500 g) soup bones (either all veal or half veal and half beef)
2 large onions, sliced
2 large tomatoes, chopped (this is a good use for overripe tomatoes)
1 medium carrot, sliced
1 celery stalk, sliced in 1-inch (2 1/2 cm) pieces
1 garlic clove
2 sprigs of fresh parsley
1 bay leaf
1 pinch of thyme
6 black peppercorns, crushed
1 cup (235 ml) dry white wine
4 quarts (4 L) cold water
Peanut oil for greasing pan

Recommended equipment

An 8-quart (8 L) stainless steel stockpot with lid, heavy roasting pan, colander, large fine-mesh sieve, large mixing bowl.

Preheat oven to 450F (232C). Lightly grease the roasting pan with peanut oil, and strew the bones around in it. Place the pan in the oven, and when the bones are lightly browned, reduce the heat to 350F (177C). Watch the bones carefully to prevent them from burning or even turning *dark* brown because this will produce a bitter-tasting stock. Add all the vegetables, herbs, and spices, continuing to roast for about 20 minutes, stirring frequently. Drain off all grease and deglaze the pan with the white wine to loosen all of the brown bits. These are juices from the bones that add excellent flavor and color to the stock.

Transfer the bones, vegetables, and seasonings to the stockpot and add the water. If necessary, add more water to cover the bones. Bring the contents to a boil *very slowly* (this may require as much as 30 minutes) to ensure that your stock stays as clear as possible. If it is brought to a boil too quickly, the stock will assume a cloudiness which is very difficult to remove. Once the boil is reached, immediately reduce heat to low, or a level where it will maintain the stock at a simmer. Set lid ajar so that some steam escapes as the stock cooks. Simmer until reduced by one-half, skimming if necessary. This will probably take 5 to 6 hours.

At the end of this period, lift meat, bones, and vegetables out of pot and place them in the colander set over the mixing bowl. Measure out the stock and return it to the stockpot for additional simmering if the amount is much greater than 2 quarts. When sufficiently reduced, pour stock

through sieve into bowl and cool to room temperature. Place in refrigerator, covered with plastic wrap, overnight. This will solidify the fat layer, making it easy to remove. Skim fat layer from top and store stock in refrigerator or freezer in desired quantities. Refrigerated stock will keep for about two weeks, frozen stock for many months.

Lamb or game stock can be made in the same way, with appropriate substitutions for the beef and veal. When making game stock, add 4 crushed juniper berries.

Thickening Agents

In this section we have listed a number of different agents which serve as intermediate or finishing steps in the preparation of other sauces. Some require cooking, some no cooking, and one (glace de viande) is made by slowly reducing brown stock. As with stocks, roux and glace de viande can be frozen in convenient quantities for later use. Remember that glace is concentrated and that a recipe may call for one or two tablespoons at the last minute, so, once prepared and frozen, a cup of glace de viande may last a long time.

Arrowroot and Cornstarch

Although not "recipes," these two thickening agents deserve brief mention in their own right. While similar, they have separate characteristics which the cook should understand. To use either of them, you should add enough cold water or other liquid to make a smooth, runny paste. Then whisk the paste into the simmering sauce and cook for several minutes. Cornstarch should be boiled but arrowroot must never be boiled—it will break down. Cornstarch, if uncooked, has a taste which distorts the final flavor of the sauce.

Arrowroot is a root starch from the West Indian *Maranta arundinacea* plant and is highly digestible. It is especially useful in recipes which require clear sauces such as the Homestead Passion Fruit Sauce (see page 101).

Derived from corn, cornstarch provides a shiny gloss when added to sauces. Although it does not produce as clear a sauce as arrowroot, it does tend to hold together a bit longer. It is used extensively in Chinese cooking and sweet and sour sauces.

Browned or Roasted Flour

We like to use browned flour for Demi-glace Brun II when the application calls for large quantities to be cooked for a long time. Using browned flour in this instance prevents the accumulation of grease on the top of the cooking liquid which occurs with butter-based roux. You must be careful while roasting the flour to pay close attention so that it does not burn or scorch. Once roasted, the flour will keep for weeks, stored at room temperature in tightly sealed glass jars.

Recommended equipment: A baking sheet or pie pan.

Preheat oven to 350F (177C). Spread a layer of flour approximately 3/4 inch (2 cm) deep in the pan and roast in the oven for about 30 minutes until light to medium brown, stirring frequently with a spatula.

Beurre Manié

This mixture, which is also the base for the roux which follow, is useful for last minute binding or adjusting of a sauce. Add a little at a time to a sauce with a whisk and simmer long enough for flour to be cooked—about 3 to 5 minutes.

Yields 1 cup

1/2 cup (60 g) flour
8 tablespoons (115 g) butter,
    softened at room temperature

Cream butter in a small bowl and gradually work in flour until mixture is smooth.

Roux

All three of these recipes are based upon Beurre Manié and vary only in length of cooking time and technique. In each case, use a 1 1/2-quart (1 1/2 L) saucepan and a wire whisk. Whenever a recipe calls for roux, it should be at room temperature.

WHITE ROUX

This is used primarily for a white sauce such as Béchamel or in cream soups.

1 recipe Beurre Manié *(see page 64)*

Stirring constantly with the whisk, cook over low heat for 4 to 5 minutes. The roux must not turn blond.

BLOND ROUX

I like to use blond roux for creamed chipped beef, Blanquette de Veau à l'Ancienne, and similar recipes.

1 recipe Beurre Manié *(see page 64)*

Stirring constantly with the whisk, cook over low heat for 6 to 7 minutes or until the color becomes blond.

BROWN ROUX

1 recipe Blond Roux *(see above)*

When the blond roux stage is reached, increase heat to medium and continue cooking and stirring until color becomes medium brown. This should take about 3 to 4 minutes. Let roux cool, and, if not to be used immediately, store in a tightly sealed glass jar in the refrigerator, where it will keep as long as two weeks.

Glace de Viande

Although this recipe is for meat glaze, other glazes can be prepared in the same fashion using the appropriate stock variation listed under Brown Stock. If you are going to prepare chicken glaze you should use brown chicken stock. Fish glaze would be made with fish stock.

Yields 2 cups

1 recipe Demi-glace Brun I
    (see page 75)

Recommended equipment

A 3-quart (3 L) saucepan, small fine-mesh sieve.

Over low heat simmer demi-glace until it acquires a dark brown syrupy appearance. As the sauce simmers, occasionally remove residue from the sides of the pan with a rubber spatula. It may be necessary to move the sauce to a smaller pan during the reduction. If so, strain the sauce as you do so. The entire process should require 2 to 2 1/2 hours of cooking. When finished, remove sauce from heat and allow it to cool. If not to be used immediately, freeze in convenient quantities, such as tablespoons.

Egg Yolk and Cream Liaison

This mixture is used to bind and enrich cream soups to a finished texture that is satin smooth. It also can be used in Sauce Suprême for a chicken fricassée and in Sauce Allemande for a Blanquette de Veau. Technique is crucial here because the egg yolk must not be allowed to curdle and therefore become visible as scrambled eggs! For the same reason, this liaison must not be used in recipes which have to be kept hot or be reheated.

1/4 cup (60 ml) whipping cream
1 egg yolk

In a small mixing bowl, blend ingredients with a whisk until smooth. This liaison should be used for 5 to 7 cups of soup or sauce. Whisk a small amount of the simmering soup or hot sauce into the bowl to warm the egg yolk and cream mixture.

Then gradually whisk this mixture into the soup or sauce until it is all incorporated. Do not allow it to come to the boil. When thickened slightly, remove from heat and serve immediately.

Crème Fraîche

Not really a sauce in its own right, crème fraîche is so indispensable that it almost belongs in the Batterie de Cuisine. Although not an exact replica because unpasteurized cream is unavailable in this country (unless you live on or near a dairy farm), this recipe will yield a product which is almost the "real thing." The uses of crème fraîche are so varied because of its slightly fermented flavor and its chemistry. Unlike whipping cream or heavy cream, it will not decompose under hard boiling in sauce reductions. And, because its fat content is lower than butter, it is an excellent finishing ingredient as well as a base for light sauces to accompany fish, poultry, and fresh vegetables such as asparagus and artichokes. The spirit of France will enliven your salads when you use crème fraîche in dressing recipes which call for whipping cream.

Yields 1 quart

1 quart (235 ml) whipping cream
1 tablespoon buttermilk

In a glass jar, bring cream to room temperature and combine it with the buttermilk, stirring thoroughly. Cover loosely and let the mixture stand at room temperature in a draft-free place for 6 to 8 hours (in winter this may take longer) or until thickened. Tighten cover and refrigerate. It will keep well for up to one month (depending on the freshness of the cream used to make it).

To start your next batch, use about 1 tablespoon Crème Fraîche to 1 quart of whipping cream and follow the same procedure. As with any culture you can keep it going ad infinitum.

Sauces Based on Roux or Stock

Sauce Béchamel

Named after the Lord Steward in the kitchen of Louis XIV, this sauce is a must in any kitchen—after you have made it a few times, you probably won't even bother to measure anymore.

Yields 3 cups

4 tablespoons (60 g) butter
1/4 cup (30 g) flour
3 cups (710 ml) milk
Salt
Freshly ground nutmeg
Freshly ground white pepper

Recommended equipment

Two 1 1/2-quart (1 1/2 L) saucepans, nutmeg grinder, wire whisk, small fine-mesh sieve.

In one of the saucepans, melt the butter, stir in the flour, and cook the roux over *low* heat, stirring for 4 to 5 minutes. *(Do not let roux take on color.)* Remove from heat and allow to cool. Bring milk, a dash of salt, and a few grinds of nutmeg and white pepper to a simmer and add to the cooled roux.

Return the mixture to medium heat and stir vigorously with whisk as mixture thickens, becomes smooth, and comes to the simmer. Reduce heat to low and allow to simmer for 6 to 8 minutes, stirring occasionally. Strain through the sieve if necessary.

To hold the sauce until serving time, sprinkle a few small pea-sized pieces of butter and a few drops of milk on top of the sauce to prevent the formation of a skin which you would have to remove later. A piece of greased waxed paper, with a couple of slits in it to let the steam escape, pressed onto the sauce will accomplish the same result.

Sauce Mornay

A staple of the commercial kitchen, this variation of Sauce Béchamel is used as a glaçage to give a golden brown color to a dish when it is run under the salamander (a high-speed broiler) at the last minute before serving. Sauce Mornay is usually implied when the word "gratinée" describes a vegetable such as broccoli or cauliflower. In poultry dishes, for example turkey Mornay or chicken tetrazini, the béchamel base would be replaced with a Sauce Suprême reduced to the consistency of béchamel.

Yields about 3 cups

2 cups (475 ml) Sauce Béchamel (see page 66)
3 egg yolks, blended with 1 tablespoon whipping cream
3 tablespoons grated Parmesan cheese
3 tablespoons grated Gruyère cheese
1/2 cup (118 ml) whipping cream
1 tablespoon grated Parmesan cheese

Recommended equipment

A 1 1/2-quart (1 1/2 L) saucepan, wire whisk, grater, rubber spatula.

Bring the sauce béchamel to a boil in the saucepan while stirring with the whisk. Remove from heat and reduce burner to low. When sauce has stopped bubbling, return saucepan to burner and whisk in the egg yolk and cream mixture, stirring constantly for 30 seconds. Remove from heat and add the 6 tablespoons of grated cheese, stirring until well blended. Set aside.

Preheat oven to 325F (163C) and place rack in top one-third position. Just before serving, whip the cream and fold it into the sauce with the spatula. Spread the sauce over the food in the dish and sprinkle the remaining tablespoon of Parmesan cheese on top. Bake until hot, then turn oven to broil and watch carefully until Mornay is golden brown.

If Gruyère is unavailable, Parmesan may be substituted in its entirety; however, you should use a good imported variety, as the domestic substitute can be raw tasting. This is also true of domestic Swiss cheese as compared to Gruyère.

Sauce Velouté de Poisson
Fish Velouté

Yields about 2 1/2 cups

4 cups (950 ml) Fish Stock *(see page 60)*
2 tablespoons Blond Roux *(see page 65)*
A 1 1/2- to 2-inch (3 3/4 to 5 cm) piece of lemon peel, all white removed
Salt and freshly ground white pepper
Knorr Aromat

Recommended equipment

Two 3-quart (3 L) saucepans, one with a lid; wire whisk.

If the stock is freshly made, keep it warm in a saucepan. If frozen, melt in a saucepan and keep warm. Put roux in the other saucepan and heat gently over low heat. Remove from heat and allow to cool slightly. Slowly pour the warm stock into the roux while stirring constantly with the whisk. Return to medium heat, stirring until velouté starts to simmer, add lemon peel, partially cover, and maintain a low simmer for 45 minutes. Skim occasionally if necessary. Velouté should thicken only slightly, so add some more hot stock if it seems too thick. Remove lemon peel. Adjust seasoning with salt, freshly ground white pepper, and a dash of Aromat.

Sauce Vin Blanc de Poisson
White Wine Fish Sauce

Yields about 3 cups

2 teaspoons chopped shallots
1/8 teaspoon freshly crushed white pepper
1/2 cup (118 ml) dry white wine
1 recipe Sauce Velouté de Poisson *(see above)*
2/3 cup (160 ml) whipping cream or Crème Fraîche *(see page 66)*

Recommended equipment

A small chef's knife, mortar and pestle, 3-quart (3 L) saucepan, wire whisk, fine-mesh sieve.

Chop the shallot, crush the pepper, put them in the saucepan, and add the white wine. Set the pan over medium heat, bring to a simmer, and cook until the liquid is reduced by one-half. Add the sauce velouté and whipping cream or crème fraîche and, stirring with the whisk, bring to a simmer over medium heat. Then reduce heat to low, and cook at a low simmer for 15 to 20 minutes or until the sauce thickens slightly and has a silky texture. Strain through the fine-mesh sieve into a clean saucepan or bowl and either keep warm over very low heat for immediate use or dot the surface with bits of butter to prevent the formation of a skin layer.

If you wish to enrich the basic sauce, at the end of the cooking time, whisk in 1 egg yolk which has been well blended with several tablespoons of whipping cream and remove immediately from heat. Do not allow to boil.

❧ Lobster Butter and Cream Sauce

Because of the lobster, fish stock, and wine base, you could think of this sauce as a distant cousin of the sauces Nantua and Américaine which follow. However, the complex aromatic intensity of Américaine differs greatly from the direct and simple richness of this sauce. As you will notice, no herbs and very little cognac are used, providing no distraction from the lobster. Quite simply, it is a mouth-watering delicacy you will believe only after you have made it for yourself. Having tasted it, the pleasure in your accomplishment will completely eclipse all of the work (and expense) in its preparation.

My toque is off to our chief saucier, Brian Puhle, who created this sauce for a Homestead Board of Directors meeting, at which it accompanied a salmon soufflé. Other serving possibilities include mousse of sole or bass and baked halibut or turbot. For an especially elegant presentation, use it to accompany Quenelles de Saumon.

Yields 6 servings

- 1/2 medium onion
- 1/2 small garlic clove
- 1/2 celery stalk
- 2 medium tomatoes
- 3 live lobsters, weighing 1 to 1 1/2 pounds (450 to 675 g) each
- 1/8 teaspoon freshly ground black pepper
- A dash of cayenne pepper
- 1/4 cup (60 ml) Cognac
- 4 cups (950 ml) Fish Stock *(see page 60)*
- 1/2 cup (118 ml) dry white wine
- 1 1/2 cups (355 ml) whipping cream
- 8 tablespoons (115 g) butter, softened at room temperature
- Olive oil for sautéing

Recommended equipment

A large chef's knife or cleaver, two 1-quart (1 L) bowls, 8-quart (8 L) stockpot or heavy-bottomed saucepan with lid, colander, wooden spoon, 1 1/2-quart (1 1/2 L) saucepan, large fine-mesh sieve, wire whisk.

Prepare the vegetables. Peel the onion and garlic and chop them coarsely. Chop the celery coarsely and reserve all three in one bowl. Halve and then quarter the tomatoes. Reserve pieces in the other bowl with their juice.

Film stockpot or saucepan with olive oil to a depth of 1/8 inch (1/3 cm) and set pan over high heat. While oil is heating, one by one, grasp the lobster tails and, using a twisting motion, separate them from the body. Drop the tails into a colander, rinse under cold running water, and reserve. With the chef's knife or cleaver, remove the claws from the body and crack them. (If you are worried about the claws, leave the rubber bands on until they are sautéing and then snip them and remove them.) Slit the body down the center, clean out intestines, and cut the body into 2- to 3-inch (5 to 7 1/2 cm) pieces and add with claws to the hot oil.

With the point of the knife, split the tails, reduce heat to medium high and sauté for about 5 minutes, stirring with the wooden spoon. When all the lobster shells have turned red, add the reserved onion, celery, and garlic along with the black pepper and cayenne. Reduce heat to medium and sauté for 2 minutes. Add brandy and flambé briefly *(see page 569)*, then add tomatoes, fish stock, and white wine. Bring to a boil, stirring occasionally, and then reduce heat and simmer, covered, for about 1 1/2 hours.

While the lobster mixture is simmering, reduce whipping cream in the smaller saucepan over low heat to 1/2 cup (118 ml) and reserve.

At the end of the cooking time, remove the lobster mixture from heat and strain through the sieve into a bowl. Clean out the saucepan, return the liquid to it, and simmer, uncovered, until reduced to 1/2 cup. Remove from heat and reserve until just before serving time.

When you are ready to finish the sauce, warm the lobster reduction and whisk in the reduced cream. When well blended, whisk in the soft butter a tablespoon at a time. When all the butter has been incorporated, taste the sauce, and if necessary season with pepper and incorporate a small additional amount of soft butter.

For the most appealing color contrast when saucing mousse or fish, do not ladle over, but rather *surround* it with the lobster sauce. When buying the lobsters for this sauce, try to find "culls," which are less expensive because they are missing one claw.

Sauce Nantua

This recipe and the following Américaine are both worthy entries in your seafood sauce repertoire. Sauce Nantua (which is traditionally made with crayfish) is easier to prepare and less costly because it uses shrimp instead of lobster. Its color gives special appeal to poached flounder fillets or a quenelle of pike. The peeled shrimp may be used as a garnish or served with the sauce over Saffron Rice.

Yields about 2 cups, for 6 servings

1 tablespoon olive oil
2 pounds (900 g) raw shrimp in the shell, heads removed
2 tablespoons chopped shallots
1/3 garlic clove
2 sprigs fresh parsley
1 tablespoon tomato paste
1/4 bay leaf
A pinch of thyme
2 1/2 cups (590 ml) Fish Stock *(see page 60)*
1/2 cup (118 ml) dry white wine
1/4 teaspoon paprika
A dash of cayenne pepper
1 tablespoon Blond Roux *(see page 65)*
1 cup (235 ml) heavy cream
2 tablespoons Cognac
Salt and freshly ground white pepper

Recommended equipment

A 4- to 5-quart (4 to 5 L) heavy-bottomed saucepan, colander, shrimp deveiner, wire whisk, large fine-mesh sieve.

Heat olive oil in saucepan over high heat until very hot. Add shrimp and sauté over medium high heat, stirring occasionally, for 5 minutes. Add shallots, garlic, parsley, tomato paste, bay leaf, and thyme, sauté for 1 minute, and then add fish stock, white wine, paprika, and cayenne. Simmer for 10 minutes. Remove about two-thirds of the shrimp, place in colander, and cool them under running cold water. With the deveiner, remove shells and return them to the sauce. Rinse the peeled shrimp to remove any shell or vein residue and reserve them for garnish or another purpose.

Add the roux to the saucepan, mixing continuously with the whisk, and then add the cream, stirring until it is completely incorporated. Bring the mixture to a simmer, and cook, stirring occasionally, for 30 minutes. Remove from heat, strain through the sieve and add Cognac. Adjust seasoning with salt and pepper.

Sauce Américaine

Typically associated with the preparation of lobster, this sauce has a past which is interesting, if difficult to document. Larousse Gastronomique tells us that the confusion began in the mid-nineteenth century, when a poached preparation called "américaine" was replaced by the Provençal version which is the basis for this recipe. Escoffier claims an anonymous French chef took it from Nice to America, from whence it was reintroduced to France. Curnonsky seems to have settled matters by attributing it to Pierre Fraisse, a Frenchman born in Sète, who was a chef in Chicago for a number of years. Upon returning to Paris, he opened Peter's, a restaurant in the Boulevard des Italiens. And, after fixing the Provençal recipe for some tourists, he responded when asked by them for its name, "homard à l'américaine." Then there is the whole school of thought which says the spelling is a misspelling of "amoricaine," after the ancient name for Brittany, Amorica.

Whatever the history, it is truly among the most elegant of the traditional sauces for seafood, whether used for poached turbot, lobster, or some other delicacy. This should be a feature of a special company dinner—one which summons from your "cave" a bottle of the best full-bodied white Burgundy. To vary the sauce, you may want to add a little whipping cream or Crème Fraîche. Or try adding a teaspoon of finely diced truffles and two tablespoons of diced lobster meat. The lobster meat used in preparing the sauce may be sliced and served with it as a separate dish or by itself in a lobster salad.

Yields about 2 cups

- 3 live lobsters, weighing about 1 to 1 1/2 pounds (450 to 675 g) each
- 1 tablespoon olive oil
- 1/2 cup (118 ml) diced onions
- 1/2 cup (118 ml) diced celery
- 1 garlic clove peeled and crushed
- 1/2 bay leaf
- 2 sprigs fresh parsley
- 1 sprig fresh tarragon
- 1/2 teaspoon coarsely ground black pepper
- A dash of cayenne pepper
- 1/2 cup (118 ml) Cognac, or other fine brandy
- 4 ripe medium tomatoes (blanched, peeled, and seeded; see page 568), coarsely chopped
- 1 tablespoon tomato paste
- 3 cups (710 ml) Fish Stock (see page 60)
- 1/2 cup (118 ml) dry white wine
- 1 tablespoon Blond Roux (see page 65)
- Salt

Recommended equipment

A 4- to 5-quart (4 to 5 L) heavy-bottomed saucepan with lid, large chef's knife or cleaver, garlic press, large fine-mesh sieve.

Place the lobster stomach-down on a cutting board, and, holding the body in one hand, twist the tail off with the other. (Or cut the tail off with the chef's knife or cleaver.) Remove claws and

Ingredients for Sauce Américaine

crack them with the back of the chef's knife or cleaver. Slit the body down the center, clean out intestines, and cut body into small pieces. Heat oil in the saucepan until very hot, add all lobster pieces, and cook, stirring, over medium to high heat until lobster is red on all sides. Then remove most of the oil by tilting the pan on its side with the lid holding the lobster back. Add onion, celery, garlic, bay leaf, parsley, tarragon, and black and cayenne pepper and sauté for 5 minutes over medium heat. Add one-half of the brandy and flambé *(see page 569)*. When flame subsides, add tomatoes, tomato paste, fish stock, white wine, and roux. Stir ingredients together and continue to stir while bringing to a boil over medium heat. Reduce heat to a low simmer and cook slowly for 15 minutes.

Remove lobster tails and claws, cool under running cold water, and remove meat. Return shells to sauce and simmer until liquid is reduced by one-half. Strain through sieve. If not to be used immediately, dot with butter to prevent formation of a skin layer. Just before serving, add rest of brandy to warm sauce and mix thoroughly. Taste and add salt if necessary.

There is no reason to be squeamish about dealing with live lobsters. The simplest way to handle them is to refrigerate them for three or four hours after you bring them home from the store. This makes them much less active and therefore very easy to handle. Make sure your chef's knife or cleaver is well sharpened and start with the point of the knife so that you can cut through the shell easily.

Sauce Velouté de Poulet
Chicken Velouté

Yields about 2 1/2 cups

4 cups (950 ml) White Chicken Stock *(see page 61)*
2 tablespoons Blond Roux *(see page 65)*
A 1 1/2- to 2-inch (3 3/4 to 5 cm) piece of lemon peel, all white removed
Salt and freshly ground white pepper
Knorr Aromat

Recommended equipment

Two 3-quart (3 L) saucepans, one with a lid; wire whisk.

If stock is freshly made, keep it warm in a saucepan. If frozen, melt it in a saucepan and keep warm. Put roux in the other saucepan and heat gently over low heat. Remove from heat and allow to cool slightly. Slowly pour the warm stock into the roux while stirring constantly with the whisk. Return to medium heat, stirring until velouté starts to simmer, add lemon peel, partially cover, and maintain a low simmer for 45 minutes. Skim occasionally if necessary. Velouté should thicken only slightly, so add some more hot stock if it seems too thick. Remove lemon peel. Adjust seasoning with salt, freshly ground white pepper, and a dash of Aromat.

Sauce Suprême

Yields about 3 cups

2 teaspoons chopped shallots
1/8 teaspoon freshly crushed white pepper
1/2 cup (118 ml) dry white wine
1 recipe Sauce Velouté de Poulet *(see page 73)*
2/3 cup (160 ml) whipping cream or Crème Fraîche *(see page 66)*

Recommended equipment

A small chef's knife, mortar and pestle, 1 1/2-quart (1 1/2 L) saucepan, wire whisk, fine-mesh sieve.

Chop the shallot, crush the pepper, put them into the saucepan, and add the white wine. Set the pan over medium heat, bring to a simmer, and cook until the liquid is reduced by one-half. Add the sauce velouté and whipping cream or crème fraîche and, stirring with the whisk, bring to a simmer over medium heat. Then reduce heat to low, and cook at a low simmer for 15 to 20 minutes or until the sauce thickens slightly and has a silky texture. Strain through the fine-mesh sieve into a clean saucepan or bowl and either keep warm over very low heat for immediate use or dot the surface with bits of butter to prevent the formation of a skin layer.

If you wish to enrich the basic sauce, at the end of the cooking time, whisk in 1 egg yolk which has been well blended with several tablespoons of whipping cream and remove immediately from heat. Do not allow to boil.

Sauce Velouté de Veau
Veal Velouté

Yields about 2 1/2 cups

4 cups (950 ml) White Veal Stock *(see page 63)*
2 tablespoons Blond Roux *(see page 65)*
A 1 1/2- to 2-inch (3 3/4 to 5 cm) piece of lemon peel, all white removed
Salt and freshly ground white pepper
Knorr Aromat

Recommended equipment

Two 3-quart (3 L) saucepans, one with a lid; wire whisk.

If stock is freshly made, keep it warm in a saucepan. If frozen, melt it in a saucepan and keep warm. Put roux in the other saucepan and heat gently over low heat. Remove from heat and allow to cool slightly. Slowly pour the warm stock into the roux while stirring constantly with the whisk. Return to medium heat, stirring until velouté starts to simmer, add lemon peel, partially cover, and maintain a low simmer for 45 minutes. Skim occasionally if necessary. Velouté should thicken only slightly, so add some more hot stock if it seems too thick. Remove lemon peel. Adjust seasoning with salt, freshly ground white pepper, and a dash of Aromat.

Sauce Allemande

Yields about 3 cups

1 recipe Sauce Velouté de Veau *(see page 74)*
2/3 cup (160 ml) whipping cream or Crème Fraîche *(see page 66)*

Recommended equipment

A 1 1/2-quart (1 1/2 L) saucepan with lid, wire whisk.

In the saucepan add the whipping cream or crème fraîche to the sauce velouté and, stirring with the whisk, bring to a simmer over medium heat. Reduce heat to low, cover partially and cook at a low simmer for 15 to 20 minutes, until sauce thickens slightly and has a silky texture. If not to be used immediately, dot surface with butter to prevent the formation of a skin layer.

If you wish to enrich the basic sauce, at the end of the cooking time, whisk in 1 egg yolk which has been well blended with several tablespoons of whipping cream and remove immediately from heat. Do not allow to boil.

Demi-glace Brun I
Brown Sauce I

The historical designation of sauces espagnole, tomate, and demi-glace as sauces grandes or sauces mères could not be more fitting. They are the source of myriad brown sauces, and this demi-glace serves as the base for the eight following recipes. Escoffier has a very meticulous description of the way in which a stock proceeds from an espagnole to a demi-glace—a process requiring several days of simmering. Yes—days. With day and night sauciers I, too, have sauces simmered for days, but the recipe you have here is a very practical variant of espagnole. Veal bones, vegetables, and wine replace roux, mirepoix, and ham, and the slow simmering of these ingredients produces a brown sauce with the flavor, texture, and color essential to a memorable Périgueux or Bordelaise.

Yields 1 quart

1 1/2 pounds (675 g) veal bones, cut into small pieces
1 small onion, sliced
1 stalk of celery, cut into 1-inch (2 1/2 cm) sections
1 ounce (30 g) tomato paste
1/2 cup (118 ml) dry white wine
1 recipe Brown Stock *(see page 63)*
Peanut oil for greasing pan

Recommended equipment

A roasting pan, 4- to 5-quart (4 to 5 L) saucepan, large fine-mesh sieve.

Preheat oven to 450F (232C). Lightly grease the roasting pan and strew the bones in it. Place in the preheated oven. When the bones begin to brown, reduce heat to 350F (177C) and add the onion, celery, and tomato paste. Roast for 10 minutes more. Remove bones and vegetables to the saucepan. Deglaze the roasting pan by bringing white wine and one-half of the brown stock to a boil over high heat and scraping bits from the bottom of the pan. Add this to the ingredients in the saucepan along with the remaining brown stock, and bring to a simmer. Cook over low heat for 3 to 3 1/2 hours, skimming if necessary. When sauce is finished, strain and cool. If not to be used immediately, freeze it for future use.

Demi-glace Brun II
Brown Sauce II

This version of demi-glace brun is made by adding 1 1/2 teaspoons of Browned or Roasted Flour *(see page 64)* to the roasting pan after reducing the oven heat. Reduce simmering time by at least 1/2 hour.

The decision as to which of these versions should be used is based on the final recipe. Demi-glace I is most desirable for such delicate entrées as veal scaloppine, as well as brown sauces such as Chasseur, Madère, and its derivative, Périgueux. Demi-glace II is more useful when large quantities are required or for braised dishes such as Sauerbraten, pot roast, and Swiss steak.

Sauce Madère

This sauce, its two variations, and the five following recipes have a common theme—homemade demi-glace. No matter what the cans and frozen packages say, your own will be better because you will not be trying to make it as cheaply as possible. Quite versatile, Madère accompanies filet of beef, ham steaks, veal scaloppine, and sautéed chicken livers extremely well.

Yields about 2 cups, for 4 to 6 servings

1 tablespoon chopped fresh shallots
1/2 teaspoon coarsely ground black pepper
1 cup (235 ml) Sercial or good dry Madeira
2 cups (475 ml) Demi-glace Brun I *(see page 75)*
1 tablespoon (15 g) butter, softened at room temperature

Recommended equipment

A 1 1/2-quart (1 1/2 L) saucepan, small fine-mesh sieve.

Combine shallots, black pepper, and Madeira in the saucepan, bring to a simmer, and cook until reduced by one-half. Add demi-glace and simmer on low heat for 10 minutes. Strain. Just before serving, add butter and stir well until completely absorbed. If sauce is not to be served immediately, dot top with one-half of the butter to prevent a skin from forming and keep hot in a double boiler. Stir in remaining butter just before serving.

Variation

🎀 Sauce Marsala

Proceed as in Sauce Madère, but replace Madeira with dry Marsala.

🎀 Sauce Périgueux

Calling for "2 to 4 truffles" is probably the greatest bit of nonchalance in the entire book. This sauce will bathe a slice of beef tenderloin with true elegance, and if you want a truly extraordinary setting for it, consult the recipe for Roast Tenderloin of Beef London House with Truffle Sauce.

Yields about 2 cups, for 4 to 6 servings

1 recipe Sauce Madère *(see page 76)*
2 to 4 canned truffles, with their juice

Drain and finely dice truffles, reserving their juice.

Following the instructions for sauce Madère, add the reserved juice from the truffles along with the demi-glace. When sauce has simmered and been strained, add diced truffles. Continue as for sauce Madère.

If you happen to be blessed with fresh truffles, do not worry about the missing juices from the can as the intense, earthy essence of the fresh "black gold" will completely permeate the sauce.

🎀 Armagnac Sauce with Green Peppercorns and Grapes

The flavor of this richly colored and textured sauce complements delicate meats such as veal and beef tenderloin. The interplay of color and taste between the grapes and peppercorns against the background of this brown, velvet sauce is a "star attraction" in itself, and you must choose a meat worthy of it. While another brandy may be substituted for Armagnac, its unique character lends distinction to this sauce. As of this writing, Armagnac is still relatively "undiscovered," and therefore has not suffered the production pressures and inevitable blending often found in Cognac.

Yields about 2 1/2 cups, for 6 to 8 servings

1 tablespoon finely chopped shallots
1 cup (235 ml) Armagnac
2 cups (475 ml) Demi-glace Brun I *(see page 75)*
1 1/2 teaspoons green peppercorns (packed in water and drained)
1/4 cup (60 ml) canned seedless white grapes, drained, or fresh (see below)
1 tablespoon (15 g) butter, softened at room temperature

Recommended equipment

A 1 1/2-quart (1 1/2 L) saucepan, small fine-mesh sieve, 8-inch (20 cm) sauté pan.

In the saucepan combine shallots and all but 2 tablespoons of the Armagnac. Bring to a simmer over medium heat and cook until reduced by one-half. Add demi-glace, reduce heat to low, and simmer for 15 minutes. Strain into a bowl and reserve. Rinse and dry saucepan.

Add remaining Armagnac and drained peppercorns to sauté pan and cook over medium heat for 1 minute. Then flambé peppercorns *(see page 569)* and when the flame dies add them to the reserved sauce. Return the mixture to the saucepan and add the grapes. Bring the sauce to a gentle simmer and cook over low heat for 2 minutes. To prevent formation of a skin on the surface, dot the top of the sauce with 1 1/2 teaspoons of the butter. When ready to serve, add the remaining butter, stirring with a spoon until completely blended.

Fresh white grapes should be used whenever possible; however, they must be peeled (and if not seedless, the seeds must be removed). Using a small paring knife, start from the stem end of grape, and peel skin in 1/3-inch (3/4 cm) pieces, down toward opposite end. Continue until all skin is peeled.

Sauce Marchand de Vins
Wine Merchant's Sauce

It is said that this sauce originated when Bordeaux wine merchants needed to rid themselves of surplus or inferior wine; however, we can't emphasize enough the importance of using a good quality wine. There are no such things as "cooking wines"—only labels trying to disguise bad wines. As with any other ingredient, an inferior wine will produce an inferior sauce.

Yields about 2 3/4 cups, for 4 to 6 servings

- 1 1/2- to 2-inch (3 3/4 to 5 cm) piece of lemon peel, all bitter white removed
- 1 tablespoon chopped fresh shallots
- 1/2 teaspoon coarsely ground black pepper
- 1/4 bay leaf
- 1 1/2 cups (355 ml) good quality dry red wine
- 2 cups (475 ml) Demi-glace Brun I *(see page 75)*
- 1 tablespoon (15 g) butter, softened at room temperature

Recommended equipment

A 1 1/2-quart (1 1/2 L) saucepan, swivel-bladed vegetable peeler, small fine-mesh sieve.

Using the vegetable peeler, remove the lemon peel and combine it with the shallots, black pepper, bay leaf, and red wine in the saucepan. Bring to a simmer and cook until reduced by one-half. Add demi-glace and simmer on low heat for 15 minutes. Then strain and skim. Just before serving, add butter and stir well until completely absorbed. If sauce is not to be served immediately, dot top with one-half of the butter to prevent a skin from forming and keep hot in a double boiler. Stir in remaining butter just before serving.

This "classical" version of marchand de vins would best accompany a roasted tenderloin. If you are sautéing steaks or filets instead, when the meat is cooked, set it aside to keep warm. Over high heat, deglaze the pan with the wine, increase the amount of chopped shallot to 1/4 cup and add it to the wine. When the wine has reduced to about 1/4 cup, add 1 cup of Demi-glace and reduce for 2 or 3 minutes. Off heat, just before serving, whisk in 3 to 4 tablespoons of softened butter and nap the steaks with the sauce.

Sauce Vinaigre de Vin Alsacienne

At home, when we wanted to give a little more "bite" to a wine sauce, I remember that we would replace some of the wine with an excellent wine vinegar. The technique of using vinegar for deglazing and sauces is associated with Alsace and the cooking of such superb Alsatian chefs as Paul Haeberlin at L'Auberge de l'Ill in Illhaeusern and André Soltner at Lutèce in New York. So, we will name this in their honor. I love this sauce as an alternative in Foies de Veau Suisse.

Yields about 2 3/4 cups, for 4 to 6 servings

1 recipe Sauce Marchand de Vins (*see page 78*)

Following the instructions for sauce marchand de vins, replace the 1 1/2 cups of red wine with 1/2 cup (118 ml) red wine vinegar and 1 cup (235 ml) red wine.

Sauce Bordelaise

Although Sauce Marchand de Vins is said to have originated when fourteenth-century wine merchants began shipping wine to England, "Bordelaise" is very specific to Bordeaux. This sauce, usually served with grilled steaks, always involves beef marrow, either in the sauce or served on the steak with a mixture of shallot and parsley.

Yields about 2 3/4 cups, for 4 to 6 servings

1 recipe Sauce Marchand de Vins (*see page 78*)
12 to 18 pieces of beef marrow, sliced 1/2 inch (1 1/4 cm) thick

Above all, be true to the spirit of the region and use only a good red Bordeaux or Cabernet.

Recommended equipment

A 3-quart (3 L) saucepan, small paring knife.

Prepare sauce marchand de vins according to instructions.

Heat slices of marrow in hot but not boiling beef bouillon or stock for 1 minute. Strain off liquid and either add marrow to sauce or carefully place marrow pieces on meat and ladle sauce over all. If marrow is added to sauce, keep warm, but nowhere near the boiling point as the marrow will dissolve.

※

Marrow from shin or thigh bones can be obtained from your butcher shop, where you should ask to have the bones sliced in 2-inch (5 cm) lengths. When you get them home, being sure that they are at room temperature, push the marrow out of the bone to remove it as nearly intact as possible. (Don't worry, some pieces will crumble!) Warm the paring knife in hot water and slice the marrow into 1/2-inch (1 1/4 cm) rounds. If not to be used immediately, the marrow pieces should be placed in a bowl of iced water. Marrow will also freeze quite successfully—it simply has to be handled a little more carefully during preparation.

Sauce Chasseur

This sauce is a country cousin of the more urbane Bordelaise and Périgueux. Literally "hunter style," the use of mushrooms and tomatoes conveys a sense of rusticity—especially if you have chanterelles close at hand. Featured in Foies de Volaille Sautés Chasseur, the sauce also sets off sautéed chicken breasts or veal cutlets quite nicely.

Yields 2 cups

8 ounces (225 g) mushrooms
1 tablespoon (15 g) butter
1 teaspoon olive oil
1 teaspoon finely chopped shallots
1/8 small garlic clove, finely chopped
1 cup (235 ml) good quality dry red wine
1 cup (235 ml) Demi-glace Brun I *(see page 75)*
2 ripe, medium tomatoes (blanched, peeled, and seeded; *see page 568*), coarsely chopped
1/2 teaspoon chopped fresh parsley
Salt and freshly ground black pepper

Recommended equipment

A paring knife, 1 1/2-quart (1 1/2 L) saucepan.

Clean the mushrooms with a paper towel or soft bristle brush. Do not wash them. Using the paring knife, slice the mushrooms 1/4 inch (2/3 cm) thick. If the mushrooms are large, use only the caps (reserve the stems for soup or stock). Otherwise, make your slices lengthwise along the stem, so that you include stem and cap in one slice.

Melt butter and olive oil in the saucepan. Add mushrooms and sauté over medium high heat for 2 to 3 minutes. Then add shallots and garlic, sauté for about 30 seconds, add the wine, and over high heat reduce liquid by one-half. Reduce heat to medium, add demi-glace and tomatoes, and simmer for 5 minutes. Before serving add parsley and adjust seasoning.

To extend the versatility of chasseur add a final touch of fresh oregano when using this sauce for a chicken dish, and when using it for veal, substitute white wine for the red. To make a version of Sauce Duxelles omit the tomatoes from the master recipe.

Basic Curry Sauce

"Basic" here means that this recipe can be adapted to numerous curried dishes, the main feature of which also determines which velouté you use. Because curry powder is a complex blend of eight to ten different spices, it is important to choose a high quality brand such as Crosse and Blackwell, Savin, or Sun. You alone can decide how much to use, depending on how "hot" you want the final dish to be (and how well you know your guests' palates). Traditionally, curry is accompanied by numerous condiments, served in separate dishes to allow each guest to make a "private mixture." Some of the more usual ones are: poppadums (lentil flour wafers); Bombay duck (dried fish fillets); mango chutney; sliced bananas, lightly sautéed in butter; diced pimiento; raisins, plumped and drained; fresh, grated coconut; diced pineapple; and diced onions, sautéed until crisp.

Yields 1 1/2 cups, for 6 servings

1 tablespoon (15 g) butter
1 tablespoon curry powder
1/2 garlic clove, peeled and chopped
1 teaspoon tomato paste
1/2 cup (118 ml) chopped onions
1/3 cup (80 ml) chopped celery
1/3 cup (80 ml) sliced apples
1 tablespoon Indian mango chutney
2 cups (475 ml) Sauce Velouté de Poulet, Veau, or Poisson *(see pages 73, 74, 68)*
Salt to taste

Recommended equipment

A 1 1/2-quart (1 1/2 L) saucepan with lid, wire whisk, large fine-mesh sieve.

In the saucepan, over medium to low heat, combine butter and curry powder, and sauté, stirring, until mixture starts to sizzle and foam—about 1 minute or less. Add garlic and tomato paste, simmer 1 minute, then add onions, celery, apple, and chutney. Simmer for 2 to 3 minutes before adding velouté. Add velouté, mixing well with the whisk, and simmer over low heat, partially covered, for 30 minutes. Strain through the sieve and correct seasoning, if necessary.

For a creamed curry dish add 1/2 cup (118 ml) whipping cream or Crème Fraîche *(see page 66)* and replace one-half of the velouté with coconut milk.

Cold Seasoned Butters and Hot Butter Sauces

Beurre Maître d'hôtel
Butter in the Style of the Maître d'hôtel

Nowadays the title maître d'hôtel generally refers to the person in charge of operating a dining room. However, this recipe harkens back to the days when proprietors of hotels and inns in the French provinces were maîtres d'hôtel, and therefore likely to create recipes for their own kitchens. Both this and the following Beurre Café de Paris lend superb touches of color and flavor to grilled meat, fish, or poultry.

Yields 1/2 cup

- 1 teaspoon finely chopped shallots
- 1 teaspoon butter
- 8 tablespoons (115 g) butter, softened at room temperature
- 1 tablespoon lemon juice
- 1/2 teaspoon chopped lemon rind (all bitter white removed)
- 1/4 teaspoon salt
- 1 tablespoon chopped fresh parsley
- 1 tablespoon finely cut chives
- 1/2 teaspoon Worcestershire sauce

Recommended equipment

A small saucepan, wooden spatula, 1-quart (1 L) bowl, hand mixer, small chef's knife, waxed paper.

In the saucepan, set over medium heat, sauté the shallots in the teaspoon of butter until soft. Then scrape them into the bowl and add the remaining ingredients, mixing until smooth and creamy.

Spread butter mixture in a thick strip down the middle of a piece of waxed paper. Shape into a cylinder 1/2 inch (1 1/4 cm) in diameter. Pull one end of waxed paper over butter and roll over and over to opposite edge of the paper. Refrigerate. When chilled and set, unwrap and cut into 1/4- to 1/2-inch (2/3 to 1 1/4 cm) thick round pieces. Extra butter, wrapped, freezes well for future use.

Variation: For tarragon-flavored butter, add to the beurre maître d'hôtel mixture 1 tablespoon finely chopped fresh tarragon.

Beurre Café de Paris
Café de Paris Butter

Our favorite, especially for a filet mignon or sirloin steak.

Yields 1 cup

- 1 small garlic clove, chopped
- 1 tablespoon chopped shallots
- 1 teaspoon butter
- 1 cup (225 g) butter, softened at room temperature
- 1/4 teaspoon Worcestershire sauce
- 1 tablespoon Escoffier sauce
- 1/4 teaspoon dry English mustard
- 1/4 teaspoon curry powder
- 1 tablespoon ketchup
- 1/4 teaspoon anchovy paste
- 1 tablespoon chopped fresh parsley
- 1 tablespoon lemon juice
- 1 teaspoon chopped lemon rind (all bitter white removed)
- 1 teaspoon chopped fresh tarragon leaves
- 1 tablespoon Cognac
- Tabasco sauce

Recommended equipment

A small saucepan, wooden spatula, 1-quart (1 L) bowl, hand mixer, small chef's knife, waxed paper.

In the saucepan, set over medium heat, sauté the garlic and shallots in the teaspoon of butter until soft. Then scrape them into the bowl, add the remaining ingredients, mix until smooth and creamy, and season to taste with a few drops of Tabasco sauce.

Spread butter mixture in a strip down the middle of a piece of waxed paper. Shape into a cylinder 1/2 inch (1 1/4 cm) in diameter. Pull one end of waxed paper over butter and roll over and over to opposite edge of the paper. Refrigerate. When chilled and set, unwrap and cut into 1/4-inch to 1/2-inch (2/3 to 1 1/4 cm) thick round pieces. Extra butter, wrapped, freezes well for future use.

Beurre au Citron
Lemon Butter

An excellent little "sauce vite," this is perfect for the last minute garnishing of fresh broccoli, cauliflower, or Asparagus.

Yields 2 1/2 tablespoons

2 tablespoons (30 g) butter
2 teaspoons fresh lemon juice

Recommended equipment

A small saucepan.

Melt the butter in the saucepan over medium to high heat while continuously moving the pan slowly back and forth. When the butter foams, immediately remove pan from heat, add lemon juice, spoon the sauce over the hot vegetable, and serve. If you like, stir in 1/2 teaspoon finely chopped fresh parsley or chives after adding the lemon juice.

Variation: For a creamy sauce au Domaine de Beauprès, melt 4 tablespoons (60 g) butter in the saucepan over medium heat. When it is melted, whisk in a pinch of salt, freshly ground white pepper, the juice of 1/2 small lemon, 1 teaspoon Dijon mustard, and 1/2 cup (118 ml) Crème Fraîche *(see page 66)*. Bring the mixture to a simmer, stirring, and adjust heat so that it simmers gently until reduced to the desired consistency. Let the sauce thicken if you want to coat the vegetable with it or serve a thinner sauce if you prefer to spoon it around the vegetable. Taste the sauce before serving and adjust seasoning if necessary. Yields enough for 4 servings of fresh asparagus or 2 servings of fresh, whole artichokes.

Gremolada

A traditional accompaniment to one of Italy's tastiest dishes—ossobuco—this butter sauce is superb with sautéed veal.

Yields 3 tablespoons

1 recipe Beurre au Citron *(see above)*
Rind of 1 lemon, all bitter white removed, finely chopped
1/2 garlic clove, finely chopped
1/2 teaspoon chopped parsley

Follow the instructions for beurre au citron, then add the chopped lemon peel and the garlic, return the saucepan to medium heat for 10 to 15 seconds, remove from heat, add the chopped parsley, and serve.

Beurre Noisette
Brown Butter

A "noisette" is a hazelnut, but there aren't any nuts in this butter—only a nutlike flavor and color from browning the butter sediment. This is a great finishing touch for sautéed fish, especially our Sautéed Mountain Trout Homestead.

Yields 2 tablespoons

2 tablespoons (30 g) butter
2 teaspoons fresh lemon juice

Recommended equipment

An 8-inch (20 cm) sauté pan.

Put butter in the sauté pan and let melt over low to medium heat while continuously moving back and forth with a light motion. After butter foams, it will settle and the sediment will slowly turn a golden brown. At this point remove pan from heat *immediately* and add the lemon juice to stabilize the color (otherwise it will brown and become beurre noir). Serve at once.

Beurre Noir
Black Butter

This sauce (which is really only dark brown) goes particularly well with sautéed veal brains, sweetbreads, or fried eggs.

1 recipe Beurre Noisette (see above)
1 teaspoon capers with their juices

Proceed as with beurre noisette, allowing the butter to turn a dark brown. Remove the sauté pan from the heat, add the capers and their juices, and serve at once.

Beurre Blanc
Basic White Butter Sauce

A classic, "rediscovered" when the nouvelle cuisine popularized lighter sauces. It is easy to prepare, but be sure to have your butter at room temperature so that you can move quickly to incorporate it into the vinegar and wine reduction.

Yields 1 cup

1 teaspoon white peppercorns, coarsely crushed
1/4 cup (60 ml) white wine vinegar
1/4 cup (60 ml) dry white wine
2 teaspoons minced shallots
1 cup (225 g) butter, softened at room temperature
Salt

Recommended equipment

A mortar and pestle, 1 1/2-quart (1 1/2 L) saucepan, wire whisk, small fine-mesh sieve, double boiler.

Using the mortar and pestle, crush the peppercorns. Simmer vinegar, wine, shallots, and pepper in saucepan until mixture is reduced to 1 1/2 tablespoons. Remove from heat and whisk in butter a tablespoon at a time, completely blending after each addition, until all the butter has been added. Strain through the sieve. Add salt to taste. If not to be used immediately, sauce may be kept warm over simmering water in a double boiler. Do not reheat sauce as it will separate. Serve as soon as possible.

❧

For a creamier sauce simmer 1/2 cup of whipping cream until thickened and reduced by one-third of its volume. Whisk reduced cream into the finished beurre blanc. The addition of cream enables the sauce to hold better.

❧ Raspberry Vinegar Butter Sauce

Truly a Homestead creation, this sauce must be made with the Homestead Raspberry Vinegar because it has a piquancy you will not find in a commercial product. We have featured this butter sauce in salmon and chicken recipes here, but the "amateur de framboise" will find countless other applications. Melba sauce is a raspberry sauce available at specialty food stores.

Yields 6 servings

2 cups (475 ml) Homestead Raspberry Vinegar *(see page 103)*
1 cup (235 ml) Crème Fraîche *(see page 66)*
1/8 teaspoon freshly crushed black pepper
8 tablespoons (115 g) butter, softened at room temperature
A pinch of sugar
1 or 2 tablespoons Melba sauce

Recommended equipment

A 3-quart (3 L) saucepan, mortar and pestle, wire whisk, large fine-mesh sieve, double boiler.

Combine the vinegar and crème fraîche in the saucepan. Crush the pepper in the mortar and pestle and whisk it into the vinegar mixture. Set the saucepan over medium high heat, bring the mixture to a boil, and cook until the liquid has been reduced to 1 cup (this should take 10 to 15 minutes). Stir occasionally with the wire whisk. Then remove saucepan from heat and whisk in the butter a tablespoon at a time. When all the butter has been absorbed, pass the sauce through the sieve into the top part of the double boiler and keep it hot over barely simmering water on low heat. Taste the sauce and, if necessary, correct the seasoning with a pinch of sugar. Add the Melba sauce if you think the color needs improvement.

Orange Cream Curry Sauce

Originally an Indian recipe, this sauce was intended to accompany grilled or sautéed meats. We reduced the amount of curry powder to make it suitable for the more subtle flavor of fish. Grilled swordfish or tuna and sautéed salmon scallops are ready companions for the fruit flavor.

Yields 2 cups

2 cups (475 ml) fresh orange juice
1 cup (235 ml) frozen orange juice concentrate
1/4 cup (60 ml) lemon juice
1/4 garlic clove, peeled
1/4 teaspoon chopped shallots
1/4 teaspoon curry powder
2 cups (475 ml) whipping cream
4 tablespoons (60 g) butter, softened at room temperature

GARNISH
Orange sections and slices of avocado or
Kiwi and mango slices

Recommended equipment

A 2-quart (2 L) saucepan, paring knife, small chef's knife, 1 1/2-quart (1 1/2 L) saucepan, wire whisk, fine-mesh sieve, double boiler.

Add the fresh orange juice, orange juice concentrate, and lemon juice to the larger saucepan. Peel the garlic clove and add it to the saucepan. Chop the shallots and add them to the saucepan with the curry powder. Set the saucepan over high heat, bring the fruit juices to a boil, and cook for about 10 to 15 minutes, until reduced to 1 cup (235 ml). Put the whipping cream in the other saucepan, bring it to a boil, and cook until it is reduced to 1 cup (about 10 minutes). When both are done, remove from heat and reserve.

Whip the soft butter into the reduced fruit juice mixture with the whisk. When the butter is absorbed, whisk in the reduced cream, strain the mixture through the sieve into the top part of a double boiler, and keep warm until ready to serve.

Herb and Vegetable Sauces

Basil Butter Sauce

For many, the thought of fresh basil conjures up thoughts of summer and pesto. This sauce is an elegant alternative to its more aggressive, uncooked cousin, and is well suited to pasta and baked or poached fish such as salmon. If you like, add some pine nuts to the finished sauce.

Yields about 1 1/2 cups, for 7 to 8 servings

4 ounces (115 g) fresh basil
1 tablespoon minced shallots
1/2 garlic clove, minced
1 tablespoon (15 g) butter
Juice of 1 lemon
1/2 cup (118 ml) dry white wine
1 cup (225 g) butter, softened at room temperature
Salt and freshly ground white pepper

Recommended equipment

A large chef's knife, 1 1/2-quart (1 1/2 L) saucepan, blender or food processor, rubber spatula, wire whisk, double boiler.

Remove the stems from the basil. Wash and dry the leaves thoroughly. With the chef's knife, roughly chop the basil, mince the shallots and garlic, and reserve all three separately.

    Melt 1 tablespoon of the butter in the saucepan, add shallots, and sauté for 2 minutes over low heat without coloring. Add garlic, stirring it in well, then add the lemon juice and white wine. Raise heat to medium and simmer, stirring occasionally, until liquid is reduced to one-third. Add the basil and simmer, stirring, for 1 minute, then remove from heat, put mixture in blender or food processor, and purée until smooth. With the spatula scrape the mixture back into the saucepan and simmer over medium heat until it has a thin puréed consistency. Remove from direct heat to a warm place next to the burner or put in a double boiler over hot, not simmering, water. (It is important that the basil mixture be hot but *not* simmering when you begin adding the butter.) With the whisk, whip in the soft butter, a tablespoon at a time, until it is completely absorbed. Adjust seasoning with salt and pepper as necessary. Keep warm until serving time, but do not allow to boil.

Green Herb Butter Sauce

Excellent with baked or poached fish, chicken, and veal, this makes a stunning taste and color contrast as a second sauce with Beurre Blanc.

Yields about 2 cups, for 8 to 9 servings

1/2 cup (118 ml) roughly chopped fresh parsley
1/4 cup (60 ml) roughly chopped fresh spinach
1/2 cup (118 ml) roughly chopped fresh watercress
1/3 cup (80 ml) roughly chopped fresh basil
1 tablespoon roughly chopped fresh tarragon
1 tablespoon minced shallots
1/2 garlic clove, minced
Juice from 1 lemon
1/2 cup (118 ml) dry white wine
1 cup (225 g) butter, softened at room temperature
Salt and freshly ground black pepper

Recommended equipment

A small chef's knife, 1-quart (1 L) bowl, 1 1/2-quart (1 1/2 L) saucepan, blender or food processor, rubber spatula, wire whisk, double boiler.

Wash all of the fresh green ingredients thoroughly under running cold water, being particularly careful to remove any grit or sand from the watercress and spinach. Dry with a towel or in a salad spinner and remove stems. Using the chef's knife, chop the ingredients, measure, and pour into the bowl.

Melt 1 tablespoon of the butter in the saucepan, add shallots, and sauté for 2 minutes over low heat without coloring. Add garlic, stirring it in well, then add the lemon juice and white wine. Raise heat to medium and simmer until liquid is reduced to one-third. Then add the chopped parsley, spinach, watercress, basil, and tarragon, and simmer, stirring, for 1 minute. Remove from heat, put mixture in blender or food processor, and process until smooth. With the spatula scrape the mixture back into the saucepan and simmer over medium heat until it has a puréed consistency. Remove from direct heat to a warm place next to the burner or put in a double boiler over hot, not simmering, water. (It is important that the herb and vegetable mixture be hot but *not* simmering when you begin adding the butter.) With the whisk, whip in the soft butter, a tablespoon at a time, until it is completely absorbed. Adjust seasoning with salt and pepper as necessary. Keep warm until serving time, but do not allow to boil.

Leek Butter Sauce

I am very partial to leeks, whether in soup, boiled in salted water and then served cold with a vinaigrette, or creamed with a Sauce Mornay (use some of the leek water to make the sauce) and baked. This sauce is especially good as an accompaniment to baked fresh salmon fillets, following the instructions for Baked Fillets of Pompano. If you desire a white sauce, do not use any of the leek greens as they will color the sauce. Save the greens for a soup.

Yields 4 to 6 servings

4 medium leeks
1 cup (235 ml) water
1/8 teaspoon salt
A dash of freshly ground white pepper
1 cup (225 g) butter, softened at room temperature

Recommended equipment

A colander, 1 1/2-quart (1 1/2 L) saucepan, blender or food processor, wire whisk.

Cut leeks in half lengthwise and then into 2- to 3-inch (5 to 7 1/2 cm) pieces. You should have about 2 cups (475 ml). Wash thoroughly under running cold water, separating the layers with your fingers to remove any sand or dirt. Drain in the colander.

Simmer the leeks in the saucepan with 1 tablespoon of the butter, the water, and salt and pepper until soft but not mushy (when the point of a knife meets slight resistance), about 15 minutes. Take off heat and allow to cool in broth. Put in blender or food processor with approximately 1/4 cup (60 ml) broth and purée until smooth. Return to saucepan and reduce to a creamy, thick consistency over low heat, stirring occasionally to prevent sticking. Remove from heat and gradually whisk in the softened butter. Adjust seasoning if necessary. Sauce may be kept warm over simmering water in a double boiler. Do not boil or it will separate.

🌿 Asparagus Butter Sauce

Great with fish or pasta—be sure to save the trimmings from the stalks for Cream of Asparagus Soup—delicious!!

Yields 4 to 6 servings

2 pounds (900 g) fresh asparagus
1 cup (235 ml) water
1/8 teaspoon salt
A dash of freshly ground white pepper
1 cup (225 g) butter, softened at room temperature

Recommended equipment

A swivel-bladed vegetable peeler, colander, 1 1/2-quart (1 1/2 L) saucepan, blender or food processor, wire whisk.

Peel the asparagus stalks and wash them under cold running water. Drain them in the colander. Cut approximately 3 inches (7 1/2 cm) from the base and cut the remainder into roughly 2-inch (5 cm) sections for the sauce.

Simmer the asparagus in the saucepan with 1 tablespoon of the butter, the water, and salt and pepper until soft but not mushy (when the point of a knife meets slight resistance), about 6 minutes. Take off heat and allow to cool in broth. Put in blender or food processor with just enough broth, approximately 1/4 cup, and purée until smooth. Return to saucepan and reduce to a creamy, thick consistency over low heat, stirring occasionally to prevent sticking. Remove from heat and gradually whisk in the softened butter. Adjust seasoning if necessary. Sauce may be kept warm over simmering water in a double boiler. Do not boil or it will separate.

🌿 Tomato Butter Sauce

Really a fresh tomato "coulis," this delightful sauce is quite versatile. Serve it with white fish such as turbot, sea bass, and pompano, or simply pour it over pasta with freshly grated Parmesan cheese. Because it is lower in butter content it is better suited to low-fat diets than its companion sauces.

Yields 4 to 6 servings

4 large tomatoes (blanched, peeled, and seeded; *see page 568*), coarsely chopped
1 tablespoon olive oil
1 teaspoon chopped shallots
1/2 garlic clove, minced or pressed
Salt and freshly ground white pepper
2 pinches of sugar
4 tablespoons (60 g) butter, softened at room temperature

Recommended equipment

A 3-quart (3 L) saucepan with lid, blender or food processor, wire whisk, double boiler.

Prepare the tomatoes and reserve.

Heat olive oil in the saucepan over low heat, add shallots and cook for 1 minute. Add garlic and cook for another minute (do not allow to brown). Add the reserved tomatoes, salt, pepper, and sugar. Bring to a lively simmer and cook, covered, for 15 minutes. Remove from heat. When cool, put in the blender or food processor and purée until fine.

(Should you wish to make extra amounts of puréed tomatoes, store in glass jars in refrigerator or freeze in plastic containers for future use.)

Just before serving, return puréed tomatoes to clean saucepan, bring to a boil, and reduce heat, simmering purée until reduced to a thick consistency. Remove from heat and whisk in softened butter, a tablespoon at a time. If necessary, sauce may be kept warm over simmering water in a double boiler. Do not boil or it will separate.

Fresh tomato gets along extremely well with herbs such as oregano, basil, and parsley so you can create any variations you like.

Red Pepper Butter Sauce

Sweet red pepper (poivron doux) *sauces became quite popular during the 1960s. This more "pointed" version is a good accompaniment for broiled chicken, veal, or fish, and, if you like it hotter still, experiment by adding fresh serrano, jalapeño, or other chili peppers.*

Yields 4 to 6 servings

4 to 5 medium to large red bell peppers
1 tablespoon olive oil
1/2 garlic clove, finely chopped
1 tablespoon finely chopped shallots
1/2 cup (118 ml) red wine vinegar
Juice of 1 lemon
1 cup (225 g) butter, softened at room temperature
Salt
A dash of freshly ground white pepper

Recommended equipment

A paring knife, colander, small chef's knife, 10-inch (25 cm) sauté pan, blender or food processor, 1 1/2-quart (1 1/2 L) saucepan, wire whisk.

Cut bell peppers in half, removing all seeds and white pulp from the inside. Wash the pieces under running cold water, drain them in the colander, and then coarsely chop them.

In the sauté pan, heat the olive oil over medium high heat, add the peppers and sauté, stirring, for 2 minutes. Reduce heat to medium, add the garlic and shallots, sauté for 30 seconds, then add the vinegar and lemon juice and simmer until peppers are partially cooked but still slightly firm. Remove from heat and cool. When mixture is cool, put in blender or food processor and purée until smooth. Then put in saucepan and reduce to a creamy, thick consistency over low heat, stirring occasionally to prevent sticking. Remove from heat and gradually whisk in the softened butter. Adjust seasoning if necessary. Sauce may be kept warm over simmering water in a double boiler. Do not boil or it will separate.

Liaisons Dangereuses: Egg Yolk Sauces

Sauce Hollandaise I

Born in exile, Hollandaise is so named because it was developed by French Huguenots living in Holland—a felicitous marriage between French sauce savoir faire and legendary Dutch butter. We prefer this version for vegetables because it is milder. The more pointed flavor of Hollandaise II is better suited to fish or poached egg dishes such as eggs benedict.

In this and the following recipes we call for a double boiler. Unless you cannot reduce your burners to a very low temperature you will find that, after making the sauce a few times, a heavy-bottomed saucepan works just as well and is less trouble. The main point is to time the preparation so that the sauce does not have to sit for a long time and get cold. As you become more experienced with cooked egg yolk sauces, you will find that you can vary the thickness of the final sauce by the way you cook the yolks. They are reasonably forgiving and can be almost scrambled and still absorb butter—producing a thicker sauce which will hold together on a hot poached egg. For vegetables, a thinner sauce is more desirable, thus the yolks should be cooked less.

Yields about 1 1/2 cups, for 4 to 6 servings

1 cup (235 ml) Clarified Butter (see page 568)
3 tablespoons white wine vinegar
1/2 teaspoon coarsely ground white peppercorns
3 egg yolks
Juice of 1/2 lemon
A dash of salt

Recommended equipment

A 1 1/2-quart (1 1/2 L) enameled or stainless steel saucepan, double boiler, wire whisk, small fine-mesh sieve.

Prepare the clarified butter. While butter is melting, make the egg yolk base by combining the vinegar, 1 tablespoon cold water, and the pepper in the top of the double boiler. Simmer until the liquid is reduced to about 1 tablespoon. Remove from heat, allowing to cool briefly. Whisk in a few drops of warm water and then the egg yolks, blending until all is well mixed. Place mixture over hot but not boiling water in the bottom of the double boiler. With the whisk whip the egg yolk mixture gently but constantly for a few minutes, and as you do so, you will get the feel of the yolks "starting to bake" (thicken) and becoming smooth and creamy. (You should begin to see the bottom of the pan between whisk strokes.)

Remove top of double boiler and set down on a cool surface. Immediately add 1 1/2 teaspoons cool water, and keep stirring with whisk until cooking process has stopped. Return top to double boiler and, pouring very carefully so as not to disturb the sediment in the bottom of the saucepan, add the clarified butter a tablespoon at a time, stirring briskly with the whisk to thoroughly incorporate the butter into the egg mixture. When about one-half of the butter has been added, stir in 1 teaspoon warm water and a few drops of lemon juice. Then continue to add the remaining butter, being sure to omit the milky residue in the bottom of the saucepan. Add remaining lemon juice, season with salt, and strain through the sieve to remove pieces of pepper and curds of egg yolk. Keep sauce warm but not hot. Hollandaise should be made no more than 20 minutes before serving and any unused amounts should be discarded as this sauce does not keep.

🎀

Should the sauce separate ("break") during cooking, put it back over hot water in the double boiler to keep warm. In another saucepan add 1 1/2 tablespoons cool water and slowly whip in separated sauce, adding a few more drops of water once or twice.

Variation

🎀 Sauce Hollandaise II

Yields about 1 1/2 cups, for 4 to 6 servings

1 recipe Sauce Hollandaise I *(see page 91)*
1 tablespoon chopped fresh shallots

Following the instructions for Sauce Hollandaise I, add the chopped shallots to the white wine vinegar before simmering, and proceed with recipe. To the finished sauce you could add a dash of cayenne pepper or a few drops of Tabasco sauce and a few drops of Worcestershire sauce.

🎀 Sauce Mousseline

This sauce really sets off a seafood mousse, particularly a lobster or shrimp timbale. If the timbale is made from a purée, I reserve a small amount of cooked lobster or shrimp, mince it finely, and fold it into the sauce at the last minute for little flecks of color.

Yields about 2 cups, for 6 to 8 servings

1 recipe Sauce Hollandaise II *(see above)*
1/3 cup (80 ml) whipped heavy cream

Follow instructions for Sauce Hollandaise II, and just before serving, fold in stiffly whipped cream with a spatula.

Sauce Maltaise

This is especially tasty with fresh Asparagus. Traditionally, this recipe calls for blood oranges ("sanguines"), which give the sauce a handsome dark orange color.

Yields about 1 1/2 cups, for 4 to 6 servings

1 recipe Sauce Hollandaise I (see page 91)
3 tablespoons fresh orange juice
Rind of 1 orange, in julienne strips

Following the instructions for Sauce Hollandaise I, omit the lemon juice, and add the orange juice to the vinegar reduction just before the egg yolks are added. When the sauce is finished, add the orange rind, which has been cut into fine julienne strips, blanched briefly in boiling water, and drained.

Sauce Béarnaise

There is no doubt that this renowned sauce is somehow involved with the southwestern French province of Béarn and its native son, Henri IV. One account has it that the recipe originated at the pavilion in St. Germain-en-Laye named after Henri IV, who completed the château begun by Henri II, son of François I. However, Larousse Gastronomique *reveals that the recipe was first found in* La Cuisinière des Villes et Compagnes *in 1818, eighteen years before the pavilion restaurant opened its doors. History aside, hot "frites" and a "bifteck grillé" resting under the green-flecked pale gold blanket of an excellent Béarnaise is one of life's basic culinary pleasures, and the color of the sauce as it mingles with the beef juices is a visual treat as well.*

Yields about 1 1/2 cups, for 4 to 6 servings

1 recipe Sauce Hollandaise I (see page 91)
3 tablespoons tarragon-flavored wine vinegar
1 tablespoon chopped fresh shallots
1 tablespoon chopped tarragon stems and pieces
1 1/2 teaspoons Glace de Viande (see page 65)
Cayenne pepper
Worcestershire sauce
1 1/2 teaspoons chopped fresh tarragon leaves

Proceed as for Sauce Hollandaise I, but replace white wine vinegar with tarragon-flavored wine vinegar. Before simmering, add the chopped shallots, tarragon stems and pieces, and glace de

viande. When sauce is finished, but before it is strained, add a dash of cayenne pepper and a few drops of Worcestershire sauce. Before serving, whisk in the chopped fresh tarragon leaves.

If fresh tarragon stems, pieces, and leaves are not available, dried tarragon may be substituted, using one-half the quantities called for.

Mayonnaise

Considered by many to be "le fond du sandwich," "mayo" requires care in the making, but rewards this care many times over because its taste is so far superior to that of the bottled variety. A classic sauce, it is thought by many to have originated on the island of Minorca, and it acquired its appellation when the French, led by the Duc de Richelieu, captured Mahon in 1757. In the following recipes you will see that, as with Sauce Hollandaise, fresh mayonnaise can either stand alone or serve as the base for many other superb sauces.

Yields 5 cups

6 egg yolks at room temperature
1/2 teaspoon salt
A pinch of freshly ground white pepper
Juice of 1 large or 2 small lemons
1 tablespoon vinegar (white wine, red wine, or cider)
1 teaspoon Dijon mustard
1 teaspoon dry English mustard
3 to 4 drops of Worcestershire sauce
4 cups (950 ml) of oil (3 of peanut oil and 1 of olive oil)
A pinch of cayenne pepper (optional)

Recommended equipment

An electric mixer with glass or stainless steel mixing bowl.

Warm mixing bowl by filling it with hot water, pouring water out, and drying *completely* with a cloth towel. Add egg yolks to bowl and mix until thickened. Then add all ingredients except oil and mix thoroughly until the mixture is smooth and all the dry mustard has been thoroughly dissolved. Begin adding oil, *in a very fine stream of droplets at first*, until 1/2 cup (118 ml) has been added. Then begin adding the oil more quickly until all of it has been added. If the sauce is too thick it may be thinned with a touch of hot water, vinegar, or lemon juice. Adjust seasoning if necessary and chill until needed. Mayonnaise will keep well for a week to ten days refrigerated in a covered glass jar.

The amount of oil called for here is less than the maximum that 6 large egg yolks will absorb, so you should have no trouble with curdling. If, however, this does happen, don't panic! Simply turn the sauce into another bowl and wash and dry the mixer bowl. Mix a small amount of dry mustard and lemon juice in the mixer bowl until fully blended. Then, starting with a small stream of droplets, gradually add all of the curdled sauce. Two critical secrets to successful mayonnaise are having warm ingredients and being very careful about the initial binding of the oil and egg yolks.

Sauce Chantilly

Master chef to the Condé household during the Louis XIV era, Vatel gave this name to a number of preparations—especially those made with the whipped and sweetened crème Chantilly. This recipe is a very light mayonnaise to serve with vegetables such as fresh Asparagus, artichokes, or with one of my favorites, cooked leeks (either hot or cold), and certainly with cold Saumon Pochée.

Just before serving, add 3/4 cup (180 ml) whipped cream to 2 cups (475 ml) fresh Mayonnaise *(see page 94)*. You may have to adjust the seasoning a bit with salt, pepper, and a few drops of lemon juice.

Curry Mayonnaise

To 2 cups (475 ml) fresh Mayonnaise *(see page 94)*, add 1 teaspoon of curry powder, 2 tablespoons chopped or puréed chutney, and 1/2 cup (118 ml) sour cream or Crème Fraîche *(see page 66)*.

Mustard Sauce

This simple sauce is excellent for dipping crisp raw vegetables or boiled shrimp.

Yields about 2 1/2 cups

2 cups (475 ml) fresh Mayonnaise *(see page 94)*
6 tablespoons Dijon mustard
2 tablespoons dry English mustard
Salt
Freshly ground white pepper
Tabasco and Worcestershire sauce to taste

Recommended equipment

A wire whisk, 1-quart (1 L) bowl.

Mixing with a whisk, combine the mayonnaise and the mustards in the bowl. Then season to taste with salt, white pepper, and drops of the two sauces. This should keep for several days under refrigeration.

Variation: Add chopped fresh dill.

Swedish Mustard Sauce

Thank you, Fred Borman. One of the best gardes-manger whom I have had the pleasure to work with, he parted with this recipe while working at the famous Scandia in Los Angeles. This sauce is best with Gravlax but can be used as a dip with appetizers such as other smoked fish and raw vegetables.

Yields about 2 1/2 cups

3 egg yolks
1/4 cup (50 g) light brown sugar
1 1/2 tablespoons Dijon mustard
1 tablespoon dry English mustard
2 1/2 cups (590 ml) fresh Mayonnaise *(see page 94)*
1/4 cup (60 ml) finely chopped fresh dill
Salt and freshly ground white pepper

Recommended equipment

A wire whisk, 1-quart (1 L) bowl.

Using the whisk, mix egg yolks, brown sugar, and mustards. When well blended, add remaining ingredients and season to taste. Chill until ready to serve. Will keep at least one week under refrigeration.

Quick Green Sauce

Every chef has a little "sauce verte" up the sleeve, and I have offered you two—this one and Green Herb Mayonnaise. Both are superb with cold seafood or seafood mousses, the difference being that this one is a more "front of the mouth" sauce, and the other is more refined. It is a matter of your time.

Yields about 3 1/2 cups

3 cups (710 ml) fresh Mayonnaise *(see page 94)*
2 tablespoons tarragon vinegar
2 tablespoons Dijon mustard
1/2 garlic clove, peeled
1/3 cup (80 ml) each roughly chopped parsley, watercress, and spinach
2 tablespoons fresh dill
2 tablespoons fresh basil

Recommended equipment

A blender or food processor, 2-quart (2 L) bowl, wire whisk.

Mix 1 cup of mayonnaise with the rest of the ingredients in the blender or food processor until smooth. Transfer to the bowl, whip in remaining mayonnaise with the whisk, and refrigerate until serving time.

Sauce Tartare

Of the mayonnaise-based sauces, the two which follow, Sauce Tartare and its variation, Sauce Remoulade, are the most commonly used and are especially well suited for hot and cold fish.

Yields about 3 1/2 cups

- 3 cups (710 ml) fresh Mayonnaise *(see page 94)*
- 3 hard-boiled eggs, chopped
- 1 teaspoon Dijon mustard
- 1 tablespoon capers, well drained, chopped
- 6 sour pickles (large cornichons) or 2 medium dill pickles, finely chopped
- 1/2 teaspoon chopped fresh parsley
- 1/2 teaspoon finely cut fresh chives
- 1/2 medium onion, minced

Mix all ingredients together in a glass or stainless steel mixing bowl and chill until serving time.

If I feel that I will not use all of the sauce at one time, I omit the eggs and onions from a portion of the sauce until it is needed.

Variation

Sauce Remoulade

Yields about 3 1/2 cups

- 1 recipe Sauce Tartare *(see above)*

Add from 1 teaspoon to 2 tablespoons of finely chopped anchovies or anchovy paste, according to your taste, to sauce tartare. To make a Creole version of this sauce reminiscent of Arnaud's, add paprika, minced shallots, and Tabasco to taste.

South of the Border Mayonnaise

A refreshing mayonnaise for cold chicken or seafood dishes. Jalapeño pepper is the secret ingredient, and you should use it according to your own palate and those of your guests.

Yields 8 servings

- 2 cups (475 ml) fresh Mayonnaise *(see page 94)*
- 2 ripe, medium tomatoes (blanched, peeled, and seeded; *see page 568*), finely diced
- 2 medium shallots, peeled and minced
- 1/2 garlic clove, minced
- 1 scallion, cut lengthwise and sliced thinly
- 1 teaspoon seeded and finely diced jalapeño pepper
- 4 drops Tabasco sauce
- 1/4 medium green bell pepper, seeded and finely diced
- 1/4 medium red bell pepper, seeded and finely diced
- A dash of chili powder
- 1 tablespoon chopped fresh parsley

Recommended equipment

A small chef's knife, paring knife, 2-quart (2 L) bowl.

Prepare the ingredients separately and then combine them. Chill in the refrigerator for 2 hours before serving.

Homestead Seafood Sauce

There really are not that many good and different cold seafood sauces. This one is unique and compliments rather than overpowers seafood—especially important for seafood salads and cocktails. The sauce originated at the former Ambassador Hotel in New York, and became very popular at its Embassy Club. Clement Grangier, a fabulous chef and great man, was executive chef, and I have a feeling he added the vodka to compliment Colonel Serge Obelensky, who was connected with the Ambassador at that time.

Yields about 2 1/2 cups

2 cups (475 ml) fresh Mayonnaise *(see page 94)*
2 2/3 tablespoons ketchup
2 2/3 tablespoons cocktail sauce
1 tablespoon chutney, chopped
2 tablespoons Cognac
2 tablespoons vodka
1 1/2 teaspoons lemon juice
1 1/2 teaspoons tarragon vinegar
1 1/2 teaspoons finely cut fresh chives
1 1/2 teaspoons chopped fresh parsley
1 1/2 teaspoons minced and peeled celery
1/2 teaspoon chopped fresh tarragon
Tabasco sauce
Salt and freshly ground black pepper

Blend ingredients well with a whisk, and add Tabasco sauce, salt, and pepper to taste. If not to be used right away, put sauce in a sealed glass jar and refrigerate. It will keep for several days.

"Another" Cold Fish Sauce

If you prefer a hotter sauce, add serrano, jalapeño, or other chili peppers.

Yields 2 cups

1/2 large red bell pepper
2 tablespoons olive oil
2 sun-dried tomatoes, drained of their oil
1/2 garlic clove, pressed
2 tablespoons Dijon mustard
1/8 teaspoon curry powder
Juice of 1 lemon
Rind of 1 lemon (all bitter white removed), finely chopped
A drop or two of Tabasco sauce
1 tablespoon ketchup
2 cups (475 ml) fresh Mayonnaise *(see page 94)*

Recommended equipment

A paring knife, 8-inch (20 cm) sauté pan, garlic press, wooden spatula, blender or food processor, 1-quart (1 L) bowl.

Rinse the pepper, quarter it, and remove the seeds and pithy white. Set the sauté pan over medium heat, add the olive oil, and, when it is hot, add the pepper and sauté for 2 minutes. Then add the sun-dried tomatoes, press in the garlic, mix well with the spatula, and sauté for 1 minute. Remove mixture from heat, and when it is cool, purée it in the blender or food processor with the mustard, curry powder, lemon juice and rind, Tabasco, and ketchup.

In the bowl, stir in puréed ingredients with the mayonnaise, and chill until serving time.

Variation: Add 3 tablespoons thinly sliced scallions or fresh chives.

Green Herb Mayonnaise

This sauce is excellent for cold salmon and crabmeat salads, and the flavor can be adjusted to suit the dish it accompanies. For example, to emphasize a pronounced flavor such as anise, substitute anise seed or fresh fennel leaves for the basil, dill, and tarragon. Similarly, for a distinctive tarragon taste increase the tarragon to one tablespoon and eliminate the basil and dill. Be sure to keep in mind the combination of the particular herbs as well as the overall taste of the sauce and seafood or poultry, and you will avoid the all too common taste disaster caused by putting herbs together which really do not get along.

Yields about 3 1/2 cups

1/2 garlic clove, minced or pressed
1 teaspoon chopped shallots
1 tablespoon olive oil
1/4 cup (60 ml) dry white wine
1/3 cup (80 ml) fresh parsley, stems removed, roughly chopped
1/3 cup (80 ml) fresh spinach, stems removed, roughly chopped
1/3 cup (80 ml) fresh watercress, stems removed, roughly chopped
2 teaspoons chopped fresh tarragon
2 tablespoons chopped fresh basil
2 tablespoons chopped fresh dill
3 cups (710 ml) fresh Mayonnaise *(see page 94)*
2 tablespoons Dijon mustard
Juice of 1 lemon
Rind of 1 lemon (all bitter white removed), finely chopped
Tabasco sauce

Recommended equipment

An 8-inch (20 cm) sauté pan, blender or food processor, 2-quart (2 L) bowl, wire whisk.

Over low heat sauté garlic and shallots lightly in olive oil in the sauté pan, then add white wine, herbs, spinach, and watercress. Bring to a simmer and cook until lightly wilted, 1 to 2 minutes. Remove from heat and cool. Put into blender or food processor and process until smooth. Turn into a bowl and whisk in the mayonnaise, mustard, lemon juice, and rind. Add a dash of Tabasco if desired. Refrigerate for 2 or 3 hours.

Before serving you may wish to add 2 tablespoons of finely cut fresh chives. The addition of a couple of finely chopped or puréed anchovies will add a different, slightly elusive, salty dimension. This sauce will keep well refrigerated for several days.

Fruited Sauces

Cumberland Sauce

If you surmise that this sauce is English, you are partially correct. It came from Germany via the Hanoverian line of English monarchs, and is named for the third son of King George II, William Augustus, Duke of Cumberland. To further complicate the international intrigue, French chefs—Escoffier among them—made it popular in England. Originally used with cold venison, we serve it with Pâté Maison, Galantine of Capon, and smoked goose, turkey, and pheasant.

Yields 2 cups

Peel of 1 orange and 1 lemon, cut into fine julienne strips, all bitter white removed
1 cup (235 ml) red currant jelly
1/2 cup (118 ml) plus 2 tablespoons Port wine
3/4 teaspoon dry English mustard
1/4 cup (60 ml) fresh orange juice
1/4 cup (60 ml) fresh lemon juice
1/4 teaspoon ground ginger
Tabasco sauce to taste

Recommended equipment

A swivel-bladed vegetable peeler, 1 1/2-quart (1 1/2 L) saucepan, wire whisk.

In the saucepan blanch the orange and lemon peel by bringing 2 cups (475 ml) water to a boil, adding the julienned peel, boiling briefly, and then draining the peel. Mixing with the whisk, combine all the ingredients in the saucepan, bring to a boil, remove from heat, and cool. Chill sauce before serving. If not to be used immediately, this sauce may be stored in the refrigerator in a tightly sealed glass jar.

Rhubarb Sauce

This sauce can be served hot or cold—hot, with Baked Virginia Smithfield Ham, it brings new life to an old favorite. And cold, with pâté, a galantine, or chilled meat such as duckling, it provides a piquant alternative to the preceding Cumberland Sauce.

Yields 6 to 8 servings

3 cups (710 ml) peeled rhubarb (about 1 1/2 pounds or 675 g), cut into 2-inch (5 cm) strips
1/3 cup (65 g) sugar
1 cup (235 ml) water
3 tablespoons red currant jelly
2 tablespoons green peppercorns (packed in water)
2 tablespoons brandy

Recommended equipment

A 1 1/2-quart (1 1/2 L) saucepan with lid, blender or food processor, rubber spatula, 2-quart (2 L) bowl, 8-inch (20 cm) sauté pan.

Put rhubarb, sugar, and water in the saucepan and cook, covered, over low heat until soft. Remove from heat and let cool slightly. Add currant jelly, put mixture into blender or food processor, and purée until smooth. With the spatula, turn the purée into a bowl.

Drain peppercorns of all but 1/2 teaspoon of the canning liquid. Over medium high heat lightly sauté the peppercorns for 30 seconds *(do not burn them)*. Add the brandy, remove from heat, flambé the peppercorns *(see page 569)* and add them to the rhubarb. Adjust seasoning to your taste. If mixture is too tart, add more currant jelly. Allow peppers to marinate in the sauce for 2 or 3 hours. Taste again, and, if you feel the sauce needs more "bite," add a dash of cayenne pepper. For garnish, you may want to add a few small pieces of peeled rhubarb that have been cooked separately in a small amount of water until soft.

Homestead Passion Fruit Sauce

In the Poultry and Game chapter you will find several sauces for roast duckling. Here is another rather unusual recipe we developed which is excellent with either roast duckling or chicken. Be sure to make it with the stock derived from the bird you are roasting. If you use the sauce for ham, chicken stock is the appropriate base, unless you have produced an aromatic stock by braising the ham. In this case, degrease the stock, and use a mixture of stock and water, depending on the saltiness of the stock.

Yields 8 to 12 servings

1 teaspoon freshly crushed black pepper
2 cups (475 ml) dry red wine
1 cup (195 g) sugar
2 cups (475 ml) White Chicken Stock or Duck Stock *(see pages 61, 62)*
1 pound (450 g) passion fruit concentrate, defrosted
1/4 cup (60 ml) orange juice concentrate, defrosted
1 1/2 tablespoons arrowroot
3 tablespoons water

Recommended equipment

A mortar and pestle, 3-quart (3 L) saucepan, wire whisk, fine-mesh sieve.

Crush the black pepper in the mortar and pestle, add the pepper with the red wine to the saucepan, set the pan over medium heat, and simmer the liquid until it is reduced to one-third. Stir the sugar into the reduced liquid and simmer until the sugar is dissolved. Add the stock, simmer for 5 minutes, add the passion fruit and orange juice concentrates, and simmer for 5 more minutes. Remove the saucepan from heat and set aside.

Blend the arrowroot with the water to make a smooth, loose paste. Whisk the paste into the sauce, blend well, and return the saucepan to medium heat. Stir constantly with the whisk while bringing the sauce to a simmer. When the simmer is reached, cook the sauce (do not let it boil) until it has a limpid, translucent appearance (about 3 minutes), and then remove from heat, strain through the fine-mesh sieve into a clean saucepan or bowl, and serve at once.

Pear Brandy Sauce

This light pear-flavored sauce, enhanced with Swiss pear brandy, is the creation of our talented chief saucier, Brian Puhle, who experimented with it a great deal until it met his approval. The first attempt was good, but after it sat for awhile, it became clear that the cloves (as is often true with strong, aromatic spices) gained strength and overpowered the subtle pear flavor. Brian then tried adding cream and to our astonishment it totally obliterated the character of the sauce we envisioned—needless to say we decided to dispense with the cream! The recipe below resulted from reducing the amount of clove and broadening the spice taste with a few green peppercorns. If you use fresh pears, which I recommend because we call for both the fruit purée and the juice, try to find Williams, and if they are not available, look for Bartlett, Comice, or Anjou, in that order. Consult the note below for poaching instructions.

This sauce enhances the old favorite, Virginia ham, and provides an elegant accompaniment for roasted stuffed quail or roasted duckling, served hot or cold. When used with quail or duckling, a garnish of lightly poached fresh apricots, combined with either dark currants or slivers of dried prunes lightly plumped in brandy, provides an attractive visual contrast to the subtle color of the sauce.

Yields about 2 cups

6 pear halves, fresh, poached (see below), or canned
1/4 cup (60 ml) poaching liquid or juice from can
2 tablespoons dry white wine
2 tablespoons Swiss pear brandy
1 small or 1/2 large clove
6 green peppercorns (packed in water and drained)
2 tablespoons (30 g) butter, softened at room temperature

Recommended equipment

A blender or food processor, 1 1/2-quart (1 1/2 L) saucepan, wire whisk.

Place pears, juice, wine, and brandy in blender or food processor and purée until very smooth. Put mixture in the saucepan, add the clove and peppercorns, and simmer over low heat for 10 minutes. Set aside and remove clove. Just before serving, whip in soft butter with the whisk. If necessary to reheat *do not* bring to a boil.

To poach fresh pears, first peel them with a swivel-bladed vegetable peeler and then cut them in half. Remove the stem, core, and seeds. Rub the pear halves with lemon juice to keep them from turning brown. Place the halves cut side down in a saucepan large enough to hold them in one layer. Cover them with a syrup made of 1 part sugar dissolved in 2 parts water (probably about 3/4 cup or 145 g sugar and 1 1/2 cups or 355 ml water). Bring the pears to a boil, reduce heat, and simmer gently for about 10 to 15 minutes, or until pears can be lightly pierced with the point of a paring knife. Carefully remove the pears with a slotted spoon and proceed with the recipe, using the poaching liquid where indicated.

Flavored Vinegars and Dressings

Sauce Mignonette

In French, mignonette means coarsely ground pepper—a prominent ingredient in this sauce and hence the reason for its name. This recipe enjoys great popularity among lovers of clams and oysters on the half shell.

Yields 1 cup

1 cup (235 ml) red wine vinegar
2 tablespoons freshly chopped shallots
1 tablespoon freshly crushed black peppercorns

Mix all together and let marinate for a few hours. (Cooking is not required.) Store in a sealed jar and refrigerate. If not used right away, this sauce may be kept for several weeks.

Homestead Raspberry Vinegar

One of our former sous-chefs, Vince Williams, experimented with this recipe until he achieved this delightful result. Use it in Canard Rôti à la Framboise and Papillons de Poulet avec Sauce Framboise as well as the following salad dressing.

Yields 1 quart

4 1/2 pints (2115 ml) very ripe fresh raspberries
3 cups (710 ml) imported red wine vinegar
3 ounces (85 g) sugar
1/2 cup (118 ml) Cognac

Recommended equipment

Two 3-quart (3 L) glass or ceramic bowls, cheesecloth, large fine-mesh sieve, wooden spoon, double boiler, fine-mesh skimmer, 1-quart (1 L) jar or bottle with lid.

Put 2 1/2 pints (1175 ml) of the raspberries in one of the bowls, add the vinegar, cover the bowl with cheesecloth, and set the bowl into the refrigerator or a cool place for 24 hours.

The next day, put the remaining raspberries in the other bowl. Pass the first batch of macerated berries through the sieve into the second bowl, stirring them down with the wooden spoon, and discard the pulp. Cover the bowl with cheesecloth and refrigerate for another 24 hours.

The third day, strain the raspberries through the sieve (discard the pulp) into the top part of the double boiler. Set the double boiler over medium heat, bring the water in the bottom part to a lively simmer, and add the sugar and Cognac to the vinegar. Maintain the simmer for 1 hour (you may need to replenish the water so keep your eye on it). The vinegar must *never* boil. As the vinegar heats, skim it from time to time as needed. When done, remove vinegar from heat, pour into a bowl, and let cool. When cool, pour it into a glass container, cover tightly, and refrigerate or keep in a cool place, where it will stay fresh for several weeks.

🌿 Raspberry Vinegar and Poppy Seed Dressing

This popular recipe is uniquely "Homestead," and came about with the increased use of natural fruit-flavored vinegars. We had made a poppy seed dressing here previously with a recipe from my friend, Eddie Hettich, then Homestead assistant executive chef. The dressing's original sweetness, however, limited its use. Replacing the white vinegar with raspberry vinegar and eliminating half the sugar made the dressing far more versatile. Use either Homestead Raspberry Vinegar or French raspberry vinegar of 7% acidity (no imitation flavors please).

Yields about 2 1/2 cups

1/4 cup (50 g) sugar
1/2 cup (118 ml) raspberry vinegar
1 1/2 teaspoons dry English mustard
3/4 teaspoon salt
2 tablespoons minced fresh onion
1 3/4 cups (415 ml) peanut oil
2 tablespoons poppy seeds

Recommended equipment

A blender or food processor.

Combine everything except oil and poppy seeds in the blender or food processor. Mix thoroughly until the onion is liquefied. With machine on, add oil slowly and continue processing until all the oil has been added. Process until thick (about two minutes). Mix in poppy seeds. Refrigerate in a covered glass jar. Will keep for one to two weeks.

🌿 Olive Oil and Lemon Juice Dressing

Yields about 3 1/2 cups

1/4 teaspoon salt
Freshly ground black pepper
1 1/2 teaspoons sugar
1 1/2 teaspoons Dijon mustard
1 1/2 teaspoons dry English mustard
1 1/2 cups (355 ml) olive oil
1 1/2 cups (355 ml) peanut oil
1/2 cup (118 ml) fresh lemon juice
1/2 garlic clove, lightly crushed

Recommended equipment

A blender or food processor.

In the blender or food processor, combine salt, pepper, sugar, and mustards. Mixing continuously, add the oils and lemon juice slowly, and then the garlic. Process until well mixed and adjust seasoning. Will keep in a covered jar in the refrigerator for at least a week.

Variations: Should you prefer a more pronounced olive oil taste, adjust the ratio of oils. For variety add 1/4 teaspoon finely chopped fresh tarragon or 1/2 teaspoon cut chives just before serving.

French walnut or hazelnut oil can be used in place of olive oil. Because of their strong flavor, however, they should be used in the proportion of 1 part hazelnut or walnut oil to 5 parts peanut oil. Although the recipe calls for lemon juice, it can be replaced by a good red, white, or tarragon-flavored wine vinegar. I would also add 1 tablespoon of freshly chopped shallots and let the dressing sit for 1 to 2 hours before serving.

Homestead Grille Hot Bacon Dressing

Yields 1 1/2 cups

4 to 5 ounces (115 to 145 g) bacon in strips
1/4 cup (50 g) sugar
1 1/2 teaspoons dry English mustard
Salt
Freshly ground black pepper
1 cup (235 ml) peanut oil
6 tablespoons red wine vinegar
1/2 garlic clove, minced

Recommended equipment

A 12-inch (30 cm) sauté pan.

In the sauté pan over low heat, cook bacon until crisp, then remove from pan leaving the fat. Add the dry ingredients, peanut oil, vinegar, and garlic to the fat in the pan. Bring to a boil, stirring occasionally, then remove from heat. Chop bacon and add to dressing just before serving. Serve hot over fresh spinach or other greens of your choice.

Homestead Sauce Vinaigrette

This dressing may be more complicated than the vinaigrette to which you are accustomed; however, this recipe is much more common to the part of Europe in which I grew up. A version of Sauce Ravigote with this base is also included as a variation below.

Yields about 3 1/2 cups

1 cup (235 ml) olive oil
1 cup (235 ml) peanut oil
1/2 cup (118 ml) red or white wine vinegar
1/2 teaspoon dry English mustard
1 1/2 teaspoons Dijon mustard
1/4 cup (60 ml) finely chopped dill pickles
1/2 cup (118 ml) finely chopped onions
1/2 teaspoon finely chopped fresh basil
1/2 teaspoon finely chopped fresh tarragon
1 tablespoon finely chopped parsley
1 1/2 teaspoons finely cut chives
1/8 teaspoon salt
A dash of freshly ground black pepper

Mixing with a whisk, combine all ingredients and adjust seasoning to your taste. The vinaigrette will keep in the refrigerator in a covered glass jar for several days. This dressing can be made in a blender or food processor if the ingredients are chopped coarsely before combining. Then purée until smooth.

Variations: Substitute shallots for onions, and if you are fond of anchovies, add a few finely chopped fillets.

For Sauce Ravigote add 2 2/3 tablespoons minced capers and 1 hard-boiled egg, finely chopped, and replace the oil and vinegar with mayonnaise. Because of the hard-boiled egg, this dressing will not keep more than 1 to 2 days, so you may want to add the egg to the amount needed just before serving.

These sauces have many diverse uses, some of which are: in salads, with fresh vegetables such as Asparagus and artichokes, and with meats such as calf's brains and headcheese.

❧ *Homestead French Dressing*

Yields about 3 1/2 cups

1 small onion, coarsely chopped
1/2 garlic clove, lightly crushed
1 cup (235 ml) Beef Bouillon
 (see page 151)
1/2 cup (118 ml) red wine
 vinegar
1 1/2 teaspoons arrowroot
2 tablespoons water (or wine
 vinegar)
1 egg yolk
1 tablespoon Dijon mustard
2 teaspoons sugar
1/4 teaspoon salt
Pinch of freshly ground white
 pepper
1/2 cup (118 ml) olive oil
1 1/2 cups (355 ml) peanut oil
1 tablespoon lemon juice

Recommended equipment

Cheesecloth, 1 1/2-quart (1 1/2 L) saucepan, whisk, medium mixing bowl, glass storage jar with lid.

Put the chopped onion and garlic in the center of a large square of cheesecloth, tie opposite corners tightly together, and add to saucepan with consommé and vinegar. Simmer for 10 minutes. Meanwhile, make a loose paste with the arrowroot and water (or wine vinegar). When the mixture has finished simmering, whisk the paste into the saucepan and simmer, stirring, 2 more minutes. Do not let it boil. Remove from heat, remove cheesecloth bag, pour mixture into the bowl, and let cool.

Mixing with a whisk, add in order the egg yolk, mustard, sugar, salt, pepper, oils, and lemon juice.

When completely blended, taste, and if too acid, whisk in a little more oil. If too bland, add lemon juice. Refrigerate in covered glass jar. This dressing will keep for at least a week.

To point up the flavor a bit, add 2 tablespoons of coarsely chopped fresh cilantro a few minutes before serving.

Fine Herbs Dressing

Yields about 3 3/4 cups

1 recipe Homestead French Dressing *(see page 106)*
1 tablespoon lemon juice
1/4 garlic clove
1/4 cup (60 ml) olive oil
1/8 teaspoon chopped fresh tarragon
1/8 teaspoon chopped fresh oregano
1 tablespoon chopped chives
1 tablespoon chopped parsley

Mixing with a whisk, combine the above ingredients except the chives and parsley. Add the chives and parsley just before serving and only to the amount of dressing needed. Refrigerate in covered glass jar; will keep at least a week.

Variation: Substitute dill or basil for tarragon and oregano.

Roquefort Dressing

Yields about 2 1/2 cups

1 cup (235 ml) fresh Mayonnaise *(see page 94)*
1 cup (235 ml) sour cream
2 tablespoons half-and-half
2 tablespoons vinegar
3/4 cup (180 ml) Roquefort cheese, crumbled
Worcestershire sauce to taste

Whisk all ingredients together. Store in a covered glass jar in the refrigerator. Will keep for several days under refrigeration.

Variation: For a stronger dressing try a mixture of 6 tablespoons of Roquefort and 6 tablespoons of Gorgonzola.

Buttermilk Dressing

Yields 2 cups

1/2 cup (118 ml) buttermilk
1/2 cup (118 ml) sour cream
1 cup (235 ml) fresh Mayonnaise
   (see page 94)
3/4 teaspoon onion powder
3/4 teaspoon garlic powder
1 teaspoon Knorr Aromat
1 tablespoon chopped fresh
   parsley
Salt and freshly ground black
   pepper

Mixing with a whisk, thoroughly combine all ingredients. Will keep in a closed jar in the refrigerator for about one week.

Cocktail Sauce

You are probably wondering why we have included one recipe, let alone two, for cocktail sauce when it is readily available at the grocery store. The answer is simple. The flavor of any bottled sauce or dressing tends to have a short shelf life—especially those containing mustard or horseradish. We do have the basic cocktail sauce made to our specifications and bottled, but because we use so much of it for receptions, buffets, and cocktail parties, it never stays in the bottle for more than a week. As you can tell, the second recipe is more highly seasoned, and you should use it when the occasion calls for Creole-style flavors.

Yields about 4 cups

3 cups (710 ml) ketchup
1 cup (235 ml) chili sauce
2 tablespoons prepared
   horseradish
1 tablespoon light brown sugar
1 teaspoon dry English mustard
1 tablespoon red wine vinegar
3 tablespoons sweet relish
A few drops Tabasco sauce
Freshly ground white pepper

Recommended equipment

A blender.

Mix all ingredients together in the order listed and then purée in the blender for 15 seconds. Store, covered, in a glass container in the refrigerator, where it will keep for weeks.

Variation

❧ *Homestead Cocktail Sauce*

Yields about 3 cups

2 cups (475 ml) ketchup
3/4 cup (180 ml) Cocktail Sauce
  (see page 108)
1/4 cup (50 g) light brown sugar
2 teaspoons curry powder
  (imported Indian is preferable)
2 tablespoons dry English
  mustard
2 to 4 drops of Tabasco sauce

Mix all together well with a whisk. Refrigerate in a sealed glass jar, and it will stay fresh for weeks.

Homestead Cantaloupe Soup at the Casino

110

Soups

It is to a dinner what a portico or peristyle is to a building; that is to say it is not only the first part of it, but it must be devised in such a manner as to set the tone of the whole banquet, in the same way as the overture of an opera announces the subject of the work.
—Grimod de la Reynière

And now it's the turn of a cold soup called *crème vichyssoise*.

This recipe, as evolved some forty years ago by Louis Diat, the French-born chef of the New York Ritz-Carlton, is, basically, every French housewife's potato and leek soup, puréed, chilled, enriched with fresh cream and sprinkled with chive. One of our troubles about reproducing this dish here in England is that leeks go out of season about the beginning, if any, of the summer, and don't normally come into the shops again until the end of it. Which means if you *must* have vichyssoise during the heat-wave period then it has to come out of a tin. Those people, however, who won't stoop to tinned soups but still want to be in the swim with their vichyssoise, have taken to using cucumbers instead of leeks, and watercress or mint instead of chives—which are hard to come by unless you grow them yourself. The mixture is still thick and rich and cold—and what's after all, in a name?

All this seems to be typical of the uneasy phase which English cooking is going through. As soon as any dish with a vaguely romantic-sounding name (you may well ask why anyone would associate Vichy with romance) becomes known you find it's got befogged by the solemn mystique which can elevate a routine leek and potato soup into what the heroine of a recent upper-class-larks novel refers to as my 'perfected vichyssoise.' Then a semi-glamorous monthly publishes a recipe in which the original few pence-worth of kitchen garden vegetables are omitted entirely and their place taken by cream of chicken soup and French cream cheese. With astounding rapidity the food processors move in, and launch some even further debased version which in a wink is turning up at banquets and parties and on the menus of provincial hotels.
—Elizabeth David

*I*n one sense, these two notes say all that needs to be said about soups—the first capturing their importance and the second their risk of becoming an endangered species. One of the oldest recognizable parts of cuisine, there are references to them at least eight thousand years before Christ—a fact Julia Child corroborates in her comments on researching lentil soup, which she traced to biblical times. I could not think of preparing a dinner menu without them—ours at the Homestead always has at least two, but somehow they seem less important to the home cook. This mystifies me because soups are an efficient way to use trimmings from vegetables, seafood, poultry, and meat. Beyond that, they have an almost infinite range of complexity and texture that allows them to be the focus of the meal or that which "set[s] the tone of the whole banquet."

I suppose there is the temptation to be elitist with soups because the seemingly easiest are actually the most complex and time consuming. English Beef Tea, for example, is an absolutely limpid pale gold liquid which has three stages and requires two to three days to prepare. Minestrone Milanese, on the other hand, has a lengthy ingredient list, but can be made in one day. By the same token, should I receive a special advance order for English Beef Tea, I know as Le Huédé said when a passenger on the *France* ordered quenelles of sole (and not pike), "*Tiens*, I said to myself, this one really knows what he wants." Obvious awareness by diners and guests of hard work in the kitchen is as welcome to the executive chef as it is to the home cook.

Because many soups have a direct relation to stocks, much of what we said concerning ingredients and cooking in the introduction to the sauce chapter is applicable here. Soups cannot be rushed. They must be simmered slowly to extract the most flavor from their ingredients. Trimmings as well as whole vegetables, seafood, poultry, and meats should be as fresh as possible—even for the Bisque of Vegetables Rosa. And, do not forget to use the bottled water available at your grocery store if your drinking water is heavily treated with chemicals. One last *conseil*: many of these recipes call for beef or chicken stock. Herein lies another reason to make your own according to the recipes in this book. Cubes or powdered stock base will inevitably lead to disappointing results. The chemical interaction which takes place in the slowly simmering stockpot cannot be had by adding water to dried or frozen ingredients—any more than Sauce Américaine can be made in the microwave.

This chapter was composed with an eye toward the seasonality of soups. Thus, you will find refreshing chilled fresh fruit or vegetable soups for summer, heavier soups for fall, hearty thick-textured soups for winter, and soups which feature fresh crops of spring vegetables.

The first quarter of the chapter is devoted to chilled soups, some of which are specific to summer, and some of which can be served either chilled in warmer months or as a hot soup course for a cold weather meal.

Three soups based solely on vegetables and their juice or fruit and their juice lead off—the Spanish classic Gazpacho (a meal in itself with a salad and French bread) is followed by a melon soup for summer gardeners and then a recipe featuring the exotic mango. A second trio, enriched with cream (two with the added tang of yogurt) and still requiring no or little cooking, follows. First comes the simple taste of cucumber, which is elaborated by a middle eastern touch of raisins and walnuts, and gives way to a curried recipe which harkens back to the spice trade routes which traversed the dangerous western waters of Africa.

The quotation from Elizabeth David is recalled by a series of recipes based on the now classic vichyssoise created by Louis Diat at the New York Ritz-Carlton. We have included four variations using other vegetables because we consider the technique an important and versatile addition to cuisine. Although there is no clear connection between this technique and Vichy, perhaps the carrot variation might be geographically the most authentic because this vegetable was considered an important part of the dietary regimen when one took the waters for liver disorders at this famous spa and resort.

The cold soup section is closed out by a colorful and tasty contribution from Russia featuring watercress, cucumber, and smoked ham and two familiar jellied soups derived from recipes which occur later in the chapter.

The portion of the chapter devoted to hot soups is generally (although not exactly) organized along the lines of a progression from more visible ingredients and less complication to completely clear consommés and broths which require considerable preparation time. The first section is composed of eleven recipes based on stock or the bouillons given near the end of the chapter. Three hearty potato-thickened soups based, respectively, on peas, lentils, and navy beans are followed by two preparations based on barley (one of which is Swiss—I just couldn't help myself).

Vegetables (with meat) simmered in stock or bouillon come center stage with a truly international collection which commences in Italy via a venerable classic from Milan and an eighteenth-century-style, rose-colored vegetable bisque. If you have always secretly thought that onion soup can be much better than that served up by most American restaurants, hop aboard for a trio of recipes which originates in France for a nostalgic visit to the famous Les Halles markets, then to Basel for a Swiss adaptation thickened and darkened with browned flour. And, as is often the case when on the trail of good food, we end up in Russia for a variation on the Swiss variation—this time flavored with caraway, enriched with sour cream, and served in a more elegant fashion. Finally, what better way to end this section than by including one of the most noted contributions of Russian cuisine—borscht. As with the onion soup, your reward for making this revered classic will be the sure knowledge of how excellent this oft-maligned soup can be.

Cream is the secret ingredient for the next section composed of six vegetable and four diverse soups, and before you mutter "calories and cholesterol," raise an eyebrow, and turn to broths and consommés, we want to make a comment. We have already stated our position on this matter in the introduction to Sauces, so we will not reiterate it here; however, we will say that, except for the Billi Bi, all of the recipes call for between 2 and 2 2/3 tablespoons of cream per person, depending on the number of servings. This is equivalent to one-half this quantity of butter, or 100 to 133 calories. In addition, save for Potage Germiny, cream and egg yolk liaisons are suggested but not mandatory. Thus, these soups should be on the list for all but those on *no-fat* diets. If it means doing some exercise to work off the cream, you should be doing that now anyhow, shouldn't you?

If you have a garden or frequent a farmers' market, the vegetable soups will be a special treat—spinach, watercress, sorrel, and asparagus are all accessible—the sorrel possibly in your yard and watercress in a nearby (unpolluted) stream. Rounding out the set of six, celery and mushroom extend the seasonal range of these soups from early spring through summer to early fall. Best of all, the overlapping seasons allow you to savor one vegetable while anticipating the arrival of another.

The sea becomes the backdrop for the last four soups in this section. First, indirectly, through curry, a symbol of the spice trade routes which took the English to the East Indies, then the peanut, native to America, transplanted to Africa, and reintroduced to Virginia and the South by the slave trade. And what cuisine has done more with seafood than French? Here are two items from classic cuisine—a post-eighteenth-century recipe featuring shrimp, and a rich specialty of the Côte d'Atlantique featuring the mollusk native to the region.

Well, the time has come to make you work for your stars. Not that the preceding recipes are child's play, but rather that bouillon, broth, and consommé demand patience, care, and, yes, skill.

By this we mean the finesse born of observation and experience which told the Sung dynasty painter when one more brush stroke would be too many, and which prevents the tiniest mote of fat from blemishing the surface of English Beef Tea. To master these recipes is to complete one of cuisine's most significant apprenticeships. At the risk of being pedantic, we will nag you one last time about water. These soups are true reductions of water and their ingredients—you will be investing far too much time and effort to end up with an elegant liquid which tastes more of chemical additives than it does of chicken, quail, or beef. Bottled spring water is relatively inexpensive and found in most grocery stores. Use it.

Simple chicken bouillon leads off, followed by a Cantonese classic which, with little assistance, can turn into one of the best hot and sour soups you have ever had. A recipe calling for quail comes next, providing you with a tour de force for those extraordinary occasions which summon forth the best efforts from your kitchen. Beef bouillon follows, and like a *sauce grande*, it stands alone, serves as the foundation for many other recipes earlier in the chapter, or is the first stage on the pilgrimage road to beef tea. A versatile clear consommé with several garnishes follows—a subtle and elegant beginning for a formal meal. Two more vegetables, celery and tomato, respectively, flavor and color a broth and a consommé, and, at last, the ne plus ultra—English Beef Tea. The *amateur de cuisine* will not be deceived by its apparent simplicity, but instead will recognize it as one of the most elegant understatements of classical cuisine. I like to reserve it for special occasions, and accordingly served it in 1981, when the Homestead was chosen to host the *Mobil Travel Guide* banquet at which the five-star awards were given to the thirty-two recipients.

Well, there you have it. This sampling of the soups we make at the Homestead will serve you well through all seasons and occasions and will also broaden your knowledge of cuisine as you add to your accomplishments. In the cooking profession, we make much of using fresh ingredients, and what better place for the bounty of the farm and the force of culinary history to meet than in the soup pot.

Cold Soups

Gazpacho

This Andalusian specialty is really a soup and salad combined—what better way to celebrate summer. To really set it off, serve in large green, yellow, red, or purple bell peppers, mixing all the colors among your guests. To make a pepper soup cup, cut the top off the pepper about 2 to 2 1/2 inches below the stem and scrape the seeds and ribs out with a teaspoon. Ladle the chilled soup into the "cups," filling them three-quarters full, and set them in a bowl with finely crushed ice as a support. Sprinkle a few sprigs of parsley or dill on the ice, garnish the cups with a lemon wedge, and call your guests to their feast of Mediterranean color.

Yields about 9 cups, for 8 to 10 servings

- 1 cup (235 ml) finely diced cucumber, peeled and seeded
- 1 cup (235 ml) finely diced celery
- 1/2 cup (118 ml) finely diced green bell pepper, seeded
- 1/2 cup (118 ml) finely sliced scallions
- 1 cup (235 ml) finely chopped tomatoes, either fresh (blanched, peeled, and seeded; see page 568) or canned
- 3 cups (710 ml) tomato juice
- 3 cups (710 ml) V-8 vegetable juice
- 1 tablespoon sugar
- A dash of freshly ground white pepper
- Salt
- A few drops of Tabasco sauce (optional)
- 2 tablespoons finely cut fresh chives
- 2 tablespoons finely chopped fresh parsley

Recommended equipment

A swivel-bladed vegetable peeler, small chef's knife, small mixing bowl.

Prepare the vegetables. Peel, seed, and dice the cucumber. Peel the celery to make it as tender and stringless as possible; remove the leaves before chopping. Seed and dice the pepper. Using the white part of the onion with several inches of green nearest the bulb, cut the scallions lengthwise into strips and then crosswise into thin slices. Prepare the tomatoes. As the vegetables are ready, put them into the mixing bowl and stir in all remaining ingredients except the chives and parsley. Refrigerate for 2 to 3 hours or until well chilled. Just before serving, adjust the seasoning and add the optional Tabasco, if desired. Stir in chives and parsley and serve.

This soup holds quite well when covered and refrigerated overnight.

Homestead Cantaloupe Soup

This colorful concoction is a wonderful way to start a luncheon or dinner in the middle of summer. It's best when made with fresh locally grown cantaloupe; otherwise make sure that the melons you buy in the store are fully ripened before you make this recipe.

Yields 6 cups, for 6 to 8 servings

2 cups (475 ml) orange juice
2 cups (475 ml) apple juice
1 cup (235 ml) dry white wine
2 tablespoons tapioca
1 ripe medium cantaloupe
Salt
Cayenne pepper
Sprigs of fresh mint

Recommended equipment

A 3-quart (3 L) saucepan, small chef's knife, blender or food processor, 2-quart (2 L) bowl.

Combine orange juice, apple juice, white wine, and tapioca in the saucepan, and simmer gently over medium heat for 10 minutes. Then cool mixture and chill. When juice mixture is chilled, prepare cantaloupe by cutting in half, removing seeds, and scooping out flesh. Divide flesh into two equal portions, coarsely chopping one and finely dicing the other. Put coarsely chopped melon into the blender or food processor with 1 cup of the chilled mixture and purée until smooth. Pour purée into the mixing bowl and add remainder of chilled juice and finely diced melon. Adjust seasoning with salt and a touch of cayenne pepper if desired.

Serve cold, with a sprig of fresh mint, in a cup set onto a bed of crushed ice. Or serve in one-half of a cantaloupe. To do this cut a whole cantaloupe in half crosswise, seed, and scoop out enough melon to hold soup. So that cantaloupe half will balance on the serving plate, cut the end straight across before filling with soup.

Refrigerated and covered, the soup will keep for 2 to 3 days.

Homestead Mango Soup

Have you ever wondered what to do with mangoes, and, not knowing, always passed them by at the produce section of your market? Well, in addition to being an important ingredient in chutney, they are a popular fruit in warm climates, and, as you will see here, can be used to make an elegant summer soup.

Yields about 6 cups, for 6 to 7 servings

1 cup (235 ml) dry white wine
2 cups (475 ml) pineapple juice
2 cups (475 ml) apple juice
2 tablespoons tapioca
5 ripe mangoes
Juice of 4 lemons

Recommended equipment

A 3-quart (3 L) saucepan, paring knife, large fine-mesh sieve, blender or food processor, 2-quart (2 L) bowl.

Combine wine and pineapple and apple juices in the saucepan and bring to a boil. Stir in tapioca, reduce heat, and simmer for 10 minutes. Remove from heat. While mixture cools, peel mangoes with a paring knife and cut into coarse pieces. Add to blender or food processor with 1 cup of the cooled juice mixture and purée until smooth. Pour purée through the sieve into the mixing bowl and stir in remaining chilled juice mixture and lemon juice. Chill thoroughly before serving.

Cucumber Soup

The next time you are tempted to belittle the cucumber or to hide when you see your neighbor coming with a gift from the summer garden, make this soup, serve it with watercress sandwiches, and remember the following words from Jane Grigson: "The cucumbers of Ur-Nammu, who lived in Mesopotamia 4000 years ago, refreshed him so well that he built a temple to the god Nanna, to save the garden where they grew from destruction. In the end Nanna could not save it, this earliest known of the world's vegetable gardens. Even the most speculative of archaeologists, with all the scientific aids available, could not place it exactly, though the site of the temple is known. Ur-Nammu paid a high price to guard his cucumbers (and his onions, leeks, lettuce and melons), though anyone eating chilled cucumber soup at the end of a hot day, may think he spent his money wisely."

Yields about 5 cups, for 6 servings

4 medium cucumbers, peeled and seeded
1/2 cup (118 ml) half-and-half
2 cups (475 ml) sour cream
2 cups (475 ml) plain yogurt
A dash of salt
Freshly ground white pepper
2 teaspoons chopped fresh dill

Recommended equipment

A swivel-bladed vegetable peeler, small chef's knife, blender or food processor, 2-quart (2 L) bowl.

Cut three of the peeled and seeded cucumbers into chunks and put in blender or food processor with the half-and-half. Purée until smooth and combine purée with sour cream and yogurt in the mixing bowl. Finely dice the remaining cucumber and stir into the mixture. Season with salt and pepper, add dill, and chill well before serving.

❧ *Persian Yogurt Soup*

This is a favorite at our al fresco buffet at the Casino. Beware of large servings as it is very rich.

Yields about 3 cups, for 4 servings

1/2 cup (118 ml) raisins
2/3 cup (160 ml) yogurt
1 cup (235 ml) half-and-half
1 hard-boiled egg, chopped
1 medium cucumber, peeled, seeded, and chopped
2/3 cup (160 ml) chopped walnuts
1/4 cup (60 ml) chopped scallions, white part only
1 teaspoon salt
1/3 teaspoon freshly ground white pepper
1/2 cup (118 ml) cold water
1 1/2 tablespoon chopped fresh parsley
1 1/2 teaspoons chopped fresh dill

Recommended equipment

A 1-quart (1 L) bowl, small chef's knife, 2-quart (2 L) bowl.

In the small bowl, soak raisins in hot water for 10 minutes and then drain. In the mixing bowl combine raisins and all remaining ingredients, mixing well. Chill for 2 to 3 hours before serving.

❧ *Senegalese Soup*

Recipes for Senegalese soup always include curry, a sure reference to the traditional importance of this part of Africa, whose Cap Vert is the westernmost point on the continent. An important landmark for the early spice traders, it was only during the fifteenth century that Portuguese sailors, under the flag of Prince Henry the Navigator, allayed fears that a dangerous uncharted sea lay beyond the bulge in the African coast.

Yields about 5 cups, for 6 servings

1 cup (235 ml) diced onions
1/2 cup (118 ml) diced celery
2 medium (or 1 large) apples, cored and chopped
4 tablespoons butter (60 g)
1 tablespoon imported curry powder
3 tablespoons flour
3 cups (710 ml) White Chicken Stock *(see page 61)*
1 tablespoon chutney
1 cup (235 ml) whipping cream
A dash of salt
Freshly ground black pepper

Recommended equipment

A small chef's knife, apple corer, 3-quart (3 L) heavy-bottomed saucepan with lid, wooden spatula, wire whisk, large fine-mesh sieve, 2-quart (2 L) bowl.

Dice the onions and celery and core and chop the apples. Melt butter in the saucepan over low heat, and add onions, celery, apples, and curry powder. Smother over low heat for about 5 minutes, stirring occasionally with the spatula. Do not allow to brown. Add flour, stirring constantly with the spatula until well mixed into a paste. Add chicken stock and chutney, increase heat, and, mixing well with the whisk, bring to a boil. Reduce heat and simmer gently, partially covered, for 45 minutes to 1 hour.

Strain through fine-mesh sieve into the mixing bowl, cool, and refrigerate until well chilled. Before serving, stir in cream and season with salt and pepper.

You may wish to garnish the soup with 1 tablespoon of whipped cream just before serving and sprinkle with either a dash of chopped parsley, fresh chives, or a teaspoon of finely chopped chutney.

Vichyssoise

In spite of the name, this recipe appears to have little to do with Vichy. It was created in the 1920s by the French-born chef of the New York Ritz-Carlton, Louis Diat, and the name may have been chosen to evoke the suave, pre–World War II grandeur of the resort. As for its origin, Craig Claiborne probably came closest in suggesting that Diat remembered the Potage Parisienne of his childhood. Vichyssoise is really a technique, and that is why it appears in the four following recipes. Although a blender is easier to use for puréeing, I prefer a food mill or fine-mesh sieve because it does not completely remove the potato texture. If you want to serve vichyssoise, recall Elizabeth David's statement and resist the temptation to use the bland dehydrated or canned versions. It's simpler than you think to make the real thing—the base can be made two to three hours ahead and the soup finished faster than you can say "canned" a few times.

Yields about 6 cups, for 6 to 8 servings

4 medium leeks, white part only
1 medium onion
1/2 celery stalk
2 pounds (900 g) boiling potatoes
1 tablespoon (15 g) butter
4 cups (950 ml) White Chicken Stock *(see page 61)*
Salt
Freshly ground white pepper
1 cup (235 ml) half-and-half
1/4 teaspoon Maggi
2 tablespoons cut fresh chives

Recommended equipment

A large chef's knife; swivel-bladed vegetable peeler; 3-quart (3 L) saucepan or casserole with cover; large fine-mesh sieve, food mill, blender, or food processor; wire whisk.

Prepare the vegetables. The leeks must be thoroughly washed of all clinging dirt by separating the stalks under running cold water. Then chop them coarsely. Peel and slice the onion. The celery stalk should be as tender and stringless as possible; remove the leaves before cutting into chunks. Rinse the potatoes, peel them, and cut them up into chunks.

When the vegetables are ready, melt the butter in the saucepan or casserole over medium heat and sauté the leeks, onion, and celery for a few minutes until softened. Then add the potatoes and the chicken stock. The stock should liberally cover the vegetables (if not, add more). Season with salt and white pepper. Increase heat to medium high, bring to a boil, then reduce heat so soup is at a medium simmer. Partially cover with the lid and cook for 30 minutes or until potatoes are soft. Remove from heat and let cool. When soup is cool enough to handle comfortably, force it through the fine-mesh sieve or food mill, or purée it in the blender or food processor. Refrigerate for 2 to 3 hours, stirring occasionally.

When soup is well chilled, whisk in the half-and-half, adjust seasoning if necessary, then stir in Maggi and the chives. Extra half-and-half may be added if soup is too thick. Serve in chilled cups.

Variation: Served hot, vichyssoise is commonly known as leek and potato soup or Potage Parisienne. Bring the soup to a simmer for a couple of minutes while adding the half-and-half and seasonings.

Homestead Watercress Vichyssoise

If you have visited us, you will understand why "Homestead" appears in the title. Two rushing streams course right through the grounds—one beside the hotel and the Casino and one between the hotel and Cottage Row. Both are literally filled with watercress the year round, and while we procure our watercress commercially, this piquant plant is as much a trademark of ours as are the local chanterelles we harvest every August. Although structurally very similar to Vichyssoise, the presence of watercress in this recipe dramatically changes the appearance of this soup to both the eye and the palate. Contrasting with the soft green hue of the soup, the tang of the watercress plays against the smoothness of Vichyssoise to provide a distinctly peppery taste.

Yields about 6 cups, for 6 to 8 servings

1 medium leek, white part only
1 medium onion
1/2 celery stalk
2 pounds (900 g) boiling potatoes
1 bunch watercress
1 1/2 tablespoons (23 g) butter
4 cups (950 ml) White Chicken Stock *(see page 61)*
Salt
Freshly ground white pepper
1 cup (235 ml) half-and-half
1/4 teaspoon Maggi

Recommended equipment

A large chef's knife; swivel-bladed vegetable peeler; 1 1/2-quart (1 1/2 L) saucepan; 3-quart (3 L) saucepan or casserole with cover; large fine-mesh sieve, food mill, blender, or food processor; wire whisk.

Prepare the vegetables. The leek must be thoroughly washed of all clinging dirt by separating the stalk under running cold water. Then chop leek coarsely. Peel and slice the onion. The celery stalk should be as tender and stringless as possible; remove the leaves before cutting into chunks. Rinse the potatoes, peel them, and cut them into chunks. Wash the watercress thoroughly under rapidly running cold water, cut off 2 to 2 1/2 inches (5 to 7 1/2 cm) from the bottoms (and discard), then pick the leaves off the stems. Using the chef's knife, in separate batches, chop the leaves finely and the stems and pieces coarsely. In the smaller saucepan over medium heat melt 1/2 tablespoon of the butter, add 2 tablespoons chicken broth, and simmer the chopped leaves for 1 minute. Remove from heat and reserve.

Prepare the soup base by melting the remaining

butter in the large saucepan or casserole over medium heat, adding the leek, onion, and celery, and sautéing for a few minutes until softened. Then add the potatoes and chicken stock. The stock should completely cover the vegetables (if not, add more). Season with salt and white pepper. Increase heat to medium high, bring to a boil, then reduce heat to a moderate simmer. Partially cover with the lid and cook for 30 minutes or until potatoes are soft. Stir in reserved watercress stems and pieces and simmer 5 more minutes. Remove from heat and let cool. When cool enough to handle, force soup through a food mill or fine-mesh sieve, or purée it in the blender or food processor. Refrigerate for 2 to 3 hours, stirring occasionally.

When soup is well chilled, whisk in half-and-half, adjust seasoning if necessary, and then stir in Maggi and the simmered leaves. If the soup is too thick, add half-and-half. Serve in chilled cups.

Variation: When this soup is served hot it is known as Potage Cressonière. To do so, bring the soup to a simmer for a couple of minutes while adding the half-and-half and seasonings.

Carrot Vichyssoise

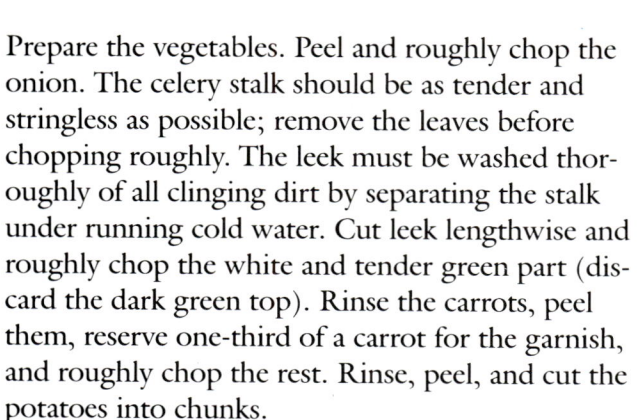

Yields 6 servings

1 medium onion
1 celery stalk
1 medium leek
3 large carrots (about 1 1/2 pounds or 675 g)
1 pound (450 g) boiling potatoes
1 tablespoon (15 g) butter
5 cups (1200 ml) Chicken Bouillon *(see page 148)*
1/4 teaspoon Maggi
Salt
Freshly ground white pepper
3/4 cup (180 ml) half-and-half

Recommended equipment

A small chef's knife; swivel-bladed vegetable peeler; 3-quart (3 L) saucepan with lid; large fine-mesh sieve, food mill, blender, or food processor; box grater; wire whisk.

Prepare the vegetables. Peel and roughly chop the onion. The celery stalk should be as tender and stringless as possible; remove the leaves before chopping roughly. The leek must be washed thoroughly of all clinging dirt by separating the stalk under running cold water. Cut leek lengthwise and roughly chop the white and tender green part (discard the dark green top). Rinse the carrots, peel them, reserve one-third of a carrot for the garnish, and roughly chop the rest. Rinse, peel, and cut the potatoes into chunks.

Set the saucepan over medium low heat, add the butter, and, when it is hot, add the onion, celery, leek, and carrots and sauté for 2 minutes. Then add the potatoes and chicken bouillon and bring to a boil. When the boil is reached, reduce heat, partially cover the saucepan, and adjust heat so that a low simmer is maintained for 45 minutes. Then remove from heat and let cool. When cool enough to handle, force soup through a food mill or fine-mesh sieve, or purée it in a blender or food processor. Adjust seasoning with Maggi, salt, and pepper and then refrigerate for 2 to 3 hours. To speed up the chilling, the soup can be set over ice and stirred from time to time.

While the soup is chilling, grate the reserved carrot into fine strips, put them into a saucepan, cover them with water, set the saucepan over medium high heat, and bring to a boil. Boil for 1 minute, remove strips from saucepan, and reserve the blanching water (allowing it to cool) for thinning the soup later if necessary. Add the strips to the soup.

When the soup is chilled, whisk in the half-and-half, adjust seasoning if needed, and, if the soup is too thick, add some of the reserved blanching water.

Variation: When you serve this vichyssoise hot it is called Potage Crécy, after the region in France known for its carrots. To serve it this way, bring the soup to a simmer for a couple of minutes while adding the half-and-half and adjusting the seasoning.

Celery Vichyssoise

Prepare this soup following the method for Carrot Vichyssoise *(see page 122)*. Substitute about 1 1/2 pounds (675 g) celery for the carrots and peel the celery before roughly chopping it. When seasoning the soup, use celery salt to taste and do not use regular salt or Maggi.

Asparagus Vichyssoise

Prepare the soup following the method for Carrot Vichyssoise *(see page 122)*. Substitute about 1 1/2 pounds (675 g) fresh asparagus for the carrots, being sure to trim it and cut off any tough, woody stems. Increase the potatoes to 2 pounds (900 g).

For a garnish, peel and trim three to four asparagus stalks, slice them into 1/4-inch (2/3 cm) thick slices, blanch them in lightly salted water for 3 minutes, drain, and add to the finished soup.

Obroschka

This interpretation of the Russian vegetable and meat soup Okroshka derives its beef flavor from the bouillon rather than from the minced beef used in the original. Traditionally, before serving, this soup would be enhanced with Kvass, an old Russian beverage made from allowing dark sour pumpernickel, malt, honey or sugar, and water to ferment for a day.

Yields about 7 cups, for 7 to 8 servings

2 hard-boiled eggs, finely chopped
1 cup (235 ml) finely diced cucumber
1 medium apple
2 tablespoons finely chopped cooked, smoked ham
2 teaspoons finely chopped fresh dill
1 1/2 bunches watercress, stems removed
4 cups (950 ml) Beef Bouillon *(see page 151)*, at room temperature
2 cups (475 ml) sour cream
Salt
Freshly ground white pepper

Recommended equipment

A 1 1/2-quart (1 1/2 L) saucepan, swivel-bladed vegetable peeler, apple corer, small chef's knife, small mixing bowl, wire whisk.

While the eggs are cooking, prepare the vegetables. Peel, seed, and finely dice the cucumber and apple. Chop the ham and wash and chop the dill and watercress leaves. Mixing well with the whisk, combine the beef bouillon and sour cream in the mixing bowl, add the ham, vegetables, herbs, and, when cool, the chopped hard-boiled eggs. Season to taste with salt and freshly ground white pepper. Chill at least two hours before serving.

Aspic

Aspic can be served as is with lemon wedges and buttered melba toast or as an elegant and tasty garnish for galantines, terrines, and pâtés. In the latter case, pour it into a flat pan (such as a small broiler pan) that will make a layer at least 1/4 inch (2/3 cm) thick. Then proceed with the chilling and, when you are ready for the garnish, take a paring knife and make vertical and horizontal lines down through the aspic to make the size you require—1/4-inch cubes would be preferable. When ready to serve, slip a spatula under the cubes, lift them out, and garnish the plates (which should be lightly chilled), moving quickly so as not to melt the aspic.

Yields 2 cups

2 cups (475 ml) Consommé Double *(see page 152)*
2 1/2 teaspoons unflavored gelatin

Recommended equipment

A 1-quart (1 L) saucepan, wire whisk.

Bring the consommé to a simmer over low heat in the saucepan, add gelatin, and stir with the whisk until it is completely dissolved, about 2 minutes. Remove the saucepan from heat, let the aspic cool, and refrigerate it, covered with plastic wrap, until it is gelled—preferably overnight. Tightly wrapped, it will keep for several days.

You may want to enhance the flavor by adding 1 tablespoon of Madeira to the mixture. If you are using the aspic for a poultry galantine or pâté, replace the Consommé Double with Chicken Bouillon, increase the gelatin to 1 tablespoon, and add 1 tablespoon Port for flavoring. Similarly, for a fish recipe, replace the Consommé Double with Fish Stock, use 1 tablespoon gelatin and 2 tablespoons of dry white wine.

 ## Jellied Madrilene

Madrilene (literally in the style of Madrid) is always associated with fresh tomatoes or tomato juice, and this lovely soup, served in chilled cups, is perfect fare for a hot day. For a final fillip, nestle a teaspoon of caviar in the sour cream garnish.

Yields 6 servings

1 recipe Consommé Madrilene *(see page 154)*
1 tablespoon unflavored gelatin

GARNISHES
Sprigs of fresh parsley or dill and lemon quarters
1 tablespoon sour cream sprinkled with freshly cut chives

Recommended equipment

A 2-quart (2 L) saucepan, wire whisk, 2-quart (2 L) bowl.

Whisk the gelatin into the warm consommé and stir until the gelatin is dissolved. Transfer the Madrilene to the bowl and set into the refrigerator to chill for several hours. If you need to speed up the process, set the bowl over crushed ice.

When ready to serve, spoon the jellied Madrilene into chilled cups, garnish to your taste, and bring it to the table right away.

Variation: Present your guests with the Madrilene served in large green, red, yellow, or purple bell peppers. To do this, follow the instructions with Gazpacho *(see page 116)*.

 # Hot Soups

Potage St. Germain
Purée of Split and Fresh Pea Soup

To be precise, this soup is a hybrid, combining Potage Purée de Pois Frais, dit Saint Germain *(purée of fresh pea soup, called Saint-Germain) and* Potage Purée de Pois Cassés *(purée of split pea soup). The split peas give texture and the fresh peas, color. And, as Roger Vergé notes elsewhere, the*

potatoes are an excellent thickening agent as well. In this and the following two preparations, a heavy-bottomed saucepan or soup pot is important to prevent the dried vegetables from sticking and burning. Should you ever find yourself with split peas, lentils, or navy beans stuck to the pot, remove

from heat immediately and scrape the bottom of the pot vigorously with a spatula. Then proceed with recipe while watching the pot very carefully. If there already is a burnt smell there is no hope of salvaging the soup—you must start over again.

Yields about 10 cups, for 8 servings   *Recommended equipment*

1 celery stalk
1 medium leek
1 large onion
8 ounces (225 g) boiling potatoes
2 cups (475 ml) split peas
2 tablespoons (30 g) bacon fat or butter
1 ham bone, or 6 ounces (170 g) smoked bacon
1/3 bay leaf
10 cups (2375 ml) White Chicken Stock *(see page 61)*
1 cup (235 ml) fresh or frozen green peas
3/4 cup (180 ml) whipping cream
Salt
Freshly ground black pepper
A few drops of Maggi

A small chef's knife, swivel-bladed vegetable peeler, large fine-mesh sieve, 5-quart (5 L) heavy-bottomed saucepan with lid, blender or food processor.

Prepare the vegetables. Wash and chop the celery; thoroughly clean the leek under running cold water, cut lengthwise and chop; peel and chop the onion; and wash and peel the potatoes and then cut into chunks. Wash the split peas in the fine-mesh sieve under running cold water, drain, and discard any debris.

Heat the bacon fat or butter until bubbly in the heavy-bottomed saucepan over medium heat. Then add the celery, leek, and onion and sauté over low heat, stirring occasionally, until vegetables have softened. Next, add ham bone or smoked bacon and the bay leaf, cook for 5 minutes, add split peas, potato chunks, and chicken stock. Bring to a boil over medium high heat, stirring from time to time, then reduce heat and partially cover saucepan so that soup maintains a slow simmer. After 1 hour check split peas for tenderness and continue cooking until they are mushy. During the last 5 or 10 minutes of cooking, add fresh or frozen green peas to soup. When soup is done, remove ham bone or bacon and bay leaf, let cool, then purée until smooth in the blender or food processor.

Wash out saucepan and return soup to it. Add cream and, while stirring soup constantly, bring to a boil over medium heat, then regulate so that soup simmers slowly for 3 to 5 minutes and develops a creamy texture. If soup is too thick add more cream or chicken stock. Adjust seasoning with salt, pepper, and a few drops of Maggi. At this point the soup may wait for a couple of hours before serving. Set aside in a cool place and dot with bits of butter to prevent formation of a skin layer. When ready to serve, reheat slowly while stirring, bring soup to a simmer for a few minutes, and ladle into serving dishes.

This soup is usually garnished with browned croutons. Cut stale bread into small dice, spread on a baking sheet, sprinkle with melted butter, and cook in a 200F (93C) oven until golden brown. Another tasty garnish is vermicelli, broken into 2- to 3-inch (5 to 7 1/2 cm) pieces before cooking. Or fresh watercress leaves, sorrel, or spinach can be lightly blanched, chopped, and added just before serving.

Lentil Soup with Frankfurters

Snow in Hot Springs means glowing fireplaces in the Great Hall, slopes full of skiers, a rink full of skaters, and voracious appetites.

That is when I put this soup on the menu. If you want a more pointed flavor, use only one-quarter cup of whipping cream and add one-half cup of dry red wine. For a heartier taste, substitute Beef Bouillon for the chicken stock.

Yields about 10 cups, for 8 servings

1 celery stalk
1 medium leek
1 large onion
1 small carrot
1/2 garlic clove
8 ounces (225 g) boiling potatoes
2 cups (475 ml) lentils
2 tablespoons (30 g) bacon fat or butter
1 ham bone, or 6 ounces (170 g) smoked bacon
1/3 bay leaf
10 cups (2375 ml) White Chicken Stock *(see page 61)*
3/4 cup (180 ml) whipping cream
Salt
Freshly ground black pepper
A few drops of Maggi
3 skinless frankfurters

Recommended equipment

A small chef's knife, swivel-bladed vegetable peeler, large fine-mesh sieve, 5-quart (5 L) heavy-bottomed saucepan with lid, blender or food processor.

Prepare the vegetables. Wash and chop the celery; thoroughly clean the leek under running cold water, cut lengthwise and chop; peel and chop the onion, carrot, and garlic; and wash and peel the potatoes and then cut into chunks. Wash the lentils in the sieve under running cold water, drain, and discard any debris.

Heat the bacon fat or butter until bubbly in the heavy-bottomed saucepan over medium heat. Then add the celery, leek, onion, carrot, and garlic and sauté over low heat, stirring occasionally, until vegetables (except carrot) have softened. Next, add ham bone or smoked bacon and the bay leaf, cook for 5 minutes, add lentils, potato chunks, and chicken stock. Bring to a boil over medium high heat, stirring from time to time, then reduce heat and partially cover saucepan so that soup maintains a slow simmer. After 1 hour check lentils for tenderness and continue cooking until they are mushy.

When soup is done, remove ham bone or bacon and bay leaf, let cool, then purée until smooth in the blender or food processor.

Wash out saucepan and return soup to it. Add cream and, while stirring soup constantly, bring to a boil over medium heat, then regulate heat so that soup simmers slowly for 3 to 5 minutes and develops a creamy texture. If soup is too thick add more cream or chicken stock. Adjust seasoning with salt, pepper, and a few drops of Maggi. At this point the soup may wait for a couple of hours before serving. Set aside in a cool place and dot with bits of butter to prevent formation of a skin layer. When ready to serve, reheat slowly while stirring. Then add the 3 frankfurters, each of which has been cut lengthwise into 4 pieces and sliced very thinly crosswise. Simmer soup with frankfurter pieces for 1 minute and serve.

Variation

Old-fashioned Navy Bean Soup

Follow the instructions for lentil soup, replacing the lentils with 2 cups of navy beans, and deleting the frankfurters. Increase the simmering time to 1 1/2 hours, check the beans for tenderness, and continue cooking until they are mushy. Before puréeing the soup, dip out 1/2 cup (118 ml) of the beans and reserve as a garnish. When ready to serve, divide the beans among the bowls and ladle in the hot soup.

For a more robust flavor and deeper color, substitute Beef Bouillon for chicken stock.

Swiss Barley Soup

What greater accolade could a product receive than the following from Escoffier for Maggi's sauce essences, "En résumé, l'Arôme Maggi, dont la capacité de conservation est illimitée, est l'auxiliaire de cuisine le plus parfait et le plus apprécié des connaisseurs." When Michael Johannes Julius Maggi, native of the Swiss canton of Thurgau, died on 19 October 1912, he left the basis of what has become an empire in the food service world. In fact, his influence was so pervasive that Hôtellerie *(1988) named him as a founder of convenience foods, specifically* Schnellen Küche *or fast food.*

But he would most want to be remembered for his sauce bases. I call for Maggi because it is a complex compound which points up the taste of a sauce or soup at the last minute—besides, one just can't make a Swiss soup without a touch of Maggi! Be sparing with it because it is concentrated.

Yields about 8 cups, for 6 to 8 servings

3 strips lean bacon weighing 2 to 2 1/2 ounces (60 to 70 g)
3 ounces (85 g) smoked ham
1 medium onion
1 small leek
1/4 celery stalk
3/4 cup (180 ml) barley
10 cups (2375 ml) Chicken Bouillon *(see page 148)*
Salt
Freshly ground white pepper
Freshly ground nutmeg
1 cup (235 ml) half-and-half
1/2 teaspoon Maggi
1 tablespoon fresh, chopped parsley

Recommended equipment

A small chef's knife, 5-quart (5 L) heavy-bottomed saucepan with lid.

Using the chef's knife, finely dice the bacon and the ham in separate batches. Next, prepare the vegetables: peel and finely dice the onion; thoroughly wash the leek under running cold water, slice lengthwise, and dice it finely; and wash and peel the celery stalk, and finely dice it.

Sauté the bacon in the saucepan over medium heat until most of the fat is melted but the bacon has not browned. Add the finely diced ham, onion, leek, and celery and the barley, and cook, stirring occasionally, for 3 minutes. Pour in the chicken bouillon, season with salt and freshly ground pepper and nutmeg, and bring to a boil. Then reduce heat, partially cover saucepan, and adjust so that soup will maintain a gentle simmer. Cook for 1 1/2 hours, stirring occasionally. Then add the half-and-half and simmer for 30 minutes more. Add the touch of Maggi, adjust seasoning if necessary with salt and pepper, stir in chopped parsley, and serve.

Rossolnik

This soup (also spelled rassol'nik *and* rossolnick*) has other variations, some of which feature cucumber juice. The pickle, however, is common to all and responsible for the unique flavor of this Russian classic.*

Yields about 6 cups, for 6 to 8 servings

6 cups (1425 ml) White Chicken Stock *(see page 61)*
1/2 cup (118 ml) barley
1/2 chicken breast, weighing 6 to 8 ounces (170 to 225 g)
1/3 bay leaf
1 1/2 medium onions
3 celery stalks
3 medium leeks
2 tablespoons (30 g) butter
1/2 large dill pickle
2/3 cup (160 ml) whipping cream
2 egg yolks
1/2 teaspoon Maggi
Salt
Freshly ground white pepper
1 tablespoon finely cut fresh chives

Recommended equipment

Two 1 1/2-quart (1 1/2 L) saucepans, small chef's knife, 3-quart (3 L) saucepan with lid, strainer, paring knife, whisk.

In one of the small saucepans, bring 3 cups (710 ml) of the chicken stock to a boil, add barley, reduce to a simmer and cook for about 1 1/2 hours or until barley is tender.

Meanwhile, put the chicken breast into the other small saucepan, cover with the remaining chicken stock, and add the bay leaf. Using the chef's knife, roughly chop the 1/2 onion and 1 of the celery stalks and add them to the saucepan. Bring to a simmer over medium heat and cook about 30 minutes or until the chicken is cooked.

While the chicken is simmering, prepare the other vegetables. Split the leeks lengthwise and wash thoroughly under running cold water, separating the stalks. Then cut them into 1-inch (2 1/2 cm) pieces. Trim the remaining celery stalks and cut into 1-inch pieces. Peel the onion and chop into pieces about 1 inch square. Melt the butter in the large saucepan over low to medium heat, add the leek and celery pieces and the chopped onion, and simmer gently, covered, without browning for 2 minutes. Remove from heat and set saucepan aside.

By now, the chicken should be done. Pour the broth through the strainer into the vegetables in the large saucepan and simmer all together for 15 minutes or until vegetables are slightly soft. While the broth simmers, skin and bone the chicken breast, cut into small dice, and reserve. When the vegetables are done, remove from heat and set aside if the barley hasn't finished cooking. When the barley is done, add it, its broth, and the reserved chicken to the vegetables in the large saucepan. At this point the soup may wait, or if you are ready to serve it, continue with the final steps.

Using the paring knife, peel the dill pickle half

lightly, slice in half lengthwise, remove seeds, and cut into thin slices crosswise. Add to soup and bring to a boil over medium heat. While soup is heating, blend the cream and egg yolks together thoroughly and then whisk mixture into boiling soup. Remove from heat and continue stirring for 15 seconds, until liaison is thoroughly incorporated and soup has thickened slightly. Add Maggi, salt and pepper to taste, and the chives. Serve at once.

As with other soups that rely on a final yolk and cream liaison, this one may be made ahead of time up to the point at which the liaison is added. Whatever you do, never let a soup boil again once the yolk and cream mixture has been whisked in.

Minestrone alla Milanese
Minestrone in the Style of Milan

Minestra *is Italian for soup and its derivative "minestrone," is usually understood to mean thick soup. Many recipes for minestrone are "revisionist" pale imitations of the real thing. This one, however, will not disappoint you. If ten servings seem like a lot, don't worry. Minestrone tastes even better reheated (or the remainder may be frozen). If the soup is too thick when it is reheated, add water (rather than stock) to regain the correct consistency.*

Yields 10 servings

2 strips bacon weighing 1 to 1 1/2 ounces (30 to 45 g)
1 cup (235 ml) chopped onion
2 whole leeks
1 medium carrot
2 celery stalks
1/2 cup (118 ml) chopped cabbage
2 tablespoons tomato paste
2 quarts (1900 ml) Beef Bouillon or White Chicken Stock *(see pages 151, 61)*
2 cups (475 ml) water
1 cup (235 ml) diced boiling potatoes
2 ounces (60 g) spaghetti
1 large (or 2 small) zucchini
3/4 cup (180 ml) chopped canned tomatoes with liquid or 3 medium, ripe tomatoes (peeled and seeded, *see page 568*), diced
1/2 cup (118 ml) lima beans
1 cup (235 ml) navy beans
1/2 cup (118 ml) fresh green peas (or frozen peas that have been thawed)
2 ounces (60 g) spinach
Salt
Freshly ground black pepper
A dash of Maggi
1 tablespoon minestrone pesto

FOR THE PESTO
6 sprigs fresh parsley
3 strips raw bacon (about 2 ounces or 60 g), or 2 ounces of salt pork
1 large garlic clove
1/8 teaspoon marjoram
1/8 teaspoon oregano
1/8 teaspoon basil

GARNISH
1/2 cup (118 ml) grated Parmesan cheese

Recommended equipment

A large chef's knife, 8-quart (8 L) stockpot, wooden spatula, swivel-bladed vegetable peeler, paring knife, strainer, small mixing bowl, 1 1/2-quart (1 1/2 L) saucepan, box grater.

Using the chef's knife, dice the bacon and sauté it in the stockpot over low heat, stirring with the spatula from time to time. While the bacon is cooking, prepare the vegetables (if you work quickly it's possible): peel and chop the onions; cut the leeks lengthwise, wash thoroughly under cold running water, and chop roughly; wash and peel the carrot and slice finely by quartering it lengthwise and then slicing into 1/8-inch (1/3 cm) thick slices; wash and peel the celery stalks, cut in half lengthwise and then into thin slices; and remove the tough outer leaves and core of the cabbage, rinse under cold water, and chop enough roughly to yield 1/2 cup (118 ml).

When the bacon has rendered its fat, add all the prepared vegetables to the stockpot and sauté for 3 minutes, stirring occasionally. Then add the tomato paste, bouillon or stock, and water, and bring to a low simmer. Cook for 45 minutes.

While the soup is simmering, prepare the other vegetables. Wash and peel the potatoes, chop into 1/4-inch (2/3 cm) dice, and cover with cold water until ready to use. Break the spaghetti into 1 1/2- to 2-inch (3 3/4 to 5 cm) pieces and reserve. Scrub the zucchini, quarter it lengthwise, and then cut into 1/4-inch thick pieces. If using canned tomatoes, drain them in the strainer set over the mixing bowl, reserving the juice. Chop the tomatoes and add them to the reserved juice. If using fresh tomatoes, simply peel, seed, and chop them and reserve in the bowl.

Meanwhile, in the saucepan, in separate batches, cook the lima and navy beans in cold water to cover until soft (about 15 minutes for the limas and 30 to 45 minutes for the navy beans). Drain and reserve. Add fresh water to the saucepan, bring it to the boil, and blanch the peas for 10 seconds. Drain and reserve. Using fresh water again, blanch the spinach for 10 seconds, drain, squeeze to remove all water, chop coarsely, and reserve.

While the beans are cooking, prepare the minestrone pesto. Wash and dry the parsley, remove the stems, and, using the chef's knife, chop it with the bacon or salt pork and the seasonings until it becomes a smooth paste. Reserve. Leftover pesto can be frozen, wrapped well in several layers of plastic wrap and labeled.

When the stockpot has simmered for 45 minutes, drain the potatoes and add them to the soup along with the spaghetti, zucchini, and tomatoes. Return the stockpot to the simmer and cook for 20 minutes, stirring occasionally. Then add the lima and navy beans, peas, and spinach, and bring to a boil. Adjust seasoning if needed with salt, pepper, and a dash of Maggi, remembering that the grated Parmesan will be an additional seasoning.

When ready to serve, heat the soup until very hot, stir in the pesto, ladle into bowls, top with grated cheese, and serve at once. (Do not let soup boil after adding pesto.)

≈ Bisque of Vegetables Rosa

Croutons lend an air of authenticity to this eighteenth-century-style soup and the tomatoes make it pink or "rosa." Known in Europe as Potage Garbûre, *it is a good "Monday" garde-manger special that can be made from cooked or raw vegetables leftover from the weekend. Just add them to the basic list given here. Also, if you prefer, substitute cooked rice for the potatoes. This excellent cool weather soup tastes just as good when reheated. If it is too thick, add some Chicken Stock, milk, or half-and-half.*

131

Yields 6 to 8 servings

2 strips bacon weighing 1 1/2 to 2 ounces (45 to 60 g)
2 medium onions
1 medium leek
1 medium carrot
1 medium turnip
4 medium broccoli spears (fresh or frozen)
3 medium boiling potatoes
1/2 cup (118 ml) chopped cabbage
1/2 cup (118 ml) lima beans (fresh or frozen)
2 sprigs of parsley
1 teaspoon dried marjoram
4 cups (950 ml) White Chicken Stock *(see page 61)*
3 cups (710 ml) water
3 medium, ripe tomatoes (blanched, peeled, and seeded; *see page 568*)
1/2 teaspoon Maggi
Salt
Freshly ground white pepper

GARNISH
1 recipe for croutons, as suggested for Potage St. Germain *(see page 125)*

Recommended equipment

A large chef's knife, 4- to 5-quart (4 to 5 L) saucepan with lid, paring knife, swivel-bladed vegetable peeler, blender or food processor.

Using the chef's knife, dice the bacon finely and sauté it in the saucepan over low heat. While the bacon is rendering its fat, work quickly to prepare the vegetables. Peel and chop the onions; cut the leek in half lengthwise, wash thoroughly under cold running water, and chop coarsely; wash, peel, and chop the carrot and turnip; rinse and chop the broccoli; rinse, peel, and chop the potatoes; remove the tough outer leaves and core of the cabbage, rinse and chop enough roughly to yield 1/2 cup (118 ml); and shell and rinse the lima beans. Remove and mince the parsley stems, reserving the leaves for garnish.

When the bacon fat has been rendered, add all the prepared vegetables and 1/2 teaspoon marjoram to the saucepan and simmer, covered, over low heat for 5 minutes, stirring occasionally. Add chicken stock and water, bring to a simmer, and adjust heat so that the soup simmers gently for 1 1/2 hours.

While the soup simmers, prepare the tomatoes, dice them, and reserve. If you are using croutons, prepare them now.

When the soup has finished simmering, remove from heat and let cool. When cool enough to handle, purée the soup in the blender or food processor until smooth. Return the soup to the saucepan, add the tomatoes, Maggi, remaining 1/2 teaspoon marjoram, and adjust the seasoning with salt and pepper if needed. Return the soup to a low simmer and cook for 3 minutes, stirring occasionally. Mince and stir in the parsley leaves, ladle into soup plates, garnish with the croutons, and serve.

Soupe à l'Oignon Gratinée
French Onion Soup

Each of the following three onion soups has its own national identity, but it is hard to find a recipe which is more commonly associated with popular French cuisine than soupe à l'oignon gratinée. A fixture on the menu of any bistro or caveau, this soup is also so common (and usually so badly prepared) in American "French" restaurants that it is in danger of being ignored. Pay careful attention to its preparation—browning (not scorching) the onions, using a first-class beef bouillon, not smothering the soup with cheese—and your guests will be transported from the first concentrated earthy scent rising from the bowl to the last spoonful.

A truly memorable onion soup can conjure up midnight in Paris at Le Chien qui Fume, Le Père Tranquille, and Le Pied de Cochon (Pied still exists, and is open around the clock), located in the legendary Les Halles (formerly the farmers' market) behind the magnificent gothic church of St. Eustache.

Yields about 8 servings

6 medium onions, weighing about 3 pounds (1350 g)
1 tablespoon (15 g) butter
2 quarts (1900 ml) Beef Bouillon *(see page 151)*
1/2 cup (118 ml) dry white wine
8 French bread croutons
Salt
Freshly ground black pepper
3/4 cup (180 ml) each of grated Swiss Gruyère and Parmesan cheese

Recommended equipment

A large chef's knife, 4- to 5-quart heavy-bottomed saucepan, baking sheet, box grater, individual ovenproof crocks or bowls.

Peel and trim the onions, cut each in half, and, using the chef's knife, mince them finely. Melt the butter over medium high heat in the saucepan, add the onions, and sauté until golden brown, stirring from time to time. Then add the beef bouillon and white wine, bring to a boil, and adjust heat so that soup simmers gently. Cook for 30 minutes.

While soup is cooking, prepare the French bread croutons. Preheat oven to 375F (190C). Use day-old bread (or leftover bread that has been frozen) and cut loaf into 1/4-inch (2/3 cm) thick slices. Plan for one or two croutons per serving, depending upon the diameter of the loaf. Arrange bread slices on baking sheet and cook in middle level of oven until they are golden brown.

When soup has finished cooking, adjust seasoning with salt and freshly ground black pepper. It is wise to underseason the soup because cheese will be added later. Soup may now wait indefinitely until serving time.

Just before serving, preheat the broiler in your

oven, grate the cheeses, and gently heat the soup if it has been waiting. When the soup is hot and your diners are ready, ladle it into the individual ovenproof crocks or bowls, float the crouton(s) on top, divide the grated cheese among the bowls, and cook under the broiler until the cheese is melted and bubbly. Serve at once.

To really give this classic "l'esprit de France," put a tablespoon of Cognac in each bowl before you add the soup.

Basler Mehlsuppe
Swiss Onion Soup

Basel (Bâle) sits directly athwart the Rhine, close to the joint border with France and Germany, so it is no surprise to find the French classic showing up with a German accent. Mehlsuppe is German for a soup thickened with flour, and the browned flour used here contributes texture, flavor, and color. For this soup you must use only imported Swiss cheese. For an unusual twist, add a touch of anise (no more than four seeds) to the soup and keep your guests in suspense.

Yields about 8 servings

6 medium onions, weighing about 3 pounds (1350 g)
1 tablespoon (15 g) butter
1/4 cup (60 ml) Browned Flour *(see page 64)*
Freshly ground nutmeg
2 quarts (1900 ml) Beef Bouillon *(see page 151)*
1/2 cup (118 ml) dry white wine
8 French bread croutons
Salt
Freshly ground black pepper
3/4 cup (180 ml) grated imported Emmentaler (Swiss cheese)

Recommended equipment

A large chef's knife, 4- to 5-quart heavy-bottomed saucepan, nutmeg grinder, baking sheet, box grater, individual ovenproof crocks or bowls.

Peel and trim the onions, cut each in half, and, using the chef's knife, mince them finely. Melt the butter over medium high heat in the saucepan, add the onions, and sauté until golden brown, stirring from time to time. Then add the browned flour and the nutmeg and stir all together well. Pour in the beef bouillon and white wine, bring to a boil, and adjust heat so that soup simmers gently. Cook for 45 minutes.

While soup is cooking, prepare the French bread croutons. Preheat oven to 375F (190C). Use day-old bread (or leftover bread that has been frozen) and cut loaf into 1/4-inch (2/3 cm) thick slices. Plan for one or two croutons per serving, depending upon the diameter of the loaf. Arrange bread slices on baking sheet and cook in middle level of oven until they are golden brown.

When soup has finished cooking, adjust seasoning with salt and freshly ground black pepper. It is wise to underseason the soup because cheese will be added later. Soup may now wait indefinitely until serving time.

Just before serving, preheat the broiler in your oven, grate the cheese, and gently heat the soup if it has been waiting. When the soup is hot, ladle it into the individual ovenproof crocks or bowls, float the crouton(s) on top, divide the grated cheese among the bowls, and cook under the broiler until the cheese is melted and bubbly. Serve at once.

Russian Onion Soup

Unlike the peasant custom observed with its French and Swiss cousins, in the service of this soup the croutons and grated cheese are passed separately—reflecting the elegance often associated with Russian cuisine.

Yields about 8 servings

6 medium onions, weighing about 3 pounds (1350 g)
1 tablespoon (15 g) butter
1/4 cup (60 ml) Browned Flour *(see page 64)*
1/8 teaspoon caraway seeds
2 quarts (1900 ml) Beef Bouillon *(see page 151)*
1/2 cup (118 ml) dry white wine
8 French bread croutons
Salt
1 teaspoon green peppercorns (packed in water and drained)
3/4 cup (180 ml) grated Emmentaler (Swiss cheese)
3/4 cup (180 ml) sour cream, at room temperature

Recommended equipment

A large chef's knife, 4- to 5-quart heavy-bottomed saucepan, baking sheet, box grater.

Peel and trim the onions, cut each in half, and, using the chef's knife, mince them finely. Melt the butter over medium high heat in the saucepan, add the onions, and sauté until golden brown, stirring from time to time. Then add the browned flour and the caraway seeds and stir all together well. Pour in the beef bouillon and white wine, bring to a boil, and adjust heat so that soup simmers gently. Cook for 45 minutes.

While soup is cooking, prepare the French bread croutons. Preheat oven to 375F (190C). Use day-old bread (or leftover bread that has been frozen) and cut loaf into 1/4-inch (2/3 cm) thick slices. Plan for one or two croutons per serving, depending upon the diameter of the loaf. Arrange bread slices on baking sheet and cook in middle level of oven until they are golden brown.

When soup has finished cooking, adjust seasoning with salt and add the green peppercorns. It's wise to underseason the soup because cheese will be added later. Soup may now wait indefinitely until serving time.

Just before serving, grate the cheese, and gently heat the soup if it has been waiting. Arrange the croutons and cheese in serving dishes to be passed separately alongside the soup. When soup is good and hot, stir in the sour cream, heat a moment or two longer, and then serve immediately in hot soup plates.

Borscht à la Russe
Beet Soup in the Style of Russia

This soup exemplifies the enrichment of fine cuisine by Russian dishes, possibly by way of Carême, when he was with Czar Alexander in Saint Petersburg. This particular recipe also reflects a Polish influence in the use of duck and beef, but the last minute addition of beet purée for color is distinctly Russian. When serving borscht cold, I omit the duck and strain the soup before ladling it into chilled plates.

Yields about 10 cups, for 8 to 10 servings

1 medium duckling, weighing 3 1/2 to 4 pounds (1575 to 1800 g)
1 strip of bacon, weighing 1/2 to 3/4 ounce (15 to 23 g)
8 medium beets
1 medium onion
1 small carrot
1 celery stalk
1 8-ounce (225 g) head of cabbage
2 medium leeks
1/2 medium green bell pepper
2 tablespoons tomato paste
1/2 bay leaf
1/8 teaspoon ground clove
A pinch of marjoram
6 caraway seeds
1 cup (235 ml) water
8 cups (1900 ml) Beef Bouillon *(see page 151)*
1 pound (450 g) lean beef brisket or short rib
1 teaspoon fresh parsley, chopped
1/2 cup (118 ml) sour cream, at room temperature
Salt
Freshly ground black pepper

Recommended equipment

A roasting pan, swivel-bladed vegetable peeler, paring knife, small chef's knife, 8-quart (8 L) stockpot, 1 1/2-quart (1 1/2 L) saucepan, blender or food processor, fine-mesh skimmer.

Preheat oven to 325F (163C). Prepare duckling for roasting *(see page 299)* and cook for 1 hour, removing fat as necessary. When duckling is roasted, set aside to cool.

Remove rind (if any) from bacon and cut into small cubes. Prepare the vegetables. Peel six of the beets (two will become the beet purée) and cut them into fine julienne strips; peel the onion and mince finely with the chef's knife; peel the carrot and cut into fine strips 1 1/2 to 2 inches (3 3/4 to 5 cm) long; wash and peel the celery stalk and cut into fine strips 1 1/2 to 2 inches (3 3/4 to 5 cm) long; wash and core the cabbage, then shred it finely; cut leeks in half lengthwise, wash thoroughly under running cold water, drain, and cut into strips 1 1/2 to 2 inches long; and halve the green pepper half, removing all the seeds.

In the stockpot, cook the bacon cubes over medium heat until nearly crisp. Then add the julienne of beet, onion, carrot, celery, cabbage, and leeks and sauté for 5 minutes. While stirring, add tomato paste, bay leaf, ground clove, marjoram, and caraway seeds. Sauté for 3 more minutes. Then add water, beef bouillon, green pepper, beef brisket or short rib, and one-half of the roast duckling (reserve remaining half for another use, such as in a salad with walnuts and raspberry vinegar and walnut oil dressing). Bring soup to a boil over medium high heat and then regulate so that soup simmers nicely. Cook for 1 1/2 hours.

Meanwhile, prepare the beet purée. Cut the remaining two beets in half, put them in the saucepan, cover liberally with water, add a dash of salt, and cook for about 30 minutes or until beets can be pierced with a knife (cooking time depends upon size and age of beets). When done, remove beets and save 2/3 cup (160 ml) of cooking liquid. When beets are cool enough to handle, slip off skins under running cold water and discard. Chop the beets coarsely and purée in blender or food processor with the reserved liquid until smooth. Pour into a bowl and reserve until soup is done.

When soup has finished cooking, remove beef, duck, and green pepper and allow soup to cool. Discard pepper. When beef is cool enough to handle, slice it, cut into matchstick-size strips, and reserve. When duck is cool enough to handle, remove skin and bones, cut meat into matchstick-size strips, and reserve. As soup cools, the fat will rise to the surface and congeal. When this process appears to have stopped, remove fat and return beef and duck to soup.

Just before serving, skim any additional fat from the surface, bring borscht to a gentle boil, and adjust seasoning if needed with salt and pepper. Add beet purée and parsley, mix well, and remove soup from heat. (If borscht simmers it will loose its lovely red color.) Serve immediately, passing the sour cream separately to each guest.

Hot Cream Soups

Like the gesso an artist uses to prepare a surface for painting, cream is used in all the soups in this section because it has a texture, color, and flavor which provide an ample foundation and elegant backdrop for the rich flavor and hue of the main ingredient, be it watercress or mussels.

Zuppa alla Modenese
Cream of Spinach Soup in the Style of Modena

In 187 A.D. the Romans demonstrated their engineering genius by constructing a 150-mile roadway from Piacenza to the Adriatic shore. Beyond this feat, the significance of the Via Emilia lies in its interconnection of great medieval cities—Piacenza, Parma, Modena, Bologna, Forlì, Cesena, and Rimini—known for treasures artistic and culinary. Roughly halfway along this road sits Modena, with its splendid Romanesque cathedral and campanile, called La Ghirlandina. Modena has much to offer the epicure as well, including zampone, *a renowned smoked sausage, encased in the lower skin of a pig's trotter, with the hoof still showing.* Tortellini modenisi *and* scaloppine *are also natives, as is the famous Zuppa alla Modenese, which follows.*

Yields about 7 cups, for 6 to 8 servings

- 8 ounces (225 g) fresh spinach
- 1 1/2 medium onions
- 1 celery stalk
- 1 medium leek
- 1 tablespoon (15 g) butter
- 6 cups (1425 ml) White Chicken Stock *(see page 61)*
- 1/4 cup (60 ml) Blond Roux *(see page 65)*
- 1 cup (235 ml) whipping cream
- 1/4 teaspoon Maggi
- Salt
- Freshly ground white pepper
- 1/8 teaspoon freshly ground nutmeg
- 1/4 cup (60 ml) grated Parmesan cheese

GARNISH
- 3 to 4 ounces (85 to 115 g) fresh spinach
- 1 1/2 teaspoons (7 g) butter
- 2 tablespoons White Chicken Stock

Recommended equipment

A large chef's knife, 4-quart (4 L) saucepan, small saucepan, wire whisk, large fine-mesh sieve, small mixing bowl, box grater, nutmeg grinder.

Prepare the vegetables. Thoroughly wash the spinach under running cold water, being careful to remove all sand and grit. Remove any tough stems, and chop roughly. Peel and coarsely chop the onions; wash the celery stalk, and chop coarsely; thoroughly clean the leek under running cold water, slice lengthwise, and chop coarsely.

In the saucepan, melt the tablespoon of butter, add the spinach, onion, celery, leek, and 2 tablespoons of chicken stock. Bring vegetables to a low simmer and cook for 10 minutes.

While the vegetables are simmering, prepare the blond roux.

Then add remaining chicken stock to the vegetables, bring to a boil, and, using the whisk, whip in the roux, mixing until completely smooth. Reduce heat to a low simmer, cook for 20 minutes, then add whipping cream, and simmer for 10 more minutes.

While soup is simmering, prepare the spinach garnish. Wash the spinach well under running cold water, removing all sand and grit. Remove stems and chop finely. Melt 1 1/2 teaspoons of butter in the small saucepan, add the chopped spinach and 2 tablespoons chicken stock, and cook gently over low heat for 1 minute. Do not let spinach brown and add a little more stock if necessary. When done, set aside and reserve.

When the soup has finished cooking, pour it through the fine-mesh sieve into the mixing bowl, wash out the saucepan and return the soup to it. If soup is too thick, add some more whipping cream or chicken stock; if too thin, cook on a low simmer another 10 minutes. When soup has desired consistency, add the reserved cooked spinach and Maggi and adjust seasoning with salt and white pepper. At this point, grind in the fresh nutmeg, stir in the grated cheese, and then serve piping hot. If you are not ready to serve it, the soup will wait comfortably if set aside in a cool place with dots of butter on the surface to prevent the formation of a skin layer. Whatever you do, do not boil the soup after adding the cheese.

Here are two additional serving suggestions. For a more "alla campagna" version omit the cream from the soup altogether, and after straining it, return it to a simmer. Whisk in two beaten egg yolks, simmering until they curdle into little shreds, and serve it garnished with croutons. For a more "alla citta" version, just before serving (and *before* adding the Parmesan), blend 1 egg yolk well with 3 tablespoons of whipping cream, bring soup to a boil, and, stirring constantly with a whisk, add yolk and cream mixture. Remove soup from heat immediately, add grated Parmesan, and do not let it boil again.

Do *not* use aluminum saucepans in this recipe as they will interact with the spinach and spoil its delicate flavor.

❧ *Cream of Watercress Soup*

An ancient and venerable green, it is said that salads of cress, endive, and lettuce were found at the banquet table of Belshazzar, the Babylonian king of Mesopotamia. Watercress is readily available all year and usually comes in bunches weighing about four ounces. If you do not see it, ask your grocer to get it. Should you be as fortunate as to have wild watercress growing in a nearby freshwater creek, hurray for you—the flavor of the wild one is like no other!

Yields about 7 cups, for 6 to 8 servings

1 bunch watercress (about 4 ounces or 115 g)
1 1/2 medium onions
1 celery stalk
1 medium leek
1 tablespoon (15 g) butter
6 cups (1425 ml) White Chicken Stock *(see page 61)*
1/4 cup (60 ml) Blond Roux *(see page 65)*
1 cup (235 ml) whipping cream
1/4 teaspoon Maggi
Salt
Freshly ground white pepper

Recommended equipment

A large chef's knife, small saucepan, 4-quart (4 L) saucepan, small saucepan, wire whisk, large fine-mesh sieve, small mixing bowl.

Wash the watercress gently but thoroughly in plenty of running cold water and drain. Cut off stems about 2 inches (5 cm) from the bottom and discard. Pick the leaves off the stems, putting the leaves in one pile and the stems in another. Using the chef's knife, in separate batches, chop the leaves finely and the stems coarsely. In the small saucepan melt 1 1/2 teaspoons butter, add 2 tablespoons chicken stock and the chopped leaves, bring to a simmer over medium heat, and cook for 3 minutes. Remove from heat and reserve.

Peel and coarsely chop the onions; wash the celery stalk, remove the leaves, and chop coarsely; thoroughly clean the leek under running cold water, slice lengthwise, and chop coarsely. In the large saucepan, melt the remaining butter, add the watercress stems, onion, celery, leek, and 2 tablespoons of chicken stock. Bring vegetables to a low simmer and cook for 10 minutes.

While the vegetables are simmering, prepare the blond roux.

Then add remaining chicken stock to the vegetables, bring to a boil, and, using the whisk, whip in the roux, mixing until completely smooth. Reduce heat to a low simmer, cook for 20 minutes, then add whipping cream, and simmer for 10 more minutes.

Pour soup through fine-mesh sieve into the mixing bowl, wash out the saucepan, and return soup to it. If soup is too thick, add some more whipping cream or chicken stock; if too thin, cook on a low simmer another 10 minutes. When soup has desired thickness, add the reserved watercress leaves and Maggi and adjust seasoning with salt and white pepper. Serve piping hot, or, if you are not ready to serve it, the soup will wait comfortably if set aside in a cool place with dots of butter on the surface to prevent the formation of a skin layer.

❧

As a further enrichment, just before serving, blend 1 egg yolk well with 3 tablespoons of whipping cream, bring soup to a boil, and, stirring constantly with a whisk, add yolk and cream mixture. Remove soup immediately from heat and do not let it boil again.

Potage Germiny
Cream of Sorrel Soup

Although you might have patches of it appearing annually in or near your lawn, the taste of this popular French green is not widely known in the United States, and its mysterious lemon-like flavor in this soup will most likely puzzle your guests. The soup may be puréed in a blender rather than put through a sieve, and, unlike the other cream soups, for this one the liaison enrichment is a must. Aluminum saucepans cannot be used in this recipe because they will cause the sorrel to turn gray in color and bitter in taste.

Yields about 7 cups, for 6 to 8 servings

2 ounces (60 g) fresh sorrel
1 1/2 medium onions
1 celery stalk
1 medium leek
1 tablespoon (15 g) butter
6 cups (1425 ml) White Chicken Stock *(see page 61)*
3 tablespoons Blond Roux *(see page 65)*
1 cup (235 ml) whipping cream
1/4 teaspoon Maggi
Salt
Freshly ground white pepper

GARNISH
2 ounces (60 g) sorrel
1 1/2 teaspoons (7 g) butter
2 tablespoons White Chicken Stock

LIAISON
3 egg yolks
1/3 cup (80 ml) whipping cream

Recommended equipment

A large chef's knife, 4-quart (4 L) saucepan, wire whisk, paring knife, small saucepan, large fine-mesh sieve, small mixing bowl, wooden spoon.

Prepare the vegetables. Thoroughly wash the sorrel under running cold water, remove any tough stems, and chop coarsely. Peel and coarsely chop the onions; wash the celery stalk, and chop coarsely; thoroughly clean the leek under running cold water, slice lengthwise, and chop coarsely.

In the saucepan, melt the tablespoon of butter, add the sorrel, onion, celery, leek, and 2 tablespoons of chicken stock. Bring vegetables to a low simmer and cook for 10 minutes.

While the vegetables are simmering, prepare the blond roux.

Then add the remaining chicken stock to the vegetables, bring to a boil, and, using the whisk, whip in the roux, mixing until completely smooth. Reduce heat to a low simmer, cook for 20 minutes, then add whipping cream, and simmer for 10 more minutes.

While soup is simmering, prepare the sorrel garnish. Wash the 2 ounces of sorrel thoroughly under cold running water, remove stems, and, using the paring knife, cut into thin julienne strips, making a chiffonade. Melt 1 1/2 teaspoons of butter in the small saucepan, add the chiffonade and the 2 tablespoons of chicken stock, and cook gently over low heat for 1 minute. Do not let the sorrel brown and add a little more stock if necessary. When done, set aside and reserve.

When the soup has finished cooking, pour it through the fine-mesh sieve into the mixing bowl, wash out the saucepan, and return soup to it. Add the reserved cooked sorrel strips and Maggi and adjust seasoning with salt and white pepper. If not to be served right away, it can wait comfortably if set aside in a cool place with dots of butter on the surface to prevent the formation of a skin layer.

Just before serving, blend the egg yolks with the whipping cream to make the liaison. Bring the soup to a boil, and, stirring with the wooden spoon, mix the liaison into the soup. Remove immediately from heat and do not let soup boil again. Serve as soon as possible.

Cream of Asparagus Soup

This soup can be made with scraps of fresh asparagus (including the tough end of the stalk if it is peeled) or, if you want to indulge yourself and your family, use the best part of each stalk and reserve the tips, lightly sautéed, for the garnish.

Yields about 6 cups, for 6 to 7 servings

2 to 2 1/2 cups (475 to 590 ml) cut asparagus pieces (about 12 to 18 stalks)
1 1/2 medium onions
1 celery stalk
1 medium leek
1 tablespoon (15 g) butter
6 cups (1425 ml) White Chicken Stock *(see page 61)*
1/2 cup (118 ml) Blond Roux *(see page 65)*
1 cup (235 ml) whipping cream
1/4 teaspoon Maggi
Salt
Freshly ground white pepper

GARNISH
12 to 14 1-inch (2 1/2 cm) asparagus tips
1 1/2 teaspoons (7 g) butter
2 tablespoons White Chicken Stock

Recommended equipment

A large chef's knife, 4-quart (4 L) saucepan, wire whisk, small saucepan, large fine-mesh sieve, small mixing bowl.

Prepare the vegetables. Wash the asparagus, cut into pieces 1 to 2 inches (2 1/2 to 5 cm) long to yield 2 to 2 1/2 cups, and set aside. Peel and coarsely chop the onions; wash the celery stalk, and chop coarsely; thoroughly clean the leek under running cold water, slice lengthwise, and chop coarsely.

In the saucepan, melt the tablespoon of butter, add the asparagus, onion, celery, leek, and 2 tablespoons of chicken stock. Bring vegetables to a low simmer and cook for 10 minutes.

While the vegetables are simmering, prepare the blond roux.

Then add remaining chicken stock to the vegetables, bring to a boil, and, using the whisk, whip in the roux, mixing until completely smooth. Reduce heat to a low simmer, cook for 20 minutes, then add whipping cream, and simmer for 10 more minutes.

While soup is simmering, prepare the asparagus garnish. Melt 1 1/2 teaspoons of butter in the small saucepan, add the asparagus tips and 2 tablespoons chicken stock, and cook gently over low heat for 8 to 10 minutes or until soft. Do not let asparagus brown and add a little more stock if necessary. When done, set aside and reserve.

When the soup has finished cooking, pour it through the fine-mesh sieve into the mixing bowl, wash out the saucepan, and return soup to it. If soup is too thick, add some more whipping cream or chicken stock; if too thin, cook on a low simmer another 10 minutes. When soup has desired thickness, add the reserved cooked asparagus pieces and Maggi and adjust seasoning with salt and white pepper. Serve piping hot, or, if you are not ready to serve it, the soup will wait comfortably if set aside in a cool place with dots of butter on the surface to prevent the formation of a skin layer.

As a further enrichment, just before serving, blend 1 egg yolk well with 3 tablespoons of whipping cream, bring soup to a boil, and, stirring constantly with a whisk, add yolk and cream mixture. Remove soup immediately from heat and do not let it boil again.

Cream of Celery Soup

This soup is a good way to use up celery scraps and pieces. You may use the celery heart, too, or save it for salad or as a vegetable, braised with a little stock.

Yields about 7 cups, for 6 to 8 servings

2 1/2 cups (590 ml) celery
1 1/2 medium onions
1 medium leek
1 tablespoon (15 g) butter
6 cups (1425 ml) White Chicken Stock *(see page 61)*
1/4 cup (60 ml) Blond Roux *(see page 65)*
1 cup (235 ml) whipping cream
1/4 teaspoon Maggi
Salt
Freshly ground white pepper

GARNISH
2 celery stalks
1 1/2 teaspoons (7 g) butter
2 tablespoons White Chicken Stock

Recommended equipment

A large chef's knife, 4-quart (4 L) saucepan, wire whisk, paring knife, small saucepan, large fine-mesh sieve, small mixing bowl.

Prepare the vegetables. Wash the celery, remove the leaves, and chop it coarsely to yield 2 1/2 cups, and set aside. Peel and coarsely chop the onions; thoroughly clean the leek under running cold water, slice lengthwise, and chop coarsely.

In the saucepan, melt the tablespoon of butter, add the celery, onion, leek, and 2 tablespoons of chicken stock. Bring vegetables to a low simmer and cook for 10 minutes.

While the vegetables are simmering, prepare the blond roux.

Then add remaining chicken stock to the vegetables, bring to a boil, and, using the whisk, whip in the roux, mixing until completely smooth. Reduce heat to a low simmer, cook for 20 minutes, then add whipping cream, and simmer for 10 more minutes.

While soup is simmering, prepare the celery garnish. Wash, trim, and peel the celery stalks, removing the leaves, and, using the paring knife, cut into thin matchstick-size strips. Melt 1 1/2 teaspoons of butter in the small saucepan, add the celery strips and 2 tablespoons chicken stock, and cook gently over low heat for 8 to 10 minutes or until soft. Do not let celery brown and add a little more stock if necessary. When done, set aside and reserve.

When the soup has finished cooking, pour it through the fine-mesh sieve into the mixing bowl, wash out the saucepan, and return soup to it. If soup is too thick, add some more whipping cream or chicken stock; if too thin, cook on a low simmer another 10 minutes. When soup has desired thickness, add the reserved cooked celery strips and Maggi and adjust seasoning with salt and white pepper. Serve piping hot, or, if you are not ready to serve it, the soup will wait comfortably if set aside in a cool place with dots of butter on the surface to prevent the formation of a skin layer.

As a further enrichment, just before serving, blend 1 egg yolk well with 3 tablespoons of whipping cream, bring soup to a boil, and, stirring constantly with a whisk, add yolk and cream mixture. Remove soup immediately from heat and do not let it boil again.

Cream of Mushroom Soup

Perhaps more than any other of the cream soups, this one will astound you if you are used to the familiar variety in the can—you may never buy it again. Use fresh mushroom stems that have been trimmed from their caps. The type of mushroom used is a matter of choice. The recipe works well with the pale white, cultivated mushrooms (champignons de Paris) available everywhere. But, where fresh seasonal mushrooms are to be had, by all means use them.

Yields about 7 cups, for 6 to 8 servings

1 pound (450 g) fresh mushrooms
1 celery stalk
1 medium onion
1 medium leek
1 tablespoon (15 g) butter
6 cups (1425 ml) White Chicken Stock *(see page 61)*
1/4 cup (60 ml) Blond Roux *(see page 65)*
1 cup (235 ml) whipping cream
1/4 teaspoon Maggi
Salt
Freshly ground white pepper
1 tablespoon finely cut chives or chopped parsley

GARNISH
6 mushroom caps
1 1/2 teaspoons (7 g) butter
2 tablespoons White Chicken Stock

Recommended equipment

A small chef's knife, large fine-mesh sieve, 4-quart (4 L) saucepan, wooden spatula, wire whisk, 8-inch (20 cm) sauté pan, blender or food processor.

Prepare the vegetables. Trim the caps from 6 mushrooms and reserve for the garnish. Using the chef's knife, chop the mushroom stems and pieces coarsely, set them into the sieve, rinse under cold running water, and let drain. Rinse the celery stalk, and chop it coarsely. Peel and chop the onion. Slice the leek lengthwise, wash it thoroughly under running cold water, and chop coarsely.

Set the saucepan over medium heat, add the butter, and, when it is hot, stir in the mushroom pieces and sauté for 3 minutes. Add the chopped celery, onion, and leek to the saucepan and sauté another 3 minutes. Add the chicken stock, bring to a boil, and adjust heat so that the soup simmers for 10 minutes.

Prepare the blond roux while the vegetables are simmering.

Remove saucepan from heat, whisk in the roux, blend well, return saucepan to heat, and simmer for 20 minutes.

While soup is simmering, prepare the garnish. Brush any clinging dirt from the mushroom caps, and dice them finely. Set the sauté pan over medium heat, add the butter, and, when it is hot, add the diced caps and chicken stock and sauté, stirring, for 3 minutes. Remove from heat and reserve.

When the soup is done, remove from heat, and, when it is cool enough to handle, either force it through the sieve or purée it in the blender or food processor. Then return it to the saucepan, add the cream and reserved mushroom garnish, and simmer gently on low heat for 5 minutes. Add the Maggi and salt and pepper to taste. Just before serving, stir in the chives or parsley.

For a stronger mushroom flavor, add 6 to 8 dried mushroom slices along with the fresh mushrooms and vegetables when starting the soup.

❧ Mulligatawney

*The precedent for this soup may reach as far back as the early seventeenth century, when England was aggressively seeking dominance in the East Indian spice trade. The word is an anglicized pronunciation of the East Indian words for pepper and water—*molagu *and* tunni. *Inevitably, the recipe changed through time, but even in the version given here it is highly seasoned, this time with curry.*

Yields 6 servings

1 1/2 teaspoons peanut oil
1 pound (450 g) chicken bones
1 large onion
1 celery stalk
1 medium apple
2 tablespoons curry powder
2 tablespoons mango chutney
1 tablespoon tomato paste
1 tablespoon flour
6 cups (1425 ml) White Chicken Stock *(see page 61)*
3 tablespoons Blond Roux *(see page 65)*
1 cup (235 ml) whipping cream
Salt
Freshly ground white pepper

GARNISH
1 medium apple
1 teaspoon butter

Recommended equipment

A small chef's knife, apple corer, 3-quart (3 L) saucepan, wooden spatula, wire whisk, large fine-mesh sieve, 8-inch (20 cm) sauté pan.

Set the saucepan over medium heat, add the peanut oil, and, when it is hot, add the chicken bones, and sauté for several minutes, stirring occasionally, until the bones are light golden brown.

While the bones are browning, prepare the vegetables. Peel and coarsely chop the onion. Rinse the celery stalk, remove any leaves, and chop coarsely. Core the apple and chop coarsely.

When the bones are brown, drain off the fat, add the curry powder, and sauté, stirring, over low heat for 1 minute. Then stir in the chopped onion, celery, and apple, and sauté, stirring, for 2 minutes. Add the chutney, tomato paste, and flour, and mix well before adding the chicken stock. Raise heat to medium and bring the soup to a simmer while stirring. Then adjust heat so that soup simmers gently for 10 minutes. Whisk in the roux, blend thoroughly, and simmer soup gently over low heat for 20 minutes. At this point, remove from heat, pour through the sieve, return to saucepan, set the saucepan over medium heat, add the cream, and adjust heat so that soup simmers gently until creamy and thick (about 5 minutes).

While soup is thickening, prepare the garnish. Peel, core, and finely dice the apple. Set the sauté pan over medium low heat, add the butter, and when it is hot, add the diced apple and sauté, stirring, for 2 minutes. Then remove from heat and reserve.

When the soup is creamy and thick, adjust the seasoning with salt and pepper and, just before serving, stir in the reserved garnish.

Cream of Chicken Soup Virginia

This is a tasty alternative to the traditional southern peanut soup, which, for some, is too rich to serve at the beginning of a meal.

Yields 6 to 7 servings

1 1/2 teaspoons peanut oil
1 pound (450 g) chicken bones
1 medium onion
1 celery stalk
1 medium leek
6 cups (1425 ml) White Chicken Stock *(see page 61)*
1/4 cup (60 ml) Blond Roux *(see page 65)*
3/4 cup (180 ml) roasted, shelled, unsalted peanuts
1 cup (235 ml) whipping cream
1/8 teaspoon Maggi
Salt
Freshly ground white pepper

Recommended equipment

A 3-quart (3 L) saucepan, wooden spatula, small chef's knife, wire whisk, large fine-mesh sieve.

Set the saucepan over medium high heat, add the peanut oil, and, when it is hot, add the chicken bones, and sauté for several minutes, stirring occasionally, until the bones are light golden brown.

While the bones are browning, prepare the vegetables. Peel and coarsely chop the onion. Rinse the celery stalk, remove any leaves, and chop coarsely. Halve the leek lengthwise, rinse thoroughly under running cold water, and chop coarsely.

When the bones are brown, add the chopped onion, celery, and leek, reduce heat to medium, and sauté for 3 minutes. Then add chicken stock, bring to a simmer, and adjust the heat so that the soup simmers gently for 10 minutes.

Meanwhile prepare the blond roux.

Remove saucepan from heat, whisk in the roux, blend it in thoroughly, return saucepan to heat, and adjust it so that the soup simmers slowly. Cook the soup for 20 minutes, stirring occasionally. While the soup simmers, finely dice the peanuts and reserve.

When the soup has finished simmering, strain it through the sieve, return it to the saucepan, and stir in the cream and diced peanuts. Set the saucepan back over heat, return soup to a simmer, and cook for 5 minutes. Then add the Maggi, taste the soup, and, if necessary, adjust the seasoning with salt and pepper. The soup can be served now, piping hot, or can wait for a couple of hours, put aside in a cool place with dots of butter on the surface to prevent the formation of a skin layer.

Variation: Omit the peanuts and serve as a plain cream soup, or, if you like, stir in cooked rice, diced chicken, or finely diced red pimiento.

Bisque of Shrimp

After the eighteenth century, a bisque usually meant crayfish were added to a soup in some form, often puréed. Now that crayfish are commercially raised, you might want to try them in place of shrimp in this recipe, but be forewarned—they are not easy to clean. An excellent fish stock and shrimp fresh from your fishmonger are de rigueur for this recipe. Elegant in structure but not time-consuming to prepare, this soup, accompanied by a full-bodied Chardonnay or Meursault, is an exquisite prelude to an early fall dinner.

Yields about 8 cups, for 8 servings

1 medium onion
1/2 celery stalk
2 medium, ripe tomatoes
1 tablespoon Blond Roux (see page 65)
1 tablespoon olive oil
3 pounds (1350 g) shrimp in the shell
1/2 cup (118 ml) Cognac
1 pinch thyme or 1 small sprig fresh thyme
1/2 bay leaf
2 tablespoons tomato paste
1 sprig fresh parsley
A dash of paprika
A pinch of cayenne pepper
1/2 teaspoon black peppercorns, crushed
2 quarts (1900 ml) Fish Stock (see page 60)
1 cup (235 ml) whipping cream
1 teaspoon butter
Salt
Freshly ground white pepper

Recommended equipment

A small chef's knife, 4- to 5-quart (4 to 5 L) heavy-bottomed saucepan, wooden spatula, mortar and pestle, wire whisk, fine-mesh skimmer, colander, shrimp deveiner, fine-mesh sieve.

Prepare the vegetables. Peel and trim the onion and chop coarsely; wash the celery stalk, trim off the leaves, and chop it coarsely; and wash and pare the tomatoes and chop them coarsely.

Prepare the blond roux.

Heat oil in the saucepan over medium to high heat, add shrimp, and sauté for 5 minutes stirring constantly with the wooden spatula. Then reduce heat, add one-half of the Cognac, simmer for a few moments, add celery, onion, thyme, and bay leaf, and sauté for 3 minutes. Next, add tomatoes, tomato paste, parsley, paprika, cayenne pepper, and crushed peppercorns, and sauté for 3 minutes. Then add roux, blend in well, and add the fish stock, stirring all together with the whisk until mixture comes to a boil. Then lower heat and maintain a constant simmer. Cook for 10 minutes, occasionally stirring with the spatula, then remove from heat.

Using the skimmer, lift about 1 cup (235 ml) of shrimp into the colander and refresh them under running cold water. Peel and devein the shrimp and finely dice enough to yield 1/2 cup (118 ml) and reserve. Return the saucepan to heat, bring to a simmer, and cook for 20 minutes. Add the cream, simmer another 10 minutes, and then strain the soup through the sieve and return to a clean saucepan. If the bisque must wait before serving, dot the top with bits of butter to prevent the formation of a skin layer.

When ready to serve, reheat bisque gently to a low simmer, stir in the remaining Cognac and diced shrimp, adjust seasoning with salt and pepper if needed, and serve right away.

Billi Bi

This elegant and delicious classic soup is more refined than its cousin, mouclade, the renowned saffron- and curry-tinged stew from Poitou-Charentes on the Côte d'Atlantique. After flavoring the broth, the cooked mussels yield an extra bonus. Two or three (without their shells) can be added to each serving, saved for a salad, or left in the shell for serving as an hors d'oeuvre with a chilled sauce such as Curry Mayonnaise, Sauce Remoulade, or Mustard Sauce. Or, for an appetizer, at another time, prepare Mussels Provençale. Whatever you do, never use aluminum saucepans while preparing this dish.

Yields about 6 cups, for 6 to 8 servings

2 quarts (2 L) mussels in the shell
2 cups (475 ml) dry white wine
2 tablespoons chopped shallots
1 tablespoon finely cut celery leaves
1/3 bay leaf
1 teaspoon crushed white pepper
1 cup (235 ml) Fish Stock *(see page 60)*
3 cups (710 ml) whipping cream
Salt
A dash of cayenne pepper
3 egg yolks
2 tablespoons finely cut fresh chives

Recommended equipment

A stiff bristle brush, small chef's knife, 4- to 5-quart (4 to 5 L) saucepan with lid, slotted spoon, colander, medium mixing bowl, strainer lined with cheesecloth or large fine-mesh sieve, 3-quart (3 L) saucepan, wire whisk.

Using the stiff bristle brush, scrub the mussels thoroughly under running cold water being careful to remove beards (or scrape them off with a paring knife). Some mussels may be partially open—if they are, touch them, and if they remain open, discard them. Drain off all the rinsing water and put mussels in the large saucepan with the wine, shallots, celery, bay leaf, pepper, and fish stock. Bring to a boil over medium heat, cover pan, and stir or shake from time to time for about 5 minutes or until shells have opened. Remove saucepan from heat. Dip mussels out with the slotted spoon into the colander set inside mixing bowl to drain completely. Discard any unopened mussels and reserve the rest for one of the uses suggested above.

Combine the cooking juices from the saucepan with the liquid in the bowl, and pour all through the strainer lined with cheesecloth or the fine-mesh sieve into the smaller saucepan. Add all but 1/4 cup (60 ml) of the whipping cream and simmer gently over medium to low heat for 10 minutes. Adjust seasoning with salt and a dash of cayenne. At this point the soup can wait for a couple of hours before serving. (Or it may be chilled and served cold, omitting the final enrichment.) Set soup aside in a cool place and dot top with bits of butter to prevent the formation of a skin layer.

When ready to serve, bring soup to a low simmer, blend egg yolks and remaining whipping cream thoroughly, and whisk mixture into hot soup while stirring constantly. Soup must not boil. Remove from heat if necessary and keep stirring until egg-yolk mixture has thickened. Then add chives and serve.

Bouillons and Consommés

These soups are a paradox. Apparently simple to the eye and subtle to the palate, these recipes are the pièces de resistance of soup making. Their understated elegance is produced only through hours of meticulous care in preparation, but, like a Venetian sunset, the limpid gold of a perfect English Beef Tea is not easily forgotten.

Chicken Bouillon

Yields about 3 quarts

4 quarts (4 L) White Chicken Stock *(see page 61)*
2 1/2 to 3 pounds (1125 to 1350 g) chicken parts (necks, wings, backs, gizzards)
1 large or 2 medium onions
2 leeks (white part only)
4 celery tops with leaves
4 large sprigs parsley
1/2 teaspoon freshly crushed white or black peppercorns

GARNISHES
Celestine or Vermicelli *(see page 153)*

Recommended equipment

An 8-quart (8 L) stockpot with lid, slicing knife, mortar and pestle, large fine-mesh sieve lined with cheesecloth, large mixing bowl, fine-mesh skimmer.

Set the stockpot over medium high heat and put the chicken stock (which should have been thoroughly and carefully degreased when you made it) into the pot. Add the chicken parts. Peel and slice the onion. Rinse the leeks under running cold water, carefully removing all sand and grit, and slice them. Rinse and slice the celery tops into 1-inch (2 1/2 cm) pieces, and add them with the onion, leeks, and parsley to the stockpot. Add the pepper and bring the stock slowly to a simmer. Adjust the heat so that the stock simmers slowly, partially covered, for 45 minutes.

At the end of the simmering period, ladle the bouillon into the cheesecloth-lined sieve set over the mixing bowl (or a saucepan if you are serving it soon). Wait a few minutes for all of the bouillon to drain through and then skim any fat from the surface. Taste and adjust the seasoning if needed with salt.

When ready to serve, bring the bouillon to a simmer, ladle it into warm cups or soup plates, and present it either plain or with one of the suggested garnishes.

Frozen chicken parts may be used, but should be blanched before adding to the stock.

Cantonese Egg Drop Soup

This nourishing soup is very appealing to the eye as it stands. However, several garnishes can be used without detracting from it in any way. Finely diced chicken (skin removed), cooked in the bouillon with the bones, or a very thin julienne of water chestnuts or thinly sliced raw mushrooms can be added. A few shrimp briefly cooked in some of the bouillon and cut into tiny dice are another colorful addition. Finally, if you are a real devotee of Szechuan cuisine, use all of these garnishes, add wine vinegar and freshly ground white pepper just before serving, and, unless you live in San Francisco or New York, you will have a "hot and sour" better than any you can find at your local Chinese restaurant.

Yields about 7 cups, for 6 servings

2 pounds (900 g) chicken bones
1/2 medium onion
1/4 celery stalk
1/4 leek, green part only
2 quarts (1900 ml) Chicken Bouillon *(see page 148)*
2 tablespoons arrowroot
6 tablespoons cool water
3 egg whites
5 scallions, green tops only

Recommended equipment

A 3-quart (3 L) saucepan, colander, large chef's knife, 4- to 5-quart (4 to 5 L) heavy-bottomed saucepan, fine-mesh sieve or coarse-mesh sieve lined with cheesecloth, large mixing bowl, wire whisk, coarse-mesh sieve.

Put the chicken bones in the smaller saucepan, cover with hot water, bring to a boil over high heat, and boil for 30 seconds. Remove from heat, pour off hot water, and run cold tap water into the saucepan to rid bones of all scum. Drain well in the colander.

While the bones are draining, prepare the vegetables. Peel and trim the onion and chop coarsely; wash the leafy celery stalk and chop coarsely; and thoroughly wash the green part of the leek under running cold water and chop coarsely. Put the clean and drained bones into the larger saucepan and add the chopped onion, celery, leek, and chicken bouillon. Bring slowly to a simmer over low heat and adjust burner so that soup simmers gently for 45 minutes. Then pour soup through the fine-mesh sieve (or coarse-mesh sieve lined with several layers of cheesecloth) into the large mixing bowl. Wash out saucepan, return soup to it, and set over medium heat to bring liquid to a low boil.

Using the whisk, blend the arrowroot with the 6 tablespoons of cool water, mixing thoroughly into a smooth, thin paste. Pour mixture into hot soup, stirring constantly with the whisk, and cook, stirring, until arrowroot has thickened the soup (about 2 to 3 minutes after soup has returned to a simmer).

When ready to serve, warm the soup plates. Briefly whip egg whites in a small bowl with a fork and, holding the coarse-mesh sieve about 10 inches above the soup, gradually pass the egg whites through the sieve into the simmering soup. Using the whisk, stir constantly with gentle, deliberate strokes to form egg drops and to keep strands of white separate. Quickly slice the trimmed scallion tops in half lengthwise and then very thinly crosswise. Distribute them among the soup plates, ladle the hot soup over, and serve immediately with fried noodles or thin pancake strips (such as the Celestine garnish, *see page 153*).

Essence de Caille Royale
Royal Essence of Quail

Browning the quail bones gives this soup a special flavor, and, ideally, only quail should be used for one-half of the bones, but pheasant may be substituted for the chicken where called for. A royal treat, this soup should set the stage for a meal which features Suprêmes de Saumon Amoureuse with either Roast Tenderloin of Beef London House with Truffle Sauce or Tenderloin of Lamb en Croûte Florentine. Be sure to use one of the three suggested garnishes, which you can prepare as the soup is cooking.

Yields about 7 cups, for 6 to 8 servings

1 1/2 tablespoons chicken fat or peanut oil
2 pounds (900 g) quail and chicken bones (1 pound of each)
1 medium onion
1/4 celery stalk
1/2 medium carrot
1/2 medium leek, green part only
1 sprig of parsley
1/3 bay leaf
2 quarts (1900 ml) Chicken Bouillon *(see page 148)*
1/2 cup (118 ml) dry white wine
1 tablespoon arrowroot
1/4 cup (60 ml) cold water

Recommended equipment

A 12-inch (30 cm) sauté pan, wooden spatula, 8-inch (20 cm) sauté pan, small chef's knife, paring knife, large fine-mesh sieve, 5-quart (5 L) saucepan, small mixing bowl, fine-mesh skimmer, small bowl, wire whisk, swivel-bladed vegetable peeler, paring knife, 1 1/2-quart (1 1/2 L) saucepan.

In the large sauté pan, heat 1 tablespoon of the chicken fat or peanut oil over medium heat, add the quail and the chicken bones, and sauté until golden brown. Stir the bones around from time to time with the wooden spatula so that they brown on all sides.

While the bones are browning, prepare the vegetables. Trim and pare the onion, cut in half, and brown in the remaining peanut oil in the small sauté pan. Wash the celery and carrot and chop coarsely. Thoroughly wash the green part of the leek, separating the leaves under cold running water, and chop coarsely. Rinse and dry the parsley.

When the bones are well browned, add the onion, celery, leek, carrot, parsley, and bay leaf, and sauté for 2 minutes, stirring from time to time. Drain in fine-mesh sieve to remove excess fat.

Pour the chicken bouillon into the large saucepan, add the bones and vegetables and the white wine, and bring to a low simmer over low heat. Cook for 45 minutes. Then strain through clean fine-mesh sieve into the mixing bowl and skim off all fat.

Wash out the saucepan, return soup to it, and, when ready to serve, bring to a low boil. Blend arrowroot with the 1/4 cup of cold water and mix completely into a smooth paste. Then, stirring constantly with the whisk, add to the boiling soup, and continue stirring until soup simmers again and arrowroot is thoroughly incorporated. Cook for 2 to 3 minutes while stirring, remove from heat, and serve immediately with one of the suggested garnishes.

GARNISHES
Vegetable
1 small celery stalk, well peeled
1 small carrot, peeled
1 medium leek, white part only

Thoroughly wash the celery and carrot and peel both. Cut the white part of the leek lengthwise and wash carefully under running cold water. Using the paring knife, cut the vegetables into thin 2-inch (5 cm) long strips, add to boiling salted water in a small saucepan, and blanch for 4 minutes. Drain well before serving.

Chestnut and chive
1 tablespoon finely cut fresh chives
4 water chestnuts

Using the paring knife, cut the chives into tiny pieces and the water chestnuts into thin slices. Then make fine strips from the slices and stir the chives and chestnuts into the soup before serving.

Egg
10 fresh quail eggs

Bring water to a slow boil in the small saucepan, add eggs, and cook for 3 minutes. (It's wise to have a few extra eggs because sometimes they are difficult to peel.) Cool the eggs under cold water for several minutes, peel, and add one egg to each cup of soup before serving.

It is easier to place the garnish in individual cups or bowls before adding the broth and serving the soup. But the garnish may go into the soup before serving if it is offered at the table from a tureen.

Beef Bouillon

For generations of travelers on the North Atlantic, eleven o'clock in the morning brought one of the most eagerly anticipated moments in the daily life of the great luxury liners. Even if you were foresighted (or lucky) enough to book a deck chair on the sunny side of the ship and were tightly bundled up in the wool blanket, the chill produced by these express mail ships traveling at 30 to 35 knots could penetrate to the bone, and no sight was more welcome than the deck steward with his tray of silver pots full of steaming beef bouillon. Save for the Queen Elizabeth II, *the great steamships are gone, but this recipe will give you a soup equal to that from Le Huédé's kitchens on the* France *(you will have to supply your own blanket and deck chair).*

Yields 2 quarts

4 quarts (4 L) water (for stock, not blanching)
2 pounds (900 g) lean beef (shank, neck, or chuck), cut into 1-inch (2 1/2 cm) cubes
4 pounds (1800 g) beef bones, cut by your butcher into pieces 4 to 5 inches (10 to 12 1/2 cm) long
2 medium onions
1 medium carrot
1 celery stalk
1 leek
1/2 small white turnip
1/2 bay leaf
1 sprig fresh parsley
1/2 teaspoon salt

Beef bouillon can be used as is, with different garnishes, or as a base in Soupe à l'Oignon Gratinée, Basler Mehlsuppe, Russian Onion Soup, Consommé Double, and Borscht à la Russe. Even though time-consuming to prepare, the serious home cook should never shy away from making it.

Recommended equipment

A 5-quart (5 L) saucepan or 8-quart (8 L) stockpot, small chef's knife, baking sheet, colander, fine-mesh skimmer, large fine-mesh sieve, large mixing bowl.

Bring 1 1/2 quarts (1 1/2 L) of water to a boil in the saucepan or stockpot, add beef and bones, bring to a boil again, and boil for 1 minute. Remove from heat, pour off all hot water, and run cold water into the pan to rid bones of all scum. Drain well in the colander.

Wash out pot, add beef, bones, and the 4 quarts of cold water. Bring to a boil over medium heat and then adjust heat so that pot simmers gently. Cook for 2 hours, skimming from time to time.

While the pot is simmering, prepare the other vegetables. Preheat oven to 425F (218C). Trim the root ends from the onions and cut in half. Do not peel. When oven is hot, put onion halves skin side down on baking sheet and roast until golden brown—approximately 3 to 4 minutes. During this time, wash the carrot and celery stalk and cut in half crosswise; wash the leek thoroughly under running cold water, separating the leaves, and cut in half lengthwise; and wash and trim the turnip half.

When bouillon has simmered for 2 hours, add the vegetables, bay leaf, parsley, and salt. Simmer all together for another hour. Remove from heat, pour stock into sieve set over the mixing bowl, and let cool to room temperature. Refrigerate when cool. When thoroughly chilled, the fat will have risen to the top of the bouillon and can be easily removed.

To serve the bouillon hot, gently warm it, pour it into soup bowls and garnish it with freshly snipped chives or minced parsley. If you are saving it for later use, ladle into freezer containers in 1-cup (235 ml) quantities and freeze. When completely frozen, unmold, wrap in plastic wrap, label, and store in freezer until needed.

❦ Consommé Double

For this special soup it is essential to use lean beef and watch the simmering very carefully. The egg whites and shells refine the bouillon by clarifying it, and the cooking with meat and vegetables improves the flavor. Your efforts will be rewarded as you savor your first spoonful and discover one of cuisine's great treasures.

Yields 7 cups, for 6 to 8 servings

1 pound (450 g) lean beef (shin or chuck)
1 medium leek, green part only
1/3 cup (80 ml) leafy celery tops
1/2 medium carrot
1 sprig fresh parsley
1 medium onion
3 egg whites
3 eggshells
2 quarts (1900 ml) Beef Bouillon *(see page 151)*, at room temperature
Salt
Freshly ground black pepper

Recommended equipment

A small chef's knife, meat grinder or grinding attachment with medium blade, medium mixing bowl, 4-quart (4 L) heavy-bottomed saucepan, wooden spatula, large fine-mesh sieve lined with cheesecloth, ladle, fine-mesh skimmer.

Using the chef's knife, trim the beef of all visible fat, then put through medium blade of the meat grinder into the mixing bowl.

Wash the green part of the leek thoroughly under cold running water and slice crosswise into thin slices. Wash the leafy celery tops and slice thinly. Scrub the carrot half and cut into thin slices. Wash the parsley. Peel the onion, cut in half, and slice it coarsely. Add the vegetables and the black pepper to the beef. Separate the eggs (reserving the yolks for another use), and add the whites and shells to the mixing bowl. Combine all ingredients thoroughly, the best way—with your hands—as if you were mixing a meat loaf.

Put the beef bouillon (which was thoroughly and carefully degreased when you made it) into the saucepan, add the beef mixture, and bring *slowly* to a gentle simmer over medium heat. While simmering point is being reached, take the wooden spatula and gently scrape it across the bottom of the saucepan, 3 to 4 times, using a very slow, deliberate motion. This procedure prevents the meat mixture from sticking and, after the simmer is reached, should be repeated once. *Do not stir* the consommé—simply move the spatula back and forth.

Cook the consommé at a very low simmer for 2 hours. The consommé should only show tiny bubbles around the inside edge of the saucepan. Adjust heat as necessary and watch the consommé carefully. At no point should the liquid bubble rapidly.

After 2 hours, take saucepan off heat, wait for simmer to stop, and ladle consommé gently into cheesecloth-lined sieve set over mixing bowl (or another saucepan if you are serving it soon). Wait a few minutes for all the consommé to drain through, then skim off any fat before reheating. If you are going to store it, let cool to room temperature before refrigerating and then skim off fat when chilled. To serve, reheat gently to a low simmer, adjust seasoning if necessary with salt, and ladle into warm cups or soup plates. Serve plain or with one of the garnishes suggested below.

GARNISHES

Julienne. Use a combination of carrots, celery, and the white part of the leek. Wash vegetables well, peel the carrot and celery stalk, and cut them and the leek into matchstick-size strips (no longer than the bowl of your soupspoon). Put into small saucepan, cover with water, add a dash of salt, and cook until tender (about 10 minutes). Drain thoroughly and pat with a kitchen towel before using. Snip fresh chives into small pieces and add to vegetables just before serving.

Brunoise. Use the same ingredients and procedure as for julienne, but add white turnips and finely dice all the vegetables.

Celestine. Make thin Crêpes *(see page 520)*, adding finely cut chives to the batter and eliminating the sugar. When cool, cut into fine strips no longer than 2 inches (5 cm).

Chasseur. Thoroughly clean fresh mushroom caps and slice into thin strips. Slice ripe tomatoes (blanched, peeled, and seeded; *see page 568*) into thin strips. Add both to finely cut fresh chives.

Vermicelli. Cook pasta until done, cool under running cold water, drain well, and add to finely cut chives.

The garnishes should be put into the serving dish first and the consommé ladled over them.

Celery Broth

Here, the lowly celery is elevated to a noble position. No longer will it wait in your produce bin to "stretch out" a chicken or tuna salad, or worst of all to be thrown out because it was forgotten.

Yields 6 servings

1 cup (235 ml) celery leaves and scraps
6 cups (1425 ml) Beef Bouillon *(see page 151)*
1 cup (235 ml) water
2 celery stalks
Salt
Freshly ground white pepper

Recommended equipment

A small chef's knife, 2-quart (2 L) saucepan, small saucepan, large fine-mesh sieve, medium mixing bowl.

Rinse the celery scraps and leaves, chop coarsely, and set aside. Set the large saucepan over medium heat, add the beef bouillon and 1/2 cup (118 ml) water, and bring to a slow simmer. Add the celery scraps and simmer gently for 15 minutes.

While the broth simmers, rinse the celery stalks, trim them, peel if necessary to make them as stringless as possible, and slice very thinly. Put the slices in the small saucepan, add the remaining water, bring to a simmer over medium heat, and cook gently for 5 minutes. When done, remove from heat and reserve.

When the broth has finished simmering, strain it thorough the fine-mesh sieve into the mixing bowl and then return it to the saucepan. Add the celery slices with their liquid, reheat gently until hot, adjust seasoning if necessary with salt and pepper, and serve.

Consommé Madrilene
Hot Tomato Broth in the Style of Madrid

Yields 6 servings

6 cups (1425 ml) Consommé Double *(see page 152)*
3 medium to large, ripe tomatoes
1/3 celery stalk
1 sprig fresh parsley
1/4 small green bell pepper
3 drops red food color (optional)

GARNISH
1 large, ripe tomato (blanched, peeled, and seeded; *see page 568*)
2 tablespoons finely cut chives

Recommended equipment

A 2-quart (2 L) saucepan, small chef's knife, paring knife, large fine-mesh sieve lined with cheesecloth, medium mixing bowl.

Set the saucepan over medium heat, add the consommé, and while bringing it to a low simmer, rinse, seed, and coarsely chop the 3 tomatoes and add them to the saucepan. Rinse and chop the celery, rinse the parsley, rinse and seed the bell pepper, and add them all to the saucepan. Prepare the tomato for the garnish. Reserve the flesh, keeping it as intact as possible, and add the pulp to the consommé. Bring the consommé back to a simmer, and adjust the heat so that it cooks gently for 15 minutes.

While the consommé simmers, cut the reserved tomato flesh into small square or diamond shapes and divide them among the serving cups or bowls.

When the consommé has finished simmering, remove from heat, add the optional food color, and strain it through the cheesecloth-lined sieve into the mixing bowl. Rinse out the saucepan and return the consommé to it, heat gently until very hot, and adjust the seasoning if necessary. Slice the chives very thinly and divide them among the serving cups or bowls. Ladle the consommé into the dishes and serve at once.

 ## English Beef Tea

Larousse Gastronomique *tells us that beef tea "is chiefly given, in small doses, . . . for . . . awakening the appetite." What an understatement! As I said in the introduction, even in the Homestead kitchen this is a very special soup. More demanding of time than ingredients, it is the third and final stage in a series beginning with Beef Bouillon. But, you will receive your own five-star award, as every spoonful brings sheer pleasure to your palate and appreciative murmurs from your guests. Save it for a special gathering of epicures and pass a plate of homemade Paillettes or plain melba toast separately. When serving this broth as a course in an elegant menu, I would advise having no other beef course in the dinner. Garnishes are definitely out of order because they would compete with the extraordinary flavor.*

English Beef Tea in the Commonwealth Room

Yields 8 cups, for 8 to 10 servings

Recommended equipment

5 pounds (2275 g) lean beef (shank or chuck)
6 cups (1425 ml) Beef Bouillon *(see page 151)*, at room temperature
A dash of salt
A dash of Knorr Aromat

A small chef's knife, meat grinder or grinding attachment with medium blade, large mixing bowl, ladle, two 1/2-gallon (2 L) wide mouth heavy duty glass jars with lids, 8-quart (8 L) stockpot, old newspaper, large fine-mesh sieve lined with cheesecloth.

Using the chef's knife, trim the beef of all visible fat and gristle, then put through the medium blade of a meat grinder into the mixing bowl.

Divide the meat between the jars and ladle the bouillon over it. Fold about twelve pages of an old newspaper to fit the bottom of the stockpot. Put the jars into the stockpot onto the newspaper, add water so that it comes two-thirds of the way up the jars, and set stockpot over low heat. Bring water to a boil and then immediately adjust heat so that a low simmer is maintained. Cook for 5 hours, checking from time to time to see if the water level needs to be replenished.

When the beef tea has finished simmering, gently lift jars from stockpot (protect your hands with a kitchen towel). Set the cheesecloth-lined sieve over the mixing bowl (or a saucepan if you are going to serve it soon), and very carefully pour the beef tea into it, leaving about 1 inch (2 1/2 cm) of liquid in the bottom of each jar. Do not disturb any solids remaining in the bottoms of the jars. It may take as long as 10 minutes for the liquid to drip through the sieve.

To serve, reheat very gently until almost hot, but just below the simmering point. Adjust seasoning if necessary with a dash of salt and Aromat. If some dots of fat are floating on the surface, draw a paper towel across the top in a continuous sweeping motion. Repeat if necessary until all visible fat is removed. Then ladle into warm serving dishes and watch your guests enjoy this unique soup.

Beef tea will keep for 2 days under refrigeration or may be poured into freezer containers, frozen, unmolded, and stored for later use.

Hors d'Oeuvres and Salads

The most entertaining element of Russian cuisine remains that of the *zakuski*, an impressive display of hors d'oeuvres related to the Scandinavian *smörgåsbord*. An upper middle-class house would present platters of smoked sturgeon, herring fillets, suckling pig in horseradish, salmon, cucumbers in brine, little warm pâtés of meat baked in pastry (*pirozhki*), and small pancakes (*blini*) filled with sour cream and the finest caviar from the Caspian Sea. It was with the *zakuski* that exuberant drinking commenced. One never drank without eating; and the rich fish and tidbits that were small meals in themselves provided a firm foundation for tot after tot of vodka. . . . And if one's purse matched his thirst, he could afterward indulge in what the Russians called *champanskoe*, served not just chilled, as in France, but half-frozen.

Herbs and condiments, in addition to being thrown into stewpots, medical preparations, and witches' brews, also played a major part in the medieval salad. A recipe for "salat" from *The Forme of Cury*, an important early cooking manual compiled by the master cooks of Richard II of England around 1390, advises, "Take parcel, sawge, garlec, chibollas [young onions], oynons, leek, borage, myntes, porrectes [a kind of leek], fenel, and ton tressis [cresses], rew, rosemarye, purslarye [purslane]; lave, and woisshe hem clene; pike hem, pluk hem small with thyn [thine] honde, and myng [mix] hem ind raw oile. Lay on vynegar and salt, and serve it forth."

—William Harlan Hale

When the King said gravely to the White Rabbit, "begin at the beginning," Lewis Carroll's readers knew what the "beginning" was. In Wonderland, yes, but in "culinaryland," yes and no. A description of a royal banquet in Mantua in 1581, with four cardinals and three dukes seated at the head table under a *baldachino* (canopy), informs us that the first course was composed of "salads decked out with various fantasies such as animals made of citron, castles of turnips, high walls of lemons; and variegated with slices of ham, mullet roes, herrings, tunny, an-

Gravlax in the Main Dining Room

chovies, capers, olives, caviar, together with candied flowers and other preserves." But contemporary French practice would have the salad placed after the entrée to cleanse the palate. That is unless it is *tiède* (warm), sautéed *foie gras* at Lutèce or Meneau's L'Esperance in Saint-Père-sous-Vézelay, *salade tiède aux crustaces* at Troisgros, *gerbe d'asperges violettes* at Vergé's Moulin de Mougins, or *salade tiède d'épinards* from our Grille. In this case it could be served first—as an hors d'oeuvre. That is, unless the diner orders it after an hors d'oeuvre. You see the problem. Then there is the general American custom of serving salad as a side dish *with* the meal. At the Homestead, we follow this practice in the Dining Room, but at formal banquets, salad is served separately following the entrée.

What all of this really reveals is flexibility and change rather than confusion. The recipes in this chapter are lighter preparations than the typical entrée, making many of them just right for fall and winter luncheons as well as hors d'oeuvres. Literally meaning "outside the work," this term usually refers to individual items which are served at cocktail parties or to accompany an aperitif. Serving as many receptions and cocktail parties as it does, the Homestead offers a wide range of hors d'oeuvres; however, because such entertaining is not the focus of this book, we have included only a few of our more popular items. For hot preparations we have selected recipes from Persia and Russia. The first one features tender tidbits of marinated chicken roasted on a skewer and the second recalls Hale's first passage at the beginning of this chapter and elegant Russian cuisine with its delicate deep-fried beef and cabbage mixture in a pastry shell. Both of these are excellent for passing on trays—in small quantities, mind you, as they must be enjoyed immediately. Beware the telltale sign of the "catered function"—a limp, tepid, soggy hors d'oeuvre which was meant to be served piping hot. Far better to make your guests wait for the next batch.

For a hot first course, two mushroom-based recipes lead off, Jim Wolfe's shiitakes being especially suited to grilled meat or poultry and the trio in vol-au-vents providing an elegant opening for a more formal occasion. Among the hot dishes, there are four mollusks and two crustaceans. In the first group, clams, mussels, scallops, and oysters are to be found—each with a distinctive treatment. The first two receive an aromatic topping: the scallops are aswim in a quick but elegant sauce, and the oysters are coated with the lightest of gratinées. Both of the crabmeat recipes are delicious, and you will probably find that before you can get the first bite of crab cake, your guests will be begging for more. Be sure to make fresh Sauce Tartare for this one.

The section of cold preparations begins with four hors

d'oeuvres which can be set out in bowls or on trays, to be replenished from the kitchen as needed. Hummus is a simple chick-pea and sesame dip which can be accompanied with raw vegetables. Marinated mushrooms and marinated shrimp need only to have a supply of toothpicks close by. Most elegant of all is the canapé, which with smoked salmon, shrimp, and caviar, should be reserved for special occasions. By the way, if you have a Middle Eastern feast in the offing, serve Persian Chicken Kebabs along with Hummus and pita bread as part of your menu.

Dining in warm weather brings the delight of alfresco meals with the double challenge of first courses which are light and able to withstand warm temperatures. Here we have provided you with five possibilities, the first being relatively simple recipes based on avocado, one with a colorful gazpacho aspic filling and one filled with crabmeat and Sauce Ravigote. The third is marinated fresh salmon with a tangy mustard sauce. The final pair is comprised of two "house" specialties which are extremely popular, but also a bit time-consuming to make. Both the pâté and the galantine, however, can be fixed well in advance, leaving you the time to savor them along with your guests—especially with a salad of crisp, fresh greens, French bread, and a well-iced Alsatian Pinot Blanc or Bordeaux Graves. Enjoyed under a natural *baldachino* such as our enormous sugar maple at the Casino, this is the perfect start for a lazy summer afternoon.

Which brings us to salads, and a paraphrase of Elizabeth Barrett Browning—"how do I fix thee, salad, let me count the ways." The proliferation of salad "bars" has transformed the concept for many from lightly dressed, delicately tossed fresh greens to MacNelly's "Perfesser's" classic reply to an inquiry about the evening's dinner—"cream of bottom shelf." We have mixed reactions to this. Obviously, we applaud a move toward the consumption of salads as traditionally conceived, but not when the greens become invisible under a mountain of cheese cubes, processed meat, bacon substitutes, and other "food" substances. Louis XIV would have banished them from the royal table. To be historically correct, salads are thought of as falling into two categories—those featuring one or two greens as vegetables (*salade simple*) and those based on vegetables and meat and/or fish (*salade composée*). To close out the chapter we have given you three of the former, five of the latter, and a delicious maverick which, according to *Larousse Gastronomique*, is not a salad at all because it lacks salt.

The simple salads feature, in order, spinach, cucumbers, and beets, each set off by a dressing particularly suited to the unique nature of the vegetable it accompanies. Being easily prepared in advance, the cucumber and beet salads are excellent picnic items as well. The spinach salad is another matter, however, and your guests should be sitting at the table, their forks poised, as you rush it in from the kitchen.

Among composed salads, few have a wider following than potato salad, and the legendary *salade niçoise*, as well as the two we have included here, pretty well cover the waterfront. First of the two is our own recipe, featured at the Casino buffet. Its mayonnaise-based dressing is more familiar to many American palates than the second recipe, which is more European in adding a vinaigrette to the warm potato slices. Somewhat in the antipasto tradition is another of our Casino favorites, this time based on tortellini. All three are good picnic items, and the complexity of the tortellini dish will easily make it the star of the table. The fisherman's salad is perfect fare for seafood lovers longing for the ocean. Keep this one well chilled and enjoy it soon after you prepare it—preferably at your own backyard picnic because it is a lot to carry to the beach.

Finally, two fruit preparations. The first fits more easily in the salad category because it does have vegetables and a dressing. Inspired by the Hawaiian islands, it is especially suited to charcoal-grilled dishes with an oriental flavor. The second recipe will surprise you if "fruit salad" automatically means Waldorf salad or bottled fruit cocktail. Offered as a real palliative for the winter "blues," the contrast of flavors, textures, and colors will be a welcome addition to your table.

In closing, let us leave you with a word about dressings. If you look at B. G. McElwee's Shopping List in the Introduction, you will see that we use great quantities of oil, vinegar, and other salad dressing ingredients every week—for one simple reason. We make our dressings every day, and there is no reason for you to do otherwise. Few recipes are easier and consume less time to make, and all a basic "o and v" requires is a bowl and a whisk. Why be enslaved to the monotony, preservatives, and tired herbs to be found in bottled or dried dressings, when you can make them at home according to the inspiration of the moment? When you are at the market, look for good French white and red wine vinegars with no more than 7 percent acidity. Don't worry about herb-flavored products, you can add your own as needed. As for oils, that is a matter of taste, but you will probably find that having two types of olive oil on hand—one more aromatic and one less so—is quite useful. And there you are, add a pepper grinder and you are in business.

Hot Hors d'Oeuvres

Broiled Persian Chicken Kebabs

In Turkish cooking, "kebab" is generally understood to mean meat cooked on skewers, as it is here. The use of "Persian" in the title reflects the many influences on Turkish cuisine, among them Greek and Persian, and the traditional prominence of Middle Eastern lands in the spice trade. Broiling produces the most authentic results, but these may be sautéed or baked according to the variations, if you prefer.

Yields 8 to 12 servings as an appetizer

5 chicken breasts, weighing about 8 ounces (225 g) each
1/2 medium onion
1 medium lemon
Salt
Freshly ground white pepper
8 to 12 saffron threads
2 tablespoons melted butter

Recommended equipment

A boning knife; slicing knife; glass, china, or stainless steel bowl; plastic wrap; small saucepan; 8-inch (20 cm) metal skewers; broiling pan; pastry brush.

Prepare each chicken breast by working with the boning knife along the breastbone and down the ribs, pulling the meat from the bone as you go and removing it in one piece. Cut the wing off at the joint (save for the stockpot) and remove the skin from the breast. Each breast is made up of two parts, the larger piece (on the top) is called the fillet and the smaller layer underneath is the filet mignon. Separate the two. In the filet mignon is a tough white tendon, visible in the meat where it lay against the ribs, which must be cut out. Cut each breast into four to six pieces (leaving the filet mignon as is), keeping in mind that each piece will be skewered so that the number of pieces depends upon the size of the breast. When all the breasts are prepared, set them aside while you prepare the marinade.

Peel the onion half and slice it as thinly as possible. Halve the lemon lengthwise. Slice one of the halves as thinly as possible and squeeze the juice from the other half over the chicken pieces. Combine the onion and lemon slices, salt, and pepper in the glass bowl. Crush 6 to 8 threads of saffron with your fingers, add them to the bowl, mix well, add the chicken pieces, and continue to mix with your hands until all ingredients are well blended. Cover the bowl tightly with plastic wrap and refrigerate for 4 to 12 hours, turning the chicken once or twice during that time.

When ready to broil, preheat the broiler to very hot. Melt the butter and add to it the liquid from the marinade and 2 to 3 threads of crushed saffron. Mix them in thoroughly. Push the chicken pieces onto the skewers, packing them tightly and adding an occasional lemon slice. Lay the skewers into a broiling pan and brush the chicken pieces with the marinade. Set the broiling pan on a rack 3 inches (7 1/2 cm) from the broiler and cook the chicken for 8 to 10 minutes, turning the skewers so that the chicken is nicely browned. When done, slide the chicken onto a warm serving dish and let your guests help themselves with toothpicks. Or, serve them on small plates with other hors d'oeuvres such as Clams Casino and Crabmeat Remick *(see pages 166 and 170)*.

Variations: The marinated chicken can be sautéed in a preheated sauté pan over medium high heat with the onion and lemon slices in 2 tablespoons each of Clarified Butter *(see page 568)* and peanut oil. Season to taste with salt and pepper and sauté, stirring occasionally, for 6 to 8 minutes until the chicken is done but not dry.

Or, blend the marinated chicken and lemon slices with 1/2 cup (118 ml) hot pepper jelly, spread in a baking dish, and bake in a preheated oven at 375F (190C) for 8 to 10 minutes or until done. Turn the broiler on for 1 or 2 minutes to lightly brown the top and then serve.

Pirojskis

*Many versions of this preparation exist (*pirozhki *is Russian for pies that are small enough to be eaten out of the hand), variously filled with fish, game, vegetables, cream cheese, and even truffles. Sometimes baked, sometimes fried, the pastry is crucial and must be carefully made. This recipe comes from the Russian kitchen of the Embassy Club of the former Ambassador Hotel in New York City. Serve them before dinner with well-iced Champagne or as an accompaniment to Borscht à la Russe.*

Yields 2 to 3 dozen

FOR THE DOUGH
1 pound (450 g) butter
2 cups (475 ml) lukewarm milk
1/2 ounce (15 g) yeast
8 egg yolks
1 teaspoon salt
1 tablespoon (12 g) sugar
2 pounds (900 g) flour
Butter for the bowl

FOR THE FILLING
6 tablespoons Sauce Béchamel
    (*see page 66*)
1/4 small head of white cabbage
2 medium onions
4 eggs
1 tablespoon peanut oil
2 pounds (900 g) ground lean
    beef
6 tablespoons Demi-glace Brun I
    (*see page 75*)
1/4 cup (60 ml) chopped fresh
    parsley
1/4 cup (60 ml) fine white bread
    crumbs
Salt
Freshly ground black pepper

Peanut oil for deep frying

Recommended equipment

Two small saucepans, 2-quart (2 L) bowl, blending fork, pastry scraper, two kitchen towels, large chef's knife, 2-quart (2 L) saucepan, 12-inch (30 cm) sauté pan, wooden spatula, meat grinder with fine blade, small mixing bowl, rolling pin, 3-inch (7 1/2 cm) biscuit cutter, electric deep fryer with thermostat, frying thermometer, fine-mesh skimmer, paper towels, heatproof serving platter.

Set one small saucepan over low heat, add the butter, and let it melt (cut the butter into chunks for even melting). Set the other small saucepan over low heat, add the milk, and heat it until it is lukewarm (110F or 44C). Then remove from heat, stir in the yeast, and let it dissolve. When the butter is melted and the yeast is dissolved, combine them in the bowl and add the egg yolks, salt, and sugar. Using the blending fork, mix in the flour a cup at a time until the dough forms a soft ball. Then turn the dough out onto a lightly floured work surface and knead the dough until it is smooth and elastic. (Work with one hand kneading and the other hand using the pastry scraper to turn the dough over.) Rinse out the bowl (or use a fresh one), butter it lightly, form the dough into a ball, and set it into the bowl. Turn the dough over (so the buttered side is up), cover the bowl with a damp kitchen towel, and set in a warm, draft-free place to rise for about 1 1/2 hours.

While the dough is rising, prepare the filling. Make the sauce béchamel and reserve. Dice the cabbage with the chef's knife. Set the large saucepan over high heat, add water and salt, and bring to a boil. Add the diced cabbage and boil for 10 minutes. Then remove from heat, drain the cabbage, refresh it under cold water, drain again, and reserve. Peel the onions and chop them finely. Rinse out the saucepan, add cold water and the eggs, bring to a simmer, and cook until they are hard-boiled (about 8 to 10 minutes). When done, put the eggs in cold water until cool, then peel and reserve.

Set the sauté pan over medium high heat, add the peanut oil, and, when it is hot, stir in the ground beef with the wooden spatula. Cook, stirring to separate the beef, until the meat begins to brown. Then stir in the onions and cabbage, reduce heat to medium, and sauté for 5 minutes. Stir in the sauce béchamel and the demi-glace, simmer for 5 more minutes, then remove from heat and allow to cool.

When the beef mixture is cool, put it through the fine blade of the meat grinder into a bowl. Rinse, dry, and chop the parsley. Chop the hard-boiled eggs. Using the blending fork, mix the parsley, hard-boiled eggs, and bread crumbs into the beef. Season to taste with salt and pepper, blend thoroughly, and reserve while you check on the dough. The dough has risen enough if two fingers poked down into it leave a depression. If the dough isn't ready, chill the beef mixture.

When the dough has risen, punch it down, turn it out onto a lightly floured work surface, and let it rest for 5 minutes under a damp towel. Then roll the dough out evenly to a 1/4-inch (2/3 cm) thickness. Using the biscuit cutter, cut the dough into circles (or using a paring knife, cut oval or other shapes, either larger or smaller, depending upon their intended use). Put about a tablespoon of the beef mixture in the center of each circle, fold the dough over the filling, pinch it tightly together, and set them on a lightly floured surface, covered with a damp cloth, to rise for 20 minutes in a warm draft-free place.

Preheat oven to 200F (93C).

Heat the peanut oil in the deep fryer to 375F (190C). When the oil is hot and the pirojskis have risen, put a few of them at a time into the hot oil (do not crowd the fryer) and cook until golden brown on all sides. Use the fine-mesh skimmer to turn them as necessary for even browning. When done, remove to a triple thickness of paper towels to drain, then put them in the serving dish, set into the oven to stay hot, and fry the next batch of pirojskis. Serve them very hot.

For a smaller quantity, prepare one-half of the recipe. Any leftover dough may be wrapped tightly and frozen for another time.

Shiitake Mushrooms with Mustard Sauce

Native to the orient, these mushrooms (pasania cuspidata), known in China as black mushrooms and in Japan as shiitake, have gained such popularity that they are now widely raised in the United States. Nearby Virginia farms supply the shiitake for this very popular appetizer prepared by Chef Jim Wolfe in our Grille. Serve them on a warm plate with the sauce in a separate dish.

Yields 4 servings

FOR THE MUSTARD SAUCE
3/4 cup (180 ml) mayonnaise
2 teaspoons Dijon mustard
Juice of 1/4 lemon
A dash of dry white wine
A dash of white wine Worcestershire sauce

1 1/4 pounds (570 g) fresh shiitake mushrooms
2 teaspoons freshly chopped shallots
1 teaspoon chopped fresh parsley
1/2 cup (118 ml) Clarified Butter *(see page 568)*
Salt
Freshly ground black pepper

Recommended equipment

A wire whisk, small bowl, paring knife, paper towels, small chef's knife, 12-inch (30 cm) sauté pan, wooden spatula, large fine-mesh sieve.

1/4-inch (2/3 cm) thick strips and reserve. Chop the shallots with the chef's knife. Rinse the parsley, pat dry, chop, and reserve.

Set the sauté pan over high heat, add the clarified butter, and, when it is hot, stir in the mushrooms. Sauté, stirring, until the shiitake are lightly browned. Stir in the shallots, blend well, and sauté, stirring, for 1 minute. Season the mushrooms to taste with salt and pepper, scrape them into the sieve to drain off excess butter, and serve hot, sprinkled with parsley, on warm plates, with the sauce on the side in a separate dish.

Prepare the mustard sauce by whisking all ingredients together in a small bowl. Refrigerate the sauce while you prepare the shiitake.

Using the paring knife, cut the stems from the mushrooms and either discard the stems or save them for the stockpot. Wash the mushrooms thoroughly under running cold water, drain, and pat dry with paper towels. Cut the shiitake into

Variation: After removing stems and washing and drying the shiitake, slice them into pieces 1/2 inch (1 1/4 cm) thick. Dust them with flour seasoned with salt and pepper, dip them into a light egg wash, roll them in yellow cornmeal, and sauté in the clarified butter, turning occasionally, until browned.

Mélange de Champignons au Vol-au-Vents
Creamed Mushrooms in a Patty Shell

The patty shells must be prepared the day you use them. Any fresh mushrooms, such as cèpes or chanterelles, will do nicely with the morels and shiitake. But, they must be fresh. With the exception of dried morels, the texture and intensity of dried mushrooms would overwhelm the delicate sauce and unbalance the dish.

Yields 6 servings

1 recipe Vol-au-Vents *(see page 514)*
1 1/2 cups (355 ml) Sauce Velouté de Poulet *(see page 73)*
6 ounces (170 g) fresh shiitake
6 ounces (170 g) fresh morels
6 ounces (170 g) fresh mushrooms
1 1/2 tablespoons (22 g) butter
2 teaspoons chopped shallots
Juice of 1/2 lemon
1/4 cup (60 ml) dry white wine
1/2 cup (118 ml) whipping cream
Salt
Freshly ground white pepper

Recommended equipment

A paring knife, 2-quart (2 L) saucepan, wooden spatula, baking sheet.

the shallots into it and sauté them for 30 seconds. Adjust heat to medium high, add all the mushrooms, sprinkle them with lemon juice, and sauté, stirring, for 3 minutes. Add the white wine, stir it in, and simmer for 2 minutes before adding the velouté and whipping cream. Bring to a brisk simmer and cook for about 5 to 8 minutes or until the sauce is reduced to a creamy consistency. Taste and adjust seasoning if necessary with salt and white pepper. Keep warm over very low heat and dot the surface with bits of butter to prevent the formation of a skin layer.

When ready to serve, preheat the oven to 250F (121C). Set the vol-au-vents on the baking sheet and put them into the middle level of the oven to heat for 5 minutes. Remove the vol-au-vents from the oven, set them on a serving plate, and divide the creamed mushrooms among them. Serve at once.

If fresh morels are unavailable, use 3/4 ounce (23 g) dried French or Swiss morels. Soak the dried mushrooms in 2 cups (475 ml) of warm water for 30 minutes, remove them gently with your hands, set into a strainer, and rinse out any remaining dirt under running water. Let drain, slice into 1/4-inch thick pieces, and use them in the recipe. The soaking liquid can be strained through several layers of cheesecloth or a paper filter and used in soups or stocks.

Variations: Use Sauce Velouté de Veau *(see page 74)* instead of velouté de poulet. Substitute imported Port for the white wine. Present the creamed mushrooms on buttered Pullman loaf toast instead of in a patty shell.

Prepare the vol-au-vents and reserve.

Prepare the velouté and reserve.

Brush the mushrooms gently of any clinging dirt. Working with the shiitake, remove the stems (save them for another use, such as in soup or stock) and slice the mushrooms into 1/4-inch (2/3 cm) thick slices. Slice the morels and other mushrooms into slices of the same thickness (do not remove the stems). Put the butter in the saucepan and set it over medium heat. Chop the shallots while the butter is melting and, when it is hot, stir

🜲 Clams Casino

This hors d'oeuvre (which, incidentally, has nothing to do with the Homestead Casino) appears frequently on the dinner menu because it is a perennial favorite of our guests. Be sure to use the leanest bacon you can find since the cooking time is short. To serve this as a luncheon entrée, allow ten clams per person.

Yields 6 servings

30 Cherrystone clams in the shell
1 tablespoon chopped shallots
1/2 medium green bell pepper
1 cup (225 g) butter, softened at room temperature
1/2 cup (118 ml) pimientos, drained
2 tablespoons chopped fresh parsley
1/2 cup (118 ml) fine white bread crumbs
6 bacon slices, weighing 2/3 ounce (20 g) each

Recommended equipment

A stiff bristle brush, clam knife, 8-inch (20 cm) sauté pan, 1-quart (1 L) bowl, wooden spatula, paring knife, small chef's knife, large baking dish (or several pie pans).

Scrub the clams thoroughly under cold running water with the stiff bristle brush. Discard any clams whose open shells will not close when touched. Using the clam knife, open the clams leaving each on the half shell. Do it this way: hold the clam firmly in your hand with the hinged side of the shell toward your palm; insert the knife blade between the shell halves; and gradually work the knife back toward the hinged side to sever the muscle. Remove top shell and discard.

With the chef's knife, chop the shallots. Trim the bell pepper of the bitter white and remove the seeds. Chop it finely. In the sauté pan, melt 2 tablespoons butter over medium low heat, add shallots and bell pepper, and sauté for 3 minutes, stirring from time to time. When done, remove from heat and let cool.

Finely dice the pimientos and chop the parsley, using the chef's knife. Blend the remaining butter, pimientos, parsley, and bread crumbs together in the bowl, mixing thoroughly with the wooden spatula. Add the sautéed shallots and peppers and blend well.

Preheat oven to 400F (204C).

Top each clam on the half shell with 2 teaspoons of butter mixture, patting it down to cover the clam. When all are stuffed, cut each slice of bacon crosswise into 5 pieces and put a piece on each clam. Set the clams into the baking dish and bake in the middle level of the oven for 7 to 9 minutes or until the bacon is crisp. Serve immediately.

Mussels Provençale

Although there is a Provence mussel, native to the Mediterranean and commercially raised in Toulon and Marseilles, this recipe calls for the black, common mussel, now readily available from farms on the northern American Atlantic coast. The preparation really combines two techniques—the initial cooking in wine à la marinière and the final aromatic dressing with bread crumbs à la provençale.

Yields 48 pieces, for 6 to 8 servings

2 quarts (1900 ml) mussels in the shell
2 cups (475 ml) dry white wine
2 tablespoons chopped shallots
1 tablespoon finely cut celery leaves
1/3 bay leaf
1 teaspoon crushed white pepper
1/4 cup (60 ml) olive oil
1 garlic clove, minced
1 cup (235 ml) fine white bread crumbs
2 tablespoons finely chopped parsley
1/4 teaspoon chopped oregano
4 tablespoons (60 g) butter, softened at room temperature

Recommended equipment

A stiff bristle brush, 4-quart (4 L) saucepan with lid, slotted spoon, colander, medium mixing bowl, 1 1/2-quart (1 1/2 L) saucepan, baking dish.

Using the stiff bristle brush, scrub the mussels thoroughly under cold running water, being careful to remove the beards (or scrape them off with a paring knife). If some mussels are partially open, try to push shells open all the way and discard any that open up. Drain off all rinsing water and put mussels in the large saucepan with the wine, shallots, celery leaves, bay leaf, and pepper. Bring to a boil over medium heat, cover pan, and stir or shake from time to time for about 5 minutes or until shells have opened. Remove saucepan from heat. Dip mussels out with a slotted spoon into the colander set inside the mixing bowl to drain completely. Discard any unopened mussels and reserve the cooking juices from the saucepan and the bowl for another use (such as Billi Bi, *see page 147*). Snap off one-half of each shell so that mussel remains on the other half.

Preheat oven to 325F (163C).

Now prepare the stuffing for the mussels. Heat olive oil in the smaller saucepan and add the garlic, bread crumbs, parsley, oregano, and butter, and blend well over medium heat for 2 minutes. Remove from heat. Set mussels on the half shell into baking dish and spread a spoonful of mixture over each (there should be enough for 48 mussels). Bake for 10 minutes or until golden brown and serve immediately while piping hot.

Coquilles Saint-Jacques au Beurre Blanc et Essence de Citron
Scallops in Vermouth and Lemon Butter Sauce

This preparation is distinguished by combining the subtly sweet taste of lightly sautéed fresh scallops with the tang of a variation on beurre blanc, *one of the simplest but most venerable sauces from classic cuisine. Be sure to watch the initial sautéing and keep it to the minimum suggested here—too much and the scallops will toughen quickly. Bake and serve them in individual scallop shells accompanied by a white Bordeaux Graves and Dinner Rolls for a superb first course. A bed of rock salt on the baking pan and serving plate will keep the shells level and steady.*

Yields 4 servings

1 pound (450 g) fresh sea (or bay) scallops
1/8 teaspoon salt
1 tablespoon minced shallots
2 tablespoons Clarified Butter (see page 568)
1 teaspoon freshly crushed white peppercorns
Juice of 1/2 lemon
1 cup (235 ml) dry vermouth
8 tablespoons (115 g) butter, softened at room temperature
1 cup (235 ml) whipping cream
1 1/2 teaspoons finely cut fresh chives
Fresh dill or parsley for a garnish

Recommended equipment

A colander, small chef's knife, 12-inch (30 cm) sauté pan, wooden spatula, slotted spoon, mortar and pestle, wire whisk, fine-mesh sieve, double boiler, 1 1/2-quart (1 1/2 L) saucepan, 1-quart heatproof serving dish or four individual ramekins or scallop shells.

Rinse the scallops under cold running water in the colander, drain, halve them crosswise, and season lightly with salt. Mince the shallots and set aside. Preheat the sauté pan over high heat, add the clarified butter and then the scallops. Sauté them for 1 1/2 minutes on each side. (For bay scallops, leave whole and cook for a total of 1 1/2 minutes while stirring with the wooden spatula.) Remove scallops with the slotted spoon to a side dish and reserve.

Add shallots to the sauté pan and cook over medium heat for 1 minute. Crush the pepper in the mortar and pestle and then add it to the sauté pan with the lemon juice and vermouth. Increase heat and cook until liquid is reduced to 1 1/2 tablespoons (about 4 minutes). Remove pan from direct heat, let cool slightly, and, using the whisk, whip in the softened butter 1 tablespoon at a time, blending completely before each addition. Strain sauce through the sieve into the double boiler and keep warm over simmering water.

In the saucepan reduce the whipping cream over medium high heat to 1/3 cup (80 ml), whisk it into the butter sauce, and add the chives.

Preheat broiler. Divide the scallops among individual ramekins (or scallop shells balanced on a baking sheet) or put into heatproof serving dish. Run under the broiler for 30 seconds to warm scallops, remove from oven, spread sauce evenly over the scallops, decorate with a sprig of fresh dill or parsley, and serve immediately.

Variation: Replace the vermouth with dry white wine, add three threads of saffron to the whipping cream before reducing, and when cream is reduced, add a small tomato (blanched, peeled, and seeded; *see page 568*), finely diced, just before cream is added to butter sauce. As a final fillip, add a dash of paprika or cayenne pepper to garnish the scallops after they have been sauced.

Baked Oysters with Crabmeat Gratinée Homestead

Even though the admonition about consuming oysters only in the "r" months is no longer taken seriously, a preparation such as this one is especially brought to mind by the chill of winter and thoughts of glowing embers as pictured here at Sam Snead's Tavern.

Yields 2 servings

3/8 cup (90 ml) Homestead Seafood Sauce *(see page 98)*
4 ounces (115 g) lump crabmeat
8 fresh oysters on the half shell
1 1/2 tablespoons grated Parmesan cheese
Rock salt for the baking dish

Recommended equipment

A small bowl, rubber spatula, box grater, baking dish.

Prepare the seafood sauce.

Preheat oven to 325F (163C).

Carefully pick over the crabmeat with your fingers to remove any pieces of shell and cartilage. Put it into the small bowl and, using the rubber spatula, gently fold in 1/4 cup (60 ml) of the seafood sauce, being careful not to break up the lumps. Spread 1 tablespoon of this mixture over each oyster on the half shell and top them off with 1/2 teaspoon of the seafood sauce.

Grate the Parmesan on the fine side of the box grater and sprinkle it over each oyster.

Spread a layer of rock salt in the bottom of the baking dish to stabilize the oysters while they bake. Nestle the oysters into the salt, bake for 6 minutes, then turn on the broiler just long enough to get a golden brown glaze. Serve at once while the oysters are piping hot.

Crabmeat Remick

Elegant but simple to prepare, this hors d'oeuvre is perfect as a first course served in ramekins or scallop shells as well as for a cocktail party when served on small, cooked artichoke bottoms or in well-washed clam or oyster shells.

Yields 5 servings as a first course or 24 pieces as an hors d'oeuvre

3/4 cup (180 ml) Homestead Seafood Sauce *(see page 98)*
1 pound (450 g) lump crabmeat
1/4 cup (60 ml) grated Parmesan cheese
Butter for the baking dish(es)

Recommended equipment

A box grater, medium mixing bowl, rubber spatula, 1-quart (1 L) baking dish or five individual ramekins or scallop shells.

Prepare the seafood sauce.

Carefully pick over the crabmeat with your fingers to remove any pieces of shell, butter your baking dish(es), and grate the Parmesan.

Preheat oven to 325F (163C).

In the mixing bowl, combine 1/2 cup (118 ml) of the seafood sauce with the crabmeat, folding together very gently with the rubber spatula to keep the crabmeat lumps together. When mixed, put into baking dish(es), spread remaining sauce on top of the crabmeat, sprinkle evenly with the Parmesan, and bake for 10 minutes. Then turn on the broiler and watch carefully until the top is golden brown.

Variation: Use baked or poached flaked halibut or add cooked shrimp to either the crabmeat or fish variation.

Homestead Crab Cakes

The Maryland shore is justly proud of its crabmeat and this recipe is the right showcase for the renowned crustacean. The only problem is making enough to go around. Once your guests start dressing each bite with some Sauce Tartare, you may find yourself surrounded by looks imploring you to go back to the deep fryer and cook up another batch. Two cakes are sufficient for a first course, but three will disappear with no trouble at a luncheon.

Yields 9, 3-ounce crab cakes

1 pound (450 g) lump crabmeat
1 tablespoon chopped shallots
1 garlic clove
4 tablespoons (60 g) butter
1 tablespoon Old Bay seafood seasoning
1 tablespoon dry English Mustard
2 tablespoons flour
1 1/2 cups (355 ml) Fish Stock (see page 60)
2 egg yolks
1/4 cup (60 ml) finely diced red bell peppers
1/4 cup (60 ml) finely diced green bell peppers
1/2 cup (118 ml) finely diced onions
2 tablespoons chopped fresh parsley
1 tablespoon water
1 cup (235 ml) fine white bread crumbs
Salt
Freshly ground black pepper
A pinch of cayenne pepper
1 cup (235 ml) Sauce Tartare (see page 97)
3 tablespoons flour
6 eggs
1 cup (235 ml) cracker meal
Peanut oil for deep frying

Recommended equipment

A large chef's knife, garlic press, 2-quart (2 L) saucepan, wire whisk, 12-inch (30 cm) sauté pan, wooden spatula, 2-quart (2 L) bowl, 1-quart (1 L) bowl, electric deep fryer with thermostat, frying thermometer, fine-mesh skimmer, paper towels, ovenproof dish.

Carefully pick over the crabmeat with your fingers to remove any pieces of shell and reserve.

Using the chef's knife, chop the shallots and either mince the garlic or wait to put it through the press. Set the saucepan over medium low heat, add 3 tablespoons butter, and, when it is hot, add the shallots and garlic and sauté for 30 seconds. Add the Old Bay seasoning, mustard, and 2 tablespoons flour, and blend together well for 30 seconds before whisking in the fish stock. Stir with the whisk until the sauce is smooth and simmering. Let simmer for 5 minutes, then remove saucepan from heat, whisk in the egg yolks, and set aside to cool.

Prepare the vegetables. Rinse, halve, seed, and finely dice the bell peppers. Peel and finely dice the onion. Rinse and chop the parsley and reserve. Set the sauté pan over medium low heat, add the remaining butter, and, when it is hot, stir in the peppers and onion, add the water, and sauté, without browning, for 3 minutes. Then remove pan from heat and set aside.

Put the crabmeat into the bowl and add the cooled sauce, the pepper and onion mixture, the parsley, and bread crumbs. Season lightly with salt and add the black and cayenne peppers to taste. Blend the mixture very gently with your hands, being careful not to overmix lest you break up too many crabmeat lumps. Then cover the bowl and set it into the refrigerator to chill for at least 30 minutes.

When the crabmeat mixture is well chilled, work quickly to form cakes weighing 2 3/4 to 3 ounces (75 to 85 g) each. You should have enough for about 9 cakes. (Use a metal ring such as a biscuit cutter to help you shape the cakes if they are difficult to handle.) Refrigerate them if you are not ready to cook them.

Prepare the sauce tartare and reserve.

When you are ready to cook, dust the crab cakes with flour and set aside. Beat the eggs together well and reserve them in the bowl. Put the cracker meal on a plate or on your work surface. Heat the peanut oil in the deep fryer to 375 to 400F (190 to 204C). Check the temperature with the thermometer and when the oil is hot, bread the crab cakes for frying. Take them one by one and dip them first into the beaten eggs and then roll them in the cracker meal. Put a few cakes into the deep fryer, being careful not to crowd the pot. Fry them to a golden brown. When done, remove with the skimmer to drain on folded paper towels.

While the cakes are frying, preheat oven to 325F (163C).

When all the cakes are cooked, arrange them in the ovenproof dish and set them into the oven for 4 to 6 minutes or until they are piping hot. Serve immediately accompanied with sauce and lemon wedges.

If you do not have a deep fryer, the crab cakes may be sautéed in Clarified Butter *(see page 568)* or oil until well browned on both sides and then heated in the oven.

Cold Hors d'Oeuvres

Hummus

Known in Arabic as hummus bi tahina *(tahina is sesame seed paste), this delicious paste is a staple food in the Middle East. There, it is either eaten as is, scooped up with little pieces of pita bread, or used as a dip for raw vegetables.*

Yields about 1 cup

1 cup (235 ml) canned cooked chick-peas
1 tablespoon chopped fresh parsley
1 garlic clove
1/3 cup (80 ml) sesame oil
1/2 cup (118 ml) lemon juice
1/4 teaspoon salt

Recommended equipment

A small fine-mesh sieve, small chef's knife, garlic press, electric blender.

Drain the chick-peas in the sieve. Rinse, dry, and chop the parsley. Press the garlic into the blender jar, add the oil, lemon juice, and salt, and blend on medium speed for a few seconds. Then add the chick-peas and 2 teaspoons parsley and purée on high speed until creamy and smooth. Chill for at least an hour before serving. Spoon into a serving bowl, sprinkle with remaining parsley, and serve.

Chick-peas are also known as garbanzo beans.

Marinated Mushrooms

This recipe and the one following for marinated shrimp are always successful as individual party hors d'oeuvres. The marinade works nicely for chanterelles or shiitake (remove the stems and discard) as well, but because their flavor is more intense, they should be marinated overnight. Be sure to use anise seeds and not the whole anise pod, known as star anise. Serve with toothpicks.

Yields about 48 pieces

1 1/2 pounds (675 g) small whole mushrooms
1/2 medium onion
1 1/2 cups (355 ml) olive oil
2 tablespoons lemon juice
2 peeled garlic cloves
1/2 cup (118 ml) red wine vinegar
A pinch of thyme
1/3 bay leaf
6 anise seeds
1 teaspoon sugar
Salt
Freshly ground black pepper

Recommended equipment

A paring knife, small chef's knife, 12-inch (30 cm) sauté pan, wooden spatula, garlic press, glass or ceramic bowl.

Brush the mushrooms of any clinging dirt, rinse gently, and set aside to drain. Peel the onion half, chop it finely with the chef's knife, and reserve.

Set the sauté pan over medium high heat, add 3 tablespoons olive oil, and, when it is hot, add the mushrooms and sauté, stirring with the spatula, for 2 minutes. Add the lemon juice to the pan, cook for 1 minute, add the onion, and press in the garlic. Sauté for 30 seconds and then add the remaining olive oil, vinegar, thyme, bay leaf, anise, and sugar. Stir well. Season the mushrooms to taste with salt and pepper. Bring the mushrooms to a boil, adjust heat so that they simmer for 8 minutes, stirring from time to time, then remove them from heat, let cool, and scrape them into the bowl. Cover the bowl and put it into the refrigerator for several hours or overnight.

In addition to being a party hors d'oeuvre, marinated mushrooms can be the center of a light salad for 6 to 8 people. Prepare the following garnishes: quartered tomatoes, sliced avocados, hard-boiled eggs, sliced scallions, and capers. Divide the mushrooms and garnishes among the plates. Sprinkle 1 tablespoon of minced parsley over the mushrooms and serve.

Marinated Shrimp

This colorful and refreshing dish could serve four for luncheon on a hot summer day. Mound the shrimp on a bed of lettuce, choose your garnish (such as hard-boiled eggs and olives), and pass crusty French Bread in a basket. If you serve them as party hors d'oeuvres, be sure to prepare more than enough—guests, like seventeen-year locusts, devour them when the platter comes into view.

Yields 6 to 8 servings

2 pounds (900 g) fresh shrimp
1/2 medium Bermuda onion
1 garlic clove
3 tablespoons olive oil
Salt
Freshly ground white pepper
1/4 cup (60 ml) dry white wine

FOR THE MARINADE
5 tablespoons olive oil
4 tablespoons white wine vinegar
1 tablespoon lemon juice
Zest of 1/2 lemon
1/2 teaspoon chopped fresh tarragon
2 tablespoons Dijon mustard
1/2 medium green bell pepper
1/2 medium red bell pepper
2 tablespoons chopped fresh parsley

Recommended equipment

A colander, shrimp deveiner, small chef's knife, 12-inch (30 cm) sauté pan, wooden spatula, garlic press, box grater, wire whisk, small mixing bowl, plastic wrap.

Rinse the shrimp in the colander under running cold water, peel and devein them, and set them aside. Peel the onion, mince it, and reserve. Peel the garlic.

Set the sauté pan over medium high heat, add the olive oil, and, when it is hot, add the shrimp and season with salt and pepper. Sauté for 2 minutes. Then stir in the onions, press in the garlic, and sauté for 30 seconds. Add the white wine and simmer gently for 4 minutes, stirring occasionally.

While the shrimp are simmering, prepare the marinade. In the mixing bowl, combine the olive oil, vinegar, and lemon juice, blending thoroughly with the whisk. Using the fine side of the box grater, zest one lemon half, being careful to leave the bitter white behind. Add the zest to the mixing bowl with the tarragon and mustard and mix well with the whisk. Rinse, seed, and finely dice the bell peppers and stir them into the marinade.

When the shrimp are done, scrape them and their juices into the bowl with the marinade and mix well. When the shrimp have cooled to room temperature, cover the bowl tightly with plastic wrap and refrigerate for at least 4 hours. Stir them once or twice during this time. Just before serving, sprinkle the chopped parsley over the shrimp.

Canapé Morgon

Usually reserved for the most elegant of hors d'oeuvres, the appellation "canapé" is derived from the bread round which is its base. So often overlooked, the quality of the bread is paramount.

You are preparing a first-class mixture, so do not cut corners on the bread—as Escoffier said, "the cheapest is the dearest in the end." If you have not made Pullman Loaf, go to your bakery and buy it or pain de mie. *If you prefer not to use bread, celery, artichoke hearts, cherry tomatoes, or hard-boiled egg halves can also be used as a base for this delicious topping.*

Yields 32 pieces

8 slices Pullman Loaf *(see page 488)*
Butter, softened at room temperature
1 medium, ripe tomato (blanched, peeled, and seeded; *see page 568*)
3 ounces (85 g) fresh shrimp in the shell
3 ounces (85 g) smoked salmon
3 medium or 4 small celery hearts
3 tablespoons Homestead Seafood Sauce *(see page 98)*
A dash of cayenne pepper
2 hard-boiled eggs
1/2 teaspoon chopped fresh parsley
2 ounces (60 g) caviar
Sprigs of fresh dill or parsley
Lemon wedges

Recommended equipment

A 2-inch (5 cm) biscuit cutter, 1-quart (1 L) saucepan, large chef's knife, shrimp deveiner, paring knife, 1-quart (1 L) bowl, small fine-mesh sieve.

Let the bread sit out unwrapped the day before you are to prepare the canapés. (Or, dry the slices slightly in a 200F [93C] oven the day of your party.) Before working with the other ingredients, toast the bread lightly and let it cool. Cut the rounds, using the biscuit cutter, and spread them with a thin layer of room temperature butter.

Prepare the tomato: remove all pulp, dice it finely, and reserve. Bring lightly salted water to a boil in the saucepan, add the shrimp, and when the water returns to a boil, immediately remove the shrimp from heat, drain, and refresh under cold water. Peel and devein the shrimp, halve them lengthwise, dice finely with the chef's knife, and reserve. Prepare the salmon by looking carefully for any bones and removing them and any skin. Then dice the salmon finely and reserve.

Trim the leaves from the celery hearts, make them as stringless as possible, rinse, and dice finely. Prepare the Homestead seafood sauce and put it into the bowl. Mix in the tomato, shrimp, smoked salmon, celery, and cayenne and refrigerate while you prepare the garnish.

Prepare the hard-boiled eggs and, when they are cool, peel them and separate the whites from the yolks. Mince the whites and yolks separately or push them through the sieve separately and reserve. Rinse, dry, and chop the parsley. Mix the parsley with the minced egg whites.

When ready to serve, spread about 1 tablespoon of the seafood mixture on each toast round. Sprinkle some egg yolk on one-half of each canapé and some egg white on the other. Place 1/4 teaspoon caviar in the center of each canapé, arrange them on a serving platter, decorate the platter with dill or parsley sprigs and lemon wedges, and serve.

🕊 Avocado Southampton

Despite the name, there is more to do here with Spain than England or Long Island. Native to the American tropics, the Aztec ahuacatl *became "avocado" in Spanish. Gazpacho is indisputably Spanish, even though there is disagreement about its etymology.* *The contrast of textures and colors, while paying due respect to the avocado's delicate flavor, creates a study in subtlety.*

Yields 4 servings

3/4 teaspoon unflavored gelatin
2 teaspoons hot water
1 cup (235 ml) Gazpacho *(see page 116)*
2 ripe avocados
1/2 lemon, juiced
4 teaspoons sour cream
1/2 lemon, quartered
Sprigs of parsley or dill

In a small mixing bowl, dissolve gelatin with 2 teaspoons of hot water. Add to gazpacho and mix well. Cut avocados in half, remove pits, and dip halves into water seasoned with the lemon juice (to prevent avocado from turning brown). Wipe avocado halves dry and distribute the gazpacho mixture evenly among them. Refrigerate for 1 to 2 hours or until mixture sets. Just before serving, top with sour cream and garnish with lemon quarters and sprigs of parsley or dill. For an *à la Russe* touch, nestle a small spoonful of black caviar in the sour cream.

🕊 Crabmeat Ravigote

You can prepare the crabmeat and the sauce ahead of time and slice and fill the avocados just before serving.

Yields 16 servings

2 pounds (900 g) lump crabmeat
1 recipe Sauce Ravigote *(see page 106)*
8 ripe avocados
1 lemon

Recommended equipment

A 2-quart (2 L) bowl, rubber spatula, paring knife.

Pick over the crabmeat carefully with your fingers to remove any pieces of shell and reserve it in a bowl in the refrigerator.

Prepare the ravigote. Gently fold 2 cups (475 ml) of sauce into the crabmeat, using the rubber spatula, trying not to break up the crabmeat lumps. The remaining sauce will be the garnish.

Halve and peel the avocados, remove the pits, and squeeze lemon juice all over them to prevent them from turning brown. Mound about 1/4 cup (60 ml) of crabmeat in each avocado half, garnish each with 1 tablespoon of the remaining sauce, and serve at once.

Gravlax with Dill and Mustard Sauce

This traditional Swedish dish (gravlax med dillsås) must be made from fresh centercut salmon and with the freshest dill for a full, piquant aroma. The process takes three days, but once marinated the salmon will keep for several days under refrigeration. Serve with Swedish Mustard Sauce, capers, finely chopped onions, and, as the Swedes do, accompany the gravlax with small potatoes boiled in their jackets.

Yields 12 servings

2 pounds (900 g) fresh centercut salmon fillet
1 1/2 tablespoons salt
1 1/2 tablespoons freshly crushed white peppercorns
1 1/2 tablespoons sugar
2 tablespoons coarsely chopped fresh dill
4 drops olive oil
1/4 cup (60 ml) aquavit
1 recipe Swedish Mustard Sauce (see page 96)

Recommended equipment

A boning knife; hemostat or needle-nose pliers; paring knife; mortar and pestle; small mixing bowl; small chef's knife; stainless steel, glass, or ceramic pan just large enough to hold the salmon; plastic wrap; slicing knife.

The skin must remain on the salmon, but all the bones must be removed. With the hemostat or pliers bone the fillet *(see page 568)*. Then turn it over and, using the paring knife, make 3 skin-deep incisions along the length or across the width of the fillet to enable the marinade to penetrate.

In the mixing bowl, combine the salt, pepper, and sugar. Chop the dill with the chef's knife and add one-half of it to the mixing bowl. Put the fillet skin side down in the pan and, using your fingers, rub the olive oil over it and pour the aquavit around it. Spread the marinade mixture evenly on top of the fillet and divide the remaining dill over it.

Cover pan tightly with plastic wrap and refrigerate for 36 hours. Turn the salmon over and refrigerate for another day. Then spoon marinade over it several times, rewrap, and return to refrigerator for 12 hours. (If the fillet is from a small salmon and thin, reduce marinating time by 24 hours.) Now the fish is ready to serve.

Prepare the mustard sauce.

To slice for serving, put the salmon skin side down on a carving board and scrape off some of the marinade. With the slicing knife cut thin slices across the bias at a 135° angle without cutting through the skin. As the knife approaches the skin turn it parallel to the skin and cut the salmon slice away (as you would for smoked salmon). Arrange several slices on each plate, add the garnishes, sauce, and potatoes, and serve to your appreciative guests.

Variations: For marinated juniper salmon, replace the dill and aquavit with 1 1/2 tablespoons of crushed juniper berries and 1/4 cup (60 ml) gin. For salmon anisette, replace the dill with 1 teaspoon of lightly crushed anise seeds and use 2 tablespoons of Pernod rather than aquavit. All of these marinades produce interesting results when fresh tuna or bluefish is substituted for the salmon.

Pâté Maison

Tightly wrapped and refrigerated, this pâté keeps very well for two weeks. So you can serve a crowd and recover in the aftermath with enough remaining for a quiet lunch or two. For each serving, present two slices of the pâté on the plate garnished with matchstick-size strips of cornichons and pass Cumberland Sauce separately. Be sure to have some crusty French Bread close at hand for those gourmands who cannot resist spreading the delicious cooked fatback on bread.

Yields 24 to 30 servings

- 1 1/2 pounds (675 g) boneless lean veal shoulder or trimmings
- 1 1/2 pounds (675 g) boneless lean pork shoulder or butt
- 1 1/2 cups (355 ml) dry white wine
- 3 tablespoons chopped shallots
- 1 garlic clove
- 1 tablespoon (15 g) butter
- 1 tablespoon green peppercorns (packed in water and drained)
- 1 pound (450 g) liver (all calf's, all pork, or 1/3 each calf's, pork, and chicken)
- 1 pound (450 g) pork fat
- 1 teaspoon pâté spices *(see below)*
- 1 teaspoon Knorr Aromat
- 2 teaspoons salt
- 1/4 cup (60 ml) Cognac
- 1/2 cup (118 ml) Madeira
- 4 crushed juniper berries
- 2 pork or veal tenderloins, weighing 8 ounces (225 g) each
- Peanut oil
- 1 to 1 1/2 pounds (450 to 675 g) sliced pork fatback
- 2 eggs
- 1 cup (235 ml) fine white bread crumbs
- 3 tablespoons coarsely chopped black truffle trimmings
- 2 bay leaves

- 1 recipe Cumberland Sauce *(see page 100)*

Recommended equipment

A small chef's knife, 2-quart (2 L) bowl, plastic wrap, garlic press, 8-inch (20 cm) sauté pan, wooden spatula, meat grinder with fine blade, two medium mixing bowls, mortar and pestle, blending fork, blender or food processor, rubber spatula, 12-inch (30 cm) sauté pan, loaf pan 12 x 5 x 3 inches (30 x 12 1/2 x 7 1/2 cm), aluminum foil, heavy roasting pan.

Cut the veal and pork into large chunks, set them into the bowl, pour in the white wine, cover tightly with plastic wrap, and put the bowl in the refrigerator. Let the meat marinate for 24 to 48 hours.

When ready to proceed, peel and chop the shallots, peel the garlic clove, and set the smaller sauté pan over medium low heat. Add the butter and the shallots to the pan, press in the garlic, and stir in the green peppercorns. Sauté for 2 minutes, then remove from heat and let cool in the pan.

Remove the veal and pork from the marinade, reserve the marinade, and grind the meats together in the meat grinder with a fine blade. Grind the liver and pork fat, each separately. Then combine all the ground meats and fat in the mixing bowl; add the sautéed shallot mixture, pâté spices, Aromat, salt, Cognac, Madeira, the reserved marinade, and juniper berries. Mix thoroughly with the blending fork and then purée in batches in the blender or food processor on high for 20 to 30 seconds. Scrape each batch into the clean mixing bowl, mix all together, and refrigerate for 30 minutes.

While the mixture is chilling, prepare the tenderloins. Trim them of all fat. Set the large sauté pan over medium high heat, film the pan bottom with peanut oil, and, when it is hot, add the tenderloins and sauté them until well browned on all sides. When browned, remove them from the pan and let cool at room temperature.

Prepare the loaf pan by lining the bottom and sides with sheets of fatback. The fatback should be sliced very thin, only 1/8 inch (1/3 cm) thick, and be in pieces about 8 x 8 inches (20 x 20 cm). It is best to have your butcher slice it for you. Any leftover fatback will keep very well if wrapped airtight and frozen.

When the pâté mixture is chilled, beat the eggs lightly and blend them into the mixture with the bread crumbs and chopped truffles. Mix well and return bowl to the refrigerator.

Preheat oven to 350F (177C).

When the tenderloins are cool enough to handle, you are ready to assemble the pâté. Remove the mixture from the refrigerator and spread one-half of it evenly in the bottom of the loaf pan. Place the tenderloins side by side lengthwise in the pan and spread the remaining meat mixture on top of them. Cover the pâté mixture with a single layer of fatback, place the bay leaves on top, and cover the pan with a double thickness of aluminum foil. Set the loaf pan into the roasting pan to make a bain-marie and add enough hot water to come one-third of the way up the side of the loaf pan.

Put the pans into the oven and bake for 10 minutes. Then reduce heat to 325F (163C) and bake for 2 to 2 1/2 hours or until the juices run clear. When done, remove the pâté pan from the roasting pan and let the pâté cool to room temperature in the pan on a rack. Then refrigerate the pâté, in its juices, overnight.

Prepare the Cumberland sauce and reserve until serving time.

When ready to serve, remove the pâté from the pan by dipping the pan into 2 to 3 inches of hot water and then running a thin-bladed knife along all sides of the pan to loosen the pâté, and unmold it onto a platter.

To serve, make thin slices with a sharp knife, being careful to leave the ring of fatback intact around each slice. You will also find that the cooking juices have congealed into a gelée, which, if you move quickly, can be diced into small pieces with a cold knife and used to garnish the slices of pâté. Serve at once.

❧

If pâté spices are unavailable you can mix your own by combining two parts each of dried sage, thyme, marjoram, and rosemary to one part each of nutmeg, ground cloves, and freshly ground white pepper.

You may divide the pâté mixture in half and bake it in two loaf pans (about 8 x 4 x 3 inches or 20 x 10 x 7 1/2 cm). In this case, reduce the baking time by 15 minutes.

Variations: When pâté has cooled to room temperature in its juices, drain off the juices and pour in Aspic seasoned with Madeira *(see page 124)* to cover pâté by a depth of 1/4 inch (2/3 cm). For a truly high feast replace the tenderloins with tinned foie gras.

❧ Galantine of Capon

Its tiny cubes of gelée sparkling like jewels, this elegant preparation is a prominent feature of the Casino cold buffet. I will be honest and say that the recipe presents a challenge, but the dedicated cook will rise to the occasion, knowing of the coming accolades around the table. Serve this with either Cumberland Sauce or, if you are as much a fan of it as I am, Rhubarb Sauce.

Yields 12 to 14 servings

- 1 pound (450 g) boneless lean veal chuck or shoulder
- 1 pound (450 g) boneless lean pork shoulder or butt
- 1 1/2 cups (355 ml) dry white wine
- 1 fresh capon, weighing 5 to 6 pounds (2250 to 2700 g)
- 3 ounces (85 g) finely chopped shallots
- 2 teaspoons butter
- 8 ounces (225 g) pork fat
- 2 teaspoons salt
- 1/4 teaspoon freshly ground white pepper
- A pinch of Knorr Aromat
- A pinch of pâté spices *(see page 179)*
- 3 tablespoons Cognac
- 3 tablespoons Madeira
- 2 eggs
- 1/4 cup (60 ml) crushed ice
- 1 cup (235 ml) whipping cream
- 2 ounces (60 g) pistachio nuts
- 4 ounces (115 g) cooked smoked beef tongue
- 4 ounces (115 g) cooked ham
- 2 ounces (60 g) black truffles
- 4 to 5 quarts (4 to 5 L) Chicken Bouillon *(see page 148)*

- 1 recipe Cumberland Sauce *(see page 100)*

Recommended equipment

A boning knife, 2-quart (2 L) bowl, plastic wrap, cheesecloth, kitchen towel, small chef's knife, 8-inch (20 cm) sauté pan, meat grinder with fine blade, blender or food processor, large mixing bowl, wooden spoon, 2-quart bowl, 1 1/2-quart (1 1/2 L) saucepan, paring knife, rubber spatula, white kitchen string, 8-quart (8 L) stockpot.

The first step is to cut the veal and pork into large pieces, place them in the bowl, add the white wine, cover the bowl tightly with plastic wrap, and set the bowl into the refrigerator. Let the meat marinate for 24 to 48 hours.

Set the capon, breast side down, on your cutting board and, using the boning knife, split the skin along the backbone and make a skin-deep cut from the neck to the tail, loosening the skin very carefully and keeping it in one piece. When the skin is cut, work the boning knife between the breast meat and the ribs and loosen the meat from one side and then the other so that the skin and breast meat come away from the bone together. (Work on one side of the capon first and then the other.) Pull the skin away from the thigh and leg meat, leaving the meat behind (this will be ground as part of the stuffing).

Cut a piece of cheesecloth 3 to 4 inches (7 1/2 to 10 cm) larger on all sides than the capon skin. Lay the cheesecloth on your work surface and center the capon skin on it with the outside next to the cheesecloth and the breast meat facing up. Cover the skin and breast meat with a damp kitchen towel to prevent them from drying out while you prepare the stuffing mixture.

Cut enough meat from the thighs and drumsticks to yield 8 ounces (225 g). Chop the shallots, cook them in the sauté pan with butter over medium low heat for 30 seconds, remove from heat, and let cool. Remove the veal and pork from the marinade, reserve the marinade, and grind the meats together with the dark meat from the capon and the shallots, using the fine blade of the meat grinder. Grind the meats together twice. Grind the pork fat once separately. Then combine the meats and pork fat with the salt, pepper, Aromat, pâté spices, Cognac, Madeira, the reserved marinade, and eggs in the large mixing bowl, and stir with the wooden spoon until well mixed. Put about one-half of this mixture along with one-half of the crushed ice in the blender or food processor and process on high just until well blended, about 30 seconds. Then add 1/4 cup (60 ml) of the whipping cream and process on high again just enough to mix well. Add up to another 1/4 cup of cream by tablespoons until the stuffing is smooth (you may not need all the cream) blending after each addition. Do not blend more than another minute or the stuffing will get warm. Turn the contents into the 2-quart bowl and refrigerate while repeating this process with the remaining meat mixture.

When the second batch of meat is blended, add it to the first and mix them thoroughly. Rinse out the large bowl and put ice in the bottom. Place the bowl with the meat mixture in the large bowl, pack ice around the sides, and keep refrigerated.

Bring water to a boil in the saucepan, add the pistachio nuts, blanch for 30 seconds after water returns to a boil, then drain the nuts, run cold water over them, drain again, and remove their skins by rubbing the pistachios between your fingers. Stir the pistachios into the stuffing and then return it to the refrigerator.

Using the paring knife, peel and trim the beef tongue, cut into 1/4-inch (2/3 cm) thick strips, and reserve. Cut the ham into 1/4-inch thick strips and reserve. Slice the truffle into strips and reserve. Remove the kitchen towel from capon and, using a sharp boning knife held parallel to the work surface, slice each piece of breast meat in half. Remove each sliced top layer of breast meat and place beside the attached breast meat on the capon skin where there is no meat. Remove stuffing from refrigerator and spread one-half of it evenly with the spatula over the breast meat. Next make a layer of strips on the stuffing by alternating with rows of ham, tongue, and truffle right next to each other. Spread the remaining stuffing mixture on top, being careful not to disturb the strips. With both hands, pull up the cheesecloth on one long side and bring over to the other long side, making a roll. The cheesecloth will hold the roll together while it cooks and should wrap completely around the breast meat and stuffing, overlapping where the roll comes together. Tie the cheesecloth tightly with kitchen string at the ends of the roll and tie the roll loosely at 3-inch (7 1/2 cm) intervals.

Set the stockpot over medium high heat, place the rolled galantine in the pot, and pour in the chicken bouillon so that it covers the galantine by a depth of several inches. Bring the bouillon to a simmer and adjust heat so that the bouillon simmers gently for 1 3/4 hours. When done, let the galantine cool completely in the bouillon and refrigerate them together until ready to serve.

While the galantine is chilling, prepare the Cumberland or rhubarb sauce and reserve.

To serve, remove the galantine from the bouillon, remove the cheesecloth and strings, and slice. Set a slice in the center of each serving plate and ladle the sauce around it.

Variation

 Galantine of Capon Jardinière

3 small whole carrots
3 small whole zucchini
3 small celery stalks
6 whole string beans
3 fresh asparagus stalks
1/2 small red bell pepper
2 ounces (60 g) black truffles

Peel the carrots, trim and scrub the zucchini, peel the celery stalks, snap the string beans, and peel and trim the asparagus stalks. Bring water to boil in a 2-quart (2 L) saucepan, add the vegetables and some salt, and boil for 1 minute. Then remove from heat, drain, cool off under running cold water, and drain well. Seed the bell pepper, remove the white pith, and slice into strips 1/4 inch (2/3 cm) wide. Slice the truffle.

The vegetables replace the layers of ham and tongue in the center of the stuffing. As you make up the layer of vegetable strips and truffle, remember that when the galantine is served you want a colorful slice, so lay the vegetables with contrasting colors next to each other.

☙

The galantine jardinière will only keep for a few days because the vegetable strips will spoil more quickly than the meat strips.

☙ Salads

☙ Salade Tiède d'Epinards
Warm Spinach Salad

In its original form, this recipe, popular in many parts of France, called for dandelion greens, but since Jean Troisgros took the idea of a spinach salad from California back home to Roanne, the French palate has been gravitating toward its more delicate flavor. The spinach must be very fresh—the leaves crisp, crunchy, and green. You can cook the bacon ahead of time but the dressing must be combined with the greens at the last minute so that its heat wilts the spinach and the salad is warm when served.

Yields 4 to 6 servings

2 pounds (900 g) fresh spinach
1 recipe Homestead Grille Hot Bacon Dressing *(see page 105)*
Freshly ground black pepper

Recommended equipment

A colander, large mixing bowl.

Wash the spinach thoroughly yet gently in several changes of cold water to rid it of all sand. Lift the spinach into the colander to drain and discard any withered leaves and tough stalks. Then either spin the leaves dry or pat them gently with a towel and refrigerate the spinach in the bowl until you are ready to serve.

Cook the bacon according to the recipe for hot bacon dressing, chop it roughly, and reserve. When you are ready to serve, remove the spinach from the refrigerator and proceed with the instructions for the dressing. Bring the dressing just to the boiling point, pour it over the spinach in the bowl, and mix gently. Divide the spinach among the serving plates, top each serving with the reserved chopped bacon and freshly ground pepper, and serve at once.

Variation: Top each serving with chopped walnuts and thinly sliced Belgian endive in addition to the bacon and pepper.

❦ Pressed Cucumber Salad

Next summer, when your garden (or your neighbor's) seems overrun with cucumbers, this recipe will come to the rescue. Although it can be prepared with cucumbers from the store, the subtle garden-fresh flavor blossoms when paired with this light marinade.

Yields 6 servings

5 medium cucumbers
3 tablespoons salt
Freshly ground white pepper
3 tablespoons vinegar
1/2 cup (118 ml) peanut oil
1 tablespoon chopped fresh parsley
1 tablespoon finely cut chives
1 teaspoon finely cut dill

Recommended equipment

A swivel-bladed vegetable peeler, teaspoon, slicing knife, large glass or ceramic bowl, plate to fit inside bowl, colander, kitchen towel.

Peel the cucumbers, halve them lengthwise, and remove the seeds by scraping them out with a teaspoon. Slice the cucumbers crosswise into very thin slices. Put the slices into the large bowl, sprinkle them with the salt, and mix it in thoroughly with your hands. Cover the cucumbers with a plate that is small enough to fit inside the bowl (about 1 1/2 inches or 3 3/4 cm smaller in diameter) and put a 3 to 4 pound (1350 to 1800 g) weight on the plate (a few large cans will do) to press the water out of the cucumbers. Set the bowl in a cool place or in the refrigerator overnight.

When ready to proceed, drain the cucumbers in the colander and squeeze them dry with your hand or in a kitchen towel. Put the cucumbers into a serving dish and add the pepper, vinegar, and oil. Rinse the parsley, pat dry, and chop. Rinse the chives and slice finely. Rinse the dill, pat dry, and cut finely. Taste the cucumbers for salt—you will probably not want to add any. Add the parsley, chives, and dill to the cucumbers, stir thoroughly, and serve.

Variation: Make a creamy dressing for the pressed cucumbers by combining 1/2 cup (118 ml) sour cream or Crème Fraîche *(see page 66)*, juice of one-half lemon, and dill, parsley, and chives.

❦ Beet Salad

For a color and flavor contrast, do as the French do to enhance midwinter salads, and mix the beets with mâche (called lamb's lettuce, field salad, or corn salad), now increasingly available in American specialty markets.

Yields 6 to 8 servings

2 pounds (900 g) beets
1/3 cup (80 ml) cider vinegar
1 cup (235 ml) peanut oil
1 tablespoon sugar
1 tablespoon prepared horseradish
1 medium onion
Salt
Freshly ground black pepper
1/8 teaspoon caraway seeds

Recommended equipment

A 3-quart (3 L) saucepan, 1-quart (1 L) bowl, wire whisk, slicing knife, medium mixing bowl, plastic wrap.

Rinse beets under running cold water, put them in the saucepan, add water to cover the beets by several inches, salt the water lightly, and set the saucepan over high heat. When the water boils, adjust the heat so that the water maintains a gentle boil. Cook the beets until they are tender. This can take from 30 to 60 minutes (or longer) depending upon the size of the beets, their age, and how they were stored. They are done when a paring knife thrust into their center meets slight resistance. When done, remove saucepan from heat, run cold water into the saucepan, and let beets cool until you can handle them. While the beets are cooking, prepare the dressing. Using the wire whisk, combine the vinegar, oil, sugar, and horseradish in the small bowl. While the beets are cooling, peel the onion, halve it, slice very thinly, and reserve.

When the beets are cool enough to handle, slip off their skins under running cold water and slice them as thinly as possible (1/8 inch or 1/3 cm thick). If the beets are very large, halve or quarter them before slicing. As the beets are sliced, put them in the mixing bowl. When all the beets are sliced, season with salt and pepper, sprinkle with caraway seeds, stir in the sliced onions, pour on the dressing, mix well, cover the bowl with plastic wrap, and set it in the refrigerator to marinate for several hours or overnight. Stir the salad once or twice during this time. If you want to enjoy the salad soon, set it in a cool place until serving time (but not in the refrigerator).

Variation: Make a sour cream or Crème Fraîche *(see page 66)* dressing with 1 cup cream to 2 tablespoons vinegar.

˚ Homestead Potato Salad

It may seem obvious, but the most critical ingredient in this salad is the potato. *Many people use baking potatoes because they are on hand and realize their mistake too late when the potatoes crumble as they are sliced. Firm boiling potatoes are de rigueur. I also call for fresh Mayonnaise instead of the bottled variety because it plays such a prominent role in the dressing.*

Yields 8 to 10 servings

2 pounds (900 g) boiling potatoes
2 cups (475 ml) Mayonnaise *(see page 94)*
1 medium onion
1 tablespoon prepared mustard
1/2 teaspoon salt
1/8 teaspoon freshly ground white pepper
1 1/2 teaspoons sugar
2 tablespoons cider vinegar
2 tablespoons sweet pickle juice
1 tablespoon chopped fresh parsley

Recommended equipment

A stiff bristle brush, 3-quart (3 L) saucepan, colander, small chef's knife, wire whisk, medium mixing bowl, paring knife, wooden spoon.

Scrub the potatoes under running cold water while you are bringing water to boil in the saucepan. Salt the water lightly, add the potatoes, return water to the boil, and cook until the potatoes are just tender (about 15 to 20 minutes).

While the potatoes are cooking, prepare the mayonnaise. Then combine the mayonnaise with the other ingredients in the mixing bowl. Peel and chop the onion and add it. Add the mustard, salt, pepper, sugar, cider vinegar, and pickle juice. Mix everything together with the whisk. Rinse the parsley, pat dry, chop, and stir it into the mayonnaise mixture. Let it season while the potatoes cook.

When the potatoes are done, drain them in the colander and let them cool until you can handle them. When cool enough, peel them with the paring knife, quarter them lengthwise, and slice into 3/4-inch (2 cm) chunks. Stir the potatoes into the mayonnaise dressing and serve. Of course, this can be chilled before serving if you wish, and it must be kept under refrigeration.

Variation: Add 2 tablespoons chopped sweet pickles or sweet pickle relish and 2 coarsely chopped hard-boiled eggs.

Ambassador Potato Salad

This salad was a favorite of Harold P. Bock, formerly general manager of the Homestead. After leaving the Homestead he became general manager of the Ambassador Hotel (later the Sheraton-East Ambassador) in New York City, where he hired me as a young chef. The French method of stirring the vinaigrette into the warm potato slices ensures a thorough absorption of the dressing, providing a slightly tart flavor which is an excellent accompaniment for goodies from the charcuterie.

Yields 6 to 8 servings

1 1/2 to 1 3/4 pounds (675 to 800 g) small to medium Red Bliss potatoes
1/4 cup (60 ml) Beef Bouillon (see page 151)
1/4 cup (60 ml) white wine vinegar
1/2 cup (118 ml) plus 2 tablespoons olive oil
1/4 teaspoon sugar
2 scallions
Salt
Freshly ground black pepper
1 tablespoon chopped fresh parsley
1 teaspoon finely cut fresh chives
1/8 teaspoon chopped fresh tarragon

Recommended equipment

A stiff bristle brush, 3-quart (3 L) saucepan, colander, small saucepan, small chef's knife, wire whisk, 1-quart (1 L) bowl, paring knife, slicing knife, medium mixing bowl, wooden spoon.

Clean the potatoes with the brush under running cold water while you are bringing water to a boil in the large saucepan. Salt the water lightly, add the potatoes, return water to the boil, and cook until the potatoes are just tender but still firm.

While the potatoes are boiling, warm the beef bouillon in the small saucepan and then pour it into the small bowl and add the vinegar, olive oil, and sugar. Mix well with the whisk. Rinse the scallions, slice them finely, stir them into the small bowl, and reserve.

When the potatoes are done, drain them in the colander and let them cool until you can handle them. Then peel them with the paring knife and, using the slicing knife, cut them into slices 1/8 to 1/4 inch (1/3 to 2/3 cm) thick. As you slice them, put them into the larger bowl. Season them with salt and pepper and while they are still warm pour on the blended dressing. Let the potatoes marinate for 10 minutes.

While the potatoes are marinating, rinse the fresh parsley, chives, and tarragon, pat dry, chop the parsley and tarragon, and slice the chives finely. When the potatoes have finished marinating, sprinkle the fresh herbs over them, stir together gently, and serve.

Tortellini Salad

Pasta has finally achieved its rightful place on the American table. It took decades for vacation travelers to realize that there is culinary life after spaghetti, and that it offers a vast and nutritious array of possibilities. Even though you can purchase dried tortellini, we urge you to buy the fresh products now widely available. Better yet, consult Marcella Hazen's Classic Italian Cook Book *and try your own. Prepare this early in the day for a summer evening meal—it would be perfect as part of a buffet dinner and may be kept covered and refrigerated for two or three days.*

Yields 8 to 10 servings

1 pound (450 g) meat tortellini
2 tablespoons olive oil
Salt
1 1/2 cups (355 ml) olive oil
1/2 cup (118 ml) red wine vinegar
2 teaspoons Dijon mustard
1/2 cup (118 ml) ripe olives
1/2 cup (118 ml) green olives
1/2 red bell pepper
1/2 yellow bell pepper
1/2 green bell pepper
1/2 cup (118 ml) pine nuts
1/2 medium onion
2 1/2 ounces (70 g) Genoa salami
4 to 6 ounces (115 to 170 g) canned artichoke hearts
1/4 teaspoon Pesto *(see page 418)*
Salt
Freshly ground white pepper
1 tablespoon finely cut chives

Recommended equipment

A 4- to 5-quart (4 to 5 L) saucepan with lid, colander, large mixing bowl, small bowl, wire whisk, paring knife, pie pan, small chef's knife.

Bring 3 to 4 quarts of lightly salted water to boil in the covered large saucepan and, when boiling, add the tortellini and 2 tablespoons olive oil. Re-cover the saucepan, return to a boil, then uncover and adjust heat so that the pasta cooks at a slow boil. Cook until the tortellini is al dente and retains a firmness in texture when chewed. Taste a piece to be sure. Fresh tortellini will take about 4 minutes and dried will take 8 to 12. When done, remove pot to sink and let cold water run briskly into the pot for 2 to 3 minutes or until the tortellini is cool. Do not let the pasta sit in water any longer than necessary. Drain it thoroughly in the colander and then put it in the large mixing bowl.

Using the wire whisk, mix the olive oil, vinegar, and mustard together thoroughly in the small bowl and pour it over the tortellini.

Prepare the other ingredients and add to the tortellini as they are ready. Pit and slice the ripe and green olives (buy them pitted if you can). Rinse, seed, and remove the pith from the bell peppers. Slice them into very thin strips. Toast the pine nuts in the pie pan in a 325F (163C) oven until lightly browned. Watch them carefully lest they burn. Peel the onion and chop it into fine dice with the chef's knife. Slice the salami into matchstick-size strips. Quarter the artichoke hearts (or, if using bottoms, cut them into 6 pieces). Add the pesto to the tortellini, season with salt and pepper, and stir everything together thoroughly. Refrigerate the salad for 2 hours, stirring it a couple of times. Just before serving, sprinkle on the chives and, if the tortellini has absorbed all the dressing, add a little more.

Variation: Make additions or substitutions according to your preference. For example, fresh ripe tomatoes (blanched, peeled, and seeded; *see page 568*) sliced into strips; ham; pepperoni; scallions; and blanched fennel, broccoli, or other vegetables.

Fisherman's Salad

This seafood salad must be made with the freshest ingredients, so use what is available at your local market. Flaked, cooked salmon, halibut, and sole are good substitutions for the mussels, oysters, and scallops. And any smoked fish—such as sturgeon, mackerel, whitefish, or trout—may be used instead of smoked salmon. Rollmops herring can replace herring in sour cream. Fresh greens—spinach, Boston lettuce, watercress—in any combination, make an attractive background for this colorful salad. And, adjust the seasoning to suit your taste by using flavored vinegars and jalapeño or other hot peppers. The separate ingredients may be prepared well in advance, with the final assembly done just before serving.

Yields 12 servings

1 pound (450 g) fresh shrimp
1/2 medium onion
2 celery stalks
1/2 medium red bell pepper
1/2 medium green bell pepper
12 small, whole fresh mushrooms
12 mussels
12 oysters
1/2 pint (235 ml) bay scallops, whole (or sea scallops, halved)
1 cup plus 2 tablespoons (250 ml) olive oil
1 small garlic clove

SPICES FOR THE BAG
1/2 bay leaf
1/4 teaspoon coriander
1 small clove
1/8 teaspoon oregano

1/2 teaspoon green peppercorns (packed in water and drained)
1/3 cup (80 ml) dry white wine
1/3 cup (80 ml) tarragon vinegar
1 tablespoon capers
12 black Greek olives
12 small (or 8 medium) new red-skinned potatoes
6 ounces (170 g) sliced smoked salmon

8 ounces (225 g) marinated herring in sour cream
2 ripe tomatoes (blanched, peeled, and seeded; *see page 568*), sliced into 1/4-inch (2/3 cm) wide strips
8 ounces (225 g) lump crabmeat
8 ounces (225 g) fresh string beans
Juice of 1/2 lemon
1 ripe avocado
2 hard-boiled eggs
4 radishes
2 lemons
1 head red leaf lettuce
Fresh dill or parsley sprigs
Salt
Freshly ground black pepper
Worcestershire sauce

Recommended equipment

A shrimp deveiner, paring knife, wooden spatula, stiff bristle brush, oyster knife, garlic press, cheesecloth, 4-quart (4 L) saucepan, 2-quart (2 L) saucepan, small bowl, paper towels, large mixing bowl, two large spoons.

Rinse the shrimp under running cold water, drain, peel, and devein them. Refrigerate and reserve.

Prepare the vegetables: Using the paring knife, peel the onion and cut into 1-inch (2 1/2 cm) dice; rinse the celery stalks, remove as many strings as possible, and cut diagonally into 1/4-inch (2/3 cm) thick slices; rinse the bell peppers, scrape out seeds and pithy white, and cut into 1-inch dice; and clean the mushrooms of any clinging dirt and trim off stems, leaving the mushrooms whole if they are small (if you are using large ones, halve them).

Scrub the mussel and oyster shells with the stiff bristle brush under running cold water, work the shells open with the oyster knife, and reserve the mussels and oysters (discard the shells). Rinse the scallops under running cold water, drain, and reserve. (If using sea scallops, halve them.)

Set the large saucepan over medium heat, add 2 tablespoons (30 ml) olive oil, and, when oil is hot, add the shrimp and sauté, while stirring with the wooden spatula, for 2 minutes. Then add the onions, celery, bell peppers, and mushrooms. Peel the garlic and press it into the mixture. While the mixture continues to simmer for another 2 minutes, prepare the spice bag by cutting a 6-inch (15 cm) square of cheesecloth, placing the bay leaf, coriander, clove, and oregano in the center, and tying the opposite corners together tightly. Add the spice bag to the saucepan, stir, and add the green peppercorns, wine, vinegar, and remaining olive oil. Bring mixture to a low simmer and cook for 2 minutes. Stir in the mussels, oysters, scallops, capers, and olives, return to a simmer, and remove from heat. Let cool to room temperature, remove the spice bag, and refrigerate if you are a few hours away from serving.

While the seafood is cooling, prepare the other ingredients. Using the small saucepan, bring lightly salted water to a boil, add the potatoes in their jackets and cook until just tender (about 10 to 12 minutes). Drain, let cool to room temperature, peel, and then slice into 1/4-inch (2/3 cm) thick slices.

Slice the smoked salmon (or other smoked fish) into 1/4-inch (2/3 cm) wide slices and reserve.

Rinse the sour cream off the herring and slice it into 1/4-inch (2/3 cm) thick strips.

Prepare the tomatoes.

Pick over the crabmeat with your fingers, removing any bits of shell, and being careful not to break up the lumps any more than necessary.

In the small saucepan, bring lightly salted water to a rolling boil. Meanwhile, trim the beans, split lengthwise, and cut into pieces about 3 inches (7 1/2 cm) long. When the water is boiling, add the string beans, boil for 3 minutes, drain, refresh under cold running water, and drain.

In the small bowl, combine 1/2 cup (118 ml) water and the juice squeezed from one-half of a lemon. Cut the avocado in half, remove the pit and peel, and slice each half lengthwise into 6 slices. Drench the slices in the lemon water and drain on paper towels (this will retard the darkening of the fruit).

Cook the eggs until they are hard-boiled and then cool, peel, and slice them into quarters. Slice the radishes very thinly. Quarter the lemons. Wash and dry the greens and prepare your herbs.

Now you are ready for the final assembly. Scrape the seafood into the mixing bowl and add the potatoes, salmon, herring, tomatoes, crabmeat, and string beans. Fold everything together carefully, using the serving spoons or your hands, until well blended. Adjust the seasoning with salt, pepper, and Worcestershire sauce. Let salad marinate for 10 to 15 minutes before arranging on the greens.

When ready, divide the greens among the plates or else serve from a platter. Mound the seafood on the greens and decorate with avocado slices, egg quarters, radish slices, the herbs, and lemon wedges.

❧ Islander Salad

We serve this with our "luau" (complete with suckling pig roasted over hot coals), but you do not have to go to such extremes. Simply present it on a platter lined with the freshest greens available—chicory or romaine, red leaf, or Boston lettuce—and garnished with black olives and kumquats to enjoy a refreshing and simple salad for a hot day.

Yields 4 to 6 servings

1/2 cup (118 ml) finely diced celery
1/2 cup (118 ml) pineapple chunks
1/2 cup (118 ml) water chestnuts
1/2 cup (118 ml) bean sprouts
1/2 cup (118 ml) chopped fresh mango
1 medium apple
2 pimientos (packed in water and drained)
4 ounces (115 g) fresh snow peas

FOR THE DRESSING
2/3 cup (160 ml) mayonnaise
1/2 teaspoon curry
2 tablespoons ketchup
Juice of 1/2 lemon
2 tablespoons pineapple juice
2 tablespoons chopped mango chutney

Recommended equipment

A small chef's knife, paring knife, small fine-mesh sieve, 1-quart (1 L) bowl, 2-quart (2 L) saucepan, small bowl, wire whisk, serving platter.

As each ingredient is prepared, add it to the larger bowl. Rinse the celery, make it as stringless as possible, and dice it finely. Drain the pineapple chunks and reserve 2 tablespoons juice for the dressing. Drain the water chestnuts and slice each. Rinse the bean sprouts and drain them. Peel the mango with a paring knife and cut into chunks. Peel and core the apple and dice it finely. Dice the pimientos finely.

Add lightly salted water to the saucepan and set it over high heat. While waiting for the water to boil, snap the blossom ends off the snow peas. When the water boils, add the snow peas, boil them gently for 2 minutes, remove from heat, cool them under running cold water, drain thoroughly, and reserve.

Using the whisk, combine the mayonnaise, curry, ketchup, and lemon and pineapple juices in the small bowl. Chop the mango chutney, add it to the dressing, and stir the dressing into the salad ingredients.

When ready to serve the salad, line a platter with the greens of your choice, mound the salad on them, and garnish the top with the reserved snow peas.

Winter Salad of Fresh and Dried Fruits

Somewhere, along about mid-January, when you have convinced yourself that Gauguin was really on to something when he moved his studio from Paris to Tahiti, think about this salad. Like his canvasses, it provides bold colors and contrasts sure to arrest the attention of the hibernating winter palate with the flavors of tropic climes.

Yields 4 to 6 servings

1/2 cup (118 ml) dried apricots
1/2 cup (118 ml) pitted dates
1/2 cup (118 ml) pitted prunes
1/2 cup (118 ml) raisins
1 cup (235 ml) apple juice
Juice of 1/2 lemon
2 tablespoons sugar
1/2 cup (118 ml) chopped walnuts
1 cup fresh pineapple cubes
1 ripe pear
1 orange
1 banana
Kirsch
10 fresh whole strawberries
1 kiwi fruit
1 apple

Recommended equipment

A 1 1/2-quart (1 1/2 L) saucepan, small chef's knife, small mixing bowl, serving bowl, apple corer.

With the chef's knife, halve the apricots and dates, and add them along with the prunes, raisins, apple juice, lemon juice, and sugar to the saucepan. Bring to a boil over medium high heat, then reduce heat and simmer for 5 minutes. Cool to room temperature, cover, and refrigerate for 2 hours.

At the end of this period, remove the bowl from the refrigerator and add the remaining ingredients as each is prepared. Chop the walnuts and add the pineapple cubes. Peel, core, and cube the pear. Peel the orange, halve it lengthwise, and cut it crosswise into 1/2-inch (1 1/4 cm) slices. Peel and slice the banana. Sprinkle the fruit with kirsch to taste, fold it all together lightly, and transfer it to the serving bowl.

Prepare the garnish. Hull and halve the strawberries. Peel the kiwi fruit and slice it thinly. Core, peel, and slice the apple. Distribute the garnish on the top of the other fruit, and spoon juice from the bowl over all of it. Cover and chill for an hour before serving. Spoon the salad into bowls or onto a bed of lettuce and serve.

Sautéed Mountain Trout Homestead

Fish and Shellfish

On another occasion, Escoffier was coaxed from his kitchen at the Savoy to the galleys of the recently launched Hamburg-America luxury liner the *Imperator*, where he produced for Kaiser Wilhelm II a phenomenal creation of salmon steamed in champagne. "How can I repay you?" asked the emperor, summoning the chef into his presence. "By giving us back Alsace-Lorraine" was Escoffier's reply.
—William Harlan Hale

On either side of the bridge at Illhaeusern, a hundred years ago, there stood a little *auberge*. There wasn't much to choose between the two of them unless you were a local who understood the nuances of Alsatian village life. On the west bank of the Ill was La Truite, run by the Mullers; on the east was L'Arbre Vert, kept by the Haeberlins. Both were peasant families with their horses, their patches of cabbage, their beds of the special reeds which were sold to tie up vines.

In both establishments the fare was much the same, *choucroute* and *écrevisses* and the famous *matelotes* of the region, for most of the villagers were fisher-folk and their *matelotes* were spoken of as far away as Colmar or Strasbourg. To the villagers of Illhaeusern, however, the fish stew at La Truite was the *matelote catholique*, at L'Arbre Vert the *matelote protestante*. They were said to be very different, but in those days no-one revealed the secrets of her cuisine and, if Madame Haeberlin were asked for her recipe, she would describe her method in the vaguest terms and add, "Then I give it my benediction."

Today, La Truite is still a bistro—a jolly enough place where the Mullers will make you a rough, peasant omelette.... It is the Alsace of the crooked beam and the stork's nest, the gnome in the garden and the fat goose postcard.

On the other side of the river, L'Arbre Vert has become L'Auberge de l'Ill, a three-star restaurant where the Haeberlins now serve some of the finest food in France.
—Quentin Crewe

Geopolitics, religion, and cuisine—what better themes could there be to begin this chapter? Before accusing Escoffier of setting too dear a price for his salmon recipe, we would do well to remember that nations still do legal battle over territorial fishing rights—a vestige of times when armada was pitted against armada for dominion over the seas. Equally important is the fish as a religious symbol. Egyptians thought them important enough to share tombs with the pharaohs, and early Christians, living among hostile pagans, cautiously scratched the simple sign of a fish in the sand to indicate their shared allegiance to Christ. Those familiar with the New Testament are aware of the use of the metaphor of fish and fishermen and fishers of men.

Religion and fish have also been intertwined from the culinary standpoint, especially in the Roman Catholic Church. In medieval times, the faithful were directed to eat fish for nearly half the days in a year, and Elizabethans dealt with similar restrictions for 145 days of the year. Only in 1966 did Pope Paul VI relax the requirements of fish as Lenten and Friday fare. Perhaps the most pervasive proof of this traditional association is the fact that your local fish market probably still gets its best supply of fresh items every Thursday—in time for the Friday shopper.

Such dietary strictures could work for or against the popularity of fish by leading to inventive cuisine or intense dislike. We certainly subscribe to the former viewpoint—as the size of this chapter indicates. Escoffier really speaks for all of us with a European background because the preparations of fish, whether simple or grand, have always played a central part in our cuisine. In fact, to be historical for just a moment, let us tell you about a ceremonial occasion, which incidentally reminds us of the sustained influence of Catherine de' Medici. Her son, King Charles IX, was to receive his bride, Elizabeth of Austria, in Paris. But 29 March 1571 was a Friday, and that meant fish. No matter, the Parisian chef and his sauciers staged a banquet which showed they had earned their postgraduate toques from the *scuola di cucina Italiana*. The party commenced after mass at Nôtre Dame and included oysters, whale meat (fifty pounds), crayfish, salmon, turbot, brill, herring (two hundred salted and two hundred fresh), carp, steamed mussels, platters of broiled lobster, trout, and one thousand pairs of frogs legs. (And there was no B. G. McElwee or Charlie Bogan to help get it there either.) The cost? Well, the public purse "contributed" 300,000 *livres*, which today would start a "Parisgate" investigation.

The point is that it was a high *meatless* feast. All well and good you say, the United States has an immense coastline, but Europe is crisscrossed with rivers—the Danube, Rhine, Rhône, Loire,

Saône, Seine, Elbe, Weser, and Neckar, for example—whereas, for its land mass, the United States has relatively few. We will concede that this was an obstacle for inland dwellers before reliable refrigerated transport, but nowadays, if I can have scallops with their roe flown in from France, I know you can find fresh fish in your market almost anywhere in this country, and probably not just on Thursdays, either. Above all, you should look for signs of quality and freshness, just as you do in selecting produce, poultry, and meat. Use the following guidelines suggested by A. J. McClane in *The Encyclopedia of Fish Cookery*:

> (1) When pressed with your finger the flesh will be firm and elastic; it must not feel so soft that your finger leaves an indentation.
> (2) The fish's eyes should be clear and full, not milky and sunken.
> (3) Its gills should be bright red rather than a muddy gray.
> (4) It will have a clean, often cucumberlike odor.
> (5) Its characteristic skin color should be unblemished by any reddish patches along the ventral area.

Finally, get to know your fishmonger so you can expect an honest answer to, "Did it come in fresh today?"

By the size of this chapter you may think that we have included a recipe for every one of the more than twenty thousand (a conservative estimate) species of fish known to exist. Actually, this chapter is large because fish and shellfish play a prominent role in our cuisine at the Homestead and they should in yours as well. If you look at B. G. McElwee's Shopping List, you will see that on average we serve more than thirty-five hundred pounds of fish a week, and this figure climbs dramatically with high guest counts. It is not a matter of being "trendy" because the concern for cholesterol has made fish an "in" food—it has always been an "in" food for cuisine, be it *truite au bleu* at streamside or *saumon soufflé "Auberge de l'Ill"* at Illhaeusern.

Our kitchen honors this tradition in the range of preparations we serve—from the very simple and "à la minute" to the intricate and time-consuming. Nowhere, however, is there richness for its own sake. Fish, above all, should never be smothered with sauce. If it takes the sauce to "fait passer le poisson," you bought the wrong "poisson." Many of the sauces in this chapter call for butter or cream as a finishing touch, but the quantity of sauce you should serve per person (rarely more than one-quarter cup) is so small as to make the cholesterol content negligible for all but those who can have no fat.

Now, on to the fish. We have selected recipes which reflect the preparations we serve here using the kinds of fish and shellfish likely to be available to you. Obviously, there are regional variations. Because there are seven species of salmon, those of you on the East Coast may find Atlantic and coho salmon, and those of you on the West Coast may find Pacific salmon. In other instances, we have tried to note substitutions where possible.

The first section of the chapter is composed of recipes for freshwater fish: three for trout, two for shad, and nine for salmon (although shad and salmon are really anadromous in that they live in salt water but reproduce in fresh water). Leading off with trout is a natural for this book because it is almost a Homestead culinary trademark. (I probably should have a sign outside my office saying "over 1 million served since 1962.") You have a choice of three techniques—sautéed, baked, or charcoal grilled—but, above all, try to get only mountain trout as we do from our own Alleghenies.

Two recipes honor the American native shad, one baked in light pastry and one quickly sautéed and dressed with lemon and capers. And then it is on to salmon. An extraordinary fish, salmon has an exceptional nutritional value because almost all of it is edible. It is a cook's dream because, like sole, it can accommodate a vast array of treatments. We have offered you a wide range of possibilities including two reasonably quick sautées of thin scallops—one featuring our own raspberry vinegar butter sauce and another with a Swiss flair featuring fresh dill. Two lightly baked fillet recipes follow, first one with a fragrant tarragon and Pernod sauce and then a page out of Escoffier's book with a visually stunning setting of caviars, saffron, and Champagne sauce. This "wonderfish" presents so many opportunities to the serious cook that we felt bound to close out the section with five quite different preparations from *la cuisine*. From this point on you will have to roll up your sleeves, but the results will be worth it. Appropriately, we begin this excursion in France.

The first one calls for pâte feuilletée, and you will find that Michel Finel's recipe is easy and reliable. Tucked inside the pâte is a salmon fillet dressed with a salmon and smoked salmon purée. Close behind is a preparation which needlessly intimidates people. In fact just think of the quenelles as salmon dumplings without the flour. When poached properly these little jewels almost seem so light as to need weights to keep them in their bowls. Carême may have had a hand in bringing the next recipe home from his days with Czar Alexander in Saint Petersburg because it is a much elevated version of the Russian peasant-style pie of the same name. Returning to France for the two-part salmon finale, we begin with the tour de force of the cold buffet—a whole poached salmon. Do not be put off by this prospect, as we have given you a good basic technique and a number of tasty and colorful serving suggestions. And speaking of colors, the last recipe is most striking in this regard. A multilayered mousse of sole, spinach laced with basil and watercress, and salmon, all surrounded by a pink moat of sauce, will defy you to even rest your fork between mouthfuls.

Being a cook and not an ichthyologist, I was stumped by grouping the next set of recipes. In turning to McClane's *Encyclopedia of Fish Cookery*, we found that "sole" is an umbrella category which includes plaice, flounder, halibut, sanddab, and turbot in addition to Dover and the ten other soles. And the problem for all of us as shoppers is that a sole is not a sole is not a sole (apologies to G. Stein). We call for Dover sole, which is flown in from Europe. If it is not available, try for petrale or sand sole on the West Coast and lemon sole (which is the market name for a winter flounder weighing more than three pounds) on the East Coast. Many other items are sold as "sole" fillets, and you must rely on your fishmonger for the true story.

Five recipes, ranging widely in method and complexity, begin the sole section. A colorful preparation poached in wine and garnished with sautéed fresh vegetables and pesto leads off, followed by a variant of the quenelle technique discussed under salmon—this one a little more painstaking but also more foolproof. Once again *la cuisine* beckons and we find ourselves on the road with an international trio—first in my hometown of Lucerne for what might be called a "peek-a-boo" soufflé, and then over the Alps and down the boot to Florence for a very attractive rolled presentation featuring Catherine's famous *spinaci*. And faster than you can say *train bleu* and *TGV*, we are pulling into the Gare de Lyon to end the "true" sole section in the City of Light with a Parisian accent of truffles, shrimp, and a tale of two sauces.

Moving on to the cousins of sole we encounter a trio of flounder, halibut, and turbot. The first recipe will be a pleasant surprise for those who, seeing "stuffed flounder" on a menu, instinctively look at the next selection. These fillets are lightly filled with a colorful and tasty crabmeat mixture instead of the usual heavily breaded "stuff." Fresh tarragon, cucumbers, and a tangy sauce set off the following halibut preparation, and not to be outdone, the English turbot, surrounded by red and white, is accompanied, not by "British Railway boiled potatoes," but with rather delicate little pommes de terre in the Parisian manner.

A genuine western Atlantic Ocean native, the pompano, is up next, and this is one instance where the European versions pale by comparison. We will not deceive you, it is rare and expensive, but the flavor and texture of pompano are second to none. Each of the three preparations offers an interesting backdrop for this exceptional fish, beginning with a relatively quick poached recipe and a balsamic vinegar butter sauce. Exotic fruit lends a tropical air to the next dish, which is sautéed, and a visually intriguing parchment-enclosed presentation associated with New Orleans, but popularized by Escoffier, rounds out the group.

To end the fish section, we have included three fish which are favorites of angler and gastronome alike. Red snapper and swordfish lead off with simple preparations, respectively broiling and charcoal grilling, each complemented by maître d'hôtel butter. Black sea bass completes the trio with a Mediterranean dish whose flavors of orange in three forms combine with the pungency of green peppercorns to bring the sunshine of Provence to your table.

Sunshine brings the beach to mind and the beach makes us think of those perennial favorites, crab, shrimp, and lobster. In general, simplicity should guide the preparation of these three, and of the eight recipes we have given you, only three are somewhat difficult. If there ever were a seasonal dish, it is soft-shelled crabs. To be at their best they must be enjoyed within hours of shedding their shells and prepared simply, either sautéed or breaded and fried lightly, as we have indicated. The third recipe, a colorful and spicy crabmeat gratinée, is a Homestead staple, and can be served all year round.

Because everyone has so many shrimp recipes, we saw no reason to confuse the issue with many more. Although we serve five to six hundred pounds of shrimp a week, it is usually featured cold at receptions or in buffet salads; however, the two warm preparations we have are a bit unusual and may interest you. The first is a southwestern dish made quite lively with the touch of jalapeño pepper, and the second is a variation of the now classic recipe created years ago at Delmonico's in New York. The latter teams shrimp with what some consider the ultimate seafood, lobster, which closes out the crustaceans in three different versions.

A genuine French classic from one of the great Parisian restaurants (alas, now closed), this elegant presentation features cooked lobsters which are halved, the meat removed and quickly worked into a scrumptious sauce, only to be returned to the shell halves, gratinéed, and served. Then comes the worldwide favorite—broiled lobster. We call for "Maine" lobster, but that is a misnomer. This recipe is excellent the world over; recommended equipment: one beach, lobsters, charcoal fire, and good companions—yields fond memories for all. Speaking of memories, the last recipe in this trio is a real culinary "sleeper." Like English Beef Tea, it is an apparently simple, understated recipe.

Just a "little lobster mousse" with a Sauce Américaine base—we dare you to say that to your guests without a hint of a (well-deserved) smile of satisfaction.

Since the other mollusk cousins—oysters, clams, and mussels—appear elsewhere, scallops have to carry this section on their own. If we may say so, each of the three recipes is excellent, and they differ greatly from each other. The first is our adaptation of the Peruvian lime juice–marinated specialty, seviche, made more colorful and tasty by additional vegetables and spices. From South America, it is nonstop to Italy for a pan-sizzled sauté finished off with garlic, lemon, and parsley. And, drawing on the imagination for a dramatic finish, the last recipe uses papillotes as display cases for scallops, colorful vegetables, and a tangy sauce.

To conclude the chapter we return to the Mediterranean, one of the world's venerable fishing grounds. Pasta, rice dishes, and aromatic stews are synonymous with many of the cuisines around this basin, and the six preparations we have given you are only a glimpse of the diversity to be found on the western and northern coastlines. Italy leads off with two fettuccine recipes, the first calling for a somewhat French-accented traditional mixture of vegetables and seafood in a cream sauce. Rather more unusual and eastward-looking is the pasta dish with oriental vegetables. Then it is up the Ligurian coast and across the border to the Côte d'Azur, where we encounter an elegantly simple technique pairing mussels with the texture and earthiness of pilaff. Moving on through Provence, Autoroute A9 branches left at Narbonne, leading straight toward the looming majesty of the Pyrenees, Catalonia, and the Spanish culinary masterpiece—paella. On one hand this recipe is a blockbuster because it calls for twenty-six ingredients. On the other hand the major effort is expended in the preparation for cooking—the actual cooking requiring only about thirty minutes. Most important, like the next recipe, paella is a culinary treasure worth the effort, even if it is not a literal transcription of the dish you had in Barcelona, Valencia, or Málaga. And now bouillabaisse—a recipe about which much, probably too much, has been said and written, and on which there is little agreement. Marseilles seems to be the home port for the preparation, but *les provençals* would probably argue about that. What is not in dispute is the fact that this version will give you a pleasing and tasty result you will be delighted to place on your table—and you might even be tempted to serve it to a Niçoise if not a Marseillaise.

Thinking back to the beginning of this introduction (if we have not lost you by now), the last recipe in this chapter—a somewhat simple fish stew from Greece—could not be more appropriate. For it was in the eastern Mediterranean that the activity of the early church, especially the teaching and letters of Saint Paul, took place, and it was from Alexandria, where the Bible was translated into Greek, that sailors carried news of the new religion.

Well, we have come a long way from the trout streams of the Alleghenies to the Aegean sea, but, in truth, this group of recipes is only a figurative minnow in the overall "fish story"—remember the twenty thousand species. Regardless of what fish or shellfish you serve, let us leave you with two *conseils*. First, we cannot overemphasize the importance of proper cooking. Overcooking fish is a cardinal culinary sin because it destroys the unique texture and flavor. In all of these recipes we have given you careful instructions and in the Ingredients and Techniques section there is a description of sautéing fish which can be used for any of the other nineteen thousand–plus species we left out. Second, *freshness* is as important here as pure water is in sauces and soups. Recall Escoffier and remember that the sauce *must not* "fait passer le poisson."

Trout

Sautéed Mountain Trout Homestead

A traditional Homestead favorite, this is a simple and delicious way to prepare any delicate fish and protect its flavor. Use only fresh trout—ours come from nearby Allegheny streams. If you have a rushing mountain stream nearby and can catch your own, your reward will be doubled.

Yields 6 servings

6 fresh trout, weighing 10 to 12 ounces each (285 to 340 g) before boning
1 tablespoon chopped fresh parsley
Juice of 3 lemons
1/2 cup (118 ml) canned or peeled fresh grapes (4 to 5 per serving)
1/3 cup (80 ml) blanched, sliced almonds
1/2 cup (118 ml) half-and-half
Salt
Freshly ground white pepper
1 cup (120 g) flour
1/4 to 1/2 cup (60 to 118 ml) peanut oil
6 tablespoons (90 g) butter
Sprigs of fresh parsley or dill
6 lemon wedges

Recommended equipment

A boning knife, small mixing bowl, waxed paper (or plate), small chef's knife, 12-inch (30 cm) sauté pan, turning spatula, paper towels, serving platter (or plates).

Mix the half-and-half in the small bowl with some salt and pepper, spread the flour on the waxed paper (or plate), and, holding the butterfly fillets carefully, dip them one by one into the cream, being sure to coat both sides. Let any excess cream drip off and then place fillets on the flour, pat lightly into flour, turn over and repeat with the other side, remove, and shake gently to dislodge the excess flour. (Do this just before you are ready to sauté the fillets, otherwise they will be pasty.)

Set the sauté pan over high heat, pour in oil to a depth of 1/8 inch (1/3 cm), and when the oil is hot put the trout into it skin side up. It is important not to crowd the pan. Cook fillets in separate batches as necessary, changing the oil after the first two. When the trout starts to sizzle, reduce heat to medium high and sauté for 3 minutes. Turn fillet over and, after sizzling starts, sauté for 2 minutes. Remove to paper towels to drain and then place on warm serving platter (or plates).

When all fillets are cooked, pour oil from pan and wipe out. Add butter and set over medium heat. Shake pan gently to swirl butter around as it melts until it begins to turn light golden brown. When this happens add the lemon juice immediately to prevent the butter from browning any further. (The butter at this stage is "beurre noisette" and has a nutlike flavor.) Stir in the parsley, almonds, and grapes, remove from heat, and pour sauce over the fish. Garnish with sprigs of parsley (or dill) and lemon wedges and serve at once.

One by one, rinse the trout thoroughly under cold running water and then, using the boning knife, butterfly them: split the trout open along the belly, leaving the halves attached along the back, and carefully remove the entrails, all bones (including the backbone), the head, and gills. Do not remove the skin. Then trim away about 1/4 inch (2/3 cm) along the belly flaps.

Rinse the parsley, spin or pat dry, chop, and reserve. Juice the lemons. Prepare the grapes *(see page 78)* and, if you wish, toast the almonds. (Preheat oven to 250F [121C] and toast the almonds on a pan until they are golden brown. When they are done, remove them from the oven and reserve.)

❧ Baked Mountain Trout with Tarragon Stuffing

I prefer Italian flat-leafed parsley for this dish because it has more flavor than the familiar curly variety. When you present trout this way, accompany them with boiled Pommes de Terre Parisienne and a tossed green or Pressed Cucumber Salad.

Yields 8 servings

2 cups (475 ml) fine white bread crumbs
2 1/2 to 2 2/3 cups (590 to 635 ml) half-and-half
1/4 teaspoon salt
1/8 teaspoon freshly ground white pepper
2 teaspoons chopped fresh tarragon
2 tablespoons chopped fresh parsley
8 fresh trout, weighing 10 to 12 ounces (285 to 340 g) each before boning
2 tablespoons (30 g) butter
1 tablespoon finely chopped shallots
1/4 cup (60 ml) dry white wine
1 1/2 cups (355 ml) Beurre Blanc *(see page 84)*
1/3 cup (80 ml) whipping cream
Fresh tarragon sprigs
Butter for the waxed paper

Recommended equipment

A 1-quart (1 L) mixing bowl, mixing fork, boning knife, enameled cast-iron baking dish or lined copper plat à sauter, large chef's knife, waxed paper, 1 1/2-quart (1 1/2 L) saucepan, wire whisk, turning spatula, paring knife, heatproof serving dish.

In the mixing bowl, combine the bread crumbs, 2 1/2 cups (590 ml) half-and-half, salt, pepper, tarragon, and parsley. Mix well with the mixing fork and then refrigerate for an hour. The mixture must be a smooth paste—add more half-and-half, a few drops at a time, as needed.

One by one, rinse the trout thoroughly under cold running water and then, using the boning knife, butterfly them: split the trout open along the belly, leaving the halves attached along the back, and carefully remove the entrails, all bones (including the backbone), the head, and gills. Do not remove the skin. Then trim away about 1/4-inch (2/3 cm) along the belly flaps. Open each trout, lay skin side down on your work surface, season lightly with salt and pepper, spread 3 tablespoons tarragon stuffing on center of one-half of trout, and fold trout back together.

Preheat oven to 375F (190 C).

Butter the baking dish or plat à sauter with 1 tablespoon of the butter. Chop the shallots with the chef's knife and strew them evenly in the bottom of the baking dish. Lay the trout into the dish, pour wine around trout, dot trout with remaining butter, and cover dish loosely with buttered waxed paper. Set the dish over medium heat until simmering point is reached, then set into the middle level of the oven and bake for 18 minutes or until fillets spring back from a light touch.

Prepare the beurre blanc while the trout are baking and reserve.

When the trout are done, take dish from oven, remove waxed paper, drain cooking liquids into saucepan, and set baking dish aside, loosely covered, in a warm (not hot) place. Add 1/3 cup (80 ml) whipping cream to the saucepan and set over medium high heat to reduce to 1/4 cup. Blend this into the beurre blanc with the whisk.

When trout have rested for 5 minutes, transfer them one at a time to the center of a piece of waxed paper, about 10 by 12 inches (25 x 30 cm). Using the paring knife, peel off the skin starting at the head end or from the back edge. Then, using both hands, lift waxed paper from one side and gently roll the trout over to the other side, using the paper as a support. Peel the skin from the second side and then transfer the trout to the serving dish. If necessary, reheat the trout in a 350F (177C) oven for 2 minutes. Then spoon sauce over the trout, garnish with tarragon sprigs, and serve at once.

Charcoal Grilled Mountain Trout

A very popular preparation at the Homestead's outdoor picnics, this will be a favorite of yours wherever your picnic may be. For indoor dining, cook the trout en papillote.

Fresh trout are de rigueur because the only seasoning is Beurre Maître d'hôtel, which allows the fragile aroma and delicate flavor of the trout to be fully enjoyed. Serve the trout with a lemon wedge and small boiled (or new) potatoes in their jackets rolled in melted butter and seasoned with a pinch of salt and snips of fresh chives.

Yields 1 serving

1 fresh trout, weighing about 12 ounces (340 g) before boning
A dash of salt
Freshly ground white pepper
Juice of 1/2 lemon
1 1/2 tablespoons (22 g) Beurre Maître d'hôtel *(see page 81)*, softened at room temperature
1 teaspoon fine white bread crumbs
Peanut oil for the foil

Recommended equipment

A charcoal grill, boning knife, aluminum foil.

Start the fire in your charcoal grill and time the following preparations so the coals will be good and hot.

Rinse trout *thoroughly* under cold running water and then butterfly it: using the boning knife, split it open along the belly, leaving the halves attached along the back. Clean out the insides, carefully remove all bones (including the backbone), the head, and gills, and trim about 1/4 inch (2/3 cm) along the belly flaps. Season with a dash of salt, a few twists of the white pepper mill, a squeeze of lemon juice, and spread the trout halves with the beurre maître d'hôtel. Sprinkle the bread crumbs over all—they will absorb some of the juices and keep the fish moist. Lightly oil a piece of foil large enough to completely wrap the trout. Then fold trout halves together, place on the foil, and fold the edges tightly together for a complete seal.

Place the foil package on the grill rack over hot coals for 2 minutes on one side, turn for 2 minutes on the other side, and then move trout to a spot over medium coals to finish cooking—about 4 more minutes. It is important not to overcook the fish.

༂

If you have never handled fresh mountain trout before, you may be surprised by their slippery natural coating. If this bothers you, it can be removed by a thorough rinse in running cold water.

For indoor cooking, place the trout papillotes *(see page 568)* on a baking pan or sheet and cook in preheated 350F (177C) oven for 8 minutes. With either cooking method the time should be increased for larger trout.

The potatoes may also be cooked in a foil pouch on the rack over the coals, for 10 minutes on a side.

Shad

Baked Shad and Roe in Phyllo Pastry

Springtime shad feasts are an American tradition observed by the native American Indian and Revolutionary soldier alike. The Winepesaukees called in their neighboring tribes and Washington and Lafayette toasted "Gentleman, charge your glasses," as the planked shad sizzled over the fire at the Fish House in Andalusia, Pennsylvania, on the banks of the Delaware. To this day, many children would still dispute the Latin name sapidissima, or "most delicious," probably substituting "most bony" instead. However, this is only a matter of proper filleting. Among the most delicate of fish flavors, shad must be carefully cooked to protect it. Phyllo pastry is perfect for this. If it is frozen, thaw it overnight in the refrigerator. Thin sheets of Pâte Feuilletée can be substituted if the phyllo is unavailable.

Yields 4 servings

4 portions of boned shad, weighing 4 to 5 ounces (115 to 145 g) each
1 set of roe, weighing 8 to 12 ounces (225 to 340 g)
Juice of 1 lemon
1 teaspoon Worcestershire sauce
Salt
Freshly ground white pepper
6 tablespoons (90 g) butter, melted
1 strip of bacon, weighing 2 to 3 ounces (60 to 85 g)
1 teaspoon chopped shallots
1 tablespoon dry white wine
8 phyllo pastry sheets, 16 x 15 inches (40 x 37 1/2 cm)
1 egg
1 tablespoon water
Butter for the foil

Recommended equipment

A large baking dish, two small bowls, small baking dish, aluminum foil, damp kitchen towel, pastry brush, 9-inch (22 1/2 cm) slicing knife, paring knife, baking sheet.

Using cold water, wash the shad fillets and roe gently and pat dry.

Preheat oven to 325F (163C).

Put shad skin side down into the large baking dish. In one of the small bowls, combine the lemon juice and Worcestershire sauce, pour over the fillets, season them with salt and pepper, and drizzle 1 tablespoon of melted butter over them. Set aside to marinate.

Cook the bacon in the small baking dish in the oven until half cooked. Turn slice over, add the shallots, wine, and roe, season with salt and pepper, cover dish with buttered aluminum foil, and set into the middle level of the oven to cook for 4 to 5 minutes. Remove dish from oven, uncover, and set aside to cool roe in the dish.

Remove phyllo pastry from refrigerator and while you are working keep a damp towel over the pastry. Spread a phyllo sheet on your work surface. Using the pastry brush, cover the entire sheet with melted butter. Place a second sheet on top of the first, butter, add a third, butter it, and finally add a fourth sheet and butter it. (If some of the phyllo sheets stick together and you use two for each layer rather than one, don't worry—a few more will not matter.) Using the slicing knife, slice the phyllo stack on the diagonal to make two pastry packages.

Repeat the above process.

Preheat oven to 350F (177C).

Divide the shad fillets among the four phyllo pastry packages. Remove roe from baking dish, divide each one lengthwise in half so that you have four pieces, and place one piece on top of each fillet. Remove bacon from dish, discard, and drizzle drippings from dish over the roe. Wrap the phyllo pastry around the fillet and roe, pressing the sheets together without folding. Trim the pastry, leaving 1 1/2 inches (3 3/4 cm) on both ends. Mix the egg and water together thoroughly in the other small bowl and brush the tops and sides of the pastry packages with the egg wash. Place on baking sheet, set into the middle level of the oven, and bake for about 12 minutes or until the pastry is golden brown. Let packages rest in a warm place for a few minutes before serving.

You can wrap the shad and roe ahead of time, cover them with a damp towel, and then refrigerate. Do not brush on the egg wash until you are ready to bake the packages. If they have been chilled, allow 2 more minutes cooking time. You will need 10 ounces (285 g) Pâte Feuilletée *(see page 513)* if you choose to use it.

Sautéed Shad and Roe Grenobloise

Downstream from the confluence of the Isère, which runs through Grenoble, and the Rhône, lies the part of Provence known as the Bouches-du-Rhône, and it is here and in the département of Var that the nonesuch or nonpareil capers grow in wild abundance. Although trout is indigenous to the waters of the high Dauphiné, we have adapted this technique to our native shad. The key to success here is moving quickly to preserve the flavor and texture of the fish. Watch the butter closely so it does not burn, work in the lemon and capers at just the right moment, and voilà—a Homestead springtime favorite.

Yields 4 servings

4 portions of boned shad, weighing 4 to 5 ounces (115 to 145 g) each
1 set of roe, weighing 8 to 12 ounces (225 to 340 g)
1/4 cup (60 ml) half-and-half
Salt
Freshly ground white pepper
1/2 cup (60 g) flour
1/4 cup (60 ml) peanut oil
2 teaspoons chopped fresh parsley
1 large lemon
1/4 cup (60 g) butter
2 tablespoons capers, with 1 to 2 teaspoons of liquid

Recommended equipment

A 2-quart (2 L) mixing bowl, waxed paper or plate, 12-inch (30 cm) sauté pan with lid, turning spatula, paper towels, small chef's knife, paring knife, wooden spoon.

Using cold water, wash the shad fillets and roe gently and pat dry.

Mix the half-and-half with the salt and pepper in the bowl and spread the flour on waxed paper on your work surface. Dip the fillets into the half-and-half, scrape excess off with your fingers, and pat each fillet gently into the flour, turning to coat both sides. Lightly shake off any excess flour and reserve the fillets. Repeat this process for each fillet and then the roe. The dipping and flouring must be done just before you are ready to sauté the fish.

Set the sauté pan over medium high heat, add the peanut oil, and heat until a drop of water sizzles vigorously when dropped into the pan. Place the fillets skin side up in the pan, sauté 1 minute, reduce heat to medium, sauté 3 minutes, turn shad with spatula, and sauté 2 more minutes. (If fillet is thick, add 1 minute to the cooking time for each side.) Remove from pan and let drain on paper towels.

Sauté the roe for 7 to 9 minutes (depending upon the size), using the lid set loosely over the pan because roe has a tendency to pop while it is cooking.

Preheat oven to 250F (121C).

While the roe is sautéing, chop the parsley with the chef's knife. Then, with the paring knife, remove the peel and bitter white of the lemon, remove a 1/2-inch (1 1/4 cm) thick slice from each side, remove seeds, and then cut lemon flesh into small dice and reserve.

When roe is done, let set 3 minutes while you warm the serving plates or platter. Arrange the shad fillets for serving and split each roe in half lengthwise so you have four servings. Set into the middle level of the oven to keep warm while you prepare the sauce.

Remove all oil from the pan and set it over medium heat. Add the butter to the pan and heat until the butter begins to foam. Let the butter cook until it turns golden brown. At this point immediately add the diced lemon and the capers with their liquid. Simmer for 30 seconds, stir in parsley, and divide the sauce among the fillets and roe. Serve at once.

Salmon

Escalopes de Saumon Homestead at the Cascades

Escalopes de Saumon Homestead
Salmon Scallops with Raspberry Vinegar Butter Sauce

In standing guard over the Loire, the great sixteenth-century châteaux were also keeping watch over one of France's greatest sources of salmon. And, there is general agreement in France that one of the best and most original treatments of this popular fish is the sautéed scallop accompanied by sorrel and butter sauce devised by the Troisgros brothers of Roanne. Our version calls for a sauce and a raspberry vinegar we created here. The contrasting pinks of the fish and sauce are set off well by the bright green of lightly blanched, tiny String Beans or pencil-thin fresh Asparagus, steamed Pommes de Terre Parisienne, and a salad of Boston or Bibb lettuce.

Yields 6 servings

1 recipe Raspberry Vinegar Butter Sauce *(see page 85)*
2 to 2 1/4 pounds (900 to 1025 g) fresh centercut salmon (5 to 6 ounces or 140 to 170 g per serving)
Salt
Freshly ground white pepper
6 to 8 tablespoons Clarified Butter *(see page 568)*
Flour
Peanut oil for the waxed paper

FOR THE GARNISH
2 kiwi fruit
Fresh raspberries

Recommended equipment

A double boiler, 12-inch (30 cm) slicing knife, hemostat or needle-nose pliers, waxed paper or aluminum foil, cleaver, paring knife, 12-inch (30 cm) sauté pan, flat turning spatula, heatproof platter.

Prepare the raspberry vinegar butter sauce and keep it warm in the double boiler.

Using the slicing knife, remove the skin, cut the salmon in two lengthwise, and remove the center bone, producing two fillets. Remove any embedded bones with the hemostat or pliers *(see page 568)*. Slicing at a 45° angle (as you would for smoked salmon), cut each fillet into three pieces of equal size, and, working with one at a time, place them between two lightly oiled pieces of waxed paper (or aluminum foil). Using the flat side of the cleaver (or the bottom of the small sauté pan), pound the salmon with light strokes until it is uniformly 1/4 to 3/8 inch (2/3 to 1 cm) thick. Season each salmon scallop lightly with salt and pepper and set aside.

Prepare the clarified butter and reserve.

Prepare the garnish now. Peel the kiwi fruit, slice thinly, and reserve. Wash enough raspberries to have three per serving—fill a small bowl with water, float the raspberries in it briefly, remove them gently, and let drain while you sauté the salmon.

Preheat oven to 250F (121C).

To sauté the salmon, set the sauté pan over medium high heat, add 1 tablespoon clarified butter, and, when it is hot, dust a salmon scallop lightly with flour, and put it into the pan. If you can sauté two at the same time without their touching, add more clarified butter and do so; otherwise, sauté them in batches, adding another tablespoon of clarified butter for each one. Watch carefully, as they will cook very quickly. Sauté the first side for 1 minute, turn with the spatula, and sauté the second side for 1 1/2 minutes. When done, remove to the heatproof platter, wipe the pan out with paper towels, add another 1 or 2 tablespoons clarified butter, and sauté the remaining salmon in batches (wiping out the pan and adding clarified butter each time).

When all the salmon has been sautéed, set the platter into the oven for 2 minutes. Remove the platter from the oven, divide the raspberry vinegar butter sauce among warm serving plates, place a salmon scallop on top, garnish with kiwi fruit slices and raspberries, and serve at once.

Variations: Prepare Orange Cream Curry Sauce *(see page 86)* or Homestead Passion Fruit Sauce *(see page 101)* for the salmon. For the former, garnish the scallops with orange and kiwi fruit slices and for the latter use avocado and mango slices.

Escalopes de Saumon Lac Léman
Salmon Scallops with Dill Sauce

Lac Léman (Lake Geneva) is the closest thing Switzerland has to an ocean—it even has a Riviera, the Vaudois. Approximately forty-five miles long from Geneva's five-hundred-foot high jet d'eau to Montreux and the castle of Chillon, whose dungeon was the unfortunate location for Lord Byron's famous prisoner, it is a breathtakingly beautiful body of water, dotted with picturesque side-wheel steamers, whose comings and goings tie together the Swiss and French sides of the lake. (Evian-les-bains, home of the world-famous spa and source of the renowned bottled spring water, is located here.) The féra, a salmonlike fish, is native to Lac Léman (and Auvergne and the Morvan in Burgundy) and herb-flavored cream sauces are part of the regional cuisine. Our adaptation features the American salmon paired with a dill sauce, and with a little bit of imagination, you can easily conjure up a sunset dinner at the water's edge in Montreux. This dish should be prepared for no more than six guests because its success depends upon the last-minute preparation of the delicate salmon scallops. New potatoes steamed in their jackets or Rice Pilaff accompanied by a mixed green salad or fresh Asparagus complete this presentation nicely.

Yields 6 servings

1 large or 2 small ripe tomatoes (blanched, peeled, and seeded; see page 568)
2 tablespoons chopped shallots
1 tablespoon freshly crushed white pepper
1 cup (235 ml) dry white wine
1/2 cup (118 ml) Fish Stock (see page 60)
Fresh dill stems
2 to 2 1/4 pounds (900 to 1025 g) fresh centercut salmon (5 to 6 ounces or 140 to 170 g per serving)
Peanut oil for waxed paper
3 tablespoons Clarified Butter (see page 568)
3 tablespoons dry white wine
2 cups (475 ml) Crème Fraîche (see page 66)
Juice of 1 lemon
1 tablespoon chopped fresh dill
Salt
Freshly ground white pepper
6 mushroom caps
1 tablespoon (15 g) butter
Juice of 1/2 lemon
2 tablespoons white wine
6 sprigs fresh dill

Recommended equipment

Two 1 1/2-quart (1 1/2 L) saucepans, large chef's knife, mortar and pestle, 3-quart (3 L) saucepan, slicing knife, hemostat or needle-nose pliers, waxed paper or aluminum foil, cleaver, 12-inch (30 cm) sauté pan, paper towels, wire whisk, fine-mesh sieve, 8-inch (20 cm) sauté pan, 1 1/2-quart (1 1/2 L) saucepan, heatproof platter.

Prepare the tomatoes so that they will be ready when you need them. Cut them into 1/2-inch (1 1/4 cm) thick strips and put them into one of the smaller saucepans.

Using the chef's knife, chop the shallots and add them to the large saucepan with the crushed white pepper, 1 cup of wine, and the fish stock. Wash the dill, gently pat it dry, and strip off enough leaves to make one tablespoon chopped and reserve. Add the stems to the saucepan and reserve 6 whole sprigs for the garnish. Bring the mixture to a medium high boil and reduce the contents to 3 to 4 tablespoons. This will take about 15 minutes. Remove from heat and reserve.

While the sauce is reducing prepare the salmon. Using the slicing knife, remove the skin, cut the salmon in two lengthwise, and remove the center bone, producing two fillets. Remove any embedded bones with the hemostat or pliers *(see page 568)*. Slicing at a 45° angle (as you would for smoked salmon), cut each fillet into three pieces of equal size, and, working with one at a time, place them between two lightly oiled pieces of waxed paper (or aluminum foil). Using the flat side of the cleaver (or the bottom of the small sauté pan), pound the salmon with light strokes until it is uniformly 1/2 inch thick. Season lightly with salt and freshly ground white pepper.

Set the large sauté pan over medium high heat, add 2 tablespoons of clarified butter, and, when hot, sauté the scallops for 1 1/2 minutes on each side. You will have to add 1 tablespoon of clarified butter to the pan when you sauté the last scallops. As they are done, remove them to paper towels drain and pour off all remaining butter. Add 3 tablespoons of white wine to the pan, simmer for 1 minute, then add to the reduction in the large saucepan.

Set the saucepan over medium heat, add the crème fraîche and juice of one lemon, and simmer until reduced about one-quarter to a creamy consistency, stirring from time to time with a whisk. This should take about 4 to 5 minutes. Strain through the sieve into the other small saucepan, add reserved chopped dill, adjust seasoning if needed with salt and pepper, and keep warm.

Preheat oven to 325F (163C).

Brush the mushroom caps of any clinging dirt. Set the small sauté pan over low to medium heat and add 1 tablespoon of butter, juice of 1/2 lemon, 2 tablespoons of white wine, and the mushroom caps. Season lightly with salt and pepper and cook for 2 minutes on a side. When done, pour off some of the liquid into the tomatoes and start warming them gently on low heat (do not boil).

Arrange the salmon on the serving platter and heat for 1 minute on the upper level of the oven. Then pour the dill sauce over the scallops, arrange the mushroom caps and tomato pieces on the platter, garnish with the reserved dill sprigs, and serve at once.

For an elegant touch, add a teaspoon of salmon caviar to each scallop before serving.

Suprêmes de Saumon Amoureuse
Fillets of Salmon with Pernod and Tarragon Sauce

Invented by a Dr. Ordinaire, a Frenchman living in Couvet, Switzerland, the formula for absinthe liqueur was sold to a M. Pernod in 1791. French soldiers returning from Algeria in the 1850s contributed to its popularity, and by the turn of the century "la Verte" was virtually the apéritif national. *However, by this time, it was clear that wormwood, its main ingredient, was responsible for much more than the amorous and euphoric moods attributed to it. In 1915 it was outlawed and replaced by* pastis *and the Pernod called for here. A handsome entrée, this dish is particularly stunning when each serving is garnished with fresh tarragon sprigs, two or three lightly blanched fresh Snow Peas, and a cooked, peeled shrimp. Boiled Pommes de Terre Parisienne are the perfect companion for this salmon. Small portions of the fish alone make a superb first course for a special dinner.*

Yields 6 servings

1 tablespoon finely chopped shallots
2 to 2 1/4 pounds (900 to 1025 g) boned and skinned fresh salmon fillets (5 to 6 ounces or 145 to 170 g per serving)
Salt
Freshly ground white pepper
1/2 cup (118 ml) dry white wine
2 sprigs fresh tarragon
3 cups (710 ml) whipping cream
1 1/2 tablespoons lobster base (for live lobster *see below*)
1 tablespoon Pernod
A dash of cayenne pepper
1 tablespoon chopped fresh parsley
Butter for the baking dish and the waxed paper

Recommended equipment

A large chef's knife, enameled cast-iron baking dish or lined copper plat à sauter, waxed paper or aluminum foil, 4-quart (4 L) saucepan, wire whisk, fine-mesh sieve, double boiler.

Preheat oven to 325F (163C).

Butter the baking dish or plat à sauter. Using the chef's knife, mince the shallots and strew them in the baking dish. Rinse the salmon fillets gently under cold water, drain, and pat dry. Season them lightly with salt and pepper and lay them in the dish. Pour the wine around the fillets, cover loosely with buttered waxed paper (or buttered foil), bring to a low simmer over medium heat, then place on middle rack in preheated oven. Bake for 8 to 10 minutes (thin fillets cook quickly) or until fish just comes apart when pulled with a fork.

While the fish is baking, rinse and dry the fresh tarragon, remove the leaves, chop, and reserve them. Put the stems and pieces into the saucepan with the cream, lobster base, and Pernod. When the fish is done, remove from oven and reserve, covered loosely with the waxed paper so the steam may escape. Set the saucepan over medium heat, bring to a boil, stirring occasionally with the whisk, reduce heat to a low simmer, add cooking liquid from the baking dish, and reduce by one-half (or until the sauce coats a wooden spoon, about 10 minutes).

Next, strain sauce through the sieve into a clean saucepan. Add the chopped tarragon leaves (or dried tarragon), simmer 1 minute, and adjust seasoning with salt, pepper, and a dash or two of cayenne. Chop the parsley and stir it into the sauce.

(If you are not quite ready to serve, pour sauce into a double boiler to keep warm and coat the surface with dots of butter to prevent the formation of a skin layer.)

When ready to serve, heat the salmon for 1 minute in the oven, put on warm serving plates, spoon the sauce over the fillets, and garnish as you wish. Serve immediately.

Lobster base is available in specialty food shops, but to give the eye and palate a real treat, try fresh lobster. If using fresh lobster, get one that weighs 1 to 1 1/4 pounds (450 to 675 g). Separate the tail from the body. Cut the tail crosswise into three pieces and bake in the same pan with the salmon. Crush the body and claws and cook in 1 tablespoon of olive oil in a hot sauté pan, stirring occasionally, until the shells turn red. Then add 1/4 cup (60 ml) dry white wine and simmer over medium heat for 3 minutes. When you are ready to reduce the cream sauce, add contents of the sauté pan to the saucepan.

The rich flavor created by using fresh lobster is enhanced by the luxurious garnish it provides. Slice the tail meat into medallions (after removing the shell) and decorate the fillets with this delightful delicacy.

Suprêmes de Saumon avec son Caviar et Sauce Champagne
Fillets of Salmon with Salmon Caviar and Champagne Sauce

On the Imperator, *Escoffier steamed Kaiser Wilhelm II's salmon in Champagne, and our preparation calls for it to be used in the sauce, which permits the flavor of the Champagne to play a more prominent role. It may take a bit of doing, but use any friendly persuasion you can with your fishmonger to obtain the fresh salmon caviar, as it is stunning against the saffron-colored sauce. Use a good French or California brut Champagne for the sauce and devise your menu to serve it throughout the meal as well.*

Yields 6 servings

1 cup (235 ml) Sauce Velouté de Poisson *(see page 68)*
1 tablespoon chopped shallots
2 to 2 1/4 pounds (900 to 1025 g) boned and skinned fresh salmon fillets (5 to 6 ounces or 145 to 170 g per serving)
Salt
Freshly ground white pepper
1/2 cup (118 ml) dry white wine
1 2-inch (5 cm) piece of lemon peel
Juice of 1 lemon
1 teaspoon freshly crushed black pepper
1 cup (235 ml) dry Champagne
1 cup (235 ml) whipping cream
4 threads saffron
6 teaspoons fresh salmon caviar
6 sprigs fresh dill or parsley
Butter for the baking dish and the waxed paper

Recommended equipment

A large chef's knife, enameled cast-iron baking dish or lined copper plat à sauter, waxed paper or aluminum foil, serving platter, mortar and pestle, 3-quart (3 L) saucepan, paring knife, fine-mesh sieve.

Prepare the velouté and set it aside.
Preheat oven to 325F (163C).

Using the chef's knife, chop the shallots. Butter the baking dish or plat à sauter and strew the shallots in the bottom. Gently wash the fillets, drain, pat dry, season lightly with salt and white pepper, and lay them in the dish. Pour the wine around the fillets, cover with the buttered waxed paper (or buttered foil), bring to a low simmer over medium heat, and then place in the oven. Bake for 8 to 10 minutes (if the fillets are thin, 6 to 8 minutes should be enough) or until the fish just comes apart when pulled with a fork. When done, remove salmon to the serving platter and keep it covered loosely with the waxed paper so the steam may escape.

Pour the cooking liquid into the saucepan. With the paring knife, remove a 2-inch-long strip of lemon peel (leaving the bitter white behind). Juice the lemon and add the juice and peel to the saucepan. Crush the black pepper in the mortar and pestle and add it to the saucepan along with the Champagne, bring to a simmer over medium heat, and adjust heat so that liquid simmers until reduced by one-half. (This may take 15 minutes.) When reduced, add the velouté, whipping cream, and saffron, bring to a gentle simmer, and cook for about 10 minutes (or until the sauce coats a wooden spoon nicely and is of a creamy consistency). Strain sauce through the sieve into a clean saucepan.

Set the serving platter into the oven for 1 minute to warm the fillets. Then remove, spoon sauce over fish, add a teaspoon of caviar to the top of each portion, and garnish the platter with fresh dill or parsley sprigs. Serve at once.

Certainly other varieties of fish such as sole, sea bass, or halibut can be prepared this way, but the salmon caviar makes this a particularly colorful choice. If you prefer, serve North American or imported beluga caviar along with the salmon caviar.

Soufflé de Saumon en Croûte
Salmon Soufflé in Puff Pastry

Puff pastry and fresh salmon are two of life's culinary delights. The now classic saumon en croûte, featuring a whole salmon wrapped in puff pastry, was devised by Fernand Point for the Aga Khan. If anything, this presentation is made both lighter and more elegant by the soufflé. To set it off properly, surround each slice with Beurre Blanc or Sauce Mousseline and garnish with fresh dill.

Yields 5 servings for a main course or 7 servings for a fish course

8 ounces (225 g) Pâte Feuilletée (see page 513)
1 boned and skinned salmon fillet, weighing about 1 1/2 pounds (675 g)
Salt
Freshly ground white pepper
3 ounces (85 g) smoked salmon
1 egg white
1 cup (235 ml) whipping cream
1 tablespoon finely crushed ice
1 egg
1 tablespoon cold water
2 cups (475 ml) Beurre Blanc (see page 84)
Butter for the baking sheet

Recommended equipment

A hemostat or needle-nose pliers, paring knife, waxed paper, cleaver, blender or food processor, rubber spatula, 1-quart (1 L) bowl, 2-quart (2 L) bowl, wooden spoon, rolling pin, baking sheet, wire whisk, pastry brush, serrated knife.

Prepare the pâte feuilletée and reserve. Refrigerate the two bowls.

Rinse the salmon fillet under cold running water, pat dry, and lay on your work surface. Remove any bones with the hemostat or pliers *(see page 568)*. Using the paring knife, trim the fillet along the flank and any thinner sections to make a uniform shape. You will need 4 to 5 ounces (115 to 145 g) of trimmings to purée with the smoked salmon. The fillet should be 1 inch (2 1/2 cm) thick—if necessary, place it between two lightly oiled pieces of waxed paper (or aluminum foil), and, using the flat side of the cleaver (or the bottom of a small sauté pan), pound the salmon with light strokes until it reaches the desired thickness. Season fillet lightly with salt and pepper and reserve.

With the paring knife, cut the salmon trimmings and the smoked salmon into thin strips 1 to 1 1/2 inches (2 1/2 to 3 3/4 cm) long. Put pieces into the blender or food processor, season lightly with salt and pepper, add the egg white, half of the whipping cream, and the crushed ice. Purée until smooth, but no longer than absolutely necessary. Scrape purée into the smaller of the two chilled bowls with the rubber spatula and set over ice in the larger bowl. Beating with the wooden spoon, blend the remaining cream thoroughly into the purée and keep on ice (or refrigerated) for at least 10 minutes before continuing. The purée should be a smooth, lightly firm paste. If it is too thick, slowly add more whipping cream until the desired consistency is obtained.

With the rubber spatula, spread the salmon purée over the fillet, mounding it up slightly from both sides to the center. Reserve.

Preheat oven to 375F (190C) and adjust the rack to the middle position.

Roll out the puff pastry into a rectangle with a thickness of 1/8 inch (1/3 cm). Lift the pastry over the salmon fillet, centering it carefully, and fold both long sides completely under the fillet. Take each of the two corners at both ends and, with the paring knife, cut out a triangle of pastry (about 3 inches or 7 1/2 cm long on each side) so that you can make a smooth, neat fold under the fillet with the remaining dough. Pinch edges to make a tight seal. Lightly butter the baking sheet and set the fillet on it.

Mix the egg and 1 tablespoon of water with the whisk, blend well, and brush the egg wash over the pastry. Set the baking sheet into the oven and bake for 25 minutes. While the salmon is baking, prepare the beurre blanc and reserve. When done, the pastry should be a light golden brown color. Remove from oven and let rest in a warm (not hot) place for 5 to 10 minutes before slicing. While the salmon is resting, bring the sauce to serving temperature. Use the serrated knife to make even slices, set on warm serving plates, surround with sauce, and serve immediately.

You can prepare this early in the day because when wrapped with pastry, the salmon fillet can be refrigerated until you are ready to bake it. If you do this, add 5 minutes to the baking time. If you use Sauce Mousseline, prepare 1 recipe *(see page 92)*.

Variation: The following smoked fish can replace the smoked salmon: trout, whitefish, or tuna. Also, when using the smoked salmon, add a little chopped fresh dill to the purée.

Quenelles de Saumon

Quenelles—to the serious food lover the very word conjures up visions of delicate palpable clouds, earthly miniatures of the great white puff balls found in the clear blue skies of spring and autumn. Properly prepared and surrounded with Sauce Américaine, Sauce Nantua, or Lobster Butter and Cream Sauce, these quenelles are a sublime creation which rivals beluga caviar as a first course. Accompany this with your best Champagne. Need we say more?

Many people are unnecessarily skittish about poaching quenelles, but in truth it is more difficult to poach a dumpling than a quenelle. The trick is to make sure the mousseline is well set in the refrigerator before forming the quenelles and poaching them.

Yields 6 to 8 servings for about 30 quenelles

1 1/2 pounds (675 g) boned and skinned fresh salmon fillets
6 egg whites
1 whole egg
1 teaspoon salt
1/4 teaspoon freshly ground white pepper
2 cups (475 ml) Crème Fraîche (see page 66)
3 quarts (3 L) Fish Stock (see page 60)

Recommended equipment

A boning knife, blender, rubber spatula, 2-quart (2 L) mixing bowl, 4-quart (4 L) plat à sauter or 12-inch (30 cm) sauté pan, wooden spoon, slotted wooden spoon.

Bone and skin the salmon *(see page 568)*. Cut the fillets in several pieces and reserve in the refrigerator until needed. Put the egg whites, whole egg, salt and pepper in the blender and purée until the mixture thickens slightly. Add the salmon and continue blending until smooth, pausing briefly if necessary to scrape down the sides of the container with the spatula. Moving quickly, add the crème fraîche to the salmon mixture and blend until completely incorporated. (Do not overblend or you will have salmon butter!) Scrape into the mixing bowl, cover tightly with plastic wrap, and chill for several hours or until mixture is well set and thick in consistency.

While the mousseline is chilling, prepare your sauce to the holding point and reserve. When you begin cooking the quenelles, bring your sauce to serving temperature so that it is ready.

When you are ready to poach the quenelles, warm your serving dishes or plates or glass bowl to hold the first batch as the second poaches. In the plat à sauter or sauté pan, add fish stock to a depth of 1 1/2 inches (3 3/4 cm) and bring to a rapid simmer over medium high heat. Reduce heat to medium to maintain a steady simmer. Remove the mousseline from the refrigerator and, working quickly with the wooden spoons, take about 2 to 3 tablespoons of the salmon mousseline, form it into rough ball-like shapes, and gently lower it into the simmering stock. Continue until you have filled the pan with quenelles, being sure that each has room around it and the pan is not crowded. Since the mixture is cold when it drops into the stock it will slow down the simmer, which is what you want to happen so the quenelles will not fall apart. Keep your eye on the stock so that it simmers just enough to shimmer.

Depending on how well the simmer is maintained, quenelles this size should be ready to turn in 5 to 6 minutes. (Unlike beignets, they will not always turn themselves over, but when it is time to turn them, they will seem to start to turn over.) Very carefully press down on one side of a quenelle with the wooden spoon and it should roll over quite easily. (A stubborn one may require a deft motion with both spoons.) Continue cooking until quenelles are done. When finished, they will have become slightly enlarged and firm in texture. (If you are in doubt, you can always sneak one from the pan to check that it is cooked all the way through.)

When the quenelles are done, remove them carefully with the slotted spoon, drain, and either distribute them among the warmed serving dishes or place into the warmed bowl while you poach the remainder. As you ladle the sauce around the quenelles, be *very careful* not to pour sauce over them to ensure the most attractive presentation.

Because it does not have a panade as do the Quenelles de Sole, this mixture may occasionally be cantankerous and not thicken sufficiently. Never fear, help is only a mousse away. Preheat your oven to 350F (177C). Butter enough ramekins or little soufflé molds for each guest to have one. Fill the molds almost to the top with the mixture and set them into a baking pan. Pour boiling water into the pan about two-thirds of the way up the mold, cover with waxed paper, and bake for about 20 minutes. The mousses will rise and pull away from the sides of the molds ever so slightly. (To check their doneness use a cake tester or toothpick.) When done, invert over serving plates, unmold and garnish with fresh dill or tarragon, sauce, and serve.

We have called for fresh salmon in this recipe, but smoked salmon also makes a superb quenelle. Add some finely minced fresh tarragon when you prepare the salmon mousseline and a small amount of Pernod to the poaching liquid. In this case we would poach the quenelles in a mixture of fish stock and water. For a sauce we would first lightly sauté two minced shallots in butter, add them to 1 cup (235 ml) dry white wine and reduce by three-quarters over moderately high heat. Add this to 4 cups (950 ml) of Sauce Velouté de Poisson *(see page 68)* and simmer for 20 minutes. Just before serving, whisk in the juice of one-half lemon and about 4 ounces (115 g) of softened butter.

Coulibiac de Saumon à la Russe

To be precise, "coulibiac" refers to a nineteenth-century Russian fish pie, usually made with salmon. The filling for the original was thickened with sturgeon marrow (viziga), *and you may do that here if you wish (see page 214). The version we have given you, although a bit complicated, is more in keeping with current culinary practice and makes this venerable recipe more accessible to the home cook. Reserve it for a special luncheon or dinner, and while the dish is settling before slicing, make a Sauce Mousseline or be traditional and melt some butter to accompany it. The dough, crêpes, and filling can be prepared in advance, and final assembly and cooking requires about an hour. Any remnants are delicious chilled and served with a fresh green salad.*

Yields 8 servings as an entrée or 12 to 16 servings as a first course

- 1 1/2 pounds (675 g) Brioche dough *(see page 490)*
- 4 hard-boiled eggs, chilled and finely chopped
- 1 teaspoon chopped shallots
- 1 3/4 to 2 pounds (800 to 900 g) centercut salmon
- A dash of salt
- Freshly ground white pepper
- 3/8 cup (90 ml) dry white wine
- 4 Crêpes *(see page 520)*, about 8 inches (20 cm) in diameter
- 3 cups (710 ml) Rice Pilaff *(see page 424)*
- 1 1/2 cups (355 ml) Sauce Velouté de Poisson *(see page 68)*
- 1 cup (235 ml) finely chopped onions
- 1 cup (235 ml) finely diced celery
- 1 cup (235 ml) finely diced mushrooms
- 2 tablespoons (30 g) butter
- 1/2 bay leaf
- A pinch of freshly ground nutmeg
- Juice of 1/2 lemon
- 6 anise seeds
- 2 tablespoons chopped fresh parsley
- Butter for the baking dish, aluminum foil, and baking sheet
- 1 egg for glaze
- 1 recipe Sauce Mousseline *(see page 92)*

Recommended equipment

A 1 1/2-quart (1 1/2 L) saucepan; timer; glass, stainless steel, or ceramic baking dish (large enough to hold salmon in one layer); large chef's knife; aluminum foil or waxed paper; medium mixing bowl; 12-inch (30 cm) sauté pan; nutmeg grinder; wooden spatula; rolling pin; baking sheet; wire whisk; pastry brush.

First, prepare the brioche dough and set it aside to rise in a warm draft-free place. Next, using the saucepan, start the eggs cooking to become hard-boiled and set a timer for them so you can prepare the filling for the coulibiac.

Preheat oven to 350F (177C).

Butter the baking dish. Chop the shallots with the chef's knife and strew them over the bottom of the baking dish. With the chef's knife, cut the salmon into two fillets lengthwise along the backbone, and add them skin side down to the baking dish. Season with salt and pepper and pour the white wine around the salmon. Cover the dish loosely with buttered foil or waxed paper and set into the oven for 10 minutes. Remove from oven and let salmon cool, uncovered, in the dish. When cool, remove skin and bones from salmon and flake fish into the mixing bowl, reserving the cooking liquid.

Make the crêpes (do not add sugar to the batter) while the salmon cooks and cools.

Prepare the rice pilaff and the sauce velouté.

Using the chef's knife, finely chop the onions, celery, and mushrooms in separate batches. In the sauté pan over medium high heat, melt the butter and, when it sizzles, add the onions, celery, mushrooms, bay leaf, and nutmeg. Squeeze lemon juice over the mushrooms and when mixture simmers reduce heat to medium low to cook it gently for 5 minutes without browning. Stir occasionally with the wooden spatula. Then add the salmon cooking liquid, the rice pilaff, and the velouté. Simmer all together gently on low heat, while stirring, for 1 minute. Add hard-boiled eggs, anise, and adjust seasoning with salt and pepper. Stir for 30 seconds or so—the filling should have a moist, paste-like consistency. Remove from heat. Chop the parsley and stir it into the filling. Let mixture cool in the pan, covered loosely with waxed paper. Remove bay leaf.

When filling is at room temperature, you can form the coulibiac. Tear off a 20-inch (50 cm) long sheet of waxed paper and lay it on the work surface. Take two of the crêpes and place them side-by-side so that they overlap across the width of the waxed paper at the center of the sheet. Spread one-half of the filling 1 1/2 inches (3 3/4 cm) thick on the crêpes, leaving a 2-inch (5 cm) crêpe border with no filling on it. (You will have a strip of filling approximately 4 inches [10 cm] wide and 10 inches [25 cm] long.) Spread salmon flakes over filling and then make another layer with the remainder of the filling. Shape the top, sides, and ends by rounding off (as you would a meat loaf). Place two more crêpes on top, overlapping, and, using the waxed paper as a support, form a loaf, roll paper around it, and refrigerate for 30 minutes or longer. The preparation up to this point can be done earlier in the day.

About an hour and a half before you want to serve the coulibiac, roll out the brioche dough in a rectangular shape about 1/4 inch thick by 14 inches wide by 18 inches long (2/3 x 35 x 45 cm). Fit this on top of the salmon loaf, turn over, and wrap remaining dough around it. Trim dough edges if necessary, leaving enough to overlap, and pinch tightly to seal. Set seam side down on a buttered baking sheet and set aside at room temperature in a draft-free spot for 20 minutes.

Preheat oven to 350F (177C).

Thoroughly mix the egg with the whisk and brush this all over the pastry. Set on rack in middle level of the oven to bake for 40 to 45 minutes or until golden brown. Remove from oven and let rest for 15 minutes in a warm place before serving. While the salmon rests, prepare the sauce mousseline, spoon onto warm serving plates, and lay a salmon slice gently on the sauce.

For an authentic touch, prepare dried *viziga* (sturgeon spine) and add it to the filling while it cools in the pan. Soak 2 ounces (60 g) of dried *viziga* in cold water for 5 hours, cook in lightly salted water for 4 hours (or until it reaches a tapioca-like consistency), cool, chop coarsely, and add to filling.

 ## *Saumon Poché*
Poached Salmon

De rigueur for publicity photographs of buffets on cruise ships or at resorts, poached salmon is one of those dishes which seems unapproachable for home cooking. This is simply not true, but you must handle the fish carefully and watch the poaching liquid temperature closely so the salmon does not overcook. The flesh must come off the bone easily but not crumble. As you will discover, this is one preparation which is equally good hot or cold. Served hot, it can be accompanied by Sauce Hollandaise II, Sauce Mousseline, Beurre Blanc, or Beurre au Citron. When chilled and presented whole for a summer luncheon or light supper, a salmon clad with wafer-thin cucumber slices as mock scales and glazed with a transparent gelée made from the poaching liquid becomes a composition worthy of a still-life portrait. Accompany this with Mayonnaise or Green Herb Mayonnaise and an excellent Meursault or Chardonnay and you will have your guests talking about it for months.

Yields 8 to 10 servings

5 to 6 quarts (4 3/4 to 5 3/4 L) Court Bouillon (*see page 60*)
1 cleaned, fresh, whole salmon, weighing 7 to 9 pounds (3175 to 4100 g)
1/2 cup (118 ml) vinegar
1 cup (235 ml) dry white wine

Recommended equipment

A stainless steel or tin-lined fish poacher with removable rack, cheesecloth, white kitchen string, thermometer, paring knife.

Prepare the court bouillon.

Rinse the salmon under running cold water and, if it is too long for your fish poacher, cut off the head and reserve it to be cooked beside the tail. Cut four large pieces of cheesecloth, being sure that each one is 6 inches (15 cm) longer than the fish. Dampen the cheesecloth, spread it out on your work surface in four layers, center the fish on it, wrap the salmon up, and tie the ends of the cheesecloth tightly with string. Also, tie string loosely around the middle of the salmon to hold the cloth in place while poaching.

Set the poacher across two burners on the stove top, pour in the court bouillon, and add the vinegar and wine. Lay the salmon on the rack and lower it into the court bouillon (if you do not have a rack, use a thin piece of board, wrapped well with aluminum foil, that will fit into the poacher). The liquid must cover the salmon with a depth of 2 inches (5 cm); add water if necessary. Hang the thermometer in the poacher, being sure the bulb is in the liquid and not touching the poacher.

Bring the court bouillon *slowly* to a very low simmer, about 185F (85C); reaching this temperature at the proper speed should take 30 to 45 minutes. Poach the salmon, uncovered, for 45 minutes (for an 8-pound fish), maintaining the temperature at about 185F. The liquid never bubbles, just shimmers slightly to ensure gentle, slow cooking of the delicate flesh. Then lower heat so that the temperature falls slowly to 140F (60C) throughout another 45-minute period. (Add 5 minutes per additional pound to the timing of each period for larger fish and decrease by 5 minutes for smaller fish.)

The salmon is now cooked and can wait for up to half an hour in the liquid if it is to be served hot. If you are serving it chilled, remove poacher from heat and let salmon reach room temperature in the liquid before draining and refrigerating. In either case, lift salmon out when ready, drain, and set onto a platter or large pan. Cut the string, unfold the cheesecloth, and, with the paring knife, peel away the skin and scrape away the dark, top layer of salmon flesh. Turn the salmon over gently but firmly, aided by the unfolded cheesecloth, then remove cheesecloth, skin, and dark flesh. With the help of two long spatulas, lift salmon to serving platter, decorate as you wish, and serve.

Another way to poach a salmon is to remove the head and fillet the salmon lengthwise into two pieces. Then remove all bones, put the two fillets together again, and wrap with cheesecloth. Proceed as in the basic recipe but reduce the simmering time by 10 minutes. If you like, spread any of these fresh herbs—fennel, dill, tarragon, basil, or parsley—between the halves before wrapping with cheesecloth.

Chaud-Froid Mousse de Sole et Saumon "Tricolor"
Tricolor Cold Mousse of Sole and Salmon

This is one of those rare instances when the name means just what it says—"hot-cold." Originally referring to something which is cooked and then served chilled under a congealed sauce, the term is said to have originated in 1759 at the Château Montmorency. After having been summoned to the king's council from a large dinner party he was hosting, the maréchal de Luxembourg returned late in the evening and, famished, demanded only one dish—a chicken fricassée with its once warm sauce now solidified. Obviously pleased with it, he asked for it to be prepared again, and although the chef attempted to rename it refroidi, *the maréchal would not hear of it, so* chaud-froid *it was, and is today. This cream-, green-, and pink-banded mousse appeals to eye and palate alike, and you should serve it for a special luncheon or as a first course for an important dinner. Accompany it with Pressed Cucumber Salad combined with fresh dill and oil and vinegar or sour cream, and for a sauce, choose "Another" Cold Fish Sauce. Spoon it around each serving before garnishing the slices with sprigs of fresh dill.*

Yields 10 to 12 servings

FOR THE SOLE LAYER
10 ounces (285 g) boned and skinned sole fillets
1/2 teaspoon salt
1/4 teaspoon freshly ground white pepper
1/2 teaspoon Knorr Aromat
1 egg white
1 1/3 cups (315 ml) whipping cream
2 tablespoons finely crushed ice

FOR THE VEGETABLE LAYER
1/2 pound (225 g) spinach
1 tablespoon chopped shallots
3 tablespoons coarsely chopped fresh basil
1/4 bunch watercress
2 tablespoons coarsely chopped parsley
1 teaspoon butter
2 tablespoons dry white wine
A pinch of freshly ground nutmeg
1/2 cup (118 ml) sole mousse

FOR THE SALMON LAYER
6 ounces (170 g) boned and skinned salmon fillets
1/4 teaspoon salt
A pinch of cayenne pepper
1/8 teaspoon freshly ground white pepper
1/4 teaspoon Knorr Aromat
1 egg white
1 cup (235 ml) whipping cream
1 tablespoon finely crushed ice

Butter for the pan and the waxed paper
2 cups (475 ml) "Another" Cold Fish Sauce *(see page 98)*

Recommended equipment

A paring knife, blender or food processor, rubber spatula, 1-quart (1 L) bowl, small mixing bowl, wooden spatula, 4-quart (4 L) saucepan with lid, colander, large chef's knife, 12-inch (30 cm) sauté pan, nutmeg grinder, a 6- to 8-cup (1 1/2 to 2 L) loaf pan or terrine mold and a larger pan into which it will fit easily to form a bain-marie, waxed paper.

For the sole layer

Wash the sole fillets under cold running water, pat dry, and, with the paring knife, slice into pieces about 1 1/2 inches (3 3/4 cm) wide. Put the sole pieces into the blender or food processor and add salt, pepper, Aromat, egg white, and 1/3 cup (80 ml) whipping cream. Purée for 30 seconds, scrape down sides of container with rubber spatula, and add the crushed ice. Purée again while gradually adding another 1/3 cup of cream until the sole is perfectly smooth. Do not purée any longer than absolutely necessary or else you will risk forming little bits of butter in the mixture. Scrape purée into the 1-quart bowl and refrigerate for 30 minutes or until set. When chilled, set bowl with purée over ice in the small mixing bowl and, by using the wooden spatula, blend in the remaining cream 2 to 3 tablespoons at a time. Keep purée on ice in the refrigerator.

For the vegetable layer

While the sole layer is setting in the refrigerator, prepare the vegetable layer. Wash the spinach in several changes of cold water, drain, and break off stems. Bring salted water to boil in the saucepan and blanch the spinach for 30 seconds. Pour into colander, run cold water over the spinach, let drain, and, by small handfuls, squeeze all water out of the spinach. Reserve.

Using the large chef's knife, chop the shallots, basil, watercress, and parsley. In the sauté pan, melt the butter over medium low heat, add the shallots and sauté for 1 minute. Then add the wine, basil, watercress, and parsley, grind in the nutmeg, blend well with the wooden spatula, and simmer 1 minute or until the greens are just wilted. Remove from heat and let cool completely. When cool, put in blender or food processor, add the spinach, and purée until very fine. Scrape mixture into bowl and thoroughly blend in 1/2 cup (118 ml) of the chilled sole purée. Refrigerate until ready to use.

For the salmon layer

Follow the technique for the sole layer, using the salmon layer ingredients.

Baking the mousse

Preheat oven to 350F (177C).

Butter the pan or mold and, using the rubber spatula (dip it into cold water before you begin), spread the sole mixture evenly in the bottom. Be sure to wipe up any excess that may cling to the sides of the pan. Spread the vegetable mixture in an even layer over the sole, followed by the salmon.

Set the pan into the larger pan, pour boiling water into the larger pan to a level two-thirds of the way up the smaller pan, cover it loosely with buttered waxed paper, and set the bain-marie into the middle level of the oven to bake the mousse for about 40 minutes or until mixture has slightly pulled away from the sides of the pan.

When done, remove from oven, remove pan from the water, and let cool completely at room temperature before setting the mousse into the refrigerator. Prepare the sauce while the mousse is chilling. When ready to serve, unmold mousse and slice. Place slices on plates, surround them with the sauce, and serve at once.

It is most important to keep the mixtures icy cold before using and chilled while blending. If they become warm they will not bind properly and the mousse will be grainy. If you have a food grinder, it is advisable to grind the fish pieces separately before puréeing. Fish varies in quality and thickness and will act differently when absorbing cream so use the proposed amounts as a guide. What you want when working in the last bit of cream is a well-blended, pudding-soft mixture.

The mousse can be made a day ahead and will keep well refrigerated for two or three days.

Variation: Before adding salmon layer, press a few slices of cooked lobster, small, cooked shrimp, or fresh scallops into the vegetable mixture, either in a line down the center or in a pattern.

Sole and Friends

In these recipes, we have made the point of calling for Dover sole, and before you think of making a substitution, you should know that history has it that Vatel, the famous maître d'hôtel, is said to have committed suicide in 1671 when he found that his sole had not been shipped for an important dinner. This fish has served as the foundation for countless legendary culinary creations, in part because of its delicate texture and flavor, and in part because of its shape, which is longer and deeper than flounder. True sole is flown in fresh or frozen from France or England and is available at good fish markets. If you cannot find imported sole, flounder fillets or lemon sole will approximate (but never duplicate) it in these recipes.

Fillets of Sole Amanda

Larousse Gastronomique lists eighty separate recipes calling for fillet of sole (not including timbales), which says two things—it is an extraordinarily versatile fish and I should not be shy about adding another. I devised this combination and named it for my daughter when she was at an age when fish is an "iffy" thing for children. Easily prepared, it is an excellent recipe when time is short, but you must use only the freshest vegetables sautéed à la minute for it to be a success. Serve with Rice Pilaff or potatoes boiled in their jackets.

Yields 6 servings

1/2 teaspoon Pesto *(see page 418)*
1 leek (white and light green
6 mushrooms
1 large (or 2 small) zucchini
4 ripe olives
1 medium red bell pepper
2 tomatoes (blanched, peeled, and seeded; *see page 568*)
1 tablespoon finely cut fresh chives
1 tablespoon finely chopped shallots
2 1/4 pounds (1025 g) boned and skinned fillets of Dover sole (6 ounces or 170 g each)
Salt
Freshly ground white pepper
1 cup (235 ml) dry white wine
Juice of 1 lemon
3/8 cup (90 ml) dry white French vermouth
2 1/2 cups (590 ml) whipping cream
4 saffron threads, chopped
1 tablespoon olive oil
Butter for the baking dish and the waxed paper

Recommended equipment

A paring knife, small chef's knife, enameled cast-iron baking dish or lined copper plat à sauter, waxed paper or aluminum foil, 1 1/2-quart (1 1/2 L) saucepan, 12-inch (30 cm) sauté pan, heatproof serving platter.

Prepare the pesto.

Prepare the vegetables and set aside until needed. Wash the leek thoroughly under running cold water, slice in half lengthwise with the paring knife, and then cut into thin 1 1/2-inch (3 3/4 cm) long strips. Brush the mushrooms of any clinging dirt and slice each one into 1/2-inch (1 1/4 cm) thick slices. Wash the zucchini and cut into strips 1 1/2 inches long and 1/4 inch (2/3 cm) thick. Pit the olives if necessary and cut into strips. Rinse the pepper, slice in half, remove seeds, and cut into strips 1 1/2 inches long. Prepare the tomatoes and cut into strips 1 1/2 inches long. Slice the chives into fine pieces. Mince the shallots with the chef's knife.

Preheat oven to 325F (163C).

Rinse the fillets of sole gently under cold water and pat dry. Spread the butter thoroughly inside the baking dish, strew the shallots on the bottom, and lay the fish into the dish. Season lightly with salt and pepper. If the fillets are not all centercuts, fold the thin ends underneath for an even thickness. Pour 1/2 cup (118 ml) of the wine around the fish and add the lemon juice. Cover the dish loosely with buttered waxed paper (or buttered foil) and set over medium heat to bring liquids to a low simmer. When simmering, put the dish into the middle level of the preheated oven and bake for 6 to 8 minutes (depending upon thickness of fish). Fish are done when they spring back from a light touch with your finger.

Remove fillets to the warm serving platter and pour off all liquid into the saucepan. Add the remaining 1/2 cup of wine and the vermouth and reduce over medium high heat to 1/3 cup (80 ml). Add the cream and saffron and reduce to about 1 3/4 cups (415 ml) or until liquid is a light creamy consistency. Set aside to keep warm.

Heat the olive oil in the sauté pan and add the leeks, mushrooms, zucchini, olives, bell pepper, and pesto, and sauté, stirring occasionally, over medium to high heat for 3 minutes. Add the tomatoes and chives, sauté for 30 seconds, and spread vegetables over the sole fillets. Return to oven for 30 seconds, remove, pour on the cream sauce, and serve.

Quenelles de Sole

The Quenelles de Saumon are made from a mousseline and therefore are just a bit trickier than these quenelles. Preparing a panade for this mixture is a more traditional and very safe method. When served hot, accompany them with Beurre Blanc, Sauce Nantua, or Sauce Amoureuse. Cold, they are excellent served with a Curry or Green Herb Mayonnaise.

Yields 6 to 8 servings

FOR THE PANADE
1/2 cup (118 ml) milk
3 tablespoons (45 g) butter
1/2 teaspoon salt
Freshly ground white pepper
A pinch of nutmeg
1/2 cup (60 g) flour
2 egg yolks

FOR THE MOUSSE
1 pound (450 g) boned and skinned sole fillets
Salt
Freshly ground white pepper
1 1/2 cups (355 ml) whipping cream
1 tablespoon crushed ice
2 eggs
2 egg whites

Peanut oil for the waxed paper
1 quart (1 L) Fish Stock (see page 60)

Recommended equipment

A 1 1/2-quart (1 1/2 L) saucepan, wire whisk, wooden spatula, paring knife, food grinder with fine blade, blender, rubber spatula, 2-quart (2 L) bowl, soupspoon, waxed paper, 4-quart (4 L) plat à sauter or 12-inch (30 cm) sauté pan, slotted spoon.

Prepare the panade first. Put the milk, butter, salt, pepper, and nutmeg in the saucepan and set the pan over medium high heat. Stir occasionally with the whisk while bringing the mixture to a low boil. When the mixture is boiling and the butter has melted, add the flour all at once, remove pan partially from heat, and, using the wooden spatula, blend the mixture thoroughly until it comes away from the sides of the saucepan and pulls together. This should take about 3 to 4 minutes. Remove pan completely from heat, let mixture cool for 1 minute, add 1 egg yolk, and blend until thoroughly absorbed. Then add the second yolk, blend until smooth, and set saucepan aside so that mixture can cool.

Now prepare the mousse. Rinse the sole fillets gently under running cold water, drain, and cut into small pieces with the paring knife. Put the pieces through the food grinder twice, using the fine blade. Chill the mixture for 15 minutes. Then put the ground sole into the blender container, season with salt and pepper, add 2/3 cup (160 ml) whipping cream, and purée on high speed until mixture thickens. Scrape down the sides of the container with the rubber spatula, add the remaining cream and the crushed ice, and blend until smooth. The blending must be done as quickly as possible and all the ingredients must be very cold or else they will not bind properly. Scrape the sole mixture into the bowl and refrigerate until the panade is cool.

When the panade is cool, beat the whole eggs and egg whites together thoroughly and reserve. Remove the sole mixture from the refrigerator and combine it with the panade by either blending thoroughly with a spatula or using a hand-held mixer. Then add one-half of the beaten eggs, blend until smooth, add the remaining eggs, blend again until smooth, and refrigerate the mousse mixture, covered with plastic wrap, until you are ready to form and cook the quenelles.

While the mousse is chilling, prepare your sauce to the holding point and reserve. When you begin cooking the quenelles, bring your sauce to serving temperature.

When you are ready, lightly oil a long sheet of waxed paper, remove the mousse from the refrigerator, and, with the help of a soupspoon dipped in warm water, make oval shapes in your palm. As they are made, set them on the waxed paper until you have used up all the mixture.

When you are ready to poach the quenelles, warm your serving dishes or plates or glass bowl to hold the first batch as the second poaches. In the plat à sauter or sauté pan, add the fish stock and enough water to bring the depth of poaching liquid to 1 1/2 inches (3 3/4 cm), and bring to a boil over high heat. Reduce heat immediately to medium to maintain a rapid simmer. Gently lower the ovals into the simmering liquid, being careful not to crowd the pan so that each quenelle has room around it. Because the mixture is cold when it drops into the liquid the simmer will slow down which is what you want to happen so the quenelles will not fall apart. Keep watching the liquid and adjusting the heat as necessary so that it simmers just enough to shimmer.

Depending on how well the simmer is maintained, quenelles this size should be ready to turn in 5 to 6 minutes. At this point, they will seem to start to turn over. Very carefully press down on one side of a quenelle with the wooden spoon and it should roll over quite easily. Continue cooking until they are done. When finished, the quenelles will have become slightly enlarged and firm in texture.

When the quenelles are done, remove them carefully with the slotted spoon, drain, and either distribute them among the warmed serving dishes or place into the warmed bowl while you poach the remainder. When you sauce the quenelles, be very careful to pour sauce around them, *not over* them, for the most appealing presentation.

❧

To serve the quenelles cold, poach them as directed but let them cool in the poaching liquid, then drain, cover tightly with plastic wrap, and refrigerate until serving time. If you like, substitute striped bass, sea bass, or pike for the sole.

Soufflé de Sole Lucernoise

Lucerne is an extraordinary place. The stunning panorama of the Voralps and magnificent Lake of the Four Cantons forms a dramatic backdrop for the cuisine of its internationally renowned hotels—the Schweizerhof, the Palace, and the National, scene of one of the collaborations between César Ritz and Auguste Escoffier. Besides, it is my hometown. I devised this soufflé when I was at the Ambassador Hotel in New York, and, as one is wont to do when a creation turns out well, I named it in honor of my culinary heritage.

Yields 6 servings

1 recipe Mousse de Sole *(see pages 219–20)*
2 cups (475 ml) Sauce Velouté de Poisson *(see page 68)*
12 boned and skinned fillets of sole, weighing 4 to 5 ounces (115 to 145 g) each
2 tablespoons minced shallots
1 tablespoon melted butter
Salt
Freshly ground white pepper
1/2 cup (118 ml) dry white wine
1 cup (235 ml) whipping cream
12 fresh mushrooms
Grated rind of 1/2 lemon (all bitter white removed)
1 tablespoon chopped fresh parsley
1 tablespoon finely cut chives
3 tablespoons grated Parmesan cheese
1 tablespoon (15 g) butter
2 egg yolks
Butter for the baking dish and the waxed paper

Recommended equipment

A large chef's knife, enameled cast-iron baking dish or lined copper plat à sauter, small saucepan, paring knife, pastry brush, waxed paper, 3-quart (3 L) saucepan, box grater, 12-inch (30 cm) sauté pan, wooden spatula, wire whisk, small bowl, electric mixer, rubber spatula, turning spatula, heat-proof serving platter.

Prepare the mousse de sole and reserve.

Prepare the sauce velouté de poisson and reserve.

Rinse the fillets gently under cold running water, pat dry, and reserve.

Preheat oven to 375F (190C).

Using the chef's knife, mince the shallots. Butter the baking dish or plat à sauter, strew 1 tablespoon shallots over the bottom (reserve the rest), and lay six fillets into it in a single layer so that they are not touching each other. Use the thicker centercut fillets for this bottom layer.

Put 1 tablespoon butter into the small saucepan to melt over low heat.

Spread 3 tablespoons of the mousse de sole on each fillet in the dish, forming a line down the center. Using the paring knife, cut an incision all the way through in each of the remaining fillets, starting in the center 1 1/2 inches (3 3/4 cm) from one end and ending 1 1/2 inches from the other end. This cut will be the "pocket." One by one, place a fillet with a pocket over a fillet in the baking dish, being sure to expose some of the mousse through the pocket. Season the top fillet lightly with salt and pepper and brush the melted butter over it with the pastry brush. Pour the wine around the fillets, cover loosely with buttered waxed paper, and set the baking dish over medium heat until the simmering point is reached. Then set dish into the middle level of the oven and bake for 15 minutes or until fillets spring back to a light touch.

Remove dish from oven, remove waxed paper, and pour off the cooking liquids into the saucepan. Add 1/2 cup (118 ml) whipping cream to the saucepan and set over medium high heat to reduce liquid by one-third. Set the fillets, loosely covered, to rest in a warm (not hot) spot until you are ready to assemble the dish.

While the cooking liquids are reducing, clean the mushrooms of any clinging dirt and cut into 1/4-inch (2/3 cm) thick slices. Using the fine side of the box grater, grate the lemon rind and reserve.

221

Chop the parsley, cut the chives, grate the Parmesan, and reserve all.

When the cooking liquids are reduced, set saucepan aside off heat.

In the sauté pan, combine the 1 tablespoon butter, remaining shallots, the mushrooms, and the lemon rind, and sauté over medium heat for 3 minutes, stirring from time to time with the wooden spatula. Then add the reduced cooking liquids and sauce velouté de poisson and simmer over medium heat for 3 minutes, stirring occasionally.

Using the whisk, blend the egg yolks with 1 tablespoon whipping cream and then whisk yolks into the sauce in the sauté pan (remove pan partially from heat before adding yolks). Whisk for 30 seconds without letting sauce simmer, remove pan from heat, and continue to mix with whisk for another 30 seconds.

When ready to finish the dish, preheat the broiler to hot. Whip remaining cream in the electric mixer until stiff, fold into sauce in the sauté pan with rubber spatula, and add parsley and chives to the sauce. Transfer the sole fillets with the turning spatula to the heatproof platter, spoon the sauce over them, sprinkle Parmesan over all, set platter 6 inches (15 cm) from broiler element, and cook until the sauce is golden brown. Serve at once.

❧ Paupiettes of Sole Florentine with Tomato Butter Sauce

The technique for this recipe and the one following derives from two classic preparations—ballottine and galantine. *The former is, strictly speaking, thinly sliced poultry, meat, or fish which is rolled, cooked, and served hot or cold. The latter calls for the slices to be rolled around a stuffing bound with a sauce, or* salpicon, *cooked, and served cold, usually in aspic. While such preparations (like our Galantine of Capon) are large enough to serve several people, paupiettes are generally individual portions. When these paupiettes are sliced, the spinach filling contrasts with the Tomato Butter Sauce to make an attractive and delicious entrée. Accompany them with boiled Pommes de Terre Parisienne. Any leftover servings can be chilled and served with a green salad for a light lunch.*

Yields 6 servings

1 1/2 cups (355 ml) Tomato Butter Sauce *(see page 89)*

FOR THE MOUSSE
1 1/2 pounds (675 g) fresh spinach
4 tablespoons minced shallots
1/2 small garlic clove
2 tablespoons grated Parmesan cheese
3 tablespoons (45 g) butter
1 1/2 teaspoons water
Salt
Freshly ground white pepper
Freshly ground nutmeg
6 ounces (170 g) Dover sole scraps and trimmings
1 egg white
1/3 cup (80 ml) whipping cream
2 crushed ice cubes

FOR THE FILLETS
1 1/2 pounds (675 g) Dover sole fillets, boned and skinned (about 4 ounces or 115 g each)
Oil for the waxed paper
1/2 cup (118 ml) dry white wine
Fresh parsley sprigs, dill, or tarragon

Recommended equipment

A colander, large chef's knife, box grater, 12-inch (30 cm) sauté pan, wooden spatula, blender, cleaver, waxed paper or aluminum foil, rubber spatula, nutmeg grinder, enameled cast-iron baking dish or lined copper plat à sauter, 1 1/2-quart (1 1/2 L) saucepan, fine-mesh sieve.

Prepare the tomato butter sauce and set aside in its saucepan until needed.

Prepare the mousse. Wash the spinach thoroughly in several changes of cold water, drain in the colander, remove any tough stems, and chop coarsely with the chef's knife. Mince the shallots and mince the 1/2 garlic clove (or put it through a garlic press).

Grate the Parmesan cheese on the fine side of the box grater and reserve.

Melt the butter in the sauté pan over low heat, add 2 tablespoons of minced shallots, stir with the wooden spatula for 1 minute, and add minced or pressed garlic. Sauté for 30 seconds without coloring. Then add chopped spinach and 1 1/2 teaspoons of water, season with salt, pepper, and nutmeg, and simmer over medium heat until spinach is well wilted but not overcooked (2 to 3 minutes). Set pan aside to cool to room temperature.

Gently rinse the sole scraps and trimmings in cold water, drain, and pat dry. Cut into 1- to 2-inch (2 1/2 to 5 cm) long pieces. Put them into the blender jar with the egg white, whipping cream, and crushed ice. Purée until very smooth (but no longer than absolutely necessary); the ice prevents the mousse from becoming too warm while blending. Refrigerate for at least 15 minutes before adding the cooled spinach mixture, then stir all together, add the reserved Parmesan, mix well, and return to refrigerator.

Preheat oven to 325F (163C).

Rinse the fillets gently under running cold water, drain, and pat dry. Lightly oil two pieces of waxed paper large enough to enclose the fillets in one layer. Using the flat side of the cleaver (or a sauté pan), flatten the fillets one by one with light but firm strokes until they are 1/4 inch (2/3 cm) thick. Remove top piece of paper and season fillets lightly with salt and pepper. Using the rubber spatula, spread about 3 tablespoons of the spinach mousse evenly on each fillet and carefully roll up, making six paupiettes.

Butter the baking dish or plat à sauter and add the paupiettes. Sprinkle with remaining shallots and add the white wine. Cover loosely with buttered aluminum foil or waxed paper and set over medium heat until the wine simmers. Put into the oven and bake for 12 minutes.

Start warming the tomato butter sauce on low heat.

When paupiettes are done, drain off liquid into the saucepan and simmer over medium heat until reduced to 3 tablespoons (45 ml). Let paupiettes set, partially covered, for 5 to 10 minutes in a warm (not hot) place. (They will slice more easily after this rest.) When liquid is reduced, strain it through the sieve into the tomato butter sauce and mix together. Slice each paupiette into three to four pieces, divide sauce among warm plates or spread on a serving dish, arrange slices on the sauce, garnish with sprigs of fresh parsley, dill, or tarragon, and serve at once.

Paupiettes de Sole Tout-Paris

"Paris" in the title usually means a more elaborate treatment, and this recipe is no exception. Two techniques are combined here—the twin luxuries of Sauce Nantua and a Parisian-style finish with Sauce Vin Blanc, truffles, and shrimp.

However, it is not an overbearing presentation. Dress it up or down with Rice Pilaff or boiled Pommes de Terre Parisienne, whip up a green salad, and—who is that waiting at the table for two next door at the Café de la Paix?

Yields 6 servings

3/4 cup (180 ml) Sauce Nantua (*see page 70*)
3/4 cup (180 ml) Sauce Vin Blanc de Poisson (*see page 68*)
6 boned and skinned sole fillets, weighing 6 ounces (170 g) each
Peanut oil
1 egg white
2/3 cup (160 ml) whipping cream
Salt
Freshly ground white pepper
2 crushed ice cubes
2 tablespoons chopped shallots
1/2 cup (118 ml) dry white wine
6 thin slices black truffle
6 peeled, deveined, cooked small shrimp
Sprigs of fresh parsley or dill
Butter for the baking dish and the foil

Recommended equipment

A paring knife, waxed paper, cleaver, blender, rubber spatula, enameled cast-iron baking dish or lined copper plat à sauter, aluminum foil, 2-quart (2 L) saucepan, fine-mesh sieve.

Prepare the sauce Nantua and the sauce vin blanc de poisson, and be sure to have the cooked shrimp on hand for the garnish.

Rinse the fillets under cold running water, pat dry, and, using the paring knife, trim 2 ounces (60 g) off of each fillet to shape them evenly. Reserve the trimmings in the refrigerator. Lightly oil two sheets of waxed paper, place a fillet between them, and, with light but firm strokes, flatten it with the cleaver until the fillet is about 1/4 inch (2/3 cm) thick. Flatten each fillet and then refrigerate, covered with the waxed paper, until ready to use.

Make the mousse for the paupiette filling with the reserved trimmings. The ingredients must be chilled thoroughly before you begin. Cut the trimmings into pieces 1 to 2 inches (2 1/2 to 5 cm) long, put into blender container, and add the egg white, 1/3 cup (80 ml) whipping cream, salt, pepper, and crushed ice. Blend on high for 15 seconds and then add remaining cream. Blend again until the mixture is a smooth paste but *no longer than necessary*. Turn into a bowl and refrigerate until ready to use.

Preheat oven to 325F (163C) and butter the baking dish or plat à sauter. Chop the shallots.

Remove fillets from refrigerator, peel away the top piece of waxed paper, season lightly with salt and pepper, and divide the mousse among the fillets. Using the spatula, spread the mousse evenly over each fillet and then roll each up into a paupiette (roll) beginning with the narrower end. (It may be helpful to use the bottom piece of waxed paper for support as you roll up the fillet.) Set the paupiettes into the buttered baking dish, strew with the chopped shallots, pour the wine around, and cover loosely with buttered foil or waxed paper. Set the dish over medium heat, bring to a simmer, and then put into the oven to bake for 12 minutes or until the flesh springs back when lightly touched.

While the paupiettes bake, start warming the sauce Nantua and sauce vin blanc de poisson very gently on the lowest heat possible, and stir from time to time.

When the paupiettes are done, remove from oven, drain off the liquid into the saucepan, and set them aside (in their dish) in a warm (not hot) spot, loosely covered, while you finish the sauce. Simmer the liquid over medium high heat until reduced to about 2 tablespoons (30 ml). Then pass the liquid through the sieve into the sauce vin blanc.

As soon as the sauces are ready, set out the warm serving plates, slice each paupiette in half, and set two halves on each plate. Cover one half with sauce Nantua and the other with sauce vin blanc. Place a slice of truffle on the halves with sauce vin blanc and a shrimp on the halves with sauce Nantua.

Garnish the plates, if you wish, with sprigs of fresh parsley or dill, and serve immediately.

Variations: A few threads of saffron can be added to the sauce vin blanc. The sauce Nantua can be replaced with Sauce Américaine *(see page 71)*.

❧ *Baked Fillets of Flounder Homestead*

We do not want to tread on any toes, but it seems that the phrase "flounder stuffed with crabmeat" is synonymous with deep-fried fish stuffed with something that, except for the mandatory piece or two of crab, could just as easily be used for a Thanksgiving turkey. We have offered you a way to set all this straight. The technique is simple, the flavors are direct, and sauced with Nantua, these alternative fillets will so impress you that on your next beach trip you will drive right by the local "grease emporium," preferring instead to go to the fishmongers to pick up the flounder to fix your own. Serve with a steamed or boiled potato and a colorful mixed green combination salad or, if you must have french fries and coleslaw because it's the beach, we will look the other way.

Yields 6 servings

1 1/2 cups (355 ml) Sauce Nantua *(see page 70)*
12 boned and skinned flounder fillets, weighing 4 to 5 ounces (115 to 145 g) each
3/4 cup (180 ml) melted butter
1/2 pound (225 g) lump crabmeat
3/4 cup (180 ml) Homestead Seafood Sauce *(see page 98)*
A dash of cayenne pepper
1/4 teaspoon Old Bay seafood seasoning
2 tablespoons finely cut fresh chives
Salt
Freshly ground white pepper
1/3 cup (80 ml) fine white bread crumbs
1/4 teaspoon Hungarian paprika
2 tablespoons grated Parmesan cheese
Sprigs of fresh parsley or dill
Butter for the baking dish

Recommended equipment

A large baking dish, small saucepan, mixing fork, 1-quart (1 L) bowl, paring knife, small mixing bowl, box grater, pastry brush.

Prepare the sauce Nantua and reserve.

Rinse the fillets gently under cold running water, pat dry, and reserve. (If the fillets are thick, flatten them lightly with a cleaver between two pieces of waxed paper.)

Preheat oven to 375F (190C).

Butter the baking dish and lay six fillets into it in a single layer. Use the thicker centercut fillets for this bottom layer.

Set the butter into the small saucepan to melt over low heat.

Carefully pick over the crabmeat with your fingers to remove any pieces of shell. With the mixing fork, blend the crabmeat with the seafood sauce, cayenne, Old Bay seasoning, and chives in the mixing bowl. Do not break up the crabmeat lumps. Spread 1/4 cup (60 ml) of the mixture on each fillet, forming a line down the center.

Using the paring knife, cut an incision all the way through each of the remaining fillets in the center starting 1 1/2 inches (3 3/4 cm) from one end and ending 1 1/2 inches from the other end. This cut will be the "pocket." One by one, place a fillet with a pocket over a fillet in the baking dish, being sure to expose some of the crabmeat stuffing through the pocket. Season the top fillet lightly with salt and pepper.

In the small bowl, mix the bread crumbs, paprika, and Parmesan. Divide this mixture among the flounder fillets, covering the exposed crabmeat and as much of the top fillet as possible. Moisten the bread crumbs with drops of melted butter and, with the pastry brush, cover the remaining exposed fillet with butter.

Set the baking dish into the middle level of the oven to bake for 15 minutes. (Remember to add 3 minutes to the cooking time if fillets were refrigerated.) While the fillets bake, start warming the sauce Nantua very gently on the lowest possible heat, stirring from time to time. When fillets are done, remove from oven, and spoon about 3 tablespoons (45 ml) of sauce Nantua onto each warmed serving plate. Set a fillet on the sauce on each plate, garnish with sprigs of fresh parsley or dill, and serve at once.

If you stuff the fillets ahead of time, refrigerate them, covered with plastic wrap, until you are ready to bake them and then add 3 minutes to the cooking time.

Suprêmes of Halibut with Sauce Doria

As Jane Grigson notes, "Doria" means cucumbers and fish. This recipe carries the usual technique a bit further by adding a tart, creamy tarragon sauce to the lightly sautéed cucumbers. All in all, it is a fitting way to highlight halibut, which deserves more attention than it receives.

Yields 6 servings

1 cup (235 ml) Sauce Velouté de Poisson (see page 68)
6 boned and skinned halibut fillets, weighing 5 to 5 1/2 ounces (145 to 160 g) each
1 1/2 tablespoons minced shallots
Salt
Freshly ground white pepper
1 cup (235 ml) dry white wine
1/4 cup (60 ml) tarragon vinegar
1 teaspoon freshly crushed black pepper
3 sprigs fresh tarragon
1 tablespoon chopped fresh parsley
1 medium to large cucumber
1/2 cup (118 ml) whipping cream
1 1/2 teaspoons (7 g) butter
Butter for the baking dish and the waxed paper or foil

Recommended equipment

A small chef's knife, enameled cast-iron baking dish or lined copper plat à sauter, waxed paper or aluminum foil, 3-quart (3 L) saucepan, mortar and pestle, fine-mesh sieve, swivel-bladed vegetable peeler, 10-inch (25 cm) sauté pan, wooden spatula.

Prepare the sauce velouté de poisson and reserve.

Rinse the halibut fillets gently under cold running water, pat dry, and reserve.

Preheat oven to 325F (163C).

With the chef's knife, mince the shallots. Butter the baking dish or plat à sauter, strew 1 tablespoon of the shallots (reserve the rest) in the bottom, place the fillets on top, season them lightly with salt and pepper, and pour 1/2 cup (118 ml) of wine around them. Cover the dish loosely with buttered waxed paper (or foil) and set over medium heat until a low simmer is reached. Put into the middle level of the oven and cook until the fillets are springy to the touch (7 to 10 minutes).

When the fillets are done, keep them warm, covered loosely with the paper, while you prepare the sauce. Pour the cooking liquids into the saucepan, add the remaining wine and shallots, the vinegar, and crushed black pepper. Rinse the tarragon gently under cold water, pat dry, and pick the leaves off the stems. Chop the leaves and reserve at least 1 teaspoon for the sauce and the rest for garnishing the plates. Add the stems to the saucepan, bring to a rapid simmer over medium heat, and cook for about 15 minutes or until reduced to about 1/4 cup (60 ml).

While the sauce is reducing, wash the parsley, pat dry, chop, and reserve. Peel the cucumber, slice in half lengthwise, remove the seeds, and cut into pieces 1 1/2 to 2 inches (3 3/4 to 5 cm) long and 1/2 inch (1 1/4 cm) wide. Set aside.

When the sauce has been reduced, add the velouté de poisson, simmer for 5 minutes over low heat, add the cream, and simmer another 5 minutes or until the sauce is a creamy consistency. If it is too thick, add a little white wine and cream. Using the sieve, strain the sauce into a clean saucepan, adjust seasoning if necessary, add the chopped parsley and 1 teaspoon tarragon leaves, and set aside in a warm place. Dot the top with butter bits to prevent the formation of a skin layer.

In the sauté pan, melt 1 1/2 teaspoons butter over medium heat, add 1 1/2 teaspoons water and the cucumber pieces, season lightly with salt and pepper, and simmer, stirring occasionally, for 4 to 5 minutes until barely soft (it must not be mushy).

When everything is ready, set fillets on warm plates, arrange cucumbers on top, spoon sauce over all, garnish with reserved tarragon leaves, and serve at once.

Whenever you have excess fresh tarragon from a recipe, or winter is approaching with tarragon still in the garden, pick the leaves carefully off the stems, wash, dry well on paper towels, and add to bottled white wine vinegar. This makes an excellent vinegar for cooking and salad dressings, and the method works equally well for basil, chervil, and oregano.

Suprêmes of English Turbot with Beurre Blanc and Red Pepper Butter Sauce

Although we have ended "sole and friends" with turbot, this is not meant to imply that it is inferior to sole. In fact, many would argue to the contrary. Be that as it may, this fish is significant enough to have a lidded poacher, the turbotière, named after it and shaped like it. For this recipe, be sure to get the European turbot and not the Pacific version, which is a much lesser flounder. Pay careful attention to saucing the plates so that the contrasting colors show on either side of the fillet.

Yields 6 servings

1 cup (235 ml) Beurre Blanc (*see page 84*)
1 cup (235 ml) Red Pepper Butter Sauce (*see page 94*)
24 pieces Pommes de Terre Parisienne (*see page 442*)
6 boned and skinned turbot fillets, weighing 5 to 6 ounces (145 to 170 g) each
Salt
1 tablespoon (15 g) butter
Freshly ground white pepper
1 tablespoon chopped shallots
1 cup (235 ml) dry white wine
Juice of 1 lemon
1 tablespoon freshly snipped chives
6 sprigs fresh dill or parsley
Butter for the baking dish and waxed paper or foil

Recommended equipment

An enameled cast-iron baking dish or lined copper plat à sauter, 3-quart (3 L) saucepan, small chef's knife, waxed paper or aluminum foil, ladle.

Prepare the beurre blanc and red pepper butter sauce and reserve.

Peel and trim the potatoes for pommes de terre Parisienne and set aside covered with cold water until it is time to boil them.

Rinse the turbot fillets gently under cold running water, pat dry, and reserve. Spread the butter thoroughly inside the baking dish.

Preheat oven to 325F (163C).

Fill the saucepan two-thirds full of water, add a little salt, set over high heat, bring to a boil, and add the potatoes. Cook until the point of a knife thrust into a potato meets little resistance (about 8 to 10 minutes). Drain, add 1 tablespoon butter to the saucepan, roll the potatoes around in it, and keep warm partially covered. Just before serving sprinkle with the chives.

While the potatoes are cooking, chop the shallots with the chef's knife, strew them in the baking dish or plat à sauter, and set the turbot fillets on top. Season the fillets with salt and pepper, pour the wine around them, add the lemon juice, and cover with the buttered waxed paper (or foil). Over medium heat bring the fillets to a low simmer and then put into the middle level of the oven to cook until the fish is springy to the touch (8 to 10 minutes). Remove from oven and set aside partially covered until ready to serve.

When ready to serve, divide the red pepper sauce and the beurre blanc among warm serving plates so that each sauce covers one-half of the plate. Place the fillets carefully in the center of the plates, garnish with fresh dill sprigs (or parsley), arrange the potatoes with their chive snips around the fillets, and serve immediately.

Variation: Try pairing Tomato Butter Sauce *(see page 89)* with either Basil Butter Sauce *(see page 87)* or Beurre Blanc enlivened with a little minced tarragon.

Pompano

Baked Fillets of Pompano with Balsamic Vinegar Butter Sauce

Surely among the most sought-after fish on the East Coast, the pompano is one of the most unusual, as A. J. McClane notes: "The silvery slab-sided pompano is one of the spookiest fish in the ocean. It's not uncommon to see a pompano 'walk' across the water in a semicircular course around a running boat, and the fish may even pancake on the surface in the way children throw a flat stone to watch it skip. When approached by a boat in shallow water a pompano can streak through the air like a rocket and on several occasions I've had pompano jump aboard—an unearned but welcome dividend."

We have given you a little bit of a dividend here as well. Pompano really is without peer and the Balsamic Vinegar Butter Sauce we devised seems to point up its unique flavor especially well.

Yields 6 servings

6 boned and skinned pompano fillets, weighing 6 ounces (170 g) each
1 tablespoon minced shallots
Salt
1/4 cup (60 ml) dry white wine
1/3 cup (80 ml) balsamic vinegar
1 teaspoon crushed black pepper
1/2 cup (118 ml) whipping cream
6 tablespoons (90 g) butter, softened at room temperature
Butter for the baking dish and the waxed paper
Fresh dill or parsley sprigs

Recommended equipment

Enameled cast-iron baking dish or lined copper plat à sauter, large chef's knife, waxed paper, two 1 1/2-quart (1 1/2 L) saucepans, mortar and pestle, wire whisk, fine-mesh sieve, 1-quart (1 L) mixing bowl.

Rinse the fillets gently under cold running water, pat dry, and reserve.

Thoroughly butter the baking dish or plat à sauter. Using the chef's knife, mince the shallots and strew one-third of them over the bottom of the dish. Lay the fillets into the dish, season lightly with salt, pour the wine around the fillets, and cover them loosely with buttered waxed paper. Set aside.

Preheat oven to 325F (163C).

In one of the saucepans, combine the vinegar, the remaining shallots, and the crushed pepper and simmer over medium heat until reduced to 2 tablespoons (30 ml). Remove from heat and reserve. In the other saucepan simmer the cream over low heat until reduced to one-third the original volume (2 2/3 tablespoons or 40 ml), remove from heat, and reserve.

Set the baking dish over medium heat and bring to a simmer. Then put it on a rack in the middle of the oven and cook the fillets for 5 minutes. Remove from oven and drain one-half the liquid into the saucepan with the reduced cream. Set baking dish aside, loosely covered, in a warm (not hot) place and reserve.

Using the whisk, whip the softened butter 2 tablespoons at a time into the vinegar reduction, blending well until all butter is absorbed. Add cream mixture, combining completely, and strain through the sieve into the mixing bowl. Set the bowl over, not in, hot water to keep sauce warm for a short time (or use a double boiler).

When all is ready, divide the sauce among warmed plates, place a fillet on each, garnish with fresh dill or parsley sprigs, and serve at once.

Sautéed Fillets of Pompano Moderne

Although pompano is caught from Brazil to Massachusetts, its devotees seem to be concentrated on the southern Atlantic and Gulf coasts. Here, fresh fruits emphasize the tropical connection and augment the fish to provide ample servings. The egg wash technique is especially suited to fragile fillets such as pompano, perch, or small sole, keeping them moist and flavorful while providing a golden crust.

Yields 6 servings

6 boned and skinned pompano fillets, weighing 4 to 5 ounces (115 to 145 g) each
1/3 cup (80 ml) plus 1 tablespoon half-and-half
Salt
Freshly ground white pepper
1/2 cup (60 g) flour
2 eggs
1/3 to 1/2 cup (80 to 118 ml) peanut oil
4 ounces (115 g) blanched, sliced almonds
3 slices fresh pineapple
1 banana
A dash of sugar
2 kiwi fruit
4 tablespoons (60 g) butter
Juice of 2 lemons
Parsley sprigs
Lemon quarters

Recommended equipment

A small mixing bowl, waxed paper (or plate), medium mixing bowl, wire whisk, 12-inch (30 cm) sauté pan, turning spatula, paper towels, serving platter or plates, baking pan.

Rinse the fillets gently under cold running water, pat dry, and reserve.

Mix the 1/3 cup of half-and-half in the small bowl with some salt and pepper, spread the flour on the waxed paper (or plate), and, handling the fillets carefully, dip them one by one into the cream, let excess cream drip off, and place them on the flour. Turn each one over, pat lightly into flour, remove, and shake gently to remove excess flour. (Do this just before you are ready to sauté the fillets, otherwise they will be pasty.)

Using the whisk, mix the eggs together thoroughly with the 1 tablespoon of half-and-half in the medium mixing bowl. Set the sauté pan over medium high heat, add oil to a depth of 1/8 inch (1/3 cm), and, when it is hot, drench the floured fillets in the egg wash and add them to the pan. Do not crowd the pan. You may have to sauté the fillets in two batches. When the fillets sizzle, reduce heat to medium and cook for 2 minutes on each side.

While fish is cooking, warm the serving platter (or plates). As each fillet is done, drain on paper towels and then place them on the warm serving platter (or plates).

Preheat oven to 250F (121C) and toast the almonds on a pan until they are golden brown. When they are done, remove them from the oven, reserve, and raise heat to 400F (204C).

Lightly butter the baking pan. Halve each pineapple slice. Peel the banana and cut it lengthwise into six pieces. Set the banana on top of the pineapple, put both into the baking pan, add a dash of sugar to the top of the fruit, and heat for 5 minutes in the oven. Meanwhile, peel each kiwi fruit and slice into six slices.

Remove all oil from the sauté pan, add the butter, turn heat to medium, and, when butter begins to sizzle, shake the pan in a back and forth motion. When butter turns light brown, immediately add the lemon juice, mix well, and pour over the fish. Decorate the top of the fillets with the cooked fruit and the kiwi slices, sprinkle the almonds over all, garnish the platter (or plates) with the parsley sprigs and lemon quarters, and serve at once.

❧ Pompano en Papillote

Cooking "en papillote" had been around a long time before Escoffier featured it in a recipe in Le Guide Culinaire. *Now a New Orleans specialty, this preparation has become popular because it retains the flavor and juices of the ingredients. Making a papillote is a simple process; however, timing the cooking accurately is of the utmost importance. Thick pieces of fish or meat should be precooked by sautéing beforehand so that 8 to 10 minutes of baking en papillote will finish the dish. Choose ingredients that will cook within the same amount of time and rush the papillotes from the oven to the table to preserve their nicely puffed appearance. Your guests will delight in the fragrant aroma when they open the paper.*

230

Yields 6 servings

1 cup (235 ml) cooked wild rice
6 papillotes *(see page 568)*
Clarified Butter *(see page 568)* or olive oil for the papillotes
1/2 cup (118 ml) Sauce Vin Blanc de Poisson *(see page 68)*
1 tablespoon finely chopped shallots
6 ounces (170 g) fresh mushrooms
1 1/2 teaspoons (7 g) butter
Juice of 1 lemon
Dry white wine if needed
1 tablespoon chopped fresh parsley
Salt
Freshly ground white pepper
6 boned and skinned pompano fillets, weighing 8 to 9 ounces (225 to 285 g) each
A dash of Worcestershire sauce
About 3 tablespoons (45 g) butter, soft, melted, or clarified

Recommended equipment

A 1 1/2-quart (1 1/2 L) saucepan with lid, parchment paper for the papillotes, pastry brush, large chef's knife, 12-inch (30 cm) sauté pan, wooden spatula, baking pan or sheet.

Using the saucepan, prepare the wild rice according to the package instructions. While rice is cooking, make the papillotes and brush them all over one side with the clarified butter or olive oil.

Prepare the sauce vin blanc de poisson.

When the rice is finished, chop the shallots finely with the chef's knife, set them aside, clean the mushrooms, and then finely dice them. Heat the butter over low heat in the sauté pan, add the shallots, and cook gently for 1 minute. Add the mushrooms, squeeze lemon juice over them, mix well with the spatula, and simmer for 2 minutes. (The lemon juice will help keep the mushrooms a light color.) Then add the wild rice and the sauce vin blanc de poisson and, while stirring, cook at a gentle simmer for 3 minutes. The mixture should be a light, moist paste. If too thick, add a little white wine; if too thin, cook a bit longer. Rinse the parsley, pat dry, chop, stir it into the mixture, adjust seasoning with salt and pepper, and remove the sauté pan from heat.

Preheat oven to 350F (177C).

Rinse the fillets gently under cold running water and pat dry. Place a pompano fillet on one-half of each papillote, season with salt, white pepper, several drops of lemon juice, and a few drops of Worcestershire sauce. Spread 1/4 cup (60 ml) of stuffing over fillet. (If two small fillets are used per serving, place the second one on top of the stuffing with the skinned side up, and season it with salt, white pepper, several drops of lemon juice, and a few drops of Worcestershire sauce.) Spread or brush some soft, melted, or clarified butter over the fillet. Following the instructions, fold the paper over and seal tightly. Place papillotes on baking pan or sheet, being sure that they are not touching each other, and bake in the middle level of the oven for 8 to 12 minutes depending on thickness of fish. When done, remove them from the oven to your serving plates and rush them to the table.

Variations: Add fresh lump crabmeat or cooked, diced shrimp to the stuffing. Or substitute brown rice for the wild rice or use wild rice and Rice Pilaff in equal amounts. When using the pilaff, blanched and diced red or green bell peppers and peas add a colorful touch. To the basic stuffing you could add a fine julienne of vegetables, strips of peeled, seeded tomato, or a pinch of basil, tarragon, or oregano. Herbs that are too strong can overpower a delicate fish like pompano so be careful. Finally, a discreet addition of a few drops of Pernod will mystify many guests and conjure up the spirit of Toulouse-Lautrec.

Ocean Anglers' Favorites

Broiled Fillets of Red Snapper Maître d'hôtel

A perennial favorite at the Homestead, red snapper ranks next to pompano as Florida's choice among diner and angler alike. Because snapper does not fare so well on the grill I have called for the fillets to be coated with a seasoned cracker meal before being quickly broiled and baked.

Yields 6 servings

2 tablespoons Beurre Maître d'hôtel *(see page 81)*
6 boned and skinned red snapper fillets, weighing about 6 ounces (170 g) each
1/2 cup (118 ml) cracker meal (or fine white bread crumbs)
1 teaspoon Hungarian paprika
1/4 cup (60 ml) peanut or olive oil
Salt
Freshly ground white pepper
1/2 lemon
Sprigs of fresh parsley
6 lemon wedges

Recommended equipment

A small bowl, broiler pan, turning spatula.

Prepare the beurre maître d'hôtel and reserve.

Adjust oven rack so it is 6 inches (15 cm) from the broiler element and preheat broiler to maximum heat.

Rinse the fillets gently under cold running water, pat dry, and reserve. Combine the cracker meal (crushed saltines are good) and paprika in the bowl. Rub 1 tablespoon of the oil around the bottom and sides of the broiler pan.

Lay the fillets into the pan, skin side down, and season lightly with salt and pepper. Sprinkle 1 1/2 tablespoons of meal mixture over each fillet and then moisten the meal with oil (to prevent burning) by dipping your fingers into oil and patting it into the meal until well moistened.

Set the pan under the broiler and cook for 3 to 4 minutes or until the meal coating is golden brown. Remove pan from broiler, turn oven heat to 375F (190C), and carry pan to your kitchen sink. While holding pan at an angle to drain liquid into sink, slowly pour 1 cup (235 ml) hot water around fillets. Repeat with another cup of hot water but keep 4 to 5 tablespoons of water in the pan. (This water bath eliminates most of the oil from the fish and provides moisture for the final baking.)

Move rack to the middle position and set the pan on it, baking for 6 minutes for 1 1/2-inch (3 3/4 cm) thick fillets. (Add 2 minutes more cooking time for every additional 1/2 inch [1 1/4 cm] of thickness.) When done, remove from oven to the serving plates, top each fillet with 1 teaspoon beurre maître d'hôtel, squeeze juice from one-half lemon over all fillets, and garnish each plate with sprigs of fresh parsley and lemon wedges.

Variation: Use a different seasoned cracker meal such as the one for Broiled Maine Lobster *(see page 243)* and accompany the fillets with Fried Parsley *(see page 238)*.

Grilled Swordfish Steak Everglades

Lest you think the "sword" is a quaint piece of equipment on this creature, you should know that throughout maritime history the swordfish has shown a proclivity for ramming ships (making substantial penetration into wooden hulls) and attacking submerged vessels. Then, consider the fact that the fish can weigh more than eleven hundred pounds. As far as I am concerned, the only swordfish I want to meet are in our coolers. As of this writing some of the best food to be had in Palm Beach, Florida, is at the Everglades Club, where my good friend and colleague, Eddie Hettich, is chef. This preparation is named in his honor. Be sure to use the marinade shown below and a charcoal grill when weather permits. If grilling the fish indoors, our Homestead Passion Fruit Sauce (as shown in the accompanying photograph) sets off the fish handsomely and is a good alternative to Beurre Maître d'hôtel.

Yields 6 servings

2 tablespoons Beurre Maître d'hôtel *(see page 81)*
6 centercut swordfish steaks, weighing 6 to 8 ounces (170 to 225 g) each, 1 1/4 to 1 1/2 inches (3 to 3 3/4 cm) thick
1 orange
1 grapefruit
1 kiwi fruit
1/2 cup (118 ml) olive oil
1/4 teaspoon Hungarian paprika
1/4 teaspoon salt
1/8 teaspoon freshly ground white pepper
Fresh parsley sprigs
Lemon wedges

Recommended equipment

A charcoal grill and hardwood charcoal, paring knife, wire whisk, 2-quart (2 L) mixing bowl, turning spatula, heatproof platter.

Prepare the beurre maître d'hôtel and reserve. Start your charcoal fire at least one-half hour before you want to cook.

Rinse the swordfish steaks gently under cold running water, pat dry, and reserve.

Peel the orange, grapefruit, and kiwi fruit. Remove the orange and grapefruit sections from between the membranes and slice the kiwi fruit into six pieces. Reserve the fruits at room temperature.

Preheat oven to 325F (163C).

Using the whisk, combine the olive oil, paprika, salt, and pepper in the bowl. When your coals are hot and you are ready to cook, dip each swordfish steak into the oil, let excess drip off, and set onto the grill. After 2 minutes, turn the fish 90° on the same side to make a crisscross pattern. Grill for 2 more minutes before turning over. Grill 4 minutes on the other side. The total time depends upon the thickness of the fish and the intensity of the charcoal fire. For a steak 1 1/4 to 1 1/2 inches (3 to 3 3/4 cm) thick, the cooking time over a hot fire will be 8 to 9 minutes. For a steak 1 to 1 1/4 inches (2 1/2 to 3 cm) thick, about 6 to 8 minutes will do.

When done, arrange the steaks on the platter, place an orange and grapefruit section and a kiwi slice on each, and top with 1 teaspoon of beurre maître d'hôtel. Put the platter into the middle level of the oven for 30 seconds, remove, garnish with parsley sprigs and lemon wedges, and serve.

You may wish to marinate the steaks for an hour on each side, refrigerated and under plastic wrap, before cooking. Mix 1 cup (235 ml) olive oil, 1 lemon sliced, 1/4 teaspoon Worcestershire sauce, 1/2 garlic clove, minced or pressed, salt, freshly ground white pepper, and 1/4 teaspoon Hungarian paprika. Add any one of these herbs: 1/2 teaspoon oregano, 1/2 teaspoon chopped fresh fennel leaves, 1/8 teaspoon anise, or 1 tablespoon chopped fresh celery leaves.

Suprêmes de Loup de Mer à l'Orange et Poivre Vert
Fillets of Sea Bass with Green Peppercorn and Orange Sauce

Passengers outbound from New York on the great North Atlantic liners knew that the voyage really was about to begin when the Ambrose Channel Lightship came into view, for it was here that the harbor pilot was dropped off and the ship's captain assumed command of the bridge. As polished brass handles set the ship's telegraphs to "all ahead standard," the lazily turning massive turbines, coaxed by high-pressure superheated steam, would come smartly to full power. Those lining the taffrail knew the ever-lengthening roiling and churning wake below meant that Southampton, Cherbourg, and Le Havre were dead ahead. They probably did not know that barely twelve miles to starboard lay one of New York's richest sources of black sea bass. George Washington was the first person on record to charter a boat to fish for sea bass and until 1832 skippers had to go no farther than this to supply the legendary Fulton Fish Market. A cook's delight, this agreeable fish is amenable to a wide variety of treatments such as this one, more reminiscent of the Provence of Outhier and Vergé than it is of lower Manhattan. This handsome dish is delicious served with Rice Pilaff and fresh Asparagus or String Beans. Or, present the fillets on a bed of Epinards Etouffés seasoned with butter and a dash of nutmeg.

Yields 6 servings

2 oranges
2 egg yolks
Juice of 1 lemon
2 teaspoons cold water
1/2 cup (118 ml) Clarified Butter *(see page 568)*
6 boned and skinned sea bass fillets, weighing 5 to 6 ounces (145 to 170 g) each
Salt
Freshly ground white pepper
1 tablespoon chopped shallots
1/2 cup (118 ml) dry white wine
2 cups (475 ml) whipping cream
3 threads of saffron
1 tablespoon (15 g) butter
18 green peppercorns (packed in water and drained)
6 sprigs fresh dill or parsley
Butter for the baking dish and the waxed paper

Recommended equipment

A swivel-bladed vegetable peeler, paring knife, 1 1/2-quart (1 1/2 L) saucepan, double boiler, wire whisk, small chef's knife, small enameled cast-iron baking dish or lined copper plat à sauter, waxed paper or aluminum foil, 3-quart (3 L) saucepan, fine-mesh sieve, 8-inch (20 cm) sauté pan, heatproof serving platter.

Peel one orange with the vegetable peeler, being careful to leave the bitter white behind. Using the paring knife, cut the peel into fine julienne strips and blanch for 1 minute in boiling water in the small saucepan. Drain thoroughly and reserve. Peel the other orange with the paring knife, removing peel and bitter white, and discard peelings. Remove the orange sections from between the membranes and reserve. Squeeze the first orange and reduce the juice to 2 tablespoons in the small saucepan. Then put juice in the top part of the double boiler and set the double boiler over medium heat.

Using the whisk, blend the egg yolks and lemon juice thoroughly into the reduced orange juice. Whip the egg yolks gently, waiting for them to thicken and become creamy. When they are thickened, remove the double boiler from heat, add the cold water to the egg mixture, mix well, and return to heat. Then add the warm clarified butter a tablespoon at a time while whipping briskly with the whisk until all butter is absorbed. Keep warm (but not hot) in the double boiler.

Preheat oven to 325F (163C).

Rinse the sea bass fillets gently under cold running water, pat dry, season lightly with salt and pepper, and reserve. Using the chef's knife, chop the shallots. Spread 2 tablespoons of butter in the baking dish or plat à sauter, strew the shallots in the bottom, lay in the fillets, pour the wine around them, and cover loosely with buttered waxed paper (or foil). Set over medium heat, bring to a simmer, and put into the middle level of the oven for 7 to 9 minutes (or until fillets feel springy to a light touch of the finger).

When fillets are done, pour the cooking liquid into the large saucepan and set the baking dish, loosely covered, aside in a warm spot. Put the saucepan over medium heat, add the cream and saffron, bring to a boil, then reduce heat so that sauce maintains a steady simmer. Reduce the liquid by one-third (about 5 minutes), strain into the clean small saucepan, and keep warm.

Set the sauté pan over medium low heat, add 1 tablespoon butter and the green peppercorns, and sauté lightly for 1 minute. Then add them to the cream in the saucepan.

When ready to serve, bring the cream to a boil, remove from heat, and whisk in the orange butter 2 tablespoons at a time. Blend carefully and add the julienne of orange peel. Arrange the fillets on the platter and set into the oven for 1 minute to heat. When warm, remove from oven, spoon the sauce over the fillets, decorate with the reserved orange sections, garnish with the fresh dill (or parsley), and serve at once.

Crustaceans: Crab, Shrimp, and Lobster

Sautéed Soft-shelled Crabs with Lemon Butter

All growing crabs must shed their shells and, when they do, there is a treat in store. Several species are edible, but blue crabs are really the only ones to look for, and they must be only hours away from having been caught. Serve with a boiled potato and a salad of mixed greens with tomato and cucumber.

Yields 4 to 6 servings

12 soft-shelled crabs (2 to 3 per serving, depending upon size)
1 tablespoon chopped fresh parsley
1/2 cup (118 ml) milk
Salt
Freshly ground white pepper
1 cup (120 g) flour
1/4 cup (60 ml) peanut oil
6 tablespoons (90 g) butter
Juice of 2 lemons
Sprigs of parsley
Lemon quarters

Recommended equipment

Scissors, small chef's knife, small mixing bowl, plate or dish for flour, waxed paper, 12-inch (30 cm) sauté pan, wooden spatula, paper towels, heatproof serving platter.

Clean the crabs just before you plan to cook them. Rinse each crab under running cold water, turn it on its back, lift up the apronlike flap and pull it away. Pull out the fleshy gills from under the flaps at each end of the crab. Cut the eyes off with the scissors, press above the legs, and remove the bile sac. Rinse the crab again and pat dry.

Rinse the parsley, pat dry, chop, and reserve.

Put the milk in the mixing bowl and season with salt and pepper. Spread the flour on the plate or dish and place a sheet of waxed paper on your work surface. Taking the crabs one by one, dip each into the milk, let excess milk drip off, then dust each crab with flour on both sides. Shake gently to remove extra flour and set aside on the waxed paper.

Heat the peanut oil in the sauté pan over medium high heat. The pan is ready when a drop of water sizzles in the hot oil. Add the crabs to the pan, bottom side down, in a single layer and sauté until brown on the bottom. The crabs will not brown if the pan is crowded. Turn the crabs with the wooden spatula, brown on the other side, and remove to drain on folded paper towels. The whole sautéing process should not take more than 4 to 5 minutes (or 3 to 4 if the crabs are very small). If more than two batches need to be cooked in the same oil, wipe out pan and start with fresh oil *(see Notes on Sautéing Fish, page 569)*.

While the crabs are being sautéed, preheat the oven to 375F (190C).

When all the crabs are cooked, arrange them on the heatproof serving platter and set them into the oven to stay hot.

Drain all the oil from the pan, wipe out with paper towels, and add the butter to the pan, shaking occasionally over medium heat until the butter begins to foam and turn golden brown. At this moment add the lemon juice to stop the browning process, remove pan from heat, add the reserved parsley, and pour the lemon butter over the crabs. Serve at once, garnished, if you like, with parsley sprigs and lemon quarters.

Breaded Fried Soft-shelled Crabs with Fried Parsley

You can agonize over whether to fry or sauté, as in the previous recipe, but these fried soft-shelled crabs, a pure pleasure by themselves when served with a simple lemon wedge, coleslaw, or Sauce Tartare, are enhanced by the addition of a Fried Parsley garnish. While the oil is hot, make it do double duty by frying the parsley after the crabs.

Yields 4 to 6 servings

12 soft-shelled crabs (2 to 3 per serving, depending upon size)
1/2 cup (118 ml) milk
Salt
Freshly ground white pepper
1 cup (120 g) flour
2 eggs
1 tablespoon water
2 cups (475 ml) fine white bread crumbs
Peanut oil for deep frying

Recommended equipment

Scissors, small bowl for milk, plate or dish for flour, small mixing bowl, wire whisk or hand-held mixer, plate or dish for bread crumbs, waxed paper, electric deep fryer with thermostat or other deep pot, frying thermometer, fine-mesh skimmer, paper towels, heatproof serving platter.

Clean the crabs just before you plan to cook them. Rinse each crab under running cold water, turn it on its back, lift up the apronlike flap and pull it away. Pull out the fleshy gills from under the flaps at each end of the crab. Cut the eyes off with the scissors, press above the legs, and remove the bile sac. Rinse the crab again and pat dry.

Put the milk in the bowl and season with salt and pepper. Spread the flour on the plate or dish. Using the whisk or mixer, beat the eggs with the water in the small mixing bowl. Spread the bread crumbs on the plate or dish and put a sheet of waxed paper on your work surface.

Now you are ready for the crabs. Take them one by one and dip them first into the milk, let excess drip off, then dust each side with flour. Shake the crab gently to remove extra flour, dip it into the egg wash, let excess drip off, then dust each side with bread crumbs, lightly patting them onto the crab. Shake gently to remove extra crumbs and set aside on the waxed paper. Arrange the crabs in a single layer to keep the crumbs intact. (Reserve the flour if you plan to fry parsley too.)

Heat the peanut oil in the deep fryer to 360 to 375F (182 to 190C). Check the temperature with the thermometer and when the oil is hot add the crabs slowly one by one. Do not crowd the pot. Using the fine-mesh skimmer to keep the crabs gently submerged in the oil, fry them to a golden brown and turn them when one side is done. This should take 4 to 5 minutes depending upon the size of the crabs. When done, remove with the skimmer to drain on folded paper towels.

While the crabs are frying, preheat the oven to 375F (190C).

When all the crabs are cooked, arrange them on the heatproof serving platter and set them into the oven to stay hot.

FOR FRYING THE PARSLEY

1 bunch parsley
1/3 cup (80 ml) milk
1 egg yolk
1/3 cup (40 g) flour
Salt
Freshly ground white pepper
1 egg white

Recommended equipment

Two small mixing bowls, wire whisk, hand-held electric mixer, rubber spatula, fine-mesh skimmer, paper towels.

Wash the parsley carefully in cold water, pat or spin dry, and break into sprigs. Reserve while the batter is prepared.

In a mixing bowl, using the whisk, combine the milk, egg yolk, and flour. Blend well and then season with salt and pepper. Using the hand-held mixer, whip the egg white until stiff and then blend into the batter with the rubber spatula.

Dust the parsley sprigs with the flour remaining from the crabs, check to see that the frying oil is still hot (360 to 375F or 182 to 190C), and spread out some fresh paper towels. Dip the sprigs one by one into the batter, let excess drip off (or wipe off gently with your fingers), and drop each sprig into the hot oil. Do not crowd the pot. Fry until golden brown, turning with the skimmer to brown evenly, for about 1 minute. Remove to drain on paper towels and, if necessary, fry another batch.

When all is ready, garnish the crab platter with the fried parsley and serve immediately.

Parsley can be fried without using a batter. Simply wash the sprigs, dry thoroughly, and drop them into the hot oil, stirring with the skimmer for 8 to 10 seconds (or until lightly crisp). Drain on paper towels before serving.

Gratinéed Lump Crabmeat Homestead

This makes a superb center for a cold weather luncheon accompanied by Sancerre or Sauvignon Blanc, crusty French Bread for dipping up the sauce, and a green salad. I insist that you not compromise on two ingredients—the crabmeat and the bread crumbs. Only lump crabmeat has the uniform white color and texture which complements this sauce. And unless you use bread crumbs made from first quality white bread such as Pullman Loaf, your sauce will be like paste. Scallop shells make lovely serving and cooking dishes and placing them on a bed of rock salt will keep them from rolling around on your baking pans and serving plates.

Yields 4 servings

1 pound (450 g) lump crabmeat
2 tablespoons finely chopped shallots
2 tablespoons finely diced green bell peppers
2 tablespoons finely diced red bell peppers
1 tablespoon (15 g) butter
2 teaspoons dry English mustard
6 tablespoons dry white wine
1/2 cup (118 ml) fine white bread crumbs
2 1/2 cups (590 ml) whipping cream
1/4 teaspoon Worcestershire sauce
A few drops of Tabasco sauce
1/4 teaspoon Old Bay seafood seasoning
A dash of Knorr Aromat
A dash of salt
Freshly ground white pepper
1 tablespoon grated Parmesan
2 tablespoons (30 g) melted butter
1 tablespoon finely sliced fresh chives
1/4 teaspoon paprika
Butter for the baking dish

Recommended equipment

A large chef's knife, 12-inch (30 cm) sauté pan, wooden spatula, 3-quart (3 L) saucepan, rubber spatula, 1-quart (1 L) baking dish or 4 individual ramekins or scallop shells, box grater, small mixing bowl.

Carefully pick over the crabmeat with your fingers to remove any pieces of shell and reserve in a bowl. Using the large chef's knife, finely chop the shallots and peppers. Put 1 tablespoon of butter in the sauté pan and heat over medium heat. When butter is hot add the shallots and both peppers and cook for 1 minute. Add the mustard and white wine and bring mixture to a boil, then reduce heat so mixture simmers and continue cooking for 2 minutes while stirring occasionally with the wooden spatula. Add the crabmeat and 1/4 cup (60 ml) of the bread crumbs and then remove pan from heat.

In the saucepan bring the whipping cream to a boil, add the Worcestershire sauce, Tabasco, Old Bay seasoning, Aromat, salt, and pepper. Reduce heat and simmer until cream is reduced to 1 1/2 cups (355 ml) (about 15 to 20 minutes). While the cream is reducing, butter your baking dish(es), grate the cheese, and melt the 2 tablespoons of butter, reserving both. When cream is reduced, add it to the sauté pan along with the chives and fold all together gently with the rubber spatula to keep the crabmeat lumps together. Scoop into buttered ovenproof dish (or scallop shells or individual ramekins).

Preheat oven to 325F (163C).

Combine remaining bread crumbs, paprika, and reserved Parmesan cheese and spread over crabmeat. Moisten crumb topping with reserved melted butter and bake in preheated oven for 10 minutes. Then turn on broiler just long enough to make a golden brown crust.

Shrimp Bahía

By the late 1970s, nearly six hundred million pounds of shrimp were being brought annually to market in the United States. "Everyman's" favorite, this crustacean is truly ubiquitous, being found in fresh and salt water the world over. The west coast of Mexico is dotted with bahías (bays), and here the shrimp encounters a major influence in American cooking—southwestern cuisine. In Hot Springs we have to be a bit cautious about using too much jalapeño, but if your guests are from Bahía de Banderas, let them be your guide—better yet, see if they will fix the shrimp, and you do the dishes. Serve this with Rice Pilaff or Saffron Rice, and a mixed green salad.

Yields 6 to 8 servings

1 medium red bell pepper
1 medium green bell pepper
1 medium onion
1 medium garlic clove
1 small jalapeño pepper
6 medium, ripe tomatoes (blanched, peeled, and seeded; see page 568) or 2 cans whole tomatoes, each weighing 14 to 16 ounces (395 to 450 g)
2 1/2 tablespoons olive oil
1/2 cup (118 ml) canned tomato juice
1/2 cup (118 ml) canned tomato sauce
1/3 bay leaf
Salt
Freshly ground white pepper
A dash of Tabasco
3 pounds (1350 g) shrimp
1 teaspoon cornstarch
2 tablespoons cold water
2 medium lemons
2 tablespoons capers with liquid

Recommended equipment

A paring knife, small chef's knife, 3-quart (3 L) saucepan, garlic press, wooden spatula, colander, shrimp deveiner, wire whisk, 12-inch (30 cm) sauté pan.

Prepare the vegetables. Rinse the bell peppers and, using the paring knife, cut both in half, remove seeds, and cut into 1-inch (2 1/2 cm) square pieces. Peel the onion and cut coarsely into 1-inch square pieces. Peel the garlic clove. Seed the jalapeño pepper and cut it coarsely. Prepare the ripe tomatoes and chop them (or the canned tomatoes) coarsely.

Heat 1 tablespoon of olive oil in the saucepan over medium heat, add all the peppers and the onion, then press the garlic into the mixture. Sauté, stirring occasionally, for 5 minutes, then add the tomatoes, tomato juice, tomato sauce, and bay leaf. Season lightly with salt, pepper, and a dash of Tabasco. Bring to a simmer over low to medium heat and cook for 15 minutes.

While the sauce simmers prepare the shrimp. Wash them well in the colander under running cold water, let drain, then shell and devein them. If you work quickly you should be able to get them all done while waiting on the sauce.

When the sauce has finished simmering, mix the cornstarch with the cold water, remove saucepan from heat, and whisk cornstarch mixture slowly into sauce. Return to heat and continue stirring until the sauce has simmered a couple of minutes. Then adjust heat so that it simmers unattended for 5 more minutes. When done, remove from heat and reserve.

Using the paring knife, remove all peel from the lemons down to the flesh. Halve them, remove core and seeds, then dice flesh into 1/4-inch (2/3 cm) cubes and reserve.

Heat 1 1/2 tablespoons olive oil in the sauté pan over medium to high heat. When the oil is hot, add the shrimp, season lightly with salt and pepper, and sauté, stirring from time to time, for 5 minutes (if shrimp are large add 2 minutes to the cooking time). Stir the Creole sauce into the shrimp, simmer for 5 minutes, add the lemon cubes and capers, and serve piping hot on warm dinner plates.

If you use canned tomatoes, use the juice from the can. If you use fresh tomatoes, use canned tomato juice.

If you have more sauce than you need, reserve it, and, after adding a few sautéed fresh mushrooms, serve over an omelet or scrambled eggs for brunch or a light supper. Or, spoon it over scrod, sole, or halibut fillets and bake in a preheated 325F (163C) oven. The sauce alone without the shrimp is a sauce Creole and will keep well for a few days under refrigeration (or it can be frozen).

Mixed Seafood Newburg

This is an adaptation of the famous lobster "Newberg" created in a chafing dish more than one hundred years ago by Captain Ben Wenberg at the Delmonico Restaurant in New York City. After a disagreement with Charles Delmonico, he left, and the dish was removed from the menu. Incessant demand by faithful clients brought it back, and we are happy to pass it on to you. Serve in Vol-au-Vents for a first course or lunch, or accompany it with Riz Valencienne and a tossed salad for dinner.

Yields 6 to 8 servings

1 pound (450 g) cooked shrimp, peeled and deveined *(see page 175)*
1/2 pound (225 g) cooked lobster meat *(see pages 242–43)*, cubed
8 tablespoons (115 g) butter
2 teaspoons Hungarian paprika
A pinch of cayenne pepper
1 teaspoon dry English mustard
3 tablespoons flour
2 cups (475 ml) half-and-half
1 cup (235 ml) Fish Stock *(see page 60)*
1 cup (235 ml) whipping cream
1 2-inch (5 cm) piece lemon peel
1 tablespoon chopped shallots
1/2 cup (118 ml) dry sherry
1 pound (450 g) bay scallops
1 tablespoon dry white wine
Salt
Freshly ground white pepper

Recommended equipment

A 2-quart (2 L) saucepan, wooden spatula, wire whisk, swivel-bladed vegetable peeler, large chef's knife, 4-quart (4 L) enameled cast-iron baking dish or lined copper plat à sauter, 12-inch (30 cm) sauté pan, large fine-mesh sieve, 1-quart (1 L) bowl.

Prepare the cooked shrimp and lobster before you begin the sauce.

Melt 6 tablespoons of the butter in the saucepan over medium heat and add paprika, cayenne, and mustard and sauté for 1 minute while stirring from time to time with the wooden spatula. Then add the flour slowly while mixing with the whisk, blend well, and cook the roux for 1 minute. Next, add half-and-half, fish stock, and whipping cream, mixing thoroughly with the whisk until the sauce is smooth and comes to a boil. Add the lemon peel to the saucepan. Adjust heat to low so that the mixture simmers slowly and cook for 20 minutes while stirring occasionally. When done, remove from heat and reserve.

While the mixture is simmering, cut the lobster meat into 1-inch (2 1/2 cm) cubes, and if the shrimp are large, cut them in half crosswise. Reserve. With the chef's knife, chop the shallots.

Preheat oven to 325F (163C).

In the baking dish or plat à sauter, melt the remaining butter over low heat, add the shallots, and sauté for 1 minute. Stir in the shrimp, lobster, and sherry and set pan into oven to heat for 5 minutes. Then remove from oven and reserve.

Rinse scallops under cold running water, drain, and if you are using sea rather than bay scallops, quarter them. Put the wine in the sauté pan, set over low heat, add the scallops, and bring to a low simmer. Cook for 2 minutes while stirring, remove from heat, pour scallops into strainer set over the bowl and reserve both scallops and liquid.

Add scallops to baking dish with lobster and shrimp. Pass the cream sauce through the strainer into the baking dish and stir together gently with the wooden spatula. Set baking dish over low heat, bring to a gentle simmer, and heat for 2 minutes. If sauce is too thick, thin with some of the reserved scallop cooking liquid. Adjust seasoning with salt and pepper and serve at once.

Variation: Use lump crabmeat instead of lobster and substitute Rainwater Madeira for the sherry.

Baked Lobster Thermidor

Café de Paris (which closed in 1955) was a Parisian culinary landmark. Open from 1822 to 1858, the first restaurant of this name was located on the boulevard des Italiens and was a favorite haunt of Balzac, Alfred de Musset, and Alexandre Dumas père. In 1878, the avenue de l'Opera opened and so did another Café de Paris.

Although many dishes were created here, this is the one which survives to the present day. According to Larousse Gastronomique, it was created by Léopold Mourier to honor the historical play Victorien Sardou. The name comes from Sardou's play, Thermidor, *which opened in 1891.*

In keeping with its origin, this is a dramatic presentation which can have feature billing or play a supporting role. For dinner, accompany the lobster halves with Rice Pilaff and a tossed green salad. For a first course, fish course, or light lunch, serve a lobster half by itself to each guest.

Yields 6 servings

1 1/2 cups (355 ml) Sauce Velouté de Poisson *(see page 68)*
3 live lobsters, weighing 2 to 2 1/2 pounds (900 to 1350 g) each
Salt
2 tablespoons chopped shallots
12 mushrooms
3/4 cup (180 ml) Sauce Mornay *(see page 67)*
2 tablespoons (30 g) butter
Juice of 1/2 lemon
1 teaspoon dry English mustard
1 teaspoon chopped fresh tarragon leaves
A pinch of cayenne pepper
1/3 cup (80 ml) dry white wine
1 tablespoon finely cut chives
2 tablespoons grated Parmesan cheese
Sprigs of parsley

Recommended equipment

A 16-quart (15 L) stockpot with lid, large chef's knife or cleaver, paring knife, 1 1/2-quart (1 1/2 L) saucepan, wooden spatula, wire whisk, baking sheet, box grater.

Prepare the sauce velouté de poisson before you start cooking the lobsters.

Fill the stockpot with water, add a handful of salt (about 3 tablespoons) or seaweed, cover, and bring to the boil. Drop the lobsters into the pot one by one, re-cover, and when water maintains a steady, lively simmer, begin timing 18 minutes.

While the lobsters are cooking, chop the shallots, brush the mushrooms of any clinging dirt, cut into 1/2-inch (1 1/4 cm) cubes, and reserve.

Prepare the sauce Mornay.

When lobsters are done, remove pot to sink and run cold water into it continuously for 10 minutes. Then drain lobsters, cut in half lengthwise with the chef's knife, remove meat from body, crack claws and remove meat, and reserve empty body shells. With the paring knife, cut the meat into 1/2-inch cubes and reserve.

Melt the butter in the saucepan over medium heat, add shallots, sauté 1 minute, add mushrooms, sprinkle with lemon juice, and sauté for 3 minutes, stirring from time to time with the wooden spatula. Then add mustard, tarragon, cayenne, and wine, and simmer for a few minutes until liquid is reduced to 2 tablespoons. Next, add lobster meat, sauté for 1 minute, then add the sauce velouté de poisson, blending well with the whisk. Simmer mixture on low for 2 minutes stirring occasionally. Cut the chives. Remove mixture from heat, add chives, let cool briefly, then fill the six lobster shells. Set shells on baking sheet and spoon 2 tablespoons sauce Mornay over each. Grate the Parmesan cheese with the box grater and sprinkle some over the sauce.

Adjust the oven rack to be 6 inches (15 cm) from the broiler unit and preheat broiler to maximum heat. Set baking sheet on rack and broil lobsters until the stuffing is golden brown, then turn off broiler and set oven heat to 350F (177C). Bake lobster for 5 minutes (or 10 minutes if you had stuffed and refrigerated them ahead of time). Remove from oven, set lobsters on individual plates or serving platter, garnish with sprigs of parsley, and serve.

Broiled Maine Lobster

Although popularly known as Maine lobster, this crustacean is actually caught in an area ranging from North Carolina to Belle Isle, in the Canadian Maritimes. This species, along with its European cousin (known in France as the Prince Noir) is typically larger than the lobsterette and spiny lobster, but surprisingly is no less tender, which may account for its popularity. In spite of the fact that lobster tanks are common in many inland supermarkets, you must choose your lobsters carefully.

Because they are not fed after they are caught, their meat tends to shrink, and if you do not choose lively (i.e., fresh) lobsters you may be shocked to crack an enormous claw, anticipating a succulent morsel, only to find it half empty. Caveat emptor! This simple classic should be presented with Fried Parsley and french fried julienne potatoes for an elegant dinner. The seasoned topping insulates the delicate lobster meat from the direct heat of the broiler.

Yields 6 servings

6 live lobsters, weighing 1 1/2 to 2 pounds (675 to 900 g) each
2/3 cup (160 ml) finely crushed saltines
1 teaspoon dry English mustard
1/8 teaspoon cayenne pepper
2 tablespoons chopped shallots
1/2 medium green bell pepper
1/2 medium red bell pepper
1 3/4 cups (395 g) butter
1 tablespoon olive oil
Juice of 1/2 lemon
Lemon quarters

Recommended equipment

A blender or food processor, large chef's knife or cleaver, paring knife, 12-inch (30 cm) sauté pan, wooden spatula, heavy roasting pan, pastry brush, 1 1/2-quart (1 1/2 L) saucepan.

Set the lobsters into the coldest part of your refrigerator to make them easier to handle.

Whir enough saltines in the blender or food processor to yield 2/3 cup, then add the mustard and cayenne pepper and blend for a few seconds. Using the chef's knife, chop the shallots. Seed the bell peppers, remove the white pith, and finely dice them. Melt 2 tablespoons (30 g) butter in the sauté pan over medium low heat, add the shallots and peppers, and sauté for 3 minutes, stirring from time to time with the wooden spatula. Then add 1 cup (225 g) butter, let it melt, stir in saltine mixture, and mix well for 1 minute. Remove from heat and reserve.

Prepare the lobsters for cooking. One at a time, place a lobster stomach down on a cutting board. Insert the tip of the chef's knife where the body joins the tail section and cut toward the head, splitting the body. Remove knife, insert point where tail joins the body, and halve the tail. Separate the lobster into two halves. Twist off the claws. Remove sand sac from head and the intestinal tract in the tail and discard. Using the back of the chef's knife (or flat side of a cleaver), whack each claw firmly to crack it.

Adjust oven rack to be 6 inches (15 cm) from broiler unit and preheat broiler to high heat.

Set lobsters into the roasting pan, shell side down, arrange claws next to them, and brush the claws with olive oil. Spread 2 tablespoons of saltine mixture over each lobster half, patting it down lightly. Put pan into oven and broil until cracker coating is golden brown, about 4 minutes. Turn off broiler, set oven heat to 375F (190C), and bake lobster on middle level of oven. The total cooking time for a 2-pound lobster is about 18 minutes and 16 minutes for a 1 1/2-pound lobster.

While the lobster is baking, melt the remaining butter in the saucepan over low heat and add lemon juice. When the lobsters are done, remove them and the claws to serving plates and accompany them with lemon wedges and individual dishes of melted butter.

Variations: Brush the lobster halves with melted butter, bake at 375F (190C) for 8 minutes, top each half with 2 to 2 1/2 tablespoons of Gratinéed Lump Crabmeat Homestead *(see page 239)*, sprinkle grated Parmesan cheese on the crabmeat, and bake for 10 more minutes. Also, vary the cracker coating with different seasonings by adding garlic, oregano, olive oil, butter, or hot peppers. Fine white bread crumbs may also be used instead of crackers.

Charcoal grilling produces a tasty dish, especially if done at the shore under a setting sun with a charcoal fire at the water's edge—whether on La Croisette, at Nauset Point, or the Outer Banks. For each lobster, cut a large piece of heavy duty aluminum foil, spread a layer of seaweed in the center, set a whole lobster on top of the seaweed, cover with another layer of seaweed, and wrap tightly, folding and pinching the foil to form a leakproof package. Set package on rack over hot coals and grill 25 minutes for a 1 1/2-pound lobster and 30 minutes for a 2-pound lobster. Turn foil packages over once during grilling and move them around so that the packages in the center are moved to the outside and vice versa. For serving, remove foil and seaweed, split lobster in half, crack claws, and accompany with lemon wedges and melted butter flavored with lemon juice.

Mousse d'Homard Américaine
Cold Mousse of Lobster

Whether the focus of an elegant luncheon or the first course of an extraordinary dinner, this mousse will provide your guests with a culinary memory that will endure forever. While time-consuming to prepare, the sauce Américaine base is one of the great legacies of haute cuisine and it will contribute a color and texture that would please Rembrandt. Many garnishes are suitable, but among the best are Boston lettuce leaves, watercress, fresh tarragon or parsley, and lemon and tomato quarters. A Pressed Cucumber Salad goes well with this as does fresh Asparagus.

Yields 8 to 10 servings

2 cups (475 ml) Sauce Américaine *(see page 71)*
1 cup (235 ml) cooked lobster meat *(see pages 242–43)*, chilled
1 1/2 tablespoons unflavored gelatin
2 tablespoons water
2 tablespoons Cognac
1 1/2 cups (355 ml) whipping cream
Salt
Freshly ground white pepper
A dash of cayenne pepper
2 cups (475 ml) Sauce Chantilly *(see page 95)*
Peanut oil for the mold

Recommended equipment

A 1-quart (1 L) bowl, double boiler, 1 1/2-quart (1 1/2 L) saucepan, blender or food processor, electric mixer, rubber spatula, medium mixing bowl, wire whisk, crushed ice, 6-cup (1 1/2 L) mold or individual ramekins, plastic wrap.

Prepare the sauce Américaine and chill.

Cook the lobster, remove shell, cut enough meat coarsely to yield 1 cup, and chill.

Soak the gelatin in the bowl in cold water to cover until soft. Then either put the gelatin into a double boiler or set bowl over very hot water, stir in 2 tablespoons water, and heat until gelatin melts.

Warm 1 cup (235 ml) of the sauce Américaine over low heat in the saucepan and, when the gelatin has melted, stir it into the sauce. Set saucepan aside.

Put the cold lobster pieces, the remaining chilled sauce Américaine, and Cognac in the blender or food processor and purée until very smooth. Whip the cream until stiff, using the electric mixer. With the rubber spatula, scrape the purée into the medium mixing bowl and add the warm sauce, mixing thoroughly with the whisk. Set the bowl over crushed ice and let cool while stirring. Adjust seasoning with salt and pepper and add the cayenne. When the mixture begins to get stiff, fold in the whipped cream.

Lightly oil the mold or individual ramekins, fill with the mousse, cover with plastic wrap, and refrigerate for several hours or, preferably, overnight.

Well before serving prepare the sauce Chantilly.

When ready to serve, unmold mousse by dipping mold in pan of hot water for a few seconds. Set serving plate upside down on top of mold and, holding both together tightly, reverse. The mousse should slip out of the mold easily. If not, run a paring knife around the edge and then reverse again. Decorate with your garnishes and serve on chilled plates accompanied by the sauce Chantilly.

Scallops

This mollusk offers another example of the rich history of seafood. Italian Renaissance painter Sandro Botticelli's *Birth of Venus* is perhaps the most eloquent visual statement of her mythical origin in a scallop shell. Legend further records that her mode of transport consisted of a scallop carriage drawn by six seahorses.

For medieval Christian pilgrims there were three main destinations: Rome, Jerusalem, and Santiago de Compostela, with its Romanesque cathedral, shrine of Saint James the Apostle. Martyred by the sword in A.D. 44 at the command of Herod Agrippa I, Saint James wore the scallop shell as his personal symbol, and, in medieval art, if you see a traveler depicted with a scallop shell on the saddle bag, it is a sure sign of a pilgrimage to Compostela. A grueling voyage—it is estimated that more than five hundred thousand people undertook the ordeal during the height of this period (the twelfth century). In cuisine, the association continues to be strong, as the appellation *Coquilles Saint-Jacques* is used for a wide variety of scallop preparations in France.

Marinated Bay Scallops

If you look at this recipe and think "seviche," you are partly correct. Peruvian in origin, seviche is really a pickling technique, and although usually associated with lime juice and scallops, it can be used with fish and other pickling solutions. The orthodox version calls for lime juice, onions, peppercorns, and bay leaf. This one is much more colorful, and we think more interesting for cook and guest alike. Pale scallops with their red and green pepper strip companions are presented in a nest of Boston lettuce and fresh watercress, and the perfect summer lunch or light dinner is on your plate.

Yields 4 servings

1/2 cup (118 ml) freshly squeezed lime juice
1 medium garlic clove
A pinch of sugar
1/2 cup (118 ml) olive oil
1 pound (450 g) bay scallops
1/2 medium red bell pepper
1/2 medium green bell pepper
2 ripe olives
1 small jalapeño pepper
1/2 teaspoon fresh oregano, chopped
1/2 medium cucumber
A dash of salt
Freshly ground white pepper
1 large ripe tomato (blanched, peeled, and seeded; *see page 568*)
1 small head Boston lettuce
1 bunch watercress
2 scallions
1/4 teaspoon chopped fresh dill

Recommended equipment

A 3-quart (3 L) glass or nonmetallic bowl, garlic press, wire whisk, colander, paring knife, swivel-bladed vegetable peeler, large chef's knife, waxed paper or plastic wrap.

Pour the lime juice into the bowl and put the garlic clove through the press into the lime juice. Add the sugar, and, stirring with the whisk, slowly add the olive oil and mix thoroughly (as you would make a mayonnaise).

Rinse the scallops in the colander under cold running water and let them drain while the vegetables are being prepared. Rinse the bell peppers, halve them, and, with the paring knife, clean out the seeds and cut the flesh of one half of each pepper into thin strips. Pit the olives if necessary and slice thinly. Rinse the jalapeño pepper, seed it, and cut into thin slices. Peel, seed, and finely dice the cucumber half.

Add the scallops to the marinade in the bowl along with the red and green peppers, olive slices, oregano, jalapeño pepper, and cucumber. Season lightly with salt and freshly ground white pepper, stir well, cover bowl with waxed paper or plastic wrap, and refrigerate for two hours. During that time stir the mixture twice.

While the scallops are marinating, prepare and chop the tomato and wash the lettuce and watercress (or whatever greens you plan to use).

When the scallops are ready, rinse the scallions, halve them lengthwise, and slice thinly. Add them with the dill and tomato to the scallops, stir, and let sit for 10 to 15 minutes. Then arrange the lettuce and watercress on the plates, divide the scallops and vegetables among them, and serve.

Variation: Fresh chives can be used instead of dill (and do not use the scallions). If bay scallops are not available, sea scallops can be used in this recipe, but they are not as tender or as sweet. If you do use sea scallops, cut them in half crosswise and increase the marinating time by 30 to 60 minutes, depending on their size.

For variety, set the scallops with their marinade against any, or a combination, of the following: fresh spinach, Belgian endive, radicchio, red leaf lettuce, chicory, or Bibb lettuce.

Sautéed Sea Scallops Gremolada with Tomato Butter Sauce

Like its buttery cousin served with Ossobuco alla Milanese, the gremolada is a piquant touch that makes the scallops a savory success. The scallops must sizzle the moment they touch the hot oil, or else their juices will be lost. Prepare all the ingredients ahead of time because the final cooking is very quick. Serve this hearty dish on warmed plates with steamed potatoes and a mixed green salad on the side.

Yields 6 servings

2 cups (235 ml) Tomato Butter Sauce *(see page 89)*

FOR THE GREMOLADA
1 medium garlic clove
Grated rind of 2 lemons
2 tablespoons chopped fresh parsley
1/8 teaspoon oregano

FOR THE GARNISH
6 sprigs parsley
6 lemon wedges
6 slices of Pullman Loaf *(see page 488)*

FOR THE SCALLOPS
24 to 30 sea scallops (about 6 ounces or 170 g per serving)
1/3 cup (80 ml) half-and-half
Salt
Freshly ground white pepper
1/2 cup (60 g) flour
1/4 cup (60 ml) peanut oil
3 tablespoons (45 g) butter

Recommended equipment

A 1 1/2-quart (1 1/2 L) saucepan, paring knife, small chef's knife, box grater, small bowl, colander, medium mixing bowl, waxed paper, 12-inch (30 cm) cast-iron or enameled cast-iron sauté pan, wooden spatula, slotted spoon, paper towels.

Prepare the tomato butter sauce and set aside in the saucepan.

Prepare the gremolada. Peel the garlic clove, mince it finely with the chef's knife, and put it in the small bowl. Grate the lemon rind on the fine side of the box grater, being careful to leave the bitter white behind, and add it to the bowl. Chop the parsley and combine it with the oregano in the small bowl. Mix the ingredients thoroughly and set aside.

For the garnish, reserve washed sprigs of parsley, slice fresh lemons into wedges, and toast the bread.

Rinse the scallops in the colander under cold water, drain, pat them dry, halve them crosswise, and put the halves into the mixing bowl. Pour on the half-and-half and season with salt and pepper. Spread the flour on waxed paper (or a plate). Taking the scallops one by one, remove them from the half-and-half, shake gently, and roll them in the flour until well coated.

Set the tomato butter over low heat to warm. Warm the plates. Heat the peanut oil in the sauté pan over medium to high heat. When the oil is hot, gently shake the excess flour from the scallops and add them to the sauté pan. Sauté, turning them as they brown, until they are nicely browned on all sides (about 4 minutes). When done, remove scallops with the slotted spoon to paper towels to drain.

Now you must move quickly to finish the dish. Set the toast on the warmed plates, pour some tomato butter sauce around each slice, and divide the scallops over the toast. Wipe out the sauté pan, removing all the oil, add the butter, and set over medium heat. When butter begins to foam, add the gremolada mixture, stir together for 15 seconds, and pour over the scallops. Garnish the plates with the parsley sprigs and lemon wedges and serve immediately.

 Coquilles Saint-Jacques en Papillote au Printemps
Scallops with Fresh Vegetables en Papillote

Our own creation, the papillote contains so much good culinary activity inside that, when opened, it is like going inside a circus tent. The lemon juice and butter combine with the scallops' own juices to create a sauce that asks to be soaked up with a crusty Dinner Roll or French Bread. You will enjoy the fragrance and presentation of this dish, and, with a green salad, it makes a perfect light luncheon. Start your stopwatch to see how long it takes the first guest to ask, "How did you do it?"

Yields 6 servings

6 tablespoons (90 g) Beurre Maître d'hôtel *(see page 81)*
18 pieces Pommes de Terre Parisienne *(see page 442)*, steamed
6 papillotes *(see page 568)*
1 large (or 2 small) zucchini
1/2 medium to large red bell pepper
1/2 medium to large yellow bell pepper
1 medium to large leek (white part only)
3 scallions
18 pods of snow peas (if large, use 12 and halve them), blanched and cooled
2 tablespoons olive oil
Salt
Freshly ground white pepper
1/8 teaspoon grated fresh ginger root
2 pounds (900 g) bay scallops
Juice of 2 lemons (3 if small)
3 fresh basil leaves, halved
Butter for the papillotes
Peanut oil for the baking sheet

Recommended equipment

Parchment paper for the papillotes, paring knife, 1 1/2-quart (1 1/2 L) saucepan, colander, 12-inch (30 cm) sauté pan, box grater, wooden spatula, baking sheet.

If you have none already stored, prepare the beurre maître d'hôtel and reserve.

Prepare the pommes de terre Parisienne and reserve.

Make the six papillotes and butter them on one side.

Prepare the vegetables. Scrub the zucchini (do not peel) and, using the paring knife, cut into matchstick-size strips 1 1/2 inches long and 1/4 inch thick (3 3/4 cm x 2/3 cm). Wash the bell pepper halves, remove seeds, and cut into matchstick-size strips. Thoroughly wash the leek under running cold water, cut in half lengthwise, and then into fine strips 1 1/2 inches long. Wash the scallions and slice thinly. Fill the saucepan with water, set over high heat, and, when it has come to a boil, blanch the snow peas for 30 seconds. Drain them in a colander and let them cool.

Set the sauté pan over medium heat, add the olive oil, and, when it is hot, add the zucchini, bell peppers, leek, scallions, and snow peas. Season lightly with salt and pepper, grate in the ginger, and sauté for 2 minutes, stirring with the spatula from time to time, then remove from heat and set aside.

Rinse the scallops under running cold water in the colander and let drain. (If you are using sea scallops cut the large ones in half crosswise.)

Preheat oven to 375F (190C).

Divide the scallops among the papillotes, season lightly with salt and pepper, then add even portions of the sautéed vegetables, pommes de terre Parisienne, beurre maître d'hôtel, and lemon juice. Place one-half of a basil leaf on each portion and fold the papillotes tightly along the edges.

Oil the baking sheet, place the papillotes on it, and set into the middle level of the oven to cook for 7 minutes (8 minutes for sea scallops). The paper should puff up and be lightly browned. Rush the papillotes to the table to preserve the beauty of this presentation.

Variation: Instead of scallops, use fillet of sole "en goujons"—boneless and skinless "fingers" of sole, 2 to 2 1/2 inches long and 1/2 inch thick (5 to 6 3/4 cm x 1 1/4 cm), cut across the grain of the fish. Cook the papillotes for 8 to 9 minutes, depending upon the size of the goujons. (Allow about 6 ounces [170 g] of fish per serving.)

Mélange Méditerranéen: Pasta, Rices, and Maritime Stews

Fettuccine Fruits de Mer

"Fruits de mer" is a general term and you could just as easily use lump or king crabmeat, oysters, mussels, and other fish. This is a favorite among Grille regulars and you may prefer to omit the cream for a lighter but still delicious presentation. Above all, use only the freshest vegetables and seafood available.

Yields 6 to 8 servings

2 tablespoons salt
1/4 cup (60 ml) olive oil
1 pound (450 g) fettuccine
4 cups (950 ml) whipping cream
8 ounces (225 g) small shrimp, peeled and deveined
1 tablespoon chopped shallots
2 celery stalks
1/2 medium carrot
1/2 bunch of broccoli
1 medium zucchini
1 medium red bell pepper
6 ounces (170 g) mushrooms
8 ounces (225 g) bay scallops (or sea scallops cut up)
8 ounces (225 g) fresh or cooked lobster
1/2 teaspoon Pesto *(see page 418)*
Salt
Freshly ground white pepper
A dash of cayenne pepper
4 ounces (115 g) snow peas
1/4 cup (60 ml) grated Parmesan cheese

Recommended equipment

An 8-quart (8 L) stockpot with lid, long-handled fork, colander, 3-quart (3 L) saucepan, shrimp deveiner, stiff bristle vegetable brush, paring knife, swivel-bladed vegetable peeler, 12-inch (30 cm) sauté pan, wooden spatula, box grater.

Bring 7 quarts water to a boil in the covered stockpot, add 2 tablespoons each of salt and olive oil, and then the fettuccine. Re-cover pot, return to a boil, then uncover and adjust heat so that pasta cooks at a slow boil. Stir occasionally with the long-handled fork to keep it from sticking together. Cook until the pasta is al dente and retains a firmness in texture when chewed. Taste a piece to be sure. Fresh pasta will be done in 3 to 4 minutes and dried pasta will take 9 to 12. When done, remove pot to sink and let cold water run briskly into it while stirring for 30 seconds. Then drain pasta into the colander and reserve.

Add the whipping cream to the saucepan and set it over medium heat to reduce to slightly less than half. Keep an eye on it while you prepare the fish and vegetables.

The final cooking of this dish goes quickly, so

keep the prepared ingredients reserved nearby. Wash the shrimp under cold running water, then peel and devein. Chop the shallots. Wash the celery stalks, trim with the paring knife so that they are as stringless as possible, and cut into matchstick-size strips. Scrub the carrot, peel it, and cut into strips 2 inches (5 cm) long and 1/8 inch (1/3 cm) thick. Wash the broccoli, break off the buds so that they are 2 inches long, and reserve. Scrub the zucchini and cut into matchstick-size strips. Wash the bell pepper, halve it, scrape out the seeds, and cut into matchstick-size strips. Brush the mushrooms of any clinging dirt and cut into thick slices. Wash the scallops under cold running water and drain. (If using sea scallops, cut into thirds or quarters, depending upon their size.) Cut the lobster meat into 1/2-inch (1 1/4 cm) cubes.

Prepare the pesto.

Add 2 tablespoons olive oil to the sauté pan and set over medium-high heat. When oil is hot, add the shrimp and cook for 2 minutes, stirring with the wooden spatula. Then add the shallots, celery, carrots, broccoli, zucchini, bell pepper, and mushrooms and sauté for 3 minutes, stirring occasionally. Next, add scallops, lobster, and pesto and sauté, stirring, for 2 minutes. Stir in the reduced cream and season to taste with salt, white pepper, and cayenne. Remove pan from heat and reserve.

The finishing of this dish should be done only when you are ready to serve it. Trim the snow peas of their blossom ends and blanch briefly in boiling water in a small saucepan, drain, and reserve. Using the box grater, grate the Parmesan cheese. Stir the cooked fettuccine into the vegetables in the sauté pan and simmer over medium heat for 2 minutes. Stir in the snow peas, remove pan from heat, and blend in the Parmesan. Serve immediately on warm plates or in pasta bowls.

If serving is delayed and the fettuccine becomes too pasty, stir in some half-and-half until the texture is satisfactory.

Variation: For a distinctly different flavor, omit the pesto and instead of celery use one-quarter of a medium fennel bulb, trimmed and cut into matchstick-size strips. Or, substitute fresh dill for the pesto and strips of smoked salmon for the lobster and/or the shrimp.

Fettuccine Orientale with Shrimp and Scallops

More than anything else, this recipe shows the great versatility of pasta. A Homestead creation, here the color and texture of oriental vegetables are paired with the coolness of mint and the fire of Cajun seasoning. An unlikely combination, you say? Well, give it a try—we think you will be pleasantly surprised.

Yields 6 to 8 servings

FOR THE SAUCE
Zest of 1/3 lemon
1 tablespoon (15 g) butter
2 teaspoons curry powder
4 cups (950 ml) whipping cream
Salt

FOR THE VEGETABLES
1/2 medium red bell pepper
1/2 medium green bell pepper
1/3 medium cucumber
4 ounces (115 g) snow peas
8 whole, canned water chestnuts
8 dried wood ear mushrooms
1 tablespoon olive oil
Salt
Freshly ground white pepper

FOR THE PASTA
1 tablespoon salt
2 tablespoons olive oil
1 pound (450 g) fettuccine

FOR THE SEAFOOD
1 pound (450 g) medium shrimp
1 pound (450 g) bay scallops
2 scallions
1 garlic clove
12 fresh mint leaves
1 tablespoon olive oil
1 teaspoon flour
1/4 teaspoon Cajun seafood seasoning or Old Bay seafood seasoning plus a pinch of cayenne pepper
Freshly ground white pepper
Salt

Recommended equipment

A paring knife, small chef's knife, 3-quart (3 L) saucepan, 8-quart (8 L) stockpot with lid, wooden spatula, swivel-bladed vegetable peeler, 1-quart (1 L) bowl, long-handled fork, colander, shrimp deveiner, fine-mesh sieve, 12-inch (30 cm) sauté pan, garlic press, serving dish.

Using the paring knife, remove the zest from one-third of the lemon, being careful to leave all the bitter white behind, chop the zest finely with the chef's knife, and reserve. Set the saucepan over medium low heat, add the butter, and, when it has melted, add the lemon zest and curry powder and sauté, stirring, for 30 seconds. Then add the whipping cream and a pinch of salt and bring to a boil, stirring occasionally. Adjust the heat so that the mixture simmers until it is reduced by one-half—about 20 minutes. When done, remove from heat and reserve.

While the cream is simmering, bring 5 to 6 quarts of water to boil in the stockpot with the lid on.

While the water is coming to a boil, prepare the vegetables and reserve all until needed. Rinse the bell pepper halves, seed them, and slice them into fine julienne strips. Rinse the cucumber, peel one-third of it, halve and seed the peeled section, and slice it into matchstick-size strips. Rinse the snow peas and snap off the blossom ends. Slice the water chestnuts as thinly as possible. Set the dried mushrooms into the bowl, cover with cold water, and let soak until softened. When soft, slice them into 1/4-inch (2/3 cm) thick strips.

When the water has come to a boil, remove the lid, add the salt, olive oil, and fettuccine, replace the lid, and return to the boil. Then remove the lid and adjust heat so that the fettuccine boils gently until done al dente—for fresh pasta, this will take about 4 minutes. While it is cooking, separate the strands as necessary with the long-handled fork. When done, remove from heat, drain pasta in the colander, run cold water over the fettuccine for 15 to 20 seconds, and let drain well.

Prepare the seafood: rinse the shrimp under running cold water, peel, and devein. Rinse the scallops in the fine-mesh sieve under running cold water and let drain. Also, rinse the scallions, slice very thinly, and reserve. Peel the garlic clove. Using the chef's knife, roughly chop the mint leaves and reserve.

Set the sauté pan over medium heat, add 1 tablespoon olive oil, the bell peppers, cucumber, snow peas, water chestnuts, and mushrooms, and season with salt and pepper. Sauté, stirring, for 5 minutes. Then remove from heat and scrape the vegetables into the reduced cream sauce in the saucepan.

Return the sauté pan to medium high heat, add another tablespoon of olive oil, and, when hot, stir in the shrimp and sauté, stirring and turning the shrimp, for 3 minutes. Quickly dust the scallops with flour and add them to the pan along with the scallions and mint leaves. Press the garlic into the pan, season with the Cajun (or Old Bay) seasoning, a pinch of salt, and pepper, and sauté for 3 more minutes. Then remove pan from heat and reserve.

Combine the fettuccine in the saucepan with the reduced cream and vegetables and blend well while bringing the mixture to a simmer over medium heat. Heat the fettuccine thoroughly, pour into a warm serving dish, spread the seafood over the top, and serve at once.

Pilaff of Mussels à la Marinière

To get any more Mediterranean we would have to staple a little bag of sand from Saint-Tropez to this page. Pilaff from Turkey and mussels from Provence prepared in the time-honored "sailor's way"—all you need is van Gogh's intense sun and azure-blue water.

Long a staple in the European diet, mussels are becoming popular in North America—so much so that they are commercially farmed on the Atlantic coast. These small mollusks deserve simple preparations to enhance their subtle, smoky flavor. Accompany the pilaff with a green or vegetable salad for a lunch or light dinner. Or, for an appetizer, offer the mussels on the half shell with the sauce spooned over them (six per serving should suffice) and some crusty French Bread on the side.

Yields 6 servings

5 dozen mussels
1 recipe Rice Pilaff *(see page 424)*
3 cups (710 ml) dry white wine
3 tablespoons chopped fresh shallots
1 teaspoon chopped celery leaves
1 teaspoon coarsely crushed white pepper
1 teaspoon Blond Roux *(see page 65)*
Juice of 1 lemon
Salt
A dash of cayenne pepper
2 tablespoons chopped fresh parsley
2 tablespoons (30 g) butter, softened at room temperature

Recommended equipment

A stiff bristle brush, paring knife, colander, 4- to 5-quart (4 to 5 L) saucepan with lid, small chef's knife, mortar and pestle, slotted spoon, large mixing bowl, 3-quart (3 L) saucepan, fine-mesh sieve lined with cheesecloth, small mixing bowl, wire whisk.

Using the stiff bristle brush, scrub mussels thoroughly under cold running water, being careful to remove beards (or scrape them off with a paring knife). If any mussels are partially open, touch them, and if they remain open discard them. Drain the mussels in the colander.

Begin cooking the rice pilaff.

Put the mussels into the large saucepan and add the wine. Chop the shallots and celery leaves with the chef's knife, crush the pepper in the mortar and pestle, and add all to the saucepan. Cover the saucepan, bring to a boil over medium high heat, and stir or shake from time to time for about 5 minutes or until the shells have opened. Remove saucepan from heat and dip mussels out with the slotted spoon into the colander set inside the mixing bowl to drain completely. Discard any unopened mussels.

Combine the cooking juices from the large saucepan and the mixing bowl in the small saucepan. Bring to a boil over medium heat and simmer until reduced by one-third (about 10 minutes). Pour the reduction through the cheesecloth-lined sieve set over the small mixing bowl, wash out the small saucepan, and return the reduction to it. Bring to a simmer over medium heat, whisk in the blond roux until well blended, add lemon juice, and simmer on low heat for 5 minutes. Adjust seasoning with salt if needed and add cayenne pepper.

While the sauce is simmering, remove mussels from their shells. Discard the shells and gently wash any mussels that are still sandy or gritty (be sure, too, that any remaining beard is disposed of). Chop the parsley. When the sauce has finished simmering, add the mussels and parsley, return to a simmer, then remove from heat, blend in the soft butter, and serve over the rice pilaff on a warm dinner plate.

Paella

This classic dish has as many variations as the Spanish coast has seaports—even the Spaniards don't agree on the ingredients that vary from province to province according to local produce and taste. Don't be intimidated by the length of the recipe. Prepare each element separately, in advance, and then the final cooking time is no more than thirty minutes. Your guests must be ready and waiting as soon as this comes from the oven—moist rice dishes wait for no one. Your effort will be rewarded by the beauty of the glistening blue-black mussel shells, red and green peppers, saffron rice, white seafood, and browned meats. Strongly contrasting flavors and textures will create a memorable feast for you and your friends, even if you are dining at home rather than beneath a Spanish moon in Valencia or Barcelona.

Yields 12 to 18 servings

8 ounces (225 g) pork shoulder
8 ounces (225 g) baked smoked ham
2 frying chickens, each weighing about 2 to 2 1/4 pounds (900 to 1025 g)
2 medium onions
2 garlic cloves
1 medium green bell pepper
1 medium red bell pepper
4 medium, ripe tomatoes (blanched, peeled, and seeded; see page 568)
8 ounces (225 g) green peas
12 artichoke hearts or 6 bottoms (canned or fresh)
24 mussels (about 1 quart or 1 L)
1 1/2 pounds (675 g) shrimp
4 medium lobster tails, weighing 6 to 8 ounces (170 to 225 g) each (or 24 crayfish tails or 4 Maine lobsters weighing 12 ounces [340 g] each)
1 pound (450 g) red snapper or grouper
1 pound (450 g) cod or halibut
5 tablespoons olive oil
1/8 teaspoon saffron threads, chopped
A pinch of thyme
1/2 bay leaf
1 tablespoon tomato paste
1 cup (235 ml) dry white wine
3 1/2 cups (830 ml) White Chicken Stock *(see page 61)*
2 cups (475 ml) raw long grain rice
4 pimiento halves (packed in water and drained), chopped
3 tablespoons capers, partially drained
1 pound (450 g) squid, cut into bite-size pieces (optional)

Recommended equipment

A large chef's knife, boning knife, stiff bristle brush, shrimp deveiner, wooden spatula, deep iron skillet or paella pan *(see below)*, 1 1/2-quart (1 1/2 L) saucepan with lid, slotted spoon, colander, medium mixing bowl, 4 quart (4 L) saucepan.

Prepare each ingredient and set aside until needed.

For the meat and poultry: With the large chef's knife, finely dice the pork and ham in separate batches. Using the boning knife, cut each chicken into eight pieces. With the chicken laying breast side up, carefully cut through the joint connecting the thighs to the body, using the sharp point of the boning knife to separate the thigh from the body without cutting either. Similarly, use the point of the boning knife to cut the leg and thigh apart at the joint without cutting through the bones. Putting the bird on its side, use the boning knife to cut the breast free, just at the point where the ribs end. Turn bird over and repeat on other side. Cut through joints at neck end of breast, releasing the breasts and wings as one section. Cut breast into two pieces lengthwise at the breast bone. Finally, cut each breast crosswise into two pieces, leaving the wing attached to one of the pieces. Reserve.

For the vegetables: Remove the skin from the onions and chop them finely with the large chef's knife. Peel and mince the garlic. Seed and dice the bell peppers. Prepare the tomatoes and quarter them. Cook the green peas in water in the small saucepan, drain, and set aside. Wash out saucepan. Prepare the artichoke hearts (cut in half) or the bottoms (cut into quarters).

For the seafood: Scrub the mussels thoroughly

with the brush under cold running water, being careful to remove the beards (or scrape them off with a paring knife). Peel and devein the shrimp. Using the large chef's knife, cut each lobster tail into five pieces. If using crayfish tails, leave them whole. If using Maine lobsters, cut them into chunks. Remove skin and bones from the fish and cut into chunks. If using the optional squid, clean and cut into small pieces.

Now, at last, you are ready to cook. In your pan over medium heat, add 3 tablespoons olive oil and when it is good and hot add the chicken, pork, and ham. Cook, stirring with a wooden spatula, until meats are lightly browned on all sides (3 to 4 minutes). Add the onions, garlic, green and red peppers, two of the tomatoes, saffron, thyme, and bay leaf to the pan and sauté for 2 minutes. Then add tomato paste and 1/2 cup (118 ml) each of white wine and chicken stock. Bring to a simmer and adjust heat to maintain a gentle simmer on low heat for 15 minutes. Then add rice and remaining chicken stock, bring back to a simmer, and cook for 8 minutes.

At the same time, when the above ingredients have reached their first simmer, begin cooking the seafood, starting with the mussels. Put the remaining 1/2 cup of white wine in the small saucepan, add mussels, cover tightly, bring to a boil, and steam for 5 minutes or until shells have opened. Remove saucepan from heat. Dip mussels out with the slotted spoon into the colander set inside a mixing bowl to drain completely. Discard any unopened mussels and reserve the cooking juices. Snap off one-half of each shell so that mussel remains on the other half. Reserve.

In the large saucepan heat 2 tablespoons olive oil over medium heat, add shrimp and lobster, and cook for 3 minutes, stirring constantly with a wooden spatula. Add the cooking juices from the mussels and simmer for 4 minutes. Set aside.

Preheat oven to 350F (177C).

When rice and meat mixture has finished the second simmer, arrange the following on top in an attractive pattern: the shrimp and lobster pieces with their cooking juices, the raw fish pieces (and optional squid), and the two remaining quartered tomatoes. Set pan over medium heat, bring to a simmer, and set into preheated oven for 8 minutes. Remove from oven, sprinkle peas, artichoke pieces, pimiento, and capers over all. Arrange the mussels in a neat pattern and return to the oven for 1 minute. Call your guests to the table.

Remove pan from the oven and check the rice: if too dry, add a little chicken stock; if too soupy, simmer over medium heat a minute or two. Rice should be slightly firm, not mushy and overcooked. When paella is perfectly cooked, carry the steaming pan to the table, delighting your diners with the fragrant and beautifully composed dish.

There are special wide, shallow paella pans available, but a good substitute would be either a deep, iron skillet or a heavy stainless steel, copper, or enameled cast-iron sauté pan. Whatever you choose, remember that the paella is cooked in the oven so the pan must have heatproof handles.

Bouillabaisse

To give you an idea of the importance attached to this dish in France, Larousse Gastronomique notes that legend gives credit for its invention to Venus. Although she is said to have created it for her husband, Vulcan, Méry's poetic account attributes it to the abbess of a convent in Marseilles. Whatever its origin, bouillabaisse is native to Provence and the most authentic versions are to be found along the Mediterranean Coast from Marseilles to Toulon. Of course, les Marseillaises would dismiss any other recipe as an imitation, and arguments over the authenticity of any given recipe have probably led to fatal duels, but, in truth, there are as many variations as there are chefs preparing them. Some add potatoes to the stew and others omit saffron. It would be presumptuous to give an exact recipe for a dish which is made with fish native to the Mediterranean and difficult to obtain elsewhere. So, we will give a basic guide for a saffron-flavored fish stew that will warm you and your guests and bring them back for more. Serve it in hot soup plates accompanied by rounds of French Bread that have been rubbed with puréed garlic, moistened with olive oil, and toasted in the oven.

Yields 8 servings

8 pounds (3600 g) whole fish or 4 pounds (1800 g) fish fillets *(see below)*
1 large leek or 2 small (white part only)
1 celery stalk
1 large onion (or 2 small)
2 large ripe tomatoes (blanched, peeled, and seeded; *see page 568*)
1/2 teaspoon chopped fresh fennel leaves (or 6 anise seeds)
2 garlic cloves
1 1/2 tablespoons olive oil
8 saffron threads, chopped
1/8 teaspoon thyme
1/3 bay leaf
1 1/2 quarts (1 1/2 L) Fish Stock *(see page 60)*
2 cups (475 ml) water
1 cup (235 ml) dry white wine
2 tablespoons chopped parsley
A dash of salt
Freshly ground white pepper
A dash of cayenne pepper

Recommended equipment

A boning knife, paring knife, small chef's knife, 8-quart (8 L) stockpot, wooden spatula.

Having chosen your fish, prepare them for cooking. If the fish are whole, you will have to clean, fillet, and bone them. Once you have the fillets, cut them into pieces 1 1/2 to 2 inches (3 3/4 to 5 cm) long, keeping the firmer-fleshed fish separate from the more delicate (they require different cooking times).

Prepare the vegetables, reserving each one. Wash the leek thoroughly under running cold water, trim, and with the paring knife, cut into fine julienne strips. Wash and trim the celery of all tough strings and cut into fine julienne strips. Peel the onion, halve it, and then mince it finely with the chef's knife. Prepare the tomatoes and cut them into strips. Chop the fresh fennel leaves if you are using them. Peel and mince the garlic cloves.

Set the stockpot over medium heat, add the olive oil, and, when it is hot, add the leeks, celery, and onion. Sauté for 1 minute and then stir in the tomatoes, garlic, saffron, thyme, bay leaf, and fennel (or anise seeds). Cook, stirring, for 1 minute and then add the fish stock, water, and white wine. Bring to a strong simmer and put the firmer fish (such as red snapper, tuna, grouper, and striped bass) into the stockpot and simmer gently for 5 minutes. Add the more delicate fish and continue gently simmering for 8 minutes. During this time chop the parsley with the chef's knife, make your toast, and heat the soup plates. (If you are adding lobster, do it during the last 2 minutes of cooking time and before the final seasoning.)

Adjust the seasoning with salt and white and cayenne pepper. Stir in the parsley and serve immediately to your eager diners.

You should choose several different varieties (five to six) from among the freshest seafood available in your area. Some possibilities are: flounder, red snapper, grouper, striped or sea bass, tuna, mackerel, halibut, sea scallops, eel, cod, monkfish, and seatrout. Use smaller amounts of oily fish such as mackerel. If you want lobster in your stew, cut tails into 1 1/2- to 2-inch (3 3/4 to 5 cm) pieces (in the shell), sauté in olive oil for about 10 minutes over low to medium heat, and add to stew during the last couple of minutes.

In Marseilles you would also find *rouille*, a last-minute sauce enhancement based on pimiento, hot pepper, garlic, and either olive oil or a thin mayonnaise, into which the hot fish broth is mixed just before serving.

When fennel is cooked for a vegetable the leaves are trimmed and can find their way into this dish, or be used as a decoration on a fish entrée.

Aegean Fisherman's Stew

Between Greece and Turkey lies the island-studded Aegean, the only area of the Mediterranean where sailors can rely on regular winds throughout the summer months. These northern winds, known as etesian (from the Greek etos, a year, thus being reliable every year), are colloquially called "meltemi" (possibly a corruption of "bel tempo," the time of good weather). Just as the meltemi nourished the merchant trade along the archipelago to Crete and Alexandria, this simple regional fish stew sustains those famished by long hours laboring at sea—or on land. We recommend striped bass, sea bass, grouper, scrod, or red snapper. When served with a mixed green salad and crackers this light, creamy stew makes a complete meal.

Yields 6 servings

2 recipes Sauce Velouté de Poisson *(see page 68)*, using only 2 tablespoons roux
3 celery stalks
2 medium onions
2 medium carrots
3 medium boiling potatoes (1 1/4 to 1 1/2 pounds or 570 to 675 g)
1 slice smoked bacon about 3/4 to 1 ounce (23 to 30 g)
1 medium garlic clove
2 1/4 pounds (1025 g) fish fillets
1/8 teaspoon dried thyme (or 1 sprig fresh thyme, chopped)
1/2 small bay leaf
8 ounces (225 g) green peas (fresh or frozen)
Salt
Freshly ground white pepper
A dash of Worcestershire sauce
2 tablespoons chopped fresh parsley

Recommended equipment

A paring knife, slicing knife, stiff bristle brush, swivel-bladed vegetable peeler, small chef's knife, 4- to 5-quart (4 to 5 L) saucepan, wooden spatula.

Prepare the sauce velouté de poisson, using only 2 tablespoons roux (i.e., one-third of the total) when binding the fish stock.

Next, prepare the vegetables, reserving each one. Wash the celery stalks and peel them with the paring knife to remove as many strings as possible. Slice the celery, on a slant, into pieces 1/4 inch (2/3 cm) thick. Peel the onions and, using the slicing knife, cut them into slices as thinly as possible. Scrub the carrots, peel them with the vegetable peeler, and slice them into pieces 1/8 inch (1/3 cm) thick. Scrub the potatoes, peel them, and slice into 1-inch (2 1/2 cm) cubes.

Cut the bacon into small cubes. Chop the garlic.

Rinse the fish fillets gently under running cold water, pat dry, and check them to be sure they have been thoroughly boned. Remove the skin, cut the fillets into 2- to 2 1/2-inch (5 to 6 1/4 cm) chunks, and reserve.

Set the saucepan over medium heat and sauté the bacon cubes until the fat has been rendered. Add the celery, onions, carrots, thyme, garlic, and bay leaf, and sauté for 1 minute, stirring occasionally with the spatula. Add the velouté de poisson, bring to a low simmer, and cook for 5 minutes, stirring from time to time. Then add potatoes and cook until they can just be pierced with a knife (8 to 9 minutes).

Meanwhile, blanch the peas, drain, and reserve. When the potatoes are just right, add the fillet pieces and simmer gently for 3 minutes. Put the peas into the saucepan and simmer another minute. Then taste carefully for seasoning and add salt, pepper, and a dash of Worcestershire sauce. If the stew is too thick add a little milk or fish stock. Just before serving, stir in the parsley.

Suprêmes de Volaille Kiev in the Grille

Poultry and Game

Poultry

Then, with a vaguely interested air, she would stop in front of the stall she had chosen, examine a couple of chickens (they were sold in pairs in those days), and verify that the comb was a healthy red, the feet smooth and white, and the eyes bright. Then she blew on the feathers in the crop, in order to separate them, and felt with her thumb to see that the crop was slim, bright, and without any white flakiness. She checked to see that the gizzard wasn't stuffed with corn, which would have artificially inflated the weight ("Why should I pay for corn which does neither the chicken nor me any good?"). Finally, she made sure that the other chicken making up the pair had the same qualities as his corn-fed brother.

Following this minute examination, my aunt's face would express a pained skepticism with regard to the unfortunate fowls, and the farmer's wife, watching my aunt out of the corner of her eye, became convinced that she had a difficult customer on her hands.

"My little woman," she would protest (my Aunt Celestine was a "little woman" of over 200 pounds), "those chickens have never eaten anything but corn. It's been over a week since they stopped running loose and were put in the *épinette*." (An *épinette* was a wicker cage in which chickens were placed for fattening.)

"My poor woman," my aunt replied with an absolutely counterfeit air of profound commiseration, "your chickens ought to have stayed another week or two in the *épinette*. In any case, at my table I can't serve birds that are nothing but skin and bones."

With that, she began a false exit, knowing full well that the farmer's wife would do everything in her power to keep her from going. It was all part of an immutable ritual, without which—for the farmer's wife as much as for my aunt—the negotiation would have had no real interest.

Aunt Celestine would then announce a firm and definitive price, which she would not exceed for anything in the world. It was a question of dignity. Her price was, for that matter, perfectly honest, which didn't prevent the farmer's wife from feigning, for the sake of principle, a deep disappointment. Magnanimously, my aunt would agree to take—at the same price—two or three other pairs of the remaining chickens. The farmer's wife, in order to have the last word, would exclaim: "Very well! But it's only because it's you—I'm losing money on the deal." This didn't fool anyone, but it provided a logical ending for the transaction.

—Roger Vergé

Although the Homestead's average weekly shopping list for fresh poultry of 1,250 pounds of chicken, 2,250 pounds of turkey, and 750 pounds of duckling exceeds Aunt Celestine's by a bit, our own B. G. McElwee is just as hard to please as she. Because he has been buying in such quantities from the same Virginia chicken and turkey poulterers for many years, the Homestead kitchen is assured of the same consistency and quality the Michelin three-star French chefs demand and receive from the famed chicken suppliers in the Bresse region. Fortunately, poultry processing plants and refrigerated transport have freed us from carrying home a squirming chicken under each arm—indeed, I don't know where we would find room in the kitchen to let several thousand birds run around loose. Ironically, even with (or because of) these conveniences, we all need more than ever to be Aunt Celestines when we shop for chicken.

Unless you happen to have a butcher who buys fresh chickens from a local producer, you have to rely on poultry which has been processed several days previously. In that case, there is no alternative to shopping around for the brand which consistently gives you the best results. Freshness should be your first concern. Poultry which is shipped any great distance is chemically treated to maintain color and retard spoilage, so you want to give these chemicals as little time to work as possible.

By the way, on the topic of color, some producers feed their chickens such items as marigold petals to produce a yellowish hue. This is false representation for sales purposes. In southwestern France, there is a definite preference for chickens raised on corn, which does produce a yellow-colored meat. In northern Europe, however, the paler color of chicken raised on other grains is preferred, and, depending on their origins, Americans reflect these preferences. There is a definite difference in flavor between the two, and, if you can get corn-fed chicken, do so. "Free-range" chicken (and free-range meat in general) is becoming easier to come by, and, depending upon the feed available in the range, can be the tastiest and most chemical-free of all.

Before moving on to a sketch of the poultry section of this chapter we will leave you with two *conseils*. Because Aunt Celestine kept her birds alive until she worked her kitchen magic on them, she had no fear of the most serious problem facing the poultry industry—salmonella. A bacteria which can be lethal, it only becomes a problem if chickens have to wait for some time between being eviscerated and being packaged. Commercial producers use a chemical bath which dramatically reduces the possibility of contamination, but, to be on the safe side, give your poultry a thorough rinse inside and out with cold running water and pat dry before proceeding with the preparation. Also, be sure to wash your work surface thoroughly after you have finished working with the uncooked bird.

One of the most beneficial by-products of the concern over heart disease has been the confrontation of the fact that "fat is bad." Initially, this meant shunning all but fish and chicken—a trend we saw very clearly here at the Homestead. But the danger of dependence on only two animal protein sources, one of which (fish) is subject to environmental forces, has been realized, and producers of poultry, pork, and beef began to bring leaner meat to market. There is an additional benefit to be gained from geese and ducks. Cooks in southwestern France have traditionally rendered the fat for baking and sautéing, and chemical analysis shows that poultry fat has only 41 percent of the cholesterol contained in a similar amount of butter. In addition, it withstands the heat of sautéing better than butter, and many claim that it gives a superior flavor. Easy to store, rendered poultry fat can be kept in a covered jar in the refrigerator for weeks or frozen for months. So much for behind-the-scenes action, it is time to move center stage with that most versatile performer, M. Poulet, alias Mr. Chicken.

Every cookbook writer seems to define poultry differently, so we will follow suit. Chicken is the obvious charter member of the club, but we have also included turkey, goose, and duck. These birds have been domesticated for a long time, and as we point out in the introduction to the game section, the recipes for their preparation are more difficult to adapt for wild game.

In the poultry section of this chapter we start our tour in Russia, with an orthodox twist on Chicken Kiev and end right here at the Homestead with the American favorite—turkey, stuffed à la française with a southern accent. Between these two there is a globe-trotting array of recipes to tempt you depending upon the season and your creative urges.

First off is a series of preparations based on chicken breasts which have been boned—an easy task which you will master by the time you have done it twice. From Kiev, our itinerary takes us to fall in the Vallée d'Auge with fresh apples and a rich Calvados-laced brown sauce, followed by a trip through Madame du Barry's secret door to the private dining room of Louis XV, and then to a dignified but spicy Indonesian preparation with curry and chutney. Back to France, we encounter a colorful and tasty duo—first, a classic papillon with a Homestead-inspired raspberry sauce, followed by a side trip to Bordeaux for a peppery dish with a luxurious mushroom sauce evocative of the forests of the French southwest. Just time enough to do your laundry and prepare for a change of scene and pace. Popular where energy is scarce, stir-frying is a technique which offers the simplicity of cooking in one pan. This method is featured in three recipes which take us first to Hungary for a rosy, paprika-flavored dish, and then to the home of stir-frying for two Far Eastern recipes, the first more Indonesian in style, and the second more Chinese.

Returning to Virginia, we conclude the chicken breast tour with seven eclectic recipes, the first three accompanied by elegant sauces enriched by simmering with chicken bones, and each of the remaining four set off by exotic or colorful stuffings. First comes a dish calling for Virginia ham and mushrooms which loves the elegance of being served under glass. An Austrian recipe flavored with caraway follows, and the trio is completed by an exciting Hawaiian dish which echoes the great Indian trade routes with curry, pineapple, chutney, and saffron.

In the final section of this group, exotic gives way to classical as we start with a taste of Hawaiian fruit and coconut. The French influence reappears, first, with an aromatic fresh tarragon stuffing and then with a high feast, à la Périgord, of foie gras and truffles. And it is on to Florence, home of Catherine de' Medici, where we alight in the shadow of Giotto's Campanile and dine on a sumptuous preparation with tomato sauce and a stuffing based on spinach.

Bidding adieu to the warm greens of summer, we welcome the vibrancy and invigorating chill of autumn with four hearty and tasty preparations. Mediterranean influence dominates the first two—a perennial Italian favorite with a rich, tomato-based sauce, followed by a venerable Spanish classic (by way of Cuba), which, with its rice, is reminiscent of jambalaya. Moving northward from the coast we encounter a French sauté set in a creamy sauce enlivened by green peppercorns. Firmly at the center of French cooking is the fourth recipe—a wine-marinated preparation which simmers in a robust mixture of smoked bacon and vegetables in true Burgundian style.

The curtain comes down on the chicken show with a trio of very different roasted birds. A good, homey, pot-roasted chicken leads off. All this one needs is a slice of Mom's apple pie and homemade vanilla ice cream. Cookbook authors wax rhapsodic about chicken roasting in the oven, and well they should because its aroma causes great anticipation among cooks and diners alike. This next French specialty will hardly disappoint you as the tarragon permeates the air, let alone when the crisp brown skin and moist meat encounter the crème fraîche in the sauce. As a finale we have included a sophisticated recipe which could even serve as a Thanksgiving or holiday dish for a small gathering. The tang and color of orange and tangerine provide a zesty backdrop for the complexity of the wild rice, hazelnut, and chicken liver stuffing in this boned and roasted bird.

Never bashful, M. Poulet returns for a short encore with a quick chicken liver sauté enhanced by a sauce chasseur—a perfect high protein lunch when the cold winter winds are blowing.

Heartier fowl fill out the poultry section as we wend our way to the great American bird. It seems that the popularity of duck is soaring as it gets more lean, and you will find recipes with a raspberry-flavored sauce (our favorite) as well as the traditional orange-flavored one. We have also included a variation with ancient roots derived from pomegranate syrup, turmeric, and walnuts. Being large birds, goose and turkey are both favorites for ceremonial holiday feasts. Because so many stuffing and sauce recipes exist, we have given the basic French goose preparation with a simple brown sauce. The turkey, however, is another story. Boned and rolled, there is a choice of two stuffings, which keeps this from being the same old bird. Our favorite here at the Homestead uses Virginia ham with apricots, pecans, and raisins. However, you may prefer the one based on veal and pork sausage, spiced with sage and Spanish olives. Either one is sure to please and is guaranteed to prevent post-turkey "leftover-itis."

Before sending you to the kitchen to earn your wings, we need to stop by the Butcher Shop for a lesson from Walker May and his colleagues on the difference between two cuts of chicken that are often called for in these recipes. Throughout this cookbook we encourage you to do your own food preparation, whether you are working with fish, meat, or vegetables. This becomes particularly important when working with poultry and game. Nowadays, unless you buy a whole, fresh chicken (and for some recipes you must) you will be buying parts—already cut up—and included in the package price is the cost of someone else doing the job for you. How much wiser to buy a whole bird, cut it up yourself, and have scraps left for the stockpot which will provide the base for your own flavorful sauces and soups.

Once you have mastered cutting up and/or boning a chicken, any fowl is easy to deal with.

Two chicken cuts, suprêmes and côtelettes, need to be defined. A suprême is a boneless and skinless piece of breast; each whole breast yields two suprêmes. A whole breast also yields two côtelettes. A côtelette is a boned piece of breast with the skin on and the first wing joint (next to the breast meat) still attached (a nice and easy way to get more chicken on your plate). Suprêmes are one of the simplest cuts to make and can become one of the most elegant presentations. The côtelette is usually called for when "baked breast of chicken" is in the recipe title. The suprêmes or côtelettes may be stuffed and the stuffing will go either in a pocket in the breast meat (a pita bread–like pocket) or between the skin and the meat.

One last *conseil*. To do all this you will need an excellent (and we mean *excellent*) boning knife. (This applies to working with fish and meat as well.) Toss out any lightweight implements masquerading as "gourmet" tools, and buy either a German or French knife, preferably stainless steel (harder to maintain a sharp edge on than carbon steel, but also nonreactive with food), and a good butcher's steel for sharpening. Now, put on your apron, sharpen up the blade, and get to work on those suprêmes and côtelettes.

 ## *Suprêmes de Volaille Kiev*
Breast of Chicken in the Style of Kiev

An important center of medieval Russia until it was conquered by the Tartars in the early thirteenth century, Kiev is rightly honored with a recipe. As with the church and the revolution there is orthodoxy and revisionism in the history of this famous preparation. Many versions call for garlic, parsley, and/or tarragon to be worked into the filling. I prefer this one because nothing stands between the flavor of the chicken and the butter. It comes by way of a Russian chef and respected colleague at the Embassy Club of the former Ambassador Hotel in New York City. Present this classic on a bed of Rice Pilaff or Riz Valencienne and accompany it with fresh Asparagus.

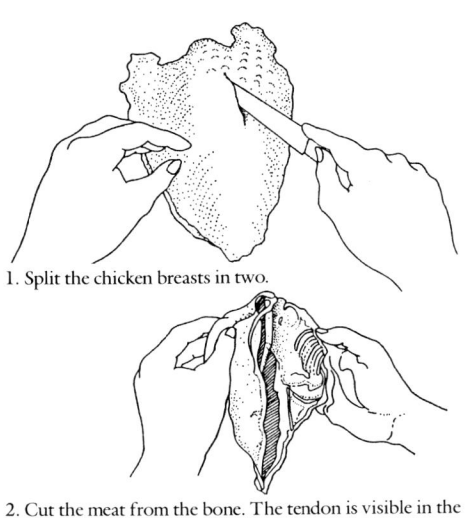

1. Split the chicken breasts in two.

2. Cut the meat from the bone. The tendon is visible in the filet mignon that lies against the larger filet.

3. Remove the tendon.

Yields 6 servings

3 whole chicken breasts, weighing 12 to 16 ounces (340 to 455 g) each
Salt
Freshly ground white pepper
8 ounces (225 g) butter in chilled quarters
4 eggs
3 tablespoons water
1/2 cup (60 g) flour
2 cups (475 ml) fine white bread crumbs
1 tablespoon melted butter
Juice of 1/2 lemon
Peanut oil for frying

Recommended equipment

A boning knife, waxed paper, cleaver, pan large enough to hold prepared chicken for chilling, 1-quart (1 L) mixing bowl, wire whisk, electric deep fryer with thermostat, frying thermometer, small saucepan.

For boned and skinned chicken breasts

Working with one whole breast at a time *(see illustration)*, rib side down on your cutting surface, split the breast in two, and cut the wings off at the beginning of the first joint (next to the breast). Remove the skin and separate the flesh from the bone, beginning at the ridge of the breastbone. For each side, use the boning knife and cut along the breastbone and then down the ribs, pulling the meat from the bone as you go and removing it in one piece. One whole breast yields two boneless and skinless pieces of meat called suprêmes. Each piece of meat is made up of two parts, the larger piece (on the top) is called the fillet and the smaller layer underneath is the filet mignon. Separate the two. In the filet mignon is a tough white tendon, visible in the meat where it lay against the ribs, which must be cut out.

Flattening the suprêmes

When all the suprêmes are ready, take the fillets, spread them smooth side down in a single layer on a large sheet of waxed paper, moisten each one with a few drops of cold water, cover with another sheet of waxed paper, and flatten them with the cleaver (or the bottom of a small sauté pan), using firm, light strokes until each piece is about 1/8 inch (1/3 cm) thick. Be careful not to tear the chicken. (The thicker part of the fillet may require a few more strokes to flatten out.) Spread out a fresh, smaller piece of waxed paper and arrange the filets mignons on it. Sprinkle them with a few drops of water, cover with another piece of waxed paper, and flatten them as you did the fillets. Now the fillets must be attached to the filets mignons. Lay each filet mignon along the thinner side of the larger fillet, overlapping it, cover with waxed paper, and attach the two pieces with a few light strokes of the cleaver. Season each suprême lightly with salt and pepper.

Next, prepare the butter. Cut each stick into thirds, cutting crosswise on the diagonal, and roll out on your work surface until it is a rounded oblong about 2 to 3 inches (5 to 7 1/2 cm) long. Place a butter oblong slightly crosswise in the center of each suprême and fold the meat over it one side at a time, making sure that there is a good overlap on the top and bottom to hold the butter in during cooking. As the suprêmes are finished, set them on the pan in a single layer and refrigerate for 30 minutes to 1 hour. (Cover with a slightly damp towel if you are chilling them longer.)

After suprêmes are chilled, beat the eggs with the water in the bowl using the whisk. Season with salt and pepper and beat until well blended. Put the flour on a plate (or your work surface) and do likewise with the bread crumbs. One at a time, roll the suprêmes in the flour and then the egg wash. Be careful to completely coat the surface with the egg. Then roll the chicken gently in the bread crumbs, remove, and look at it closely to make sure that bread crumbs are completely covering the surface. (If not, use your fingers to dab on some egg wash and then sprinkle with more crumbs.) Roll the chicken packages gently in your hand, pressing each end lightly to securely seal them. Then return chicken to egg wash, coat thoroughly, roll in bread crumbs a second time, and refrigerate until you are ready to cook.

Preheat the peanut oil in the deep fryer to 350F (177C). Place as many of the rolled suprêmes in the wire frying basket as will fit comfortably in a single layer without touching. (An average basket will hold three.) Lower the basket slowly into the hot oil, and as soon as the chicken starts to cook, count 8 minutes, cooking the chicken to a golden brown. Preheat oven to 200F (93C). Lift basket from oil, remove suprêmes to a dish, and set them into the oven to keep warm while the other pieces are frying. Cook each batch the same way, being sure that the oil maintains an even heat.

While the remaining suprêmes are cooking, melt the butter in the small saucepan and keep it warm. Juice the lemon and, just before serving, combine the juice with the butter. Season the chicken lightly with salt, drizzle butter and lemon mixture over it, and serve immediately.

Suprêmes de Volaille Normande
Breast of Chicken Normandy

For D-Day veterans, Normandy will forever conjure up memories of "Omaha" and "Utah" beaches and the beachheads of "Sword," "Juno," and "Gold." Long before World War II, this stunning corner of France was known for art, geography, and cuisine. The Bayeux tapestries are here, as are Rouen cathedral, the Norman abbey of Caen, and the spectacular complex of Mont-Saint-Michel, dating from the Carolingian period. It is also marked by deep valleys, which have given rise to the designation of some areas as "alpine"—there is even a Suisse Normande. Most important for us is the Pays d'Auge, the celebrated region of apple trees, Calvados, and cider as well as Camembert, Pont-l'Evêque, and Livarot cheeses—not to mention cream and beurre d'Isigny.

Now, all you have to do to bring fall in Normandy to your table is to follow the instructions, add a crisp autumn evening, and serve. The elements of this dish can be prepared an hour ahead of time, with the final simmering done at the last minute. Serve it with angel hair pasta and fresh Brussels Sprouts, String Beans, or Asparagus. (Oh yes, if you get to Mont-Saint-Michel and are starved, an excellent omelette is still to be had at Mère Poulard.)

Yields 6 servings

1 quart (1 L) Brown Chicken Stock *(see page 62)*
3 whole chicken breasts, weighing 12 to 16 ounces (340 to 455 g) each
2 medium apples (preferably Granny Smith or Winesap)
1 teaspoon butter
1/2 teaspoon sugar
1/4 cup (60 ml) Calvados
Salt
Freshly ground black pepper
1 tablespoon chopped shallots
2 tablespoons Clarified Butter *(see page 568)*
1/4 cup (60 ml) dry white wine
1/2 cup (118 ml) Calvados
1 cup (235 ml) Crème Fraîche *(see page 66)*
Zest of 1/3 lemon

Recommended equipment

A 3-quart (3 L) saucepan; boning knife; swivel-bladed vegetable peeler; apple corer; broiler pan; small chef's knife; an enameled cast-iron baking dish or lined copper plat à sauter with lid, large enough to hold the chicken in a single layer; wooden spatula; platter; large fine-mesh sieve; wire whisk; serving platter; 1 1/2-quart (1 1/2 L) saucepan.

Set the large saucepan over medium high heat, add the chicken stock, and cook at a lively simmer until reduced to 1 cup. When done, remove from heat and reserve.

While the stock is reducing, prepare the chicken for cooking. Put each whole breast on your work surface with the rib side down and spread the two halves apart with your hands. Cut along each side of the breastbone with the boning knife to release the breast halves. The rib bones and skin will be removed just before the final simmer. When they all have been split, set the breasts aside while you prepare the apples.

Preheat the oven broiler to maximum heat.

Peel the apples, core them, and slice each one into eight sections. Butter the broiler pan, arrange the apple slices in it in a single layer, and sprinkle them with sugar. Pour 1/4 cup Calvados around the apples, set the broiler pan on the oven rack a few inches from the broiler, and cook until the slices are lightly browned. When done, remove from oven and reserve until needed.

Season the chicken breasts lightly with salt and liberally with pepper. Chop the shallots and reserve.

Set the baking dish or plat à sauter over medium heat, add the clarified butter, and, when it is hot, add the chicken breasts, skin side down, in a single layer. Sauté them until browned and then turn them over to brown the other side (this should take 3 to 4 minutes per side). When the chicken is browned, add the shallots to the pan, stir for 15 seconds, and then add the white wine and 1/2 cup Calvados. Bring the liquid to a simmer for 3 minutes, add the stock, return liquid to a simmer, cover the pan, and adjust heat so that the chicken simmers gently for 20 minutes. (You can cook the chicken in 350F [177C] oven, if you prefer, after returning it to a simmer.)

When done, remove the chicken to a platter to cool and pass the sauce through the sieve into the remaining saucepan. Mince the lemon zest. Blend the crème fraîche into the sauce with the whisk, stir in the lemon zest, set the saucepan over medium high heat, and simmer the sauce until it is reduced to a light creamy consistency and can coat the back of a spoon. When done, remove from heat and keep at room temperature until the final simmer.

When the chicken is cool, remove the bones and skin and add the suprêmes to the sauce in the saucepan. At this point the dish may wait for up to an hour before serving. When ready to serve, set the saucepan over medium heat, bring the chicken to a simmer for a couple of minutes to heat it thoroughly, then arrange the chicken breasts on a warmed serving platter (or plates), spoon the sauce over them, garnish with the apple slices, and serve at once.

Variation: For suprêmes with Bourbon sauce, substitute 1/2 cup Jack Daniels Green or Black Label for the Calvados (after the chicken has browned). The Bourbon gives the chicken a fine flavor and this preparation has become very popular on our menu. For those who do not enjoy Bourbon, call this dish "southern style" and surprise their palates with the deliciously aromatic sauce—they *will* like it. We know that Jack Daniels is "Tennessee sippin' whiskey" so if you are a Bourbon purist, use Wild Turkey instead.

Suprêmes de Volaille Cordon Bleu
Breast of Chicken Cordon Bleu

The term cordon bleu *comes from the Royal Order of Saint Esprit and was first connected with cuisine when a woman—not a man—under Madame du Barry's direction prepared a dinner for King Louis XV that was such a success that the king wanted to hire the chef for himself. Madame du Barry saw to it that her* cuisinière *received the* cordon bleu *in recognition of her prowess. Today,* cordon bleu *is synonymous with ham and cheese enclosed by either chicken or veal. (Unless you have a meat slicer, be sure to have your butcher or delicatessen department slice the cheese and ham for you to ensure the required uniformity.) Here they are wrapped in a* suprême *of chicken and gently sautéed, melding the flavors into a luscious mouthful. Serve this with either Fettuccine Alfredo or Primavera and your guests will be delighted.*

Yields 6 servings

- 3 whole chicken breasts, weighing 12 to 16 ounces (340 to 455 g) each
- 3 ounces (85 g) cooked, smoked ham (6 slices, 1/2 ounce each)
- 3 ounces (85 g) imported Swiss (Emmentaler) cheese (6 slices, 1/2 ounce each)
- Salt
- Freshly ground white pepper
- 4 eggs
- 2 tablespoons water
- 6 tablespoons flour
- 1 cup (235 ml) fine white bread crumbs
- Peanut oil for sautéing
- 2 tablespoons (30 g) butter, melted
- Juice of 1/2 lemon

Recommended equipment

A boning knife, waxed paper, cleaver, pan large enough to hold prepared chicken for chilling, 1-quart (1 L) mixing bowl, wire whisk, 12-inch (30 cm) sauté pan, wooden spatula, slotted spoon, paper towels, heatproof serving platter.

Prepare the chicken breasts according to the instructions for Suprêmes de Volaille Kiev *(see page 264)*; however, cut out the white tendon without separating the large and small pieces of the suprême.

When all the suprêmes are ready, work carefully with the boning knife to make a pocket in each one: make a lengthwise cut into, *but not through*, the meat. Begin at the thicker side, about 1 to 2 inches (2 1/2 to 5 cm) from where the wing was attached, and cut to the other end. Spread the pocket open with your fingers and set the suprêmes in a single layer between two pieces of waxed paper. Flatten them with the cleaver (or the bottom of a small sauté pan), using firm, light strokes until each piece is about 1/4 inch (2/3 cm) thick. Be careful not to tear the chicken. (The thicker part of the fillet may require a few more strokes to flatten out.)

Cut each ham slice into strips about 2 1/2 to 3 inches (6 1/4 to 7 1/2 cm) long and 1 1/2 inches (3 3/4 cm) wide and stack them in six piles. One at a time, wrap a slice of cheese around each ham stack, surrounding the ham completely, set it in the pocket of a suprême, and pull the chicken around it. As each one is finished, set it on a pan, and when all are ready set them to chill in the refrigerator for 20 to 30 minutes. (If you chill them longer than that, cover them with plastic wrap.)

After chilling, remove packages from refrigerator

and season them with salt and pepper. Mix the eggs with the water in the bowl using the whisk. Put the flour on a plate (or your work surface) and do likewise with the bread crumbs. One at a time, roll the suprêmes in the flour, covering them completely, dip them into the egg wash, and then roll them in the bread crumbs. Press the edges lightly together to ensure a good seal. (If there are any spots with no bread crumbs, use your fingers to dab on some egg wash and then sprinkle with more crumbs.) Refrigerate on the pan in a single layer until you are ready to sauté them.

When ready to cook, preheat oven to 325F (163C).

Set the sauté pan over medium high heat and add peanut oil to a depth of 1/4 inch (2/3 cm). When oil is hot, add the suprêmes to the pan in a single layer without touching each other. (If you need to, cook them in batches rather than crowd the pan.) When they begin to sizzle, lower heat so that they cook to an even, golden brown on the first side. This will take 4 to 5 minutes. Turn with the wooden spatula and cook on the other side for 3 to 4 minutes or until nicely browned. When done, remove with slotted spoon to an ovenproof dish and set into the oven for 10 minutes. While suprêmes are cooking, melt the butter slowly and add the lemon juice. Remove dish from oven, set suprêmes on paper towels to drain, then remove them to a warm serving platter. Drizzle the melted butter over them and serve at once.

Variations: Use Gruyère, mozzarella, or raclette cheese instead of the Emmentaler. Rather than use bread crumbs, dredge the suprêmes in flour and then dip into egg wash which has been seasoned with four medium sage leaves, cut into fine strips.

Papillons de Poulet avec Sauce Framboise
Butterfly Chicken Breasts with Raspberry Vinegar Butter Sauce

The term papillon *(butterfly) refers to the shape of the whole breast when it is boned and flattened. Grilled indoors or out and served with the aromatic raspberry sauce, like butterflies, these delicate morsels will flit off your guests' plates in the twinkling of an eye. The Homestead Raspberry Vinegar imparts a piquancy to the sauce not attainable with commercial brands. Remember to start it at least forty-eight hours in advance, for it is well worth the effort and will keep for several weeks under refrigeration. Rice Pilaff and fresh Snow Peas nicely round out the color and texture of this unusual presentation.*

Yields 6 servings

6 whole chicken breasts, weighing 12 to 16 ounces (340 to 455 g) each
Salt
Freshly ground white pepper
1/2 cup (118 ml) olive oil
1/8 teaspoon ground ginger
1 tablespoon grated fresh ginger
1/2 medium garlic clove
1 recipe Raspberry Vinegar Butter Sauce *(see page 85)*
Peanut oil for the grill

FOR THE GARNISH
1 ripe avocado
1 ripe mango

Recommended equipment

A boning knife, waxed (or freezer) paper, cleaver, flat dish large enough to hold chicken in one layer, small bowl, wire whisk, stainless steel box grater, garlic press, plastic wrap, paring knife, charcoal grill or broiler pan with rack, flat turning spatula, serving platter.

Working with one whole breast at a time, set it skin side down on your work surface with the thicker end pointing toward you. To make the "butterfly," you must keep the two halves of the breast meat attached to each other while you remove the meat from the bone. To do this, insert the tip of the boning knife where the wing is attached (at the first wing joint next to the breast). From this point, draw the knife along the rib cage, loosening the meat from the bone. Repeat for the other side of the whole breast. Turn the breast over so the skin side is up. Now you must remove the meat from the bones. Hold the rib cage firmly with one hand and pull the meat away from it with your other hand. Now all you need to do is cut the wings off, remove the skin, cut out the white tendon (which is visible in the meat where it lay against the ribs), and you will have a chicken "butterfly" ready to be flattened.

To flatten the chicken, work with one double breast at a time. Put the chicken "butterfly" between two pieces of waxed paper on your work surface and flatten it with the flat side of a cleaver (or the bottom of a small sauté pan), to a thickness of 3/8 to 1/2 inch (1 to 1 1/2 cm), using firm but easy strokes. When all the double breasts have been flattened, set them into the flat dish in a single layer, season them lightly with salt and pepper, and reserve.

In the small bowl, combine the olive oil and ground ginger with the whisk. Using the fine side of the box grater, grate the fresh ginger and add it to the bowl. Peel the garlic clove and press it into the oil mixture. Combine the ingredients thoroughly with the whisk, pour the marinade over the chicken breasts, cover the dish with plastic wrap, and put the chicken in the refrigerator to marinate for 1 to 4 hours. Prepare the raspberry vinegar butter sauce about half an hour before you plan to grill the chicken.

For cooking the chicken

Before cooking the chicken, prepare the garnish and reserve, wrapped in plastic, until needed. Peel the avocado, slice it, and discard the pit. (Drizzle lemon juice on the slices if the wait will be longer than the time it takes to cook the chicken.) Peel the mango and slice it.

If you are grilling the chicken, start your charcoal fire about 45 minutes before you want to cook so that the coals are hot and well adjusted. Assuming the coals are hot, grilling and broiling times should be about the same.

To grill the chicken, place chicken breasts smooth side down on oiled grates and grill for 1 1/2 minutes. Rotate the chicken 90° around on the grates and grill 2 more minutes. Then turn chicken over and grill for 3 minutes.

To broil the chicken, wipe the broiler pan rack with peanut oil. Preheat broiler to maximum heat and adjust the oven rack to the highest position. Set the rack in the pan and place chicken breasts with their smooth (top) side down on the oiled rack and broil for 3 1/2 minutes. Turn chicken over and broil for 3 minutes. Remove from oven. Stir any cooking juices from the chicken into the raspberry sauce and spoon it on the serving platter (or plates), place the chicken breasts smooth (top) side up on the sauce, garnish with avocado and mango slices, and serve at once.

Breast of Chicken Homestead with Essence of Wild Mushroom Sauce

Crushed pepper is the dry marinade, Port deglazes the pan, and the result is the essence of Bordeaux on your plate. The sauce is prepared separately with wild mushrooms gathered throughout the mountains, hills, and trails near the Homestead by our Kitchen Department. This annual tradition yields morels and cèpes in the spring, chanterelles in August, and delights our guests who are offered part of the harvest on our menu. When there are bumper crops, we dehydrate the rest for future use in soups and sauces. Serve this with String Beans or Carottes Glacées and a generous supply of French Bread or Dinner Rolls to soak up the sauce. The sauce also goes well with Canard Rôti, Medallions of Venison, or Scaloppine di Vitello.

Yields 6 servings

FOR THE CHICKEN
3 whole chicken breasts, weighing 12 to 16 ounces (340 to 455 g) each
Salt
2 tablespoons black peppercorns
2 tablespoons Clarified Butter *(see page 568)*
1 tablespoon olive oil
1/2 teaspoon chopped shallots
3 tablespoons imported Port

FOR THE SAUCE
1 pound (450 g) chicken bones
1 quart (1 L) White Chicken Stock *(see page 61)*
3/4 ounce (23 g) dried cèpes
1/4 ounce (7 g) dried morels
1 teaspoon chopped shallots
1/2 cup (118 ml) imported Port
5 tablespoons Crème Fraîche *(see page 66)*

Recommended equipment

A boning knife, waxed paper, cleaver, mortar and pestle, pan large enough to hold chicken in single layer, plastic wrap, roasting pan, colander, 4-quart (4 L) saucepan, fine-mesh sieve (or cheesecloth-lined strainer), 2-quart (2 L) saucepan, small chef's knife, 2 small saucepans, wire whisk, 12-inch (30 cm) enameled cast-iron baking dish or lined copper plat à sauter, heatproof platter.

Prepare the chicken for cooking. Follow the instructions for boned and skinned chicken breasts in the recipe for Suprêmes de Volaille Kiev *(see page 264)*; however, keep the fillet pieces together. Then flatten them according to the instructions in the same recipe. Season the chicken lightly with salt, crush the pepper coarsely in the mortar and pestle, and pat the pepper onto the chicken. Lay the chicken on a pan in a single layer, cover with plastic wrap, and refrigerate until you are ready to cook.

While the chicken marinates, prepare the sauce. Preheat oven to 350F (177C). Rinse the chicken bones thoroughly in cold running water if they are fresh (i.e., have not been frozen) and then let them drain in the colander. Spread the bones in the roasting pan and set them into the oven to roast until they are light brown (about 10 to 15 minutes). When the bones have begun a good sizzle, stir them about once or twice so they brown evenly and do not burn. When they are brown remove them from the pan to the colander to drain them of all grease.

Set the large saucepan over medium high heat and add the chicken stock. Wash the cèpes and morels gently and thoroughly under cold running water and add them to the chicken stock. Put the drained chicken bones into the stock, bring it to a boil, and adjust heat so that the stock simmers steadily until the liquid is reduced to 1 cup (235 ml). This will take about 1 1/2 hours. When done, strain the liquid through the fine-mesh sieve into the 2-quart saucepan and skim off any grease. Discard the bones. The cèpes and morels can be saved and frozen for another use such as in stocks, soups, or egg dishes. Reserve the sauce base while you prepare the other components.

Peel and chop the shallots and put them in one of the small saucepans. Add the Port, set the saucepan over medium high heat, bring to a simmer, and cook until the liquid is reduced to 1 tablespoon. Put the crème fraîche into the other small saucepan, set it over medium high heat, bring to a simmer, and cook until reduced by one-half. When the Port and crème fraîche are reduced, whisk them into the reserved sauce base and keep warm while you cook the chicken. If the sauce must wait, set it aside and dot the surface with bits of butter to prevent the formation of a skin layer.

When ready to cook, remove the chicken from the refrigerator and unwrap. Preheat oven to 325F (163C). Set the baking dish or plat à sauter over medium high heat, add the clarified butter and olive oil, and, when it is hot, add the chicken. Sauté until golden brown, turn over, brown the other side, and set the pan into the oven to bake for 5 minutes. Chop the shallots. Remove the pan from the oven, put chicken on the heatproof platter, and keep it in a warm (not hot) spot. Drain the grease from the pan, add the shallots, sauté, stirring, for 15 seconds, and then add the Port. Bring the Port to a simmer and deglaze the pan, scraping up all the brown bits on the pan bottom. Add the deglazed liquid to the reserved sauce base in the saucepan, blend together with the whisk, and set the saucepan over medium heat. Bring the sauce to a simmer, adjust seasoning if necessary, and cook for 5 minutes. Skim any fat from the sauce and strain it through the sieve into a clean saucepan. Divide the chicken among warm serving plates, pour the sauce over and around it, and present at once to your guests.

Fillets of Chicken Breast Hungarian

Mention Hungarian cuisine to most people and two words usually come to mind—paprika and goulash (gulyás). Although now one the major exporters of high quality paprika (especially from Szeged), Hungarians did not know of the Indian sweet red pepper from which it comes until the invading Turks brought it along in the sixteenth century. Moreover, paprika did not really take hold in their cuisine until the eighteenth century. Paprikáscsirke is a Hungarian favorite, and our version differs primarily in omitting fresh green peppers and using a bit more paprika. Serve the fillets over hot noodles that have been seasoned lightly with salt, pepper, and bits of butter.

Yields 6 servings

FOR THE SAUCE
1 cup (235 ml) finely chopped onions
3 cups (710 ml) White Chicken Stock *(see page 61)*
6 tablespoons (90 g) butter
1 small garlic clove
3 tablespoons Hungarian paprika
1/4 bay leaf
1 piece lemon peel, about 2 x 2 inches (5 x 5 cm)
1 tablespoon tomato paste
2 tablespoons flour
1 cup (235 ml) sour cream at room temperature

FOR THE CHICKEN
5 half chicken breasts, weighing 6 to 8 ounces (170 to 225 g) each
Salt
Freshly ground white pepper
1 1/2 teaspoons flour
1 tablespoon olive oil
1 tablespoon chopped shallots
1/2 cup (118 ml) dry white wine

Recommended equipment

A large chef's knife, 2-quart (2 L) saucepan, 3-quart (3 L) saucepan, garlic press, wooden spatula, wire whisk, boning knife, 1-quart (1 L) mixing bowl, fine-mesh sieve, waxed paper, cleaver, 12-inch (30 cm) sauté pan, paper towels.

Chop the onions finely with the chef's knife. In the small saucepan, bring the chicken stock to a boil over medium heat as you proceed with the next steps. Set the large saucepan over medium heat, add the butter, and, when it is melted, add the onions and sauté for about 4 minutes or until they are soft, golden in color, but not browned. Peel the garlic and then press it into the onions, blend with the wooden spatula, and add the paprika, bay leaf, and lemon peel, and cook, stirring, for 2 minutes. Add the tomato paste, blend well, and simmer mixture another 2 minutes. Then add the 2 tablespoons flour, stirring to mix well, and cook for another minute before adding the boiling chicken stock. Blend thoroughly with the wire whisk, until the sauce is smooth and simmering. Simmer sauce for 30 minutes, then strain through the sieve into a clean saucepan, whisk in the sour cream, and adjust the seasoning if necessary.

While the sauce is simmering, prepare the chicken breasts for cooking following the instructions for boned and skinned chicken breasts in the recipe for Suprêmes de Volaille Kiev *(see page 264)*. When they are ready, follow the instructions for flattening the fillets between waxed paper, being sure to flatten them just enough to even them out.

After flattening, cut each fillet into six pieces and combine them with the filets mignons in the mixing bowl. Season the chicken with salt and pepper and dust lightly with the remaining flour.

Set the sauté pan over medium high heat, add the olive oil, and, when it is hot, add the chicken pieces. Stir occasionally, turning the chicken, and cook about 4 to 5 minutes until the pieces are golden brown. Remove chicken to paper towels to drain. Add the shallots to the pan, cook without browning for 30 seconds, and then add the white wine and simmer until wine is reduced by one-half. Strain through the sieve into the saucepan which contains the sauce, add the chicken fillets, and simmer gently for 10 minutes. Remove from heat and serve immediately with hot noodles.

"Some Like It Not So Hot" Chicken Breast Fillets

As with any fad, when Cajun was "ragin'," everyone seemed to clamor for pan-blackened this and hot-seasoned that. ("But novelty is the cry.") Cajun and Creole cooking are important parts of our culinary tradition, but in perspective. In the same vein, here, ancient Chinese stir-frying and vegetables combine with Indian seasonings to produce a result that is spicy in its own right. If you want an even hotter taste, add jalapeño or other hot peppers and a few drops of Tabasco sauce. As with any stir-fry, the ingredients are prepared ahead of time, allowing for easy last-minute cooking. Serve this next to a Rice Pilaff and accompany it with a salad of Boston, Bibb, or red leaf lettuce mixed with thinly sliced cucumbers that have been marinated with fresh chives, dill, or tarragon.

Yields 6 servings

5 half chicken breasts, weighing 6 to 8 ounces (170 to 225 g) each
1/4 teaspoon grated fresh ginger
Salt
Freshly ground white pepper
4 ounces (115 g) cooked smoked ham
1 small carrot
3 Chinese cabbage stalks
6 medium mushrooms
6 scallions
1/2 medium green bell pepper
6 ounces (170 g) snow peas
4 ounces (115 g) pimiento (packed in water and drained)
2 medium tomatoes (blanched, peeled, and seeded; *see page 568*)
1/2 cup (118 ml) White Chicken Stock *(see page 61)*
1/2 teaspoon arrowroot
1 tablespoon olive oil
Peel from 1/2 lemon, grated
1/4 teaspoon curry powder
1 tablespoon chopped mango chutney
2 tablespoons Indonesian soy sauce

Recommended equipment

A boning knife, waxed paper, cleaver, 1-quart (1 L) mixing bowl, box grater, mixing fork, paring knife, swivel-bladed vegetable peeler, 12-inch (30 cm) sauté pan, wooden spatula.

Follow the instructions for boned and skinned chicken breasts in the recipe for Suprêmes de Volaille Kiev *(see page 264)*, and, when they are ready, follow the instructions for flattening the fillets between waxed paper, being sure to lightly flatten them so they are just evened out.

After flattening, cut each fillet into six pieces and combine them with the filets mignons in the mixing bowl. Grate the fresh ginger over the chicken, season with salt and pepper, and mix all together well.

Now, prepare the other ingredients and reserve. Cut the ham into 2-inch (5 cm) long julienne strips. Rinse the carrot, peel it, and cut into 2-inch long julienne strips. Rinse the cabbage, cut in half lengthwise and then into 2-inch long julienne strips. Brush the mushrooms of any clinging dirt and slice thinly. Rinse the scallions, trim if necessary, and slice thinly. Seed the bell pepper half and cut into 2-inch long julienne strips. Pull the blossom end from the snow peas, blanch them, drain, and set aside. Cut the pimiento into fine strips. Prepare the tomatoes, cut them into fine strips, and see to it that the chicken stock is ready. Blend the arrowroot with enough cold water to make a smooth paste.

When you are ready to cook, set the sauté pan over medium high heat, add the olive oil, and when the pan is hot add the chicken pieces. Sauté, while stirring with the wooden spatula, for 3 minutes. Then reduce heat to medium and add strips of ham, carrot, cabbage, mushroom, scallion, and green pepper. Grate the lemon peel into the sauté pan, add the curry powder, and sauté for 3 minutes. Add the chutney, soy sauce, and chicken stock and bring to a simmer for 1 minute. Slowly add arrowroot mixture while stirring constantly and simmer for another minute. Stir in snow peas, the pimiento and tomato strips, blend well, and simmer another minute. Then remove from heat and serve immediately.

Variation: Use small, raw shrimp instead of chicken, or else a mixture of the two, and follow the same cooking time.

Homestead Sweet and Sour Lemon Chicken

As with the preceding recipe this stir-fry can be done at the last minute once all the ingredients are prepared. If you recoil at the super-sweet sauces to be found at some Chinese restaurants, take heart. This one plays three taste sensations against each other—sweet, sour, and tart. Combined with the ginger on the chicken it becomes a winning entry in the Oriental "derby," which can also be prepared with some of the delicious baby vegetables available today, such as corn, yellow squash, eggplant, and carrots. Serve this with Steamed or Exotic Fried Rice or Rice Pilaff.

Yields 6 servings

FOR THE SAUCE
2 cups (475 ml) canned pineapple juice
3 tablespoons vinegar
1/4 cup (50 g) light brown sugar
1/4 cup (60 ml) pomegranate syrup or concentrate
2 tablespoons ketchup
Juice of 1 large lemon
Rind from 1 lemon
3 tablespoons arrowroot

FOR THE VEGETABLES
4 Chinese cabbage stalks
18 whole water chestnuts
3 scallions
2 medium zucchini
1 medium red bell pepper
6 ounces (170 g) snow peas

FOR THE CHICKEN
5 half chicken breasts, weighing 6 to 8 ounces (170 to 225 g) each
1 teaspoon grated fresh ginger
Salt
Freshly ground black pepper
1 tablespoon peanut oil

Recommended equipment

A 2-quart (2 L) saucepan, wire whisk, small bowl, paring knife, stiff natural bristle brush, boning knife, waxed paper, cleaver, 2-quart mixing bowl, stainless steel box grater, 12-inch (30 cm) sauté pan, long-handled cooking fork, slotted spoon, paper towels, wooden spatula.

For the sauce, combine all the ingredients except 3 tablespoons pineapple juice, the lemon peel, and arrowroot in the saucepan, whisk together well, bring to a simmer over medium heat, and cook for 10 minutes. While the sauce is cooking, remove all bitter white from the lemon rind, cut into fine julienne strips, blanch in a small saucepan, and reserve. When the sauce is ready, blend the arrowroot with the reserved pineapple juice in the small bowl until it has the consistency of a thin paste. Add mixture slowly to the simmering sauce, stirring constantly with the whisk, and simmer for 3 minutes. The sauce should be syrupy so that it can coat the chicken and vegetables without being pasty. (If it is too thin, make up an additional 1 1/2 to 2 teaspoons of the arrowroot mixture, add it to the sauce, and simmer some more; if too thick, whisk in a small amount of pineapple juice.) When done, remove from heat and reserve.

Prepare the vegetables. Rinse the cabbage under cold running water and cut in half lengthwise and then into strips about 2 inches by 1/4 inch (5 x 2/3 cm). Open the tin of water chestnuts, drain them, slice into pieces, and reserve. Rinse the scallions, trim the tops, slice coarsely, and reserve. Scrub the zucchini well with the bristle brush under running cold water and cut into strips about 2 inches by 1/4 inch. Rinse the bell pepper, halve it, remove the seeds and white pith, and cut it into thin, 2-inch long strips. Rinse the snow peas, snap off the blossom ends, and, if large, cut in half on the diagonal, and reserve.

Prepare the chicken for cooking. Follow the instructions for boned and skinned chicken breasts in the recipe for Suprêmes de Volaille Kiev *(see page 264)*; however, keep the fillet pieces together. Then flatten them according to the instructions in the same recipe. Cut each fillet diagonally into six pieces. Grate the fresh ginger. Combine the chicken in the mixing bowl with the ginger, salt, and pepper. Using your fingers, roll the fillet pieces around in the seasonings to coat them completely.

Set the sauté pan over medium heat, add the peanut oil, and, when it is hot, put the chicken pieces into the pan. Stir them around constantly with the fork, keeping them separate, until they are well browned on all sides. This will take about 4 minutes. When brown, remove the chicken pieces to paper towels and reserve.

Set the sauté pan back over medium heat, add a little more peanut oil if necessary, and, when it is hot, put the vegetables and the lemon julienne, reserved when the sauce was made, into the pan all at once, and stir constantly with the wooden spatula for 3 minutes. Stir in the chicken pieces, add enough sauce to cover them and the vegetables, and gradually bring to a gentle simmer. Heat thoroughly, about 2 minutes, before serving.

❧

If pomegranate syrup is unavailable, substitute 1 cup (235 ml) pomegranate juice simmered separately to reduce it to 1/4 cup before making the sauce.

Baked Breast of Chicken Virginia

The Gauls devised the method for curing pork legs, paving the way for such gastronomic delights as jambon de Bayonne, Schwarzwaldschinken, *and* prosciutto, *but if you are from Virginia, you know there is only one ham. A tradition dating from the Jamestown colony, ham curing is taken very seriously here—in fact one of our suppliers has been in business since 1779. Need we say that Virginia ham is de rigueur for this recipe to be authentic. If you must substitute, use only first quality (i.e., not boiled) ham because it is the ham and mushroom combination which gives this dish its distinctive flavor. For special appeal, present it under a glass bell-shaped cover (*sous cloche*), served with Rice Pilaff.*

Yields 6 servings

FOR THE SAUCE
1/2 celery stalk
1/4 medium onion
1 to 1 1/2 pounds (450 to 675 g) chicken bones
1 teaspoon peanut oil
1/2 cup (118 ml) White Chicken Stock *(see page 61)*
1 cup (235 ml) Sauce Velouté de Poulet *(see page 73)*
3/4 cup (180 ml) whipping cream

FOR THE CHICKEN
3 whole chicken breasts, weighing 12 to 16 ounces (340 to 455 g) each
Salt
Freshly ground white pepper
1 tablespoon chopped shallots
1/4 cup (60 ml) dry white wine
12 medium mushroom caps
2 tablespoons (30 g) butter
Juice from 1/2 lemon
1 teaspoon chopped fresh parsley
6 very thin slices uncooked Virginia ham, weighing 1 1/2 ounces (45 g) each

Butter for the baking dish and serving platter

Recommended equipment

A large chef's knife, 12-inch (30 cm) enameled cast-iron baking dish or lined copper plat à sauter, wooden spatula, 4-quart (4 L) saucepan, boning knife, 10-inch (25 cm) sauté pan, ovenproof serving platter, large fine-mesh sieve.

Preheat oven to 350F (177C). Chop the celery and onion coarsely with the chef's knife. Rinse the chicken bones thoroughly in running cold water if they are fresh (i.e., have not been frozen). Let them drain. Then set the baking dish or plat à sauter over medium high heat, add the peanut oil and the chicken bones, and cook, stirring with the wooden spatula, for 3 to 4 minutes. Add the celery and onion, stir them in, and set the baking dish into the oven for 5 minutes, or until the bones are slightly browned.

Remove baking dish from the oven, pour off excess fat, and set the dish over medium high heat. Add the chicken stock and simmer for a few minutes to deglaze the pan. Then transfer the bones and their rendered juices to the saucepan, being sure to scrape the bottom of the baking dish thoroughly. Wipe out the dish and reserve it for baking the chicken. Add the sauce velouté and cream to the saucepan and bring to a low simmer. Maintain the low simmer for 20 minutes and stir occasionally. When done, set aside.

While the sauce is simmering, prepare the chicken for cooking by cutting it into côtelettes. Follow the instructions for boned and skinned chicken breasts in the recipe for Suprêmes de Volaille Kiev *(see page 264)*; however, leave the skin on, keep the fillet pieces together, and cut the wing off at the second joint, keeping the bone in between the first and second joints, thus making a côtelette. When the côtelettes are ready, season them with salt and pepper and reserve.

Butter the reserved baking dish, chop the shallots, and strew them in the bottom of the dish. Set the chicken pieces into the dish, skin side up, add the white wine, and set the dish into the oven. Bake for 15 minutes, reduce heat to 325F (163C), and continue baking another 10 minutes. Remove dish from oven, turn chicken over (skin side down), and let set for 10 minutes out of the oven.

While the chicken is resting, prepare the mushrooms. Brush them of any clinging dirt, remove stems (reserve for another use), and sauté the whole caps in the remaining butter over medium low heat, stirring, for 3 minutes. Remove from heat, squeeze lemon juice over the caps, stir, and set aside.

Chop the parsley and preheat the broiler to maximum heat.

Lightly butter the ovenproof serving platter and arrange the slices of ham on it. Set the platter under the broiler for 2 minutes. While ham is heating, remove skin from chicken. Remove platter from broiler and set aside momentarily. Drain any juices from the mushroom caps into the reserved sauce in the saucepan, taste for seasoning, and strain through the sieve into a clean saucepan. Start warming the sauce to serving temperature.

Set a piece of chicken on each ham slice, top with two mushroom caps, and run back under the broiler just long enough to rewarm the chicken. Remove from broiler and spoon the warmed sauce over the chicken. Sprinkle the parsley on top and serve immediately.

Baked Breast of Chicken with Caraway Sauce

Josef Schelch, our executive sous-chef, brought us this recipe from his Austrian grandmother. Actually, we never were as successful as she must have been in balancing all the complex flavors of the original, so I have divided the recipe in two—a main preparation, followed by a variation. The sauce used here is the foundation for several recipes, which vary according to the seasonings used. Noodles, Spätzle, or Rice Pilaff suit this dish well.

Baked Breast of Chicken with Anisette Sauce at Sam Snead's Tavern

277

Yields 6 servings

FOR THE SAUCE
1 celery stalk
1/2 medium onion
1 1/2 to 2 pounds (675 to 900 g) chicken bones
1 teaspoon peanut oil
1/2 cup (118 ml) dry white wine
2 cups (475 ml) Sauce Velouté de Poulet *(see page 73)*
1 tablespoon Glace de Viande *(see page 65)*
1 piece lemon peel, about 1 x 2 inches (2 1/2 x 5 cm)
1/2 cup (118 ml) whipping cream

FOR THE CHICKEN
3 whole chicken breasts, weighing 12 to 16 ounces (340 to 455 g) each
Salt
Freshly ground white pepper
1 tablespoon finely chopped shallots
1/2 cup (118 ml) dry white wine
1/4 teaspoon caraway seeds

Butter for the baking dish

FOR THE GARNISH
Peel from 1/2 lemon
3 canned artichoke bottoms or hearts
1/2 medium red bell pepper
1/2 teaspoon butter

Recommended equipment

A large chef's knife, 12-inch (30 cm) enameled cast-iron baking dish or lined copper plat à sauter, wooden spatula, 4-quart (4 L) saucepan, boning knife, large fine-mesh sieve, 8-inch (20 cm) sauté pan.

Preheat oven to 350F (177C). Chop the celery and onion coarsely with the chef's knife.

Rinse the chicken bones thoroughly in cold running water if they are fresh (i.e., have not been frozen). Let them drain. Then set the baking dish or plat à sauter over medium high heat, add the peanut oil and the chicken bones, and cook, stirring with the wooden spatula, for 3 to 4 minutes. Then add the celery and onion, stir them in, and set the baking dish into the oven for 5 minutes, or until the bones are slightly browned.

Remove the baking dish from the oven, pour off excess fat, and set it over medium high heat. Add the white wine and simmer for a few minutes to deglaze the pan. Then transfer the bones and their rendered juices to the saucepan, being sure to scrape the bottom of the baking dish thoroughly. Wipe out the dish and reserve it for baking the chicken. Add the sauce velouté, the glace de viande, lemon peel, and cream to the saucepan and bring to a low simmer. Maintain a low simmer for 20 minutes and stir occasionally. When done, remove from heat and reserve.

While the sauce is simmering, prepare the chicken for cooking by cutting it into côtelettes. Follow the instructions for boned and skinned chicken breasts in the recipe for Suprêmes de Volaille Kiev *(see page 264)*; however, leave the skin on, keep the fillet pieces together, and cut the wing off at the second joint, keeping the bone in between the first and second joints, thus making a côtelette. When the côtelettes are ready, season them with salt and pepper and reserve.

Butter the reserved baking dish, chop the shallots, and strew them in the bottom of the dish. Set the chicken pieces into the dish, skin side up, add the remaining white wine, and set the dish into the oven. Bake for 15 minutes, remove dish from oven, turn chicken over (skin side down), and let set for 10 minutes. Then remove skin from the chicken pieces, strain the liquid from the saucepan through the sieve over the chicken (the chicken should be covered by at least 1/2 inch or 1 1/4 cm of sauce—and a little more white wine and half-and-half if needed), add the caraway seeds, and bring to a low simmer over medium low heat. Simmer gently for 10 minutes.

While the chicken simmers, prepare the garnish. Cut the lemon peel into julienne strips, blanch, and drain. Quarter the artichoke bottoms or, for the hearts, cut them in half. For the pepper half, trim it of white pith and remove seeds, cut into fine julienne strips, and sauté for 3 minutes in 1/2 teaspoon butter in the sauté pan.

When the chicken is ready, check the sauce for thickness and seasoning. If too thick, add a little more cream (or half-and-half); adjust seasoning if needed. Stir in the lemon peel, artichoke pieces, and bell pepper, blend well, and serve immediately.

Variation

Baked Breast of Chicken with Anisette Sauce

Substitute four pieces of star anise for the caraway seeds and julienne strips of red and yellow peppers, lightly sautéed, for the lemon julienne and artichoke pieces.

Baked Breast of Chicken Maharajah

Although we have traditionally used this name to reflect the curry and chutney, it would probably be more accurate to name it after the great Hawaiian ruler, Kamehameha. Late eighteenth-century British traders are no doubt responsible for introducing the spices, but a curry made with coconut milk is indigenous to Hawaii. A favorite at Homestead buffets, the rice should be served separately and combined on the plate with the chicken and curry sauce.

Yields 6 servings

FOR THE SAUCE
1/2 medium onion
1/2 celery stalk
1 1/2 pounds (675 g) chicken bones
1 teaspoon peanut oil
1 to 2 teaspoons curry powder
1/2 cup (118 ml) dry white wine
1 1/2 cups (355 ml) Basic Curry Sauce *(see page 80)*
1/2 cup (118 ml) coconut milk or Crème Fraîche *(see page 66)*
1/2 cup (118 ml) White Chicken Stock *(see page 61)*

FOR THE CHICKEN
3 whole chicken breasts, weighing 12 to 16 ounces (340 to 455 g) each
Salt
Freshly ground white pepper
1 tablespoon chopped shallots
1/3 cup (80 ml) dry white wine
2 cups Saffron Rice *(see page 424)*
1/2 cup (118 ml) raisins
1 banana
3 slices fresh pineapple
1 teaspoon sugar
1/2 cup (118 ml) coconut flakes
2 tablespoons mango chutney
2 pimiento halves (packed in water and drained)
3 whole maraschino cherries (or 3 strawberries)

Butter for the baking dish and baking sheet

Recommended equipment

A large chef's knife, 12-inch (30 cm) enameled cast-iron baking dish or lined copper plat à sauter, wooden spatula, 4-quart (4 L) saucepan, boning knife, large fine-mesh sieve, baking sheet, pie pan, heatproof serving platter.

Preheat oven to 375F (190C).

Peel the onion, chop coarsely, and reserve. Rinse the celery stalk, trim to make as stringless as possible, chop coarsely, and reserve.

Rinse the chicken bones thoroughly in cold running water if they are fresh (i.e., have not been frozen). Let them drain. Then set the baking dish or plat à sauter over medium high heat, add the peanut oil, and, when it is hot, stir in the chicken bones and cook, stirring, for 3 minutes. Stir in the onion and celery and set the pan into the oven for 5 minutes, browning the bones lightly. When the bones are brown, remove from oven and set over medium heat. Drain off excess grease, add curry powder, stir for 30 seconds, add the white wine, and simmer for 3 minutes to deglaze pan. Then transfer the bones and their juices to the saucepan, scraping the bottom of the baking dish thoroughly. Wash out the dish and reserve it for baking the chicken. Add the curry sauce, coconut milk (or crème fraîche), and chicken stock to the saucepan with the bones, and bring to a low simmer. Simmer for 20 minutes, stirring from time to time. The sauce should have a smooth, creamy consistency. If it is too thick, add a little more chicken stock; if too thin, let it simmer longer. When the sauce is done, remove from heat and set aside.

While the sauce is simmering, prepare the chicken for cooking by cutting it into côtelettes. Follow the instructions for boned and skinned chicken breasts in the recipe for Suprêmes de Volaille Kiev *(see page 264)*; however, leave the skin on, keep the fillet pieces together, and cut the wing off at the second joint, keeping the bone in between the first and second joints, thus making a côtelette. Season the chicken lightly with salt and pepper.

Reduce oven heat to 350F (177C).

Butter the reserved baking dish. Chop the shallots with the chef's knife, strew them in the bottom of the dish, arrange the chicken skin side up on the shallots, and add the remaining white wine.

Set into the oven to bake for 15 minutes, then remove from oven, turn chicken over (skin side down), and let set for 10 minutes.

While the chicken is resting, start the saffron rice. When done, take off heat and reserve.

When the chicken has rested, remove the skin, pour the juices from the baking dish into a bowl, and then pass them through the sieve over the chicken. Strain the reserved curry sauce over the chicken. Set the dish over medium heat, bring the chicken and its sauce to a low simmer, and cook gently for 10 minutes. Taste the sauce and adjust seasoning if necessary. Keep warm.

Set the raisins in a small bowl and cover with hot water. Let soak for at least 10 minutes, then drain and reserve.

Preheat broiler to maximum heat.

While the chicken and sauce simmer, prepare the fruit. Peel the banana and cut it crosswise into six pieces. Peel and core a fresh pineapple, make three slices 1 1/4 to 1 1/2 inches (3 to 3 3/4 cm) thick, and cut each ring in half. Butter the baking sheet and set the fruit pieces into it in a single layer. Sprinkle the sugar over the fruit and set the dish under the broiler for 3 to 4 minutes or until lightly browned. Spread the coconut flakes on the pie pan and set into the oven until they are toasted to a light brown. When done, remove from oven and reserve.

Chop the mango chutney and cut the pimiento into fine dice. Cut the cherries (or strawberries) in half. Stir the drained raisins, chutney, and pimiento into the saffron rice and reheat if necessary over low heat for a few minutes. Warm the serving platter. When all is ready, make a bed of rice on the platter, arrange the chicken on it, spoon about 3 tablespoons of the curry sauce over each côtelette, and top with a piece of pineapple, banana, a cherry or strawberry half, and a sprinkling of the reserved coconut flakes. Serve at once and offer the remaining curry sauce separately.

Baked Breast of Chicken Kaunaoa

Bananas, mangos, pineapples, and coconuts all flourish in Hawaii, but this name takes on added significance from its geographical location. In Hawaiian, "Kona" generally means the leeward side of an island, and when speaking of the "big island," Hawaii, it refers to the Kona coast. Bounded on the southwest by Kaunaoa Point, for which the recipe is named, this area is fertile ground for banana cultivation as well as for the Kona coffee bean raised in the hills one to two thousand feet above the lava shoreline.

Here, we have attempted to capture some of the profuse colors and tastes of Hawaii, but if you wish you may also add slices of Kiwi fruit and maraschino cherries to elaborate the tropical motif. Wild rice and fresh String Beans are a good accompaniment for this treat from the islands.

Yields 4 servings

FOR THE CHICKEN
2 whole chicken breasts, weighing 12 to 16 ounces (340 to 455 g) each
1 ripe mango (or papaya)
1/4 cup (60 ml) Clarified Butter *(see page 568)*
Salt
Freshly ground white pepper
1/4 cup (30 g) flour
2 eggs
1/2 cup (118 ml) coconut flakes
1 tablespoon peanut oil
3 tablespoons half-and-half

FOR THE GARNISH
1/2 medium pineapple
1 banana
1 1/2 teaspoons sugar
2 medium strawberries

Recommended equipment

A boning knife, paring knife, 2-quart (2 L) mixing bowl, wire whisk, 12-inch (30 cm) enameled cast-iron baking dish or lined copper plat à sauter, metal tongs, paper towels, baking sheet, heatproof serving platter.

Prepare the chicken for cooking by cutting it into côtelettes. Follow the instructions for boned and skinned chicken breasts in the recipe for Suprêmes de Volaille Kiev *(see page 264)*; however, keep the fillet pieces together and cut the wing off at the second joint, leaving the bone in between the first and second joint, thus making a côtelette. When they are ready, make a pocket in the meat for the stuffing: using the paring knife, insert the tip 1 to 2 inches (2 1/2 to 5 cm) from the wing joint and make a shallow, lengthwise cut down the center, stopping 1 to 2 inches from the opposite end. Do not cut through to the opposite side. (If necessary, run your finger around the inside of the pocket, gently smoothing and enlarging it.)

Peel the mango with the paring knife and cut into eight strips. Stuff two of these, folded if necessary, into each côtelette pocket and press edges together to close the opening. Set the côtelettes in a single layer on a pan and refrigerate for 15 to 20 minutes. (You can stuff them hours ahead of time. They will wait nicely if covered with plastic wrap.)

While the chicken is chilling, prepare the clarified butter and then the remaining fruit for the garnish. Peel and core the pineapple half and slice it into four rings. Peel the banana, halve it lengthwise, and cut each in half again to make four pieces. (Sprinkle lemon juice on the banana pieces if they are to sit for any length of time.) Wash, hull, and halve the strawberries.

When you are ready to finish the dish, season the côtelettes with salt and pepper and roll them in the flour. Using the whisk, whip the eggs, 1/4 cup coconut flakes, peanut oil, and half-and-half together in the mixing bowl. Set the baking dish or plat à sauter over medium high heat, add the clarified butter, and, when it is hot, dip the floured côtelettes into the batter in the mixing bowl and then set them into the dish. When the chicken is sizzling, lower heat to medium and sauté, turning once, until the chicken is a light golden brown on both sides.

Preheat oven to 325F (163C).

When the chicken is browned, set the baking dish into the oven and bake for 15 minutes. While the chicken is baking, finish the fruit by arranging the pineapple slices and banana pieces on a baking sheet, sprinkling them with the sugar, and browning them lightly under the broiler. Also, separately, brown the remaining coconut flakes under the broiler.

When the chicken is baked, remove it from the oven, remove the skin, arrange the chicken on the warm serving platter or plates, and top each piece with a pineapple slice, banana quarter, coconut flakes, and strawberry half. Serve at once.

If you would like to serve a sauce along with the chicken, prepare this one. Simmer 1/2 cup (118 ml) Sauce Suprême and 1 tablespoon Glace de Viande *(see pages 74 and 65)* together with 2 tablespoons dry sherry for a few minutes and serve it around, *not on*, the chicken.

Baked Breast of Chicken with Tarragon Stuffing

Tarragon is a relative newcomer to the spice and herb scene, having been introduced to Europe via western Asia and Russia by thirteenth-century Arabs. Its name derived from the corruption of Arabic for "little dragon," this herb, which comes from the daisy family, is a real kitchen workhorse, either as part of a Sauce Béarnaise, or tout seul, as it is here. Dried herbs simply will not do, for there is no substitute for the delicate aroma and bright color of fresh tarragon. Fortunately, it is readily available at farmers' markets or many supermarkets, and, if you are diligent enough to raise your own, how much greater is the reward from preparing this dish. Accompany these aromatic morsels with fresh String Beans, Asparagus, new peas, or Carottes Glacées.

Yields 6 servings

2 cups (475 ml) fine white bread crumbs
2 1/2 to 2 2/3 cups (590 to 635 ml) half-and-half
Salt
Freshly ground white pepper
2 teaspoons chopped fresh tarragon leaves
2 tablespoons chopped fresh parsley
3 whole chicken breasts, weighing 12 to 16 ounces (340 to 455 g) each
2 tablespoons chopped shallots
2/3 cup (160 ml) dry white wine
1/3 cup (80 ml) dry white vermouth
1 cup (235 ml) Crème Fraîche (see page 66)
1 1/2 teaspoons Glace de Viande (see page 65)
Butter for the baking dish

Recommended equipment

A 1 1/2-quart (1 1/2 L) mixing bowl, blending fork, large chef's knife, boning knife, baking dish, heatproof serving platter, 1 1/2-quart (1 1/2 L) saucepan, fine-mesh sieve.

In the mixing bowl, using the blending fork, thoroughly combine the bread crumbs and 2 1/4 cups (535 ml) half-and-half. Season lightly with salt and pepper and blend well. Wash the tarragon and parsley, pat or spin dry, and chop finely with the chef's knife. Mix the tarragon and 1 1/2 tablespoons parsley, reserving the rest, into the bread crumb mixture and set the bowl into the refrigerator to chill for at least an hour. After chilling, you may need to add a little more half-and-half to make a smooth paste.

While the stuffing is chilling, prepare the chicken for cooking by cutting it into côtelettes. Follow the instructions for boned and skinned chicken breasts in the recipe for Suprêmes de Volaille Kiev *(see page 264)*; however, leave the skin on, keep the fillet pieces together, and cut the wing off at the second joint, keeping the bone in between the first and second joints, thus making a côtelette. When they are ready, make a place for the stuffing in each one. With the narrow, lengthwise edge facing you, run your finger between the meat and the skin, going to 1 inch (2 1/2 cm) from the wing joint and 1 to 1 1/2 (3 3/4 cm) inches from the bottom (skinless) side. Do not separate the skin all the way to the thick edge, but stop 1 to 1 1/2 inches away from it.

When the stuffing is chilled and the chicken ready, preheat oven to 350F (177C). Butter the baking dish. Stuff each chicken piece with 1/4 cup (60 ml) of stuffing, pull skin completely over the stuffing, and season lightly with salt and pepper. Chop the shallots with the chef's knife, strew them in the baking dish, and set the chicken into the dish skin side up. Pour in the wine and vermouth and set the dish into the oven to bake for 15 minutes. Then reduce heat to 325F (163C) and bake for another 15 minutes.

Remove chicken from oven, transfer it to a serving platter, and keep warm. Scrape all liquids and shallots from the baking dish into the saucepan, set over medium high heat, and reduce to 2 tablespoons. Then add the crème fraîche and glace de viande and simmer about 10 minutes or until the sauce is a light creamy consistency. Strain sauce through sieve, adjust seasoning if necessary, and spoon the sauce around the chicken. Sprinkle the reserved parsley over the dish and serve at once.

The chicken can be stuffed several hours ahead and kept under refrigeration. If you do this, add 5 minutes to the baking time.

Baked Breast of Chicken Ambassador

In la cuisine *the traditional* ambassadrice *garnish calls for chicken livers and shredded truffles, among other things. Here the focus is sharpened and enriched with foie gras—no herbs, only minimal seasonings, and the receptiveness and reflectiveness of fresh chicken.*

And with ingredients such as these the chicken must *be fresh, lest you would have Aunt Celestine turn in her grave. We will not repeat the extensive discussion of truffles and foie gras to be found under Roast Tenderloin of Beef London House, but we will say that chicken and truffle seem to work an earthy magic together which is neither to be believed nor duplicated. If you are fortunate enough to have foie gras and black truffles in hand at the same time, to paraphrase Olivier Messiaen, here is truly an "apparition of culinary heaven."*

Yields 6 servings

FOR THE STUFFING
1/2 cup (118 ml) fine white
   bread crumbs
2/3 cup (160 ml) whipping
   cream
Salt
Freshly ground white pepper
6 ounces (170 g) foie gras,
   softened at room temperature
4 ounces (115 g) black truffles

FOR THE CHICKEN
3 whole chicken breasts,
   weighing 12 to 16 ounces
   (340 to 455 g) each
Salt
Freshly ground white pepper
1 tablespoon chopped shallots
2/3 cup (160 ml) dry sherry

Butter for the baking dish

FOR THE SAUCE
6 medium mushrooms
1 tablespoon (15 g) butter
Truffle strips
Juice of 1/2 lemon
1 tablespoon Glace de Viande
   (see page 65)
1 cup (235 ml) Crème Fraîche
   (see page 66)

Recommended equipment

A 1-quart (1 L) mixing bowl, blending fork, boning knife, paring knife, baking dish, heatproof serving platter, fine-mesh sieve, 1 1/2-quart (1 1/2 L) saucepan, 2-quart (2 L) saucepan, wooden spoon.

In the mixing bowl combine the bread crumbs, cream, salt, pepper, and softened foie gras, mixing thoroughly with the blending fork. Refrigerate until ready to use.

Prepare the chicken for cooking by cutting it into côtelettes. Follow the instructions for boned and skinned chicken breasts in the recipe for Suprêmes de Volaille Kiev *(see page 264)*; however, leave the skin on, keep the fillet pieces together, and cut the wing off at the second joint, keeping the bone in between the first and second joints, thus making a côtelette. Then, with the paring knife, make a pocket in the meat for the stuffing by holding the knife parallel to your work surface and inserting the knife point into the wide edge of the breast, 1 to 2 inches (2 1/2 to 5 cm) from the wing joint. Cut lengthwise along the edge toward the other end. Stop the cut 2 inches from the end, and cut to within 1 1/2 to 2 inches of the other side, making a pocketlike incision. Run your finger around the inside of the pocket, smoothing and enlarging it, and then season the chicken lightly inside and out with salt and pepper.

Preheat oven to 350F (177C).

Drain the truffles and reserve their liquid for the sauce. With the paring knife, cut twelve thin slices of truffle and the remaining pieces into thin strips. Reserve the strips. Stuff about 2 1/2 tablespoons of the foie gras mixture into the breast pocket and slip two truffle slices between the skin and the meat, setting them side by side. Pull and fold the skin over the pocket opening and press the edges together.

Butter the baking dish. Chop the shallots and strew them in the dish. Set the chicken into the dish, skin side up, add the sherry, and put into the oven to bake for 15 minutes. Then reduce the heat to 325F (163C) and continue cooking for another 15 minutes. Remove from oven, transfer the chicken to a warm serving platter, and let it rest in a warm (not hot) spot.

Strain the juices from the baking dish into the smaller saucepan, add the reserved truffle juices, and simmer over medium heat until they are reduced to 2 tablespoons. Remove from heat and reserve.

Brush the mushrooms of any clinging dirt, slice them, and then cut the slices into strips and reserve.

Melt the butter in the other saucepan over medium heat, add the mushrooms, reserved truffle strips, and lemon juice and simmer for 30 seconds before adding the reduced liquid from the baking dish, glace de viande, and crème fraîche. Bring to a simmer over medium low heat and simmer about 10 minutes or until the sauce is light and creamy. Adjust seasoning if necessary with salt and pepper, spoon sauce over the chicken, and serve at once.

❧

Canning truffles regrettably removes some of their unforgettably rich, earthy aroma, but open the can a few hours in advance, pour them into a dish with their juices, and add 1 or 2 tablespoons of sherry or Madeira. This will restore them somewhat and make the sauce all the more interesting. Foie gras comes in numerous forms, from fresh to tinned with various added meats and truffles. Try to get fresh if you can and if you happen to have the tinned with the truffle in the middle . . . well, a little extra truffle never hurt anybody!

❧ Baked Breast of Chicken Florentine

In A.D. 647, more than eight hundred years before the Medici moved into the Palazzo Medici-Riccardi, the great T'ang emperor T'ai Tsung received spinach as a gift from the King of Nepal, who believed it was the best plant grown in his country. But spinach was not native to Nepal—it came from Persia. From the Persian word aspanākh *we derive our name for this versatile vegetable that has an extraordinary affinity for some of life's other pleasures—butter, cream, nutmeg, olive oil, ham, anchovies, bacon, and several cheeses. In addition to political intrigue, Florentines were also skilled in the cultivation of spinach, which is why any dish "Florentine" is synonymous with "spinach."*

Yields 6 servings

FOR THE STUFFING
1 pound (450 g) fresh spinach
2 tablespoons (30 g) butter
1 tablespoon chopped shallots
1 tablespoon grated Parmesan cheese
Salt
Freshly ground white pepper
A dash of freshly ground nutmeg
4 ounces (115 g) ricotta cheese

FOR THE CHICKEN
3 whole chicken breasts, weighing 12 to 16 ounces (340 to 455 g) each
1 tablespoon chopped shallots
Salt
Freshly ground white pepper
1/2 cup (118 ml) dry white wine

Butter for the baking dish

FOR THE TOMATO SAUCE
8 medium, ripe tomatoes (blanched, peeled, and seeded; *see page 568*)
1 tablespoon olive oil
1 tablespoon (15 g) butter
1 tablespoon chopped shallots
1 small garlic clove
1/2 cup (118 ml) tomato juice
1 piece of lemon peel, 1 1/2 to 2 inches (3 3/4 to 5 cm) long
A pinch of oregano
A pinch of sugar
Salt
Freshly ground white pepper

FOR THE FINISHING OF THE DISH
1 cup (235 ml) Sauce Mornay (*see page 67*)

Recommended equipment

An 8-quart (8 L) stockpot, wooden spoon, colander, large chef's knife, 12-inch (30 cm) sauté pan, nutmeg grinder, wooden spatula, stainless steel box grater, 2-quart (2 L) mixing bowl, boning knife, baking dish, garlic press, fine-mesh sieve, heatproof serving platter.

Break the stems off the spinach and wash thoroughly in several changes of cold water. While washing the spinach, bring water in the stockpot to a full boil over high heat, add spinach, and when water returns to a boil time 15 seconds. Stir the spinach down with the wooden spoon to keep it submerged. When done, remove pot to sink, pour contents into colander, and, when the hot water has drained out, set the colander under cold running water to refresh the spinach. Stir a few times to speed the process. When cool, let drain, and squeeze tightly by small handfuls to rid the spinach of all excess moisture. Then chop it roughly with the chef's knife.

Set the sauté pan over medium heat, add the butter, and, while it is heating, chop the shallots and grate the Parmesan cheese. Then add the shallots to the pan and cook for 30 seconds. Next, add the spinach and season with salt, pepper, and nutmeg. Mix thoroughly with the wooden spatula, remove from heat, add the ricotta and Parmesan cheeses, mix well, scrape into the mixing bowl, and reserve. Wash out the sauté pan so it will be ready when you make the tomato sauce.

Prepare the chicken for cooking by cutting it into côtelettes. Follow the instructions for boned and skinned chicken breasts in the recipe for Suprêmes de Volaille Kiev *(see page 264)*; however, leave the skin on, keep the fillet pieces together, and cut the wing off at the second joint, keeping the bone in between the first and second joints, thus making a côtelette. When they are ready, make a place for the stuffing in each one. With the narrow, lengthwise edge facing you, run your finger between the meat and the skin, going to 1 inch (2 1/2 cm) from the wing joint and 1 to 1 1/2 (3 3/4 cm) inches from the bottom (skinless) side. Do not separate the skin all the way to the thick edge, but stop 1 to 1 1/2 inches away from it.

Preheat oven to 350F (177C). Butter the baking dish. Chop the shallots with the chef's knife and strew them in the bottom of the dish.

Stuff each chicken piece with 1/4 cup (60 ml) of the spinach mixture, packing it in between the skin and meat, and pulling the skin completely over the stuffing. Season the chicken lightly with salt and pepper and set it into the baking dish skin side up, add the white wine, and put it in the oven to bake for 15 minutes. Then reduce heat to 325F (163C) and cook for 15 more minutes.

While the chicken is baking, prepare the sauce Mornay and make the tomato sauce. Prepare the ripe tomatoes and cut them up coarsely into pieces about 1 inch (2 1/2 cm) long. Reserve. Set the sauté pan over medium heat, add the olive oil and butter, and, while it is heating, chop the shallots. When the pan is hot, add the shallots and cook, stirring, for 30 seconds. Press in the garlic, stir, and add the tomato pieces, tomato juice, lemon peel, oregano, sugar, salt, and pepper. Bring to a simmer and cook for 15 to 20 minutes or until the tomato sauce is reduced to one-third of its original volume and the tomato pieces are bound together by the thickened sauce. When done, remove from heat, discard lemon peel, and set aside until the chicken is out of the oven.

When the chicken is ready, remove it from the

oven, drain off the cooking juices, and then pour them through the sieve into the tomato sauce. Mix well. Raise the oven heat to 400F (204C). Spread the tomato sauce on the heatproof serving platter, arrange the chicken on top, and cover each piece of chicken with 2 tablespoons of sauce Mornay. Set into the oven to bake for about 6 to 8 minutes or until the sauce Mornay is golden brown. Serve at once.

You may stuff the chicken well in advance and keep it under refrigeration until you are ready to prepare the dish. In this case, add 5 minutes to the baking time. The tomato sauce may also be prepared in advance, but the sauce Mornay should be made within an hour of using it lest it separate.

Pollo alla Cacciatora
Chicken in the Style of the Hunter

*Throughout this book there are references to Catherine de' Medici, which is a shorthand way of referring to the substantial influence of Italian cuisine. Even though related to its French cousin, chasseur, this sauce has flavors that are more immediate, reflecting what, in many instances, is a main difference between the two national cuisines. Unlike risotto or ossobuco, this seems to be a truly pan-Italian dish, with regional variations to be sure, but a dish to be found wherever there are good native cooks. Interestingly enough, you will find both masculine and feminine references (*cacciatore *and* cacciatora) *for this rustic recipe. Perhaps as with Venus and Bouillabaisse, it can be traced back to Diana, goddess of the hunt. Saffron Rice is an appropriately colorful and tasty companion.*

Yields 6 to 8 servings

3 chickens, weighing 2 1/4 to 2 1/2 pounds (1025 to 1125 g) each
Salt
Freshly ground white pepper
Flour
1/4 cup (60 ml) olive oil
2 tablespoons chopped fresh shallots
1 garlic clove
1 pound (450 g) small mushrooms
1/4 teaspoon fresh oregano
1/3 bay leaf
1 tablespoon tomato paste
2 cups (475 ml) red wine
3 medium, ripe tomatoes (blanched, peeled, and seeded; see page 568)
1 1/2 cups (355 ml) Demi-glace Brun II *(see page 76)*
1 teaspoon chopped fresh parsley

Recommended equipment

A boning knife, two 12-inch (30 cm) sauté pans with lids, metal tongs, metal slotted spoon, paper towels, wooden spatula, large chef's knife, paring knife, basting spoon, heatproof serving dish or plates.

With the boning knife, disjoint each chicken into four pieces: leg-thighs and breasts (cut as côtelettes). Begin by inserting the knife point into the ball joint where the thigh meets the body and separating the two. Leave the thigh and leg together. Repeat for the other side. Then cut the wing tips off at the second joint (leaving the bone in between the first and second joints) and, beginning with one side, cut along the breastbone and down the ribs, separating the meat from the bone as you go and removing it in one piece. Repeat for the other side and reserve the bones for another use. Season the chicken pieces with salt and white pepper and dust lightly with flour.

Set each of the sauté pans over medium high heat, add 2 tablespoons olive oil to each pan, and, when it is hot, divide the chicken pieces between the pans so that they fit into them in a single layer. Sauté for 8 to 10 minutes, browning the chicken well on both sides, and turning it once.

While the chicken is browning, chop the shallots and the garlic with the chef's knife, brush the mushrooms of any clinging dirt and, if they are large, quarter them, using the paring knife. Reserve.

When the chicken is brown, remove it with the slotted spoon to paper towels and drain the excess grease from the pans, leaving only 1 tablespoon behind. With the sauté pans over medium heat, add the garlic, shallots, mushrooms, oregano, and bay leaf and sauté for 2 minutes, stirring with the wooden spatula. Then stir in the tomato paste and red wine and simmer for about 10 minutes or until the liquid is reduced by half.

While the sauce simmers, prepare the tomatoes and chop coarsely.

When the sauce is reduced, stir in the demi-glace, return chicken pieces to the pans, cover, and simmer gently for 30 minutes. When done, remove all grease from the pans with the basting spoon, stir in the tomatoes, and simmer uncovered for 5 minutes. Chop the parsley. Adjust seasoning if necessary, arrange the chicken on a warm serving dish or plates, sprinkle with parsley, and serve at once.

This dish may be prepared hours ahead and reheated very slowly. Chanterelles or other mushrooms may be used to enhance the flavor. If fresh tomatoes are unavailable, substitute an 8-ounce (225 g) can of whole or plum tomatoes, drained, and coarsely chopped.

Arroz con Pollo
Chicken with Spanish Rice

When I was night sous-chef at the former New York City Ambassador Hotel, we had fun making this dish for our late-night snack before the after-theater crowd arrived and kept us busy. The Cuban saucier was very good, having received his training in pre-Castro Havana, and this dish was a favorite of his. Because the ingredients may be prepared hours in advance, this is an excellent dish for entertaining. Use the recipe as a guide and once you are comfortable with the technique, vary the ingredients to suit your taste. Serve this with a mixed green salad tossed with oil and vinegar.

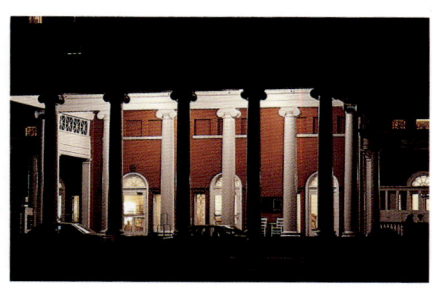

Yields 6 to 8 servings

3 chickens, weighing 2 1/4 to 2 1/2 pounds (1025 to 1125 g) each
Salt
Freshly ground white pepper
4 ounces (115 g) smoked, cooked ham
1 medium green bell pepper
1 medium onion
2 tablespoons olive oil
1 medium garlic clove
A pinch of thyme
1/3 bay leaf
6 ounces (170 g) Italian sausage, either mild or hot
1 tablespoon tomato paste
3 1/2 cups (830 ml) White Chicken Stock (see page 61)
1/8 teaspoon chopped saffron threads
4 ripe tomatoes (blanched, peeled, and seeded; see page 568)
6 pitted black olives
1 1/2 cups (355 ml) raw long grain rice
2 tablespoons capers
6 ounces (170 g) shelled peas
3 pimiento halves (packed in water and drained)
6 artichoke hearts, canned
1 medium, ripe avocado
Juice of 1/2 lemon
12 green asparagus stalks (or white canned)

Recommended equipment

A boning knife, paring knife, large chef's knife, Dutch oven with lid, garlic press, metal tongs, wooden spatula, 1 1/2-quart (1 1/2 L) saucepan, 1-quart (1 L) mixing bowl, swivel-bladed vegetable peeler, long-handled cooking fork.

With the boning knife, disjoint each chicken into four pieces: leg-thighs and breasts (cut as côtelettes). Begin by inserting the knife point into the ball joint where the thigh meets the body and separating the two. Leave the thigh and leg together. Repeat for the other side. Then cut the wing tips off at the second joint (leaving the bone in between the first and second joints) and, beginning with one side, cut along the breastbone and down the ribs, separating the meat from the bone as you go and removing it in one piece. Repeat for the other side and reserve the bones for another use (such as making stock). Season the chicken lightly with salt and pepper and reserve.

Using the paring knife, cut the ham into 1/2-inch (1 1/4 cm) cubes. Rinse the bell pepper, halve and seed it, and cut into 1-inch (2 1/2 cm) pieces. Peel the onion and chop it finely with the chef's knife.

Set the Dutch oven over medium high heat, add 2 tablespoons olive oil, and, when it is hot, add chicken pieces in a single layer. Sauté for about 10 minutes, turning the chicken once with tongs, or until both sides are golden brown. Sauté the remaining chicken pieces the same way until all are finished. (If the oil becomes too dark, drain it from the pan and replenish it with fresh oil.) Drain off the fat, leaving about 2 tablespoons in the pan. Reduce heat to medium and add the ham, bell pepper, and onion, press in the garlic, and then mix in the thyme and bay leaf. Sauté for 2 minutes, stirring once or twice. During this time, slice the sausage into 1-inch thick pieces, and then add it to the chicken along with the tomato paste, chicken stock, and saffron. Bring to a gentle simmer, cover pan, and simmer for 10 minutes.

While the chicken simmers, prepare the tomatoes and cut each olive into several pieces.

Preheat oven to 325F (163C).

When the simmering time is over, add the rice, tomatoes, and olives to the pan, stir, re-cover, and set into the oven. Bake for 18 minutes.

While the chicken is baking, prepare the vegetables and set aside until needed. Measure out the capers, including some of their vinegar. Bring salted water to boil in the saucepan, add the peas, return water to the boil, then remove from heat, drain the peas, and cool under cold water. Quarter the pimiento halves. Cut the artichoke hearts in half. Halve the avocado, remove peel and pit, quarter each half, and put pieces into the mixing bowl. Squeeze the lemon juice over the avocado, covering all surfaces. If you are using fresh asparagus, peel the woody part of the stalk and cook in salted water until the point of a knife just pierces the stalk easily. Cool under cold running water, drain, and reserve.

When the chicken is done, remove pan from oven, uncover, and fluff the rice with the fork. The rice should be moist—if dry, add a little more chicken stock, re-cover pan, and return to the oven for a few minutes. If the rice is too wet, re-cover pan and set into the oven again. Check after 3 minutes. When the rice is ready, lightly mix the capers and peas into it and add the pimiento, artichoke, avocado, and asparagus. Serve from the Dutch oven at the table, or arrange the chicken, rice, and vegetables on a warm serving platter. In either case, have your guests at the table waiting to savor this colorful dish.

Poulet Mode de Meurice
Chicken in the Style of Meurice

This was a fixture on the menu when I joined the kitchen staff at the New York City Ambassador Hotel and was brought from his native France by our distinguished executive chef, Clement Grangier. Both extremely talented, he and his brother Raymond had served in kitchens on legendary French Line ships—he as a chef on the Ile de France, *and Raymond as chef des cuisines of the* Liberté *and* Flandre. *The distinctly Parisian feel about this dish leads me to believe that there may be a connection to the venerable landmark hotel of the same name on the Rue de Rivoli. The sauce, finished with two creams, is delicious served with plain, buttered noodles, Rice Pilaff, Spätzle, or Pommes de Terre Parisienne Rissolées.*

Yields 6 servings

3 chickens, weighing 2 1/4 to 2 1/2 pounds (1025 to 1125 g) each
Salt
Freshly ground white pepper
Flour
1/2 cup (118 ml) Clarified Butter *(see page 568)*
2 tablespoons chopped shallots
12 small mushrooms
1 piece of lemon peel, about 2 x 1 inches (5 x 2 1/2 cm)
Juice of 1 lemon
1 1/2 cups (355 ml) dry white wine
1 tablespoon Glace de Viande *(see page 65)*
1/2 cup (118 ml) White Chicken Stock *(see page 61)*
3 slices Pullman Loaf *(see page 488)*
6 artichoke hearts, halved (or 4 bottoms, quartered)
1 cup (235 ml) whipping cream
1 cup (235 ml) sour cream or Crème Fraîche *(see page 66)*, at room temperature
1 teaspoon green peppercorns (packed in water and drained)
2 teaspoons chopped fresh parsley

Recommended equipment

A boning knife, two 12-inch (30 cm) sauté pans with lids, metal tongs, wooden spatula, large chef's knife, paring knife, 10-inch (25 cm) sauté pan, metal slotted spoon, paper towels, fine-mesh sieve, basting spoon, 2-quart (2 L) mixing bowl, heatproof serving platter.

With the boning knife, disjoint each chicken into four pieces: leg-thighs and breasts (cut as côtelettes). Begin by inserting the knife point into the ball joint where the thigh meets the body and separating the two. Leave the thigh and leg together. Repeat for the other side. Then cut the wing tips off at the second joint (leaving the bone in between the first and second joints) and, beginning with one side, cut along the breastbone and down the ribs, separating the meat from the bone as you go and removing it in one piece. Repeat for the other side and reserve the bones for another use. Season the chicken pieces with salt and white pepper and dust lightly with flour.

Set each of the large sauté pans over medium high heat, add 3 tablespoons clarified butter to each pan, and, when it is hot, divide the chicken pieces between the pans so that they fit into a single layer. Sauté for about 5 minutes, turning the chicken once to brown it on both sides, and then reduce heat to medium low and continue cooking another 3 minutes.

While the chicken is browning, chop the shallots with the chef's knife, brush the mushrooms of any clinging dirt and, if they are large, cut them in half. Cut the piece of peel with the paring knife, squeeze the lemon, and reserve the juice and peel.

When the chicken is ready, drain the excess grease from the sauté pans, divide the shallots between them, stir for 30 seconds, then divide the mushrooms, lemon juice, and lemon peel between the pans. Simmer, stirring, for 1 minute before adding the white wine, glace de viande, and chicken stock. Bring the pans to a low simmer, cover, and maintain a simmer for 30 minutes, turning the chicken pieces once after about 15 minutes.

While the chicken simmers, prepare the croutons from the bread slices. Trim off the crusts and cut each slice into pieces that are 2 inches long and 1/2 inch wide (5 x 1 1/4 cm). Heat the remaining clarified butter in the smaller sauté pan over low heat, add the croutons, and cook, stirring, until they are golden brown. When done, remove from pan with the slotted spoon and drain on paper towels. If necessary, add some more butter to the pan, set over medium low heat, add the artichoke hearts (or bottoms), and cook gently without browning for 2 or 3 minutes.

After the chicken has simmered for 30 minutes, remove the chicken and mushrooms with a slotted spoon and keep in a warm (not hot) place. Pour the liquid from the pans through the sieve into the bowl, and remove grease from the top with the basting spoon. Return the liquid to one of the sauté pans, add the cream, sour cream (or crème fraîche), and green peppercorns, bring to a simmer, and reduce the liquid by about one-half, or until the sauce is light and creamy.

While the sauce is reducing, chop the parsley.

When the sauce is ready, divide it and the chicken and mushrooms between the pans, bring to a simmer, adjust the seasoning if needed, then arrange on the warm serving platter (or plates), arrange the artichoke hearts (or bottoms) on top, sprinkle the croutons and parsley over all, and serve at once.

❧

If you use canned artichoke hearts (or bottoms) they may be used as is. For fresh ones, precook them in boiling water until just tender, refresh under cold running water, drain, and then proceed with the recipe.

Variation: Try marinating the chicken pieces before cooking them, following the instructions in Coq au Vin Mode de Bourgogne *(see below)*, but using a dry white wine instead of a red wine.

❧ *Coq au Vin Mode de Bourgogne*
Chicken in the Style of Burgundy

Solidly rooted in French bourgeois country cuisine, this chicken and its beef companion, Boeuf à la Bourguignonne, are true harbingers of the approach of cold weather. The pillowy hills of the Burgundian countryside outlined by borders of changing leaves and the aroma of smoke from fires of wood and culled grape vines set the scene for the much awaited appearance of this classic. We marinate the chicken because we think it enhances the meat and the sauce. Although you can use white wine, tradition calls for red, which produces a more robust sauce. Above all, use only a top quality wine for the marinade and accompany the dish with a full-bodied Côtes du Rhône or Burgundy. Incidentally, you should use a good smoke-cured bacon for the lardons to impart a genuinely rustic flavor in the sautéing. Serving two or three parsleyed new potatoes per person will give your guests all the excuse they need to soak up any remains of the sumptuous sauce.

Yields 6 servings

3 chickens, weighing 2 1/4 to 2 1/2 pounds (1025 to 1125 g) each
Salt
Freshly ground black pepper

FOR THE MARINADE
1 medium onion
1 celery stalk
1/2 medium carrot
1/4 bay leaf
A dash of thyme
1/2 garlic clove
1 bottle red Burgundy

FOR COOKING THE CHICKEN
Flour
4 to 5 ounces (115 to 145 g) slab bacon or salt pork in one piece
1 1/2 cups (355 ml) Demi-glace Brun II *(see page 76)*

FOR THE VEGETABLE AND CROUTON GARNISH
12 whole small onions or 48 pearl onions
12 whole small mushrooms
3 tablespoons Clarified Butter *(see page 568)*
1/2 teaspoon sugar
3 slices Pullman Loaf *(see page 488)*
1 1/2 teaspoons chopped fresh parsley

Recommended equipment

A boning knife, large ceramic or glass bowl, large chef's knife, stiff bristle brush, plastic wrap, paring knife, paper towels, two 12-inch (30 cm) sauté pans, Dutch oven, wooden spatula, 2-quart (2 L) saucepan, 10-inch (25 cm) sauté pan, slotted spoon, large fine-mesh sieve, 2-quart (2 L) mixing bowl, basting spoon, small chef's knife.

Rinse the chickens under cold running water, drain, and, with the boning knife, disjoint each chicken into four pieces: leg-thighs and breasts (cut as côtelettes). Begin by inserting the knife point into the ball joint where the thigh meets the body and separating the two. Leave the thigh and leg together. Repeat for the other side. Then cut the wing tips off at the second joint (leaving the bone in between the first and second joints) and, beginning with one side, cut along the breastbone and down the ribs, separating the meat from the bone as you go and removing it in one piece. Repeat for the other side and reserve the bones for another use. Season the chicken lightly with salt and pepper and set it into the ceramic or glass bowl.

Peel the onion and chop it coarsely with the chef's knife. Rinse the celery stalk and trim to make it as stringless as possible, then chop it coarsely. Scrub the carrot and chop it coarsely. Add the three vegetables to the bowl with the chicken, followed by the bay leaf, thyme, and garlic. Pour on the wine, adding more if needed to cover the chicken. Cover the bowl with plastic wrap and set in the refrigerator to marinate for 18 to 24 hours.

The next day, remove the chicken from the marinade, drain on paper towels, and pat dry, reserving the marinade. Dust the chicken pieces with flour.

Remove the rind from the bacon and cut it into 1/2-inch (1 1/4 cm) cubes or lardons. (If you use salt pork, parboil in water for 10 minutes before cubing.) Set the sauté pans over medium high heat, divide the lardons between them, and sauté, stirring, until they are crisp. Remove lardons to paper towels to drain and divide the chicken pieces between the pans. Brown the chicken well on all sides, turning as necessary (this should take 8 to 10 minutes).

Preheat oven to 325F (163C).

When the chicken is brown, add the onions, celery, and carrots from the marinade and sauté the vegetables with the chicken pieces for 3 minutes. Remove the chicken and vegetables and place them in the Dutch oven. Drain the fat from both sauté pans and deglaze each with a little of the marinade, scraping the liquid into the Dutch oven with the wooden spatula. Add the demi-glace and remaining marinade to the chicken and bring the mixture to a simmer over medium heat, cover, and set into the middle level of the oven to bake for 35 minutes.

While the chicken is cooking, bring lightly salted water to boil in the saucepan, add the whole small onions, return to the boil, and cook for 10 minutes. (If using pearl onions, blanch them for 2 minutes.) Remove from heat, drain, and run cold water into the pan. Drain the onions again, peel them with the paring knife, and reserve.

Prepare the mushrooms by brushing them gently of any clinging dirt. If they are large, halve them, otherwise leave them whole. Set the 10-inch sauté pan over medium heat, add 1 1/2 teaspoons of the clarified butter and, when it is hot, stir the mushrooms into the butter and sauté, stirring, for 3 minutes. Remove the pan from heat, season the mushrooms lightly with salt and pepper, scrape them into a bowl, and set aside.

Add another 1 1/2 teaspoons clarified butter to the sauté pan, set over medium heat, and stir in the sugar and the cooked small onions. Sauté, stirring from time to time, until the onions are lightly browned and glacéed. Drain off excess butter, add the onions to the mushrooms, and wash out the sauté pan.

Cut the bread slices into croutons about 2 inches long and 1/2 inch wide (5 x 1 1/4 cm). Set the sauté pan over medium low heat, add the remaining clarified butter, and, when it is hot, stir in the croutons and sauté, stirring, until they are golden brown. Then remove from heat, drain on paper towels, and reserve.

When the chicken and vegetables are done (a heavier chicken may need 10 more minutes for cooking), remove them to a dish with the slotted spoon. Strain the cooking liquid through the sieve into a bowl and let cool for a few minutes. Skim the fat from the top with the basting spoon and return the sauce to the Dutch oven. Bring to a boil over high heat and cook until it is reduced by one-half its volume. When reduced, return the chicken to the sauce and add the reserved mushrooms and onions. Bring to a simmer, heat for 2 minutes, adjust seasoning if necessary, skim any remaining grease from the surface, and transfer to a heated serving dish.

Rinse the parsley, spin or pat it dry, and chop it with the chef's knife. Sprinkle the lardons over the chicken and then the croutons and the parsley. Serve at once.

If fresh small onions are unavailable, use canned or frozen onions, omit the boil, and go directly to browning them in butter. For a more robust, "country" flavor, blanch the bacon rind in simmering water for 10 minutes and add it to the Dutch oven to cook with the chicken and vegetables.

Variation: Reduce the strained sauce by one-third and then blend in 1/3 to 1/2 cup (80 to 118 ml) room-temperature sour cream or Crème Fraîche *(see page 66)*, stirring until well mixed. If you prefer, omit the bacon (or salt pork) and brown the chicken in a few tablespoons of peanut oil.

🌿 Chicken in the Pot Homestead

Chicken in the pot or La Poule au Pot, supposedly traces its roots to Henri IV, who promised his countrymen "a chicken in every pot every Sunday." Thus began the unending love affair between a casserole-roasted fowl and peasant and noble alike (including the ravishing Empress Eugénie, wife of Napoleon III). Our version is a good luncheon or family dinner dish during a cold spell or when you (or a dear one) are feeling under the weather and in need of a "pick-me-up" meal.

Yields 4 servings

A roasting chicken, weighing 3 1/4 to 3 1/2 pounds (1465 to 1575 g)
1 medium onion
1 teaspoon peanut oil
1 very small clove
2 quarts (1900 ml) White Chicken Stock *(see page 61)*
1 cup (235 ml) water
1/6 small bay leaf
1 1/2 medium carrots
2 celery stalks
1 medium leek, white part only
1/2 medium turnip
4 ounces (115 g) shelled peas (or frozen)
6 ounces (170 g) noodles
Salt
Freshly ground white pepper
8 slices French Bread *(see page 487)*
2 tablespoons grated Parmesan cheese
1 tablespoon finely cut fresh chives

Recommended equipment

White kitchen string, trussing needle, 8-quart (8 L) stockpot, paring knife, 8-inch (20 cm) sauté pan, Dutch oven (or other ovenproof pot with lid to hold chicken snugly with room for vegetables), swivel-bladed vegetable peeler, basting spoon, 2-quart (2 L) saucepan, baking sheet, stainless steel box grater.

Rinse the chicken well under running cold water, inside and out, drain, and truss it *(see pages 568–69)* using the white string and trussing needle. Set the chicken in the stockpot, cover well with hot tap water, and set to boil over high heat. When the boil is reached, maintain it for 30 seconds, then remove stockpot to the sink, pour off the hot water, and run cold water into the pot to rinse any scum off the chicken. Drain and reserve.

Peel the onion with the paring knife and halve it. Set the sauté pan over medium heat, add the peanut oil, and set the onion halves into it with the cut side down. Sauté until the onion is golden brown on the cut side. Then remove pan from heat, remove onion from pan, and stick the clove into one of the onion halves.

Set the chicken into the Dutch oven and add the chicken stock, water, onion halves, and bay leaf. More (or less) liquid may be needed depending upon the size of the chicken and the pot—the liquid should cover the chicken by several inches. Set the pot over medium high heat, bring to a boil, then reduce heat so that the liquid maintains a steady simmer, and cook for 30 minutes.

While the chicken simmers, prepare the vegetables. Wash the carrots, celery stalks, leek, and turnip under running cold water. Peel the carrot and the turnip half. Trim the leek of the green top and the celery of its "strings." Cut all four vegetables into matchstick-size strips about 1 1/2 inches long by 1/4 inch wide (3 3/4 x 2/3 cm) and reserve. Blanch the peas in boiling water in the saucepan, drain, and reserve. Rinse out the pan, bring water to a boil in it, add the noodles, and cook them until they are al dente. Remove from heat, drain, and reserve.

When the chicken has simmered for half an hour, skim off any fat or scum from the broth, remove the onion half with the clove, add all the matchstick vegetables, bring back to the simmer, and continue cooking for 35 minutes. Then remove chicken from broth and let it cool while the

294

broth continues to simmer. Using the basting spoon, remove all grease as it rises from the simmering broth. Adjust seasoning if needed with salt and pepper. Disjoint the chicken into breasts, thighs, legs, and wings, and remove all the skin and as many bones as possible. (If the chicken is too hot to handle, cool it under running cold water.)

Preheat oven to 375F (190C).

Return the chicken pieces to the pot, add the peas and noodles, and bring to a simmer for a few minutes. While the chicken is warming, toast the bread, grate the Parmesan cheese, set the toast on the baking sheet, sprinkle with cheese, and set the sheet into the oven to bake until golden brown (or run it under the broiler). Snip the chives. When the toast is ready and the chicken is hot, remove it from heat, stir in the chives, and serve at once alongside the toast on warm serving plates.

Variation: Substitute dumplings for the noodles, but get the recipe from your grandmother because I can never make them come out!

Poulet Rôti à l'Estragon
Chicken Roasted with Tarragon

There is something comforting about a plump chicken roasting in the oven, its delicious aroma filling the kitchen with promise—especially an aroma infused with fresh tarragon. Serve this classic with Whipped Potatoes, Spätzle, or noodles, and the tiniest green beans you can find sautéed in butter at the last minute. If by chance you have a market with imported produce, look for haricots verts *from France.*

Yields 4 to 6 servings

2 chickens, weighing 2 1/4 to 2 1/2 pounds (1025 to 1125 g) each
16 fresh tarragon leaves
1/2 teaspoon plus a large pinch coarsely chopped fresh tarragon leaves and stems
Salt
Freshly ground black pepper
1 tablespoon olive oil
1/2 medium onion
1 celery stalk
2/3 cup (160 ml) dry white wine
1 teaspoon Glace de Viande *(see page 65)*
1 cup (235 ml) Crème Fraîche *(see page 66)*

Recommended equipment

A small chef's knife, white kitchen string, trussing needle, heavy roasting pan, wooden spatula, wooden spoon, large fine-mesh sieve.

Rinse each chicken inside and out under running cold water, drain, pat dry, and set on your work surface.

Rinse the tarragon, pat dry, pull off sixteen leaves, and set them aside. Chop enough stems and leaves together for 1/2 teaspoon plus a large pinch and reserve.

Set each chicken on its back with the cavity facing you. Gently loosen the skin from each side of the breast and for each half slip four tarragon leaves in a single layer between the skin and the meat. Pull the skin back to its original position. Then divide the 1/2 teaspoon chopped stems and leaves between the cavities, truss the chickens with the white string *(see pages 568–69)*, and season them lightly with salt and pepper. Chop the giblets and neck bones coarsely and set aside. (Save the liver for another use.)

Preheat oven to 350F (177C).

Set the roasting pan over medium high heat, add the olive oil, and, when it is hot, add the chickens, setting them each on one side to begin with, and strew the chopped giblets and neck bones around them. When the pan sizzles, set it into the oven and roast the chickens for 15 minutes. Then turn the chickens over to their other side and roast for another 15 minutes.

While the chicken roasts, peel the onion and

chop it coarsely. Wash the celery stalk, trim to make it as stringless as possible, and chop it coarsely. Reserve both.

When the chickens have finished roasting on their second side, turn them over onto their backs, strew the onion and celery around them, add 1/3 cup (80 ml) white wine, and return them to the oven. Reduce the oven temperature to 325F (163C) and roast the chickens for 25 minutes, basting occasionally. To see if the chickens are done, pierce the leg joint and if the juices run clear they are ready. When done, remove the chickens to a warm serving platter, set them breast side down, and let them rest for 10 minutes before removing the trussing strings.

Add any escaped juices on the platter to the roasting pan, set the pan over medium heat, bring to the simmer, and cook until the liquid is nearly evaporated and quite thick. *Do not let the vegetables burn*. Pour off all grease from the pan, add the remaining white wine, and deglaze the pan while scraping up all the brown bits with the wooden spatula. When the pan is deglazed, add the glace de viande and crème fraîche and mix well with the wooden spoon. Simmer for 3 minutes or until the sauce is thickened and creamy. Then strain sauce through the sieve, add the remaining large pinch of chopped tarragon, spoon the sauce over and around the chicken and serve. (If you prefer, carve the chicken for individual servings before you nap it with the sauce.)

Roast Boned Chicken with Wild Rice and Hazelnut (or Chestnut) Stuffing

The year 1812 was not a banner one for Napoleon—at least on his northern flank. However, he fared better on the Iberian peninsula as his general, Maréchal Suchet, won rather handily at Oropéza, Murviedro, and Valencia. To express his gratitude, Napoleon named Suchet the Duc d'Albuféra, giving him control over a territory which included rice fields surrounding a lake (of the same name) connected to the bay of Valencia. The "D'Albuféra" preparation was created (probably by Carême) to honor this event, and, when used with poultry, usually means a boned bird stuffed with rice, foie gras, and truffles, and served with a touch of pimiento in the sauce, to reflect the Spanish origin. Our version features a roasted bird with a wild rice, hazelnut, and chicken liver stuffing (to lighten the load on your pocketbook). The Spanish flair is still evident in the orange sauce, in which you will probably use Valencia oranges. An elegant presentation for a fall or winter dinner, it should be served with fresh String Beans, Brussels Sprouts, or Asparagus. Garnish each portion with tangerine sections.

Yields 6 servings

FOR THE STUFFING
4 ounces (115 g) wild rice
1/2 medium onion
1 celery stalk
6 ounces (170 g) chicken livers
1 tablespoon Clarified Butter *(see page 568)*
1 egg yolk
2 tablespoons Demi-glace Brun I *(see page 75)*
2 tablespoons hazelnut paste
1/4 cup (60 ml) fine white bread crumbs
Salt
Freshly ground black pepper

FOR THE CHICKEN
3 chickens, weighing 2 1/4 to 2 1/2 pounds (1025 to 1125 g) each
3 tablespoons Clarified Butter

Butter for the roasting pan

FOR THE SAUCE
1 recipe orange sauce from Canard Rôti à l'Orange *(see page 300)*

FOR THE GARNISH
3 tangerines

Recommended equipment

A 2-quart (2 L) saucepan with lid, fine-mesh sieve, paring knife, large chef's knife, 10-inch (25 cm) sauté pan, wooden spatula, blending fork, boning knife, kitchen scissors, aluminum foil, roasting pan.

Bring 1 1/2 quarts (1 1/2 L) lightly salted water to boil in the saucepan, add the wild rice, and simmer for 50 minutes or until tender. When done, drain into sieve, run cold water over rice, drain, and reserve.

Peel the onion half and chop it into fine dice using the chef's knife. Rinse the celery stalk, trim it with the paring knife, make it as stringless as possible, and dice it finely with the chef's knife. Rinse the chicken livers, trim them of any stringy bits, and chop them coarsely.

Set the sauté pan over medium heat, add the clarified butter, and, when it is hot, add the onion and celery and sauté for 1 minute before adding the chicken livers. Stir in the livers, sauté for 2 minutes, then remove pan from heat and mix in the wild rice, egg yolk, demi-glace, hazelnut paste, and bread crumbs. Season with salt and pepper, blend together well with the fork, and reserve.

To prepare the chickens for roasting, rinse off each one under cold running water and split them in half along the backbone and breastbone, using the boning knife. For each half, remove the meat from the bones by cutting and scraping it away, being careful to keep the cutting edge of the knife against the bones. Insert the tip of the knife into the ball joints that connect the thighs to the body, sever the joint to loosen the thigh bone, cut the meat from the thigh bone, and remove the bone. Sever the leg joint and leave the bone in the leg. Now you should have six halves that are boneless except for the leg bone and ready to be stuffed. Put the chicken halves skin side down on your work surface, spread each one open, and season lightly with salt and pepper. Divide the stuffing among the halves, using 4 or 5 tablespoons for each, and mound it into a ball in the center of each chicken piece. Fold the breast meat over the stuffing and make a neat package with the leg bone extended to one side. With the scissors, cut six strips of aluminum foil that are 2 inches wide (5 cm) and as long as the width of the roll of foil. Wrap a strip around each chicken package to help hold it together while roasting.

Preheat oven to 375F (190C).

Butter the roasting pan and set the chicken into it in a single layer with the skin side up. Sprinkle the clarified butter over the chicken, put the pan into the middle level of the oven, and cook for 5 minutes. Then reduce heat to 325F (163C) and roast for 40 minutes, basting occasionally with the pan juices.

Prepare the orange sauce.

Peel the tangerines carefully, remove the fruit sections, and reserve.

Near the end of the cooking time, pierce the chicken legs with a fork, and if the juices run clear the chicken is done. Remove the pan from the oven and let the chicken rest for 5 minutes before removing the foil strips. While the chicken rests, warm the orange sauce, then set the chicken halves on warm dinner plates, spoon the sauce around, and garnish the top with tangerine sections.

Hazelnut paste is available at specialty food stores. Two tablespoons finely ground hazelnuts may be substituted for the paste.

Variation: Substitute raspberry sauce from the Canard Rôti à la Framboise *(see page 298)* for the orange sauce and/or a chestnut purée for the hazelnut paste.

Foies de Volaille Sautés Chasseur
Sautéed Chicken Livers in the Style of the Hunter

This nourishing dish is a snap if the Sauce Chasseur is prepared in advance. The Italians discovered the sympatico nature of parsley, garlic, and lemon and I use it (gremolada) here as the final fillip for a classic French preparation. Serve the foies de volaille with Rice Pilaff or pasta, such as spaghetti or angel hair noodles.

Yields 5 servings

2 cups (475 ml) Sauce Chasseur (see page 80)
1 1/2 pounds (675 g) fresh chicken livers
3 tablespoons olive oil
Salt
Freshly ground black pepper
2 teaspoons chopped fresh parsley
1/4 clove garlic chopped
Peel from 1/3 lemon, all bitter white removed

Recommended equipment

Paper towels, 12-inch (30 cm) sauté pan, wooden spatula, metal slotted spoon, large fine-mesh sieve, paring knife, small chef's knife.

Prepare the sauce chasseur and keep it warm while you cook the livers.

Rinse the chicken livers gently under cold water, drain on paper towels, and pick them over, removing any stringy filaments.

Set the sauté pan over medium high heat, add half of the olive oil, and, when it is hot, add half of the livers to the pan and season lightly with salt and pepper. Brown the livers well on all sides, stirring with the spatula, then remove them with the slotted spoon to the sieve to drain. Add remaining olive oil and livers to the pan, season with salt and pepper, and brown them as you did the first batch. When done, remove to sieve to drain.

Using the chef's knife, chop the parsley, garlic, and lemon peel together until well blended. Bring the sauce chasseur to a boil over medium high heat, then reduce heat and simmer for 2 minutes. Stir in the chicken livers, return sauce to the boil, remove immediately from heat, spoon onto warm plates, and sprinkle each serving with some of the chopped parsley mixture.

Canard Rôti à la Framboise
Roast Duckling with Raspberry Sauce

It certainly is no overstatement to say that duck is to southwest France what chicken is to Bresse. Obviously integral to foie gras production, ducks (and geese) are a bulwark of the cuisine of Gascogne, Languedoc, and Guyenne. Like the salmon, almost every part of a duck can be (and is) used for culinary purposes—even the feathers bound together with string are useful for basting. As you can tell from the fact that we use an average of seven hundred and fifty pounds a week, duck is an important feature on our menus, and it should be a staple of your kitchen as well. Because it is important to master, I have given you the traditional preparation for roasting an entire bird, but when quartered, as we typically serve it, the cooking time is significantly reduced without losing any flavor. I could go on and on about this fabulous fowl because I love it, but I must get back to the kitchen. Once very difficult to locate, fresh duckling is now available in many supermarkets or butcher shops and is superior to a frozen bird. In addition, commercial farms in North Carolina and elsewhere have been producing a larger and leaner duck than its northern cousin, thus increasing the number of servings per bird. Serve this and the two variations with wild rice and fresh String Beans for a perfect fall dinner. If you have made Homestead Raspberry Vinegar, by all means use it in the sauce.

Yields 4 to 6 servings

Recommended equipment

FOR ROASTING THE DUCKS
2 ducklings, weighing 5 1/4 to 5 1/2 pounds (2400 to 2500 g) each
Salt
Freshly ground black pepper
1 medium onion
1 celery stalk
1 small carrot
1 1/4 cups (295 ml) dry white wine

FOR THE RASPBERRY SAUCE
1/4 cup (60 ml) Melba sauce
1/4 cup (60 ml) raspberry vinegar
1/4 cup (60 ml) Brown Chicken Stock or Duck Stock *(see page 62)*
2 teaspoons Glace de Viande *(see page 65)*
2 juniper berries
1/4 teaspoon freshly ground white pepper
A dash of cayenne pepper
Juice of 1 lemon
2 teaspoons arrowroot
3 tablespoons Chambord liqueur

FOR THE GARNISH
4 ounces (115 g) fresh raspberries
Fresh mint sprigs

A boning knife, trussing needle, white kitchen string, heavy roasting pan, paring knife, small chef's knife, bulb baster, heatproof platter, wooden spatula, fine-mesh sieve, 1-quart (1 L) bowl, 1 1/2-quart (1 1/2 L) saucepan, wire whisk, small dish.

Preheat oven to 425F (218C).

For each duck, remove the giblets and liver (save it for another use such as a pâté or sauté lightly with a vinaigrette in a *salade tiède*) from the duck cavity and hold the duck under running cold water, rinsing it inside and out. Let drain briefly and then pull or trim away all excess fat from inside the duck near the tail, around the neck, and under the skin. Using the boning knife, cut off any excess neck bone and the wings at the first joint and reserve. Season the duck inside and out with salt and pepper. Using the trussing needle, poke the duck skin all over but especially around the legs to enable the fat to escape during roasting. Truss the ducks *(see pages 568–69)* with white kitchen string and set them on their side in the roasting pan.

Set the pan into the oven and roast the ducks for 10 minutes or until you hear them sizzling. Then reduce the heat to 350F (177C) and roast 30 minutes on each side.

Meanwhile, prepare the vegetables. Peel the onion with the paring knife and cut it into eight pieces. Rinse the celery stalk and the carrot and chop them roughly with the chef's knife. Also, rinse the giblets and chop them into 1/2-inch (1 1/4 cm) long pieces.

When the ducks have roasted for 60 minutes, remove the pan from the oven, remove them from the pan, drain off all fat from the pan, and then return ducks to the pan with the breast side up. Spread the onion, celery, carrot, giblets, neck pieces, and wing tips around the ducks and set into

the oven for 10 minutes. Then add 1 cup (235 ml) wine, reduce heat to 325F (163C), and roast for 35 minutes. Baste with the pan juices every 10 minutes. When the roasting time is ended, insert the trussing needle into the leg joint. If the juices run clear, remove the ducks from the oven. If the juices are pink or red, return the ducks to the oven and roast 10 to 15 minutes before checking again.

When the ducks are cooked, remove them to the platter, breast side down, and let them rest in a warm (not hot) spot for at least 15 to 20 minutes before carving. It is important that the juices have time to retreat into the breast meat.

While the ducks are resting, set the roasting pan over medium heat and simmer the cooking juices until they have been reduced to a brown syrupy liquid, clinging to the vegetables and bones, and the fat in the pan is clear. Tip up the pan, spoon out the fat, and discard. Lower heat, add the remaining wine, and dissolve the reduced juices by simmering gently while scraping and stirring with the wooden spatula. When the juices are dissolved, remove from heat and reserve.

For the raspberry sauce, combine all the ingredients except the arrowroot and Chambord in the saucepan. Set the saucepan over medium heat and stir occasionally with the whisk while bringing the sauce to a simmer. Let the sauce simmer on low for 10 minutes. Blend the arrowroot and Chambord together in the small dish and mix until it is a smooth paste. Then whisk the paste into the simmering sauce and continue to stir while the sauce simmers for another 3 minutes. (Do not boil.) Stir in the reduced cooking liquids and strain through the sieve into a clean saucepan. Keep the sauce warm while you crisp the duck.

To crisp the duck just before serving, set the oven to 400F (204C). Either carve the duck or leave it whole and set it on a pan in the oven for 5 minutes. Remove duck from oven, spoon the raspberry sauce on a warm serving platter or plates, and set the crisp duck on the sauce (or pass the sauce separately). If you wish to serve the duck without the skin, remove it after the duck has rested and just before carving. Garnish the plates or platter with the fresh raspberries and mint sprigs.

If you must use frozen duckling, let it thaw very slowly in the refrigerator for 24 hours before preparing it. A 4 1/4- to 4 3/4-pound bird will serve two people. If the ducks are lighter than called for in the recipe, check for doneness 15 minutes earlier. Save the carcass and make duck stock from it for future use.

Melba sauce is a commercially prepared raspberry sauce that is available in specialty stores.

Variation

 Canard Rôti à l'Orange
Roast Duckling with Orange Sauce

For many this is the classic, if overworked, roast duckling recipe. Historically, the sauce is well rooted in antiquity because the orange and juice you will use probably are direct descendants from the tree Vasco da Gama planted in Lisbon on returning from China early in the sixteenth century.

Yields 4 to 6 servings

2 tablespoons sugar
1/4 cup (60 ml) red wine
3/4 cup (180 ml) fresh orange juice
1/4 cup (60 ml) red currant jelly
A dash of cayenne pepper
Juices from the roasting pan
1 large orange
1 tablespoon arrowroot
1/4 cup (60 ml) Curaçao or Grand Marnier
4 drops red food color (optional)

Recommended equipment

A 2-quart (2 L) saucepan, swivel-bladed vegetable peeler, paring knife, 1 1/2-quart (1 1/2 L) saucepan, fine-mesh sieve, small dish, wire whisk.

Following the recipe for Canard Rôti à la Framboise *(see pages 299–300)*, roast the ducks, set them to rest, reduce the roasting juices, strain, and reserve.

Put the sugar in the saucepan, set it over medium low heat, and cook until the sugar is a light brown caramel color. Then add red wine and simmer until the sugar is dissolved. Add the orange juice, jelly, cayenne, and juices from the roasting pan and bring the mixture to a low simmer. Simmer for 10 minutes.

While the sauce simmers, use the vegetable peeler to peel one-half of the orange, being very careful to leave the bitter white behind. Cut the peel into very fine, thin strips with the paring knife, put the strips into the small saucepan, cover with water, set the saucepan over medium high heat, and bring to a boil. Let boil 5 minutes, drain into the fine-mesh sieve, and reserve the strips.

Peel the rest of the orange, remove all the white pith, cut the orange into sections, and reserve.

When the sauce has finished simmering, blend the arrowroot and Curaçao or Grand Marnier in the small dish until they make a smooth paste. Then remove the sauce from the heat and whisk in the arrowroot mixture. Set the saucepan back over the heat and stir until the sauce simmers. Add the blanched orange zest and let the sauce simmer on low heat for 3 minutes before serving. If you like, strictly for appearance, add four drops of red food color to the sauce. Decorate the serving plates or platter with the orange sections.

Variation

Roast Duckling with Walnut and Pomegranate Sauce

This might as well be called canard à l'ancienne. *Turmeric (*curcuma *or "saffron of the Indies"), source of the bright yellow in curry powder, dates from the Middle Ages. Walnuts were known in fourth century B.C. Greece, and the pomegranate, widely used in France and known as* grenade, *can be found prominently displayed in a Theban wall painting of a garden dated B.C. 1400. This is an unusual and excellent way to serve duck—especially in the twentieth century.*

Yields 4 to 6 servings

2 tablespoons rendered duck fat
1 medium onion
1/4 teaspoon turmeric
1/4 teaspoon freshly ground black pepper
1 cup (235 ml) coarsely chopped walnuts
Juices from the roasting pan
1/4 cup (60 ml) pomegranate syrup
1/3 cup (80 ml) lemon juice

Recommended equipment

A small chef's knife, 10-inch (25 cm) sauté pan, wooden spatula.

Following the recipe for Canard Rôti à la Framboise *(see pages 299–300)*, roast the ducks, set them to rest, reduce the roasting juices, strain, and reserve.

Set the sauté pan over medium heat, add the duck fat, and while the fat is heating, peel and finely chop the onion. When the fat is hot add the onion, turmeric, and pepper and sauté, stirring with the wooden spatula, until the onions are golden brown. Then add the walnuts, sauté 1 minute, add the juices from the roasting pan, the pomegranate syrup, and lemon juice, and adjust the heat so that the sauce maintains a low simmer for 15 minutes. Taste and correct the seasoning before serving.

If pomegranate syrup is unavailable, use 1 cup of pomegranate juice, simmered separately until reduced to 1/4 cup before adding it to the sauté pan.

Oie Rôtie au Jus Lié
Roast Goose with Brown Sauce

A stone carving in Berlin's Staatliches Museum attests to the fact that, long before foie was being made gras by the gaveuses *of Périgord, ancient Egyptians force-fed geese to produce this culinary treasure. Furthermore, history tells us that goose was a staple in the diet of Egyptian priests. Inroads by the native American gobbler notwithstanding, goose is still a European favorite, this status having been forever ensured in England, when on 29 September 1588 (Michelmas Day) Queen Elizabeth, who happened to be dining on roast goose, was informed of Drake's victory over the Spanish Armada. The Toulouse goose (*grosse*), usually weighing twenty-two pounds or more, is truly a* usine de foie gras, *but the* petite goose *used here, weighing about eight to eleven pounds, is an excellent roasting fowl, amenable to many treatments, beginning with this simple but classic one. You will have the best results with fresh, young domestic goose. Braised Red Cabbage or sauerkraut and Whipped Potatoes or Spätzle would be traditional accompaniments.*

Yields 5 to 6 servings

A fresh goose, weighing 8 to 10 pounds (3650 to 4550 g)
Rendered goose fat
Salt
Freshly ground black pepper
1 medium onion
1 celery stalk
1 1/2 cups (355 ml) dry white wine
6 juniper berries
2 cups (475 ml) Brown Chicken Stock *(see page 62)*
1 1/2 teaspoons flour

Recommended equipment

A paring knife, small saucepan, white kitchen string, trussing needle, heavy roasting pan, small chef's knife, bulb baster, aluminum foil, platter, basting spoon, 8-inch (20 cm) sauté pan, wooden spoon, wire whisk, fine-mesh sieve.

Preheat oven to 400F (204C).

Remove the neck and giblet package from the cavity of the goose and reserve both. Then rinse the goose inside and out under running cold water, let drain, and pat dry. Using the paring knife, cut out as much excess fat as you can find, put it in the small saucepan, and set the saucepan over low heat to render the fat. Season the goose inside and out with salt and pepper and truss it with the string *(see pages 568–69)*. Put 1 tablespoon rendered fat in the roasting pan, lay the goose on its side in the pan, and set the pan into the oven. When the goose begins to sizzle, time 15 minutes and then reduce oven heat to 325F (163C) and roast for 30 minutes. Using the bulb baster, remove nearly all the fat from the pan, turn goose over to other side, and roast for 45 minutes. Take the pan out of the oven, remove fat from the pan again, and turn goose on its back.

Peel and trim the onion, coarsely chop it, and

add it to the pan. Rinse the celery stalk, trim it of any leaves, chop it coarsely, and add it to the pan. Rinse the reserved neck and giblets under cold water, roughly chop them, and add them to the pan. Pour the wine around the goose, strew the juniper berries in the pan bottom, cover the goose breast loosely with foil, and return the goose to the oven to roast for 1 hour. During this time, baste the goose with the pan juices three times. Then remove foil and roast the goose another 30 minutes, for a total cooking time of 3 hours. Prick the leg joint with a fork and if the juices run clear the goose is done.

Remove goose from oven, set it on the platter with the breast side down, remove trussing strings, and let goose rest for 15 minutes before carving. Skim the fat from the roasting pan with the basting spoon, add chicken stock, set the pan over medium high heat, and bring to a simmer. Reduce heat and let the stock simmer gently while you prepare the roux. Set the sauté pan over medium heat, add 1 tablespoon rendered goose fat, stir in the flour, and cook, stirring, until the flour turns light brown. Remove pan from heat, let cool for 1 minute, then scrape the roux into the simmering stock in the roasting pan and whisk constantly until well blended and smooth. Simmer the sauce gently for 10 minutes then strain into a clean saucepan, add any juices from the platter, taste, and adjust seasoning if necessary. Keep the sauce warm over low heat while you carve the goose and arrange the dinner plates.

This is the most basic preparation for goose and can be elaborated by various stuffings such as fresh sausage and apples, chestnuts, or a most elegant and festive combination of plumped, pitted prunes stuffed with foie gras.

Roast Double Breast of Turkey with Ham, Apricot, and Pecan Stuffing

Culinary history like any other is often full of conflicting origins, but there is no doubt about this one—turkey is truly the American bird. Native to an area ranging from the isthmus of Panama to the Pacific Northwest, it made its European debut in 1511 as ten "well-guarded" turkeys were brought to Spain by Miguel de Passamonte under orders from the Bishop of Valencia. By the early seventeenth century, the bird Brillat-Savarin called "one of the finest gifts made by the New World to the Old," was commonplace in Europe and had been introduced to the Middle East via the Indian port of Goa.

Turkey seems to suffer from its role as a "high feast" bird, causing it to be forgotten for the rest of the year except as an ignoble filler in a club sandwich. As you can tell by the fact that we use more than a ton a week, it is extremely popular at the Homestead and we serve it in many guises. We especially recommend this one and its variation because they are so attractive, tasty, and unusual that you will probably want to serve them year-round as we do (except possibly at Thanksgiving, when you may have to break out the cranberry sauce for visitors from New England). As with a galantine, it is also superb cold served with Cumberland Sauce and a salad, or sliced thinly in a sandwich with fresh watercress as in our Shenandoah at the Café Albert.

Yields 8 to 10 servings

1 fresh turkey, weighing 8 to 12 pounds (3550 to 5450 g)

FOR THE STUFFING
8 ounces (225 g) Virginia ham
2 celery stalks
1/2 medium onion
1 tablespoon peanut oil
1 pound (450 g) veal trimmings, shoulder, or chuck
1/4 cup (60 ml) chopped fresh parsley
4 ounces (115 g) dried apricots
4 ounces (115 g) pecans
2 ounces (60 g) raisins
1/2 cup (118 ml) fine white bread crumbs
1 cup (235 ml) half-and-half
Salt
Freshly ground white pepper

FOR ROASTING
Salt
Freshly ground white pepper
1/2 teaspoon fresh rosemary
2 tablespoons peanut oil
1/2 medium carrot
1 celery stalk
1 medium onion
1 cup (235 ml) dry white wine

FOR THE SAUCE
1 1/2 tablespoons Dijon mustard
1 1/2 cups (355 ml) whipping cream
2 tablespoons Glace de Viande (*see page 65*)

Recommended equipment

A large chef's knife, 10-inch (25 cm) sauté pan, meat grinder with fine blade, 2-quart (2 L) bowl, rubber spatula, boning knife, white kitchen string, heavy roasting pan, two wooden spatulas, platter, aluminum foil, 1 1/2-quart (1 1/2 L) saucepan, fine-mesh sieve, slicing knife.

Remove the neck and giblet package from the cavity of the turkey and reserve both. Rinse the turkey inside and out under running cold water, let drain, and pat dry. Set aside while you prepare the stuffing.

Using the chef's knife, dice the ham into 1/4-inch (2/3 cm) cubes. Wash the celery stalks, make them as stringless as possible, and dice them finely. Peel the onion and chop it into fine dice. Put the sauté pan over medium heat, add the peanut oil, and, when it is hot, add the diced ham, celery, and onion. Sauté, stirring occasionally, for 2 minutes, then remove pan from heat and let cool.

While the ham mixture cools, put the veal through the meat grinder twice, using the fine blade. Rinse the parsley, pat dry, chop, and reserve. Slice each apricot into several pieces. Put the veal in the mixing bowl and add the apricots, pecans, raisins, bread crumbs, half-and-half, reserved parsley, and sautéed ham mixture. Blend all together with the rubber spatula and season with salt and pepper (remembering that the ham may be salty so season carefully). Set the bowl into the refrigerator to chill the stuffing while you bone the turkey.

Set the turkey breast side down on your work surface. Using the boning knife, make a skin-deep incision on the top of the backbone from neck to tail, loosening the skin as you go. For each side, run the boning knife, point down, from the backbone along the ribs, pulling the breast meat and skin away from the bones as you go. Try not to damage the skin. Bone the other side. Then pull away as much skin as possible from the thighs and legs, keeping it intact as much as you can. (See below for uses of the leg and thigh meat.) Lay the breast meat skin side down on your work surface and spread out the skin from the thighs and legs. Holding the knife parallel to the work surface, slice the breast meat in half lengthwise, remove the top layer of meat, and set on extra skin gained from thighs and legs. Spread the stuffing on the center of the breast meat and form a roll by folding the skin over the stuffing from both sides. Tie the roll with kitchen string at 2-inch (5 cm) intervals, season with salt and pepper, and rub in the rosemary.

Preheat oven to 400F (204C).

To roast the turkey roll, put the peanut oil in the roasting pan, lay the roll in the pan with the breast meat down, and set the pan into the oven. When the turkey is sizzling, let it roast for 10 to 15 minutes. Reduce oven heat to 325F (163C) and cook for 45 minutes. Meanwhile, rinse the carrot and celery stalk and chop both coarsely. Peel and quarter the onion. At the end of the 45-minute roasting period, turn the roll over with the two spatulas, strew the carrot, celery, and onion around the turkey, and add the white wine.

Roast the turkey for 30 more minutes, turn again, and continue cooking for another 15 minutes. Remove pan from oven, set the turkey on a platter, cover it loosely with aluminum foil, and let it rest for 15 minutes.

Transfer the juices and vegetables from the roasting pan to the saucepan, set the pan over medium heat, add the mustard, cream, and glace de viande, and bring the sauce to a boil. Cook until the sauce is reduced by one-half or has reached a creamy consistency (this should take 10 to 15 minutes). When done, pass the sauce through the sieve into a clean saucepan, adjust the seasoning if necessary, and keep warm. Cut the strings on the roast, add any juices on the platter to the sauce, and slice the turkey in 1/4-inch slices. Spoon the sauce onto a plate or serving platter, place a turkey slice or two on top, and serve at once.

If your butcher bones the turkey for you, be sure that you get the skin from the thighs and legs. The meat from the legs and thighs may be used instead of veal trimmings in the stuffing. If you do this, add enough pork to bring the meat weight up to 1 pound (450 g) before grinding. If the thigh and leg meat is not used for the stuffing, boil it and use it in a turkey salad. The bones can be used for stock. The same boning, stuffing, and cooking procedure can be used with two to three large roasting chickens. In this case, the total cooking time would be 1 hour.

For a more unusual texture and color combination, add 3/4 cup (180 ml) cooked wild rice to the basic stuffing.

Variation

❧ Roast Double Breast of Turkey with Olive Stuffing

- 1 pound (450 g) veal trimmings, shoulder, or chuck
- 8 ounces (225 g) pork trimmings, shoulder, or butt
- 2 tablespoons chopped fresh parsley
- 1 cup (235 ml) fine white bread crumbs
- 1 cup (235 ml) half-and-half
- 1/2 cup (118 ml) dry white wine
- 1/8 teaspoon finely chopped fresh sage
- 4 tablespoons (60 g) butter, softened at room temperature
- Salt
- Freshly ground white pepper
- 3/4 cup (180 ml) Spanish olives stuffed with pimientos

Prepare this stuffing ahead of time so that it can chill for 30 minutes. Grind the veal and pork twice, separately, with the fine blade of the food grinder. Combine them in a mixing bowl and add the parsley, bread crumbs, half-and-half, wine, sage, and butter. Mix all together thoroughly, season with salt and pepper, and refrigerate. Just before using, chop the olives and stir them in. The stuffing should be moist and soft. If it is too dry, add a little half-and-half.

Game

Game is a healthy, warming, and savory food, fit for the most delicate palate and easy to digest. In the hands of an experienced cook, game can provide dishes of the highest quality which raise the culinary art to the level of a science.

There is game of all sorts. Certain types of game from Périgord will not have the same flavor as similar game killed at Sologne. Whereas a hare killed near Paris will make dull eating, a leveret from the Haut Dauphiné or the Burgundy district will be more deliciously flavored than any other of its kind.

—Brillat-Savarin

His legal colleagues could attest to Brillat-Savarin's expertise vis-à-vis game because he often absent-mindedly carried recent trophies of the hunt in the pockets of his great coat when he sat on the bench. He would probably applaud the fact that refrigerated transport has made game much more widely available, but he most likely would argue that, by definition, it cannot be domesticated. To be strictly correct, game is traditionally either hunted or trapped in the fall, winter, or spring and Brillat-Savarin would insist, as do partisans of the hunt (with justification in many cases), that the flavor of farm-raised game is a pale reflection of the wild game taste. Of course, if you have ever tried to marinate out the strong fishy taste of wild waterfowl, you may prefer the "pallid" version. In either case you are at the mercy of the animal's diet, whether natural or commercially controlled—and there are differences among producers on this crucial item.

Hunting enthusiasts will also insist, rightly, that nothing can take the place of the ancient hunting rituals. Whether waiting patiently at daybreak in blinds at the water's edge in near-freezing temperatures, or assuming a motionless stance for hours in a tree platform, or moving stealthily in the crisp autumn air through a stubble-filled cornfield, the hunter is always hopeful, driven by the anticipation of fragrant aromas arising from succulent, freshly prepared game at the camp fire or dinner table.

Roast Pheasant with Green Olives and Raspberry Vinegar Sauce in the Commonwealth Room

The following recipes, while used for domesticated game at the Homestead, can be easily adapted for wild game (possibly even the wild turkey Walter Rhett has been stalking for years on Warm Springs Mountain).

You will notice that, even though duck and goose can be considered game, we have already treated them in the poultry section, primarily because the domesticated fowl are most commonly available and the greatest variance in size and taste is likely to be found between domestic and wild waterfowl. Wild ducks and geese tend to be much smaller than their farm-raised cousins, and unless they migrated over a great many cornfields on their journeys, they will tend to have a fishy smell which can only be tempered through "spirited marination" for two or three days. Quail, pheasant, and venison are much less problematic and the recipes here work equally well with domesticated or wild animals.

Venison is particularly popular at the Homestead and, except for the months of July and August, we feature it on our menu weekly. Low in fat and easy to digest, it also stores well, especially frozen. Because it is low in fat, one must be particular about cooking methods. For example, the saddle (sometimes referred to as the tenderloin), which consists of the whole back, saddle, and rib, is preferable for sautéing, whereas the rack and leg pieces are better roasted. The shoulder and leg braise well, and the neck, shoulder, shank, brisket, and leg parts should be used in stews.

Marination should not be automatic. For mature animals, marinating in wine for several days, covered and refrigerated, produces a tenderizing effect. The marinade and cooking method are the same as that for Sauerbraten, and, while back, leg, and shoulder parts can all be used, the back parts will cook more quickly. You do not need to marinate young animals, although there are those who feel that a wine marinade creates its own "wild" flavor. If you are not using them right away, put scallops and medallions in an oil marinade, but be cautious with the herbs and spices lest you overwhelm the natural flavor of the meat.

Roast Stuffed Quail Virginia

These delicate little birds, whose popularity began with Egyptians of the Old Kingdom, are a favorite of Homestead guests and hunters alike. Fortunately, domestic quail farms have made frozen quail readily available, and in some markets, fresh, boned quail (which we use at the Homestead) are easy to find. If you have to bone them yourself, consult your neighborhood hunter or follow the simple instructions below. If you have any on hand, use Homestead Raspberry Vinegar to add aromatic intensity to the quail roasting liquid.

Yields 6 servings

FOR THE STUFFING
- 4 ounces (115 g) wild rice
- 1/2 medium onion
- 1 medium apple
- Peel of 1/2 lemon
- 4 ounces (115 g) fresh quail, duck, or chicken livers
- 2 teaspoons chopped parsley
- 1 tablespoon (15 g) butter
- 1 egg yolk
- 2 ounces (60 g) fine white bread crumbs
- 3 tablespoons whipping cream
- 2 tablespoons whole cranberry sauce
- Salt
- Freshly ground black pepper

FOR ROASTING THE QUAIL
- 12 quail
- Salt
- Freshly ground black pepper
- 2 tablespoons Clarified Butter *(see page 568)*
- 1 tablespoon chopped shallots
- 1/2 teaspoon crushed black pepper
- 1/4 cup (60 ml) dry red wine
- 1/4 cup (60 ml) raspberry vinegar
- 2/3 cup (160 ml) Demi-glace Brun II *(see page 76)*

FOR BAKING THE APPLE SLICES
- 3 medium Rome apples
- 2 teaspoons butter
- 1 teaspoon sugar
- Juice of 1 lemon
- 2 tablespoons dry white wine

Recommended equipment

A 2-quart (2 L) saucepan, fine-mesh sieve, paring knife, large chef's knife, swivel-bladed vegetable peeler, apple corer, box grater, 12-inch (30 cm) sauté pan, wooden spatula, boning knife, mortar and pestle, aluminum foil, heavy roasting pan, pastry brush, heatproof platter, fine-mesh sieve, baking dish.

Bring 1 1/2 quarts (1 1/2 L) lightly salted water to boil in the saucepan, add the wild rice, and simmer for 50 minutes or until tender. When done, drain the rice into the sieve, run cold water over it, let drain, and reserve.

While the rice is cooking, prepare the other stuffing ingredients. Peel the onion, chop it finely, and reserve. Peel and core the apple and dice it finely. (Cover with a damp cloth if necessary to prevent it from drying out.) Grate the peel of 1/2 lemon on the fine side of the box grater, being careful to leave the bitter white behind, and reserve. Rinse

the livers with cold water, pat dry, chop roughly, and reserve. Rinse the parsley, pat dry, chop, and reserve.

Set the sauté pan over medium heat, add the butter, and, when it is hot, add the onions and sauté for 1 minute. Add the reserved diced apple and the lemon rind and mix well with the onions before adding the chopped livers. Sauté, stirring with the wooden spatula, for 1 minute, then remove from heat and let cool in the pan.

When the rice is cooked and has cooled, add it to the sauté pan along with the egg yolk, bread crumbs, cream, parsley, and cranberry sauce. Season lightly with salt and pepper, blend together thoroughly, and reserve.

Prepare the quail for roasting by partially boning them if you could not buy them preboned. Using a sharp boning knife, cut each quail down its back and split it open. Remove the breastbone and backbone and spread the quail out on your work surface with the skin side down. Season lightly with salt and pepper. When all the quail are partially boned, stuff each one with a golf-ball-size lump of stuffing, fold the quail around the stuffing, and reshape to its original form. Wrap the base of each quail with a 1-inch (2 1/2 cm) wide strip of foil to help hold its shape during cooking.

Preheat oven to 375F (190C).

Brush 1 tablespoon clarified butter on the bottom and sides of the roasting pan, arrange the quail in the pan, and brush them with the remaining clarified butter. Set the pan over medium high heat and when the quail begin to sizzle set the pan into the oven. Roast for 13 to 15 minutes depending upon the size of the quail; they should be slightly underdone. When cooked, remove pan from oven, set the quail on the platter, and keep in a warm spot.

Wipe the butter out of the roasting pan. Chop the shallots, crush the black pepper in the mortar and pestle, and add them both to the pan. Set the pan over medium heat and stir the shallots and pepper for 1 minute before adding the wine and vinegar. Deglaze the pan, scraping up the brown bits on the bottom, and simmer until the liquid has been reduced to about 2 tablespoons. Add the demi-glace and simmer gently for 10 minutes.

While the sauce simmers, prepare the apple slices. Peel and core the apples and cut each one into four rings about 1/4 inch (2/3 cm) thick. Butter the baking dish, arrange the slices in it, sprinkle them with sugar, lemon juice, and white wine, and set them to bake at 375F for about 6 minutes or until they are cooked but still firm. When done, remove from the oven and keep warm.

When the sauce has simmered, strain it into a clean saucepan and keep warm. When you are ready to serve, set the apple slices on warm serving plates or a platter, place a quail on each apple ring, and spoon the sauce over each quail.

Variation: Try the quail with the stuffing for Roast Boned Chicken with Wild Rice and Hazelnut (or Chestnut) Stuffing *(see page 296)*.

Suprêmes de Faisan au Madère
Roast Breast of Pheasant with Madeira Sauce

History tells us that thirty-three of these colorful birds (along with quail, peacocks, swans, cranes, capons, guinea hens, and chickens) were featured at a party given by Catherine de' Medici in 1549 for fifty dinner guests. No wonder, because their delicate flavor, described by Brillat-Savarin as being reminiscent of both poultry and venison, is a culinary treasure which serves as an excellent showcase for so many delicious sauces. I have chosen Sauce Madère for this basic preparation, but you will note that there are also three variations, not the least of which is Périgueux—truffles and pheasant go together like ducks and water. Serve this with wild rice and a salad of fresh mixed greens with a nut oil dressing.

Yields 6 servings

3 young, fresh pheasants, weighing 2 1/2 to 2 3/4 pounds (1125 to 1250 g) each
Salt
Freshly ground black pepper
3 slices pork fatback, 6 x 8 inches (15 x 20 cm) and 1/8 inch (1/3 cm) thick
2 tablespoons peanut oil
1 medium onion
1 celery stalk
3/4 cup (180 ml) Madeira
2 cups (475 ml) Demi-glace Brun II *(see page 76)*

Recommended equipment

White kitchen string, wooden toothpicks, heavy roasting pan, paring knife, large chef's knife, platter, boning knife, heatproof serving dish, wooden spatula, fine-mesh sieve, aluminum foil.

For each pheasant, remove the giblets and liver, if any, from the cavity and reserve, then hold the pheasant under cold running water, drain, and pat dry. Season the cavity and the outside with salt and pepper. Tie the pheasant with string so it will hold its shape during roasting. Place a sheet of fatback over the breast of each bird, being sure to cover the narrow part toward the legs, and secure it with the wooden toothpicks. Spread the peanut oil in the roasting pan and arrange the pheasants on their side in the pan.

Preheat oven to 350F (177C).

Peel the onion and chop it roughly with the chef's knife. Trim the celery stalk, rinse under cold water, and chop it roughly. Spread the onions and celery around the pheasants in the pan and if you have any excess neck or wing parts add them too. Set the pan over medium high heat and bring the pheasants to a good sizzle. Then set the pan into the oven to roast for 15 minutes. Turn the pheasants over to the other side for another 15 minutes and then turn them onto their backs and continue roasting for 10 more minutes. When done, remove pan from oven and set the pheasants breast side down on a platter for 20 to 30 minutes or until cool. When cool, use a boning knife to separate the breast from the bones, remove the skin, and arrange the breasts in a heatproof serving dish (reserve the leg-thighs for another use; *see below*). The breast meat should be a pale pink color.

Remove all fat from the roasting pan and add the breastbones and backbones to the pan. Set it over medium high heat, add the Madeira, and deglaze the pan, scraping up the brown bits on the bottom with the wooden spatula. Bring the Madeira to a simmer and cook until it has been reduced by one-half. Then add the demi-glace and maintain a low simmer for 20 minutes. Pass the sauce through the sieve, skim off all fat, and pour over the pheasant breasts. Cover the dish with aluminum foil and set into the oven at 250F (121C) for 10 minutes to thoroughly heat the pheasant. Be sure that the sauce does not boil. When hot, serve at once.

ple of minutes in butter with a chopped shallot, then stir into the wild rice before serving. The leg-thighs can finish roasting by themselves and then be used in a salad.

If you do have the pheasant livers (or you may use some chicken livers) dice them and sauté for a cou-

Variation

 Suprêmes de Faisan au Périgueux

Prepare the sauce Périgueux *(see page 77)* and substitute it for the Madeira sauce. As an additional refinement, if you have any foie gras, use it to enhance the dish. If tinned, place thin slices, topped with bits of truffle, on the pheasant breasts. If fresh, you have the basis for a stunning first course. Slice the foie gras, sauté quickly in butter, and serve warm, with a simple vinaigrette, accompanied by thin apple slices sautéed in butter.

Variation

 Suprêmes de Faisan avec Sauce Vinaigre de Vin et Poivre Vert

Add 1/2 cup (118 ml) dry red wine and 1/4 cup (60 ml) red wine vinegar to the roasting pan instead of the Madeira. Deglaze the pan, scraping up the brown bits on the bottom with the wooden spatula. Bring the liquid to a simmer and cook until it has been reduced by one-half. Then add the demi-glace and maintain a low simmer for 20 minutes.

While the sauce simmers, sauté 1 ounce (30 g) green peppercorns (packed in water and drained) in 1/2 teaspoon butter for 1 minute, add 2 tablespoons Cognac to the pan, deglaze the pan, remove pan from heat, and reserve.

When the sauce has finished simmering, pass it through the sieve, skim off all fat, add the reserved green peppercorns, and pour over the pheasant breasts. A nice balance is achieved by adding a few drained canned white grapes to the sauce before heating the pheasant. Heat the pheasant according to the instructions in the basic recipe.

Variation

Suprêmes de Faisan au Bordelaise

Add 3/4 cup (180 ml) dry red wine, 2 tablespoons chopped shallots, and 1 tablespoon crushed black pepper to the roasting pan instead of the Madeira. Deglaze the pan, scraping up the brown bits on the bottom with the wooden spatula. Bring the liquid to a simmer and cook until it has been reduced by one-half. Then add the demi-glace and maintain a low simmer for 20 minutes. Pass the sauce through the sieve, skim off all fat, and keep the sauce warm in a double boiler.

The pheasant suprêmes must be heated without the sauce. Brush a little soft butter on them, pour

2 tablespoons Cognac around them, cover tightly with aluminum foil, and set the dish into the oven at 250F (121C) for 10 minutes.

While the suprêmes are heating, mince three raw pheasant livers and three raw chicken (or duck) livers, and press them through a fine-mesh sieve. Melt 2 teaspoons butter in an 8-inch (20 cm) sauté pan over low heat, add the strained liver, blend well with the butter, add 1 tablespoon Cognac, and mix well. Do not allow the mixture to boil. Scrape the livers into the sauce in the double boiler and blend them into the sauce.

When the suprêmes are hot, serve them at once with the sauce Bordelaise passed separately in a sauce boat.

🦅 Roast Young Pheasant with Green Olives and Raspberry Vinegar Sauce

In Bouquet de France, *Samuel Chamberlain writes that "the inevitable olive tree, a gnarled dwarf flashing its silvery mantle, constitutes the hallmark of Provence." For the seasoned traveler this recipe will stir memories of meals at La Regalido and Cabro d'Or featuring the direct tastes of the green picholines and raspberry vinegar, with the distinctly Provençal aroma of thyme. Serve the pheasant with small potatoes sautéed until crisp and brown in olive oil with a few garlic cloves.*

Yields 4 servings

4 fresh young pheasants, weighing 1 pound (450 g) each
Salt
Freshly ground black pepper
A pinch of ground thyme
4 slices pork fatback, 4 x 4 inches (10 x 10 cm) and 1/8 inch (1/3 cm) thick
1 medium onion
1 celery stalk
1 teaspoon peanut oil
2 juniper berries
1/2 cup (118 ml) raspberry vinegar
3 cups (710 ml) Demi-glace Brun I *(see page 75)*
1 teaspoon tomato paste
20 French green olives (Picholine du Gard)
1 tablespoon (15 g) butter, softened at room temperature

Recommended equipment

Wooden toothpicks, heavy roasting pan, small chef's knife, two wooden spatulas, platter, fine-mesh sieve, 2-quart (2 L) saucepan, paring knife, ovenproof serving dish, wire whisk, aluminum foil.

For each pheasant, remove the giblets and liver, if any, from the cavity and reserve, then hold the pheasant under cold running water, drain, and pat dry. Season the cavity with salt, pepper, and thyme. Cover the breast with a piece of fatback and attach it with four wooden toothpicks. The fatback should be sliced as thinly as possible and be in a square piece, about 4 by 4 inches (10 x 10 cm). It is best to have your butcher slice it for you, and any leftover fatback will keep for months if wrapped airtight and frozen.

Preheat oven to 325F (163C).

Peel and trim the onion and chop into large dice. Rinse the celery stalk, trim it of any leaves, and chop into large dice.

Set the roasting pan over medium heat, add the peanut oil and, when it is hot, set the pheasants into the pan on one side. When the pheasants are sizzling in the pan, sauté for 2 minutes, turn them on their other side for 2 minutes, turn them on their backs, and add the onion, celery, and juniper berries. When the vegetables are sizzling, set the pan into the oven and roast for 12 minutes. Remove pan from oven, remove pheasants from pan, and set them breast side down on a platter to allow the juices to retreat back into the meat. At this point the pheasants should be lightly pink at the bone so they will be ready for the final saucing and heating. An overcooked pheasant will be tough and stringy.

Drain all fat from the roasting pan, set it over medium high heat, add the raspberry vinegar, bring to the simmer, and cook for 3 minutes. Then add demi-glace and tomato paste and simmer until liquid is reduced by one-half. Strain sauce through the sieve into the saucepan, add the olives, dot the top of the sauce with bits of butter to prevent the formation of a skin layer, and set aside.

When the pheasants have rested and are cool enough to handle (about 20 minutes), remove the fatback and toothpicks. Bone and skin each pheasant by running the paring knife along the backbone to separate the breasts. Bone each breast but leave the wing and wing joint attached. Remove the leg-thighs. Peel the skin from the breast and most of the skin from the leg-thighs. Place the pheasant pieces in a single layer in the ovenproof serving dish. If the pheasant must wait, cover the dish with a damp towel.

When you are ready to finish the dish, set the oven heat to 250F (121C). Bring the sauce to a low boil over medium high heat, remove saucepan from heat, whisk in the softened butter, pour the sauce over the pheasant pieces, and cover the dish tightly with foil. Set the dish into the oven for 4 to 5 minutes or until the pheasant is hot. Do not let the sauce boil. Serve at once.

Variation: Quail may be prepared in the same way, but reduce the roasting time to 8 minutes. The sautéing time, before they go into the oven, is the same for quail and pheasant.

Hasenpfeffer
Braised Marinated Rabbit

Known in England as "jugged hare" and in France as civet de lièvre, *the German version of this dish, given here, is very popular at home in Lucerne, and I feature it every week during high season for luncheon at the Casino. Personally, I advise marinating the rabbit to produce the flavor of the original recipe, but it is not mandatory. It is crucial, however, to use young, fresh (not frozen) rabbit for a tender result. Serve it with Spätzle, as we do back home in the "old country."*

Yields 6 servings

2 fresh rabbits, weighing 1 3/4 to 2 3/4 pounds (790 to 1250 g) each

FOR THE MARINADE
1 medium onion
1 celery stalk
1/2 medium carrot
1/2 bay leaf
A pinch of thyme
6 juniper berries
1 teaspoon crushed black peppercorns
1 small clove
1/2 garlic clove
2 cups (475 ml) dry red wine
3 tablespoons red wine vinegar

FOR BRAISING
1/2 cup (60 g) flour
1/2 teaspoon salt
1/2 teaspoon freshly ground black pepper
4 to 5 ounces (115 to 145 g) slab bacon or salt pork in one piece
The strained marinade
1 1/2 cups (355 ml) Demi-glace Brun II *(see page 76)*

FOR THE MUSHROOMS
12 fresh mushrooms
1 1/2 teaspoons Clarified Butter *(see page 568)*
Salt
Freshly ground black pepper
Juice from 1/2 lemon

FOR THE ONIONS
12 small whole white onions or 48 pearl onions
1 1/2 teaspoons Clarified Butter
1/2 teaspoon sugar

FOR THE CROUTONS
3 slices Pullman Loaf *(see page 488)*
2 tablespoons Clarified Butter

FOR SERVING
1 teaspoon chopped fresh parsley

Recommended equipment

A boning knife, large ceramic or glass bowl, large chef's knife, stiff bristle brush, mortar and pestle, plastic wrap, paper towels, two 12-inch (30 cm) sauté pans, Dutch oven, wooden spatula, large fine-mesh sieve, 10-inch (25 cm) sauté pan, 2-quart (2 L) saucepan, paring knife, slotted spoon, platter, basting spoon.

Rinse the rabbits under running cold water, drain, and, with the boning knife, disjoint each into six pieces: two forelegs with shoulders, two loin sections ("rable"), and two hind legs. Set the pieces into the ceramic or glass bowl.

Peel the onion and chop it coarsely with the chef's knife. Rinse the celery stalk, remove any leaves, make it as stringless as possible, and chop it coarsely. Scrub the carrot and chop it coarsely. Add the three vegetables to the bowl with the rabbit. Then add the bay leaf and thyme. Lightly crush the juniper berries and the black peppercorns in the mortar and pestle and add them to the bowl. Add the clove, peel the garlic, and add it. Pour on the wine and the vinegar, mix all together well, cover the bowl tightly with plastic wrap, and set it into the refrigerator to marinate for two to three days. (If the rabbit is not covered by the marinade, either add more wine or after the first day turn the rabbit pieces over.)

When you are ready to cook, remove the rabbit from the marinade and let the pieces drain on paper towels. Reserve the marinade. Pat the rabbit dry. Combine the flour with the salt and pepper on your work surface, roll the rabbit pieces in it to dust them thoroughly, and reserve.

Remove the rind from the bacon and cut it into 1/2-inch (1 1/4 cm) cubes or lardons. (If you use salt pork, parboil in water for 10 minutes before cubing.) Set the sauté pans over medium high heat, divide the lardons between them, and sauté, stirring, until they are crisp. Remove lardons to paper towels to drain and reserve them. Divide the rabbit pieces between the pans. Brown the rabbit well on all sides, turning as necessary (this should take 8 to 10 minutes).

Preheat oven to 325F (163C).

Remove the rabbit to the Dutch oven. Drain excess fat from sauté pans. Strain the marinade into a bowl and add all the vegetables to the Dutch oven. Divide the marinade between the sauté pans, bring to a simmer, and deglaze the pans, scraping up all the brown bits. Remove pans from heat and reserve. Set the Dutch oven over medium heat, sauté the rabbit and vegetables for 3 minutes, and then add the liquid from the sauté pans. Bring the rabbit to a simmer and cook for 10 minutes. Add the demi-glace, return to a simmer, cover the pot, and set it into the oven to braise the rabbit for 40 minutes.

While the rabbit is braising, prepare the mushrooms, onions, and croutons. Brush the mushrooms gently of any clinging dirt. If they are large, cut them in half, otherwise leave them whole. Set the 10-inch (25 cm) sauté pan over medium heat, add the butter, and, when it is hot, stir in the mushrooms, season them lightly with salt, pepper, and lemon juice, and sauté them for 3 minutes. Scrape them from the pan into a small dish and reserve.

For the onions, bring lightly salted water to boil in the saucepan, add the whole onions, return to a boil, and cook for 10 minutes. (If using pearl onions, blanch them for 2 minutes.) Remove from heat, drain, and run cold water into the pan. Drain the onions again and peel them with the paring knife. Set the sauté pan over medium heat, add the butter, sugar, and onions, and sauté until they are light brown and glacéed. This should take 4 to 5 minutes. When done, drain off all excess fat and add the onions to the mushrooms. Wash out the sauté pan and reserve.

Cut the bread slices into croutons about 2 inches long and 1/2 inch wide (5 by 1 1/4 cm). Set the sauté pan over medium low heat, add the butter, and, when it is hot, stir in the croutons and sauté, stirring, until they are golden brown. Then remove from heat, drain on paper towels, and reserve.

The rabbit is done when a knife can be easily inserted into the meat and it comes away from the bone. When done, remove from oven and take the rabbit out of the pot with a slotted spoon. Let it rest on a platter while you finish the sauce. Set the Dutch oven over medium heat and bring to a simmer. Skim off the fat as it rises to the surface. Then pour the sauce through the sieve into the saucepan, set it over medium high heat, and simmer until the sauce is reduced by one-third. Then add the rabbit, mushrooms, and onions, and simmer gently for 2 minutes. Rinse the parsley, spin or pat dry, and chop it with the chef's knife. Adjust the sauce seasoning if necessary and skim off any fat. When ready to serve, either present the hasenpfeffer in a serving dish or on dinner plates. In either case, sprinkle with the reserved lardons, croutons, and the parsley.

Variation: Stir in 1/4 cup (60 ml) Crème Fraîche *(see page 66)* or sour cream (at room temperature) to the finished sauce.

Southern Fried Rabbit

Before you snicker too much at the thought of serving this at the Homestead, listen to what Roger Vergé has to say about the appropriateness of serving rabbit in aspic at the Moulin de Mougins: "I agree that it is not, perhaps, entirely within the ambience of a three-star restaurant, new clients may say that it is 'worth the detour,' but not completely 'worth the trip.' But you must remember that I put this into my menu years ago, before I had even one star. . . . And it is truly authentic Provençal." Well, in truth, this dish is "truly authentic" Swiss, because it was a regular feature back home, where no one had ever even heard of southern fried chicken. Of course, this technique differs from that for chicken because it bakes slowly in the oven after having been lightly fried. Even with fresh, young rabbit (which is de rigueur—no frozen allowed) this is necessary to have "tender vittles." Now y'all serve up a heap of Whipped Potatoes, String Beans Country Style, and Baking Powder Biscuits.

Yields 6 servings

2 fresh rabbits, weighing 1 3/4 to 2 3/4 pounds (790 to 1250 g) each
1/4 cup (60 ml) milk
1/2 cup (60 g) flour
1 teaspoon salt
1/2 teaspoon freshly ground black pepper
1/4 cup (60 ml) peanut oil

FOR THE GRAVY
2 tablespoons flour
2 cups (475 ml) milk
A dash of freshly ground nutmeg
1 chicken bouillon cube or 1/4 teaspoon chicken base
1/8 teaspoon Maggi

Recommended equipment

A boning knife, shallow dish, waxed paper, 12-inch (30 cm) sauté pan, metal tongs, roasting pan, paper towels, basting spoon, wooden spoon, wire whisk, nutmeg grinder, fine-mesh sieve.

Rinse the rabbits under cold running water, drain, and, with the boning knife, disjoint each into six pieces: two forelegs with shoulders, two loin sections ("rable"), and two hind legs. Set the pieces into the shallow dish, pour the milk around them, and let them soak for 30 minutes. Combine the flour with the salt and pepper on your work surface. One piece at a time, let extra milk drip off rabbit and roll it around in the flour, patting it on. Gently shake off any excess flour, and as each piece is dusted, lay it on a sheet of waxed paper in a single layer.

Set the sauté pan over medium high heat and add the peanut oil. The oil will be hot when a drop of water added to the pan sizzles and pops. When the oil is hot, add the rabbit pieces in a single layer. Do not crowd the pan, and, if necessary, sauté the rabbit in two batches. Cook the rabbit until golden brown on all sides, turning with the tongs as necessary. After the first side is browned, adjust heat to medium so that the rabbit cooks evenly.

Preheat oven to 325F (163C).

When all the rabbit pieces are browned, set them into the roasting pan in a single layer (reserve the sauté pan) and put the pan into the oven to bake the rabbit for 40 minutes. Turn the pieces over halfway through the cooking period. When done, remove the rabbit from the oven, put the pieces on several layers of paper towels, and scrape any juices from the roasting pan into the reserved sauté pan. Set the sauté pan over medium heat and remove fat with the basting spoon, except for 3 to 4 tablespoons for the gravy. Put the flour into the pan and mix it with any brown bits in the pan bottom, stirring constantly with a wooden spoon, and cook until the flour has taken on a light golden color. Move pan off heat, add the milk all at once, return pan to heat, and stir together with the whisk until a simmer is reached. Grind in the nutmeg, add the chicken bouillon and Maggi, and simmer on low for 5 minutes. Adjust seasoning if necessary and if gravy is too thick add more milk a little bit at a time until a light creamy consistency is obtained. If too thin, simmer the gravy a few minutes longer. Strain the gravy into a warm sauceboat and pass it separately. Serve the fried rabbit immediately to preserve its full flavor.

Variation: Season the flour for dusting the rabbit with garlic, sage, thyme, celery seed, or hot pepper.

French Venison Stew

We pondered at length the matter of including three recipes for venison in this book. Many recent books confine "game" to quail, pheasant, or an occasional rabbit. However, just as the hunt was of great significance in the forests surrounding the châteaux of the Loire, so it is in our mountains. Deer are more than abundant in Bath County, so the hunting season serves the dual purpose of keeping the herds in balance with their food supply and providing bounty for the hunter's table. Here, the rich tradition of Bourgogne, Nivernais, and Bourbonnais is reflected in a savory stew for the cold time. Begin your preparations two to six days in advance, and when you serve it, present this hunter's classic with Spätzle or noodles to enable your guests to soak up every bit of the flavorful sauce.

Yields 6 to 8 servings

3 pounds (1350 g) boneless venison shoulder, chuck, or leg

FOR THE MARINADE
1 medium onion
1 celery stalk
1/2 medium carrot
1 garlic clove
6 juniper berries
1/2 bay leaf
1 small clove
A pinch of thyme
2 cups (475 ml) dry red wine
3 tablespoons red wine vinegar

FOR BRAISING
4 to 5 ounces (115 to 145 g) slab bacon or salt pork in one piece
2 tablespoons peanut oil
Salt
Freshly ground black pepper
2 tablespoons flour
1 tablespoon tomato paste
The strained marinade
1 1/2 cups (355 ml) Demi-glace Brun II *(see page 76)*

FOR THE MUSHROOMS
12 fresh mushrooms
1 1/2 teaspoons Clarified Butter *(see page 568)*
Salt
Freshly ground black pepper
Juice from 1/2 lemon

FOR THE ONIONS
12 small whole white onions or 48 pearl onions
1 1/2 teaspoons Clarified Butter
1/2 teaspoon sugar

FOR THE CROUTONS
3 slices Pullman Loaf *(see page 488)*
2 tablespoons Clarified Butter

FOR SERVING
1 teaspoon chopped fresh parsley

Recommended equipment

A boning knife, large ceramic or glass bowl, large chef's knife, stiff bristle brush, plastic wrap, large fine-mesh sieve, paper towels, Dutch oven, wooden spatula, 10-inch (25 cm) sauté pan, 2-quart (2 L) saucepan, paring knife, slotted spoon, 3-quart (3 L) saucepan, basting spoon.

Using the boning knife, trim the venison, cut it into 1 1/2-inch (3 3/4 cm) cubes, and put them into the ceramic or glass bowl. Peel the onion, chop it coarsely with the chef's knife, and add it to the bowl. Rinse the celery stalk, remove any leaves, make it as stringless as possible, chop it coarsely, and add it to the venison. Scrub the carrot, chop it coarsely, and add it to the bowl. Peel the garlic clove and put it into the bowl with the juniper berries, bay leaf, clove, and thyme. Pour on the wine and add the vinegar. Add more wine if necessary to completely cover the venison. Mix all together well, cover bowl with plastic wrap, and set it into the refrigerator to marinate for two to six days.

When the venison has been marinated, remove bowl from refrigerator, set the sieve over a bowl, and strain the meat and vegetables from the marinade. Reserve the marinade liquid. Separate the meat from the vegetables, reserving both. Lay the venison out on paper towels to drain thoroughly (pat dry if necessary before browning).

Remove the rind from the bacon and cut it into 1/2-inch (1 1/4 cm) cubes or lardons. (If you use salt pork, parboil in water for 10 minutes before cubing.) Set the Dutch oven over medium high heat, add the lardons, and sauté, stirring, until they are crisp. Remove lardons to paper towels to drain and reserve them. Add the peanut oil to the bacon fat, turn heat to high, and, after lightly seasoning the venison with salt and pepper, sauté it by batches until all of the meat is nicely browned. When the venison is browned, return all of it to the pan, add the reserved vegetables from the marinade, sprinkle on the flour, and sauté, stirring, until the flour is brown. Stir in the tomato paste, mix well, and sauté 1 minute. Add the marinade liquid, deglaze the pot, scraping up all the brown bits on the bottom, and simmer until the sauce is smooth (about 5 minutes). Add the demi-glace, return sauce to a simmer, cover pot, and adjust heat so that a gentle simmer is maintained for 1 to 1 1/2 hours (or until venison is tender).

Meanwhile, prepare the mushrooms, onions, and croutons. Brush the mushrooms gently of any clinging dirt. If they are large, halve them, otherwise leave them whole. Set the sauté pan over medium heat, add the butter, and, when it is hot, stir in the mushrooms, season lightly with salt, pepper, and lemon juice, and sauté them for 3 minutes. Scrape them into a small dish and reserve.

For the onions, bring lightly salted water to boil in the smaller saucepan, add the whole onions, return to a boil, and cook for 10 minutes. (If using pearl onions, blanch them for 2 minutes.) Remove from heat, drain, and run cold water into the pan. Drain the onions again and peel them with the paring knife. Set the sauté pan over medium heat, add the butter, sugar, and onions, and sauté until they are light brown and glacéed. This should take 4 to 5 minutes. When done, drain off all excess fat and add the onions to the mushrooms. Wash out the sauté pan and reserve.

Cut the bread slices into croutons about 2 inches long and 1/2 inch wide (5 x 1 1/4 cm). Set the sauté pan over medium low heat, add the butter, and, when it is hot, stir in the croutons and sauté, stirring, until they are golden brown. Then remove from heat, drain on paper towels, and reserve.

When the venison is tender, remove it with a slotted spoon to the large saucepan. Pour the sauce through the sieve into a bowl and discard the vegetables. If you have the time, let the fat rise to the top as the sauce cools and then skim it off. Otherwise, return the sauce to a simmer in the Dutch oven and skim off the fat with the basting spoon. When the sauce is degreased, adjust the seasoning if necessary, pour it over the venison, set the saucepan over medium low heat, add the mushrooms and onions, and bring the stew to a gentle simmer for a few minutes to heat it through. Rinse the parsley, spin or pat dry, and chop it with the chef's knife. When ready to serve, either present the venison in a serving dish or on warm dinner plates. In either case, sprinkle with the reserved lardons, croutons, and the parsley.

Variation: For more of a "hunter's stew," do not discard the vegetables, but rather leave them in to contribute a touch of color and a slightly more robust taste. Alternatively, in the method above, use only 1 tablespoon flour after the venison has been browned and then after the sauce is strained, whip in 1/2 cup (118 ml) Crème Fraîche *(see page 66)* and simmer for a few minutes until the sauce has the desired consistency.

Medallions of Venison with Juniper Cream Sauce

Unless you can obtain the venison saddle from your butcher shop, make sure that, by the time deer season starts, you have obligated your neighborhood hunter by having him over for several meals. In that way, he just might contemplate giving you this most precious treasure of the hunt. Or, at the very least, you could invite him to this meal if he furnishes the venison. Present this prize cut with wild rice, Navets Glacés, sautéed wild mushrooms (shiitake, chanterelles, or morels), and, if you like, cranberry or lingonberry sauce nestled in a peach half. If your butcher bones the saddle, be sure to bring the bones home for the sauce.

Yields 6 servings

2 1/2 pounds (1125 g) boneless venison saddle

FOR THE MARINADE
2 teaspoons freshly ground black pepper
6 juniper berries
A sprig of rosemary
1/2 lemon
1 cup (235 ml) olive oil
1 cup (235 ml) peanut oil

FOR THE SAUCE
Bones from the saddle
1 tablespoon oil from marinade
2 tablespoons chopped shallots
1/2 cup (118 ml) dry red wine
1 cup (235 ml) Demi-glace Brun II *(see page 76)*
4 juniper berries
2 cups (475 ml) whipping cream

FOR COOKING THE MEDALLIONS
Salt
Freshly ground black pepper
Flour
3 tablespoons oil from marinade
1 teaspoon butter
1 tablespoon chopped shallots
1/2 cup (118 ml) dry red wine

Recommended equipment

A boning knife, large glass or ceramic bowl, mortar and pestle, paring knife, plastic wrap, cleaver, enameled cast-iron baking dish or lined copper plat à sauter, small chef's knife, wooden spatula, 12-inch (30 cm) sauté pan, platter, wooden spoon, large fine-mesh sieve.

Using the boning knife, bone the saddle of venison, reserving the bones, and trim the meat of excess fat and the silver skin. Set the meat into the bowl. Crush the pepper and juniper berries separately in the mortar and pestle and add them to the bowl. Chop the rosemary and sprinkle it over the venison. Slice the lemon thinly and lay the slices directly on the meat. Pour on the olive and peanut oils, adding some extra, if needed, to cover the meat. Cover the dish tightly with plastic wrap and refrigerate for at least 3 hours (or as long as three days if the venison is from a very mature animal, turning the venison over after the second day). Wrap the bones and refrigerate them if you choose a long marinating time.

When you are ready to cook, the sauce must be started first. Preheat oven to 375F (190C). Remove the bones from the refrigerator and chop them with the cleaver into pieces about 2 inches (5 cm) long. Put the oil into the baking dish or plat à sauter, add all the bones, and set them into the oven to brown. When they are golden brown, remove from oven, degrease the pan, and set it over medium heat. Chop the shallots, add them to the bones, and sauté, stirring, for 1 minute. Add the wine and simmer until it is reduced by one-half. Add the demi-glace and bring it to a simmer, stirring up all the brown bits from the pan bottom. Crush the juniper berries in the mortar and pestle and add them to the sauce along with the cream. Bring the sauce to a simmer and cook until it is reduced by one-half and has a creamy, smooth consistency. This may take 30 to 45 minutes, depending upon the thickness of the cream. When done, remove from heat and reserve.

When the sauce is ready, the venison can be cooked. Remove the venison from the marinade, reserve the marinade, and slice the meat into twelve medallions, about 1 1/2 to 2 inches (3 3/4 to 5 cm) thick and weighing 2 1/2 to 3 ounces (70 to 85 g) each. Season the medallions lightly with salt and pepper, dust with flour, and reserve. Set the sauté pan over high heat until very hot. Add 3 to 4 tablespoons oil from the marinade and sauté the medallions in two batches, cooking them until well browned, about 1 3/4 to 2 minutes on each side for medium. The medallions must not be cooked well done. As they are done, remove them to the platter, arrange them in a single layer, and keep them in a warm (not hot) spot while you chop the shallots and deglaze the pan. Remove all oil from the pan, add butter and shallots to the pan, and sauté over medium heat for 1 minute. Add the wine and simmer until it is reduced to 2 to 3 tablespoons. Add the reduction to the reserved juniper cream sauce, mixing well with the wooden spoon, and strain the sauce into a clean saucepan. Reheat gently if the sauce has cooled. Add any juices on the platter to the sauce, mixing well with the spoon, arrange the venison on the serving plates, spoon some of the sauce over each medallion, and serve at once.

Roast Stuffed Tenderloin of Venison with Cream Mustard Sauce

If you have been in Manhattan during the cold seasons of the year, your spirits have undoubtedly been lifted by the aroma of the charcoal fires used by sidewalk vendors to roast chestnuts and pretzels in their pushcart grills. Even better, you may have emerged from a visit to the Metropolitan Museum, purchased a bag of hot chestnuts, and enjoyed their warmth during a brisk stroll down Fifth Avenue toward midtown. One of the true harbingers of winter, chestnuts round out the ingredients of the colorful and tasty stuffing to make this roast a perfect fireside dish. Serve this with Brussels Sprouts and Spätzle.

Yields 6 servings

3 pounds (1350 g) boneless
   venison tenderloin

FOR THE STUFFING
6 chestnuts
2 ounces (60 g) wild rice
12 fresh cranberries
2 pineapple rings
2 ounces (60 g) dried apricots
2 ounces (60 g) walnuts
1/4 cup (60 ml) fine white bread
   crumbs
2 tablespoons Cognac
Salt
Freshly ground black pepper

FOR THE SAUCE
2 to 3 pounds (900 to 1350 g)
   venison bones and trimmings
1 tablespoon peanut oil
1/2 medium onion
1/2 celery stalk
6 juniper berries
A sprig of rosemary
1/4 cup (60 ml) dry white wine
2 cups (475 ml) Demi-glace
   Brun II *(see page 76)*

FOR ROASTING THE
TENDERLOIN
Salt
1 teaspoon crushed black pepper
6 slices pork fatback, 5 x 5 inches
   (12 1/2 x 12 1/2 cm) and 1/8
   inch (1/3 cm) thick
2 tablespoons peanut oil

2 tablespoons chopped shallots
1/4 cup (60 ml) dry white wine
1/4 cup Cognac
1/2 cup (118 ml) Demi-glace
   Brun II
2 tablespoons Dijon mustard
1/2 cup (118 ml) Crème Fraîche
   (see page 66)

Recommended equipment

A boning knife, cleaver, 1 1/2-quart (1 1/2 L) saucepan, large chef's knife, large fine-mesh sieve, mixing fork, 1-quart (1 L) bowl, plastic wrap, butcher's steel, metal bulb baster, white kitchen string, enameled cast-iron baking dish or lined copper plat à sauter, mortar and pestle, heavy roasting pan, platter, wire whisk.

Using the boning knife, bone the venison tenderloin, reserving the bones, and trim the meat of excess fat and the silver skin. Using the cleaver, cut the bones into 2-inch (5 cm) pieces and set aside (or refrigerate if it will be a while before you make the sauce). Trim about 1 1/2 inches (3 3/4 cm) off either end of the tenderloin and add these trimmings to the bones when you make the sauce.

Set the tenderloin aside (or refrigerate it if you have trimmed it ahead of time) while you prepare the stuffing. For the chestnuts, buy them roasted in vacuum-packed jars (available in specialty food stores), chop them coarsely, and proceed with the recipe. (Or, wait until early winter, when you can buy them fresh; *see below*.) Bring 1 quart (1 L) lightly salted water to boil in the saucepan, add the wild rice, and simmer for 50 minutes or until tender. When done, drain into sieve, run cold water over rice, drain, and reserve. Bring water to boil in the saucepan, add the cranberries, and after the water returns to a boil, cook for 1 minute, then drain and set aside. Dice the pineapple rings (use either canned or fresh) and put them into the mixing bowl. Dice the apricots, chop the walnuts coarsely, and add them both to the bowl. Using the mixing fork, stir the fruits together and add the bread crumbs, Cognac, and the reserved chestnuts, wild rice, and cranberries. Taste the mixture and season with salt and pepper. Then cover bowl tightly with plastic wrap and refrigerate until needed.

When you are ready to stuff the tenderloin, make a cavity lengthwise in the center of the tenderloin. With the help of a butcher's steel (or larder), begin at one end and make an opening all the way to the other. Remove the steel, and using the metal baster, with bulb removed, enlarge the hole by pushing it through. Then, grasping the small end of the baster, slowly pull it out while filling the cavity immediately with the stuffing as you withdraw the baster. Season the tenderloin lightly with salt and pepper. Wrap a piece of fatback over each end of the tenderloin and cover the top with the remaining slices of fatback. Tie the fatback securely with kitchen string, cover the tenderloin loosely with plastic wrap, and refrigerate it while you prepare the sauce.

Preheat oven to 375F (190C).

Put the peanut oil into the baking dish or plat à sauter, add the reserved bones and trimmings, and set the dish into the oven until the bones are brown. While the bones are browning, peel the onion, chop it coarsely, and reserve. Rinse the celery stalk, trim it of any leaves, chop coarsely, and reserve. Crush the juniper berries in the mortar and pestle. When the bones are brown, add the reserved onion and celery, and the rosemary and juniper berries. Mix the vegetables and bones together well and roast for 5 minutes. Then remove pan from oven and drain off any excess fat. Set the pan over medium heat and add the white wine, stirring well to scrape up the brown bits from the pan bottom, and then add the demi-glace. Mix well while bringing the sauce to a simmer. Cook the sauce until it has been reduced by one-half. When done, remove from pan and reserve.

To roast the tenderloin, set the roasting pan over high heat, add the peanut oil and, when it is hot, add the tenderloin with the top side (the fatback side) facing down. Sear the tenderloin well on that side (3 to 4 minutes) and then turn it over to sear the other side. When the tenderloin is well browned, set it into the oven to roast for 15 minutes, turn it, and roast another 15 minutes. This timing will give you a tenderloin that is medium (just a touch of pink). Remove the roast from the oven and set it, with the top side facing down, on a platter to rest for 15 minutes while you finish the sauce. Chop the shallots. Drain the excess fat from the roasting pan, set it over medium heat, add the shallots, and sauté, stirring, for 1 minute. Add the white wine and Cognac and deglaze the pan. Stir in the demi-glace and simmer until reduced by one-half. Strain the reserved sauce into the roasting pan and, mixing with the whisk, stir in the mustard and crème fraîche and blend well. Bring the sauce to a simmer and cook for about 5 minutes or until the sauce is creamy and smooth. Adjust the seasoning if needed, strain the sauce into a clean saucepan, add any juices from the platter, and keep the sauce warm over low heat while you serve the tenderloin. Cut the string from the tenderloin, remove the fatback, and slice the venison into serving slices. Spoon some of the sauce onto the warm dinner plates and arrange the slices on top (or pass the sauce separately, if you wish).

❧

Fresh chestnuts must be peeled before cooking. To peel them, take a small, sharp knife and slash the shells on one side. Then you may either roast them or boil them. To roast them, set them on a pan and put them in a 400F (204C) oven for 8 to 10 minutes. One by one, peel off their shells and inner skin, keeping the chestnuts warm in the turned-off oven. They must be warm or they will not peel. To boil them, set them in a pot of water, bring to a boil, and boil for 1 minute. Remove pot from heat and peel the chestnuts one at a time, keeping the others warm in the pot. When all the fresh chestnuts have been peeled, set them in a saucepan, add water and a little salt, and simmer them until cooked but still firm, about 10 minutes. Then drain the chestnuts, chop them coarsely, and continue with the recipe.

Medallions of Veal Picante

 Veal

> Never mind if your butcher screams at you, you must insist on getting exactly the cut you want. Also get, at the same time, some veal kidneys, each surrounded by its white fat—about one for each person—since they seem to complement the flavor of the main piece of meat. Oh, but it's difficult to explain exactly how to cook veal. It's an almost secret way, which grandmother taught to her daughter and the daughter, in time, passed on to *her* daughter, on and on, generation to generation. . . . It's hard to put it into words on paper. The skill is in your fingers—in the judgment of your eyes.
>
> Veal cooks itself well or badly in the first ten minutes. If you don't do it right at once, you can't save it later. You go wrong if it gets ten degrees too hot—equally wrong if it stays ten degrees too cold. You must brown it dead right, but if you burn it to the slightest degree, you're lost. You can't explain, you have to do it. You have to learn by eye, by nose, by touch of the finger, by tasting with the tip of the tongue.
>
> —Jean Troisgros

Why a whole chapter devoted to veal, when the old favorites beef, lamb, and pork have to be content with a three-way billing? Well, first of all, I like veal, but more to the point is the fact that its popularity has crossed the Atlantic. Historically an Italian favorite, veal was one of the countless enrichments Catherine brought over the Alps on her journey to marry Henri II in 1533. Ever since then it has enjoyed a prominent place in European cuisine.

If we had written this book twenty years ago, we probably would have been reluctant to include anything but veal chops or roasts—for two reasons. First, most American producers were marketing what was, for all intents and purposes, baby beef. Almost red in color, it was meat from large animals, usually grain fed, and occasionally so mature that light marbling of fat was visible. Second, it was hard to convince American butchers to cut slices for scaloppine the correct way. Now, however, many producers (some right here in Virginia) sell veal which certainly all but the fussiest purist would agree equals the best northern Italian meat, which comes from milk-fed calves never more than three months old. Retailers have kept pace with the times, so your butcher will no longer grimace when you ask for scaloppine cut from the top round *across* the grain. Even so, we have taken no chances here and usually call for a loin which you cut up yourself.

Veal has an important place in this book for two other reasons— many of the cuts are quickly prepared and it is a meat with little fat and therefore low in cholesterol. Notice that we said "quickly prepared," *not* easily prepared—at least, not at first. As the late Jean Troisgros states clearly in the quote above, there is a very particular technique to cooking veal. Once mastered (and this comes quickly with practice), the tricks will become second nature to you, and long-lost relations from Milano, Firenze, and Verona will be dropping in for your legendary scaloppine *alla casa*. If I may add my own *conseil* here, it is that you must always respect the natural delicate flavor of veal. Perfectly cooked and set off with just the right touches of spice and color, veal is fare fit for Valhalla, but smothered under a thick blanket of nondescript sauce, it might as well be school cafeteria "mystery meat."

Like chicken, veal is amazingly versatile, and we chose these recipes to reflect that and thus provide you with an ample selection. Because veal sautés so well, the opening section contains a collection of fifteen quite different preparations for scaloppine, or scallops. Leading off is a personal favorite in honor of Eddie Hettich, long-time friend, colleague, and chef at the Everglades Club in Palm Beach. Eclectic in style, its curry and ginger give a distinctly Indian flavor, but what do you say about banana, dill pickle, and watercress? All I can say is try it, and you will definitely like it.

On to more classical fare and Italy for a group of recipes which are sure to find their way into your repertoire. Mies van der Rohe, the world-famous Bauhaus architect, said "less is more," and one can argue that the first preparation, with its simple, delicate, lemon-enlivened sauce, is the best of the whole lot. Simplicity gives way to historical controversy dating to 1134 in the next pair of offerings. Because two powerful branches of the Hapsburg dynasty lay claim to Wienerschnitzel, we gave you two versions: the Austrian, garnished with anchovies and capers, and the Italian, infused with the piquancy of deep-fried sage leaves. Leaving family quarrels behind, we hop around the boot a little bit with a Roman presentation featuring prosciutto and sage, followed by a recipe calling for a richly colored brown sauce flavored by Marsala—a famous Sicilian native. Before following Catherine across the Alps, we stop in Verona, home of star-crossed lovers, for a recipe requiring that you be as agile as

Mercutio to capture the lively flavors and colors of the accompanying vegetables.

Heading northward in Europe inevitably brings thoughts of colder climes, and the final group of scaloppine-based dishes is more suited to fall and winter. Germany leads off with a recipe for a luscious cream-based sauce featuring fresh mushrooms, and then it is on to old Russia, where the mushrooms are set aside for the tartness of pickles, deep red of fresh tomatoes, and dark luxury of black caviar—reminding us anew of the important role this vast country has played in the history of elegant cuisine. Not to be outdone, France calls us back, first to Normandy for apples and Calvados, and then to Franche-Comté or Jura (which just happens to border Switzerland) for that extraordinary springtime treasure from mountain forests—morels.

Intense flavor and complex texture become the rule as we close out this section with four very different preparations. A quick foray back to Italy yields hearty rolled scaloppine with sausage and prosciutto stuffing. Then it is to France once again for two cheese lovers' delights—a roquefort and prosciutto filling, followed in turn by a classic from haute cuisine—the *cordon bleu* enclosed ham and cheese technique originated by Madame du Barry's chef. At last, the "cutlet express" comes to a stop in snowy Moscow for a classic *côtelette fausse*, which is here simplified to make your life a little easier.

Changing scale and preparation style we jump from the sauté pan—not into the fire—but into the roasting pan, for two roasts and three braises. Both roasts use the entire loin—the first in an elegantly simple presentation calling for pan juices to be reduced with wine, cream, and tarragon, and the second in a German-inspired recipe with a veal and kidney stuffing sauced with a wine and demi-glace–enriched reduction. From here it is straight to the French family kitchen for "Mom's veal stew." Certainly a national culinary treasure, a good blanquette is one of those recipes Jean Troisgros meant when he talked about daughters handing them down to daughters. Our version walks the imaginary tightrope between haute cuisine and *minceur* by using only cream to smooth out the sauce at the last minute instead of the traditional egg yolk and cream liaison with butter.

Rustic and hearty are the key words as we close out this section with two regional preparations—one French and one Italian. Burgundy is synonymous not only with fine wine but also with some of the best cooking to be had in France. This recipe captures the Burgundian spirit, with an earthy wine and demi-glace sauce as a perfect foil for mushrooms, pearl onions, and smoky bacon. And finally, ossobuco. The very name will cause native northern Italians and seasoned travelers to call their travel agents and reach for their passports. A deservedly legendary specialty, this recipe returns us to "less is more." There are very few ingredients, but they must be excellent and well cooked. Careful braising with just a few aromatic vegetables, a light wine and demi-glace reduction, just a hint of lemon, garlic, and parsley—what more could one ask than perhaps a side dish of Risotto Milanese at a small table in the Galleria Vittorio Emanuele off the Piazza del Duomo?

And now we come to the section for adults and venturesome children only—liver and sweetbreads. For those of us who love liver and sweetbreads, extolling their virtues is preaching to the converted. For others there is always hope. The Swiss calf's liver presentation offers a choice of sauces, one based on a green peppercorn and wine vinegar reduction, and a sweeter one using Madeira. The choice is yours, but whichever you choose, use only the freshest liver and sauté it at the very last minute.

The fact that sweetbreads come last definitely does not mean they are least. We would be deceiving you if we said they were easy to prepare. Blanching and cleaning them can be quite tedious, but the memory of all that fades when you see the ecstatic smiles of delight on your guests' faces as they savor their first mouthful. The first of the recipes is a Homestead favorite, braised with aromatic vegetables, white wine, and stock, sauced with sherry and cream, and garnished with colorful peppers and prosciutto. The second is a very special preparation reserved for true epicures—sautéed sweetbreads stuffed with foie gras and truffles and set off with a touch of tart lemon butter. C'est formidable!

Medallions of Veal Picante

Gautier and other late nineteenth-century French writers tried to popularize a technique called "synesthesia," in which colors could be heard, music tasted, and other modes of experience likewise intermixed. The opening photograph should suggest a true synesthetic experience in that this dish "tastes" as colorful as it appears. It is piquant, to say the least, and even though the combination may strike you as unusual, I can assure you that it is at the top of the veal list here. Eddie Hettich, my good friend, and chef at the Palm Beach Everglades Club, is especially fond of this and I hope I got it close enough to suit him. To carry out the Middle Eastern theme established by the spices, serve it with Turkish Rice and a mixed green salad, or simply with tabouli.

Yields 6 servings

1 1/2 pounds (675 g) boned and trimmed veal loin
3 tablespoons flour
Salt
Freshly ground white pepper
1/2 teaspoon curry powder
1/2 teaspoon grated fresh ginger root
3 tablespoons peanut oil
2 tablespoons chopped shallots
1 tablespoon (15 g) butter
1/2 cup (118 ml) dry white wine
1 cup (235 ml) Basic Curry Sauce *(see page 80)*
2 tablespoons Glace de Viande *(see page 65)*
1/2 cup (118 ml) whipping cream
1 large banana
1 medium dill pickle
1 whole canned pimiento (packed in water and drained)
1/3 bunch watercress

Recommended equipment

A boning knife, kitchen towel, cleaver, small dish for flour, box grater, 12-inch (30 cm) sauté pan, turning spatula, small chef's knife, paring knife, heatproof platter, wooden spatula, wire whisk, 10-inch (25 cm) sauté pan, fine-mesh sieve.

Using the boning knife, cut off the flank from the loin and reserve it for another use (such as stew, stuffings, or stock). Cut the trimmed loin in half lengthwise and then cut twelve pieces that are 1 inch (2 1/2 cm) thick and weigh about 2 ounces (60 g) apiece. To flatten the medallions, dampen a kitchen towel lightly with cold water, set it down on your work surface, and place a medallion just above the center of the towel. Fold the top of the towel over the medallion and then fold in the sides. Grab the towel firmly so that it is tight around the veal and, using the flat side of the cleaver, flatten the medallions to a thickness of 3/4 of an inch (2 cm), using light but firm strokes. Repeat this for each piece of veal so they will all be of uniform size.

Blend the flour, salt, pepper, and curry powder together in the small dish. Peel the fresh ginger root, grate what you need into the flour mixture, and stir it in. Set the large sauté pan over medium high heat, add the peanut oil, and, when it is hot, coat enough medallions for a first batch with the flour mixture, shake off excess flour, and add them to the pan. Do not crowd the pan—cook them in two batches. When the veal starts to sizzle, reduce heat to medium and sauté until golden brown (about 3 or 4 minutes). Then turn the medallions over and sauté another 3 minutes.

When the first batch is done, remove the medallions to the heatproof platter, add a little more peanut oil to the sauté pan if needed, coat each remaining medallion with flour, and sauté the veal as you did the first batch. When they are done, remove the medallions from the pan to the platter and reserve while you prepare the sauce.

Chop the shallots. Drain the oil from the sauté pan but leave all the brown bits in the pan. Set the pan over medium heat, add 2 teaspoons butter, and, when it is hot, add the shallots and sauté, stirring with the wooden spatula, for 1 minute. Then add the white wine and deglaze the pan, scraping up all the brown bits from the pan bottom. Simmer until the mixture has been reduced to 2 to 3 tablespoons. Then add the curry sauce, glace de viande, and cream while blending well with the whisk. Bring to a simmer and adjust heat so that the sauce simmers gently for 10 minutes.

Preheat oven to 325F (163C).

While the sauce simmers, peel the banana and slice it into twelve slices 1/4 inch (2/3 cm) thick. Set the remaining sauté pan over medium heat, add 1 teaspoon butter, and, when it is hot, add the banana slices and sauté them on both sides, stirring them, for a total time of 1 minute. When done, remove from heat and set pan aside while you prepare the pickle and pimiento. Peel the skin from the pickle, slice in half lengthwise, remove all seeds, and cut into matchstick-size strips. Seed the pimiento and cut it into matchstick-size strips. Reserve both until the final step.

Rinse the watercress in cold water, spin or pat dry, and reserve.

When the sauce has finished simmering, drain the juices from the veal platter into it and stir together. Arrange the medallions on the platter with a banana rondelle on each one. Set the platter into the oven to heat for 3 minutes. Strain sauce through the sieve into a clean saucepan, stir in the pickle and pimiento strips, spoon sauce over the medallions, garnish with the watercress, and serve at once.

Scaloppine di Vitello al Limone
Veal Scallops with Lemon

In The Classic Italian Cookbook, Marcella Hazen notes: "Italian cooking is an expression of convenience rarely used by Italians. The cooking of Italy is really the cooking of its regions, regions that until 1861 were separate, independent, and usually hostile states." Nevertheless, in her superb recipe collection she includes al limone as one of her three scaloppine offerings because, like Pollo alla Cacciatora, it is found throughout Italy. Also seemingly ubiquitous in Italian cuisine is the lemon, and you simply cannot come away from Sicily without vivid memories of the fragrance and profusion of citrus trees. Here, the confluence of French sauce and Italian veal technique creates a dish more likely to be found along the Franco-Italian border in Liguria or the Piedmont. It is the simplest of the scaloppine preparations and thus the best with which to learn your technique, and we would not be surprised if, having mastered all the others, you return to this as your favorite. Fettuccine Alfredo is a natural companion.

Yields 4 servings

2 cups (475 ml) White Veal Stock *(see page 63)*
12 ounces (340 g) boned and trimmed veal loin
2 tablespoons flour
Salt
Freshly ground white pepper
2 tablespoons Clarified Butter *(see page 568)*
2 tablespoons olive oil
1 tablespoon chopped shallots
1/2 cup (118 ml) dry white wine
Juice of 1 medium lemon
1 teaspoon chopped fresh parsley
1 lemon, quartered
4 tablespoons (60 g) butter, softened at room temperature
Sprigs of fresh parsley

Recommended equipment

A 2-quart (2 L) saucepan, boning knife, waxed (or freezer) paper, cleaver, small dish for flour, 12-inch (30 cm) sauté pan, turning spatula, heatproof platter, small chef's knife, wooden spatula, fine-mesh sieve, 1 1/2-quart (1 1/2 L) saucepan, wire whisk.

Set the saucepan over medium heat, add the veal stock, bring to a simmer, and adjust heat so that the stock simmers until reduced to 1/4 cup (60 ml). This will take about 20 to 30 minutes. When done, remove stock from heat and reserve.

While the sauce reduces, prepare the veal. Using the boning knife, make sure that the veal loin is well trimmed and then slice it into eight cutlets weighing 1 1/2 ounces (45 g) each. Lay a sheet of waxed (or freezer) paper on your work surface, put a cutlet on the paper, sprinkle the veal with a few drops of cool water, cover it with a second sheet of paper, and, using the flat side of the cleaver (or a mallet), flatten the cutlet to a thickness of 1/8 inch (1/3 cm) with firm, light strokes. Repeat this until all the cutlets have been flattened.

Mix the flour in the small dish with the salt and pepper and dredge each scaloppina with a coat of flour that will protect the delicate veal while cooking. Shake off excess flour.

Set the sauté pan over medium high heat, add 1 tablespoon clarified butter and 1 tablespoon olive oil, and, when the pan is hot, gently add as many veal slices as will fit easily into the pan without touching. You will have to sauté them in two batches. Sauté the scaloppine until light brown—about 45 seconds—turn them with the spatula and sauté another 30 to 45 seconds. When done, remove them to a platter (in a single layer) and sauté the second batch of scaloppine in the same way, adding the remaining clarified butter and olive oil to the pan first.

When all the veal has been sautéed and is resting on the platter, chop the shallots. Pour the olive oil and butter out of the sauté pan, set pan over medium heat, add the shallots and stir for 30 seconds before adding the wine. Deglaze the pan, scraping up all the brown bits from the pan bottom, and simmer until the wine has been reduced to 2 to 3 tablespoons. Then add the reduced veal stock and the lemon juice and bring to a simmer while stirring. Blend well before straining the sauce through the sieve into the remaining saucepan.

Preheat oven to 250F (121C).

Add any juices that have escaped from the veal on the platter to the sauce in the saucepan, adjust the seasoning if necessary, and set over medium low heat. Set the platter into the oven for 1 minute to warm the scaloppine. Rinse and chop the parsley and quarter the lemon. Remove the veal from the oven. Bring the sauce to the simmer, remove from heat, whisk in the soft butter, pour the sauce over the veal, sprinkle with chopped parsley, garnish with lemon quarters and parsley sprigs, and serve at once.

Wienerschnitzel
Veal Scallops with Anchovy and Caper Garnish

Few recipes have as lengthy a past as this one and its variation. William Harlan Hale notes: "Wiener Schnitzel and its Italian counterpart, Cotoletta Milanese, involved two Hapsburg domains in a culinary quarrel. Both branches of the family, Austrian and Italian, claimed credit for the invention of the dish, the latter branch tracing their claim all the way back to a banquet given in 1134 for the canon of Milan's St. Ambrogio Cathedral."

The cutlets should be cut from a boned and trimmed veal leg round or veal loin, and may be breaded a few hours ahead of time (they will keep perfectly if refrigerated in a single layer covered with plastic wrap). The garnish can be prepared in advance as well, making this an easy dish, in spite of its intimidating history!

Yields 6 servings

6 veal cutlets, weighing 4 to 5 ounces (115 to 145 g) each
3 tablespoons flour
Salt
Freshly ground white pepper
2 eggs
2 tablespoons cold water
1 1/2 cups (355 ml) fine white bread crumbs
1/3 cup (80 ml) peanut oil
2 tablespoons Clarified Butter *(see page 568)*
2 tablespoons (30 g) butter, softened at room temperature
Juice of 1/2 lemon

FOR THE GARNISH
6 slices peeled lemon
6 anchovy fillets rolled around capers
2 hard-boiled eggs
6 lettuce leaves
6 sprigs fresh parsley

Recommended equipment

A boning knife, waxed (or freezer) paper, cleaver, small dish for flour, 1-quart (1 L) mixing bowl, wire whisk, small chef's knife, 1 1/2-quart (1 1/2 L) saucepan, 12-inch (30 cm) sauté pan, turning spatula, paper towels.

Take the cutlets one at a time, sprinkle with a few drops of cool water, and place between two sheets of waxed (or freezer) paper on your work surface. Using a cleaver (or mallet), flatten the cutlets with firm yet light strokes to a thickness of 1/8 inch (1/3 cm).

Mix the flour together in the small dish with the salt and pepper. Break the eggs into the mixing bowl and mix them well with the cold water, using the whisk. Put the bread crumbs on your work surface (or a plate or in a bowl). Dredge the cutlets one by one in the flour, dip into the beaten egg, and then coat thoroughly with the bread crumbs using your fingers to press them into the egg coating so that they will stick. Gently shake off any loose crumbs and continue breading the cutlets until they are all done. Then either wrap and refrigerate the cutlets or proceed with the recipe.

When ready to cook, prepare the garnish first: peel and slice the lemon, prepare the anchovy fillets (or buy them already rolled), and cook the eggs until they are hard-boiled, cool in cold running water, then separate the whites from the yolks and finely chop each separately. Wash and dry the lettuce and parsley and reserve all parts of the garnish until needed.

Set the sauté pan over medium high heat, add the peanut oil and the clarified butter, and, when hot, add as many veal scallops as will fit easily into the pan. They must not overlap or be crowded. Sauté the cutlets until golden brown (about 2 minutes), turn, and sauté until golden brown on the other side (2 more minutes). When done, remove from pan and let drain on paper towels before placing on a serving platter. Sauté the remaining cutlets in the same way. You may have to add a little more oil and clarified butter for the second batch. (If you do more than two batches, discard the oil and butter which by then will contain blackened bread crumbs, wipe out the pan, and begin again with fresh oil and clarified butter.)

When all the cutlets are sautéed, discard the oil and butter in the sauté pan, wipe it out, set it over medium heat, add the soft butter, and heat until the butter is foamy and beginning to turn light brown. Immediately add the lemon juice, remove pan from heat, and spoon the sauce over the veal scallops. Place a lemon slice in the center of each scallop and an anchovy roll in the center of each lemon slice. Decorate the platter with the lettuce leaves and place some chopped white and yolk of egg in each leaf. Garnish with sprigs of parsley and serve at once.

Variation

Scaloppine di Vitello Milanese
Veal Scallops in the Style of Milan

Follow the directions for Wienerschnitzel, but add 4 ounces (115 g) grated Parmesan cheese to the bread crumbs and substitute olive oil for the peanut oil. Serve with a lemon slice and fried fresh sage (omit the rest of the garnish). This veal is traditionally served with pasta on the side and a fresh tomato sauce, such as Tomato Butter Sauce, is either passed separately or spooned onto the plate to receive the veal.

FRIED FRESH SAGE
12 to 18 fresh sage leaves
1/3 cup (80 ml) milk
1 egg yolk
1/3 cup (40 g) flour
Salt
Freshly ground white pepper
1 egg white
Peanut oil for deep frying

Recommended equipment

Two small mixing bowls, wire whisk, hand-held electric mixer, rubber spatula, electric deep fryer with thermostat or other deep pot, frying thermometer, fine-mesh skimmer, paper towels.

Wash the sage leaves gently in cold water, pat or spin dry, and reserve while the batter is prepared.

In a mixing bowl, using the whisk, combine the milk, egg yolk, and flour. Blend well and season with salt and pepper.

In the other mixing bowl, using the hand-held mixer, whip the egg white until stiff and then blend into the batter with the rubber spatula.

Heat the peanut oil in the deep fryer to 360 to 375F (182 to 190C). Check the temperature with the thermometer and, when it is hot, dip the sage leaves one by one into the batter, let excess drip off, and drop each leaf into the hot oil. Do not crowd the pot. Fry until golden brown, turning with the skimmer to brown evenly, for about 1 minute. Remove to drain on paper towels and, if necessary, fry another batch.

Variation: The milk in the batter may be replaced with an equal amount of dry white wine.

Saltimbocca alla Romana
Veal Scallops in the Roman Style

Distinctly Roman because of the sage and prosciutto, this veal preparation, which translates as "jump in the mouth Roman style," must be quickly sautéed to keep the ham from being overdone. Unless you have a meat slicer you will probably want your butcher to make the thin slices necessary to keep the natural saltiness of prosciutto under control. Serve the cutlets with Risotto alla Milanese, Tomatoes Provençale, and either fresh Asparagus, String Beans, or peas.

Yields 6 servings

18 to 20 ounces (510 to 570 g) boned and trimmed veal loin (or leg round)
12 fresh sage leaves
4 ounces (115 g) prosciutto
2 tablespoons flour
Salt
Freshly ground white pepper
1 tablespoon chopped shallots
2 tablespoons Clarified Butter *(see page 568)*
2 tablespoons olive oil
1/2 cup (118 ml) Marsala
1 cup (235 ml) Demi-glace Brun I *(see page 75)*
2 teaspoons butter, softened at room temperature

Recommended equipment

A boning knife, waxed (or freezer) paper, cleaver, wooden toothpicks, 12-inch (30 cm) sauté pan, turning spatula, heatproof platter, small chef's knife, wooden spatula, fine-mesh sieve, 1 1/2-quart (1 1/2 L) saucepan, wire whisk.

Using the boning knife, make sure that the veal is well trimmed and then slice it into twelve cutlets weighing about 1 1/2 ounces (45 g) each. Lay a sheet of waxed (or freezer) paper on your work surface, put a cutlet on the paper, sprinkle the veal with a few drops of cold water, cover with a second piece of paper, and, using the flat side of the cleaver (or a mallet), flatten the cutlet to a thickness of 1/8 inch (1/3 cm) with firm, light strokes. Repeat this until all the cutlets have been flattened.

Lay all the veal scallops out on your work surface and put a sage leaf in the center of each one. Slice the ham paper thin if you have not already had it sliced by your butcher. Lay a piece of ham over each scaloppina and attach it with two toothpicks. Put a piece of waxed paper on your work surface, spread the flour out on it, and season lightly with salt and pepper. Dredge each scaloppina on the veal side with flour and reserve.

Chop the shallots with the chef's knife and reserve.

Set the sauté pan over medium high heat, add the clarified butter and the olive oil, and, when it is hot, add as many scaloppine, ham side down, as will fit easily into the pan. Reduce heat to medium (too high a heat will toughen the tender veal), sauté 20 seconds, turn, and sauté for 1 minute. Remove the scaloppine from the pan and lay them in a single layer, with the ham side up, on the platter. Sauté the second batch of veal in the same manner as the first.

When all the scaloppine have been sautéed and are resting on the platter, pour the butter and olive oil from the sauté pan, set the pan back over medium heat, add the shallots, and sauté, stirring, for 30 seconds. Do not brown the shallots. Add the Marsala to the pan and deglaze it while simmering for 1 minute and scraping up all the brown bits from the pan bottom. Add the demi-glace, simmer for 10 minutes, and then strain the sauce through the sieve into the saucepan, and keep warm.

Remove the toothpicks from the scaloppine and add any juices on the platter to the saucepan. Bring the sauce to a simmer, remove from heat, and whisk the soft butter into the sauce. Spoon the sauce onto warm dinner plates, arrange the scaloppine on top, and serve at once.

Scaloppine di Vitello al Marsala
Veal Scallops with Marsala Sauce

Freighters outbound from the Sicilian port of Marsala normally have on their cargo manifest some of the island's most famous culinary export, Marsala wine. A blended wine, usually sweet enough to be served with dessert, it owes its present popularity in large part to the English. Said to have been a favorite of Lord Nelson, it gained international recognition only after nineteenth-century English wine merchants went to Sicily and actively turned it into a serious competitor with Port on the British home market. Its complex, faintly acid taste (due in part to the grapes being raised in volcanic soil), combined here with demi-glace, produces a sauce whose rich intensity of flavor is evocative of the mosaic-bejeweled interior of Monreale cathedral. Rice Creole or Fettuccine Alfredo is just right with the aromatic brown sauce, and Tomatoes Provençale with Fried Fresh Sage would round out the menu very nicely.

Yields 4 servings

1/2 cup (118 ml) Demi-glace Brun I *(see page 75)*
12 ounces (340 g) boned and trimmed veal loin
2 tablespoons flour
Salt
Freshly ground white pepper
2 tablespoons Clarified Butter *(see page 568)*
2 tablespoons olive oil
2 tablespoons chopped shallots
1/2 cup (118 ml) Marsala
1 teaspoon chopped fresh parsley
4 tablespoons (60 g) butter, softened at room temperature

Recommended equipment

A 1 1/2-quart (1 1/2 L) saucepan, boning knife, waxed (or freezer) paper, cleaver, small dish for flour, 12-inch (30 cm) sauté pan, turning spatula, heatproof platter, small chef's knife, wooden spatula, fine-mesh sieve, 1 1/2-quart (1 1/2 L) saucepan, wire whisk.

Set the saucepan over medium heat, add the demi-glace, bring to a simmer, and adjust heat so that the stock simmers until reduced to 1/4 cup (60 ml). This will take about 20 to 30 minutes. When done, remove from heat and reserve.

While the sauce reduces, prepare the veal. Using the boning knife, make sure that the veal loin is well trimmed and then slice it into eight cutlets weighing 1 1/2 ounces (45 g) each. Lay a sheet of waxed (or freezer) paper on your work surface, put a cutlet on the paper, sprinkle the veal with a few drops of cool water, cover it with a second sheet of paper, and, using the flat side of the cleaver (or a mallet), flatten the cutlet to a thickness of 1/8 inch (1/3 cm) with firm, light strokes. Repeat this until all the cutlets have been flattened.

Mix the flour in the small dish with the salt and pepper and dredge each scaloppina with a coat of flour that will protect the delicate veal while cooking. Shake off excess flour.

Set the sauté pan over medium high heat, add 1 tablespoon clarified butter and 1 tablespoon olive oil, and, when the pan is hot, gently add as many veal slices as will fit easily into the pan without touching. You will have to sauté them in two batches. Sauté the scaloppine until light brown—about 45 seconds—turn them with the spatula and sauté another 30 to 45 seconds. When done, remove them to a platter (in a single layer) and sauté the remaining scaloppine in the same way, adding the remaining clarified butter and olive oil to the pan first.

Preheat oven to 250F (121C).

When all the veal has been sautéed and is resting on the platter, chop the shallots. Pour the olive oil and butter out of the sauté pan, set pan over medium heat, add the shallots and stir for 30 seconds before adding the Marsala. Deglaze the pan, scraping up all the brown bits in the pan bottom, simmer for 1 minute before adding the reserved demi-glace, simmer for 3 minutes, and then strain through the sieve into the clean saucepan.

Add any juices that have escaped from the veal on the platter to the sauce in the saucepan, adjust the seasoning if necessary, and set over medium low heat. Set the platter into the oven to warm the veal for 1 minute. Rinse and chop the parsley. Remove the veal from the oven. Bring the sauce to the simmer, remove from heat, whisk in the soft butter, pour the sauce over the veal, sprinkle with chopped parsley, and serve at once.

 ## *Piccata di Vitello Veronese*
Veal Scallops in the Style of Verona

A la minute is definitely the key to success in this colorful elaboration of Scaloppine al Marsala. Have your guests at the ready, for like a fritto misto, the vegetables and veal will be at their flavor peak just as they leave the pan. Because of its affinity with tomato, we have called for oregano (known as sweet marjoram by some) here instead of marjoram, which would be more common to the Veneto Euganea region of Italy. However, were you preparing this in Verona, you would undoubtedly find any herb you sought in the Piazza delle Erbe (herbs), where they have been sold for more than two thousand years. One conseil, be sure that your tomato is not too ripe so that it will hold together when sautéed.

Yields 4 servings

FOR THE VEAL

1/2 cup (118 ml) Demi-glace Brun I *(see page 75)*
12 ounces (340 g) boned and trimmed veal loin
1 tablespoon chopped shallots
2 tablespoons flour
Salt
Freshly ground white pepper
2 tablespoons Clarified Butter *(see page 568)*
2 tablespoons olive oil
1/2 cup (118 ml) Marsala
1 teaspoon chopped fresh parsley
4 tablespoons (60 g) butter, softened at room temperature

FOR THE VEGETABLES

1 ripe tomato
1 small zucchini
2 tablespoons flour
1 egg
1 teaspoon cool water
1/3 cup (80 ml) cracker meal
A generous pinch of oregano
1 teaspoon chopped fresh parsley
1/2 garlic clove
2 tablespoons olive oil
2 tablespoons Clarified Butter

Recommended equipment

A 1 1/2-quart (1 1/2 L) saucepan, boning knife, waxed (or freezer) paper, cleaver, small chef's knife, two small dishes for flour, two 1-quart (1 L) mixing bowls, garlic press, two 12-inch (30 cm) sauté pans, turning spatula, heatproof platter, paper towels, baking sheet, wooden spatula, fine-mesh sieve, 1 1/2-quart (1 1/2 L) saucepan, wire whisk.

Set the saucepan over medium heat, add the demi-glace, bring to a simmer, and adjust heat so that the stock simmers until reduced to 1/4 cup (60 ml). This will take about 20 to 30 minutes. When done, remove from heat and reserve.

Meanwhile, prepare the veal. Using the boning knife, make sure that the veal loin is well trimmed and then slice it into eight cutlets weighing 1 1/2 ounces (45 g) each. Lay a sheet of waxed (or freezer) paper on your work surface, put a cutlet on the paper, sprinkle the veal with a few drops of cool water, cover it with a second sheet of paper, and, using the flat side of the cleaver (or a mallet), flatten the cutlet to a thickness of 1/8 inch (1/3 cm) with firm, light strokes. Repeat this until all the cutlets have been flattened. Reserve the veal until needed.

Rinse the tomato and make four 1/4-inch (2/3 cm) thick slices. Rinse the zucchini and, holding the knife at a 45° angle, make four 1/4-inch diagonal slices. Sprinkle the zucchini with a few drops of milk to moisten it. Put the flour in one small dish and whisk the egg and water together in one bowl. In the other bowl, mix the cracker meal with the oregano. Chop the parsley with the chef's knife and add it with the pressed garlic to the meal, mixing all together thoroughly.

Chop the shallots and reserve.

Lay out enough waxed paper on your work surface to accommodate the veal and vegetable pieces in one layer.

Mix the flour for the veal in the other small dish with the salt and pepper and dredge each scaloppina with a coat of flour that will protect the delicate veal while cooking. Shake off excess flour and lay pieces in a single layer on the waxed paper.

Dust the vegetable slices with flour, drench in egg, and dredge in the cracker meal mixture, patting it on gently with your fingers. Lay the slices in a single layer on the waxed paper.

Preheat oven to 250F (121C).

Set one sauté pan over medium high heat, add

1 tablespoon each of clarified butter and olive oil, and, when it is hot, gently add as many veal slices as will fit easily into the pan without touching. You will have to sauté them in two batches. Sauté the scaloppine until light brown—about 45 seconds—turn them with the spatula and sauté another 30 to 45 seconds. When done, remove them to a platter (in a single layer) and sauté the remaining scaloppine in the same way, adding the remaining clarified butter and olive oil to the pan first. Add the second batch of scaloppine to the platter and take the sauté pan off heat briefly.

For the vegetables, set the other sauté pan over medium high heat and add the olive oil and clarified butter. When the pan is hot, slip the vegetable slices into it and sauté until they are golden brown on both sides. Put three layers of paper towels on the baking sheet, place the sautéed vegetables on the towels in a single layer, and let drain.

Meanwhile, pour the olive oil and butter out of the veal sautéing pan, set over medium heat, add the shallots, and stir for 30 seconds before adding the Marsala. Deglaze the pan, scraping up all the brown bits on the pan bottom, simmer for 1 minute before adding the reserved demi-glace, and then simmer for 3 minutes. As sauce finishes simmering, set the veal platter into the oven to heat for 2 minutes. Put fresh paper towels under the vegetables and set their baking sheet into the oven with the veal. When the sauce is done, strain it through the sieve into the clean saucepan.

Remove the veal from the oven. Add any juices that have escaped from the veal on the platter to the sauce in the saucepan, adjust the seasoning if necessary, and set over medium low heat. Rinse and chop the parsley. Bring the sauce to the simmer, remove from heat, and whisk in the soft butter.

Remove the vegetables from the oven, spoon the Marsala sauce on warmed serving plates, set a scaloppina on the plate, then a tomato slice, another scaloppina, and a zucchini slice, in an overlapping arrangement *à cheval*. Serve at once.

Rahmschnitzel
Veal Scallops with Cream Sauce

Truly an international quartet, this German recipe and its three variations—one Russian and two French—are particularly suited to cool weather menus. The sauce is sumptuously smooth (Rahm translates as cream) and affords an excellent opportunity for Spätzle, fresh buttered noodles, or Roesti.

Yields 6 servings

2 cups (475 ml) White Veal Stock *(see page 63)*
18 to 20 ounces (510 to 570 g) boned and trimmed veal loin (or leg round)
1 1/2 cups (355 ml) whipping cream
1 tablespoon Glace de Viande *(see page 65)*
1 2-inch (5 cm) piece lemon peel (all bitter white removed)
8 ounces (225 g) fresh mushrooms
1 tablespoon (15 g) butter
Juice of 1/4 lemon
Salt
1/4 cup (30 g) flour
Freshly ground white pepper
3 tablespoons Clarified Butter *(see page 568)*
3 tablespoons peanut oil
1 tablespoon chopped shallots
1/2 cup (118 ml) dry white wine

Recommended equipment

A 2-quart (2 L) saucepan, boning knife, waxed (or freezer) paper, cleaver, paring knife, 10-inch (25 cm) sauté pan, wooden spatula, small dish for flour, 12-inch (30 cm) sauté pan, turning spatula, heatproof platter, small chef's knife, wire whisk, fine-mesh sieve, 1 1/2-quart (1 1/2 L) saucepan.

Put the veal stock in the saucepan, set over medium heat, and simmer until reduced to 2/3 cup (160 ml). This should take 20 to 30 minutes. When done, remove from heat and reserve.

While the stock is reducing, prepare the veal. Using the boning knife, make sure that the veal loin is well trimmed and then slice it into twelve cutlets weighing about 1 1/2 ounces (45 g) each. Lay a sheet of waxed (or freezer) paper on your work surface, put a cutlet on the paper, sprinkle the veal with a few drops of cool water, cover it with a second sheet of paper, and, using the flat side of the cleaver (or a mallet), flatten the cutlet to a thickness of 1/8 inch (1/3 cm) with firm, light strokes. Repeat this until all the cutlets have been flattened. Reserve the veal scaloppine.

When the veal stock is reduced, add the cream, glace de viande, and lemon peel and continue simmering until you have 2 cups (475 ml) of a creamy, ivory-colored liquid. This should take about 10 to 15 minutes. When done, remove from heat and reserve.

While the sauce simmers, prepare the mushrooms. Brush them of any clinging dirt and slice them into 1/4-inch (2/3 cm) thick slices. Set the smaller sauté pan over medium high heat, add the butter, and, when it is hot, add the mushrooms, sprinkle them with lemon juice, season lightly with salt, and sauté, stirring, for 3 minutes. Remove pan from heat and keep the mushrooms in a warm (not hot) spot until needed.

Season the flour with salt and pepper and dredge each scaloppina in it so it is well covered and will be protected from drying out during sautéing. Shake off any excess flour before putting them in the pan.

Set the remaining sauté pan over medium high heat, add 1 tablespoon each of clarified butter and peanut oil, and, when the pan is hot, gently add as many veal slices as will fit easily into the pan without touching. You will have to sauté them in three batches. Sauté the scaloppine until light brown—about 45 seconds—turn them with the spatula and sauté another 30 to 45 seconds. When done, remove them to a platter (in a single layer) and sauté the remaining scaloppine in the same way, adding the remaining clarified butter and olive oil to the pan first.

When all the veal has been sautéed and is resting on the platter, chop the shallots. Pour the oil and butter out of the sauté pan, set pan over medium heat, add the shallots and stir for 30 seconds before adding the wine. Deglaze the pan, scraping up all the brown bits on the pan bottom, and simmer until the wine has been reduced to 2 to 3 tablespoons. Then add the reserved veal stock, cream, and glace de viande mixture, blend well with the whisk, and adjust seasoning if needed. Strain the sauce through the sieve into the remaining saucepan and keep warm.

Preheat oven to 250F (121C).

Add any juices that have escaped from the veal on the platter to the sauce in the saucepan. Spread the mushrooms evenly over the scaloppine and set the platter into the oven to heat for 1 minute. Then remove from oven, spoon the sauce over all, and serve at once.

Variation

Escalopes de Veau à la Russe

As it does in Rossolnik, dill pickle here dramatically changes the nature of the sauce. By replacing mushrooms in the basic Rahmschnitzel recipe, the pickle "points up" the sauce and makes it the perfect foil for the finishing Russian garnish of lightly grilled tomato and black caviar.

1 dill pickle
2 ripe tomatoes
Butter for baking sheet
6 teaspoons imported black caviar

Peel and seed the pickle, cut into fine 1-inch (2 1/2 cm) julienne strips, and reserve.

Peel the tomatoes *(see page 568)* and slice each into six slices that are 1/8 to 1/4 inch (1/3 to 2/3 cm) thick. Put them on a lightly buttered baking sheet and set them under a broiler until they are just barely grilled. Then remove and reserve.

When ready to serve the veal, stir the pickle strips into the sauce, spoon the sauce over the veal, and top each piece with a tomato round. Garnish each tomato with 1/2 teaspoon caviar and serve at once.

Variation

Escalopes de Veau au Calvados

This preparation replaces the mushrooms in the basic Rahmschnitzel recipe with apples, white wine, and Calvados. Although cold storage makes apples available all year round, fresh apples mean fall of the year and, combined with Calvados, they mean Normandy and the Vallée d'Auge. If you do serve this when apples are just off the trees, recall l'esprit normande at dessert by offering bourdelets, *which are apple turnovers in a pastry crust.*

3 large apples (preferably Winesap or Granny Smith)
Juice of 1 lemon
2 tablespoons dry white wine
6 tablespoons Calvados

Preheat oven to 325F (163C).

Butter a baking dish large enough to hold twelve apple rings in a single layer. Peel and core the apples and cut them crosswise into rings. Trim them neatly, set into the dish, sprinkle each ring with a few drops of lemon juice, add the wine and 2 tablespoons Calvados to the dish, and set into the oven to bake for 5 minutes. When done, remove to a warm place and reserve.

When ready to serve the veal, arrange the apple rings on the platter with the veal and stir 1/4 cup (60 ml) Calvados into the sauce before spooning it over the veal.

Variation

🙵 *Escalopes de Veau aux Morilles*

Although the basic Rahmschnitzel recipe calls for the white mushrooms (champignons de Paris) available in any grocery store, if dried French or Swiss morels are available, you will find that they completely transform the sauce. Somehow, cream, veal (or chicken), and morels combine to produce an earthy, yet sophisticated flavor which will make you want to sit right down and eat the dish all over again. Depending on the rainfall, fresh morels are available in the forests around the Homestead, and they may grow in your area as well. If so, or if you have imported fresh ones in your market, they can be used with equal success, although my personal preference is for the more intense flavor of the dried ones. Be sure to get genuine French or Swiss morels, because they are the only ones guaranteed not to be packed with grasses or weeds to inflate the weight.

1 1/2 ounces (45 g) dried French or Swiss morels

Put the morels in a glass or china bowl, cover with warm water, and let soak for a few hours. Then drain them and rinse them well in a sieve under running cold water to rid them of any sand or grit. Pat the morels dry with paper towels and reserve.

When the basic veal sauce for the Rahmschnitzel has been strained into the saucepan, add the morels and simmer on low heat for 10 minutes. If the sauce is too thick, add a little white wine and veal stock. When ready, spoon the sauce over the veal and serve.

🙵

If fresh morels are available, use 8 ounces (225 g). Before cooking, cut them in half and rinse the hollow insides of any dirt. Pat dry and proceed as above.

🙵 *Rollatini di Vitello*
Stuffed Veal Rolls

Along with Italian produce, local sausage, whether dry-cured salami or cooked salsiccia, *takes no backseat to French charcuterie. Unfortunately, importation laws limit the sampling of mortadella in Bologna, salamini in Padova, salami from Felino (near Parma), and salsiccia di fegato from the Adriatic port of Pescara to the fortunate traveler. However, take heart, because some American packers with Italian backgrounds take great pride in preparing such delicacies in the traditional way (we buy our mortadella and salami from them), and many local butcher shops make a version of Italian sausage which by all means you should use here. The choice of mild, hot, or sweet is up to you. Spinach noodles go well with this dish, and for a more substantial pasta in very early spring, serve Fettuccine Primavera.*

Yields 6 to 8 servings   *Recommended equipment*

1 1/4 to 1 1/2 pounds (570 to 675 g) boned and trimmed veal leg round
6 ounces (170 g) veal trimmings or boned veal shoulder
1/3 cup (80 ml) fine white bread crumbs
4 ounces (115 g) pork sausage
2 teaspoons chopped fresh parsley
12 fresh sage leaves
6 tablespoons half-and-half
Salt
Freshly ground white pepper
3 ounces (85 g) prosciutto
3 tablespoons flour
3 tablespoons peanut oil
1 tablespoon chopped shallots
1/2 cup (118 ml) Marsala
1 1/2 cups (355 ml) Demi-glace Brun I *(see page 75)*

A boning knife, waxed (or freezer) paper, cleaver, meat grinder with fine blade, 2-quart (2 L) mixing bowl, small chef's knife, blending fork, slicing knife, white kitchen string, 12-inch (30 cm) sauté pan with lid, wooden spatula, heatproof platter, fine-mesh sieve, 2-quart (2 L) saucepan.

Using the boning knife, make sure that the veal is well trimmed and then slice it into twelve cutlets weighing 1 1/2 to 2 ounces (45 to 60 g) each. Lay a sheet of waxed (or freezer) paper on your work surface, put a cutlet on the paper, sprinkle the veal with a few drops of cool water, cover with a second piece of paper, and, using the flat side of the cleaver (or a mallet), flatten the cutlet to a thickness of 1/8 inch (1/3 cm) with firm, light strokes. Repeat this until all the cutlets have been flattened. Reserve the cutlets.

Grind the veal trimmings in the meat grinder using the fine blade and put them in the mixing bowl. Add the bread crumbs and sausage. Rinse the parsley and sage separately, pat dry, chop, and put into the bowl. Stir in the half-and-half, using the blending fork, salt the mixture lightly, and add white pepper to taste. Blend everything together well and spread about 2 tablespoons of the mixture on each cutlet. Slice the prosciutto as thinly as possible (or have your butcher do it for you) and cut the slices into julienne strips. Divide the prosciutto among the cutlets, roll each cutlet up, and tie them securely with string.

Dust the rollatini lightly with flour. Set the sauté pan over medium high heat, add the peanut oil, and, when it is hot, add the veal. Sauté until the rollatini are well browned on all sides, turning them from time to time. This should take 6 to 8 minutes. Meanwhile, chop the shallots.

Preheat oven to 325F (163C).

When the veal has browned, drain off excess fat, add the shallots, stir for 10 seconds, and add the Marsala and demi-glace. Bring to a simmer, cover the pan, and set into the oven to bake for 20 minutes.

When done, remove the pan from the oven, remove the rollatini from the pan to the platter, skim any fat from the sauce, and strain it through the sieve into the saucepan. Remove the string from the rollatini, pour the warm sauce over them, and serve at once.

Roulades de Veau au Roquefort
Veal Rolls Stuffed with Roquefort

In the experience of many, Roquefort cheese is confined to service on a cheese tray, appearance in a salad dressing, or worst of all (and illegal in most places), use as a descriptive decoy to the innocent diner in the following exchange. Diner: "What dressings do you serve here?" Answer: "Thousand Island, Ranch, French, and Roquefort." The first three are a story we will leave for another time, but unless you are in a first-class hotel or restaurant, you can be sure that "roquefort" means the cheapest generic blue cheese the local food service can provide. Well, not so here and not so in France either.

Although the French make more than four hundred different types of cheese, only that which comes from the Gascon village of Roquefort-sur-Soulzon can be shipped in the familiar silver-wrapped wheels bearing the world-renowned Roquefort symbol of the sheep. This village perches, almost precariously, against the Rocks of Combalou, where vast caves, eleven stories below, have housed this industry for centuries. The caves, publicized by Pliny in the first century A.D., *have a continuous airflow whose force and humidity work the requisite magic on fresh ewe's milk curd, inoculated with* Penicillium roquefortii, *to produce this gastronomic treasure.*

Because the best Roquefort is de rigueur here we want you to look closely before you buy it. If the cheese has large cavities, or the mold has turned greenish from its natural dark blue, pass it up, no matter what your cheese merchant tells you. (Don't take any discounts either. Remember Escoffier—the "cheapest is the dearest in the end.") If, however, a good Gorgonzola from Gorgonzola or elsewhere in Lombardy is available, by all means use it. To balance the cheese flavor in this dish we suggest serving Spätzle or Roesti and a green salad laced with walnuts or pecans and tossed with a nut oil dressing.

Yields 6 to 8 servings

- 1 1/4 to 1 1/2 pounds (570 to 675 g) boned and trimmed veal leg round
- 2 tablespoons chopped fresh parsley
- 6 ounces (170 g) Roquefort cheese
- 2 ounces (60 g) cream cheese
- 1/4 cup (60 ml) bread crumbs
- 4 ounces (115 g) prosciutto
- 3 tablespoons flour
- Salt
- Freshly ground white pepper
- 3 tablespoons peanut oil
- 1 tablespoon chopped shallots
- 1/2 cup (118 ml) dry white wine
- 3/4 cup (180 ml) Demi-glace Brun I *(see page 75)*
- 3/4 cup (180 ml) whipping cream

Recommended equipment

A boning knife, waxed (or freezer) paper, cleaver, small chef's knife, 1 1/2-quart (1 1/2 L) mixing bowl, blending fork, slicing knife, white kitchen string, small dish for flour, 12-inch (30 cm) sauté pan with lid, wooden spatula, heatproof platter, fine-mesh sieve, 2-quart (2 L) saucepan.

Using the boning knife, make sure that the veal is well trimmed and then slice it into twelve cutlets weighing 1 1/2 to 2 ounces (45 to 60 g) each. Lay a sheet of waxed (or freezer) paper on your work surface, put a cutlet on the paper, sprinkle the veal with a few drops of cool water, cover with a second piece of paper, and, using the flat side of the cleaver (or a mallet), flatten the cutlet to a thickness of 1/8 inch (1/3 cm) with firm, light strokes. Repeat this until all the cutlets have been flattened and reserve them until needed.

Rinse the parsley, pat or spin dry, chop, and reserve.

In the mixing bowl, blend together with the blending fork the Roquefort, cream cheese, bread crumbs, and 1 tablespoon chopped parsley. Refrigerate the mixture while you slice the prosciutto into 12 paper-thin slices (or have your butcher slice it for you). Remove the cheese mixture from the refrigerator, put it on your work surface, and divide it into 12 equal portions. Using your hands, form each portion into an oblong shape. Lay the prosciutto slices on your work surface, center a cheese oblong on each slice, and fold all sides of the prosciutto around the cheese to make a tight package. Lay the veal cutlets on your work surface, center a ham package on each, and roll the veal around the ham to make a stuffed roulade. Tie both ends of each roll with string. Refrigerate the roulades, well wrapped, if you are not cooking them now.

When ready to cook the roulades, combine the flour with the salt and pepper in the small dish and roll the roulades in it so they are lightly dusted.

Set the sauté pan over medium high heat, add the peanut oil, and, when it is hot, add the roulades in a single layer so that the pan is not crowded. You may have to sauté them in two batches. Sauté until the roulades are well browned on all sides (about 6 to 8 minutes), turning them gently with the wooden spatula.

While the roulades are browning, chop the shallots and reserve.

Preheat oven to 325F (163C).

When all the roulades are browned, drain off excess fat, reduce heat to medium, add the shallots, stir for 10 seconds, add the wine, and deglaze the pan, stirring up all the brown bits from the pan bottom. Simmer until the liquid has been reduced by one-half. Then add the demi-glace and cream, bring to a simmer, cover the pan, and set into the oven to bake for 10 minutes.

When the roulades are done, remove pan from the oven, remove the roulades to the platter, and keep them warm. Skim off any fat from the sauce, pour it through the sieve into the saucepan, set the saucepan over low heat, taste the sauce, and adjust the seasoning if necessary. When the sauce is warm and ready, remove the strings from the roulades, pour the sauce over them, sprinkle with the remaining parsley, and serve at once.

If you and your guests are true cheese lovers, replace the cream cheese with either Roquefort or Gorgonzola. And, if there is a baker in the house, request a loaf of *pain aux noix* made with walnuts. Toast it, pass it in a basket, and your guests will be hard put to choose between simply spreading some of the cheese filling on the bread or being so forward as to ask when you will invite them back for the same meal.

Escalopes de Veau Cordon Bleu
Veal Scallops Cordon Bleu

Unfortunately, veterans of package tours both here and abroad can vouch for the abysmal scene awaiting them at too many dinners. Steam table or individual service—it doesn't really matter, because there it is, the "dreaded veal cutlet." Soggy, tough, and tasteless, what should be one of cuisine's best offerings is relegated to jokes among the diners to the effect of, "what do you think this was in its last life?" Well, prepare this dish and you will dread cutlets no more. Derived from the classic Suprêmes de Volaille Cordon Bleu, here strips of ham encased by thinly sliced cheese are surrounded by delicate veal, which is breaded and gently sautéed. Pommes de Terre Parisienne Rissolées, Tomatoes Provencale, and either fresh Asparagus or String Beans are fitting accompaniments.

Yields 4 servings

12 ounces (340 g) boned and trimmed veal loin
4 ounces (115 g) cooked, smoked ham (4 slices, 1 ounce each)
4 ounces (115 g) imported Swiss (Emmentaler) cheese (4 slices, 1 ounce each)
Salt
Freshly ground white pepper
4 eggs
2 tablespoons water
6 tablespoons flour
1 cup (235 ml) fine white bread crumbs
1/2 cup (118 ml) Clarified Butter *(see page 568)*
1/2 cup (118 ml) peanut oil
2 tablespoons melted butter
Juice of 1/2 lemon

Recommended equipment

A boning knife, waxed (or freezer) paper, cleaver, paring knife, pan large enough to hold prepared veal for chilling, 1-quart (1 L) mixing bowl, wire whisk, 12-inch (30 cm) sauté pan, wooden spatula, slotted spoon, paper towels, heatproof serving platter.

Using the boning knife, make sure that the veal loin is well trimmed and then slice it into eight cutlets weighing 1 1/2 ounces (45 g) each. Lay a sheet of waxed (or freezer) paper on your work surface, put a cutlet on the paper, sprinkle the veal with a few drops of cool water, cover it with a second sheet of paper, and, using the flat side of the cleaver (or a mallet), flatten the cutlet to a thickness of 1/8 inch (1/3 cm) with firm, light strokes. Repeat this until all the cutlets have been flattened and reserve them until needed.

Cut each ham slice into strips about 2 1/2 inches (6 1/4 cm) long and 1 inch (2 1/2 cm) wide and stack them in four even piles. One at a time, wrap a slice of cheese around each ham stack, surrounding the ham completely, set it on the center of a veal scallop, and cover it with another scallop. Press the edges together to make a complete package and as each scallop is finished set it on the pan. When all the scallops are ready, set them into the refrigerator for 20 to 30 minutes. (If you chill them longer than that, cover them with plastic wrap.)

After chilling, remove the veal from the refrigerator and season each package lightly with salt and pepper. Mix the eggs with the water in the bowl using the whisk. Put the flour on a plate (or your work surface) and do likewise with the bread crumbs. One at a time, dust the veal packages with the flour, covering them completely, dip them into the egg wash, and set them into the bread crumbs. Press the edges lightly together to ensure a good seal. (If there are any spots with no bread crumbs, use your fingers to dab on some egg wash and then sprinkle with more crumbs.) Refrigerate on the pan in a single layer until you are ready to sauté them.

When ready to cook, preheat oven to 350F (177C).

Set the sauté pan over medium heat and add 1/4 cup (60 ml) each of clarified butter and peanut oil. When the oil is hot, add as many of the veal packages in a single layer as will fit comfortably in the pan without touching. Do not crowd the pan. (You may have to sauté them in two batches.) When they begin to sizzle, lower the heat and sauté the veal until brown on the first side, turn with the spatula, and sauté until brown on the other side (about 1 1/2 minutes per side). When done, remove to paper towels on the heatproof platter to drain. (Sauté the second batch in the same way, adding the remaining clarified butter and peanut oil to the pan first.)

When ready to serve, remove the towels and set the platter into the oven to heat for 3 minutes. While the veal heats, melt the butter and when it is foamy and nut brown in color, add the lemon juice, remove from heat, stir to mix, and set aside. When the veal is hot, arrange a veal package on each warm serving plate, drizzle the melted butter over them, and serve at once.

Côtes de Veau Pojarski
Veal Cutlets in the Style of Pojarski

You have some historical leeway here because this dish was named either for General Pojarski, who liberated Moscow from the Poles in the seventeenth century, or for a tavern between Moscow and Saint Petersburg that was a coach stop. I call for the veal to be finely ground, seasoned, shaped into cutlets, and sautéed. Another version calls for saving loin chop bones and then reshaping a ground veal "chop" around the bone. Whatever the presentation, this is worthy of Sauce Périgueux or the sauce for the Tenderloin of Beef Stroganoff. Serve with a crisp potato, such as Roesti, and fresh Asparagus or Tomatoes Provençale.

Yields 6 to 8 servings

2 pounds (900 g) boned veal from shoulder, leg round, or loin
1 cup (225 g) butter, softened at room temperature
1 1/2 cups (355 ml) fine white bread crumbs
1 to 1 1/2 cups (235 to 355 ml) half-and-half
Salt
Freshly ground white pepper
1/4 cup (60 ml) Clarified Butter (see page 568)
1/4 cup (60 ml) peanut oil
2 teaspoons chopped fresh parsley
Juice of 2 lemons

Recommended equipment

A meat grinder with fine blade, large mixing bowl, plastic wrap, wooden spoon, waxed paper, 12-inch (30 cm) sauté pan, heatproof platter, 8-inch (20 cm) sauté pan.

The veal must be thoroughly chilled before grinding. Put the veal by chunks through the fine blade of the meat grinder, divide the ground veal into two equal parts, and regrind one of the portions. Put the ground veal into the mixing bowl, add all but 4 tablespoons (60 g) of the soft butter, 1 cup (235 ml) each of bread crumbs and half-and-half, salt, and pepper. Using your hands, blend the mixture thoroughly. Then cover the bowl with plastic wrap and put it into the refrigerator to chill and set for 20 to 30 minutes. The veal may be prepared up to this point several hours ahead.

When ready to cook the veal, remove the bowl from the refrigerator and, stirring with a wooden spoon, mix in enough of the remaining half-and-half so that the veal has a soft doughlike consistency. The mixture must not be runny. Lay waxed paper on your work surface and spread the remaining bread crumbs on the paper. Divide the veal into six or eight equal portions, shape each one into an oblong cutlet (or whatever shape you desire), about 1 to 1/4 inch (2 1/2 to 3 cm) thick, and roll each in the bread crumbs until thoroughly coated. (Refrigerate the veal again at this point if you are not ready to cook it.)

Preheat oven to 325F (163C).

Set the large sauté pan over medium high heat, add the clarified butter and peanut oil, and, when it is hot, add the veal cutlets and sauté until they are browned on one side. Turn them over and brown the other side (about 2 minutes per side). When they are nicely browned, set the pan into the oven to bake for 8 minutes.

While the veal is baking, wash the parsley, pat dry, and chop. Squeeze the lemons.

When the cutlets are baked, remove them from the oven, set them on the platter, and keep warm. Set the small sauté pan over medium heat, add the remaining butter, and when the butter is hot and foamy add the lemon juice and stir in the parsley. Remove from heat, pour over the cutlets, and serve them at once.

Roast Loin of Veal with Tarragon Cream Sauce

One of the most common complaints about roast veal is that it is overdone and therefore most unappetizing in appearance. However, if you watch your cooking time carefully, and are sure to let the meat rest before carving, you may be in danger of having no leftovers. Sautéed mushrooms and Tomatoes Provençale would provide excellent color contrast, and Spätzle or angel hair noodles will make the sauce vanish before your eyes.

Yields 6 to 8 servings

1 boned veal loin with flanks attached, weighing about 5 pounds (2250 g)
Salt
Freshly ground white pepper
2 slices pork fatback, 8 x 8 inches (20 x 20 cm) each and 1/8 to 1/4 inch (1/3 to 2/3 cm) thick
2 pounds (900 g) veal bones
4 sprigs fresh tarragon
1 medium onion
1/2 medium carrot
1 celery stalk
1 small garlic clove
A 2-inch (5 cm) piece of lemon peel
1 1/2 cups (355 ml) dry white wine
2 cups (475 ml) whipping cream
2 tablespoons Glace de Viande (see page 65)

Recommended equipment

White kitchen string, heavy roasting pan, cleaver, small chef's knife, swivel-bladed vegetable peeler, paring knife, aluminum foil, heatproof platter, wooden spatula, fine-mesh sieve, 2-quart (2 L) saucepan, slicing knife.

The veal loin must have the flanks attached so it can protect the very tender veal during cooking *(see illustrations)*. Season the inside of the loin lightly with salt and pepper, roll the flanks tightly around the loin, and tie it securely with string at 2-inch (5 cm) intervals. Wrap each end of the loin with a piece of the fatback and tie them on securely. Season the outside of the roast with salt and pepper and set it into the roasting pan with the flank side facing down.

Preheat oven to 375F (190C).

Using the cleaver, cut up the veal bones into 2-inch pieces and spread them around the roast. The bones and the roast should cover the bottom of the roasting pan. Set the roast into the oven to roast for 20 minutes, then reduce heat to 325F (163C) and roast another 20 minutes.

Meanwhile, prepare the vegetables. Rinse the tarragon sprigs gently, pat dry, pick off the leaves, reserving the stems, chop the leaves, and reserve. The stems will go into the pan with the other vegetables. Peel and halve the onion; peel and halve the carrot half; rinse and halve the celery stalk; peel the

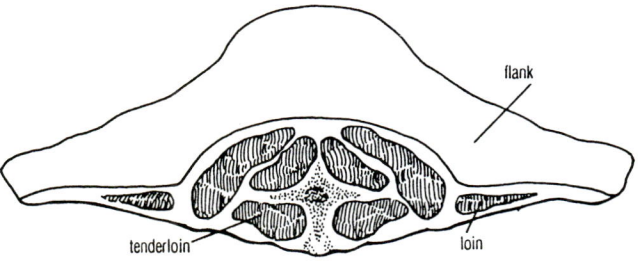

1. Top side of veal loin with bone, untrimmed flanks, loin, and fillet.

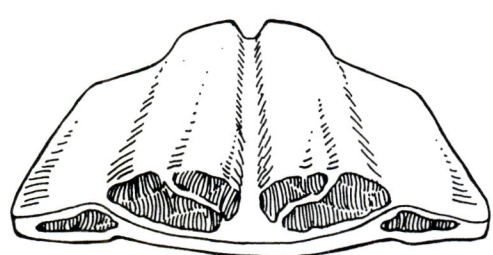

2. Bottom side of boned veal loin with flanks trimmed and fillet removed.

garlic clove; and cut a 2-inch strip of lemon peel (leaving the bitter white behind).

At the end of the roasting period, strew the tarragon stems, onion, carrot, celery, garlic clove, and lemon peel around the veal, and pour one-half of the wine around it. Cover the roast loosely with foil and set it back into the oven for 1 3/4 hours. Baste the roast with the pan juices two or three times and halfway through the cooking time pour the remaining wine around the roast. The bottom of the pan should be covered with liquid all the time, so you may have to add more wine than what is called for before the roast is finished cooking.

When the roast is done, remove it from the oven and set it on a platter, flank side facing down, to rest for 20 minutes in a warm (not hot) place.

Set the roasting pan over medium heat and remove all grease. Add the cream and glace de viande to the bones and vegetables, bring to a simmer, and cook, stirring and scraping up any brown bits from the pan bottom, until the liquid has been reduced to a creamy consistency. This should take about 10 to 15 minutes. Then strain the sauce through the sieve into the saucepan and keep warm. Adjust the seasoning if needed and stir in the reserved tarragon leaves. Add any juices from the platter to the sauce. Remove the strings and fatback from the roast, trim off the flank pieces, and slice into 1/8- to 1/4-inch (1/3 to 2/3 cm) thick slices. Spoon the sauce onto warm serving plates, arrange the slices on top, and serve at once.

The glace de viande should be veal based so as to keep the sauce as near a café au lait color as possible.

 ## *Rognonnade de Veau*
Roast Loin of Veal with Kidney Stuffing

This great Old World favorite is distinguished by the pattern created by its veal and kidney stuffing and the flavor imparted to the sauce by the bones roasting along with the meat. Be sure to give your butcher plenty of advance notice because the kidney, which makes the dish, is hard to come by. Since the flanks are rolled around the loin, they must be well trimmed, with all fat and gristle removed.

Yields 8 to 10 servings

1 boned veal loin with flanks attached, weighing about 5 pounds (2250 g)
1 veal kidney
6 ounces (170 g) veal trimmings or boned veal shoulder
1/3 cup (80 ml) fine white bread crumbs
6 tablespoons half-and-half
Salt
Freshly ground white pepper
2 slices pork fatback, 8 x 8 inches (20 x 20 cm) each and 1/8 to 1/4 inch (1/3 to 2/3 cm) thick
1 sprig fresh thyme
2 pounds (900 g) veal bones
1 medium onion
1/2 medium carrot
1 celery stalk
1 small garlic clove
1 1/2 cups (355 ml) dry white wine
1 1/2 cups (355 ml) Demi-glace Brun I *(see page 75)*

Recommended equipment

A boning knife, meat grinder with fine blade, 2-quart (2 L) mixing bowl, white kitchen string, heavy roasting pan, cleaver, small chef's knife, paring knife, swivel-bladed vegetable peeler, aluminum foil, heatproof platter, wooden spatula, fine-mesh sieve, 2-quart (2 L) saucepan, slicing knife.

Spread out the veal flanks *(see illustrations)* and be sure that they are well trimmed. Using the point of the boning knife, make 1/8-inch (1/3 cm) deep incisions on the inside of the flanks in a crisscross pattern. Trim all fat from the kidney and cut in half lengthwise. Prepare the veal stuffing by putting the veal trimmings through the fine blade of the meat grinder into the mixing bowl. Stir in the bread crumbs and half-and-half and season with salt and pepper. Place the kidney halves end to end next to the loin and pack the veal stuffing around them. Roll the flanks tightly around the loin and tie it securely with string at 2-inch (5 cm) intervals. Wrap each end of the loin with a piece of the fatback and tie them on securely. Season the outside of the roast with salt and pepper, rub with the thyme, and set it into the roasting pan with the flank side facing down.

Preheat oven to 375F (190C).

Using the cleaver, cut up the veal bones into 2-inch pieces and spread them around the roast. The bones and the roast should cover the bottom of the roasting pan. Set the meat into the oven to roast for 20 minutes, then reduce heat to 325F (163C) and cook another 20 minutes.

While the veal is roasting, prepare the vegetables. Peel and halve the onion; peel and halve the carrot half; rinse and halve the celery stalk; and peel the garlic clove.

When the veal has roasted for 40 minutes, remove it from the oven, strew the vegetables around the roast, turn it over, and pour one-half of the wine around it. Cover the roast loosely with foil and set it back into the oven to cook for 2 hours. Baste the roast with the pan juices two or three times and halfway through the cooking time pour the remaining wine around the roast. The bottom of the pan should be covered with liquid all the time, so you may have to add more wine than what is called for before the roast is finished cooking.

When the roast is done, remove it from the oven and set it on a platter, flank side facing down, to rest for 20 minutes in a warm (not hot) place.

Degrease the pan juices and set the roasting pan over medium high heat. Add the demi-glace, bring to a simmer, and cook for 10 minutes while stirring and scraping up any brown bits from the pan bottom. Then strain the sauce through the sieve into the saucepan, degrease, adjust seasoning if necessary, and keep warm. Add any juices from the platter to the sauce. Remove the strings and fatback from the roast, slice into 1/4-inch (2/3 cm) thick slices, spoon the sauce onto warm serving plates, arrange the slices on top, and serve at once.

Blanquette de Veau à l'ancienne
French Veal Stew in the Old Style

The traditional importance of this preparation in France is probably best summarized by Michelin three-star chef Michel Guérard, who noted that it is a "dish that evokes a strong emotional response because it has a very special meaning for many French people, who probably had it first at home made by Mother." As one would expect from the founder of la cuisine minceur, his recipe omits the egg yolks, cream, butter, and flour found in the ancient formulation. Here is another approach, which retains the old "bonne femme" method, while lightening it at the same time. No egg yolks are used, just a touch of roux thickens the sauce, and less than one-third of a cup per serving of cream provides the final sheen which we feel is simply a part of the tradition. Not minceur, but not likely to give you gout either, especially if you take a brisk stroll down the North Walking Trail right after lunch. Worthy of a Sunday family dinner or company meal, it can be served with noodles, Spätzle, or Riz Valencienne. For a lovely luncheon dish offer the veal in Vol-au-Vents, accompanied with a salad of mixed greens.

Yields 6 servings

2 to 2 1/4 pounds (900 to 1025 g) boneless veal shoulder
1 medium onion
1 celery stalk
1/3 bay leaf
1 sprig fresh parsley
1 quart (1 L) White Veal Stock (see page 63)
12 small white onions
12 medium mushrooms
1 1/2 teaspoons butter
1/2 cup (118 ml) dry white wine
1 1/2 tablespoons Blond Roux (see page 65)
A 1 1/2-inch (3 3/4 cm) piece of lemon peel (all bitter white removed)
1 cup (235 ml) whipping cream
1 teaspoon chopped fresh parsley
Salt
Freshly ground white pepper

Recommended equipment

A boning knife, 4- to 5-quart (4 to 5 L) saucepan with lid, colander, paring knife, cheesecloth, 3-quart (3 L) saucepan with lid, 1 1/2-quart (1 1/2 L) saucepan with lid, 10-inch (25 cm) sauté pan, wooden spatula, slotted spoon, swivel-bladed vegetable peeler, wire whisk, large fine-mesh sieve, small chef's knife.

Using the boning knife, trim the veal of all fat and gristle, cut it into 1 1/2-inch (3 3/4 cm) cubes, put them into the largest saucepan, cover them with hot water, and set the saucepan over high heat. Bring the pot to a boil, stir well, and boil for 10 seconds. Remove saucepan from heat, run cold water into it to rinse the veal thoroughly, and then drain the veal in the colander while you prepare the vegetables. Rinse out the saucepan and reserve.

Using the paring knife, peel and quarter the onion and halve the celery stalk. Rinse the parsley. Cut a piece of cheesecloth large enough to hold the vegetables, set them into it, add the bay leaf and parsley sprig, and tie the corners together. Put the drained veal into the 3-quart saucepan, set it over medium high heat, and add the cheesecloth bundle and the veal stock. Cover the saucepan, bring the veal to a boil, then adjust the heat so that the veal will maintain a steady simmer for about 1 to 1 1/4 hours, or until the veal is tender but not mushy.

While the veal is simmering, prepare the onions and mushrooms. For the onions, bring lightly salted water to a boil in the remaining saucepan, add the onions, and boil for 8 to 10 minutes or until tender. When done, drain the onions, refresh under cold running water, drain again, peel, and reserve.

For the mushrooms, brush them gently of any clinging dirt and halve them. Set the sauté pan over medium heat, add the butter, and, when it is hot, add the mushrooms, season them lightly with salt and pepper, and sauté, stirring, for 3 minutes. Remove pan from heat, scrape the mushrooms from the pan, and reserve them.

When the veal is tender, remove and discard the cheesecloth bundle and remove the veal with a slotted spoon to the reserved saucepan and set aside. Add the onions and mushrooms to the veal. Add the white wine to the sauce in the first saucepan and cook over medium high heat until the liquid is reduced to 2 cups (475 ml). While the sauce is reducing, prepare the blond roux and lemon peel. When the sauce is reduced, whisk in the roux, add the lemon peel, and bring the sauce to a boil, stirring constantly with the whisk. Add the cream, stir it in, and adjust the heat so that the sauce simmers gently for 10 minutes or until it has thickened to a creamy consistency. Strain the sauce through the sieve over the reserved veal, mushrooms, and onions in the saucepan, set the pan over medium heat, and bring the mixture to a gentle simmer for

3 minutes. While the veal is heating, rinse, dry, and chop the parsley and reserve. When the veal is hot, adjust the seasoning if necessary. If the sauce is too thin, simmer it a few more minutes; if too thick, add some more veal stock (or half-and-half). Serve the veal on warm plates and sprinkle each portion with parsley.

Côtes de Veau Bourguignonne
Veal Chops in the Style of Burgundy

This Burgundian preparation amply demonstrates that flavorful and hearty dishes are the hallmark of bourgeois country cooking. Earthy colors and textures abound, with red wine, tomato, mushrooms, and bacon set off by a simple but satisfying sauce. Because the dish can be made ahead of time, it also does well as a buffet offering. Be sure to serve noodles or Spätzle to soak up the sauce and have fresh String Beans, Carottes Glacées, or Asparagus on a side dish.

Yields 6 servings

6 veal rib or loin chops, 1/2 inch (1 1/4 cm) thick
3 tablespoons flour
Salt
Freshly ground black pepper
1/2 cup (118 ml) peanut oil
1/2 medium onion
1/2 celery stalk
1 medium garlic clove
1/4 teaspoon fresh thyme
1/2 medium bay leaf
1 tablespoon tomato paste
4 cups (950 ml) red Burgundy
2 cups (475 ml) Demi-glace Brun II *(see page 75)*
12 fresh mushrooms
2 tablespoons (30 g) butter
Juice of 1/4 lemon
12 whole pearl onions
1/2 teaspoon sugar
6 ounces (170 g) slab bacon
3 slices Pullman Loaf *(see page 488)*
2 teaspoons chopped fresh parsley

Recommended equipment

A boning knife, cleaver, small dish for flour, 12-inch (30 cm) sauté pan, turning spatula, paring knife, 4-quart (4 L) enameled cast-iron baking dish or lined copper plat à sauter, wooden spatula, aluminum foil, 10-inch (25 cm) sauté pan, small bowl, 1 1/2-quart (1 1/2 L) saucepan, slotted spoon, paper towels, heatproof platter, fine-mesh sieve, small chef's knife.

The veal chops should be cut either from the rack of veal or you can use veal steak cut from the loin. It is preferable to have the butcher do this for you because he will have a saw, but you can do this yourself with a sharp cleaver, boning knife, and sturdy cutting board.

For the veal chops: using the cleaver, split the rack of veal, remove the backbone, cut into chops and trim off the rib bones so they are 2 to 2 1/2 inches long (5 to 6 1/4 cm). With the boning knife, cut away the excess fat and flank around the bones.

For the veal steak: using the cleaver, remove the backbone from the veal loin and cut into 1/2-inch (1 1/4 cm) thick chops. With the boning knife, cut off excess flank, leaving 2 to 2 1/2 inches above the loin meat. Trim away excess fat.

Put the flour in the small dish and season with salt and pepper. Set the large sauté pan over medium high heat, add one-half of the peanut oil, and, while it is heating, dust three of the chops lightly with flour and shake off the excess. Reserve the other chops. Add the floured chops to the pan, and when they start to sizzle well, reduce the heat to medium and sauté until golden brown (4 to 5 minutes on each side). When done, remove from pan and set into the baking dish or plat à sauter. Dust the remaining chops with flour and sauté them in the same way in the remaining peanut oil.

While the last chops are sautéing, prepare the vegetables. Peel and quarter the onion; rinse and quarter the celery stalk; and peel the garlic clove. When the second batch of chops is done, set them in with the others. Degrease the sauté pan, add the onion, celery, garlic, thyme, and bay leaf, and sauté, stirring with the wooden spatula, for 1 1/2 minutes. Then add the tomato paste, blend well, add the red wine, bring to a simmer, and simmer over high heat until reduced by one-half, scraping up the brown bits from the pan bottom.

When the sauce is reduced, add the demi-glace, bring the sauce back to a simmer, and then add the sauce and vegetables to the veal chops.

Preheat oven to 300F (149C).

Set the chops over medium low heat, bring to a simmer, cover the baking dish or plat à sauter loosely with aluminum foil, and set into the oven to bake for 30 minutes.

While the chops are baking, prepare the mushrooms, pearl onions, bacon lardons, and croutons. Brush the mushrooms gently of any clinging dirt; if they are small, leave whole, and if large, halve them. Set the smaller sauté pan over medium heat, add 1/2 teaspoon butter, lemon juice, a pinch of salt, and the mushrooms. Sauté, stirring, for 3 minutes and then scrape the mushrooms into a small bowl and reserve.

For the pearl onions, fill the saucepan two-thirds full with water, add a little salt, set over high heat, and bring to a boil. Add the onions, cook them for 10 minutes, drain, and run cold water over them. When cool enough to handle, peel the onions with the paring knife. (If you use canned onions, do not boil them, and proceed with the recipe at this point.) Add 1/2 teaspoon sugar and 1 1/2 teaspoons butter to the small sauté pan and set over medium heat. Simmer the butter and sugar together for 1 minute before adding the onions and then sauté them over medium high heat until they are glacéed and golden brown. When done, remove the onions with the slotted spoon and reserve them in the bowl with the mushrooms.

For the lardons, trim off the rind (reserve it for the bean pot, soup, or a stew) and cut the bacon into pieces 1/4 inch thick and 1 inch long (2/3 by 2 1/2 cm). Wash out the small sauté pan, set over medium low heat, add the lardons, and sauté them until crisp. When done, remove with the slotted spoon to drain on folded paper towels.

For the croutons, cut the bread slices into strips 2 inches long and 1/2 inch wide (5 by 1 1/4 cm). Add 1 tablespoon butter to the bacon fat in the sauté pan, set over low heat, add the croutons, and sauté until golden brown, stirring and turning them as necessary. When done, remove them from the pan to drain on paper towels and reserve.

When the chops have finished baking, remove the dish from the oven and remove the chops to a heatproof platter. Skim all fat from the sauce in the pan and strain it through the sieve into a clean saucepan. Taste and adjust seasoning if necessary. If the sauce is too thick, add a little red wine or veal stock. If you are not ready to serve the chops, keep them uncovered at room temperature and dot the sauce with bits of butter or a few drops of red wine to prevent a skin from forming. When you are ready to serve, heat the oven to 275F (135C). Pour the sauce over the chops on the heatproof platter and arrange the mushrooms, onions, and bacon on top. Set the chops into the oven for 2 to 3 minutes (or longer if they have been waiting for you) and heat. While they are heating, rinse the parsley, pat dry, chop with the chef's knife, and reserve. When the chops are hot, remove from the oven, arrange the croutons on top, sprinkle with the parsley, and serve at once.

Variation: For a different flavor, use a dry white wine instead of the red Burgundy and 1 cup (235 ml) of demi-glace, and whisk in 3/4 cup (180 ml) Crème Fraîche *(see page 66)* after degreasing and straining the sauce.

Ossobuco alla Milanese
Veal Shank in the Style of Milan

"Osso" means bone, and "buco" means hole, and that is where you find the marrow which is the reason to prepare and enjoy this nourishing Italian gift to cuisine. Known colloquially in Milan as oss bus, *the meat for this comes from the shank (which in Trieste is prepared whole and known as* schinco*)—specifically the hind shank—which while it may be difficult to obtain, is preferable to the foreshank because it is more tender and has more meat. Have your butcher saw the center section of each shank into serving portions and save the sawn-off ends to bring home for the stockpot. To be really authentic, serve Risotto alla Milanese, perhaps a Bardolino from the Lago di Garda region, and prepare to be rewarded by this northern Italian feast.*

Yields 6 servings

2 to 3 veal shanks, weighing 3 to 4 pounds (1350 to 1800 g) each, cut into pieces 1 3/4 to 2 1/4 inches (4 1/2 to 6 1/4 cm) thick
1/3 cup (40 g) flour
Salt
Freshly ground white pepper
3 tablespoons olive oil
1 medium onion
1/2 stalk celery
1/3 carrot
1 garlic clove
1 medium tomato
1 tablespoon tomato paste
2 cups (475 ml) dry white wine
2 cups (475 ml) Demi-glace Brun II *(see page 76)*

FOR THE GREMOLADA
1 tablespoon chopped fresh parsley
Peel of 1/2 lemon
1/3 garlic clove
A pinch of oregano

Recommended equipment

Dutch oven with lid, paring knife, small chef's knife, garlic press, wooden spatula, basting spoon, heatproof serving platter, fine-mesh sieve, 1 1/2-quart (1 1/2 L) saucepan.

Season the flour with salt and pepper on your work surface, dredge the shank pieces in the flour, shake off the excess, and reserve the pieces.

Set the Dutch oven over medium high heat, add the olive oil, and, when it is hot, add the first batch of shank pieces. When the veal begins to sizzle well, adjust the heat to medium and sauté until well browned on all sides and a good crust has formed. This will take at least 10 minutes, and cannot be hurried because the crust is essential for a full-flavored sauce.

While the veal is browning, prepare the vegetables. Peel the onion and chop it coarsely with the chef's knife. Rinse the celery, chop it coarsely, and do likewise with the carrot. Peel the garlic clove. Halve the tomato and seed and quarter it. Reserve the vegetables.

When the first batch of veal is browned, remove the pieces to a plate, add oil to the Dutch oven if necessary, and brown the rest of the veal. When it is finished, remove the meat and add it to the plate with the first batch. Pour off all but about 1/2 tablespoon of fat from the Dutch oven, set over medium high heat, add the onion, celery, and carrot, and press in the garlic. Sauté, stirring with the wooden spatula, for 2 minutes before adding the tomato and tomato paste. Blend well and add the wine, stirring for 5 minutes and scraping up all the brown bits from the pan bottom. Return the shank pieces to the Dutch oven, along with any juices from the plate.

Preheat oven to 325F (163C).

Set the Dutch oven over medium high heat, add the demi-glace, and bring to a simmer. Then cover the pot and set into the oven to cook for 1 1/2 to 2 hours or until the meat is fork tender. Skim the fat from the surface twice with the basting spoon while the veal is braising.

When the veal shanks are done, remove them from the Dutch oven, set them on the heatproof platter, and keep in a warm (not hot) spot until ready to serve. Strain the sauce from the Dutch oven through the sieve into a clean saucepan and set over low heat. If needed, skim the sauce and adjust the seasoning. Keep the sauce warm while you prepare the gremolada.

Rinse the parsley, pat dry, and chop what you need. Remove the peel of 1/2 lemon, leaving the bitter white behind, and chop it finely. Chop the garlic finely. Mix the parsley, lemon peel, and garlic together and season with a pinch of oregano.

When ready to serve, pour the warm sauce over the veal, sprinkle the gremolada over all, and carry to the table at once.

The ossobuco can be prepared hours ahead of time and heated gently over low heat until ready to serve. In this case, when the veal has finished cooking, cover it with the finished sauce, dot the sauce with bits of butter to prevent a skin from forming, and set aside in a cool spot until ready to reheat. Sprinkle the gremolada over the veal just before serving.

Foies de Veau Suisse
Calf's Liver in the Swiss Style

In Switzerland we are very particular about preparing this dish. The liver must be calf's, not beef, be very fresh, and kept refrigerated until the last moment before it is sautéed very quickly over high heat in peanut oil. (Butter will burn and leave a bitter aftertaste.) The shallots must be just barely cooked with the peppercorns before the vinegar deglaze and simmering with demi-glace. When the sauce and accompanying garnish or vegetable are ready (and only then) you sauté the liver because it does not hold well, not even for a few minutes. If you serve this with crisp bacon and Roesti, you may have to prepare more the next time for those sheepish little customers who were heard to say before dinner, "Aw, Mom, not liver."

Yields 6 servings

1 1/2 pounds (675 g) calf's liver
2 tablespoons chopped shallots
1 tablespoon (15 g) butter
1 teaspoon green peppercorns (packed in water and drained)
1/4 cup (60 ml) red wine vinegar
2/3 cup (160 ml) Demi-glace Brun I *(see page 75)*
1 tablespoon chopped fresh parsley
1/3 bunch watercress
3 tablespoons flour
Salt
Freshly ground white pepper
6 tablespoons peanut oil

Recommended equipment

A paring knife, slicing knife, small chef's knife, 1 1/2-quart (1 1/2 L) saucepan, wooden spatula, fine-mesh sieve, small bowl for flour, waxed paper, 12-inch (30 cm) sauté pan, turning spatula.

Rinse the liver gently under cold running water and trim it of all skin with the paring knife. Using the slicing knife, cut the liver into twelve pieces about 1/4 inch (2/3 cm) thick or less, and refrigerate, wrapped, until needed.

Chop the shallots. Set the saucepan over medium heat, add 2 teaspoons butter, and, when it is hot, add the shallots to the pan. Stir in the peppercorns and sauté, stirring with the wooden spatula, for 1 minute without browning the shallots. Then add the vinegar and deglaze the pan for 2 minutes before adding the demi-glace. Adjust heat so that the sauce maintains a low simmer for 10 minutes. Then remove from heat, strain through the sieve into a clean saucepan, dot the top of the sauce with the remaining butter (to prevent the formation of a skin), and keep the sauce warm.

Rinse the parsley, pat dry, chop what you need, and reserve. Rinse the watercress, pat dry, and reserve.

Season the flour with salt and pepper in the small bowl and dredge the liver pieces in the mixture one by one. Pat the flour on both sides of each piece, shake off any excess flour, and lay the pieces on a sheet of waxed paper.

Set the sauté pan over high heat and add 3 tablespoons peanut oil. Heat until the oil is almost smoking, then add some liver slices—do not crowd the pan—and reduce the heat to medium high. The liver must be sautéed in batches, adding more oil as needed, so that the pan and oil stay hot. Within 15 seconds a brown crust should have formed on one side, so turn the liver pieces over, sauté another 15 seconds, and remove them immediately to a warm platter. For liver that is medium to well done, add 5 to 10 seconds to the sautéing time for each side. When all the liver has been sautéed, spoon the sauce on a warm serving dish or plates, set the liver on the sauce, sprinkle with parsley, garnish with watercress sprigs, and serve immediately.

Variation

Sauté de Foies de Veau au Madère
Sautéed Calf's Liver with Madeira Sauce

Rinse and trim the liver as described above. Then either slice or mince it. If you mince the liver, the cooking procedure differs slightly: dust the liver with flour rather than dredge it, and use Clarified Butter *(see page 568)* instead of oil. When sautéing, do not crowd the pan and stir the liver with a fork to turn the pieces over and over for 15 seconds. Then scrape the liver into a fine-mesh sieve set over a bowl to drain. Remove all but 1 tablespoon of fat from the pan, add the shallots, and sauté, stirring until they are light brown. Omit the vinegar and green peppercorns, but add 1/4 cup (60 ml) Madeira and the demi-glace, and simmer for 3 minutes. Remove the sauté pan from heat, stir the liver into the sauce, and serve at once.

Braised Sweetbreads with Sherry Favorite

Here is yet another example of the major role Catherine de' Medici played in bringing sophisticated culinary tastes to France. Along with truffles and artichokes, she introduced sweetbreads, and indeed veal probably enjoys its popularity north of the Alps because of her. Sweetbreads are not for everybody, but for those who appreciate them, a meal centered around this preparation or the more elegant one which follows can provide one of cuisine's greatest moments.

Yields 6 to 7 servings

FOR BLANCHING THE SWEETBREADS
2 pairs calf sweetbreads, weighing about 2 to 2 1/2 pounds (900 to 1125 g) each
1 tablespoon salt
Juice of 1/2 lemon

FOR BRAISING THE SWEETBREADS
1 small onion
1 celery stalk
1/2 medium carrot
1/3 bay leaf
Salt
Freshly ground white pepper
1/2 cup (118 ml) White Veal Stock or White Chicken Stock *(see pages 63 and 61)*
1/2 cup (118 ml) dry white wine
Butter for the baking dish

FOR THE SAUCE
1/2 cup (118 ml) dry sherry
2/3 cup (160 ml) whipping cream
3 tablespoons Glace de Viande *(see page 65)*
2 teaspoons Blond Roux *(see page 65)*

FOR THE GARNISH
3 ounces (85 g) ham, boiled, Virginia, or prosciutto
1 celery stalk
1/2 medium red bell pepper
6 mushrooms
1 leek
2 teaspoons butter
1 tablespoon dry sherry

Recommended equipment

A 5-quart (5 L) saucepan, 3-quart (3 L) saucepan, paring knife, nonmetallic baking dish 11 x 7 x 2 inches (27 1/2 x 17 1/2 x 5 cm), swivel-bladed vegetable peeler, aluminum foil, heatproof platter, fine-mesh sieve, 2-quart (2 L) saucepan, wire whisk, 10-inch (25 cm) sauté pan, wooden spatula.

Set the sweetbreads into the largest saucepan, cover them with cold water, and let them soak for several hours. Change the water twice during this period. (As an alternative, set the pot under running cold water for 30 minutes.)

After the sweetbreads have finished soaking, set them into the 3-quart saucepan, cover with fresh, cold water, add the salt, lemon juice, and the squeezed lemon half. Set the saucepan over medium high heat, bring to the boil, and then adjust heat so that the pot simmers for 5 minutes. When done, remove pan from heat and run cold water into the pot until the sweetbreads are completely cool. Then drain water off, set the sweetbreads on your cutting board, and, using the paring knife, trim away the white membranes, gristle, fat, and all skin. Split the large sections of the sweetbreads in half lengthwise (leave the smaller pieces whole) and reserve.

Preheat oven to 325F (163C).

Rub your baking dish with butter and set aside while you prepare the braising vegetables. Using the paring knife, peel the onion and cut into slices 1/4 inch (2/3 cm) thick. Rinse and trim the celery stalk and slice into pieces 1/4 inch thick. Rinse and peel the carrot half and cut into slices 1/4 inch thick. Strew the vegetables in the baking dish, add the bay leaf, and arrange the sweetbreads, split sides facing up, over the vegetables. Season the sweetbreads lightly with salt and pepper, pour the stock and wine around them, cover the dish with aluminum foil, and set into the oven to bake for 15 minutes. Then remove foil and bake another 15 minutes.

When the sweetbreads are done, remove them from the oven, set them on the heatproof platter, and keep them warm. Press the liquid from the baking dish through the sieve into the small saucepan. (Discard the solids.) Add the sherry, cream, glace de viande, and roux. Set the saucepan over medium heat and bring the sauce to a boil, while stirring with the whisk. Then adjust heat so that the sauce simmers and cook, stirring occasionally, until it has been reduced by one-half and has a smooth, creamy consistency. This should take about 10 to 15 minutes. Then taste, adjust seasoning if needed, and keep the sauce warm.

While the sauce is simmering, prepare the garnish. Trim the ham of any fat and slice into julienne strips. Rinse and peel the celery and slice into julienne strips. Seed the pepper half and slice into julienne strips. Brush the mushrooms of any clinging dirt and slice both caps and stems into 1/4-inch wide strips. Rinse the leek under running cold water while separating the layers to rid it of all sand. Let drain briefly and then slice the leek into julienne strips.

Set the sauté pan over medium heat, add the butter, and, when it is hot, add the ham, sauté for 30 seconds, and then add the celery, red pepper, mushrooms, and leek. Sauté, stirring, for 1 minute, add the sherry, simmer for 30 seconds, and remove from heat.

To serve, arrange the sweetbreads on warm serving plates (or leave them on the platter), spread the ham and vegetable julienne garnish with its liquid over the sweetbreads, cover with the sauce, and serve at once. (If the sweetbreads need to be rewarmed, heat them, covered with the garnish and sauce, for a minute or two in a 325F oven before serving.)

Variation

Braised Sweetbreads Catherine de' Medici

It is fitting to name a recipe after this legendary figure, for, political machinations aside, she is somewhat of a patron saint of our culinary tradition. Her influence made spinach synonymous with Florence, and the elegance captured here is evocative of such gastronomic watering holes as Sabatini on via de' Panzani or Doney on via de' Tornabuoni.

Braise the sweetbreads as above, then arrange them on a bed of blanched spinach, garnish with mushrooms, and nap with either the sherry sauce or a Madeira sauce. For the spinach, blanch two 10-ounce (285 g) bags of fresh, well-washed spinach, squeeze the water from it, season with salt, freshly ground white pepper, and nutmeg to taste, and sauté it in several tablespoons of butter. For the mushrooms, use twelve mushrooms sliced into 1/4-inch (2/3 cm) thick pieces and sauté them in 2 teaspoons butter with 2 teaspoons chopped shallots until the mushrooms are lightly browned. For the Madeira sauce, follow the instructions for the sherry sauce but use 1/4 cup (60 ml) Madeira rather than sherry.

Sautéed Sweetbreads Souvaroff

A Souvaroff preparation means truffles and foie gras—usually associated with chicken breasts—but this recipe poses the ultimate contrast of voluptuous textures punctuated with bits of black diamond. For a truly Lucullan presentation you can replace the Beurre au Citron with Sauce Périgueux, but I think the tartness of the lemon sauce is the best contrast for the richness of the sweetbreads. If you prefer a less opulent stuffing, try the Cordon Bleu variation, and for no stuffing at all, the Gismonda may suit your purposes. Serve fresh Asparagus with Carottes Glacées or Tomatoes Provençale as accompaniments for any of these.

Yields 6 to 7 servings

FOR BLANCHING THE SWEETBREADS
2 pairs calf sweetbreads, weighing about 2 to 2 1/2 pounds (900 to 1125 g) each
1 tablespoon salt
Juice of 1/2 lemon

FOR STUFFING AND SAUTÉING
4 ounces (115 g) foie gras
1 ounce (30 g) truffle
1/2 cup (60 g) flour
Salt
Freshly ground white pepper
2 eggs
3 tablespoons water
2 cups (475 ml) fine white bread crumbs
3 tablespoons peanut oil
2 tablespoons Clarified Butter *(see page 568)*

2 recipes Beurre au Citron with parsley *(see page 83)*

Recommended equipment

A 5-quart (5 L) saucepan; 3-quart (3 L) saucepan; paring knife; platter, sheet pan, or tray; 1-quart (1 L) mixing bowl; wire whisk; 12-inch (30 cm) sauté pan; wooden spatula; nonmetallic baking dish 11 x 7 x 2 inches (27 1/2 x 17 1/2 x 5 cm); paper towels or rack; 8-inch (20 cm) sauté pan.

Set the sweetbreads into the largest saucepan, cover them with cold water, and let them soak for several hours. Change the water twice during this period. (As an alternative, set the pot under running cold water for 30 minutes.)

After the sweetbreads have finished soaking, set them into the 3-quart saucepan, cover with fresh, cold water, add the salt, lemon juice, and the squeezed lemon half. Set the saucepan over medium high heat, bring to the boil, and then adjust heat so the the pot simmers for 5 minutes. When done, remove pan from heat and run cold water into the pot until the sweetbreads are completely cool.

When the sweetbreads are cool, drain them and set them on a cutting board. Using the paring knife, trim away the white membranes, gristle, fat, and all covering tissues. For the larger sweetbread sections, use your finger to loosen the covering tissues. Place the larger sections on a platter (reserve the small pieces for another use, such as in a cream sauce served over rice or toast). Cover them with a damp kitchen towel (wrung out in cold water) and set a sheet pan (or tray) on top of the towel. Put several heavy cans or other weight to equal about two pounds on top of the pan and set the sweetbreads into the refrigerator for 30 minutes.

Remove the sweetbreads from the refrigerator, remove the weight and towel, and, using the paring knife, make a pocket in each sweetbread by cutting lengthwise into the front by 2 to 2 1/2 inches (5 to 6 1/4 cm). Slice the foie gras into pieces 1/8 to 1/4 inch (1/3 to 2/3 cm) thick and slice the truffle very thinly. Fill the pockets with foie gras and truffle slices, press the sweetbreads back together, and dust lightly with the flour, which has been seasoned with salt and pepper. Mix the eggs and water thoroughly with the whisk in the bowl. Spread the bread crumbs on your work surface. One at a time, dip each sweetbread piece in the egg mixture and then roll it around in the bread crumbs. Pat the crumbs on gently to make them stick. Dip the pocket side a second time in the egg wash and bread crumbs for a secure seal.

Preheat oven to 275F (135C).

Set the large sauté pan over medium heat and add the peanut oil and clarified butter. Heat the pan until a drop of water sizzles when dropped into it. When the pan is hot, add the sweetbreads in a single layer and do not crowd the pan. (Sauté them in two batches if necessary, adding more oil and butter as needed.) Sauté the sweetbreads until golden brown (about 4 to 5 minutes) and then turn over gently to sauté for 3 to 4 more minutes.

Then remove them from the pan and sauté the second batch in the same way. Or, if you had only one batch, set the sauté pan with the sweetbreads in it into the oven to bake for 10 minutes. (If the sweetbreads are large, bake for 15 minutes.) If you have two batches, let the first wait in the baking dish until the second is done and bake them both at the same time. When done, remove the sweetbreads from the oven, lift them from the pan or dish, and set them on a rack or paper towels to drain while you prepare the beurre au citron.

Set the small sauté pan over medium heat, and prepare the sauce.

Divide the sweetbreads among warm serving plates, spoon the lemon butter sauce over them, and serve at once.

Variation

Sautéed Sweetbreads Cordon Bleu

Prepare the sweetbreads as in the main recipe. Fill the pockets with a thin slice of Emmentaler cheese wrapped around a thin slice of ham. Do not allow the ham to come into contact with the sweetbread because the ham cure discolors the meat. Then bread and sauté the sweetbreads according to the recipe.

Variation

Sautéed Sweetbreads Gismonda

Prepare the sweetbreads as in the main recipe. Split the sweetbreads in half (rather than making a pocket) and bread them with 1 1/4 cups (295 ml) bread crumbs and 3/4 cup (180 ml) grated Parmesan. Then sauté the sweetbreads according to the recipe. As an alternative to the beurre au citron, deglaze the sauté pan with sherry, add 1 or 2 teaspoons of drained capers, and whisk in a few tablespoons of softened butter.

Roast Tenderloin of Beef London House with Truffle Sauce

Beef, Lamb, and Pork

> To be free-minded and cheerfully disposed at hours of meat and of sleep and of exercise is one of the best precepts of long lasting.
>
> —Francis Bacon

Sir Francis Bacon probably could have written the promotional fliers that were distributed in neighboring colonies had he been living when Thomas Bullitt constructed the first lodge in Hot Springs, for no Madison Avenue phrase sculptor can better describe the philosophy of the Homestead. Of course, "meat" in sixteenth-century England was a more general term for food as was the French *viande*, drawn from *vivenda*, Latin for "that which maintains life." For Upper Paleolithic man, however, this meant the hunt, as the magnificent Lascaux paintings tell us. Located in the Dordogne, these cave paintings (dating from 15,000 to 13,000 B.C.) are powerful and energetic depictions of bulls, who were clearly hunted for meat to sustain life. And French hunting language still sustains this ancient connection between meat and sustenance in using *viander* to describe the pasturing of wild animals.

Along with its substantial vegetable, flower, dairy, and poultry operations, the Homestead, at one time, raised or purchased much of its meat in the Warm Springs Valley, and one look at B. G. McElwee's Shopping List will convince you that "hours of meat" are still a serious business in our kitchen. The total weekly average weight of beef, lamb, and pork in the meat cooler is about seven thousand pounds, to which must be added an additional eighteen hundred pounds of ribs of beef for the aging cooler. Add the veal from the previous chapter, and you will arrive at nearly five tons of meat per week. *Very* serious business indeed.

If you have read our introductions to the other chapters, it is probably obvious by now that we advocate moderation in culinary matters. Perhaps, like many of our colleagues here and abroad, we feel that there is a tradition we must honor and nourish—in spite of what some of our publicized confrères are doing. We were saddened, for example, to see a recent cookbook, written by an eminent author in the field, omit recipes for pork and make only a passing nod in the direction of veal, lamb, and beef.

This book does contain a large number of preparations for fish and poultry but it is as much a matter of illustrating important techniques as it is of dietary importance. We respect absolutely a moral or religious position which forbids consuming meat, but we neither agree with nor have any patience for the extremists who preach to us one day about eating X and a few years later about not eating X any more and eating Y instead. To extend Escoffier a bit, we should perhaps also be wary of "novelty" in nutrition. Do not misunderstand my position. In our kitchen, we are innovating and modifying preparations every day, but we are not willy-nilly going to stop serving beef, for example. As a case in point, this book goes to press just as some research suggests that lean beef contains some chemical compounds that actually help to control cholesterol. The main conclusion is that dietary common sense combined with daily exercise has served millions for centuries and is likely to continue to do so. Like Craig Claiborne, we cannot understand those who "live in mortal dread of high-calorie foods . . . while mindlessly gorging themselves on all sorts of . . . junk foods." Well, class dismissed, let us go back to the meat cooler.

One word about selection in this chapter. This is an eclectic group of beef, lamb, and pork recipes, based on my personal preferences as well as the awareness that there is a surfeit of cookbook preparations for steaks and chops, let alone those dog-eared family favorites in your recipe box. You may be surprised that we have no recipe for roast standing ribs of beef, even though we serve vast quantities of it. The reason for this is simple and one instance in which we actually outdo our Michelin three-star French colleagues. They rightly insist on Charolais beef and we insist on (and pay a premium for) only the best beef our dealers can find. Then it is dry-aged to our specifications, and, upon arrival at the Homestead, is kept in our aging cooler for another week—a process requiring facilities and space most restaurants can ill afford. So, having said this, if you do want to cook a standing rib roast, let us refer you to *Julia Child and Company* for an excellent fail-safe technique. But for the flavor, you will have to come to Hot Springs.

As you look through these recipes you will find more entries for beef and lamb than pork. This is due to the fact that some of the pork we serve is either in the form of charcuterie for buffets or various kinds of cold weather luncheon preparations using European-style sausages not always available outside major urban areas. In all three groups, we have included recipes ranging from simple to complex so you have a choice depending upon your guests and the occasion—be it backyard barbecue or a candlelit feast in the baronial hall. So, thumb through the chapter, plan some "hours of meat," and give your butcher a call.

❧ Beef

> Further away, we stepped into the butchers' department. Men with white aprons stood around sides of beef and legs of veal. Some were cutting steaks. At full capacity the *France* needed over two thousand pounds of meat daily. If more steak orders than expected would come in, the butchers would quickly cut additional portions and send them to the grill station.
>
> One butcher worked on a side of American beef. The meat, from a fattened animal, was handsomely marbled. It would be easy to eat and also less flavorful to eat than steaks from Charolles that were prepared nearby. The meat had a thin yellowish crust, it looked tougher, and when Le Huédé pressed his thumb in, one didn't see the imprint as clearly as in the American meat. Inevitably, comparisons were made. They were as pointless as arguments among opera lovers over the respective virtues of Verdi versus Wagner. Both can be wonderful.
>
> —Joseph Wechsberg

As a matter of record, one of the butchers on the *France* baited Joseph Wechsberg by asking him to choose between French and American beef, which he tried to sidestep as gingerly as possible. Chef Le Huédé, however, finally settled the matter by saying that first-class source of supply rather than "narrow-minded chauvinism" was the rule in any good kitchen, which meant buying French beef in Le Havre, English beef in Southampton, and American beef in New York. We do the same, and so should you. If you have a local butcher shop, patronize it if you can because you will most likely get fresher and better meat there than in a large chain, not to mention having it trimmed to order.

Our beef tour starts, appropriately, in the backyard, where some of the best meals are often to be had. In fact, we will go so far as to say that an *excellent* hamburger is one of cuisine's greatest challenges, but that is for another book. In any event we start with barbecue—yes, barbecue. Because there are so many lovely, outdoor locations in the environs of Hot Springs, picnics are very popular among our guests. And the two marinated rib recipes which begin this section are among their favorites. The first is orientally inspired and is infused with the pungency of ginger. The second receives a more complex sweet and sour marinade and is finished off with a honey glaze. Before getting on to the tenderloin recipes, there are two classic, and we mean *classic*, stews from the Old World—one for a whole piece of beef and one for stew beef. Germany leads off with a vinegar and wine marinated specialty characteristic of the Palatinate and France follows suit with a richly flavored dish which is as much a part of Burgundy as a boiled dinner is of New England. All four of these dishes are drawn from simple bourgeois cuisine (country cooking, if you like). They are hearty, intensely flavored, and meant to be enjoyed around the family table or in a gemütlich setting with close friends. Now we begin to move indoors to the crystal, fine china, and nappery which awaits us at the end of the section.

First comes a real favorite of ours, which actually can be grilled, broiled, or sautéed—steak. We know what we said above about there being too many steak recipes but this one is too good to pass up. The secret is the marinade, and, before you say, "What? Marinate steaks? *Never!*" read it through. We think you will be quite surprised. The remaining preparations call for tenderloin, which is a paradox because it is at once the most expensive and tender cut of beef, but, by itself, the least flavorful. Purchase the whole tenderloin, known in England (and America) as a "fillet" and in France as a "filet" (hence the term "filet mignon"), because these recipes will allow you to use every bit of it.

The tenderloin quintet begins in Imperial Russia, this time in Saint Petersburg, where a French accent (possibly Carême's) enlivens a traditional beef sauté with mushrooms and a sour cream sauce made rosy with concentrated tomatoes. The French influence asserts itself in the two following sliced tenderloin sautés, both of which prominently feature fresh vegetables. In the first they simmer with demi-glace to produce a dark and richly flavored sauce. In the second, a last minute wine deglaze with demi-glace added yields a more pointed sauce and the vegetables are cooked only al dente so their color and texture play well against the sauce. Two quite different roasted tenderloins conclude the quintet. The first preparation and its variation illustrate that pepper and beef can be an extraordinary combination without having to taste like five-alarm chili. Three different kinds of pepper form the dry marinade for the tenderloin in the first recipe, and the beef is finished with an Armagnac sauce. In the variation, black pepper and Armagnac play a more pronounced role, but they are held in check by the flavor and texture of raisins, the end result being a sauce you will be sure to make many times. The finale for this quintet, like English Beef Tea, is elegant and intense. Foie gras fills the tenderloin and a Périgueux-style sauce accompanies it, producing an entrée which should be the center of a winter ingathering of gastronomes.

Well, Charolais, County Durham Shorthorn, Black Angus, or Kobe (especially for the recipe that follows), buy some good short ribs, go to your local produce market for some fresh Silver (or Golden) Queen corn, dust off the picnic basket and cloth, and get ready to cook. I'll meet you in the kitchen.

Teriyaki Marinated Short Ribs of Beef Homestead

Short ribs are well worth waiting for when you follow such a simple preparation, and if you wish to observe the Japanese origin of the sauce, grill the ribs slowly over a hibachi. The marinade is equally good for chicken or spareribs. Adjust the marinating time accordingly and cook them by either method. Any leftover marinade will keep well, covered tightly, in the refrigerator (or it can be frozen).

Yields 6 servings

6 beef short ribs, weighing about 6 pounds (2700 g) in all

FOR THE MARINADE
1 1/2 cups (355 ml) soy sauce
1 1/2 cups (355 ml) teriyaki sauce
1 cup (195 g) light brown sugar
1/2 cup (100 g) sugar
1/2 cup (118 ml) water
1 tablespoon Aromat
4 garlic cloves
5 tablespoons chopped or grated fresh ginger

Recommended equipment

A paring knife; 4-quart (4 L) glass, ceramic, or stainless steel bowl; 2-quart mixing bowl; garlic press; small chef's knife; wire whisk; plastic wrap; broiler pan; aluminum foil; rack for draining ribs.

With the paring knife, trim excess fat from the beef ribs and put them into the marinating bowl.

Measure out the first six ingredients of the marinade and put them into the other bowl. Peel the garlic cloves and crush them into the bowl. Peel the ginger root and either chop or grate it, add it to the bowl, and blend all ingredients thoroughly with the whisk. Then pour the marinade over the ribs, cover tightly with plastic wrap, and set into the refrigerator to marinate for three to four days. Turn the ribs over once during this period.

When the ribs are ready to cook, preheat the oven to 300F (149C). Remove the ribs from the marinade and lay them in the broiler pan in a single layer. Spoon on enough marinade to cover the bottom of the pan by 1/2 inch (1 1/4 cm). Cover the dish tightly with aluminum foil and set into the oven to bake until tender, about 2 to 2 1/2 hours depending upon the size and thickness of the ribs.

When the ribs are done, let them rest for 10 minutes, covered, in the pan, and then remove them to a rack set over another pan to drain them of all grease. If the ribs seem too cool, they can be reheated in the oven before serving.

Barbecued Short Ribs of Beef Homestead

When packing these ribs for a picnic, you will appreciate having prepared them ahead of time. All you need to do when you are hungry is to reheat them on a charcoal grill. Be sure to include Ambassador Potato Salad and Pressed Cucumber Salad, whether for a tailgate away from home or in your own backyard. Above all, fix more than enough, because even then, the plates will be picked clean. Unfortunately, the best phrase for describing these ribs was patented by a certain Kentucky colonel years ago, but you get the idea.

Yields 6 servings

6 beef short ribs, weighing about 6 pounds (2700 g) in all

FOR THE MARINADE
1 cup (235 ml) ketchup
1/3 cup (80 ml) soy sauce
1 tablespoon grated fresh ginger
3 garlic cloves
1 tablespoon dry English mustard
1/3 cup (80 ml) white vinegar
1/2 cup (118 ml) pineapple juice
1/4 cup (50 g) light brown sugar
3/8 cup (90 ml) dry sherry
A few drops Tabasco sauce
Salt
Freshly ground black pepper

FOR THE GLAZE
1/4 cup (60 ml) honey

Recommended equipment

A paring knife; 4-quart (4 L) glass, ceramic, or stainless steel bowl; 1-quart (1 L) mixing bowl; garlic press; box grater; wire whisk; plastic wrap; broiler pan; aluminum foil; rack with pan for glazing ribs; pastry brush.

With the paring knife, trim excess fat from the beef ribs and put them in the marinating bowl.

Put the ketchup and soy sauce in the mixing bowl. Peel the fresh ginger root and grate it into the bowl. Peel the garlic cloves and crush them into the bowl. Add the remaining ingredients except the Tabasco, mix well with the whisk until the mustard is dissolved, then add Tabasco to your taste, and pour the sauce over the short ribs. Cover tightly with plastic wrap and refrigerate for two to three days. Turn the ribs over once during this period.

When the ribs are ready to cook, preheat the oven to 300F (149C). Remove the ribs from the refrigerator and lay them and the marinade in the broiler pan in a single layer. Set the pan over medium heat, bring to a simmer, then cover tightly with foil, and set into the oven to bake for 1 1/2 to 2 1/2 hours until the short ribs are tender.

When the ribs are done, remove them from the oven, remove the foil, and set the ribs on a rack over another pan. Raise oven heat to 350F (177C). Take 1/3 cup (80 ml) of the marinade from the baking dish, mix it with the honey, and brush this mixture over the ribs. Return the ribs to the oven and bake for 8 to 10 minutes, brushing them with the honey mixture several times, until they have a light brown glaze.

When the ribs are glazed, serve them at once on warm serving plates.

Any leftover marinade can be refrigerated or frozen for later use. If the mixture is too thick, add a little more pineapple juice or water.

Variation: This same marinade and procedure works well for spareribs and chicken. If using

chicken, buy ones that weigh 2 1/4 to 2 1/2 pounds (1025 to 1125 g), split them in half, marinate for one to two days, and bake for 45 to 50 minutes or until tender. When brushing on the honey mixture, do so on both sides. One chicken yields two servings; if you prepare more than six portions, increase the marinade proportionately.

❧ Sauerbraten

A strictly orthodox version of this Rhineland specialty would call for much more vinegar in the marinade, producing a tartness in the final sauce-making stage which is offset by adding sugar. I prefer this feine Küche *version (similar to an old-style French* daube*) because the beef flavor is left more intact. Although I have called for red Burgundy, if you can find a Spätburgunder from the Ahr or Baden regions, use it for the marinade. This venerable German dish goes well with Braised Red Cabbage, Spätzle, Whipped Potatoes or potato pancakes (*kartoffelpuffer*), and either a good robust imported beer or the same type of wine used for the marinade.*

Yields 8 to 10 servings

3 to 4 pounds (1400 to 1800 g) boneless chuck roast, either top or bottom round

FOR THE MARINADE
5 cups (1175 ml) red Burgundy wine
1/4 cup (60 ml) red wine vinegar
1/2 medium onion
1/2 carrot
1/2 celery stalk
1/2 bay leaf
1 small clove
12 whole black peppercorns
1 small garlic clove

FOR COOKING THE BEEF
Salt
Freshly ground black pepper
2 tablespoons peanut oil
1 tablespoon flour
1 tablespoon tomato paste

2 cups (475 ml) Demi-glace Brun II *(see page 76)*

Recommended equipment

A paring knife; white kitchen string; 5-quart (5 L) glass, stainless steel, or china bowl; mortar and pestle; plastic wrap; paper towels; large fine-mesh sieve; Dutch oven; wooden spatula; basting spoon; small mixing bowl.

Trim the excess fat from the beef and tie it in at least three places with string around the circumference of the roast. Set it into the large bowl and add the wine and vinegar. Peel the onion half and add it with the carrot and the celery stalk to the beef. Next, add the bay leaf, clove, and lightly crush the peppercorns in the mortar and pestle before adding them to the marinade. Peel the garlic clove and add it to the bowl. Then cover the bowl tightly with plastic wrap and refrigerate it for three to four days; turn the beef over once during this time.

Prepare the demi-glace before the beef is ready to be cooked.

Lift the meat from the marinade, let it drain, and pat dry with paper towels. Season the beef lightly with salt and pepper and reserve. Strain the marinade through the sieve and reserve both the liquid and the vegetables separately.

Preheat oven to 300F (149C).

Set the Dutch oven over high heat, add the peanut oil, and when it is hot put the beef into it and brown the meat well on all sides until it has a good crust. This should take about 10 minutes. When the meat is browned, reduce heat to medium, drain off all excess fat, add the reserved vegetables and spices from the marinade, and sauté for 3 minutes.

Then add the flour and stir with the wooden spatula until the flour is lightly browned (about 3 minutes). Stir in the tomato paste and cook for 1 minute before adding the reserved marinating liquid. Bring to a simmer, stirring occasionally and scraping the sediment up from the bottom of the pan. Simmer for 10 minutes, add the demi-glace, return to the simmer, cover the pot, and set it into the middle level of the oven for 2 1/4 to 3 hours. The level of the liquid should come at least three-quarters up the side of the beef. If more liquid is needed, add enough red wine or demi-glace to make up the difference.

While the beef is cooking, skim off the grease once or twice before it is done. To judge if the beef is tender, insert a paring knife into the center. If the knife meets only slight resistance then the beef is done.

When the beef is done, remove from heat and let it sit in the sauce for 10 to 15 minutes before removing it to a heated platter. Then skim all grease from the sauce with the basting spoon and strain the sauce through the sieve into the bowl. Return sauce to Dutch oven, taste, adjust seasoning if necessary, and keep warm. Remove string from beef and slice for serving. Set the slices onto the dinner plates, spoon the sauce over the beef, and serve.

Boeuf à la Bourguignonne
Beef Stew in the Style of Burgundy

You may be aware that there are two other Burgundian recipes in this volume, one for veal and one for chicken, but when it comes to the cuisine of this extraordinary province, there is always room for one more. Home of such architectural treasures as Bernard of Clairvaux's abbey at Fontenay, Abbots Hugh and Peter the Venerable's Cluny III, the Romanesque basilica at Vézelay, and the cathedral at Autun, it is at once a (if not the) culinary cradle of France. The wines are legion, as are the escargots who happily munch on the vine leaves in early autumn, making way for the sun to work its ripening magic on the grape clusters. Dijon is the mustard capital, Bresse is the world's most celebrated outdoor chicken coop, and Charolles is the village to which all of the magnificent white cattle you encounter in the Warm Springs Valley trace their lineage. And this is no small matter because Charolais beef, along with their russet-hided cousins from Limousin province, are responsible for much of the high-quality lean beef found in butcher shops today.

So here, in one pot, are two of Burgundy's greatest gifts to the gastronome—wine and beef. Be hard-nosed about selecting both because the result will be the better for it—especially as the marinade is the base for the sauce. Spätzle or noodles and a tossed green salad are all you need to complete this classic, along with some excellent Burgundy, of course.

Yields 6 servings

2 1/2 pounds (1125 g) lean, boneless beef, chuck, or top or bottom round, cut into 1-inch (2 1/2 cm) cubes

FOR THE MARINADE
1/2 medium onion
1/2 celery stalk
1/2 carrot
4 cups (950 ml) red Burgundy
1 garlic clove
1/2 medium bay leaf
1/8 teaspoon thyme

FOR COOKING THE BEEF
Salt
Freshly ground black pepper
1/4 cup (60 ml) peanut oil
1 tablespoon flour
2 cups (475 ml) Demi-Glace Brun II *(see page 76)*

FOR THE ONIONS
12 small white onions
1 1/2 teaspoons butter
1/2 teaspoon sugar

FOR THE MUSHROOMS
12 small, fresh mushrooms
1 1/2 teaspoons butter
Juice of 1/4 lemon
A dash of salt

FOR THE CROUTONS AND GARNISH
3 slices Pullman Loaf *(see page 488)*
2 tablespoons (30 g) butter
1 teaspoon chopped fresh parsley

Recommended equipment

A paring knife; 3-quart (3 L) glass, ceramic, or stainless steel bowl; plastic wrap; large fine-mesh sieve; two 2-quart (2 L) mixing bowls; 4-quart (4 L) enameled cast-iron baking dish or lined copper plat à sauter with lid; wooden spatula; slotted spoon; 2-quart (2 L) saucepan; 10-inch (25 cm) sauté pan; paper towels; basting spoon; small chef's knife.

Trim the beef of all fat and gristle, cut into 1-inch (2 1/2 cm) cubes, and put them into the 3-quart bowl. Prepare the vegetables for the marinade and add them to the beef: peel and quarter the onion half; trim the celery to make it as stringless as possible and quarter it; and peel and quarter the carrot half. Add the wine to the beef. Peel the garlic clove and add it along with the bay leaf and thyme. Cover the bowl tightly with plastic wrap and refrigerate for one or two days, stirring two or three times during the period.

Prepare the demi-glace and have it ready when you cook the beef.

When the beef has finished marinating, let it drain well in the sieve set over one of the 2-quart bowls. Then season the beef lightly with salt and pepper and reserve the marinade and its vegetables.

Set the enameled cast-iron baking dish or lined copper plat à sauter over high heat, add 2 tablespoons peanut oil, and, when it is hot, add one-half of the beef. Brown the beef thoroughly, stirring and turning it often, until all sides are well browned (this should take 8 to 10 minutes). Then remove beef with the slotted spoon to the other 2-quart bowl, add the remaining peanut oil to the pan, and, when it is hot, add the rest of the beef and brown it as you did the first batch. When the beef is nicely browned, drain all but 1 tablespoon of fat from the pan and add the browned beef from the bowl as well as the onion, celery, carrot, and garlic from the reserved marinade. Sauté, stirring, for 3 minutes before sprinkling on the flour. Continue to sauté, stirring and turning the beef, for another 3 minutes before adding the marinade liquid with the bay leaf and thyme. Bring the beef to the simmer and cook until the marinade is reduced by one-half, stirring from time to time and scraping up the browned bits from the bottom of the pan. When the marinade is reduced, add the demi-glace to the beef, adjust heat so that the pan maintains a low simmer, cover pan, and cook gently until the beef is tender. This should take about 1 1/2 hours.

While the beef is cooking, prepare the onions, mushrooms, and croutons. For the onions, bring lightly salted water to a boil in the saucepan, add the onions, and boil for about 10 minutes. When tender, drain the onions, refresh under cold running water, peel, and reserve.

For the mushrooms, brush them gently of any clinging dirt, and leave them whole if they are small (halve them if they are large). Set the sauté pan over medium heat, add 1 1/2 teaspoons butter, lemon juice, a dash of salt, and the mushrooms, and sauté, stirring, for 3 minutes. Scrape them from the pan and reserve.

To finish the onions, return sauté pan to medium heat, add 1 1/2 teaspoons butter and the sugar and cook for 30 seconds before adding the onions. Sauté, stirring occasionally, until the onions are light brown in color and glacéed. Then remove pan from heat, drain the onions, and reserve them. Wash out the sauté pan.

For the croutons, slice the bread into pieces 2 inches long and 1/2 inch wide (5 x 1 1/4 cm). Set the sauté pan over low heat, add the 2 tablespoons butter, and, when it has melted, add the croutons and cook, stirring and turning them, until the bread is golden brown. Remove pan from heat and let the croutons drain on paper towels until needed.

When the beef is tender, remove it with a slotted spoon to a clean 2-quart bowl, being sure to leave the vegetables and spices behind, and reserve. Degrease the sauce with the basting spoon and then pass it through the fine-mesh sieve into the bowl with the beef. Wipe out the cooking pot and return the beef and sauce to it. If the sauce is too thick, add a little red wine and beef stock; if too thin, let it simmer some more. Taste the sauce and adjust the seasoning if needed.

When you are ready to serve the beef, add the onions and mushrooms and bring the stew to a gentle simmer over low to medium heat and heat it thoroughly. While the stew is warming, rinse the parsley, pat it dry, and chop it. When the stew is hot, serve at once on warm dinner plates and garnish each serving with the reserved croutons and the parsley.

❧ Marinated Steaks

There is no major historical background here, just a recipe for good times. Those who insist that steak cannot be improved by marinades or who must put a prepared sauce on their beef before eating it are bound to be converted by this preparation. Sautéing the steaks yields drippings which enhance the sauce. Grilling produces the unique charcoal flavor. The choice is yours. As an accompaniment to the charcoal-grilled steaks, brush thick slices of French Bread with a mixture of melted butter, pressed garlic, and a pinch of salt, and grill until golden on each side. Voilà le Texas toast.

Yields 6 servings

FOR THE MARINADE
1 medium green bell pepper
4 pimiento halves (packed in water and drained)
1 sun-dried tomato
2 tablespoons chopped shallots
1 tablespoon freshly crushed black peppercorns
2/3 cup (160 ml) olive oil

FOR THE STEAKS
6 well-trimmed sirloin, tenderloin, or top sirloin steaks, 1 to 1 1/2 inches (2 1/2 to 3 3/4 cm) thick, weighing 8 to 10 ounces (225 to 285 g) each
1 garlic clove
Salt

FOR THE SAUCE
Oil from marinade
Vegetables from marinade
1/2 cup (118 ml) dry red wine
1 teaspoon Glace de Viande *(see page 65)*

Recommended equipment

A paring knife; small chef's knife; mortar and pestle; 1-quart (1 L) mixing bowl; garlic press; china, glass, or stainless steel platter large enough to hold the steaks in a single layer; plastic wrap; fine-mesh sieve; 12-inch (30 cm) sauté pan, broiling pan, or charcoal grill and charcoal.

Prepare the marinade. Rinse the bell pepper, halve and seed it, remove the pithy white, and dice the pepper finely with the chef's knife. Drain the canned pimiento halves and dice them finely. Dice the sun-dried tomato. Peel the shallots and chop finely. Crush the black pepper in the mortar and pestle. Put the olive oil in the mixing bowl, add all the above ingredients, and blend them together.

Spread one-half of the marinade on the platter and lay the trimmed steaks on top. Press the garlic clove over them and rub it onto the meat. Then spread the remaining marinade evenly over the steaks, cover with plastic wrap, and refrigerate for several hours or overnight.

When you are ready to cook, scrape the marinade off the steaks and strain it through the sieve into a bowl, reserving the liquid in one bowl and the vegetables in another. Season the steaks lightly with salt, and either sauté, broil, or grill them over charcoal. If you sauté them, heat a few tablespoons of oil from the marinade in the sauté pan over high heat and, when it is hot, add the steaks in a single layer and sauté for 3 to 4 minutes on a side, turning once. Keep the first batch in a warm place, uncovered, while you sauté the rest. If you broil the steaks, preheat the broiler to maximum heat and broil them 3 to 4 inches away from the heat, turning them once. Room temperature steaks will require 3 to 4 minutes on a side for rare, 5 to 6 minutes on a side for medium. To grill the steaks over charcoal, start your fire about half an hour before you plan to cook, and when the coals are just starting to ash over set the steaks on a rack about 6 inches (15 cm) above the flame (3 inches or 7 1/2 cm if your grill has a hood you can lower). Follow broiling instructions for timing.

However the steaks are cooked, be sure to let them rest uncovered in a warm, not hot, place for 3 to 5 minutes before serving. While the steaks are resting, prepare the sauce. If you sauté the steaks, add the drained vegetables from the marinade to the pan after the last batch is finished, and sauté the vegetables over medium high heat with 1 1/2 teaspoons oil from the marinade for 2 minutes. Add the wine and deglaze the pan, scraping up the brown bits from the pan bottom.

Then add the glace de viande, bring to a simmer, and cook, stirring, until the sauce is reduced to one-third. Add any juices that may have escaped from the steaks to the sauce, set the steaks on warm dinner plates, pour the sauce over them, and serve at once.

If the steaks are broiled or grilled, follow the sauce instructions using a 10-inch (25 cm) sauté pan.

Tenderloin of Beef Stroganoff

The exact history of this distinguished recipe is unclear. We know that its origin is Imperial Russia, having been named after one of the most prominent merchant/noble families in Saint Petersburg. We also know that Carême worked for Czar Alexander in Saint Petersburg. Thus, it is a reasonable supposition that this preparation, which is distinctly French in technique, could have evolved from his Russian experience. If you were cooking this in France, Crème Fraîche would replace the sour cream, giving the sauce a slightly lighter texture and providing anticurdling insurance to boot. Be sure to use the best beef you can find, and present Rice Pilaff, Riz Valencienne, or fresh noodles as the appropriate complement for this Russian classic.

Yields 5 to 6 servings

FOR THE SAUCE
3 cups (710 ml) White Chicken or Veal Stock *(see pages 61 and 63)*
8 tablespoons (115 g) butter
2 medium onions
1/4 cup (60 ml) tomato paste
1/8 teaspoon oregano
1/4 small bay leaf
A pinch of thyme
2 tablespoons flour
8 ounces (225 g) mushrooms
1 1/2 teaspoons butter
Juice of 1/2 lemon
1 cup (235 ml) sour cream, at room temperature
Worcestershire sauce
Salt
Freshly ground white pepper

FOR THE BEEF
1 1/2 pounds (675 g) beef tenderloin
Salt
Freshly ground black pepper
3 tablespoons peanut oil

Recommended equipment

A 1 1/2-quart (1 1/2 L) saucepan, 2-quart (2 L) saucepan, wooden spatula, wire whisk, slicing knife, 8-inch (20 cm) sauté pan, large fine-mesh sieve, 2-quart (2 L) mixing bowl, 12-inch (30 cm) sauté pan, long-handled fork, slotted spoon.

Set the smaller saucepan over medium heat and bring the stock slowly to a boil so it will be ready when you need it.

While the stock is heating, add butter to the other saucepan, set over medium low heat, and, while it is getting hot, peel and dice the onions. When the butter is hot, stir in the onions with the wooden spatula and sauté them without browning for about 4 minutes or until they have softened and are golden. Then stir in the tomato paste, oregano, bay leaf, and thyme and simmer on low, stirring occasionally, for 3 minutes. Add the flour and mix thoroughly. Pour in the boiling stock, stirring constantly with the whisk, and blend thoroughly. Adjust heat so that sauce simmers gently for 30 minutes.

Brush the mushrooms of any remaining dirt and cut them into slices 1/4 inch thick. Set the small sauté pan over medium heat, add the butter, and, when it is hot, stir in the mushrooms. Sprinkle them with the lemon juice and sauté, stirring, for several minutes or until the mushrooms are golden brown. Then remove from heat, scrape the mushrooms into a dish, and reserve.

Prepare the beef for cooking. Cut the meat you need from the head and tail of the fillet, reserving the centercut for another use such as a roast or filet mignon. Trim the silver membrane from the beef you are using and slice it into strips that are 1/4 to 1/2 inch (2/3 to 1 1/4 cm) thick. Season lightly with salt and pepper and reserve.

When the sauce has finished simmering, strain it through the sieve into the mixing bowl. Rinse out the sieve. Then return the sauce to the saucepan and, using the whisk, blend the sour cream in thoroughly and then add the mushrooms. Stir in the Worcestershire sauce, taste, and adjust the seasoning with salt and pepper if needed. Keep the sauce warm on low heat.

Set the large sauté pan over high heat, add 1 1/2 tablespoons peanut oil, and, when it is hot, stir in half of the beef slices and sauté them, stirring with the fork, until they are well browned. This should take 1 to 3 minutes. When the beef is browned, remove it with the slotted spoon to the sieve to drain. Immediately add the remaining peanut oil to the sauté pan and when it is hot stir in the remaining beef. Sauté as you did the first batch, and drain when done.

Then set beef into a warm serving dish, bring the sauce to a simmer, spoon the sauce over the meat, mix gently, and serve without delay.

Tenderloin of Beef Café Martin

Formerly one of the great gastronomic watering holes in Lyon, the Restaurant Morateur was founded by François Morateur in the 1840s. Early on in the restaurant's history, Morateur had a young protégé named Martin, who was intent on making his name in the United States. This he most certainly did by going to New York City and opening Martin's, which had become a culinary landmark by the time he returned home to Lyon in 1900. Morateur had a way with a sautéed beef tenderloin, which was elaborated by his pupil and is presented here in our version. Brown the beef ever so carefully so that it is still pink inside, and serve it with Rice Pilaff, Fettuccine Alfredo, or hashed brown potatoes.

Yields 6 servings

FOR THE SAUCE
2 1/2 cups (590 ml) Demi-glace Brun I *(see page 75)*
3 medium, ripe tomatoes (blanched, peeled, and seeded; *see page 568*)
1/2 medium onion
1/2 medium red bell pepper
1/2 medium green bell pepper
8 ounces (225 g) mushrooms
1 1/2 teaspoons butter

FOR THE BEEF
2 pounds (900 g) beef tenderloin
Salt
Freshly ground black pepper
1/2 garlic clove
1 tablespoon chopped shallots
3 tablespoons olive oil
1 teaspoon butter
2/3 cup (160 ml) red Burgundy

Recommended equipment

A paring knife, large chef's knife, two 12-inch (30 cm) sauté pans, slicing knife, wooden spatula, long-handled fork, slotted spoon, large fine-mesh sieve, garlic press.

Prepare the demi-glace and reserve.

Prepare the tomatoes and chop roughly into 1-inch (2 1/2 cm) square dice. Pare the onion half and cut into 1-inch squares. Trim and seed the bell pepper halves, remove the pithy white, and cut them as you did the onion. Brush the mushrooms of any clinging dirt and cut into 1/4-inch (2/3 cm) thick slices.

Prepare the beef for cooking by cutting from the head and tail of the fillet the meat that you need. Reserve the centercut for another use such as a roast or filet mignon. Trim the silver membrane from the beef you are using and slice it into strips that are 1/4 to 1/2 inch (2/3 to 1 1/4 cm) thick, season them lightly with salt and pepper, and reserve. Peel the garlic, chop the shallots, and reserve both.

Set one of the sauté pans over medium heat, add the butter, and, when it is hot, stir in the onion, bell peppers, and mushrooms and sauté, stirring occasionally with the wooden spatula, for 3 minutes. Then add the demi-glace, bring to a slow simmer, and cook for 5 minutes. Add the tomatoes, simmer for 30 seconds, remove the pan from the heat, and set aside.

Set the other sauté pan over high heat, add 1 1/2 tablespoons olive oil, and when it is hot add half of the beef and sauté, stirring with the fork, until the beef is well browned. This should take 1 to 3 minutes. It is important to keep the pan hot so the beef will brown but remain pink on the inside. When done, remove beef with the slotted spoon to drain in the sieve. Add the remaining oil to the sauté pan, and, when it is hot, stir in the remaining beef and sauté as you did the first batch. When done, remove to drain in the sieve.

Remove the fat from the sauté pan, set it over medium heat, add the butter, and when it is hot stir in the shallots. Sauté, stirring with the wooden spatula, for 30 seconds and then press in the garlic clove, mix well, and add the wine. Simmer until the liquid is reduced to 3 to 4 tablespoons. Scrape the reduction out of the pan and put it through the sieve into the reserved sauce and vegetables in the other sauté pan. Set the pan over medium heat and bring the mixture to a simmer for 2 to 3 minutes. Put the meat into a warm serving dish, spoon the sauce and vegetables over it, and serve at once.

Sauté de Mignonettes de Boeuf à la Printanière
Sautéed Filets of Beef with Fresh Vegetables

If you have wondered why culinary history is as confused as any other, here is a case in point. In French kitchens, mignonette *is usually taken to mean a tournedo or filet mignon as it does here.* Mignonette *is also applied to coarsely ground black pepper as it is here.* A la printanière *(springlike) usually refers to a garnish of new carrots and onions, spring peas, and tiny asparagus. Here the only remnant is the julienne of carrot, but the idea is the same in that the vegetables must be* very fresh *in order to capture the feeling and color of spring. One* conseil. *I never subscribed to the "burned-out" pepper fad so the amount of black pepper is left to your discretion. Remember, too much will obscure the fragile freshness contributed by the vegetables. Because this has a touch of the Orient about it, try serving it with* Exotic Fried Rice.

374

Yields 6 servings

FOR THE BEEF
12 small filets mignons, each weighing 3 to 3 1/2 ounces (85 to 100 g)
1 small garlic clove
1/4 teaspoon salt
Freshly crushed black pepper
3 tablespoons peanut oil

FOR THE VEGETABLES
2 medium, ripe tomatoes (blanched, peeled, and seeded; *see page 568*)
1/2 medium onion
1/2 medium green bell pepper
1/2 medium red bell pepper
1 medium carrot
8 ounces (225 g) fresh mushrooms
2 Chinese cabbage stalks
1 teaspoon butter
1 teaspoon olive oil
Salt
Freshly ground white pepper

FOR THE SAUCE
2 tablespoons chopped shallots
2 teaspoons butter
1/2 cup (118 ml) red Burgundy wine
2/3 cup (160 ml) Demi-glace Brun I *(see page 75)*
2 teaspoons chopped fresh parsley

Recommended equipment

A paring knife, garlic press, small bowl, mortar and pestle, slicing knife, swivel-bladed vegetable peeler, 10-inch (25 cm) sauté pan, wooden spatula, 12-inch (30 cm) sauté pan, fine-mesh sieve, 1 1/2-quart (1 1/2 L) saucepan, heatproof platter, wire whisk.

With the paring knife, trim the filets of any fat and reserve. Peel the garlic clove, crush it in the garlic press, and mix it in the small bowl with the salt. Rub the filets with this mixture. Crush black pepper in the mortar and pestle, season the filets with it, and reserve.

Prepare the vegetables and reserve until you are ready to cook them. Cut the blanched, seeded, and peeled tomatoes into 1/4-inch (2/3 cm) thick strips. Peel the onion half and slice it thinly with the slicing knife. Rinse the bell pepper halves, trim and seed them, remove the pithy white, and slice them into fine strips. Peel the carrot and cut it into very thin strips that are 1 1/2 inches (3 3/4 cm) long. Brush the mushrooms of any clinging dirt and slice them into pieces 1/4 inch thick. Rinse the cabbage stalks and slice crosswise into 1/4-inch thick strips.

Set the smaller sauté pan over medium heat, add the butter and the olive oil, and, when they are hot, add the onions, bell peppers, carrot, mushrooms, and cabbage. Season lightly with salt and pepper and sauté, stirring occasionally, until the vegetables have softened but are still al dente (about 4 minutes). Then add the tomato pieces, stir, sauté 30 seconds, remove pan from heat, and set aside.

Set the remaining sauté pan over high heat, add 1 1/2 tablespoons peanut oil, and, when it is smoking hot, add as many of the filets as will comfortably fit in the pan in a single layer without touching. Sauté until well browned, then turn them over to brown the other side (about 1 1/2 minutes for each side). When they are done, remove at once to a pan (or platter) and let them sit, in a single layer, in a warm (not hot) spot. Sauté the remaining filets by batches in the same manner, adding more peanut oil as needed.

When all the filets are cooked (and resting), drain all fat from the sauté pan. Chop the shallots. Set the sauté pan over medium heat, add 1 teaspoon butter and the shallots, and sauté, stirring, for 30 seconds. Then deglaze the pan with the Burgundy, scraping up any brown bits from the pan bottom, and simmer until the wine is reduced to one-third of its original volume. Add the demi-glace and simmer the sauce for 3 minutes.

While the sauce simmers, reheat the vegetables by setting their sauté pan over low heat and stirring them from time to time.

Wash the parsley, pat it dry, chop, and reserve.

When the sauce has simmered, skim off any fat and pass the sauce through the sieve into the saucepan. When ready to serve, bring the sauce back to a simmer, remove from heat, and whisk in the remaining butter. Do not let the sauce come back to a boil. Divide the sauce by spoonfuls among warm serving plates or platter and arrange the filets on the sauce. Add any juices from the pan where the meat was resting to the sauté pan with the warmed vegetables, stir, and arrange the vegetables next to or over the filets, sprinkle with the parsley, and serve at once.

Variations: Add 1/8 teaspoon caraway seeds when the vegetables are sautéed. Substitute sirloin steaks or minced beef tenderloin for the filets mignons.

Roast Three-Pepper Tenderloin of Beef with Armagnac Sauce

As I mentioned in the Mignonettes recipe, I am less taken than others with the pepper steak preparation which calls for a great deal of crushed pepper to be worked into the cut surface of the meat. Beef fillet, while naturally bland, has a sweetness which must not be overpowered—otherwise there is little point in going to the expense of purchasing it. Here I offer an alternative approach which combines the complexity of black, white, and green peppercorns, but confines their activity to the side of the meat, permitting the delicate flavor of the beef to stand side by side with the "bite" of the pepper. Let the pepper work on the beef overnight or, better yet, for a full day before roasting. Serve with Pommes de Terre Parisienne Rissolées and Navets Glacés.

Yields 6 to 7 servings

2 to 2 1/4 pounds (900 to 1025 g) centercut beef tenderloin
2 tablespoons freshly crushed black peppercorns
1 tablespoon freshly crushed white peppercorns
1 ounce (30 g) green peppercorns (packed in water and drained)
1 cup (235 ml) Demi-glace Brun I *(see page 75)*
Salt
About 8 ounces (225 g) thinly sliced pork fatback, 6 x 8 inches (15 x 20 cm) and 1/8 inch (1/3 cm) thick
1 tablespoon peanut oil
1 tablespoon chopped shallots
2 teaspoons butter
6 tablespoons (90 ml) Armagnac

Recommended equipment

A paring knife, mortar and pestle, waxed paper, pan or platter, white kitchen string, heavy roasting pan, small chef's knife, wooden spatula, fine-mesh sieve, 2-quart (2 L) saucepan, basting spoon.

Trim the tenderloin of all fat and remove the silver skin.

Crush the peppercorns in the mortar and pestle. Lay a piece of waxed paper on your work surface, spread the pepper on it, and roll the tenderloin in the pepper, coating it thoroughly and applying enough pressure so that the pepper sticks to the beef. Cover the tenderloin with waxed paper (or plastic wrap), set it on the pan or platter, and refrigerate for 12 to 24 hours.

While the beef marinates, prepare the demi-glace and refrigerate until needed.

When you are ready to roast the beef, remove it from the refrigerator, unwrap it, season it lightly with salt, and bard it with the fatback. It is best to have your butcher slice it for you, and any leftover fatback will keep very well if wrapped airtight and frozen. Cover both ends and the top of the tenderloin with a layer of fatback and then tie it with string at 2- to 2 1/2-inch (5 to 6 1/4 cm) intervals. Let the meat rest at room temperature for at least an hour. The fatback will protect the vulnerable tenderloin from the heat during roasting and will keep it juicy. (When meat is wrapped with fat the method is called "barding"; meat is "larded" when strips of fat are inserted into the meat with a larding needle.)

Preheat oven to 400F (204C).

Put the peanut oil in the roasting pan, set the tenderloin into it with the top (fatback) side down, and set the pan over medium high heat. When the beef has begun to sizzle, set the pan into the oven, roast for 10 minutes, turn the tenderloin over (so the fatback is on top), reduce heat to 325F (163C), and roast for 10 minutes for rare beef (20 minutes for medium rare).

When the tenderloin is done, remove from the oven and set the beef on a pan or platter with the fatback side down and let it rest uncovered for 15 to 20 minutes in a warm (not hot) place.

While the beef is resting, chop the shallots with the chef's knife. Drain all the fat from the roasting pan, set it over medium heat, and add 1 teaspoon butter and the shallots. Stir with the wooden spatula for 30 seconds. Add the Armagnac and deglaze the pan, being sure to scrape up all the brown bits from the bottom of the pan. Then add the demi-glace, bring to a simmer, and cook for 5 minutes before straining the sauce through the sieve into the saucepan.

When the beef has rested, remove the string and fatback, pour any rendered juices into the saucepan, and bring the sauce to a gentle simmer. Skim off any remaining grease with the basting spoon, remove saucepan from heat, and blend in the remaining butter. Slice the tenderloin into serving pieces. Spoon the sauce onto warm serving plates, lay the slices on top, and serve at once.

Variation

 Roast Black Pepper Tenderloin of Beef with Armagnac Sauce, Green Peppercorns, and Raisins

I am rather fond of green peppercorns, and in this adaptation of Roger Vergé's Provençal recipe the pointing of the flavors moves from the meat to the sauce.

6 tablespoons (90 ml) Armagnac
4 ounces (115 g) golden raisins
1/2 teaspoon butter
1 teaspoon green peppercorns (packed in water and drained)
2 tablespoons Armagnac

1 cup (235 ml) Demi-glace Brun I *(see page 75)*

377

Omit the three-pepper marinade in the basic instructions, seasoning the tenderloin instead only lightly with salt and freshly ground black pepper. Bard it with fatback *(see page 377)* and let the meat rest at room temperature for an hour. Follow the instructions for roasting and, while the tenderloin is cooking, pour the 6 tablespoons Armagnac into a small saucepan, add the raisins, and reserve. Melt the butter in a small sauté pan, add the green peppercorns, sauté for 2 minutes, add the 2 tablespoons Armagnac, and flambé. Remove from heat and reserve.

When the beef is roasted and resting, bring the Armagnac and raisins to a simmer and pour the Armagnac through the sieve into the roasting pan, reserving the raisins, to deglaze the roasting pan. Then add the demi-glace, bring to a simmer, and cook for 5 minutes before straining the sauce through the sieve into the saucepan.

When the beef has rested, remove the string and fatback, pour any rendered juices into the saucepan, and bring the sauce to a gentle simmer. Skim off any remaining grease with the basting spoon and stir in the raisins and the green peppercorns to warm them. Slice the tenderloin and place it on the plates, spooning the sauce around the meat.

Roast Tenderloin of Beef London House with Truffle Sauce

How felicitous that the cold of winter brings this most luxurious and Lucullan of entrées to mind. For, while tinned truffles and foie gras can be had year-round, nothing captures la gloire culinaire française *as well as the winter harvest of black diamonds from Périgord and the coming to market of the gentle gold from Périgord and Gascogne. Juxtaposing these two treasures here is not an ostentatious exercise, but rather the consummation of a natural marriage. Indeed, in Bordeaux it is said that "to put a truffle in a foie gras is to give it a soul."*

Freshly harvested black truffles from France are available in major American food markets from mid-December through February. Flash freezing extends this period by several months without the customary loss of flavor associated with the bottled and canned variety. Their extraordinary expense is due to the fact that they defy easy cultivation and must be harvested by cavage—*a venerated procedure in which the trained dogs or pigs who locate the truffles by scent are restrained while their owners* (trufficulteurs) *hand dig them from the soil, traditionally at the base of oak, beech, or hazelnut trees. As of this writing, French and American investigators report increased success at cultivation experiments, which should make truffles accessible to many more serious cooks. This effort is not misguided for, Colette not withstanding, the truffle's "supreme flavour" extends beyond the truffle, rendering transcendent such preparations as Baked Breast of Chicken Ambassador and Sautéed Sweetbreads Souvaroff.*

As the truffle seemingly depends on the vagaries of nature, so does foie gras depend on the persistence of the gaveuse—*the farmwife of southwest France whose exclusive province it is to force-feed, care for, and ultimately slaughter the geese who produce the pale golden culinary treasures. In late winter the foie gras market towns in Périgord and Gascogne feature competitions among the gaveuses for the largest goose livers, which will usually weigh at least one kilo or two-and-one-half pounds.*

Among les amateurs de foie gras *there is some disagreement over the flavor of tinned foie gras as compared to fresh, or* mi-cuit, *which is lightly cooked and vacuum packed. The former is said to have a superior flavor, the latter a superior texture. Because importation of raw goose and duck liver into the United States is illegal, this debate used to be highly academic. However, a domestic foie industry using mullard ducks has developed and is thriving in part through the dedicated promotion of such noted chefs as André Soltner and Jean Louis Palladin. For this recipe, either type of foie can be used.*

Now, all that remains is to withdraw some funds from your savings account, go to the market in search of truffles and foie gras, and gather some very special guests around your table. Begin this sumptuous feast with Quenelles de Saumon, accompany the beef with Roesti and tiny String Beans (haricots verts), *and serve the Gâteau Chambord with iced* liqueur de framboise *for an unforgettable finish.*

Yields 7 to 8 servings

1 whole foie gras weighing about 8 ounces (225 g)
2 to 2 1/4 pounds (900 to 1025 g) centercut beef tenderloin
Salt
Freshly ground black pepper
About 8 ounces (225 g) thinly sliced pork fatback, 6 x 8 inches (15 x 20 cm) and 1/8 inch (1/3 cm) thick
1 tablespoon peanut oil
1 tablespoon chopped shallots
A fresh black truffle weighing about 1 ounce (30 g)
2 teaspoons butter
3/8 cup (90 ml) Madeira
1 cup (235 ml) Demi-glace Brun I *(see page 75)*

Recommended equipment

A paring knife, butcher's steel, metal bulb baster, white kitchen string, heavy roasting pan, small chef's knife, wooden spatula, fine-mesh sieve, 2-quart (2 L) saucepan, basting spoon, wire whisk, slicing knife.

Slice the foie gras into long strips about 1 inch (2 1/2 cm) thick and reserve.

Trim the tenderloin of all fat and remove the silver skin. Using the butcher's steel (knife sharpener), make a hole in the center of the tenderloin, lengthwise, from one end to the other. Remove the steel, and using the metal baster with bulb removed, enlarge the hole by pushing it through. Then, grasping the small end of the baster, slowly pull it out of the tenderloin, while stuffing the foie gras strips into the cavity left by the retreating baster. Season the meat lightly with salt and pepper and bard it with the fatback. It is best to have your butcher slice it for you, and any leftover fatback will keep very well if wrapped airtight and frozen. Cover both ends and the top of the tenderloin with a layer of fatback and then tie it with string at 2- to 2 1/2-inch (5 to 6 1/4 cm) intervals. Let the meat rest at room temperature for at least an hour. The fatback will protect the vulnerable tenderloin from the heat during roasting and will keep it juicy. (When meat is wrapped with fat the method is called "barding"; meat is "larded" when strips of fat are inserted into the meat with a larding needle.)

Preheat oven to 400F (204C).

Put the peanut oil in the roasting pan, set the tenderloin into it with the top (fatback) side down, and set the pan over medium high heat. When the beef has begun to sizzle, set the pan into the oven, roast for 10 minutes, turn the tenderloin over (so the fatback is on top), reduce heat to 325F (163C), and roast for 20 more minutes for medium-rare beef.

When the tenderloin is done, remove from the oven and set the beef on a pan or platter with the fatback side down and let it rest uncovered for 15 to 20 minutes in a warm (not hot) place.

While the beef is resting, chop the shallots and truffle finely and reserve separately. Drain all the fat from the roasting pan, set it over medium heat, and add 1 teaspoon butter and the shallots. Stir with the wooden spatula for 30 seconds before deglazing the pan with the Madeira. Scrape up all the brown bits from the bottom of the pan and then add the demi-glace. Bring to a simmer and cook for 5 minutes before straining the sauce through the sieve into the saucepan.

When the beef has rested, remove the string and fatback, pour any rendered juices into the saucepan, and bring the sauce to a gentle simmer. Skim off any remaining grease with the basting spoon. Add the chopped truffle, simmer for another minute or two, remove from heat, and blend in the remaining butter. Slice the tenderloin into serving pieces. Spoon the sauce onto warm serving plates, lay the slices on top, and serve at once.

This preparation is also known as Fillet of Beef Prince Albert or Fillet of Beef Prince of Wales.

Lamb

> Refined or classic French cookery—call it haute cuisine if you must—and French regional, provincial, farmhouse and peasant styles of cookery cannot arbitrarily be isolated and set apart one from the other. All are interdependent and to a certain extent intermixed. Each borrows and learns from the other.
>
> A poor Provençal family might find their great son's version of a familiar dish lacking in savour, although in its original form it would have made, with a saucerful of olives and perhaps a dish of fresh figs, an entire meal. To the customers of the Provençal village boy who is now the renowned and glorious Auguste Escoffier, potatoes, artichokes and truffles do not even make one course. They belong with a joint of meat. So Escoffier uses his vegetables as a foundation upon which to bake a choice little cut of spring lamb, a loin or best end of neck. For a festival or a wedding feast a very similar dish, a *gigot* of mutton on a bed of sliced potatoes, might have been taken by Madame Escoffier senior to the village baker's oven to cook. It could be no more, and no less, than the ancient *gigot boulangère* with a midi accent. Madame Escoffier's son gives it a more elegant name. To honour his compatriot, the Provençal poet Frédéric Mistral, he calls his creation *carré d'agneau Mistral*. He publishes the recipe in a book; and another of the myriad dishes of France has entered the repertory of *la cuisine classique*.
>
> —Elizabeth David

There can be no question that these lamb recipes run from the provincial to the urbane—each *does* borrow and learn from the other, and we have attempted to reflect this by giving you some of each. Before getting to the recipes, however, we have a very important *conseil*. We are well aware that mutton has a great following in many places, England among them. However, it does have a strong flavor, which we do not care for in our kitchen. When buying lamb, be sure to look for fresh, young lamb from six to eight months old. (You can identify it by its cover of white fat on the rosy pink, textured flesh.) Lamb much younger than this is very tender, but the cuts will be smaller so you must reduce the cooking time accordingly. We prefer fresh American lamb, graded either choice or prime, to frozen, imported lamb, which has a mutton-like flavor.

Carré d'Agneau Persillé

381

Above all, be wary of lamb which was "aged" in cryovac. To cut costs, many packers will pack meat this way immediately after cutting instead of letting it age for a few days. The assumption is that it is aging in cryovac. What it is really doing is coming close to turning rancid or "high" as Brillat-Savarin would have said. Be sure to ask your butcher about how the meat was aged because prolonged cryovac storage can produce a very unpleasant odor.

Beef started in the backyard, but lamb takes it a step further back to the flickering light of ancient Middle Eastern nomadic campfires. Lamb has always had a central place in this vast area of dramatic ethnic and geographic contrasts, and we have chosen three very tasty preparations to reflect this heritage. The first is a sautéed patty, very well seasoned, accompanied by one of several sauces, and the next two are perfect for spit roasting over a charcoal (or camp) fire. Any one of them would serve perfectly as the entrée for a backyard *méchoui*.

Moving to more substantial fare, you will find three braised preparations for cooler weather. Still under the influence of the Middle East and the spice trade, we first meet up with curry powder, clove, and coconut milk. Curry also flavors the sauce, but just enough, leaving an overall impression of smoothness often lacking in curried dishes. Then, to reflect the great affection for lamb in the British Isles, we offer you two stews. But, so as not to get caught in the middle of any culinary debates, there is a Scotch version and an Irish version. The former bears the inevitable mark of barley, and the latter, potatoes and onions. So, look up your family tree and make your choice accordingly.

Now we come to the more festive and elegant preparations calling for various roasted "joints of meat." When we were talking about beef, part of our rationale for not including a roast standing rib recipe was due to the fact that this cut is widely prepared—usually quite well, occasionally superbly—in hotels, restaurants, and private clubs. Alas, this is still not so for leg of lamb in this country, Escoffier's *gigot* not withstanding. As you will see from the recipe note, Julia Child had her go at setting matters right in her writings, and we think it important enough to offer a recipe here. It is simply seasoned, as it should be, for the roasting technique is the proper focus here. Join the movement and help stamp out tough and gray lamb.

Having mastered cooking a leg, you should be ready to confront the four roasts that conclude the lamb section. First comes a preparation that ranks with cold poached salmon in conjuring up images of haute cuisine. Actually, rack of lamb is more elegant in appearance than it is complicated in preparation, but we will not tell your guests. Most of all, do not overcook it, or all is lost. Saddle of lamb comes up next, in three different guises. Leading off is one of the best statements we have seen for *fresh mint*, and not mint-flavored apple jelly, with lamb. Ginger marinade, fresh mint, and a wine and cream sauce combined with perfectly roasted pink tenderloin slices will yield flavors savored long after the last forkful—especially if you cook this over charcoal.

In the final preparations, technique becomes more demanding, but the rewards are commensurate. First the saddle is stuffed with an aromatic and colorful filling featuring green peppercorns, then it is coated with fresh rosemary. Roasting proceeds with wine, demi-glace, and more rosemary in the roasting liquid, the whole producing a sauce which perfectly sets off this piquant roast. And, for the last offering, you will have to prevail upon the house baker to prepare Michel Finel's Pâte Feuilletée. This time lamb becomes the stuffing, along with spinach and walnuts, in a new ring on the venerable Medici theme, created by our talented Grille chef, Jim Wolfe. And how appropriate to end this section in the city wherein resides the *Palazzo dell'Arte della Lana* (palace of the guild of wool workers), home of one of the most powerful mercantile guilds in thirteenth-century Florence.

✣ *Muslin Kababs*

While working the opening of the Sheraton Tel Aviv in Israel, I frequented street stands and cafés for luleh kababs, *which are eaten for snacks and meals as we enjoy hamburgers. "Luleh" means "rolled," and the meat is rolled into a roll or around a skewer, grilled, and served without any sauce. The kababs in this recipe are lamb patties. The name, Muslin, may mean that they were indigenous to the town of Mosul, in Iraq, where muslin, a delicate woven fabric, was formerly made. Or the name may refer to the lightness of a gently formed patty, perfectly sautéed. Serve them with Sauce Chasseur or the mustard sauce used for Shish Kebab. For a cocktail party, make bite-size balls, sauté in Clarified Butter, and serve them with toothpicks for dipping in the sauce.*

Yields 6 servings

2 pounds (900 g) lamb shoulder
1 medium onion
1 teaspoon butter
1/4 teaspoon curry powder
Juice of 2 lemons
3/4 cup (180 ml) yogurt
1/2 cup (118 ml) sour cream
1 1/2 cups (355 ml) fine white bread crumbs
2 teaspoons chopped fresh parsley
Salt
Freshly ground black pepper
2 tablespoons Clarified Butter *(see page 568)*
1/4 cup (60 ml) peanut oil

Recommended equipment

A boning knife, meat grinder with fine blade, small mixing bowl, paring knife, small chef's knife, 8-inch (20 cm) sauté pan, blending fork, plastic wrap, waxed paper, 12-inch (30 cm) sauté pan, turning spatula, ovenproof pan.

Trim the fat from the lamb with the boning knife and cut the meat into manageable chunks for grinding. Using the fine blade of the meat grinder, grind the lamb once and then grind one-half of it a second time. Chill the meat, covered, in the mixing bowl until needed.

Trim the onion with the paring knife and mince it finely with the chef's knife. Set the small sauté pan over low heat, add the butter, and, when it is hot, cook the onions in it without browning until they are softened and golden (about 3 minutes). Remove from heat and let the onions cool before adding them to the ground lamb. When cool, scrape the onions into the mixing bowl with the lamb and add the curry powder, lemon juice, yogurt, sour cream, and 1 cup (235 ml) of the bread crumbs. Rinse the parsley, spin or pat dry, chop, and add it to the bowl. Season with salt and pepper and mix thoroughly with the blending fork. Then cover the bowl with plastic wrap and refrigerate the mixture for 30 minutes.

While the mixture chills, prepare the mustard sauce *(see page 385)* if you are using it.

When the lamb is cold, you can shape the patties. Spread the remaining bread crumbs on waxed paper, divide the lamb into twelve equal portions (by weight, if you like), roll each portion in the bread crumbs, and shape it into a round patty about 1 1/2 inches (3 3/4 cm) in diameter. Use a metal ring, such as a biscuit cutter, as a guide.

Preheat oven to 325F (163C).

Set the large sauté pan over medium high heat, add the clarified butter and the peanut oil, and, when it sizzles, add the patties. Sauté until brown, turn, and continue to cook (about 2 minutes on each side). When done, set the patties into the ovenproof pan and set them into the preheated oven for 5 minutes to finish cooking. When the patties are ready, remove them from the oven and serve piping hot, accompanied by their sauce on the side.

Shashlik Caucasian

The tradition of cooking this dish on skewers is more than a display for the guest. A staple throughout the Middle East and Eastern Europe for centuries, these pieces of lamb were skewered on nomad's swords and broiled over an open fire. The version below is from the southern side of the Caucasus Mountains, which divide the Georgian, Armenian, and Azerbaijan republics from the rest of the U.S.S.R. to the north. Shish Kebab, the variation which follows, reflects a Turkish influence. A well-trimmed young leg of lamb can be used for this popular preparation, but a saddle of lamb is preferable and always fork tender. Serve shashlik or shish kebab on a bed of Riz Valencienne accompanied by Tomatoes Provençale.

Yields 6 to 8 servings

- 1 saddle of lamb, weighing 8 to 10 pounds (3600 to 4500 g) before boning
- 1/2 medium onion
- 1/2 medium lemon
- 1/2 teaspoon freshly crushed black pepper
- Salt
- Olive oil

Recommended equipment

A boning knife, slicing knife, mortar and pestle, glass or ceramic bowl, plastic wrap, metal skewers, pastry brush, charcoal grill and charcoal.

Using the boning knife, trim nearly all the fat from the saddle of lamb and remove the silver skin entirely. Cut the meat into cubes about 1 1/2 by 2 inches (3 3/4 x 5 cm) and put them in the glass bowl.

Peel the onion and slice it very thinly. Rinse the lemon and slice it thinly, leaving the peel on. Crush the pepper in the mortar and pestle and add the onion, lemon, and pepper to the bowl with the lamb. Mix thoroughly using your hands, cover bowl with plastic wrap, and refrigerate for 18 to 24 hours.

When ready to cook, either preheat the broiler to very hot or start the charcoal fire in the grill. In either case, the lamb should be cooked 3 inches (7 1/2 cm) from the heat source. Stick the lamb pieces on skewers, salt the meat lightly, and brush it with olive oil. For pink lamb, cook it for 3 minutes and then turn over and cook for 3 more minutes. Serve at once.

Variation

Shish Kebab

1 recipe Shashlik Caucasian *(see pages 384–85)*
2 green bell peppers
2 red bell peppers
2 medium onions
18 large mushroom caps
1 tablespoon olive oil

Marinate the lamb and then prepare the vegetables to be cooked with it.

Preheat oven to 400F (204C).

Rinse the peppers, halve and seed them, and trim away the white pith. Cut them into 2-inch (5 cm) square pieces. Peel the onions and cut them in the same way. Brush the mushroom caps of any clinging dirt and set them with the peppers and onions into an ovenproof pan. Sprinkle the vegetables with the olive oil and set the pan into the oven for 3 to 4 minutes or until the vegetables have softened and are partially cooked. Remove from oven and when cool enough to handle, alternate the vegetables, three of each per skewer, with the lamb pieces and then cook as in the shashlik recipe.

If you wish, add thyme, bay leaves, and garlic to the marinade, but I prefer to serve the following uncomplicated mustard sauce on the side with both the shashlik and the shish kebab. Blend 1 part Escoffier Sauce Diable, 1/3 part Dijon mustard, 1 1/2 parts whipping cream, and 1/4 part Worcestershire sauce together with a whisk in a 1-quart (1 L) saucepan, set over moderate heat, bring to a low boil, and simmer for 3 minutes. Serve the sauce while it is hot.

Curry of Lamb Madras

The English word "curry" evolved from the Hindi word turcarri, *and the coconut palm, native to the tropical shores of the Indian and Pacific oceans, gives us coconut milk and cream. The curries from Sri Lanka, formerly Ceylon, almost always contain coconut milk and cream and, most likely, traders from Madras, India, were exchanging culinary secrets along with their famous cloth in Ceylon.*

Turkish Rice, sautéed eggplant strips (see below) and fried poppadums (lentil flour wafers) will provide authentic accompaniments.

Yields 6 servings

3 pounds (1350 g) lamb shoulder
Salt
Freshly ground white pepper
1 tablespoon flour
3 tablespoons peanut oil
1 medium onion
2 teaspoons curry powder
1 garlic clove
1/2 bay leaf
1 tablespoon tomato paste
3/4 cup (180 ml) dry white wine
3 cups (710 ml) Basic Curry Sauce *(see page 80)*
1 piece lemon rind, about 2 inches (5 cm) long (all bitter white removed)
1 cup (235 ml) canned or fresh coconut milk

Recommended equipment

A boning knife, waxed paper, 12-inch (30 cm) sauté pan, wooden spoon or spatula, long-handled fork, small chef's knife, garlic press, slotted spoon, 3-quart (3 L) saucepan with lid or Dutch oven, basting spoon.

Using the boning knife, bone and trim the lamb and cut into pieces about 1 inch (2 1/2 cm) square.

Spread waxed paper on your work surface and put the lamb cubes on top of it in a single layer. Season lightly with salt and pepper, dust with flour, and mix well.

Set the sauté pan over medium high heat, add the peanut oil, and when it is hot, add the lamb and sauté, stirring with the wooden spoon, until the meat is golden brown. If necessary, separate the pieces with the fork and turn them over so that they brown evenly.

While the meat is browning, peel the onion and mince it finely with the chef's knife.

When the meat is browned, reduce heat to medium, add the onion and the curry powder, and sauté, stirring, for 1 minute before pressing in the garlic and stirring in the bay leaf. With the slotted spoon holding back the lamb, drain off all the fat. Blend in the tomato paste and then deglaze the pan with wine, scraping up any brown bits from the pan bottom. Bring to the simmer and cook for 1 minute before adding the curry sauce, lemon peel, and coconut milk. Bring to a low boil for 2 minutes and then transfer the lamb to the saucepan or Dutch oven. Simmer gently while removing any fat with the basting spoon. Cover the saucepan loosely with lid and maintain a low simmer for 1 to 1 1/2 hours (or until the meat is fork tender). If you prefer, set the lamb into a 300F (149C) oven to cook.

When the lamb is tender, remove the bay leaf and lemon peel and serve while piping hot.

🙢

For sautéed eggplant strips, use the peel with 1/4 inch pulp attached, cut into 1/8-inch thick (1/3 cm) strips, and sauté in olive oil until crisp.

Scotch Lamb Stew

As early as the fourth century A.D. we find a recipe in Apicius' De Re Coquinaria for a soup featuring barley. An important staple in England, it was, along with rye, the common grain used in bread baking until the mid-nineteenth century. The base for flat Scotch grille cakes called bannocks, barley is also the ingredient without which Scotch broth cannot be made. So it is here. Simmering the lamb and barley together before the vegetables are introduced imparts a flavor unique to this stew. For an authentic touch, serve it with new potatoes boiled in their jackets, and dotted with butter—known in Scotland as "stoved tatties" or "stovies." Boiled carrots would also be appropriate for a springtime meal.

Yields 6 to 7 servings

3 pounds (1350 g) boneless lamb chuck
6 to 8 cups (1425 to 1900 ml) lamb stock *(see below)*
1 cup (235 ml) barley
2 large onions
2 celery stalks
1/2 medium turnip
1 medium carrot
1 medium leek
1/3 bay leaf
1/2 cup (118 ml) fresh (or frozen) green peas, blanched
1 teaspoon Worcestershire sauce
Freshly ground white pepper
2 teaspoons cornstarch
2 tablespoons cold water

Recommended equipment

A boning knife, 3-quart (3 L) saucepan with lid, colander, paring knife, slicing knife, stiff bristle brush, swivel-bladed vegetable peeler, basting spoon, 1-quart (1 L) saucepan, small bowl.

Using the boning knife, bone the lamb, trim it of all excess fat, and cut into 1- to 1 1/4-inch (2 1/2 to 3 1/4 cm) cubes. Put the lamb into the large saucepan, cover with warm water, set the saucepan over high heat, cover, and bring to the boil quickly. When the boil is reached, remove saucepan from heat, set it into the sink, and run cold water into it to cool the lamb. Then drain the lamb in the colander and rinse out the saucepan. Return the lamb to the saucepan, add the lamb stock, and set the pan over high heat. When the boil is reached, add the barley, cover saucepan, and adjust heat so that a steady simmer is maintained for 45 minutes.

While the lamb simmers, prepare the vegetables. Peel the onions, halve them, slice very thinly, and reserve. Rinse the celery stalks, peel them, cut into matchstick-size strips, and reserve. Scrub the turnip, peel and halve it, cut one-half into matchstick-size strips (reserve the other half for another use), and set aside. Scrub the carrot, peel it, cut into matchstick-size strips, and reserve. Cut the green top off the leek and discard (or use in a soup). Wash the white part under cold running water, separating the layers with your fingers to remove any sand or dirt, let drain briefly, cut into matchstick-size strips, and reserve.

When the lamb has simmered for 45 minutes, skim the liquid with the basting spoon, add the reserved vegetables and bay leaf, and continue simmering for another 35 to 45 minutes or until the lamb is tender and the barley is cooked. While the stew is cooking, blanch the fresh peas: bring water to boil in the small saucepan, add the peas, return to a boil, remove from heat, and run cold water into the saucepan to cool the peas. Let them drain and reserve until needed. (If you are using frozen peas, blanch them now and reserve.)

When the stew is done, season with Worcestershire sauce and pepper. Add salt if needed. Put the cornstarch in the small bowl and add the water slowly while mixing into a smooth paste. Remove stew from heat, blend cornstarch mixture well into stew, return saucepan to heat, and simmer, stirring, for 3 minutes. If stew is too thin, make some more cornstarch mixture and stir it into the stew. If stew is too thick, add some stock or water. When the consistency is just right, stir in the reserved peas and serve the stew at once.

For lamb stock, follow the procedure for White Chicken Stock *(see page 61)*. Substitute 2 to 2 1/2 pounds (900 to 1125 g) lamb bones cut into small pieces and 1 pound (450 g) lamb trimmings or lamb shank for the chicken. Omit the leeks. Simmer the stock for at least 6 hours, skimming the scum from the surface from time to time.

If there is any stew left over, it can be reheated over low heat for another meal or successfully frozen.

Irish Lamb Stew

According to Larousse Gastronomique, *I have been on the right track with this recipe all these years because both of its versions for Irish stew* (Ragoûts de Mouton à l'anglaise I and II) *are similar in calling for onions and potatoes (the Incan gift to the Old World). However, let me offer one* conseil. *Should you be so fortunate as to have an Irish grandmother, disregard the following recipe and put in a call to her instead.*

Yields 6 to 7 servings

3 pounds (1350 g) boneless lamb chuck
6 to 8 cups (1425 to 1900 ml) lamb stock *(see below)*
3 large onions
1/2 medium turnip
1/8 small white cabbage
1 medium leek
1/2 small garlic clove
3 large Idaho baking potatoes
1/3 bay leaf
1 teaspoon Worcestershire sauce
Salt
Freshly ground white pepper
1 teaspoon chopped fresh parsley

FOR THE GARNISH
1/2 cup (118 ml) fresh or frozen green peas, blanched
12 pearl onions
1/2 medium turnip
1/2 medium carrot

Recommended equipment

A boning knife, 3-quart (3 L) saucepan with lid, colander, paring knife, slicing knife, stiff bristle brush, swivel-bladed vegetable peeler, basting spoon, two 2-quart (2 L) saucepans (one with a lid), blender or food processor, wooden spoon.

Using the boning knife, bone the lamb, trim it of all excess fat, and cut into cubes about 3/4 to 1 inch (2 to 2 1/2 cm). Put the lamb into the large saucepan, cover with warm water, set the saucepan over high heat, cover, and bring to the boil quickly. When the boil is reached, remove saucepan from heat, set it into the sink, and run cold water into it to cool the lamb. Then drain the lamb in the colander and rinse out the saucepan. Return the lamb to the saucepan, add the lamb stock, and set the pan over high heat. When the boil is reached, cover the saucepan and adjust the heat so that the lamb maintains a steady simmer until the meat is tender but still firm (about 1 1/2 hours). When done, remove saucepan from heat and let lamb cool in the stock.

While the lamb cools, prepare the vegetables. Peel the onions, slice them thinly, and reserve. Scrub the turnip, peel and halve it, and cut one half into thin slices. Reserve the other half for the garnish. Cut the small cabbage wedge into thin slices. Cut the green top off the leek and discard (or use in a soup). Wash the white part under cold running water, separating the layers with your fingers to remove any sand or dirt, let drain briefly, slice thinly, and reserve. Peel the garlic and reserve. Scrub the potatoes, peel them, slice thinly, and reserve.

When the lamb has cooled, skim the liquid with the basting spoon, drain off the broth into one of the smaller saucepans, add all the reserved vegetables and the bay leaf to the broth, set the saucepan over medium high heat, bring to a simmer, cover pot, and adjust heat to maintain a steady simmer for 30 minutes. When done, let cool for half an hour in the saucepan.

While the vegetables simmer, prepare the garnish. Blanch the peas: bring water to boil in the remaining saucepan, add the peas, return to a boil, remove from heat, and run cold water into the saucepan to cool the peas. Then drain them and reserve until needed. Put fresh water into the saucepan, add some salt and the pearl onions, and simmer until the onions are just tender (about 15 minutes). When done, remove from heat, drain the onions, peel them, and reserve. (If using canned onions, drain them and set aside.) Peel the reserved turnip half, cut into matchstick-size strips, and cook them in lightly salted water to cover until just done and still firm. Drain the turnip strips and set aside. Scrub the carrot half, peel it, cut into matchstick-size strips, and cook them in lightly salted water to cover, with a pinch of sugar, until just done. When done, drain, refresh under cold water, and reserve.

When the vegetables and broth have cooked and cooled, remove the bay leaf and discard. Put the vegetables and broth by batches into the blender or food processor and purée until smooth. Then add the purée to the lamb in the saucepan, set over medium low heat, and bring to a gentle simmer while stirring. Season with Worcestershire sauce, salt, and pepper. Rinse the parsley, pat or spin dry, chop, and reserve. Stir in the reserved vegetable garnish, heat thoroughly, and serve in warm bowls, sprinkled with the parsley.

For lamb stock, follow the procedure for White Chicken Stock *(see page 61)*. Substitute 2 to 2 1/2 pounds (900 to 1125 g) lamb bones cut into small pieces and 1 pound (450 g) lamb trimmings or lamb shank for the chicken. Omit the leeks. Simmer the stock for at least 6 hours, skimming the scum from the surface from time to time.

The lamb and vegetables can be cooked at the same time in one saucepan, in which case you would remove the meat before puréeing the vegetables.

Roast Leg of Lamb au Jus

In the 1960s, when Julia Child began her crusade to elevate the American culinary consciousness, she drew a bead on some of this country's more abysmal kitchen practices—miscooking lamb being one of them. Puzzling over the apparent aversion to lamb held by some Americans, she asked "Is it because they scorn their old-world beginnings and consider lamb to be peasant food? Is it because they grew up on old gray roasts with thick gravy and mint sauce, or heavy stews reeking of mutton fat?" Noting that she too had grown up on "gray legs and heavy stews," she writes that her own conversion began with a trip to France in the late 1940s. For the entire delightful description we refer you to From Julia Child's Kitchen, *but listen as she is "waiting for gigot." "It was on a flowered terrace at a comfortable and informal restaurant near Saint-Paul-de-Vence that we saw, Paul and I, our first gigot à ficelle, a large leg of lamb hung by a string tied to its shank, slowly revolving in front of a banked up wood fire. Every once in a while, a waiter, going by, would give it a twist to keep it revolving, until it was finally brown and crisp and ready to carve. If you ordered lamb, and few diners could refuse its temptation, Alex, the headwaiter, would bring the whole leg to the table."*

She concludes with an account of carving by Alex and cooking instructions, but most of all the serious reader is left with an insight into the way leg of lamb is most enjoyed—lightly pink, juicy, and full of flavor—just as it is here. Two favorite French companions for gigot rôti au jus *are Flageolets Bretonne or Pommes de Terre Boulangère.*

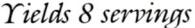

Yields 8 servings

1 leg of lamb, weighing 6 to 7 pounds (2700 to 3200 g)
1 medium garlic clove
2 shallots

FOR THE SEASONED COATING
1/2 teaspoon salt
1/2 teaspoon freshly ground black pepper
1/2 teaspoon chopped fresh rosemary
1/2 garlic clove
Grated lemon rind

FOR ROASTING
2 teaspoons peanut oil
1/2 medium onion
1 celery stalk
1/2 carrot
1 cup (235 ml) dry white wine

1 1/2 cups (355 ml) Demi-glace Brun I *(see page 75)*

Recommended equipment

A boning knife, white kitchen string, paring knife, small chef's knife, garlic press, box grater, small bowl, heavy roasting pan, stiff bristle brush, 2 wooden spatulas, bulb baster, serving platter, fine-mesh strainer, 1-quart (1 L) saucepan.

Bring the lamb to room temperature, and, using the boning knife, remove the hip bone from the large end of the leg by working around the joint and cutting it loose. Do not remove the skin or fat, unless there are areas where the fat is more than 1/4 inch or 2/3 cm thick, because both will keep the meat moist during roasting. (You may wish to remove the shank and braise it separately or use it in a stew, but the leg is more difficult to carve without it.) Tie the boned part of the leg with string every 2 inches (5 cm). Using the paring knife, peel the garlic clove and cut it into thirds. Peel the shallots and halve them. Work open a space with your finger around the bone on both ends of the leg and divide the garlic and shallot pieces between the spaces, pushing them up as far as possible. Do not make incisions with a knife.

Preheat oven to 400F (204C).

Prepare the seasoned coating. Put the salt and pepper into the small bowl; rinse, pat dry, and chop the rosemary and add it to the bowl; peel the garlic clove and press it into the bowl; and, using the fine side of the box grater, take a whole lemon, grate the rind from one half of it (leaving the bitter white behind), and blend the rind with the other ingredients in the bowl. Rub the seasoning mixture all over the leg.

Oil the roasting pan with the peanut oil, put the leg into it, skin side up, and set it into the oven for 20 minutes. Reduce the oven temperature to 325F (163C) and roast the leg for 30 minutes.

Meanwhile, prepare the vegetables. Peel and quarter the onion half and reserve. Scrub the celery stalk, quarter it, and reserve. Scrub the carrot half, cut into thirds, and reserve.

At the end of this 30-minute period, baste the lamb with the fat in the pan and strew the vegetables around it. Roast 15 minutes. Then pour in the wine and roast another 35 minutes, basting the lamb from time to time with the pan juices. (The total cooking time should be about 1 hour and 40 minutes for pink lamb and 2 hours for medium lamb.)

When the lamb is done, remove it from the oven and set it on a serving platter, skin side down, and let it rest for at least 15 minutes in a warm, not hot, place before carving. While the roast rests, add the demi-glace to the roasting pan, set over medium low heat, and simmer gently while scraping up the brown bits from the pan bottom. After 15 minutes, strain the sauce into the saucepan, skim off all fat, and add any juices from the platter that have escaped while the lamb was resting.

With the sauce ready, you may turn the leg over and carve it into neat slices. Serve them on a warm dinner plate with the sauce spooned over them.

The cooking times given above are for a pink or medium roast. For a medium well done roast (perish the thought!) increase the cooking time to 15 to 16 minutes per pound. To ease the task of carving, try the French tour de main of trimming about 3 inches (7 1/2 cm) of the meat and sinews away from the end of the shank. This gives you a handle around which you can wrap some aluminum foil to hold the leg while carving it. If you have a *manche à gigot* (lamb holding sleeve), so much the better! Then, following Alex's lead, take a sharp long knife and start midway between the large end and the shank. Holding the knife almost parallel to the surface, make successive slices, moving about 1/4 to 3/8 of an inch (2/3 to 1 cm) toward the large end each time.

Carré d'Agneau Persillé
Rack of Lamb with Parsley Crust

Rack of Lamb—the very name conjures up visions of elegant dinners in private houses, first-class restaurants and hotels, or exotic culinary settings such as the Orient Express *and the* France's *legendary Salle Chambord, where Henri Le Huédé records that he often roasted as many as two hundred racks for a single sitting. Although featured in the Grille, table-side carving by a maître d'hôtel is not crucial to the success of this dish. But you must pay careful attention to the cooking and presentation of this delicate roast; overcook it, and your effort and expense will have been wasted. Be sure not to crowd your guests' plates. Because these are rib chops and smaller than those from the loin, if you end up with three per serving, use a small side plate for the vegetables. Pommes de Terre Dauphine will enhance this venerable dish. Prepare pencil-thin fresh Asparagus, tiny String Beans, and Carottes Glacées, then gather a few of each together in a bouquet to garnish each plate* à la bouquetière.

Yields 5 to 6 servings

1 whole (7 rib) rack of lamb, weighing 6 1/2 to 7 1/2 pounds (3000 to 3500 g)
Salt
Freshly ground black pepper
2 teaspoons peanut oil

FOR THE PERSILLADE
2 tablespoons chopped shallots
1 small garlic clove
2 tablespoons chopped parsley
1/2 teaspoon chopped fresh rosemary leaves
2 tablespoons (30 g) butter
2 tablespoons olive oil
2/3 cup (160 ml) fine white bread crumbs
Salt
Freshly ground black pepper

FOR ROASTING
1/2 medium onion
1/2 celery stalk
1/3 carrot
Fresh rosemary stems

1/2 cup (118 ml) dry white wine
1/2 cup (118 ml) brown lamb stock *(see pages 63–64)*

A table for two in the Grille

Recommended equipment

A boning knife, garlic press, small chef's knife, roasting pan, 8-inch (20 cm) sauté pan, wooden spatula, fine-mesh sieve, serving platter.

Have your butcher split and trim the rack. (If you do it yourself, split the rack down the middle with a sharp cleaver and trim off all excess fat and tissue.) The trimmed weight should be about 2 3/4 to 3 pounds (1250 to 1350 g). Using the boning knife, take each side of the rack in turn and remove about 1 inch (2 1/2 cm) of fat and skin from around the ends of the bones. (This is known as "Frenching.") Trim the fat layer so that it is 1/8 to 1/4 inch (1/3 to 2/3 cm) thick, and, on the last two to three ribs on the top side (toward the shoulder), trim off the top layer of meat and fat called "deckel" (German for "cover"). Season the racks lightly with salt and pepper.

Preheat oven to 375F (190C).

Spread the peanut oil in the roasting pan, put the two lamb rack halves into it with the fat side down, and set the pan over medium high heat. When the racks are sizzling, remove from heat and set the pan into the oven to roast for 20 minutes.

Prepare the persillade. Peel and chop the shallots. Peel the garlic. Rinse the parsley, pat dry, chop, and reserve. Rinse the rosemary, pat dry, strip off the leaves, chop them, and reserve the stems separately from the leaves. Set the sauté pan over medium low heat, add the butter and olive oil, and, when they are hot, add the shallots and sauté for 1 minute before pressing in the garlic. Stir together well with the spatula, stir in the bread crumbs and rosemary leaves, and season lightly with salt and pepper. Mix well, then remove from heat and let the mixture cool before stirring in the parsley. Reserve the persillade until needed.

When the rack has finished the first roasting, remove it from the oven and transfer it to the platter to cool slightly. Reduce the oven heat to 325F (163C). When the lamb is cool enough to handle, pat the persillade evenly on the fat sides of the racks, making sure that it will adhere. Return the racks to the roasting pan (persillade side up), set aside, and prepare the roasting vegetables. Peel the onion half and cut into 1/2-inch (1 1/4 cm) chunks. Wash the celery and carrot and cut into 1/2-inch thick slices. Strew the vegetables and the reserved rosemary stems in the bottom of the roasting pan around the racks and set the pan into the oven to roast for 15 minutes (or 20 to 25 minutes for well-done lamb). When the lamb is done to your taste, remove from oven, transfer to the platter, and let rest in a warm (not hot) spot for 8 to 10 minutes before carving.

While the lamb rests, remove the fat from the roasting pan, set over medium high heat, add the white wine to the pan, and simmer to deglaze the pan while scraping up the brown bits with the wooden spatula. When the wine is reduced by one-half, add the lamb stock, continue simmering for 5 minutes, and then strain the sauce into a small, warm bowl. Slice the racks into individual "chops," each with its bone, and present them, overlapping in a semicircle, on a warm dinner plate, with the sauce spooned over them.

Variation

 ## *Carré d'Agneau Diable*
Rack of Lamb with Mustard and Parsley Crust

When the racks are cool enough to handle, just before patting on the persillade, spread 4 teaspoons of Dijon mustard evenly on the fat sides.

Broiled Marinated Tenderloin of Lamb with Fresh Mint Cream Sauce

If you are a bit blasé about roast lamb and feel that legs and racks are old hat, we suggest you try a postgraduate course with the three following preparations. Personally, we have never felt that the all-too-automatic pairing of mint-flavored apple jelly with lamb was a happy culinary event. Perhaps it is a good way of disguising mutton which is past its prime, but the delicacy of mint is all but lost. Here, we feel, is the proper marriage of fresh lamb and fresh mint (under no circumstances use dried). Moreover, marinating the lamb in ginger and garlic produces an end result which will revive any sleeping tastebuds you might have. Prepare the mint sauce while the lamb marinates. Broil the saddle or grill it over very hot coals—either way, the sauce enhances rather than obscures the distinctive lamb flavor. Serve accompanied with fresh sautéed mushrooms and peas.

Yields 6 to 7 servings

1 saddle of lamb, weighing 7 to 9 pounds (3200 to 4100 g)

FOR THE MARINADE
3 ounces (85 g) fresh ginger
1 garlic clove
1/4 teaspoon crushed black pepper
1 cup (235 ml) olive oil
1/8 teaspoon salt

FOR THE MINT SAUCE
Lamb bones from the saddle
1/2 medium onion
1/2 celery stalk
1 small garlic clove
1 1/2 cups (355 ml) dry white wine
1 cup (235 ml) lamb stock *(see below)*
1 teaspoon chopped fresh mint leaves
1 tablespoon fresh mint stems and pieces
1 1/2 cups (355 ml) whipping cream
2 tablespoons Crosse and Blackwell mint sauce

Recommended equipment

A boning knife, paring knife, box grater, small bowl, garlic press, mortar and pestle, pan for marinating lamb, cleaver, roasting pan, wooden spatula, small chef's knife, 2-quart (2 L) saucepan, fine-mesh sieve, 1-quart (1 L) bowl, broiler pan with rack, serving platter.

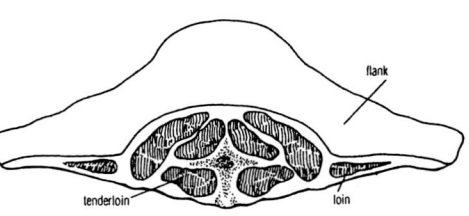

Top side with bone, untrimmed flanks, loin, and fillet.

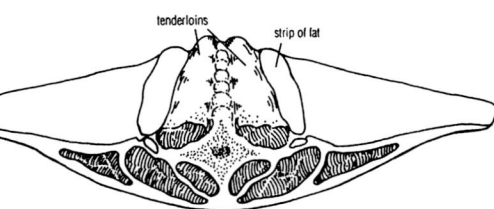

Bottom side of saddle with flank, loin, fillets, and strips of fat.

Using the boning knife, carefully remove the two loins and fillets so that you have four long pieces of meat. Completely trim the skin, the fat, and flank pieces from the loins and fillets and reserve the bones for the sauce *(see illustrations above)*. Set the lamb aside while the marinade is made.

Peel the fresh ginger with the paring knife and grate it on the fine side of the box grater into the small bowl. Peel the garlic clove and press it into the bowl. Crush the pepper in the mortar and pestle and add to the bowl. Pour in the olive oil, add the salt, and stir to combine the marinade ingredients. Set the lamb pieces into the pan, pour on the marinade, and marinate for 4 hours.

During the last hour of the marinating period, begin the mint sauce. Preheat broiler to 325F (163C). Using the cleaver, cut the reserved lamb bones into pieces about 1 to 1 1/2 inches (2 1/2 to 3 3/4 cm) long. When the oven is hot, put the bones into the roasting pan and set it into the oven to roast until they are nicely browned. Be careful not to let them scorch because the sauce will be bitter. While the bones are browning, prepare the vegetables. Peel and quarter the onion half; rinse the celery stalk and cut into thirds; and peel the garlic clove.

When the bones are brown, remove from the oven, drain the fat from the pan, add the onion, celery, and garlic to the bones, and return them to the oven to roast for 2 minutes. Then remove pan from the oven, set over medium high heat, add the wine and lamb stock, and simmer, scraping up the brown bits from the pan bottom, until the liquid has been reduced to 1/2 cup (118 ml). Rinse the fresh mint, spin or pat dry, strip off the leaves, chop them, and reserve 1 teaspoon. Chop enough stems and pieces for 1 tablespoon. Transfer the pan contents to the saucepan, set over medium low heat, and add the cream, mint stems and pieces, and the commercial mint sauce. Simmer the sauce, stirring from time to time, until it has been reduced to 1 cup (235 ml) and is creamy and smooth. Strain the sauce through the sieve into a bowl (or another saucepan), add the reserved chopped fresh mint leaves, and adjust the seasoning. If you are not cooking the lamb right away, dot the top of the sauce with bits of butter to prevent a skin from forming. Otherwise, rinse out the saucepan, scrape the sauce into it, and keep warm over very low heat (or use a double boiler) until the lamb is broiled.

To cook the lamb, adjust the oven rack to the highest position (about 3 inches or 7 1/2 cm from heat source) and preheat the broiler to maximum heat. Set the lamb on the rack in the broiler pan and broil for 3 minutes on each side for medium rare. For medium, add 1/2 minute more for each side. (Do not use this recipe for well-done lamb because the meat will be dry.) When the lamb is done, remove it from the broiler pan and set it on the platter to rest for 5 minutes in a warm (not hot) spot. When ready to serve, be sure the mint sauce is warm and add any lamb juices from the platter to it. Slice the lamb on a slant into slices 1/4 inch (2/3 cm) thick. Spoon the sauce onto warm serving plates or platter, arrange the slices on top, and serve at once.

For lamb stock, follow the procedure for White Chicken Stock *(see page 61)*. Substitute 2 to 2 1/2 pounds (900 to 1125 g) lamb bones cut into small pieces and 1 pound (450 g) lamb trimmings or lamb shank for the chicken. Omit the leeks. Simmer the stock for at least 6 hours, skimming the scum from the surface from time to time.

The French and American versions of a saddle of lamb differ considerably—the former (*selle d'agneau*) typically considered to be the rump or sirloin and the latter the entire loin and tenderloin. Save for the "baron" of lamb, there is no more special cut, and these recipes are intended for occasions which demand the best from your kitchen. The illustrations above are intended to help you either to trim the meat yourself or to give the butcher instructions, and you should refer to them as needed.

Roast Saddle of Lamb with Green Peppercorns and Rosemary

Save for the roasting technique, this preparation could almost be called a ballottine of lamb. Its appearance is certainly as stunning as one, with parsley and green peppercorns stippling every slice with colorful pinpoints of green. Nor does the flavor play second fiddle to the appearance. Sauce, meat, and aromatic stuffing constantly interact until you have chased the last peppercorn around your plate and bid fond adieu to the one remaining fleck of rosemary. The whole loin is a luxurious roast for a special dinner party. Serve it garnished with sprigs of fresh rosemary and accompanied by Pommes de Terre Boulangère or Parisienne Rissolées, Tomatoes Provençale, and fresh String Beans.

Yields 8 servings

1 saddle of lamb, weighing 7 to 9 pounds (3200 to 4100 g)
1 teaspoon coarsely chopped fresh rosemary
1/2 teaspoon salt
1/2 teaspoon freshly ground black pepper
Lamb bones from the loin

FOR THE STUFFING
1 medium onion
1 celery stalk
1 garlic clove
1 teaspoon butter
1 teaspoon water
8 ounces (225 g) lamb trimmings
8 ounces (225 g) veal or pork trimmings
1 tablespoon chopped parsley
2/3 cup (160 ml) fine white bread crumbs
2/3 cup (160 ml) half-and-half
1/4 teaspoon salt
3 tablespoons green peppercorns (packed in water and drained)

FOR ROASTING
1/2 onion
1/2 celery stalk
1/2 carrot
1 tablespoon fresh rosemary stems and pieces
1 cup (235 ml) dry white wine

2 cups (475 ml) Demi-glace Brun I *(see page 75)*

Recommended equipment

A boning knife, cleaver, small chef's knife, small bowl, paring knife, garlic press, 10-inch (25 cm) sauté pan, wooden spatula, meat grinder with fine blade, 2-quart (2 L) mixing bowl, rubber spatula, white kitchen string, heavy roasting pan, platter, fine-mesh sieve, 2-quart (2 L) saucepan, basting spoon.

Using the boning knife, completely bone the saddle, reserving the bones and all the trimmings *(see illustrations page 394)*. Remove the skin and excess fat from the flanks but leave at least 1/4 inch (2/3 cm) over the loin to protect it while roasting. Using the cleaver, cut the bones into pieces roughly 1 1/2 inches (3 3/4 cm) long. Chop the rosemary with the chef's knife, mix it with the salt and pepper in a small bowl, and reserve.

Prepare the stuffing. Peel the onion and chop it finely. Rinse the celery stalk, make it as stringless as possible, and dice it finely. Peel the garlic clove. Set the sauté pan over low heat, add the butter, water, onion, celery, and press in the garlic clove. Sauté gently without browning for 3 minutes, scrape into mixing bowl, and let cool while you grind the meat. Remove most of the fat from the lamb trimmings and grind them twice, using the fine blade. Chill the ground lamb while you grind the veal or pork trimmings twice in the same fashion. Rinse the parsley, pat dry, and chop. Add the ground meats to the mixing bowl with the sautéed vegetables and then add the parsley, bread crumbs, half-and-half, and salt. If you are not ready to stuff the saddle, chill the stuffing until needed.

When you are ready to stuff the saddle, lay it out on your work surface with the skin side down. Salt the saddle lightly. Spread one-half of the stuffing over the loin sections and between them. Arrange the green peppercorns between the two loins, spread the remaining stuffing over the peppercorns, and roll the saddle together, folding the flank tightly around the loins. Tie the rolled saddle with string at 2- to 3-inch (5 to 7 1/2 cm) intervals. Rub the saddle with the salt, pepper, and rosemary blend reserved in the small bowl.

Preheat oven to 375F (190C).

Set the saddle into the roasting pan, top side up, strew the bones around the saddle, and set it into the oven to roast for 25 minutes. Then reduce heat to 325F (163C) and roast an additional 20 minutes.

While the saddle is roasting, prepare the vegetables needed in the next step. Peel and quarter the onion half. Trim and quarter the celery and the carrot halves. When the 20-minute roasting period is finished, add the vegetables and the rosemary pieces to the roasting pan and cook another 10 minutes. Then pour the wine into the pan and roast the saddle another 20 minutes. The total cooking time will be 75 minutes for pink lamb. (If the saddle weighs more than 7 1/2 pounds before boning, add 10 to 15 minutes to the cooking time; if it weighs less than 7 pounds, subtract 10 minutes from the total time.)

When the roast is done, remove from oven and set it skin side down on a platter to rest in a warm (not hot) spot for 15 minutes before carving. While the roast rests, set the pan over medium low heat, add the demi-glace, bring to a simmer, and cook, stirring up the brown bits from the pan bottom, for 10 minutes. Then pass the sauce through the sieve into the saucepan. Skim any fat from the sauce with the basting spoon, add any juices from the platter that have escaped from the roast, adjust seasoning if needed, and keep warm while you carve the saddle.

Cut the strings and remove from the roast. Unroll the flank, cut most of it off, and discard before carving the saddle into slices 1/2 to 3/4 inch (1 1/4 to 2 cm) thick. Spoon some sauce onto each warm dinner plate, arrange the slices on top, and serve at once.

Tenderloin of Lamb en Croûte Florentine

The original version of this preparation, which I still have in my recipe box, called for a tarragon-flavored stuffing, listed below as a variation so you can try it. However, Jim Wolfe, our innovative Grille chef, came up with this tasty alternative, which is very popular among his diners. Along with Michelin three-star Chef Georges Blanc of Vonnas, who prepares cannelloni stuffed with baby Swiss chard and walnuts, Jim realized that spinach, walnuts, cheese, and cream could provide a stuffing which perfectly complemented young lamb. Be sure to taste the stuffing mixture before using it, as the fresh nutmeg should point up, but not dominate, the spinach. If the stuffing seems a bit flat, add a few more grinds of nutmeg. Serve this with Sauce Béarnaise, the mustard sauce for Shaslik Caucasian, or simply au jus using browned lamb bones simmered with lamb stock. Small vegetables gathered à la bouquetière *on the plate with the lamb and a salad of Boston lettuce, endive, and radicchio with a walnut oil dressing would handsomely complete this elegant entrée.*

Yields 6 to 7 servings *Recommended equipment*

1 saddle of lamb, weighing about 7 to 9 pounds (3200 to 4100 g)

FOR THE STUFFING

8 ounces (225 g) fresh spinach
3/4 cup (180 ml) fine white bread crumbs
3/8 cup (90 ml) chopped walnuts
1 tablespoon grated Parmesan cheese
1 tablespoon grated imported Swiss (Emmentaler) cheese
1 cup (235 ml) whipping cream
Salt
Freshly ground white pepper
Freshly ground nutmeg

FOR ROASTING

4 pieces pork fatback, about 5 inches (12 1/2 cm) square and 1/8 inch (1/3 cm) thick
2 tablespoons peanut oil
12 ounces (340 g) Pâte Feuilletée *(see page 513)*
2 egg yolks
2 tablespoons water

A boning knife, 3-quart (3 L) saucepan with lid, colander, small chef's knife, box grater, rubber spatula, 1-quart (1 L) bowl, nutmeg grinder, plastic wrap, butcher's steel, metal bulb baster, white kitchen string, 12-inch (30 cm) sauté pan, platter, rolling pin, wire whisk, pastry brush, baking pan.

Using the boning knife, carefully remove the two loins and fillets so that you have four long pieces of meat *(see illustrations page 394)*. Completely trim the skin, the fat, and flank pieces from the loins and fillets and reserve the fillets for another use. Set the lamb aside while the stuffing is made.

Fill the saucepan with water, set over high heat, and bring to a boil. While waiting, pick over the spinach and wash it thoroughly in a sinkful of cold water, plunging it up and down several times, to rid it of all sand. Let drain in a colander. When the water is boiling, add the spinach and cook 3 to 4 minutes, stirring occasionally. Then drain spinach in the colander and run cold water over it for 1 minute to cool the spinach. Let the spinach drain while you prepare the other stuffing ingredients.

Measure out the bread crumbs into the bowl. Chop the walnuts with the chef's knife and add them. Grate the cheeses into the bowl. Wring the spinach out by small handfuls, chop it finely, and stir it into the ingredients in the bowl, using the rubber spatula. Pour the whipping cream into the bowl, while mixing with the spatula, until the mixture has a loose consistency. Season with salt, pepper, and nutmeg, cover the bowl with plastic wrap, and refrigerate for 30 minutes to 1 hour to allow the bread crumbs to absorb the cream and set.

When ready to stuff the tenderloins, take them one at a time and with the help of a butcher's steel (knife sharpener) make a hole straight through the center of the loin from one end to another. To enlarge the hole, use a metal bulb baster (with bulb removed) and push it through. Push as much spinach filling as possible into the opening, working from both sides, and reserve whatever is left over. Then cover both ends of each loin with a piece of fatback and tie them on with kitchen string at 2-inch (5 cm) intervals. Be sure the string is not too tight.

Set the sauté pan over medium high heat, add the peanut oil, and, when it is hot, sear the lamb on all sides to seal in the juices. This should take no more than 5 minutes. Remove pan from heat and set the lamb loins on a platter to cool with the top side facing down.

When the lamb is cool, divide the pâte feuilletée into two equal pieces, and roll out each piece into a rectangle about 10 by 6 inches (25 x 15 cm) and 1/8 to 1/4 inch (1/3 to 2/3 cm) thick. Blend the egg yolks and water together well, using the whisk. With the pastry brush, brush the egg wash in a 2-inch (5 cm) band around the edges of the pastry rectangles.

Preheat oven to 375F (190C).

Divide the leftover stuffing into two equal portions and spread down the center of each pastry rectangle. Remove the strings and fatback from the lamb loins and place a loin on the stuffing with the smooth top side facing down. Fold the pastry up and around the lamb, press together, and seal the pastry with more egg wash. Turn each lamb loin over, so that the stuffing spread on the pastry is on the top, and set them into the baking pan. Brush the tops and sides of each pastry package with more egg wash and set into the oven to bake for 20 minutes for pink lamb. If the saddle of lamb weighed less than 7 pounds (or if you used a rack instead), reduce the baking time by 5 to 8 minutes. When the loins are done, let them rest in a warm (not hot) spot for 5 to 10 minutes before serving.

When ready to serve, carve the loins with either a serrated or well-sharpened carving knife so as not to break the pastry. Set the slices on warm serving plates with the sauce by their side.

If a saddle of lamb is unavailable, a whole rack may be substituted. In this case, the yield would be 5 to 6 servings.

Variation

Tenderloin of Lamb en Croûte à l'Estragon

Use this tarragon stuffing for the tenderloins instead of the spinach stuffing called for above.

1 cup (235 ml) fine white bread crumbs
1 1/4 to 1 1/3 cups (295 to 315 ml) half-and-half
1/8 teaspoon salt
A pinch of freshly ground white pepper
1 teaspoon chopped fresh tarragon
1 tablespoon chopped fresh parsley
1 egg yolk

Recommended equipment

A 1-quart (1 L) mixing bowl, mixing fork, plastic wrap.

In the mixing bowl, combine the bread crumbs, 1 1/4 cups half-and-half, salt, pepper, tarragon, parsley, and egg yolk. Mix all together well with the fork, cover the bowl with plastic wrap, and set it into the refrigerator for an hour. The mixture must be a smooth paste—add more half-and-half, a few drops at a time, as needed.

Pork

> Thus this custom of firing houses continued, till in process of time, says my manuscript, a sage arose, like our Locke, who made a discovery that the flesh of swine, or indeed of any other animal, might be cooked (burnt, as they called it) without the necessity of consuming a whole house to dress it. Then first began the rude form of a gridiron. Roasting by the string or spit came in a century or two later, I forget in what dynasty. By such slow degrees, concludes the manuscript, do the most useful, and seemingly the most obvious, arts make their way among mankind—
>
> Without placing too implicit faith in the account above given, it must be agreed that if a worthy pretext for so dangerous an experiment as setting houses on fire (especially in these days) could be assigned in favour of any culinary object, that pretext and excuse might be found in ROAST PIG.
>
> Of all the delicacies in the whole *mundus edibilis*, I will maintain it to be the most delicate—*princeps* obsoniorum.
>
> —Charles Lamb

Ah, the porker, truffle hunter par excellence and source of countless toothsome treats. If Charles Lamb is correct (and who for a moment could doubt his ancient Chinese source), we owe a special debt to Bo-bo, the careless son of Ho-ti the swineherd. For it was in a moment of inattention that he burned down the pigsty, unwittingly creating the first recorded barbecue. If you are from the South, this touches your culinary heart. If you are not from the South, there is no way to try to explain it.

As we noted earlier, I serve a vast variety of pork not represented here because there is no way to duplicate it at home. I mean, a York ham steak is not worth discussing unless accompanied by our buckwheat cakes, Vermont maple syrup, butter, freshly squeezed orange juice, and special Homestead blend coffee—all rolled onto your porch by Room Service as the sun is just coming over Warm Springs Mountain. Or, what about coming in from a vigorous December hike on Deerlick Trail, chilled and faint with hunger, and slipping into the richly paneled Commonwealth Room for a lunch of smoked loin of pork on sauerkraut with Swiss farm sausage and parsleyed potatoes? Sorry, but I just cannot pack a piece of our mountain landscape with every copy of this book. And as for barbecue, not a chance. We serve what I think is a pretty fair one at Sam Snead's Tavern.

Roast Loin of Pork Stuffed with Apricots

But, down the road at Covington or in Prosperity, West Virginia, people would turn their noses up at it. (I do recall that my North Carolina coauthors once politely ate a sandwich made of it.) So seriously is this matter taken in the South that a recent regional survey actually used type of barbecue sauce as a demographic variable for differentiating among various regions. But, if you are southern, you already know that.

One great development on the pork scene is the appearance of lean pork. Not about to be outdone by beef and lamb, pork producers have switched to very lean breeding stock—so successfully so that you may have difficulty finding the sliced fatback called for as a protective wrapping elsewhere in this book. But, overall, this is extremely good culinary news because not only does reducing fat have dietary implications but it also minimizes the digestibility problems so long associated with this delicious meat. So, go out and buy a pork roast, but follow our cooking method and not Bo-bo's.

Our brief excursion starts with a very safe, noncontroversial (unless you are from Hunan province) Chinese-style preparation for spareribs. An excellent picnic item, the ribs can be oven baked or charcoal grilled depending on your preference. Next comes a Roman-inspired recipe which more than anything else can serve as a general technique just as scaloppine does for veal. Pounded into thin slices, as it is here, pork tenderloin can be served in as many ways as can veal, with sauces ranging from the hunter style called for in this preparation to the lightest of pan deglazes. As a final entry in the sauté division, we have included a very tasty marinated tenderloin which is sliced, sautéed, and served with a cream sauce based on the reduced marinade and demi-glace.

Two preparations for larger cuts end the section and the chapter. Apricots in the center and rosemary on the outside dress up a loin and provide an elegant roast which, sauced with a mustard cream, is excellent served hot, or, sliced thinly, makes a superb item for a cold luncheon. Finally, is there a meat which says "Virginia" any more than ham? Even chefs in France will call for our home-cured product in preference to Bayonne or Black Forest for some recipes. Here, we have offered you one of our traditional favorites, featuring a colorful fruit dressing and a light sugar glaze as well as several alternatives. One thing is sure, you will be sad indeed to see how fast this ham bone disappears from the refrigerator.

Well, there you have it. Teriyaki beef short ribs to Homestead Virginia ham and lots of good "hours of meat" in between. Remember the other parts about sleep and exercise in the words of Sir Francis and you will be well on the way to mastering the "precepts of long lasting."

Chinese Barbecued Spareribs

What really happened at Ho-ti's pigsty is a matter of conjecture, but we do know that during the Han period, just before 100 B.C., the Emperor Wu Ti entered an expansionist phase which extended his influence west toward Persia and south toward Canton. With him came the pomegranate, whose syrup is an important ingredient in this sauce, a favorite of ours in the Hunan sweet and sour style. For tender, moist, spareribs, whether broiled indoors or grilled outdoors, I prefer to preboil them. (Whatever flavor may be lost is negligible when compared with the pleasure of a dish that is perfectly prepared every time.) Steamed Rice is the perfect background for these ribs.

Yields 6 servings

5 pounds (2250 g) pork spareribs

FOR THE BARBECUE SAUCE
2 cups (475 ml) ketchup
2 tablespoons soy sauce
1 tablespoon white vinegar
2 tablespoons grated fresh ginger root
2 garlic cloves
1 tablespoon dry English mustard
1/2 cup (118 ml) pineapple juice
1/2 teaspoon Worcestershire sauce
Peel of 1 lemon grated
1 tablespoon pomegranate syrup
1/2 cup (100 g) light brown sugar
1/4 cup (60 ml) dry sherry
Salt
Freshly ground white pepper
1 tablespoon honey

Recommended equipment

An 8-quart (8 L) stockpot with lid; fine-mesh skimmer; 1-quart (1 L) mixing bowl; paring knife; box grater; small chef's knife; wire whisk; 5-quart (5 L) glass, ceramic, or stainless steel bowl; plastic wrap; aluminum foil; broiler pan; pastry brush.

Put the spareribs in the stockpot, add lightly salted hot water to cover, put the pot over high heat, and bring pot to a boil. Then lower the heat and simmer gently for about 50 minutes to an hour or until the ribs are tender yet still firm. Skim the pot from time to time, and after the first skimming cover the pot with the lid. When the ribs are done, remove the pot from the heat, let ribs cool in the broth, then remove ribs from the pot, and let drain thoroughly. Set the ribs into the large bowl.

While the ribs are simmering, prepare the barbecue sauce. Put the ketchup, soy sauce, and vinegar into the small mixing bowl. Then peel and grate the ginger and add it to the bowl. Peel the garlic clove, chop with the chef's knife, and add it to the bowl along with the mustard, pineapple juice, and Worcestershire sauce. Then grate the peel of the lemon on the fine side of the box grater and add it to the sauce along with the pomegranate syrup, brown sugar, and sherry. Mix well with the whisk and taste before adding salt and white pepper.

When the ribs have cooled, pour the marinade over them, cover the bowl with plastic wrap, and refrigerate for 2 to 8 hours, turning occasionally.

When the ribs are ready to cook, preheat oven to 300F (149C). Line the broiler pan with aluminum foil. Remove the ribs from the marinade and lay them in the pan in a single layer with the meaty side up. Reserve 1/2 cup marinade, pour the rest over the ribs, and set them into the oven to bake. Mix the reserved marinade with the honey and brush this over the ribs during the first 15 minutes. When the ribs are nicely glazed and piping hot (after about 30 minutes), remove them from the oven and serve at once.

If pomegranate syrup is unavailable, substitute 1 cup (235 ml) pomegranate juice simmered separately to reduce it to 1/4 cup (60 ml) before making the sauce. Any leftover marinade can be refrigerated or frozen to be used again.

Variation: This barbecue sauce works well for chicken. Buy one that weighs 2 1/4 to 2 1/2 pounds (1025 to 1125 g), split in half, marinate for one to two days, and bake at 300F, covered with foil, for 30 minutes, remove foil, and bake another hour, or until tender. Baste with the sauce several times during cooking. If you grill the chicken, use a low fire and baste frequently to keep the meat moist. One chicken yields 2 servings.

Piccata of Pork

The term "piccata" is also applied to veal and typically refers to a scaloppina which is pounded thin. This recipe is particularly for those skeptics who feel that pork is always tough and dry. But, you must move very quickly in the sautéing to make sure the pork is kept tender and juicy. Savor the Roman reminiscence of sage and complete the vision by serving Fettuccine Alfredo.

Yields 6 servings

- 3/4 cup (180 ml) Sauce Chasseur (see page 80)
- 1 boneless pork loin, weighing 1 1/2 to 2 pounds (675 to 900 g)
- 1/4 cup (30 g) flour
- Salt
- Freshly ground black pepper
- 3 eggs
- 2 tablespoons water
- 1 tablespoon grated Parmesan cheese
- 5 medium, fresh sage leaves, chopped
- 1/2 cup (118 ml) peanut oil
- 2 teaspoons chopped fresh parsley

Recommended equipment

A slicing knife, waxed paper, cleaver, wire whisk, small bowl, box grater, small chef's knife, 12-inch (30 cm) sauté pan, turning spatula, wire rack for draining pork, heatproof platter.

Prepare the sauce chasseur and keep warm over very low heat (or in a double boiler) while you prepare the pork.

Trim the pork loin of excess fat, leaving only a very thin layer (or remove all fat, if you wish). Slice the loin into twelve cutlets and, one at a time, using the flat side of the cleaver (or the bottom of a small sauté pan), flatten them between two pieces of waxed (or freezer) paper to a thickness of 1/8 inch (1/3 cm), with firm, light strokes.

Preheat oven to 300F (149C).

Mix the flour with salt and pepper on your work surface. Using the whisk, beat the eggs well with the water in the small bowl. Grate the Parmesan cheese on the fine side of the box grater and add it to the bowl. Rinse the sage leaves, pat dry, chop coarsely, and add them to the egg mixture.

Set the sauté pan over medium heat and add 1/4 cup (60 ml) peanut oil. While the oil is heating, dredge the cutlets in the seasoned flour one at a time. When the oil is hot, dip the first batch of floured cutlets into the egg wash and immediately set them into the hot pan. (Do not crowd the pan.) Sauté until the pork is golden brown, turn, and sauté on the other side (about 3 minutes per side).

When done, remove to a rack to drain and proceed with the second batch of cutlets, adding the remaining peanut oil to the pan and following the same method. When the cutlets are drained, remove them to the platter (in a single layer) and, when they are all cooked, set the platter into the oven until the cutlets are hot.

While the cutlets are heating, wash the parsley, pat or spin dry, chop, and reserve. When the pork is hot, spoon the sauce chasseur on warm dinner plates, divide the cutlets among them, sprinkle the pork with the parsley, and serve at once.

Variation: Prepare some Gremolada *(see page 83)* and sprinkle 2 teaspoons of it over the pork just before it is heated in the oven.

Noisettes de Porc en Sanglier
Marinated Tenderloin of Pork with Game Sauce

"Sanglier" literally means wild boar, and, if you happen to hunt one down on your wooded estate, this recipe will work just as well for it as it will for the "tame" version I have called for here. Wild rice or Spätzle go well with the marinated noisettes, and peach or pear halves filled with cranberry sauce provide the color and taste which complete this presentation.

Yields 6 to 8 servings

3 fresh boneless pork tenderloins, each weighing about 12 to 16 ounces (340 to 450 g)
3/4 cup (180 ml) dry red wine
1 tablespoon red wine vinegar
4 juniper berries, crushed
1/2 teaspoon freshly crushed black peppercorns
1/3 bay leaf
1/3 carrot
1/2 celery stalk
1/2 medium onion
1/2 garlic clove
2 1/2 tablespoons flour
1/4 teaspoon salt
1/4 teaspoon freshly ground black pepper
4 to 5 tablespoons peanut oil
1/2 cup (118 ml) Demi-glace Brun I *(see page 75)*
2/3 cup (160 ml) whipping cream
1 tablespoon chopped fresh parsley

Recommended equipment

A paring knife, large glass or china bowl, mortar and pestle, plastic wrap, paper towels, slicing knife, cleaver, small dish, 12-inch (30 cm) sauté pan, wooden spatula, ovenproof serving platter, fine-mesh sieve, 2-quart (2 L) saucepan.

Using the paring knife, trim the excess fat and silver skin from each tenderloin and set aside while you prepare the marinade. Put the red wine and the vinegar in the bowl. Crush the juniper berries and the peppercorns in the mortar and pestle, add them to the bowl, and add the bay leaf. Rinse the carrot and celery stalk, cut them into pieces 1/2 inch (1 1/4 cm) wide, and add them to the marinade. Peel the onion half, cut it into 1/2-inch chunks, and add them to the bowl. Peel the garlic clove and stir it into the marinade. Set the pork tenderloins in the bowl, cover the bowl tightly with plastic wrap, and refrigerate for 18 to 24 hours, turning the meat once during this period.

When you are ready to cook the pork, remove the tenderloins from the marinade, reserving the vegetables and liquid separately, and pat the pork dry with paper towels. Using the slicing knife, cut each tenderloin into five noisettes weighing 2 1/2 to 3 ounces (75 to 85 g) each. Flatten each lightly with the cleaver.

Mix the flour, salt, and pepper in the small dish. Dust each noisette lightly with this mixture.

Set the sauté pan over medium high heat, add 2 tablespoons peanut oil, and, when it is hot, add as many of the noisettes as will comfortably fit into the pan without crowding. You will have at least two batches to sauté. Brown the pork well on both sides, and then reduce heat to medium and sauté for 3 minutes on each side for a total of 6 minutes. When done, remove the noisettes to the ovenproof platter and sauté the next batch, adding a little more peanut oil if necessary.

When all the noisettes have been sautéed and are resting in the platter, drain the oil from the sauté pan and add the vegetables and spices from the marinade. Sauté, stirring with the wooden spatula, for 2 minutes. Then add the liquid from the marinade, deglaze the pan while scraping up the brown bits from the bottom, and simmer until the liquid is reduced by one-half. When the sauce is reduced, add the demi-glace and cream and simmer until it is again reduced by one-half.

While the sauce is reducing, rinse, dry, and chop the parsley.

Preheat broiler to maximum heat.

When the sauce has been reduced and has a creamy consistency, pass it through the sieve into the saucepan and keep it warm over low heat. Adjust the seasoning if necessary. Set the noisettes under the preheated broiler for about 1 minute to heat, remove from oven, and arrange on warmed plates. Spoon the sauce over the meat, sprinkle with the parsley, and serve at once.

🌿 Roast Loin of Pork Stuffed with Apricots

Native to Armenia, the apricot was discovered by the Romans while on a military campaign. By the first century A.D., *it had been successfully transplanted to Rome and named* praecocia *because it ripens early in June. The first mention of combining pork and apricots came from Apicius in* De Re Coquinaria, *wherein apricots, dried dill and mint, and cumin were simmered along with the meat. Here, apricots fill the center of the roast, and rosemary (also known to Apicius) seasons the outside, providing a taste contrast that is as appealing as the visual one pictured at the beginning of this section. Any leftover pork, sliced thinly, is delicious for a cold luncheon plate.*

Yields 6 to 8 servings

1 boneless pork loin, weighing about 3 pounds (1350 g)
4 ounces (115 g) dried apricots

FOR THE SEASONING BLEND
1/2 teaspoon salt
1/2 teaspoon freshly ground black pepper
Grated rind of 1 lemon
1/2 teaspoon coarsely cut fresh rosemary

1/2 medium onion
1 celery stalk
1/2 carrot
1 cup (235 ml) dry white wine
1 cup (235 ml) whipping cream
1 tablespoon Dijon mustard
1/2 cup (118 ml) Demi-glace Brun I *(see page 75)*
Sprigs of fresh rosemary

Recommended equipment

A boning knife, butcher's steel, metal bulb baster, white kitchen string, stainless steel box grater, small bowl, heavy roasting pan, swivel-bladed vegetable peeler, small chef's knife, wooden spatula, serving platter, wire whisk, fine-mesh sieve, 2-quart (2 L) saucepan.

With the boning knife, trim the pork loin of all but 1 inch (2 1/2 cm) of flank. Using the butcher's steel, make a hole in the center of the loin all the way through from one end to the other. To enlarge the hole, use a metal bulb baster (with bulb removed) and push it through the opening. (Or, working with the boning knife, insert it into the loin from either side and twist it around to make a deep hole.) With your fingers, push as many of the dried apricots (do not soak them) as possible into the cavity from both sides to make a compact stuffing. Tie the pork loin at 2-inch (5 cm) intervals with the kitchen string.

Preheat oven to 350F (177C).

Mix the seasoning blend together in the small bowl by stirring the salt and pepper together, then grate the lemon rind on the fine side of the box grater (being careful to leave the bitter white behind) into the bowl, and, finally, coarsely cut the fresh rosemary and stir it in. Rub the seasoning all over the pork loin, working it into the fat and meat.

Set the loin fat side up into the roasting pan, set it into the oven, and roast for 20 minutes. Then reduce heat to 325F (163C) and roast for another 20 minutes.

While the loin roasts, prepare the vegetables: peel the onion half and roughly chop it; rinse the celery stalk and roughly chop it; peel the carrot half and roughly chop it; and reserve them all.

When the second 20-minute roasting period is finished, drain the fat from the pan, strew the vegetables around the loin, and roast for another 20 minutes. Then pour the wine around the loin and continue to roast for 25 minutes. (The total roasting time is about 85 minutes or 25 to 30 minutes per pound.)

When the roast is done, remove it from the oven, cut away the strings, and set the roast top side down on a platter to rest in a warm, not hot, place for 15 to 20 minutes while you prepare the sauce. Set the roasting pan over medium heat, and using a wire whisk, blend the cream, mustard, and demi-glace into the wine and vegetables. Adjust heat so that a simmer is maintained and reduce the liquid by almost one-half or until it has a light creamy consistency. This should take about 10 minutes. When the sauce is reduced, strain it into the saucepan, adjust seasoning if necessary, add any juices on the platter that have escaped from the roast, and keep warm on low heat.

Slice the loin for serving, spoon sauce on a warm plate, arrange the slices neatly on the sauce, garnish with sprigs of fresh rosemary, and serve at once.

Variation

Roast Loin of Pork Stuffed with Prunes in the Style of Sweden

Stuff the loin with dried, pitted prunes instead of the apricots. Do not soak the prunes. Use fresh sage rather than rosemary in the seasoning blend and for the garnish, and omit the mustard in the sauce. Either pork preparation is delicious with a sweet and sour sauce *(see pages 274–75)* augmented with a handful of raisins.

Baked Virginia Smithfield Ham with Homestead Southern Fruit Dressing

Smithfield, England, was a market center for meat in eighteenth-century London and Smithfield, Virginia, is for many Virginians the center of "hamdom." Located in Southampton County and therefore near the peanut growing area which extends into North Carolina, it has been a traditional destination for porkers raised on this famous groundnut. Until recent times "Smithfield" meant locally raised pork that had a unique flavor due to peanut-rich diets. However, demand for these products has so outstripped supply that, while cured in Smithfield (or certainly in Virginia), the pork may have just as easily come from the Midwest. There are many Smithfield hams, and, personally, I prefer the six-month cure of the country-style smoked Virginia ham rather than the regular cure of nine to twelve months. The milder cure leaves more moisture in the ham and is less salty, but if you prefer the longer cure, you probably should soak the ham in water overnight to draw off some of the salt. Begin working on the ham early in the day for an ample reward at dinner. Sweet Potatoes Duchesse are an authentic, colorful, and tasty complement to this "cavalier" favorite. And, if there are any large slices left on the ham bone, fire up the broiler for a Homestead breakfast specialty—York ham steaks.

Yields 12 to 18 servings

FOR THE HAM
1 whole smoked Virginia ham, weighing 15 to 20 pounds (7000 to 9000 g)
1/2 cup to 3/4 cup light brown sugar (100 to 145 g)
1 dozen or more whole cloves
2 cups (475 ml) dry sherry

FOR THE FRUIT DRESSING
1 16-ounce (570 g) can sliced yellow cling peaches (or halves)
1 16-ounce (570 g) can sliced pears (or halves)
1 16-ounce (570 g) can pineapple chunks
1 16-ounce (570 g) can apricot halves
3 ounces (85 g) raisins
6 ounces (170 g) walnuts
5 slices Pullman Loaf *(see page 488)*
3/4 cup (145 g) light brown sugar
1 teaspoon vanilla
8 ounces (225 g) butter, melted

Recommended equipment

A 16-quart (15 L) stockpot or roaster for boiling ham, paring knife, roasting pan, colander, 2-quart (2 L) mixing bowl, 1 1/2-quart (1 1/2 L) saucepan, rubber spatula, shallow baking dish (11 x 7 x 2 inches or 27 1/2 x 17 1/2 x 5 cm), basting spoon.

Wash the ham thoroughly under running cold water and then set it skin side down in the stockpot or in roaster. Set the pan on the burner and fill it with cold water to cover the ham by a depth of 2 to 3 inches (5 to 7 1/2 cm). Then bring the water to a boil and adjust heat to maintain a simmer. Cook the ham for 20 minutes per pound and start timing when the simmer is maintained. Halfway through the cooking period change the water completely, bring the fresh water to a simmer, and continue your timing when the simmer is reached. Watch the ham carefully to see that it is covered with water throughout the cooking period. When the ham is cooked, remove it from the pan or stockpot and let it rest undisturbed for 30 minutes. Discard the cooking water.

While the ham is resting, prepare the fruit dressing. Drain the peaches, pears, and pineapple chunks in the colander and put them in the mixing bowl. (If you are using peach and pear halves, slice them in half before adding them to the bowl.) Drain the apricots and reserve. Add the raisins and walnuts to the bowl. Toast the bread, cut into 1/2-inch (1 1/4 cm) cubes, and add them to the fruit along with 1/2 cup (100 g) brown sugar and vanilla. Blend together with the spatula, using gentle strokes so that the fruit is not crushed. Melt the butter in the saucepan and use some of it to lightly butter the baking dish.

Preheat one oven to 325F (163C) and one to 300F (149C).

Pour the fruit mixture into the baking dish, arrange the reserved apricots in a single layer on top, sprinkle with the remaining brown sugar, pour the melted butter evenly over the dish, and set into the 300F oven to bake for 30 minutes.

When the ham has finished resting, trim off the skin and excess fat with the paring knife, leaving only 1/8 to 1/4 inch (1/3 to 2/3 cm) of fat. Sprinkle the top of the ham with the light brown sugar, dot with cloves, and set the ham back into the roasting pan with the skin side up. Add the sherry to the roasting pan and set the ham into the 325F oven to bake until it is well browned and glacéed (about 15 to 20 minutes), basting it twice during this period.

When the ham has finished baking, remove it from the oven and let it rest uncovered for 15 minutes before slicing.

When the dressing is finished baking, remove it from the oven and spoon it onto plates with the sliced ham.

❧

There are many flavorful glazes for a baked ham, and here are some I have found to be successful. 1) Spreading 2 to 3 tablespoons Dijon mustard over the ham before the brown sugar and cloves. 2) Adding grated orange rind to the brown sugar. 3) Spreading the ham with honey mixed with powdered ginger or grated fresh ginger root. 4) Spreading the ham with maple syrup instead of sugar. 5) Spreading the ham with ginger-flavored marmalade and soy sauce.

As far as sauces are concerned, either Cumberland Sauce or Orange Sauce *(see pages 100 and 301)* are natural companions to this classic.

Pasta, Rice, and Potatoes

Throughout the world, any meal, served at any time, most likely includes pasta, rice, or potatoes in one form or another. Whether boiled, steamed, baked, or fried, served hot or cold, in combination with other ingredients or alone, these staples have served mankind well, appearing in soups, side dishes, main courses, salads, and desserts. Prepared in innumerable ways, pasta, rice, and potatoes share a history, versatility, and popularity matched only by bread.

The beginnings of pasta took myriad forms in many countries. Noodles in China have evolved differently from those in Italy, yet western and eastern culinary traditions developed from a similar base. Whether Marco Polo really brought the secret of spaghetti in his saddlebags upon his return to Venice is unimportant. What matters is that mankind throughout history has made the most from the least, working with what was plentiful and at hand. To ensure a supply of food for cold and uncertain times, what better way than to make a paste from wheat and preserve it through drying.

The origins of rice are easier to trace because the first written Chinese mention of rice dates back to 2800 B.C., when it was listed as one of the five principal and sacred crops. Historians suspect that rice was probably cultivated in India before then. The grain was introduced into Egypt and Greece, where it was highly prized during the time of Theophrastus, a philosopher and naturalist, ca. 372–287 B.C. From thence its popularity spread to Portugal, Italy, and America. In Japan, the word for rice, *gohan*, is also used to describe a complete meal.

The potato was an Incan gift from the New World to Europe, brought by Spanish explorers around 1570. Shunned at first, especially in France, it became a curiosity and ultimately a staple of the German and Irish diets. The first crop in Ireland was raised by Sir Walter Raleigh at his country estate in Youghal, and by 1666, English aristocrats enjoyed potatoes at their tables.

These sustaining foods—pasta, rice, and potatoes—have existed almost forever, and the numerous ways they can be enjoyed today are testimony to the ingenuity of mankind. At present, we have the advantage of history and can profit from the legacy of those who have gone before us. Enjoy the fruits of their labor and yours too—get into the kitchen and do your best for your family and friends.

Pasta

> I never get tired of pasta, any more than I get tired of bread. I eat it when I'm exhausted and want a quick meal that will give me a lift. I eat it when I'm in an ambitious mood, looking for something pleasant and different to compliment a guest. . . . Pasta is always the same, yet always different. It has a comforting familiarity, with its pale golden color and chewy, wheaten taste.
> —James Beard

At present, the average Italian consumes sixty-five pounds of pasta a year—more than twice that of any other nationality—and who can blame him? The Italian cuisine, one of the oldest in Europe, has had plenty of time to develop the natural taste affinities of basil, rosemary, oregano, and garlic for tomatoes, olive oil, prosciutto, and Parmesan. And pasta is the perfect transporter for any of these combinations. Thick or thin, flat or curled, stuffed or plain, the varieties of pasta are as limitless as the Italian imagination.

It is somehow fitting that hilly Tuscany, which nourished Giotto and Leonardo alike and cradled the Renaissance, should also provide the mother earth from which pasta is derived. The hardest wheat, durum, grows well in the area between Fiesole and Arezzo. When durum is milled, the product is semolina—a coarse flour that makes a very stiff unleavened dough that holds precise shapes during cooking. The characteristic stiffness of semolina dough makes it less desirable for breadmaking—bakers want a responsive, elastic dough and anyone who has made pasta dough knows that it is anything but flexible. The availability of semolina must have contributed to the dominance of pasta as the sustaining carbohydrate in the Italian diet.

The three fettuccine recipes show off the versatility of one variety of pasta. The first is deceptively simple. There really was an Alfredo who put butter and Parmesan together—his advantage was having the freshest ingredients available. Your advantage is the addition of cream—use cream with a 36 percent butterfat content and do whatever is necessary to secure that extraordinary dry, salty cheese from Parma. No substitutes will do. Watch the fettuccine very carefully while it is cooking, keeping the water at a rolling boil and testing strands for doneness. It must be al dente—firm to the bite—soft on the outside and resilient on the inside. Whether you use dried, fresh, or fresh-frozen fettuccine does not matter as long as whatever you use is of the best

Fettuccine Carbonara in the Grille

quality. Pasta made from semolina (the one flour that is never bleached) is naturally light yellow, so let the color be your guide when selecting pasta, and check the list of ingredients for semolina flour just to be sure.

Once you have mastered cooking the fettuccine, anything is possible. With Alfredo's basic recipe you can celebrate spring with primavera or fall with carbonara. The former makes use of the first fresh vegetables of the season, and, if you like, you can omit the cream sauce. Choose your favorite vegetables, sauté them lightly, and enjoy your own ode to spring. (During the winter you may create a spring memory by using frozen vegetables.) Carbonara combines tissue-thin shreds of prosciutto with zucchini, mushrooms, and red bell peppers for an autumnal allegory of seasonal change.

The pesto recipe gives you an excuse (if you need one) to enjoy pasta throughout the year. When fresh basil is available, prepare pesto and freeze it in one-cup quantities. With pesto put up for the cold time, the fragrance of a sunny summer garden can be called to mind whenever you toss pasta and pesto together. And, a spoonful can be scraped from the frozen sauce to enliven a hot soup, stew, or even a salad dressing.

Whenever pasta is mentioned, Italy comes to mind, yet there are pastalike foods in China, France, Greece, Germany, and England. The recipe for the German spätzle makes tiny freeform dumplings that retain whatever shape they had when they landed in the boiling water. The rich egg dough is beaten well, forced through a colander or spätzle sieve, and cooked in an instant. Spätzle are welcome as part of a hearty meal in winter and can be served chilled during warmer months. The spinach spätzle variation is as versatile as the plain.

The word "noodle" comes from the German, *Nudel*, and this noodle pudding is simplicity itself. Cook the noodles until just done because they will be baked with cream, nutmeg, and fruit. This pudding is sweet enough to qualify for a dessert and is often enjoyed that way by our guests at the Homestead.

Fettuccine Alfredo

Mary Pickford and Douglas Fairbanks, Jr., were so taken with this specialty that they gave the proprietor of Alfredo all'Augusteo at 31 Piazza Augusteo Imperatore a gold spoon and fork with which to serve it. Now, many Roman imitators claim the name, the fettuccine, and the golden serving sets. You need not match their calisthenics; all that is required for success is a deft touch for tossing the pasta in cream. And, speaking of cream, the original called strictly for slabs of butter and mounds of grated Romano or Parmesan. You can make it that way if you wish, but we prefer the smoother texture of cream, as well as the reduced calories. Whatever your choice, use the freshest Italian Parmesan available. Serve this with a salad of mixed greens and crunchy grissini (bread sticks).

Yields 4 to 6 servings

4 cups (950 ml) whipping cream
Freshly ground nutmeg
Salt
Freshly ground white pepper
2 tablespoons olive oil
1 pound (450 g) fettuccine
4 ounces (115 g) grated Parmesan cheese
2 tablespoons (30 g) butter

Recommended equipment

A 3-quart (3 L) saucepan, nutmeg grinder, 5-quart (5 L) saucepan with lid, long-handled fork, box grater, colander, mixing fork and spoon.

Set the smaller saucepan over medium high heat, add the whipping cream, bring it to a boil, stirring occasionally, and then adjust heat so that the cream simmers steadily. Grind in the nutmeg to taste, add a pinch of salt (remember the cheese you will add is salty) and pepper, and simmer until the cream is reduced by one-half (about 20 minutes).

Fill the large saucepan with hot water, set it over high heat, cover, and bring the water to a rolling boil. Add 1 tablespoon salt and the olive oil to the water and when it is boiling again stir in the fettuccine, using the long-handled fork to separate the strands, and re-cover the saucepan. When the water returns to a boil, uncover and cook at a lively boil until the fettuccine is just barely al dente. For fresh pasta, start checking after 3 minutes, and, for dried, check after 8 minutes.

While the pasta is cooking, grate the Parmesan and reserve.

When the fettuccine is done, pour into the colander, run cold water over the pasta for 15 to 20 seconds to stop the cooking, and let drain.

Wipe out the large saucepan, set it over low heat, add the butter, drained pasta, a pinch of salt, pepper, and the reduced cream. Toss the fettuccine with the cream, bring it to a low simmer, and heat for 2 minutes. If the sauce is too thick, add more cream, and if too thin, simmer another minute or two. Remove from heat, stir in the Parmesan, and serve at once on warm serving plates.

If there is a delay in serving, half-and-half may be added to thin out the sauce.

Fettuccine Primavera

The colors and flavors of this dish will bring the delights of spring to your table. Prepare this when the earliest fresh vegetables are available at the market and serve with crusty bread or grissini *(bread sticks).*

Yields 4 to 6 servings

FOR THE VEGETABLES
4 stalks fresh asparagus
1/2 small zucchini
1/2 small yellow squash
1/2 medium carrot
1/2 small celery stalk
12 snow pea pods
2 stalks of broccoli, cut into flowerettes
1/2 red bell pepper
1 small leek
6 medium mushrooms
2 scallions, white part only
1 tablespoon olive oil
2 tablespoons water
1/2 teaspoon Pesto *(see page 418)*

4 cups (950 ml) whipping cream
Freshly ground nutmeg
Salt
Freshly ground white pepper
2 tablespoons olive oil
1 pound (450 g) fettuccine
4 ounces (115 g) grated Parmesan cheese
2 tablespoons (30 g) butter

Recommended equipment

A swivel-bladed vegetable peeler, paring knife, 12-inch (30 cm) sauté pan, wooden spatula, 3-quart (3 L) saucepan, nutmeg grinder, 5-quart (5 L) saucepan with lid, long-handled fork, box grater, colander, mixing fork and spoon.

Choose about six vegetables from among those listed, basing your choice upon their freshness, taste, and color. Prepare each for cooking. For asparagus, use the top two-thirds of the stalk, peel, and cut into 1-inch (2 1/2 cm) long pieces. Cut the zucchini (unpeeled) into matchstick-size pieces. Lightly peel the yellow squash and cut into matchstick-size pieces. Peel the carrot and cut into matchstick-size pieces; do likewise with the celery. If the snow peas are large, halve them, otherwise leave whole. Use the smallest of the closed broccoli flower-heads, rinse, and slit the stem for even cooking. Seed the bell pepper half, remove the pithy white, and cut into very thin strips. Rinse the leek thoroughly under cold running water, separating the layers to rid them of any dirt, and cut into matchstick-size strips. Do not wash the mushrooms but gently brush them of any clinging dirt before slicing thinly. Slice the scallions into 1/2-inch (1 1/4 cm) long pieces.

Set the sauté pan over medium high heat, and, when it is hot, add the olive oil, water, and vegetables, and sauté, stirring with the spatula, for 3 minutes. Stir in the pesto, remove pan from heat, and reserve the vegetables.

Set the smaller saucepan over medium high heat, add the whipping cream, bring it to a boil, stirring occasionally, and then adjust heat so that the cream simmers steadily. Grind in the nutmeg to taste, add a pinch of salt (remember the cheese you will add is salty) and pepper, and simmer until the cream is reduced by one-half (about 20 minutes).

Fill the large saucepan with hot water, set it over high heat, cover, and bring the water to a rolling boil. Add 1 tablespoon salt and the olive oil to the water and when it is boiling again stir in the fettuccine, using the long-handled fork to separate the strands, and re-cover the saucepan. When the water returns to a boil, uncover and cook at a lively boil until the fettuccine is just barely al dente. For fresh pasta, start checking after 3 minutes, and, for dried, check after 8 minutes.

While the pasta is cooking, grate the Parmesan and reserve.

When the fettuccine is done, pour into the colander, run cold water over the pasta for 15 to 20 seconds to stop the cooking, and let drain. Wipe out the large saucepan, set it over low heat, add the butter, drained pasta, a pinch of salt, pepper, and the reduced cream. Stir in the reserved vegetables. Toss the fettuccine with the cream, bring it to a low simmer, and heat for 2 minutes. If the sauce is too thick, add more cream, and if too thin, simmer another minute or two. Remove from heat, stir in the Parmesan, and serve at once on warm serving plates.

You may omit the cream sauce and toss the fettuccine with the vegetables alone.

Fettuccine Carbonara

Some versions of carbonara call for bacon and beaten egg to be added at the last minute, others for ham. I prefer very thin shreds of prosciutto sautéed in butter with the vegetables and stirred into the cream sauce.

Yields 4 to 6 servings

FOR THE VEGETABLES
8 medium mushrooms
1 small zucchini
1/2 small red bell pepper
4 ounces (115 g) prosciutto
2 tablespoons (30 g) butter
1 tablespoon olive oil

4 cups (950 ml) whipping cream
Freshly ground nutmeg
Salt
Freshly ground white pepper
2 tablespoons olive oil
1 pound (450 g) fettuccine
4 ounces (115 g) grated
  Parmesan cheese
2 tablespoons (30 g) butter

Recommended equipment

A paring knife, slicing knife, 12-inch (30 cm) sauté pan, wooden spatula, 3-quart (3 L) saucepan, nutmeg grinder, 5-quart (5 L) saucepan with lid, long-handled fork, box grater, colander, mixing fork and spoon.

Brush the mushrooms of any clinging dirt, slice them thinly, and reserve. Slice the zucchini into matchstick-size strips and reserve. Halve the pepper, remove the seeds and pithy white, slice into very thin strips, and reserve. Slice the prosciutto into paper-thin shreds (or have your butcher do it for you) and reserve.

Set the sauté pan over medium high heat, add the butter and olive oil, and, when the oil is hot, add the mushrooms and sauté, stirring, until they are dark brown in color and most of their moisture has evaporated. When done, scrape out of the pan and reserve. Add a little more oil or butter to the pan if needed, return the pan to heat, and add the reserved zucchini, pepper, and prosciutto. Sauté, stirring, for 3 minutes, then remove pan from heat and reserve the vegetables.

Set the smaller saucepan over medium high heat,

add the whipping cream, bring it to a boil, stirring occasionally, and then adjust heat so that the cream simmers steadily. Grind in the nutmeg to taste, add a pinch of salt (remember the cheese you will add is salty) and pepper, and simmer until the cream is reduced by one-half (about 20 minutes).

Fill the large saucepan with hot water, set it over high heat, cover, and bring the water to a rolling boil. Add 1 tablespoon salt and the olive oil to the water and when it is boiling again stir in the fettuccine, using the long-handled fork to separate the strands, and re-cover the saucepan. When the water returns to a boil, uncover and cook at a lively boil until the fettuccine is just barely al dente. For fresh pasta, start checking after 3 minutes, and, for dried, check after 8 minutes.

While the pasta is cooking, grate the Parmesan and reserve.

When the fettuccine is done, pour into the colander, run cold water over the pasta for 15 to 20 seconds to stop the cooking, and let drain. Wipe out the large saucepan, set it over low heat, add the butter, drained pasta, a pinch of salt, pepper, and the reduced cream. Stir in the reserved vegetables and prosciutto. Toss the fettuccine with the cream, bring it to a low simmer, and heat for 2 minutes. If the sauce is too thick, add more cream, and if too thin, simmer another minute or two. Remove from heat, stir in the Parmesan, and serve at once on warm serving plates.

Pesto

Basil flourishes abundantly in the Ligurian hills along the coast of the Bay of Genoa. The Genoese invented pesto, an intense, uncooked sauce that envelops pasta in an unctuous aura or can add a subtle undercurrent to a fragrant bowl of Minestrone alla Milanese.

Yields about 1 cup

3 large garlic cloves
3/4 cup (180 ml) olive oil
1 cup (235 ml) fresh Italian parsley
1 1/2 cups (355 ml) fresh basil leaves
1/4 teaspoon salt
Freshly ground black pepper
2 ounces (60 g) pine nuts

Recommended equipment

A paring knife, electric blender, rubber spatula.

Put the ingredients in the blender jar in the order listed and blend on high speed until the sauce is smooth. Scrape down the inside of the jar as needed. When done, the sauce will keep well for several weeks in a tightly covered glass jar in the refrigerator, or it may be frozen.

This recipe yields enough pesto for six servings of pasta.

Spätzle

A European favorite that came from Swabia, the medieval county in southwest Germany that today comprises Baden-Württemberg and west Bavaria and is known for excellence in cuisine and automobiles, these egg dumplings are delicious with chicken, venison, pork, lamb, or veal, especially when the meat has a creamy sauce. Prepare the spätzle ahead of time and brown them in butter just before serving. If you make them as often as we do, you probably will want to buy a spätzle maker at your local kitchen store—it fits right over the pot and makes dropping the dough into the boiling water a snap.

Yields 6 servings

1 cup (235 ml) lukewarm milk
1 pound (450 g) flour
1/4 teaspoon salt
1/8 teaspoon freshly ground white pepper
1/4 teaspoon freshly ground nutmeg
5 eggs
2 tablespoons (30 g) butter

Recommended equipment

A small saucepan, scale, 2-quart (2 L) bowl, nutmeg grinder, mixing fork, 1-quart (1 L) bowl, wire whisk, wooden spoon, 3-quart (3 L) saucepan, rubber spatula, colander with large holes or spätzle maker, skimmer, large fine-mesh sieve, large flat pan or baking sheet, 12-inch (30 cm) sauté pan, wooden spatula.

Put the milk in the small saucepan and set it to warm over low heat.

Weigh out the flour and put it in the mixing bowl. Add the salt, pepper, and nutmeg and stir together with the fork. When the milk is warm (110F or 44C), put it in the smaller bowl and add the eggs one at a time, mixing thoroughly with the whisk. Make a well in the center of the flour, pour in the milk and egg mixture, and stir the flour into it. Mix thoroughly with the wooden spoon until the dough is smooth. Then stir the dough with continuous strokes until a few bubbles begin to form on the surface. (You may use a dough hook on an electric mixer if you like.) Reserve the dough.

Fill the large saucepan with hot water, set it over high heat, cover, and bring to a boil. When the boil is reached, uncover the saucepan, lightly salt the water, and adjust the heat so that the water maintains a steady boil. Set the colander (or spätzle maker) over the pot and force the dough through the holes in batches, pushing it through with the rubber spatula. When the spätzle float to the surface, immediately remove them with a skimmer, set them into a sieve, run cold water over them for 5 seconds, let drain, and put them into a large flat pan. As the spätzle are cooked and cooled, be sure that they are thoroughly drained and spread out no more than 1 inch (2 1/2 cm) deep on the pan. Do not hold them in a deep dish under any circumstances. They will wait happily at room temperature for an hour before serving.

When ready to serve, set the sauté pan over medium heat, add the butter, and, when it is hot, add the spätzle and sauté them, stirring, until lightly browned and heated through. Adjust seasoning if necessary and serve at once.

Any leftover spätzle can be chilled and served as the foundation of a luncheon salad.

Variation

ᛞ Spinach Spätzle

8 ounces (225 g) well-washed
and trimmed spinach

Blanch the spinach in lightly salted boiling water for 1 minute, cool in sieve under cold running water, drain, squeeze by small handfuls to rid spinach of water, and purée in blender until smooth (or mince finely with a knife). Prepare the spätzle dough using only 3/4 cup milk and add the spinach with the milk and eggs when you add them to the flour. If the dough seems dry, add more milk slowly until the dough is smooth and pliable. Cook according to the directions in the master recipe.

ᛞ Homestead Noodle Pudding

An excellent companion for ham or fried chicken, this favorite of Homestead guests is a frequent feature at our buffets.

Yields 10 to 12 servings

1 pound (450 g) noodles, cooked
7 eggs
2 cups (475 ml) sour cream
4 cups (950 ml) half-and-half
1/3 cup (65 g) sugar
1 teaspoon salt
1/2 teaspoon nutmeg
1/2 cup (118 ml) raisins
1/2 cup (118 ml) mandarin orange sections, drained
Butter for the baking dish

Recommended equipment

A medium mixing bowl, wire whisk, nutmeg grinder, baking dish 11 x 7 x 2 inches (27 1/2 x 17 1/2 x 5 cm).

Prepare the noodles according to the package directions, drain well, and reserve.

Preheat oven to 300F (149C).

Combine the eggs, sour cream, and half-and-half in the mixing bowl, beating well with the whisk. Add the sugar and salt, grind in the nutmeg, and blend thoroughly.

Put the raisins in a small dish, add hot water to cover, let them plump for at least 5 minutes, then drain, and reserve.

Lightly butter the baking dish, spread the noodles evenly in the bottom, sprinkle the raisins and mandarin orange sections over the noodles, pour on the egg mixture, and set the dish into the oven to bake for 45 minutes or until the liquid has been absorbed and a knife plunged into the custard at several points comes out clean. Serve as soon as possible.

Rice

> In Java it is related that Shiva, a Hindu god, took a fancy to the goddess Retna Dumila, who agreed to submit to him only after he had created the perfect food. Failing, Shiva enlisted the help of his lieutenant, Kala Gumerong, who in turn was thwarted by another reluctant goddess, Dewie Srie. Virginal to their deaths, the two enchantresses were buried by their grieving suitors, and from their tombs sprang the perfect food, Rice.
> —William Harlan Hale

The cultivation of rice requires heat, humidity, and more water than any other cereal crop. Grown in paddies, where the flooding drowns out the seedlings' competition, enabling two harvests a season, and in upland areas, this grain is the principal food crop for approximately half of the world's population. But this is not the gods' gift to man of "the perfect food"—rice alone lacks the protein needed for a complete food. It is an excellent carbohydrate and a good energy food, but when milled, about 15 percent of the protein is lost. The milling process begins with the removal of the hull, leaving brown rice (an intact kernel with the bran layer). The bran and germ are removed in the second step, leaving milled, unpolished rice. In the final stage a layer of high fat content is removed (to prolong storage life), leaving polished rice. Each part of the milling process produces a slightly different product, giving rise to the usual confusion on the subject of rice: what kind to buy and how to cook it. Brown rice takes about forty minutes to cook, or twice as long as unpolished or polished rice. All three types absorb slightly more than twice their volume of liquid, so one cup of rice yields three and one-half cups of cooked rice.

In addition to the differences in the milling process, you can choose among several types of rice: long grain, short grain, and converted. The long grain rice is usually marketed under the name of Carolina, harkening back to the days when, for nearly two hundred years, Carolina Gold was the preferred variety in England and on the Continent. (Now, most "Carolina" rice is grown in Arkansas and Louisiana.) The short grain, native to California, is available as pearl, Spanish, or Japanese rice. Converted rice is the most nutritious because before milling it is parboiled, forcing the B vitamins to be diffused throughout the kernel, so they cannot be completely removed by milling. (This partial precooking process, known and practiced by Indians and

Pakistanis for two thousand years, enabled them to escape the late nineteenth century beriberi epidemic in Asia.) Long grain rice is the favored all-purpose rice; short grain, especially the Italian Arborio rice, is chosen for pilaff and risotto; and converted is a safe choice for cooking a large quantity of rice in one pot. And then there is wild rice, which is not a rice at all but a grass seed, native to the Great Lakes region of North America, that requires about an hour to cook. Before cooking, rice may be rinsed or soaked in cold water but this is not necessary—and if you have bought a polished rice that has been fortified with vitamins and protein you will be sending these nutrients down the drain. In some culinary traditions—notably the Chinese and Japanese—washing and soaking raw rice in several changes of cold water before cooking is the first of several ritual steps. The average Chinese consumes a pound of rice a day (average American consumption per person is seven pounds per year) so they may know more than we do.

The recipe for steamed rice instructs you to rinse the rice first—in true Oriental fashion. Use the steamed rice plain, as is, for a companion to well-seasoned main dishes such as Homestead Sweet and Sour Lemon Chicken and Chinese Barbecued Spareribs. Or, add a generous pat of butter to each serving and enjoy simplicity itself.

The Moors brought their love of saffron-flavored rice to Spain, where, in the eighth century, they cultivated the grain in large quantities. The trade routes that carried saffron from Mesopotamia also brought the pilaff of the Middle East that became the paella of Iberia, and Spanish rule carried it to New Orleans—where mixed with ham (jambon and paella), it became jambalaya. When you prepare each of these rice dishes you are participating in the ancient adventures of mankind. Riz Valencienne comes, of course, from Valencia. And Turkish Rice, with pilaff as its base, exemplifies the facility rice has for showing off combinations of spicy and hearty flavorings.

For a change of pace, the rice "à la créole" is a preparation to use when a dry, fluffy rice is your choice. Or cook rice this way as the first step in Exotic Fried Rice (you may also use steamed rice or a pilaff). The important point here is that the rice must be cooked and at room temperature or chilled so that the individual grains can be separated and will not absorb the oil and butter when fried.

The basic risotto technique, when mastered, provides endless variations on a theme. Closely related to a pilaff, the Italians took it one step further. Today, Italy is Europe's only major producer of rice (there are rice plantations in France in the Camargue, but cultivation has fallen off since World War II). The Po River valley grows an abundance of Arborio rice—a thick, short grain that is very absorbent. This is part of the secret of a good risotto. Each grain absorbs enough hot, flavorful broth to swell without bursting and form a creamy liaison with the other plump grains, and, *ecco*—risotto. The Italians add (among other choices) finely grated Parmesan cheese, diced beef marrow, sliced mushrooms, chopped ripe tomatoes, or saffron. You may choose to add curry alone or any one of the following spices to the onions and butter or a combination of two or three mixed in small amounts: minced fresh coriander, ground cumin, cinnamon, grated fresh ginger, chili powder, or oregano. Fresh vegetables cut into matchstick-size pieces and lightly sautéed in butter and oil can be stirred into the risotto just before serving.

Steamed Rice

Rice is life in China. (We celebrate its symbolic fertility when we toss raw rice at a newly married couple.) Traditionally used in making paper and wine, rice is most important at the heart of a meal. Perfectly steamed rice is fluffy, fragrant, delicious, and the following method is foolproof.

Yields 6 servings

2 cups (475 ml) raw long grain rice
4 quarts (4 L) water
1 tablespoon salt

Recommended equipment

A 5-quart (5 L) saucepan with lid, colander or sieve, kitchen towel.

Rinse the rice in a sieve under running cold water, drain, and reserve.

Fill the saucepan with water, set it over high heat, cover, and bring to a boil. When the water boils, remove lid, add salt and rice, and stir until the water returns to a boil. Then adjust heat so that the water simmers steadily and cook the rice uncovered for 10 minutes. Drain rice into the colander or sieve. Fill the saucepan half full with water, return to a boil, and, when boiling, set the colander or sieve with the rice over the boiling water. Be sure that the water does not touch the rice. Cover the rice with a white kitchen towel and put a lid over the towel to hold it down. Steam the rice for 15 minutes or until fluffy and serve at once.

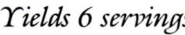 Saffron Rice

Saffron is the rarest and most colorful of kitchen spices, and the following words from Elizabeth David make clear why: "It was somewhere on the way up to Córdoba that we saw the first purple patches of autumn-flowering saffron crocuses in bloom. On our return we called on Mercedes, the second village girl who works at La Alfarella, to tell her that we were back. Her father was preparing saffron—picking the orange stigmas one by one from the iridescent mauve flowers heaped up in a shoe box by his side and spreading them carefully on a piece of brown paper to dry."

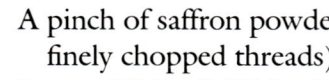

Yields 6 servings

A pinch of saffron powder (or finely chopped threads)
3 cups (710 ml) White Chicken Stock *(see page 61)*
2 cups (475 ml) raw long grain rice
2 teaspoons salt

Recommended equipment

A 1 1/2-quart (1 1/2 L) saucepan with lid.

Add a pinch of saffron to the chicken stock in the saucepan, cover, and bring to a boil over high heat. When the stock boils, uncover the saucepan, add rice and salt, re-cover the saucepan, and adjust heat to very low so that the stock barely simmers. Cook the rice gently until the stock is absorbed (about 20 to 30 minutes). When done, take off heat and leave covered until ready to serve.

 Rice Pilaff

"Pilaff" (or pilau) means that the raw rice is lightly sautéed in fat before being cooked in stock, which is completely absorbed by the grain. The result is irresistible—plump, fluffy, flavorful grains of rice, the perfect accompaniment to savory dishes.

Yields 4 to 6 servings

1/2 medium onion
2 tablespoons (30 g) butter
2 cups (475 ml) White Chicken Stock *(see page 61)*
1 cup (235 ml) raw long grain rice
1/4 small bay leaf
1 teaspoon salt
1 tablespoon (15 g) butter, softened at room temperature
Butter for the waxed paper

Recommended equipment

Waxed paper, small chef's knife, 2-quart (2 L) saucepan with lid, 1-quart (1 L) saucepan, wooden spatula.

Cut a circular piece of waxed paper the same size as the diameter of the 2-quart saucepan. Cut a cross in the center of the circle for a steam vent, butter one side of the paper, and set it aside.

Peel the onion and dice it very finely with the chef's knife. Set the 2-quart saucepan over medium low heat, add the 2 tablespoons butter and the onion, and sauté, stirring, without browning, for 3 minutes. Meanwhile, put the chicken stock in the smaller saucepan and set it over medium heat to warm. When the onions are soft and golden, add the rice to the pan, blend well, and sauté, stirring, until the rice is translucent (about 2 minutes). Pour in the hot stock, add the bay leaf and salt, increase heat to medium, and bring the stock to a simmer. Cover the rice with the waxed paper, buttered side down, cover the saucepan with the lid, and adjust heat so that the rice simmers gently for 18 minutes. Do not stir the rice while it is cooking.

When the rice is done, remove saucepan from heat, remove lid and paper, stir rice lightly with a fork, mix in the soft butter, remove bay leaf, and serve at once.

The rice may wait for you if you remove it from the hot saucepan and let it cool, uncovered, on a dish or platter. Fluff it occasionally with a fork so the grains do not steam and stick together. When cool, cover with waxed paper. To reheat, add a tablespoon or two of chicken stock to the saucepan, return rice to saucepan, set it over medium heat, cover the pan, and heat for 2 to 3 minutes or until the rice is hot.

Variation

 ## Riz Valencienne
Rice in the Style of Valencia

Near Valencia, rice fields surround Lake Albuféra, and anything "Valencienne" usually means rice (cooked in meat stock) mixed with finely diced peppers.

1 recipe Rice Pilaff *(see page 424)*
1/2 cup (118 ml) fresh (or frozen) green peas
4 ounces (115 g) canned pimiento (packed in water and drained)
2 teaspoons butter
Salt
Freshly ground white pepper
A pinch of sugar

While the rice pilaff cooks, prepare the peas by boiling them in lightly salted water for 2 minutes, then drain them in a sieve and cool briefly under running cold water. Set aside to drain while you dice the pimiento. Just as the rice is done, warm the peas in melted butter, season them with salt, pepper, and sugar to taste, and stir them with the pimiento into the cooked rice, after fluffing it with a fork. Serve at once.

Variation

Turkish Rice

1 recipe Rice Pilaff *(see page 424)*
A pinch of saffron powder (or finely chopped threads)
1/2 cup (118 ml) raisins
1/4 cup (60 ml) mango chutney
4 ounces (115 g) canned pimiento (packed in water and drained)

Prepare the rice pilaff and when you heat the chicken stock add the saffron to it before combining the stock and the rice.

While the pilaff is cooking, plump the raisins by soaking them in hot water for 5 minutes, then drain, and set aside. Chop the chutney coarsely and reserve. Dice the pimiento and reserve. When the pilaff is cooked, fluff it with the fork, mix in the raisins, chutney, and pimiento, and serve at once.

Rice Creole

Rice cooked "à la créole" is plunged into boiling water, cooled under cold water, and the result is al dente—each grain of rice is separate and firm to the bite.

Yields 6 to 8 servings

4 quarts (4 L) water
1 tablespoon salt
2 cups (475 ml) raw long grain rice
2 tablespoons (30 g) butter
Butter for the baking dish

Recommended equipment

A 5-quart (5 L) saucepan with lid, wooden spoon, large fine-mesh sieve, ovenproof baking dish, waxed paper.

Bring the water to boil in the covered saucepan over high heat. Stir in the salt and rice and continue stirring until the water boils again. Do not cover the pan. Adjust the heat so that the rice simmers steadily for 17 minutes, stirring occasionally.

When done, pour rice in the sieve and run cold water over it until the rice is cool. Set aside to drain thoroughly. Preheat oven to 300F (149C) and butter the baking dish. Spread the rice in the dish, dot it with the remaining butter, cover the rice loosely with waxed paper, and heat in the oven for 5 to 6 minutes. Serve immediately.

Exotic Fried Rice

If you have ever wondered what to do with leftover rice, you are in good company. The Chinese have this problem too, with the result that last night's steamed rice becomes today's fried rice, a favorite fast food snack at roadside stands and train stations. They would leave it white, seasoning with salt rather than soy sauce, but the principle is the same. Once the ingredients are assembled, the actual cooking is very quick and the result, served with a salad and bread, would make a complete luncheon or light supper dish.

Yields 4 to 6 servings

    4 cups (950 ml) cooked long grain rice, cooled
    6 to 8 ounces (170 to 225 g) peeled raw shrimp
    2 ounces (60 g) ham
    1/2 medium red bell pepper
    1/4 medium green bell pepper
    1 small garlic clove
    3 scallions, white part and some of the green
    1 Chinese cabbage stalk
    6 canned water chestnuts
    1 tablespoon (15 g) butter
    1 tablespoon peanut oil
    1/8 teaspoon ground ginger
    1/4 cup (60 ml) soy sauce
    3 tablespoons dry sherry
    Salt
    Freshly ground black pepper

Recommended equipment

A shrimp deveiner, large chef's knife, paring knife, garlic press, 12-inch (30 cm) sauté pan, wooden spatula.

Cook the rice according to the recipe for Steamed Rice, Rice Pilaff, or Rice Creole *(see pages 423, 424, and 426)*. Be certain that the rice is not overcooked and that it is at room temperature or chilled before you stir-fry it.

As each of the remaining ingredients is prepared, set it aside separately and reserve until you are ready to cook. Rinse the shrimp under cold running water, peel, devein, and finely dice with the chef's knife. Dice the ham finely. Rinse the bell peppers, seed them, remove the pithy white, and finely dice them. Peel the garlic clove. Rinse the scallions, trim, and finely dice. Rinse the cabbage stalk and dice it finely. Dice the water chestnuts.

Set the sauté pan over medium high heat, add the butter and oil, and, when it is hot, add the shrimp and sauté, stirring, for 1 minute. Add the ham and sauté, stirring, for 1 minute. Add the bell peppers, press in the garlic clove, and add the scallions, cabbage, water chestnuts, and ginger. Sauté, stirring, for 2 minutes and then add the rice, soy sauce, and sherry. Reduce the heat to medium and continue stirring for 2 to 3 minutes or until the rice is well blended with the other ingredients, all liquid has been absorbed, and the rice is sizzling. Season with salt and pepper and serve at once on warm plates.

Variation: Beat 2 eggs lightly and stir them into the rice just before serving. Serve when the eggs are cooked.

🕊 Risotto

A perfect risotto is a creamy union of tender yet al dente rice grains. I prefer to prepare risotto in two steps so other dinner preparations can be done. When cooking risotto, minutes do matter and you should wait for the risotto because the risotto will not wait for you.

Yields 4 to 6 servings

FOR STEP ONE
1 1/2 cups (355 ml) White Chicken Stock (see page 61)
1/2 medium onion
2 tablespoons (30 g) butter
1 cup (235 ml) raw Italian Arborio rice
1/4 small bay leaf
1/2 teaspoon salt
Butter for the waxed paper

FOR STEP TWO
1 1/2 cups (355 ml) White Chicken Stock
1/4 cup (60 ml) dry white wine
5 tablespoons grated Parmesan cheese
1 tablespoon (15 g) butter

2 ounces (60 g) beef marrow (see page 79), diced (optional)

Recommended equipment

A 1 1/2-quart (1 1/2 L) saucepan with lid, waxed paper, small chef's knife, enameled cast-iron baking dish or lined copper plat à sauter with lid, wooden spatula, box grater.

If you plan to use the beef marrow, prepare it first.

For step one, put the chicken stock in the saucepan, cover, and let it warm over low heat.

Preheat oven to 350F (177C).

Cut a circular piece of waxed paper the same size as the diameter of the baking dish or plat à sauter. Cut a cross in the center of the circle for a steam vent, butter one side of the paper, and set it aside.

Peel the onion half and dice it very finely with the chef's knife. Set the baking dish or plat à sauter over medium low heat, add the butter, and, when it is hot add the onions, and sauté without browning, stirring occasionally with the wooden spatula, for 3 minutes. Add the rice, mix thoroughly with the butter and onions, and sauté, stirring, until rice is translucent (about 2 minutes). Then increase heat to medium, add the hot stock, bay leaf, and salt, and bring the stock to a simmer. Cover the rice with the waxed paper, buttered side down, cover the pan, and set it into the oven for 12 minutes or until the liquid is absorbed.

When the liquid has been absorbed, remove pan from oven, remove lid and waxed paper, and fluff the rice with a fork so the steam can escape. At this point, if you are not ready to finish the risotto, transfer the rice to a flat dish or platter and spread it out to cool. When cool, cover with waxed paper.

To finish the risotto, begin with step two. Heat the remaining chicken stock. Return the rice to the pan, add the hot stock and the wine, and bring to a simmer over medium heat. Cover the pan and adjust the heat so that the stock simmers gently for 5 minutes.

While the risotto is finishing, grate the Parmesan and reserve.

When the risotto is done, remove from heat, remove the bay leaf, stir in the butter, Parmesan, and optional beef marrow, mix well, and serve immediately.

🕊

Arborio rice is the best choice for risotto, but a long grain polished or unpolished rice will give very good results. Never boil the rice after the Parmesan and marrow have been added because the rice will become gummy and greasy.

Variation

Risotto alla Milanese
Risotto in the Style of Milan

Risotto is identified with Milano almost as much as Bouillabaisse is with Marseilles—which means two things—(1) only a Milanese can have the "true" recipe, and (2) there are as many versions as there are Milanesi. I do know this: most recipes call for saffron, mushrooms, and prosciutto, so my "risotto alla milanese Alberto" is reasonably authentic. And, when you pair it with the Ossobuco recipe, even guests from northern Italy will be so busy polishing their plates that they will forget to argue over the culinary pedigree.

6 to 8 threads of saffron, chopped
6 to 8 mushrooms, sliced thinly

In step one of the basic risotto recipe, add the saffron to the chicken stock while it is heating, and stir the mushrooms into the butter and onions before the rice is added. Then proceed with the recipe.

Another variation is to add coarsely diced raw prosciutto to the butter and onions in step one instead of or along with the mushrooms.

Variation

 ## Risotto con Pomodori
Risotto with Tomatoes

2 tablespoons tomato paste
3 ripe tomatoes (blanched, peeled, and seeded; *see page 568*), diced

In step one of the basic risotto recipe, add the tomato paste to the butter and onions before the rice is added. While the risotto cooks in the oven, prepare the tomatoes and stir them into the rice at the beginning of step two before proceeding with the recipe.

Potatoes

> I find that the potato is a much more delicately smooth thickening agent—as well as being only about one-sixth as rich as the standard butter-flour roux. We use the potatoes raw, peeled, of course, then ground extremely fine, passed through a very fine sieve to eliminate all graininess, and worked carefully into the sauce. It is an old Provençal way, and still one of the best.
>
> —Roger Vergé

Often maligned as a "fattening" food, a plain potato is very nutritious. Trust the French to have discovered a way to thicken sauces without the standard roux by relying on the starch in the potato. (When processed and sold in bags as "potato starch," it contributes body to those airy French cakes that contain hardly any flour.) Potatoes are about 3 percent protein, contain B and C vitamins, and have only 100 calories per 4 ounces (115 grams). This is a high energy food, rich in carbohydrates and easily digested. The potato is well established on all continents, in temperate, subtropical, and tropical climates, and, today, is the most important vegetable in the world.

The potato had to go a great distance to achieve this distinction. Cultivated by the Incas more than four thousand years ago in mountainous areas where corn would not grow, the potato was brought to Europe by Spanish explorers, probably around 1570. By 1610, most likely, England and Ireland were growing potatoes and they recrossed the ocean from Ireland to what would become the United States in 1719. The French, suspicious of the new vegetable and reluctant to see its value and enjoy its virtues, were finally convinced by a historic public relations event. In 1787, Antoine Parmentier presented Marie Antoinette with a bouquet of potato flowers, thereby ensuring a perpetual place of honor for the potato on French tables. The potatoes cultivated by Parmentier propelled the vegetable to instant celebrity status. He had survived on potatoes while a Prussian prisoner during the Seven Years' War and knew the potential significance of this new crop. Parmentier planted roughly an acre of potatoes on some poor soil near Paris, guarded the field by day, and left it unguarded by night. The curious Parisians quickly spread the word and the success of that crop produced the colorful bouquet. Today, anything "Parmentier" (a soup, chicken, or beef) means "potatoes," one way or another.

Potatoes, clockwise from top; Potato Croquettes, Roesti, Pommes de Terre Dauphine, Pommes de Terre Duchesse, Pommes de Terre Parisienne Rissolées in the center

431

In France, the liaison between cuisine and the produce of the land has elevated the lowly potato from a satisfying subsistence starch to the realm of distinctive dishes. The Irish, although decimated by the devastating potato blight from 1845 to 1849, and the English, who embraced potatoes long before the French, have yet to grow potatoes that will stand up in interesting dishes rather than collapse. In the United States, several good varieties of potatoes are available. Shop where you can choose them from a bin of loose, unwashed potatoes and buy the appropriate potato for the dish you are making. There are two types from which to choose: the moist, waxy, boiling potato and the dry, mealy, baking potato. The boiling potato is appropriate for dishes where the shape must be retained throughout cooking, so choose this type when slicing and dicing potatoes for gratins, salads, or when you want a boiled or steamed potato. The baking potato, either Idaho or Maine Russet, is your choice for mashing and roasting.

The first three recipes call for baking potatoes. The classic whipped potato begins by boiling the baking potatoes until just done, draining them, and mashing them with cream and butter. The baked stuffed potatoes combine the best of two favorites—a crisp skin filled with flavorful mashed potatoes. Roesti require forethought, but by baking the potatoes the day before, you are a step ahead in your preparations. This Swiss specialty is a sophisticated relative of that American cousin, hashed brown potatoes.

The boiling potato is in the spotlight for a substantial performance in the pommes de terre Boulangère and the Swiss stewed potatoes. The former has sliced potatoes baked gently with flavorful stock and the latter has bite-size cubes simmered with seasonings and served au naturel, with Knackwurst, or disguised as Hungarian with tomato paste and paprika.

The duchesse recipe is an enriched whipped potato that plays several roles. Standing alone, the duchesse technique can be applied to baking potatoes or sweet potatoes. The basic baking potato mixture becomes pommes de terre Macaire when minced ham, onion, chives, and parsley are added, and then it is formed into patties which are sautéed until golden brown. The potato croquettes are another starring role for the duchesse. Cooled and rolled into shapes, the mixture is lightly breaded and deep fried until golden.

The duchesse performance finished, a substantial relative, Mme Dauphine, takes center stage. This time the baking potatoes are enriched by a pâte à choux before chilling, shaping, and deep frying.

A different and elegant presentation is made by the last, but not least, member of the troupe. For the pommes de terre Parisienne rissolées, boiling potatoes are neatly scooped into round or oval shapes, sautéed in clarified butter, finished in the oven, and sprinkled with fresh chopped parsley just before serving. This dish is a worthy companion to your most formal entrée.

Whipped Potatoes

Children enjoy watching a pat of butter melt into a tepid pool surrounded by a potato dam. You will please young and old alike when serving these fluffy potatoes.

Yields 4 to 6 servings

2 pounds (900 g) baking potatoes
Salt
3/4 to 1 cup (180 to 235 ml) half-and-half
Freshly ground white pepper
A pinch of nutmeg
8 tablespoons (115 g) butter, softened at room temperature

Recommended equipment

A 3-quart (3 L) saucepan with lid, stiff bristle brush, swivel-bladed vegetable peeler, small chef's knife, colander, baking sheet, small saucepan, large fine-mesh sieve or potato ricer, wooden spoon, 2-quart (2 L) saucepan, nutmeg grinder, wire whisk.

Bring lightly salted water to boil in the large saucepan, covered, over high heat. Meanwhile, scrub and peel the potatoes and cut each one into three pieces. When the water is boiling, drop the potatoes into it (the water should cover them by 1 1/2 inches or 3 3/4 cm) and when the water returns to a boil adjust heat so that the potatoes will cook, uncovered, at a lively boil.

Preheat oven to 300F (149C).

After 15 minutes begin testing the potatoes for doneness with the tip of a knife. They are done when the knife meets slight resistance (this may take 20 minutes). Do not overcook them. As soon as they are done drain the potatoes in the colander, set it on the baking sheet, and put the colander and sheet into the oven for 3 minutes to dry the potatoes.

While the potatoes are drying, heat the half-and-half in the small saucepan until it is scalded (about 180F or 82C) and then remove it from heat.

Set the sieve over the 2-quart saucepan and, with the wooden spoon, push the potatoes through it (or use a potato ricer) into the saucepan. Set the saucepan over low heat, season the potatoes with salt, pepper, and nutmeg, and whisk in the butter. Add 1/2 cup (118 ml) half-and-half, mixing thoroughly with the whisk. If you are ready to serve the whipped potatoes, continue adding half-and-half, while stirring, until they are fluffy and smooth. If the potatoes must wait more than a few minutes, keep them warm in a double boiler and, just before serving, add the remaining half-and-half while whipping them briskly with the whisk for 2 minutes.

Add as much half-and-half as you need for a fluffy potato.

Baked Stuffed Potatoes

Whether you call these twice-baked potatoes, potato boats, or by the name above, they are delicious.

Yields 4 servings

4 large baking potatoes
4 strips bacon, weighing 3/4 ounce (23 g) each
6 tablespoons sour cream
4 tablespoons (60 g) butter
2 tablespoons finely cut chives
A pinch of nutmeg
Salt
Freshly ground white pepper
2 teaspoons cracker meal
1/8 teaspoon paprika
1 teaspoon grated Parmesan cheese
1 tablespoon (15 g) butter, melted

Recommended equipment

A stiff bristle brush, 10-inch (25 cm) sauté pan, paper towels, small chef's knife, paring knife, soupspoon, mixing bowl, nutmeg grinder, wooden spoon, baking dish or pan, small bowl, box grater, small saucepan.

Preheat oven to 350F (177C).

Scrub the potatoes under cold running water, pat dry, and set them on a rack in the middle of the oven to bake for 45 to 50 minutes or until a fork poked into them meets no resistance. While the potatoes are baking, fry the bacon in the sauté pan until crisp, drain it on paper towels, let cool, chop finely with the chef's knife, and reserve.

When the potatoes are done, remove them from the oven, reduce heat to 325F (163C), and let the potatoes cool until you can handle them. Using the paring knife, cut a slice about 1 1/2 inches (3 3/4 cm) wide, and nearly as long as the potato, from the top. (Dotted with butter and seasoned to your taste, this slice is an excellent snack if dinner is far away.) Scoop out the potato pulp with the soupspoon, being careful to leave the skin intact, and put the pulp into the mixing bowl. Add the sour cream, butter, reserved bacon, chives, and nutmeg. Season carefully with salt (remember the bacon) and pepper and blend all together well with the wooden spoon, breaking up the larger lumps. The potato mixture should be smooth and not too loose. If it seems too dry, add a little more butter and sour cream. Stuff the potato skins with the mixture and arrange them in the baking dish.

Combine the cracker meal and paprika in the small bowl with the Parmesan cheese and sprinkle this mixture over the potatoes. Melt the butter and drizzle it over the topping. Set the potatoes into the oven to bake for about 10 minutes or until very hot and then serve at once.

The potatoes may be stuffed hours before serving and kept covered and refrigerated until the final baking. In this case, allow 2 to 3 minutes more for them to get hot.

Roesti

Swiss cuisine is known for chocolate, cheese, and this potato cake.

Yields 4 servings

6 large baking potatoes
2 tablespoons (30 g) butter
1 tablespoon (15 g) bacon fat
Salt
Freshly ground white pepper

Recommended equipment

A stiff bristle brush, paring knife, box grater, 12-inch (30 cm) sauté pan, turning spatula, long-handled fork.

Preheat oven to 350F (177C).

Scrub the potatoes under cold running water, pat dry, and set on a rack in the middle level of the oven. Bake them until a fork meets no resistance when plunged into the center of a potato (about 45 to 50 minutes). When done, let the potatoes cool at room temperature and then refrigerate them for several hours or, preferably, overnight.

About half an hour before serving, peel the potatoes with the paring knife and grate them on the coarsest side of the box grater (if possible, you should get pieces 1/4 inch [2/3 cm] long). Set the sauté pan over medium high heat, add the butter and bacon fat, and, when hot, add the grated potatoes, spreading them evenly in the pan. Season them with salt and pepper and sauté until the potatoes are golden brown. Turn them over with the spatula, break up the browned side with a fork, and sauté until the bottom is golden brown. Turn again with the spatula and additionally brown the side you broke up with the fork, adding more butter if the potatoes are too dry. The top and bottom must be a crisp golden brown. When done, serve immediately.

The potatoes may be boiled in their skins in lightly salted water, drained well, and chilled.

Variation: For a light meal or late-night snack, make individual portions of roesti (allow 1 1/4 to 1 1/2 potatoes per serving) and put them on an ovenproof platter. Broil thin slices of ham until hot, arrange them on the roesti, and top each serving with slices of Emmentaler or raclette cheese. Heat the roesti under the broiler until the cheese melts and serve immediately. If you are really hungry and want a Swiss version of Roger Vergé's *oeufs à la minuit*, top each serving with one or two fried eggs after the cheese is melted, and serve with a salad of mixed greens, tomato wedges, and cucumber slices.

Pommes de Terre Boulangère
Potatoes in the Style of the Baker's Wife

Throughout the French countryside it was customary for casseroles to be carried to the baker's oven to be cooked in the heat retained after the first bread of the day was done. These potatoes were usually cooked with a joint of meat in one dish, but were also cooked separately as they are here.

Yields 4 to 6 servings

2 pounds (900 g) boiling potatoes
2 medium onions
1 tablespoon (15 g) bacon fat
2 tablespoons (30 g) butter
1/4 teaspoon salt
Freshly ground white pepper
3/4 cup (180 ml) White Chicken Stock *(see page 61)*
Butter for the baking dish

Recommended equipment

A swivel-bladed vegetable peeler, slicing knife, 2-quart (2 L) bowl, 3-quart (3 L) saucepan with lid, large sieve or colander, 10-inch (25 cm) sauté pan, wooden spatula, baking dish 11 x 7 x 2 inches (27 1/2 x 17 1/2 x 5 cm).

Rinse the potatoes under cold running water, peel them, and slice into 1/4-inch (2/3 cm) thick pieces. Keep the slices covered with cold water in a bowl until you are ready to blanch them.

Bring water to boil in the covered saucepan over high heat. Drain the potato slices, drop them into the boiling water, and when the water returns to a boil, cook them for 10 seconds. Drain the potatoes immediately into the sieve or colander.

Preheat oven to 350F (177C).

Peel the onions, halve them, and slice thinly. Set the sauté pan over medium heat, add the bacon fat and butter, and, when it is hot, stir in the onion slices and sauté, stirring with the wooden spatula, for 3 minutes. When done, remove from heat and stir in the drained potato slices. Butter the baking dish. Season the potatoes with salt and pepper and spread them in the baking dish. They should have a depth of 2 to 2 1/2 inches (5 to 7 1/2 cm) in the dish. Pour in the chicken stock, set the dish into the oven, and bake until the potatoes have no resistance to the point of a knife (about 20 minutes). The dish can wait for a short while in the turned-off oven with the door ajar.

When serving the potatoes with beef, lamb, or veal, use the corresponding stock.

Variation: Sprinkle the potatoes with grated Parmesan cheese before baking and use less salt when seasoning them to compensate for the saltiness of the cheese.

Swiss Stewed Potatoes

My mother's and my family's favorite potato dish, especially when prepared with Knackwurst. A few minutes before the potatoes are cooked, stir in two to three peeled Knackwurst which have been halved lengthwise and sliced into 1/4-inch thick slices. Serve with a salad for a simple lunch or light supper.

Yields 4 to 6 servings

3 large boiling potatoes, total weight 1 1/2 to 1 3/4 pounds (675 to 790 g)
1/2 medium onion
1 1/2 tablespoons (22 g) butter
1 1/2 tablespoons flour
1/4 teaspoon Maggi
2 beef bouillon cubes
1/8 teaspoon caraway seeds
Salt
Freshly ground black pepper
2 teaspoons finely cut fresh chives

Recommended equipment

A swivel-bladed vegetable peeler, small chef's knife, 2-quart (2 L) bowl, 2-quart (2 L) saucepan with lid, colander, wooden spatula.

Rinse the potatoes under cold running water, peel, slice in half lengthwise, cut them into 1/2- to 3/4-inch (1 1/4 to 2 cm) cubes, put them into the bowl, cover with cold water, and reserve. Peel the onion half, dice it finely with the chef's knife, and reserve.

Set the saucepan over medium low heat, add the butter, and, when it is melted, stir in the flour and cook, stirring with the wooden spatula, until the flour begins to turn golden. Add the onion and cook, stirring, without browning the onion, for 1 to 2 minutes or until the flour is light brown.

Drain the reserved potatoes in the colander, put them into the saucepan, and add enough water to cover them by 1 inch (2 1/2 cm). Bring the water to a simmer, stirring constantly until the flour and water are smoothly blended. Add the Maggi, bouillon cubes, caraway seeds, salt and pepper, cover the saucepan, and adjust heat so that the potatoes simmer gently until done (about 20 to 25 minutes). Stir the potatoes once or twice while they are simmering. When done, adjust the seasoning if needed with salt, pepper, and a touch of Maggi, remove from heat, chop the chives, stir them in, and serve the potatoes at once.

Variation

🌿 *Hungarian Potatoes*

Use 2 1/4 teaspoons flour and 1 tablespoon (15 g) butter and cook until the flour starts to turn golden. Add the onions, 1 1/2 tablespoons tomato paste, and 1/4 teaspoon paprika and then proceed with the recipe.

🌿 *Pommes de Terre Duchesse*

A presentation of the potato that is worthy of a duchess—or your family for Sunday dinner or a holiday celebration. In addition to serving them individually, they can be piped onto a platter as a decorative, edible garnish for an entrée.

Yields 4 to 6 servings

3 large baking potatoes, total weight 1 1/2 to 1 3/4 pounds (675 to 790 g)
Salt
Freshly ground white pepper
A pinch of nutmeg
4 egg yolks
1 tablespoon (15 g) butter
1 egg
2 teaspoons water
Butter for the baking sheet

Recommended equipment

A stiff bristle brush, swivel-bladed vegetable peeler, paring knife, 2-quart (2 L) saucepan, colander, baking sheet, large fine-mesh sieve or potato ricer, 1 1/2-quart (1 1/2 L) saucepan, nutmeg grinder, wooden spatula, pastry bag with number 8 or 9 star tube, wire whisk, small bowl, rubber spatula, pastry brush.

Scrub the potatoes under cold running water, peel, and slice each one into thirds. If you are not going to cook them right away, put them in a bowl and cover them with cold water. When ready to cook, bring lightly salted water to boil in the large saucepan, add the potatoes, return to a boil, and cook, uncovered, until there is no resistance to a knife plunged into the center of a potato chunk (about 20 minutes). When done, drain the potatoes immediately into the colander—they must not be overcooked.

Preheat oven to 200F (93C).

When the potatoes have been drained, set the colander on the baking sheet and put the potatoes into the oven for 5 minutes to dry them out. Remove them from the oven, raise oven heat to 375F

(190C), and pass them through the sieve or ricer into the smaller saucepan. Season with salt and pepper, grind in the nutmeg, and set the saucepan over medium heat. Stir the potatoes with the wooden spatula until they are very hot. Reduce heat to very low, remove pan partially from heat, and add the egg yolks one by one, beating and blending well after each addition. Remove from heat, beat in the butter and let the potatoes cool to lukewarm. Whisk together the egg and water in the small bowl and lightly butter the baking sheet.

Using the rubber spatula, pack the lukewarm potato mixture into the pastry bag fitted with the star tube and pipe it onto the baking sheet, making swirled pyramid shapes for individual servings. Brush the potatoes with the egg wash and set the baking sheet into the oven until the potatoes are golden brown (about 8 to 10 minutes). When done, remove the potatoes from the oven and serve at once.

The potatoes may wait on the baking sheet for 1 to 2 hours before browning.

Sweet Potatoes Duchesse

The Caribbean Indian word for the native sweet potato, batata *(derived from* Ipomoea batatus*), gave its name to the potato. The sweet potato is a true root in the morning glory family and is cultivated in most subtropical areas of the world.* *(Yams, native to Africa—*nyami *is "to eat" in Senegalese—are often confused with sweet potatoes. Both are raised in the South, and, while differing in nutritional value and water content, can usually be interchanged.) The moist, golden flesh provides more calories, minerals, and vitamin A than the white potato, and has a natural affinity for baked ham, turkey, and pork.*

Yields 6 servings

2 pounds (900 g) sweet potatoes
4 tablespoons (60 g) butter
2 tablespoons sugar
A pinch of salt
A pinch of ginger
A pinch of cinnamon
2 egg yolks
2 tablespoons whipping cream
Butter for the baking sheet

Recommended equipment

A blender or food processor, 12-inch (30 cm) sauté pan, wooden spatula, wire whisk, small bowl, baking sheet, rubber spatula, pastry bag with number 8 or 9 star tube.

Preheat oven to 350F (177C).

Rinse the potatoes, pat them dry, and set them on a rack in the middle of the oven. Bake until soft, about 45 to 55 minutes, depending upon their size. When done, remove from oven and when cool enough to handle, cut the potatoes in half, scoop out the pulp, and put it in the blender jar (or food processor container) with the butter (discard the skins). Purée until smooth. Then scrape potatoes into the sauté pan, set the pan over medium heat, season the potatoes with sugar, salt, ginger, and cinnamon, and cook, stirring with the wooden spatula, until the potatoes are hot and bubbling. Reduce heat to low and partially remove sauté pan from heat. With the whisk, combine the egg yolks and cream in the small bowl and then stir the mixture into the potatoes, combining them well. Let the mixture cool.

Butter the baking sheet and when the potatoes are cool enough to handle, pack them into the pastry bag fitted with the star tube. Pipe them onto the baking sheet, making circular shapes for individual servings, and set the sheet into the middle level of the oven to bake for 10 minutes or until the potatoes are lightly browned. Serve at once.

The potatoes may wait on the baking sheet for 1 to 2 hours before browning.

Pommes de Terre Macaire

Serve these savory potato cakes with roast beef, chicken, lamb, or pork.

Yields 4 to 6 servings

1 recipe Pommes de Terre Duchesse *(see page 437)*
4 ounces (115 g) finely minced boiled or smoked ham
1 small onion
1 tablespoon bacon fat or peanut oil
1 tablespoon finely cut chives
1 tablespoon chopped fresh parsley
Flour
3 tablespoons Clarified Butter *(see page 568)*

Recommended equipment

A paring knife, small chef's knife, 8-inch (20 cm) sauté pan, wooden spatula, 12-inch (30 cm) sauté pan.

Prepare the duchesse potato recipe, following it through the point of beating the butter into the hot potato mixture. (Do not pipe it onto the baking sheet.)

Trim the ham of any fat with the paring knife, mince it finely with the chef's knife, and set aside. Peel the onion, mince it, and set aside. Put the small sauté pan over medium low heat, add the bacon fat (or peanut oil), and, when it is hot, add the minced ham and onion to the pan and cook, stirring occasionally, for 2 minutes. Remove pan from heat, scrape the ham and onion into the duchesse mixture, and stir it in. Rinse the chives and parsley, spin or pat dry, mince with chef's knife, and stir them into the potatoes, mixing well. Let the mixture cool.

Preheat oven to 325F (163C).

When the potato mixture is cool, form it into patties about 2 by 1 inches (5 x 2 1/2 cm), working on a floured surface. Set the large sauté pan over medium heat, add the clarified butter, and sauté the patties until golden brown on both sides. Do not crowd the pan. If you sauté the patties in batches, let the first batch rest on a baking sheet while you sauté the remainder. Just before serving, set the patties on the baking sheet and put them into the oven for 3 to 4 minutes or until hot.

If you are a devotee of corned beef hash and poached eggs, try Macaire patties as a substitute for the corned beef hash. Make the patties about 3 inches (7 1/2 cm) across. Top them with poached eggs, whip up a salad of fresh greens, and you have a tasty lunch or "emergency" dinner.

Potato Croquettes

Sometimes there is no hope for it but to yield to the yearning for a fried potato. True french fries, even good ones, are easier to come by in restaurants than they are at home because of the two-stage frying technique required. However, this recipe will satisfy your craving for "fries," and these elegant, melt-in-the-mouth puffs of potato go well with any entrée.

Yields 4 to 6 servings

1 recipe Pommes de Terre Duchesse *(see page 437)*
2 eggs
1 tablespoon water
Flour
Cracker meal
Peanut oil for frying

Recommended equipment

A paring knife, wire whisk, small bowl, electric deep fryer with thermostat or other deep pot, frying thermometer, fine-mesh skimmer, paper towels.

Prepare the duchesse potato recipe, following it through the point of beating the butter into the hot potato mixture. (Do not pipe it onto the baking sheet.)

Let the potatoes cool, divide the mixture into four or five parts, dust each lightly with flour, and, working on a floured surface, roll one by one into a sausage shape about 1 1/4 inches (3 3/4 cm) in diameter. Cut each length into pieces 2 inches (5 cm) long. Whisk the eggs together with the water in the small bowl and set the cracker meal and flour out separately on your work surface. Dust each potato croquette lightly with flour, dip into the egg wash, roll in the cracker meal, and set aside.

Preheat oven to 200F (93C).

Heat the peanut oil in the deep fryer or pot to 350F (177C). When the oil is hot, add the croquettes a few at a time. Do not crowd the pot. Fry them in batches and drain the croquettes on paper towels as they are done. Keep them hot in the oven and be sure to serve them as soon as possible while piping hot.

Variation

 ## Potato Croquettes with Almonds

Use a mixture of finely chopped almonds and fine white bread crumbs for the breading.

 ## Pommes de Terre Dauphine

The Dauphiné, an Alpine province on the Italian border, was added to France in 1349 and given to the king's eldest son who became known as the Dauphin. Do not confuse this with that other classic—pommes de terre Dauphinoise, a gratin of sliced potatoes with Gruyère.

Yields 8 servings

3 baking potatoes, total weight 1 1/2 pounds (675 g)
Salt
Freshly ground white pepper

FOR THE PÂTE À CHOUX
1 cup (235 ml) milk
8 tablespoons (115 g) butter
Salt
Freshly ground white pepper
A pinch of nutmeg
1 cup (235 ml) flour
4 eggs

Peanut oil for frying

Recommended equipment

A stiff bristle brush, swivel-bladed vegetable peeler, paring knife, 2 1/2-quart (2 1/2 L) saucepan with lid, 1 1/2-quart (1 1/2 L) saucepan, nutmeg grinder, wooden spatula, colander, baking sheet, large fine-mesh sieve or potato ricer, 2-quart (2 L) bowl, shallow dish, waxed paper, electric deep fryer with thermostat or other deep pot, frying thermometer, fine-mesh skimmer, paper towels.

Scrub the potatoes under cold running water, peel, and cut each into two or three chunks. Bring lightly salted water to boil in the large saucepan, covered, over high heat. When the water is boiling, add the potatoes, and cook, uncovered, until a knife can pierce them with little resistance (about 20 minutes). When done, drain them immediately into the colander.

While the potatoes are cooking prepare the pâte à choux. Set the smaller saucepan over medium high heat, add the milk, butter, salt, and pepper, and grind in the nutmeg. Bring to a boil, stirring occasionally, and as soon as the milk boils and the butter is melted, reduce heat to low, add the flour all at once, and stir constantly until the mixture comes together and no longer clings to the pan. This will take several minutes. Remove pan from heat and add the eggs one by one, beating well to blend completely after each addition. Set pan aside.

Preheat oven to 200F (93C).

When the potatoes are done and have been drained in the colander, put the colander on the baking sheet and set it into the oven for 5 minutes to dry the potatoes. Then remove them from the oven and while they are still hot put them through the sieve or ricer into the bowl. Add the reserved pâte à choux, blend thoroughly with the wooden spatula, and adjust the seasoning with salt and freshly ground white pepper. Scrape the mixture into the shallow dish, cover with a piece of lightly oiled waxed paper, and set the dish into the refrigerator to chill for several hours. (The mixture will keep well for several days under refrigeration.)

When you are ready to fry the potatoes, preheat the oven to 200F (93C) and heat peanut oil in the deep fryer or pot to 350F (177C). Shape the potato mixture into small balls or oval shapes with a teaspoon or small soupspoon and set them on lightly oiled waxed paper until you are ready to fry them. Or, use a pastry bag with a star tip to make ring shapes. When the oil is hot, cook a few of the potato shapes at one time (do not crowd the pot) until they are brown. When done, remove with the skimmer to paper towels to drain, put them on a pan, and set into the oven to keep warm while you fry the rest of the potatoes. When they are all done, serve at once.

Pommes de Terre Parisienne Rissolées

This elegant preparation is pleasantly deceptive because it requires less time than you might think. Having cooked them once, you will find that they automatically come to mind when you want that perfect little potato to serve with tenderloins and roasts of beef or lamb.

Yields 4 to 5 servings

4 large boiling potatoes, total weight 2 to 2 1/2 pounds (900 to 1125 g)
4 tablespoons Clarified Butter (see page 568)
1 teaspoon chopped fresh parsley
Salt
1 teaspoon butter

Recommended equipment

A swivel-bladed vegetable peeler, 2-quart (2 L) bowl, paper towels, round melon scoop, 2-quart (2 L) saucepan, large fine-mesh sieve, enameled cast-iron baking dish or lined copper plat à sauter large enough to hold potatoes in a single layer, wooden spatula, small chef's knife.

Rinse the potatoes under cold running water, peel them, and, as they are done, drop them into cold water in the bowl. Keep them covered with water until you are ready to make the potato balls. Using the melon scoop, cut out the balls with a back-and-forth and circular motion, making them as uniform as possible. Keep the potato balls in fresh cold water until you are ready to blanch them. (*See below* for uses of the potato scraps.)

To blanch the potato balls, drain them, put them into the saucepan, cover with hot water, set the saucepan over high heat, and bring the water to a boil. Boil the potatoes for 10 seconds, drain immediately in the sieve, and pat dry with paper towels.

Preheat oven to 400F (204C).

Set the baking dish or plat à sauter over medium heat and add the clarified butter and the potato balls. Sauté the potatoes, stirring occasionally, until they begin to brown. Then set the pan into the oven and bake until the potatoes are golden brown and cooked through (about 10 minutes). Stir them around two or three times so that they brown evenly.

While the potatoes are in the oven, rinse the parsley, pat or spin dry, chop, and reserve.

When the potatoes are done, remove them from the oven, pour off any excess butter, set the pan over medium heat, season the potatoes with salt, add the butter, sauté for 30 seconds, stirring, sprinkle on the parsley, and serve at once.

The potato scraps will keep well for 1 to 2 days covered with cold water and refrigerated. The scraps may be used in a soup or, blanched, drained, and chopped coarsely, they can become hashed brown potatoes. A dish of creamy potatoes may be made by blanching the scraps, draining them, chopping roughly, and mixing them with half-and-half. Spread the potatoes in a buttered baking dish, season with salt, freshly ground white pepper, and nutmeg, sprinkle with grated Parmesan cheese, and broil until golden brown.

Variation

❧ *Pommes de Terre Noisette Rissolées*

Use an oval scoop to make nutlike shapes and follow the recipe for pommes de terre Parisienne. Either shape may be boiled rather than sautéed, a preparation that goes well with seafood. Bring lightly salted water to boil over high heat, add the potatoes, and adjust heat so that the potatoes boil gently until done. Drain them immediately and keep warm in a saucepan over low heat. If you like, season with salt and pepper, a pat of butter, and add chopped parsley just before serving.

Vegetables

> Louhans is a sleepy agricultural town with an arcaded shopping street which would delight any artist. Its outskirts consist of extensive truck farms, incredibly fertile, well-tended acres which produce vegetables such as are seen only in the seed catalogues. The day's pick of green beans, peas, cauliflowers, tomatoes, baby turnips, eggplant, carrots, and celery is rushed to Paris by fast freight in time to appear in the gray dawn at Les Halles, where discriminating restaurant buyers snap them up.
> —Samuel Chamberlain

Louhans, near Bresse (the home of the celebrated M. Poulet), represents the best of all possible worlds—fertile ground producing perfect vegetables that are rushed to markets, before the dew dries, and bought by astute shoppers. All too often the reality is that any one of the links in the chain may be weak and the vegetables on your plate will be a mere shadow of their former selves. The grower, shipper, grocer, buyer, and cook must each do his very best—vegetables are fragile and demand care.

The fragility of fresh produce has always been a concern. Monks at thirteenth-century monasteries sold huge quantities of food at the kitchen door—as a way around an edict forbidding them to participate in worldly fairs—and were among the most efficient growers and sellers of all time. Of course, you had to live within a short distance of such a monastery to take advantage of this system. By the middle of the sixteenth century, Paris was a bustling center of commerce, and great food fairs were held on Wednesdays and Saturdays. More than two thousand heavily laden carts rumbled into the city to be unloaded and whatever remained unsold at the end of one day was not allowed to be held over until the next. Here were the beginnings of the central Paris market that would be known as Les Halles. Today the biweekly market is fundamental to the rhythm of life in most larger villages as well as cities throughout Europe. Whenever I go home to Lucerne, I make several visits to the open-air market along the quai of the Reuss River. There the *Kapelbrücke* with its water tower connects both sides of the market which is alive with the sights and smells that only seasonal fruits, vegetables, flowers, and farm-raised chickens and rabbits can provide. Here in America, in addition to the traditional farmers' markets in the cities, roadside stands have always supplied fresh vegetables to discerning buyers who demand the freshest produce possible.

Systems of distribution today are well advanced from what they were even a generation ago. Not long ago the Homestead had its own self-contained farming operation in part of what is now the Lower Cascades Golf Course. Twelve acres (not including the "potato patch") were under irrigated cultivation and the greenhouses furnished orchids, heliotrope, sweetpeas, carnations, geraniums, daffodils, lilies, pansies, snapdragons, salpiglosses, stock, and many other flowers for public spaces and private rooms alike. Even today, we make a point of purchasing produce from local valley farmers when it is at its summer peak. But our kitchen operates all year round, and to meet this demand, we have our own distribution system, which starts with B. G. McElwee.

He expects only the best from our suppliers and he accepts nothing less. Once the orders have been confirmed, Charlie Bogan and the Homestead's refrigerated tractor trailer are on the road to Washington, D.C., to pick up our fresh produce (in addition to the meats and other items), a trip he makes twice a week or more often during our busy seasons. Produce arrives at our suppliers from New York, California, Europe, or South America—wherever the vegetable is at its best the Homestead will get it. To give you an idea of our weekly vegetable consumption, for an approximate guest count of 650, we would most likely use four thousand pounds of produce, running the gamut from artichokes to watercress. If you want a thorough tour of the vegetable cooler, be sure to look at B. G. McElwee's Shopping List.

Once at the hotel, produce is stored according to its requirements for temperature and humidity. When needed, it is brought to the vegetable preparation area where the department responsible for cleaning, trimming, and cooking the vegetables takes over. Vegetables that are fresh to begin with, handled correctly, and cooked properly are delicious. Anytime someone says that throughout his lifetime he has never liked such-and-such a vegetable, we find it is usually the case that the vegetable has been improperly cooked. Overcooking is the most common mistake—vegetables should retain a slight resistance to the bite (like al dente pasta). There should be an agreeable texture rather than a mushy mouthful. Most vegetables are best if blanched, uncovered, in lots of boiling water, refreshed in cold water, and then finished just before serving by warming gently with your chosen seasoning. Also, be sure to use stainless-steel cooking pots or pots made of any nonreactive metal (never use iron).

When deciding what vegetables to serve, first check with your grocery store or farmers' market. The season usually dictates what fresh vegetables are available, although with modern transportation being what it is, the home cook can enjoy occasional happy surprises during the otherwise drab winter months. The flavors, textures, and colors of each season used to be more clearly defined than they are today, yet a fresh, garden-ripe tomato probably says "summer" better than any other vegetable. When planning your menu, consider the color of the vegetables and how they will look next to each other or the entrée itself. Do not repeat the same vegetable from one course in another—if you serve a tomato salad, stay away from Tomatoes Provençale or a dish with a tomato sauce. Vegetables within the same category should not be used twice, such as broccoli and cauliflower or Brussels sprouts and cabbage. A vegetable garnish can be the enticing touch and groups of compatible vegetables such as String Beans, Carottes Glacées, and Navets Glacés, can be gathered into small bunches and arranged around the serving plate or platter *à la bouquetière*. Take a lesson from the skillful produce sellers who arrange displays as tempting to the eye as the palate. The art of presentation begins in the market stalls and ends at your table.

The vegetable recipes are arranged alphabetically by type of vegetable, so asparagus leads off. Asparagus can be green, white, or blushed with purple and the most favored is from Argenteuil in France. Enjoyed for thousands of years, asparagus was considered by the well-to-do Egyptians a royal vegetable, and during the reign of Louis XIV in France it became very popular. Quintinie was the man able to grow it and supply the royal kitchens all year round. The best way to enjoy asparagus is the simplest—cook it until just done and serve with melted butter or a flavorful sauce. The sensible British (and other devotees) eat asparagus with their fingers, stalk by precious stalk. Try to serve it the day it is bought—most likely the asparagus has traveled a distance to reach your kitchen. If you must hold it over a day or two, trim about one-half inch off the ends of the stalks, set them upright in a glass with an inch of water in it, cover loosely with plastic wrap, and refrigerate.

Green beans came to Europe in the sixteenth century with returning Portuguese and Spanish explorers. The beans, native to Central America, were cultivated in Mexico more than seven thousand years ago. The generic term, *haricot*, that in French means "bean," appears to be derived from the Mexican word for bean, *ayacotl*. Like the potato, Europeans brought the green beans back across the Atlantic to North America. Edible pod beans go by several names: green beans, string beans, pole beans, or French beans. They are not to be confused with kidney, pinto, navy, or pea beans, each of which also came from the American continent and are often dried so they need a long, slow cooking to develop their hearty flavor. Try the Flageolets Bretonne for a taste of history.

Brussels sprouts are small buds that grow many to a tall, thick stalk, protected by an outcropping of leaves at the top. A member of the cabbage family, they profit from a blanching in briskly boiling water before finishing with seasoning. Most any flavoring that goes well with cabbage will go well with Brussels sprouts. They became popular in Europe only after World War I although they were recorded as growing around Brussels in 1213. The sprouts were under cultivation in French and English gardens at the end of the eighteenth century, and Thomas Jefferson planted them in his garden at Monticello in 1812.

Cabbage is native to the Mediterranean seaboard and has been cultivated for more than twenty-five hundred years. The Romans were very fond of it and brought cabbage to Britain from whence it spread to become a staple in the European diet. At the same time cabbage traveled in the opposite direction—the middle European "sauerkraut" can be traced to the Chinese "sour cabbage," cabbage soaked in rice wine to preserve it during the winter. In France, cabbage became acceptable when Charles V was coaxed into eating his first one by Taillevent, the squire and master of the king's kitchen garrisons. In 1375, Taillevent wrote the oldest French cookbook, *Le Viandier*, which detailed the tastes and manners of the medieval court and became one of the first books to be printed in France. The recipe for Braised Red Cabbage develops the nutty flavor with slow, moist cooking and, if you dislike cabbage, this should make you a cabbage convert.

Native to Afghanistan, the carrot was known to the Greeks and Romans and like spinach and eggplant it was brought by the Moors along the African coast to Europe. From Spain, carrots spread into Holland, France, and England and were used widely throughout Europe in the Middle Ages. The colonists brought carrots to the New World where they escaped from cultivation and became the wildflower known as Queen Anne's lace (regarded by many as a weed in spite of its lovely crown of white flowers).

Celery is a member of the carrot family and was first recorded as a food plant in France in 1623. Its relative, celeriac (celery root or celery knob), stores starch in the lower stem and looks somewhat like a turnip. Used in soups, salads, and braised or blanched for serving hot as a vegetable, celery and celeriac should be enjoyed more often than they are. Celery is generally available throughout the year and celeriac is a fall and winter vegetable. The method for cooking the celery hearts is called *blanc à légumes* and is a classical technique that should be used whenever the purity of a white vegetable needs protection. (Use this method also for Belgian Endive, Hearts of Fennel Parmesan, white asparagus, and Swiss chard.) *Blanc à légumes* may seem fussy at first, but it will be your preference after you become accustomed to it. The Purée of Celery gives you the chance to use celery and celeriac in one preparation and you will enjoy the enhanced celery flavor lent by the celeriac.

Corn was the New World's most important contribution to man's diet. Cultivated in Central America and the dietary staple of native Indians in South and North America since 3500 B.C., corn is, today, second only to wheat in the acreage planted. Columbus carried corn to Europe, where it was known as Indian corn or maize, the term used by natives of the West Indies. The word "corn," denoting maize, is used solely in the United States and was first used to describe grainlike or granular objects such as salt, used, for example, in corned (salted) beef. The sweet corn so loved in the United States stores more sugar than starch and as soon as the ear is off the stalk, the sugar begins to turn into starch. So when you are serving corn-on-the-cob, cook it as soon as possible—anything short of boiling your water in the cornfield would be about right. The Homestead Corn Pudding recipe calls for canned corn, already processed, so you can take your time. This is simplicity itself. Corn is enjoyed in all its forms—fresh (on or off the cob) or dried and then processed by either grinding into cornmeal or soaking in an alkali solution (to remove the hulls) yielding hominy, which, when dried and ground, becomes grits. The recipes for Polenta alla Milanese and Spoon Bread are made with cornmeal. Making polenta has been a rite of daily life in northern Italy for centuries. Cooked in a copper kettle reserved solely for that purpose, the polenta was enjoyed by itself or as an accompaniment to meat or fowl. Today, the combination of polenta with any roasted meat, game, or fowl, is as delicious as it is on the family hearths in Lombardy and Venetia. Spoon bread, indigenous to North America, is a cornmeal soufflé that emerged from the confluence of two great cuisines—French and African. Browned on top and soft in the center, spoon bread is perfect with pork and grilled meats. Gnocchi alla Romana, served fresh with butter, baked, or fried, can be enjoyed for breakfast, lunch, or dinner. We call for grits in this recipe because they are more readily available than semolina, a milled product of durum wheat, which is available in specialty food stores. The grits, ground from dried hominy, are a suitable substitute. If you can get the semolina, by all means use it. Grits, always white because of the alkali treatment that produces them, have been a staple of the southern table for generations. Most southerners prefer white corn and thus white cornmeal, believing that yellow corn is feed for cattle. Cornmeal is either creamy white or yellow because it is ground from the endosperm which contains the coloration of the corn kernel. Use either white or yellow cornmeal, whichever is fresh, and you will enjoy the results.

The eggplant is native to India and like so many other plants it was carried along trading routes. Arabs brought it to northern Africa and Spain in the Middle Ages, from whence the eggplant reached Italy, where it was cultivated in the fifteenth century, and France, where it was cultivated in the eighteenth century. When baked, the Asian variety of eggplant exudes a dark, sticky substance that should be saved and enjoyed. Buy eggplant that is firm to the touch, has a glossy and shining skin with no blemishes, and, to be perfectly sure that you will have a sweet rather than a bitter eggplant, look for an elongated blossom scar rather than a round one. If you want to fry the eggplant in oil, slice and salt it, letting it sit for an hour in a colander. Then rinse the slices under cold running water, pat dry, and follow your recipe. The eggplant absorbs less oil when salted before frying. Baked Eggplant Niçoise combines the simplest of ingredients for a taste of Provence on your plate.

Endive, from which the Belgian variety was developed, was native to India and known by Egyptians, Greeks, and Romans. Traditionally enjoyed raw as a salad, endive is a treat braised and served as a hot vegetable. We are all indebted to the enterprising and imaginative gardener who has given us Belgian endive. The method, *blanc à légumes*, for cooking this delicate vegetable is ideally suited for Hearts of Fennel Parmesan. Fennel, sometimes called Florentine fennel to distinguish it from the herb, is less well known in America than in Europe. The Italian name, finocchio, is becoming familiar to Americans who live near farmers' markets or specialty food stores. Fennel looks like a flattened bulb—like a short, squat stalk of celery. It has overlapping stalks and bright green shoots with feathery, dill-like leaves. The strong anise flavor of fennel is refreshing when the bulbs are trimmed, halved or quartered, and sliced thinly for a salad. Or cook the fennel whole, chill, and serve as part of a cold plate. During the fall and winter months, take advantage of the fennel supply and serve it hot, often, with any grilled meat, fish, or fowl.

A member of the lily family which includes asparagus and onions, leeks were native to the Mediterranean region and distributed by the Romans throughout Europe. The Welsh are known for two events associated with leeks. In 640, the last Briton king, Cadwallader, was victorious over the Saxons in a battle during which the Welsh wore leeks in their hats to distinguish themselves from the enemy. Also, during the annual spring plowing cooperative, or *cymmortha*, each Welsh farmer tossed a leek into the communal stew to symbolize his participation. Once known as "poor man's asparagus," leeks today are readily available in local markets and appreciated on their own merits—added to stocks, soups, or stews, they provide a subtle and haunting hint of onion. Or prepare our own favorite Leek Butter Sauce. Cooked alone, baked or braised, they are a welcome addition to any lunch or dinner.

Turnips were cultivated four thousand years ago in Eurasia as a staple, starchy food. They traveled where mankind went and flourished, even in fiercely cold and forbidding climates, enabling man's survival. Turnips are often unfairly maligned. Look for young, white turnips, known as navets to the French, available in spring and early summer. These are the best. After a brief blanching they can be mashed for a soufflé or combined with potatoes for a creamy soup. The Navets Glacés offered here is the most versatile preparation because it is the ideal companion for beef, lamb, duck, pork, or fowl of any kind. Other turnips—like rutabagas—require extended blanching and heavy peeling to make them palatable. During winter months when tender turnips are unavailable you could prepare kohlrabi, the turnip-rooted cabbage, for turnip flavor.

Peas, native to western Asia, were cultivated by the Greeks and Romans, and throughout history have been an important dried food. Fresh peas became fashionable during the sixteenth century in Europe where they were enjoyed as a delicacy and luxury. Today, sugar peas and snow peas are varieties eaten very young for the tender pods. The French call them *mange tout* (or "eat all") and among the Chinese they are known as Holland peas. It is believed that this edible-pod variety was developed in Holland where there was a traditional emphasis on farming as far back as the seventeenth century, when the Low Countries were rich in vegetables and fruits because of the limited grazing area for beef cattle. Snow peas are planted early and grow well under brisk conditions. Choose pods that are crisp and flat with a thin, light-green skin. Avoid frozen snow peas at all costs—you should change your menu rather than face the disappointment of a mushy mess on your plate.

Fresh spinach is the most versatile green vegetable. Enjoyed raw or cooked, it absorbs the flavor of whatever is served with it rather than imposing its own flavor on a dish. Originating in Persia, spinach was brought by the Arabs to North Africa and from there to Spain where spinach was cultivated near Seville by the end of the eleventh century. By the sixteenth century spinach had reached England. Today, anyone who is serious about food—either the preparation or the enjoyment of it—will sing the praises of this delicious leaf. Spinach is integral to the cuisine of France, China, Italy, and India, and is enjoyed throughout the world, from East to West, wherever man has traveled. Prepare the Creamed Spinach and even your children will ask for seconds. An excellent source of vitamin A, spinach actually contains less iron than sorrel, leek, and lettuce, Popeye myths notwithstanding. Frozen spinach exists for soups. Buy only fresh spinach for all other preparations.

Winter squashes have been cultivated for nine thousand years. In the New World, native Americans grew them with gourds, pumpkins, and corn. Carried to Europe by returning explorers, the squashes took root—both the winter squash, such as acorn, and summer squash, such as zucchini. The winter squashes are mature, hard-skinned varieties that keep very well during the winter after harvest in the late fall. The summer varieties have a soft skin and need to be eaten shortly after harvesting. The word "squash" is derived from an American Indian Algonquinian word which in a transliterated form is *askootasquash*. The Italian word for zucchini is *zucchine*—the diminutive plural of the feminine noun *zucca*, meaning "pumpkin"—meaning "little pumpkins." Zucchini are actually cylindrical pumpkins and will be as large as a watermelon if allowed to mature. Best when about five to six inches long, zucchini are known as Italian marrows in England and *courgettes* in France. The recipe for acorn squash baked with honey is the simplest and most delicious treatment of an excellent winter vegetable. (Other winter squashes can be treated the same way.) The recipes for zucchini state the lineage of this popular vegetable. Baked with tomatoes, green bell peppers, thyme, and garlic, the traditional ratatouille from Provence combines the new (zucchini, tomatoes, and sweet peppers) with the old (thyme and garlic). The sautéed zucchini is flavored with oregano, an herb known to the Greeks (the word in Greek means "mountain brightness" or "mountain joy"). Oregano enhances the flavor of zucchini so skillfully that one is grateful they were joined together. The baked zucchini combines tomatoes and red and green peppers, native to the New World, with olive oil and oregano from its adoptive land (in this case Italy).

Tomatoes were another gift to Europe from the New World. Indigenous to the Andes, they were domesticated in Mexico and arrived in Europe in 1523. Initially a novelty item, tomatoes were cultivated as ornamental plants in England by the end of the sixteenth century. Curiously, during the next two centuries, they were common only in Italy—in other areas, people were superstitious about tomatoes, calling them "love apples" and associating them with Adam and Eve's fabled departure from the Garden of Eden. Tomatoes do have poisonous relatives—the deadly nightshade, for example—and the leaves of tomato plants are poisonous. Happily, today prejudice has been overcome by good sense and tomatoes are a significant part of man's diet. Fresh tomatoes from the garden (yours or your neighbor's) are an unparalleled treat. Presented sliced on a plate with a light vinaigrette or a grinding of black pepper, fresh tomatoes need nothing else—other than you to enjoy them. Off season, tomatoes can be prepared as they were at the Fassifern Tavern or as Stewed Tomatoes. Garden-ripe tomatoes can also be used for the stewed recipe whenever you have a surfeit of fresh tomatoes and can be content to find them in your sauté pan rather than on your salad plate. The Tomatoes Provençale must be prepared with firm, perfectly ripe tomatoes. The trick here is to bake and brown them just before serving because if they wait for you they will become soggy and unworthy of your grilled meat or fowl.

Vegetables were man's first food and they deserve a place of honor at your table. All too often vegetables receive little attention in many restaurants and less in many homes. This does not have to be. Demand fresh produce at your market and you will be well on your way to discovering what La Varenne and Carême knew so long ago—that vegetables can and should enliven every meal and be an integral part of your daily diet.

Asparagus

Asparagus is a treat any way it is served—cold with a simple vinaigrette or hot with melted butter. Try hot asparagus with any one of these sauces: Hollandaise I, Maltaise, Mousseline, Mornay, or Beurre Noisette. Enjoy fresh asparagus often lest the spring crop be gone before you have had a chance to enjoy all of these sauces.

Yields 4 servings

2 pounds (900 g) fresh asparagus
Salt
2 tablespoons (30 g) butter

Recommended equipment

A swivel-bladed vegetable peeler, paring knife, white kitchen string, 8-quart (8 L) stockpot with lid, long-handled fork, kitchen towels, heatproof serving platter or plates.

Rinse the asparagus thoroughly, yet gently, in cold running water, to rid it of all sand.

Fill the stockpot with water, add about 1 tablespoon salt, and bring it to a boil, covered, over high heat.

While the water is coming to a boil, peel and trim the asparagus (save the trimmings for soup, such as Cream of Asparagus). Working with one stalk at a time, lay the asparagus flat on your work surface, hold it firmly below the tip, and, using the vegetable peeler, peel off a thin layer beginning about 2 inches (5 cm) below the tip and peeling toward the stem end. When all the stalks are peeled, arrange them in bunches with 6 to 8 stalks in each and line up the tips. Trim the stems with the paring knife, removing the lower 2 to 3 inches of the stalk where the stem is tough and woody. Tie each bundle in two places with the kitchen string.

When the water is boiling, add the asparagus bundles, return the water to a boil, and adjust the heat so that the asparagus cooks, uncovered, at a rapid simmer until just tender. This will take 6 to 10 minutes, depending upon the size of the asparagus. To test for doneness, catch a bundle with the long-handled fork, lift it out of the water, and stick the point of the paring knife into the thickest part of the stalk. There should be a slight resistance.

When done, set the pot under cold running water to cool the asparagus and immediately stop the cooking process. (If you plan to make soup, pour off about one-third of the cooking water before adding cold water and reserve.) Let the asparagus cool for 30 seconds, then remove the bundles and lay them on folded kitchen towels to drain.

Preheat oven to 250F (121C).

When ready to serve, arrange the bundles on the heatproof platter or plates, cut the strings, and remove them. Dot the asparagus with butter and set it into the oven to heat for 5 minutes or until hot. Serve at once.

To serve the asparagus cold, leave it in the cold water for 2 to 3 minutes, drain thoroughly on the towels, and refrigerate, wrapped in plastic, until needed. Serve chilled asparagus with Mayonnaise or Homestead Sauce Vinaigrette.

Variation

Asparagus Parmesan

Blend 5 tablespoons butter at room temperature with 4 tablespoons grated Parmesan cheese until they are combined into a paste. Spread this over the top 3 inches of the asparagus stalks after they have been arranged in the ovenproof dish, set the dish into the middle level of a preheated 350F (177C) oven, and bake for 6 to 8 minutes or until golden brown. Serve at once. If you want to serve a luncheon or light supper dish, present the asparagus with fried or poached eggs on top.

Beans

String Beans

Fresh vegetables are at their best when simply seasoned and served at once. The variation with toasted almonds or water chestnuts enhances the beans with a contrast in texture.

Yields 6 to 8 servings

2 pounds (900 g) fresh string beans
Salt
2 tablespoons (30 g) butter
Freshly ground white pepper

Recommended equipment

A 5-quart (5 L) saucepan with lid, colander, 12-inch (30 cm) sauté pan, wooden spatula.

Fill the saucepan with water, add about 1 tablespoon salt, and bring it to a boil, covered, over high heat.

While the water is coming to a boil, snap the beans at both ends and pull off any strings (do not cut them with a knife—you will miss the "string" if you trim the beans this way). If the beans are longer than 3 inches (7 1/2 cm), snap them in half so they can be eaten easily. Wash the beans well in the colander under cold running water.

When the water is boiling, add the beans all at once and return the water to a boil as quickly as possible. Then adjust heat so that the beans cook, uncovered, at a rapid simmer until tender but still crisp. This will take 8 to 10 minutes. To test for doneness, remove a bean, cool under cold water, and bite into it. When the beans are done, remove saucepan from heat and put it under cold running water to stop the cooking process. Remove the beans when they are tepid and drain them in the colander.

When ready to serve the beans, set the sauté pan over medium low heat, add the butter, and, when it is melted, add a pinch of salt, grind in the pepper, stir in the beans, and sauté them until they are hot (3 to 4 minutes). Serve at once.

Variation: Add toasted sliced almonds or thinly sliced water chestnuts to the butter when heating the beans.

If string beans are to be used as part of a *bouquetière* of vegetables, trim them with a paring knife to equal lengths after they have been cooked and cooled. Butter a baking pan, arrange the beans in it in rows or bunches, drizzle melted butter over them, and set the pan in a preheated 250F (121C) oven until hot. Serve at once.

String Beans Country Style

A hearty preparation for cold months when older beans are available. Serve this with Chicken in the Pot Homestead, Southern Fried Rabbit, Sauerbraten, or Scotch Lamb Stew.

Yields 6 to 8 servings

1 recipe String Beans *(see page 455)*
2 to 3 ounces (60 to 85 g) bacon
1 medium onion
1 tablespoon flour
3 cups (710 ml) water
1 chicken bouillon cube (or 1 teaspoon chicken base)
1/4 teaspoon Maggi
Salt
Freshly ground black pepper

Recommended equipment

A paring knife, small chef's knife, 3-quart (3 L) saucepan, wooden spatula, wire whisk.

Prepare the string beans so that they are cooked, cooled, and drained. Reserve them.

Using the paring knife, cut the bacon into matchstick-size strips and set aside. Peel the onion, chop it finely with the chef's knife, and reserve. Set the saucepan over medium heat, add the bacon strips, and cook, stirring with the spatula, until the fat has been rendered (1 to 2 minutes). Stir in the reserved chopped onion, and sauté, stirring, for 1 minute. Add the flour and blend it in thoroughly before adding the water while mixing with the whisk. Add the bouillon cube, Maggi, and season lightly with salt and pepper. Bring the mixture to a simmer, stirring with the whisk, and simmer for 2 minutes, stirring occasionally. Raise heat to medium high, add the string beans all at once, return to a simmer, and cook for 4 to 6 minutes (or until beans are tender), stirring from time to time. Serve while the beans are very hot.

You can add well-washed and drained raw beans to the sauce mixture and simmer until the beans are tender. This method will discolor the beans but improve the flavor.

Flageolets Bretonne
White Beans in the Style of Brittany

Navy beans traveled from North America to Europe, where they found their way into peasant cooking. Soak the beans overnight, cook them slowly the next day, and enjoy them with a Roast Leg of Lamb au Jus for a hearty dinner on a cold night.

Yields 8 to 10 servings

1 pound (450 g) dried navy beans
2 quarts (1900 ml) water
Salt
Freshly ground white pepper
1/2 carrot
1/2 medium onion
1 small clove
1/2 celery stalk
4 to 6 ounces (115 to 170 g) slab bacon

FOR THE TOMATO SAUCE
4 medium, ripe tomatoes (blanched, peeled, and seeded; see page 568)
1/2 medium onion
2 tablespoons (30 g) butter
1 garlic clove
1 tablespoon chopped fresh parsley

Recommended equipment

A 2-quart (2 L) glass, china, or stainless steel bowl; colander; 3-quart (3 L) saucepan with lid; fine-mesh skimmer; 10-inch (25 cm) sauté pan; wooden spatula; small chef's knife; garlic press.

Pick the beans over, remove any debris, and put them in the bowl. Cover them with cold water to a depth of 2 inches (5 cm) and set the beans aside to soak overnight.

The next day, drain the beans into the colander, transfer them to the saucepan, set it over medium high heat, and add the 2 quarts of water. Salt the beans lightly and grind in the pepper. Wash the carrot, halve it lengthwise, and add one half to the beans. Peel the onion half (save the other half for the tomato sauce), stick the clove into it, and add it to the beans. Rinse the celery stalk, make it as stringless as possible, halve it, and add one half to the saucepan. Add the bacon to the beans (leave the rind attached). Bring the beans to a boil, skimming as necessary, then adjust heat so that they will simmer gently, covered, until tender, about 1 1/2 to 2 hours. Do not overcook the beans into a mushy mixture.

While the beans are cooking, prepare the tomatoes, cut them into 1/2-inch (1 1/4 cm) chunks with the chef's knife, and reserve.

When the beans are done, peel the reserved onion half and dice it finely. Set the sauté pan over medium low heat, add the butter, and, when it is hot, stir in the diced onion, sauté for 1 minute, press in the garlic, sauté for 30 seconds, and stir in the reserved tomato chunks. Adjust heat so that tomato mixture simmers gently for 5 minutes. When done, adjust seasoning with salt and pepper.

While the tomatoes simmer, remove any excess liquid from the beans (more than 1/2 cup or 118 ml is too much) and the carrot, celery, onion, and bacon. When the tomatoes are done, stir them into the beans, bring to a simmer, and cook gently on low heat, stirring occasionally, for 10 minutes.

Rinse the parsley, pat or spin dry, chop, and reserve.

When the beans are ready, stir in the chopped parsley and serve. If you wish, slice the carrot, celery, onion, and bacon very thinly and garnish the servings with some of each.

The beans are delicious when rewarmed the next day.

Brussels Sprouts

At holiday time these are often served with chopped pecans or cooked chestnuts stirred into the butter. You may add Crème Fraîche, enough to make a creamy coating, when warming and seasoning them. An excellent vegetable for Suprêmes de Volaille Normande.

Yields 4 to 6 servings

1 pound (450 g) Brussels sprouts
Salt
2 tablespoons (30 g) butter
Freshly ground white pepper

Recommended equipment

A 4-quart (4 L) saucepan with lid, paring knife, colander, 10-inch (25 cm) sauté pan, wooden spatula.

Fill the saucepan with water, add about 1 tablespoon salt, and bring it to a boil, covered, over high heat.

While the water is coming to a boil, trim the Brussels sprouts of any wilted leaves and slice a sliver off the bottom of each sprout with the paring knife.

When the water is boiling, add the Brussels sprouts and return the water to a boil as quickly as possible. Then adjust heat so that the Brussels sprouts cook, uncovered, at a rapid simmer until tender but still crisp. This will take 8 to 10 minutes. To test for doneness, remove a sprout, cool under cold water, and bite into it. The sprout should have a little resistance. When the sprouts are done, remove saucepan from heat and put it under running cold water to arrest the cooking process and refresh the sprouts. Remove the Brussels sprouts when they are tepid and drain them in the colander.

When ready to serve, set the sauté pan over medium low heat, add the butter, and, when it is melted, add a pinch of salt, grind in the pepper, stir in the Brussels sprouts, and sauté them, stirring, for 3 to 4 minutes or until hot. Serve as soon as possible.

Braised Red Cabbage

You will like the classic combination when this is served with Sauerbraten, Roast Stuffed Tenderloin of Venison, or Roast Loin of Pork.

Yields 4 to 6 servings

1 head of red cabbage, weighing about 2 1/2 to 3 1/2 pounds (1125 to 1575 g)
Salt
Freshly ground black pepper
3 tablespoons sugar
1 small clove
1/3 bay leaf
A pinch of cinnamon or cumin
3 juniper berries
1 cup (235 ml) dry red wine
1/4 cup (60 ml) red wine vinegar

FOR BRAISING
1 medium onion
1 small apple
3 tablespoons bacon, goose, duck, or chicken fat

Recommended equipment

A paring knife; slicing knife; 2-quart (2 L) glass, china, or stainless steel bowl; wooden spoon; china plate to fit inside bowl; plastic wrap; swivel-bladed vegetable peeler; enameled cast-iron baking dish or lined copper plat à sauter with lid.

Trim any blemished leaves from the cabbage, quarter it, and remove the core and large ribs. Using the slicing knife, slice the cabbage thinly into pieces 1/4 inch (2/3 cm) thick. Put the cabbage into the bowl, season with salt and pepper, and add sugar, clove, bay leaf, cinnamon (or cumin), juniper berries, red wine, and red wine vinegar. Blend well. Set the china plate inside the bowl on top of the cabbage, cover the bowl with plastic wrap, and refrigerate for 18 to 24 hours. Stir the cabbage once or twice during this time.

When you are ready to braise the cabbage, preheat oven to 325F (163C). Peel the onion, halve it, and slice very thinly. Peel and halve the apple, remove the core, and slice thinly. Set the baking dish or plat à sauter over medium low heat, add the bacon (or other) fat, and, when it is hot, stir in the apple and onion slices and sauté without browning for 3 to 5 minutes or until soft and translucent. Add the cabbage with its marinade, bring to a simmer, and cook, stirring occasionally, for 5 minutes. Put the lid on the baking dish and set it into the oven. Braise the cabbage, stirring a few times, until tender. This will take 1 to 1 1/2 hours. Adjust the seasoning if needed before serving.

This dish can be prepared well ahead of time and reheated. Save any leftovers to be enjoyed again—if anything, it is better the second time around.

Carottes Glacées
Sugar-glazed Carrots

Buy firm, unblemished carrots and have patience while waiting on the sugar and butter to glaze. The Vichy variation derives from the popularity of carrots in Vichy where they were consumed daily as part of the cure.

Yields 6 servings

2 1/4 to 2 1/2 pounds (1025 to 1125 g) carrots
1 tablespoon sugar
1 1/2 tablespoons (22 g) butter
1/4 teaspoon salt

Recommended equipment

A stiff bristle brush, swivel-bladed vegetable peeler, paring knife, 2-quart (2 L) saucepan, wooden spoon.

Scrub the carrots under cold running water, peel them, and cut into sticks about 1 to 1 1/4 inches (2 1/2 to 3 3/4 cm) long and 1/3 inch (5/6 cm) thick. Using the paring knife, round off the edges of each stick into an olive-like shape. (Save the trimmings for a soup or stock.)

Set the carrots into the saucepan and add enough water to barely cover them. Add the sugar, butter, and salt. Set the saucepan over medium high heat, bring to a boil, and adjust heat so that the carrots are cooking at a brisk simmer. Do not cover the saucepan. Cook the carrots until the liquid has been reduced to 4 to 5 tablespoons of syrupy liquid. Remove from heat until you are ready to serve them. To serve the carrots, reduce the liquid further over medium heat, stirring the carrots gently, until they are covered with a shiny glaze. You must watch the carrots every second at this point because unattended they will burn and be ruined. Serve them as soon as possible.

Variation

 ## Carottes Vichy
Carrots in the Style of Vichy

Slice the carrots less than 1/8 inch (1/3 cm) thick, put them into the saucepan, and add Vichy water (or other spring water) to a depth of 1/2 inch (1 1/4 cm) below the level of carrots. Add the seasonings as in the Carottes Glacées and cook according to the method in that recipe.

 ## Purée of Carrots

We receive more requests for this recipe than any other. You will know why when you prepare this purée.

Yields 4 to 6 servings

2 pounds (900 g) carrots
Salt
8 tablespoons (115 g) butter, softened at room temperature
1 1/2 tablespoons sugar

Recommended equipment

A stiff bristle brush; swivel-bladed vegetable peeler; paring knife; 1 1/2-quart (1 1/2 L) saucepan with lid; colander, blender or food mill with fine disc; wire whisk.

Scrub the carrots under cold running water, peel them, and cut each into thirds. Put them into the saucepan (they should fit snugly) and cover them with water to a depth of 1/2 inch (1 1/4 cm). Salt lightly. Set the saucepan over medium high heat, bring to a boil, and adjust heat so that the carrots simmer, partially covered, for 30 to 45 minutes or until they are tender. Do not overcook them. To test for doneness, push the point of a knife into the thickest part of a carrot; if it meets slight resistance, the carrots are done. Remove from heat, drain carrots into colander, and reserve 1/4 cup (60 ml) cooking liquid for the purée. Wash out the saucepan. Let the carrots cool and then purée them in the blender or food mill.

When you are ready to serve the carrots, set the clean saucepan over medium low heat, add the purée, butter, sugar, and a pinch of salt, and stir all together with the whisk while heating the purée. If the purée is too thick, add some of the reserved cooking liquid to thin it out. Adjust the seasoning if necessary and serve at once.

Variation: Add a pinch of ground ginger when heating the purée.

 ## Hearts of Celery Parmesan

If you are one of those for whom celery hearts have had absolutely no attraction, this preparation may change your mind.

Yields 6 servings

3 bunches celery
Salt
1/2 lemon
2 tablespoons flour
1/4 cup (60 ml) cold water
8 ounces (225 g) veal kidney fat (*see below*)

3 tablespoons grated Parmesan cheese
4 tablespoons (60 g) butter, at room temperature
Butter for the baking dish

Recommended equipment

A 4-quart (4 L) saucepan with lid, paring knife, swivel-bladed vegetable peeler, wire whisk, small bowl, box grater, baking dish large enough to hold celery in a single layer, colander.

Fill the saucepan with water, add about 1 tablespoon salt, and bring it to a boil, covered, over high heat. While the water is coming to a boil, remove the leaves and tough or wilted stalks from each bunch of celery. Trim the base and cut a 1/4-inch (2/3 cm) deep incision across it. Peel the tough strings away on the outside stalks of each bunch and trim the tops so that the bunches are 6 to 7 inches (15 to 17 1/2 cm) long. Wash each bunch thoroughly under cold running water, keeping the stalks attached at the base yet removing any dirt on the inside. Let the bunches drain and set aside.

When the water is boiling, add the lemon half. Blend the flour with the cold water in the small bowl, mixing with the whisk, until it is a loose paste. Whisk the mixture into the boiling water, remove saucepan from heat, and continue mixing with the whisk until the flour is absorbed. Return saucepan to heat, bring liquid back to a boil, add the celery all at once with the kidney fat, and return water to a boil as quickly as possible. Then adjust heat so that the celery cooks, uncovered, at a rapid simmer until just done. This will take 10 to 15 minutes. To test for doneness, remove a celery heart from the saucepan and insert the point of a knife into the thickest part. It should meet slight resistance. Do not overcook the celery so it is mushy. When the celery is done, remove saucepan from heat and let the celery cool to room temperature in the cooking liquid. When cool, remove celery, cut each in half, and let drain in the colander.

When ready to serve the celery, preheat oven to 325F (163C). Grate the Parmesan cheese and mix it thoroughly with the soft butter to make a paste. Butter the baking dish. Arrange the celery in the dish in a single layer and spread some of the cheese mixture over each half. Set the dish into the middle level of the oven and bake for 10 to 12 minutes or until golden brown. Serve while very hot.

Veal kidney fat can be gotten from a cooperative butcher. Otherwise, substitute 2 tablespoons butter, oil, or chopped suet. Do use some fat. It will prevent the delicate white celery pieces from coming into contact with the air while roiling around in the saucepan as they cook.

🐚 *Purée of Celery*

The celeriac contributes an assertive celery flavor to the purée. The variation is a colorful garnish for any roast.

Yields 4 to 6 servings

2 bunches celery
3 small celeriac
2 medium baking potatoes, total weight 10 to 12 ounces (285 to 340 g)
1/4 cup (60 ml) half-and-half
8 tablespoons (115 g) butter, softened at room temperature
A pinch of celery salt
Salt
Freshly ground white pepper

Recommended equipment

A swivel-bladed vegetable peeler; paring knife; 3-quart (3 L) saucepan with lid; colander, blender, or food mill with fine disc; small saucepan; 1 1/2-quart (1 1/2 L) saucepan; wire whisk.

Remove the outside stalks from the celery bunches, trim the bases, and lightly peel the tough strings away on the outside stalks of each bunch. Quarter each bunch and cut into 3-inch (7 1/2 cm) long pieces. Peel the celeriac and quarter them. Put all the celery and celeriac pieces into the larger saucepan, cover them with water, add about 1 teaspoon salt, and bring to a boil over high heat. Adjust heat so that the celery cooks at a lively simmer for 15 minutes.

While the celery simmers, peel and quarter the potatoes and add them when the celery has simmered for 15 minutes. Simmer the potatoes and celery together until both are tender (about 15 minutes), then drain them in the colander, reserving 1/4 cup (60 ml) cooking liquid for the purée. Let the celery and potatoes cool and then purée them in the blender or food mill.

When you are ready to serve, heat the half-and-half in the small saucepan until hot. Set the 1 1/2-quart saucepan over low heat, add the purée, butter, celery salt, salt, and pepper, and stir in the hot half-and-half while mixing with the whisk. If the purée is too thick, add some of the reserved cooking liquid bit by bit until the desired consistency is reached. If the purée is too thin, let it simmer gently. Adjust the seasoning if necessary and serve at once while very hot.

Variation: Choose as many ripe, firm, small tomatoes as you need for each serving, slice one-third of the tomato off at the top, scoop out the seeds and pulp very carefully with a teaspoon (keeping the tomato intact), fill the cavity with the celery purée, and arrange the tomatoes in a single layer in a buttered baking dish. Bake in the middle level of a 325F (163C) oven until the tomatoes are cooked but not mushy, about 10 minutes. Serve at once.

 ## Corn

 ## Homestead Corn Pudding

Served often at the Casino buffet, corn pudding is welcomed by young and old alike.

Yields 10 servings

3 1/2 cups (830 ml) milk
1 cup (235 ml) yellow cornmeal
3 tablespoons sugar
2/3 teaspoon salt
3 large eggs
1/4 teaspoon vanilla
1 teaspoon baking powder
1 8-ounce (225 g) can whole kernel corn, including liquid
4 tablespoons (60 g) butter, softened at room temperature

Recommended equipment

A 1 1/2-quart (1 1/2 L) saucepan, wire whisk, 1-quart bowl, baking dish 11 x 7 x 2 inches (27 1/2 x 17 1/2 x 5 cm).

Preheat oven to 300F (149C).

Heat the milk to the boiling point over medium high heat in the saucepan. Then, stirring constantly with the whisk, mix in the cornmeal, sugar, and salt, reduce heat so that mixture simmers, and cook, stirring, for 5 minutes. Remove from heat. Beat the eggs well in the mixing bowl and add them to the saucepan along with the vanilla, baking powder, corn (including its liquid), and 2 tablespoons butter. Mix thoroughly, pour into the baking dish, dot top with remaining butter, and set into the oven to bake for about 20 minutes or until the top is nicely browned. Serve at once while piping hot.

Polenta alla Milanese
Polenta in the Style of Milan

The Italians made their own version of Spoon Bread and Corn Pudding. Their translation of these American favorites is perfect when paired with Pollo alla Cacciatora, Tenderloin of Beef Café Martin, or Ossobuco alla Milanese.

Yields 4 to 6 servings

4 cups (950 ml) Chicken Bouillon *(see page 148)*
1 cup (235 ml) cornmeal
6 ounces (170 g) grated Parmesan cheese
6 tablespoons (90 g) butter
Salt
Freshly ground white pepper
A touch of Maggi

Recommended equipment

A 2-quart (2 L) saucepan, wire whisk, wooden spoon, box grater, 1-quart (1L) baking dish, spatula, small saucepan.

Set the saucepan over medium high heat, add the chicken bouillon, and bring to a boil. Add the cornmeal to the boiling liquid in a thin, steady stream, stirring constantly in one direction with the whisk. Continue stirring until the liquid returns to a simmer and begins to thicken with the cornmeal. Then adjust heat to low so that the polenta cooks very slowly until it is thick and pulls away from the sides of the saucepan as you stir. While the polenta is cooking, stir from time to time with the wooden spoon. After 20 to 30 minutes the polenta should be done, and you may either serve it right away or prepare it for baking. Meanwhile, using the finest side of the box grater, grate the Parmesan cheese and reserve.

To serve: Remove saucepan from heat and stir in the butter and grated Parmesan. Season the polenta to taste with salt, pepper, and a touch of Maggi. Serve while very hot.

To bake: Remove saucepan from heat and stir in one-half the butter and 2 ounces (60 g) grated Parmesan cheese (reserve the remaining butter and cheese). Season with salt, pepper, and a touch of Maggi. Butter the baking dish. Pour the polenta into the dish, smooth the top with a spatula, sprinkle the surface lightly with cold water, and set the dish aside where it can wait happily for a few hours.

When ready to bake the polenta, preheat oven to 325F (163C). Heat the reserved butter in the small saucepan until it has a nut-brown color, pour it over the polenta, sprinkle the top with the reserved grated Parmesan, and set the baking dish in the middle level of the oven. Bake until the polenta is well heated through and the top is golden brown (10 to 15 minutes). Serve at once.

Spoon Bread

Sometimes our guests request this for breakfast or lunch. Although not on our dinner menu, we do prepare it for theme affairs such as southern or country family dinners. Serve with any grilled meat.

Yields 4 servings

FOR THE SOUFFLÉ DISH
2 teaspoons butter
1 tablespoon cornmeal

FOR THE SPOON BREAD
1/2 cup (118 ml) cornmeal
1/2 teaspoon salt
2 teaspoons sugar
3/4 cup (180 ml) boiling water
1 tablespoon (15 g) butter
3/4 cup (180 ml) buttermilk
2 eggs
1 1/2 teaspoons baking soda

Recommended equipment

A 1-quart (1 L) glass or ceramic soufflé dish, mixing fork, 1-quart (1 L) bowl, small saucepan, wire whisk, 2-quart (2 L) bowl.

Preheat oven to 325F (163C).

Butter the soufflé dish, dust with cornmeal, and set aside. Using the mixing fork and the smaller bowl, combine the cornmeal, salt, and sugar. Bring the water to a boil and pour into the dry ingredients, mixing with the fork, and then stir in the butter until it has melted. Using the whisk, combine the buttermilk and eggs in the remaining bowl and stir them into the cornmeal. Mix in the baking soda, pour the batter into the prepared soufflé dish, and set it into the middle level of the oven to bake for 30 to 35 minutes. The spoon bread is done when the top is nicely browned and the center is still soft.

Variation: For a lighter result, separate the eggs, beat the whites until firm, and fold them into the batter after mixing the yolks and buttermilk with the cornmeal.

Gnocchi alla Romana
Gnocchi in the Style of Rome

Gnocchi can be made with chou paste, customary in Austro-Hungarian cooking; potatoes, a prevalent practice in Germany; or semolina porridge, indigenous to Rome. If you are unable to find bags of milled semolina, you can come close by using grits, and, if you are from the southern United States, you will realize that gnocchi are cheese grits in disguise. Derived from a recipe written by Apicius during the days of Imperial Rome, today you can enjoy your gnocchi made with grits in the Roman style but with a savory rather than sweet seasoning.

Yields 6 servings

4 cups (950 ml) water (or milk)
1 teaspoon salt
1 cup (235 ml) grits
Freshly ground white pepper
Freshly ground nutmeg
4 tablespoons (60 g) butter

FOR BAKING THE GNOCCHI
4 ounces (115 g) Parmesan cheese, grated
2 ounces (60 g) imported Swiss (Emmentaler) cheese, grated
1 tablespoon (15 g) butter
Butter for the baking dish

FOR SAUTÉING THE GNOCCHI
2 egg yolks
2 ounces (60 g) Parmesan cheese
2 ounces (60 g) imported Swiss (Emmentaler) cheese
Flour
2 eggs
1 tablespoon water
4 tablespoons Clarified Butter (see page 568)

Recommended equipment

A 2-quart (2 L) saucepan, wire whisk, wooden spoon, nutmeg grinder, box grater, baking dish, sheet pan, waxed paper, 2-inch (5 cm) biscuit cutter, small bowl, 12-inch (30 cm) sauté pan, baking sheet.

Put the water in the saucepan and bring it to a boil over high heat. When the water is boiling, add the salt and then pour in the grits in a continuous, steady stream, stirring constantly with the wire whisk. When all the grits have been added, reduce the heat to very low so that bubbles barely break the surface, and cook, stirring occasionally with the wooden spoon, for about 20 minutes or until the grits are thick and creamy. Remove from heat and season with pepper, nutmeg, and butter. At this point, you may either serve them with more butter (they are an excellent breakfast side dish) or follow one of the preparations below.

To bake gnocchi: Preheat oven to 325F (163C). Butter the baking dish. Grate the Parmesan and Emmentaler cheeses separately on the finest side of the box grater. Stir one-half of the Parmesan into the grits, mixing thoroughly, and reserve the rest of both cheeses. Pour the grits into the baking dish, smooth them out, dot the top with butter, and sprinkle on the reserved grated cheeses. Set the dish in the middle level of the oven to bake for 10 to 15 minutes or until the grits are very hot and nicely browned. Serve at once.

To sauté gnocchi: After the seasonings have been added, beat in the egg yolks. Grate the Parmesan and Emmentaler cheeses separately on the finest side of the box grater, reserve 1 tablespoon grated Parmesan, and mix the rest of the grated cheese into the grits. Lightly butter the sheet pan, pour the grits into it, and smooth them out to a depth of 1 inch (2 1/2 cm). Cover loosely with a sheet of waxed paper and set the pan into the refrigerator for at least one-half hour.

When the grits are chilled, remove them from the refrigerator, cut out round shapes with the biscuit cutter, and dust them lightly with flour. In a small bowl, mix the eggs with the water and stir in the reserved grated Parmesan. Set the sauté pan over medium heat, add the clarified butter, and, when it is hot, dip each floured round into the egg mixture and put them into the pan. Sauté until golden brown on each side. If you have to sauté them in batches, keep the first ones warm on a baking sheet in a 325F oven. Serve while still very hot.

Baked Eggplant Niçoise

A simple way to say "Provence" when you crave an earthy experience, and the perfect complement for Roast Leg of Lamb au Jus.

Yields 6 servings

3 medium eggplants
1/4 cup (60 ml) olive oil
2 1/2 to 3 cups (590 to 710 ml) Stewed Tomatoes *(see page 476)*
Salt
Freshly ground black pepper

Recommended equipment

A swivel-bladed vegetable peeler, small chef's knife, baking dish 11 x 7 x 2 inches (27 1/2 x 17 1/2 x 5 cm).

Preheat oven to 350F (177C).

Rinse the eggplants under cold running water, peel them, and cut into 1/2-inch (1 1/4 cm) cubes. Spread the cubes in the baking dish, drizzle with olive oil, and set the dish into the middle level of the oven to bake for 10 minutes. Remove the dish from the oven, lower heat to 325F (163C), and stir the stewed tomatoes into the eggplant. Season the vegetables lightly with salt and pepper, return the dish to the oven, and bake for 30 to 45 minutes. Serve immediately.

Variations: Stir in some sliced, pitted black olives when you add the tomatoes. Or, add a sliced red pepper, a pinch of thyme or oregano, and top with some grated Parmesan cheese before the final baking.

Belgian Endive

In the 1840s, the head gardener of the Brussels botanical garden discovered that by cutting off the natural foliage of chicory and forcing the roots in darkness he got a "new" plant that became known as Belgian endive. Today, a thriving family industry grows endive during the winter in beds warmed by pipes and darkened with tin roofs and straw mounds. Endive is also grown successfully in the United States so we can offer it almost year-round to our guests.

Buy only the freshest endive you can find—firm, white leaves tinged with pale yellow—and keep them cool and well-wrapped against the light, which will turn them green and bitter.

Yields 4 to 6 servings

12 Belgian endive
Salt
1/2 lemon
2 tablespoons flour
1/4 cup (60 ml) cold water

8 ounces (225 g) veal kidney fat *(see below)*
3 tablespoons grated Parmesan cheese
4 tablespoons (60 g) butter, softened at room temperature
Butter for the baking dish

Recommended equipment

A 4-quart (4 L) saucepan with lid, paring knife, wire whisk, small bowl, colander, box grater, baking dish large enough to hold endive in a single layer.

Fill the saucepan with water, add about 1 tablespoon salt, and bring to a boil, covered, over high heat.

While the water is coming to a boil, remove any wilted leaves from the endive and trim a slice from the root end. Rinse gently under cold running water, let drain, and set aside.

When the water is boiling, add the lemon half. Blend the flour with the cold water in the small bowl, mixing with the whisk, until it is a loose paste. Whisk the mixture into the boiling water, remove saucepan from heat, and continue mixing with the whisk until the flour is absorbed. Return saucepan to heat, bring water back to a boil, add the endive and the kidney fat, and return to the boil as quickly as possible. Then adjust heat so that the endive cooks, uncovered, at a rapid simmer until just done. Begin testing for doneness after 10 minutes by inserting the tip of a knife into the thickest part. The knife should meet slight resistance. When the endive is done, remove saucepan from heat and let the endive cool to room temperature in the cooking liquid. When cool, remove endive and let drain in the colander.

When ready to serve the endive, preheat the oven to 325F (163C). Grate the Parmesan cheese on the finest side of the box grater and mix it thoroughly with the soft butter to make a paste. Butter the baking dish. Arrange the endive in the dish in a single layer and spread some of the cheese mixture over each one. Set the dish into the middle level of the oven and bake for 10 to 12 minutes until golden brown. Serve immediately while very hot.

Veal kidney fat can be gotten from a cooperative butcher. Otherwise, substitute 2 tablespoons butter, oil, or chopped suet. Do use some fat. It will prevent the white endive from coming into contact with the air while roiling around in the saucepan as they cook.

Variation: Omit the Parmesan cheese and simply heat the endive with butter.

Hearts of Fennel Parmesan

The anise flavor may be enhanced by adding a few drops of Pernod to the baking dish or an accompanying sauce. Fennel always brings good comments from our guests.

Yields 6 servings

3 medium fennel
Salt
1/2 lemon
2 tablespoons flour
1/4 cup (60 ml) cold water
8 ounces (225 g) veal kidney fat (see below)
3 tablespoons grated Parmesan cheese
4 tablespoons (60 g) butter, softened at room temperature
Butter for the baking dish

Recommended equipment

A 4-quart (4 L) saucepan with lid, paring knife, swivel-bladed vegetable peeler, wire whisk, small bowl, colander, box grater, baking dish large enough to hold fennel in a single layer.

Fill the saucepan with water, add about 1 tablespoon salt, and bring to a boil, covered, over high heat.

While the water is coming to a boil, trim the fennel leaves to within 1 inch (2 1/2 cm) of the knob. (Save the lacy leaves for another use, such as seasoning a soup or sauce, or decorating a serving platter.) Trim a slice from the root end and cut a 1/4-inch (2/3 cm) deep incision across it. If the fennel bulbs are large, remove the outermost branches on each side. With the vegetable peeler, lightly trim the stringy outside of the bulbs, wash them well, let drain, and set aside.

When the water is boiling, add the lemon half. Blend the flour with the cold water in the small bowl, mixing with the whisk, until it is a loose paste. Whisk the mixture into the boiling water, remove saucepan from heat, and continue mixing with the whisk until the flour is absorbed. Return saucepan to heat, bring water back to a boil, add the fennel bulbs and the kidney fat, and return to the boil as quickly as possible. Then adjust heat so that the fennel cooks, uncovered, at a rapid simmer until just done. Begin testing for doneness after 15 minutes by inserting the tip of a knife into the thickest part. The knife should meet slight resistance. Do not overcook the fennel. When done, remove saucepan from heat and let fennel cool to room temperature in the cooking liquid. When cool, remove the fennel (reserve 2 tablespoons liquid for the next step) and let drain in the colander.

When ready to serve the fennel, preheat oven to 325F (163C). Grate the Parmesan cheese on the finest side of the box grater and mix it thoroughly with the soft butter to make a paste. Butter the baking dish. Slice the fennel bulbs in half (or quarter them if they are large) and arrange them cut side up in the baking dish in a single layer. Drizzle the reserved cooking liquid over them and spread some of the cheese mixture over each one. Set the dish into the middle level of the oven and bake for 10 to 12 minutes until golden brown. Serve at once while very hot.

Veal kidney fat can be gotten from a cooperative butcher. Otherwise, substitute 2 tablespoons butter, oil, or chopped suet. Do use some fat. It will prevent the fennel bulbs from coming into contact with the air while roiling around in the saucepan as they cook.

Variation: Omit the Parmesan and add 1/2 cup (118 ml) Demi-glace Brun I *(see page 75)* and 1/4 cup (60 ml) Madeira to the baking dish before putting it in the oven. Or, rather than baking, dust the cooked fennel lightly with flour and sauté in Clarified Butter *(see page 568)* over medium high heat until golden brown. Remove fennel from pan, wipe out sauté pan, add 2 tablespoons butter, and sauté until the butter is nut brown in color. Pour the Beurre Noisette over the fennel and serve at once.

Gratin of Leeks

Leeks are more popular now that people are becoming familiar with them. An excellent vegetable, they are a lively addition to any soup.

Yields 6 servings

6 to 8 large leeks
Salt
1 1/2 cups (355 ml) Sauce Mornay *(see page 67)*
3 tablespoons grated Parmesan cheese
Butter for the baking dish

Recommended equipment

A 4-quart (4 L) saucepan with lid, paring knife, white kitchen string, long-handled fork, slotted spoon, colander, baking dish large enough to hold leeks in a single layer, box grater.

Fill the saucepan with water, add 2 teaspoons salt, and bring to a boil, covered, over high heat.

While the water is coming to a boil, work with one leek at a time and trim off the bushy roots, remove any wilted or tough leaves, and trim the green tops so each leek is 6 to 7 inches (15 to 17 1/2 cm) long. Halve each leek lengthwise, beginning 2 inches (5 cm) from the root end and cutting toward the top. Wash each leek thoroughly under cold running water, separating the leaves as much as possible to get rid of all sand and dirt. When rinsed, put three to four leeks together in a bundle and tie each one in two places with kitchen string.

When the water is boiling, add the leeks and boil for 12 to 18 minutes or until the leeks are just tender. Test for doneness by inserting the tip of a knife into the thickest white part of a leek. There should be some resistance. When done, remove the bundles with the help of the fork and slotted spoon to a basin or bowl full of cold water to cool. After a few minutes, remove the leeks to the colander to drain. Remove the strings.

While the leeks are cooking and cooling, prepare the sauce Mornay and reserve. Or, if you have time, prepare the sauce after the leeks have finished cooking and replace one-half of the milk called for with leek cooking liquid.

When you are ready to serve the leeks, preheat oven to 375F (190C). Butter the baking dish. If the leeks are large, finish slicing them in half and, if they are small, leave them as is. Fold them in half end-to-end by placing the dull side of a knife across the leek at the center, and, with the help of a spatula, fold it over (this will make them easier to serve). Grate the Parmesan cheese. Arrange the leeks in a single layer in the baking dish, pour on the sauce Mornay, sprinkle with the Parmesan, and set the leeks into the middle level of the oven to bake for 6 to 8 minutes or until golden brown. Serve immediately.

Navets Glacés
Sugar-glazed White Turnips

Having prepared this once, you will do it again—soon. These turnips stand alone very well or you can combine them with String Beans and Carottes Glacées à la bouquetière in an elegant presentation for the most formal menu.

Yields 4 to 6 servings

2 pounds (900 g) small white turnips
Salt
3 tablespoons (45 g) butter
2 tablespoons sugar

Recommended equipment

A swivel-bladed vegetable peeler, paring knife, 3-quart (3 L) saucepan with lid, large fine-mesh sieve, 12-inch (30 cm) sauté pan, wooden spoon.

Rinse the turnips under cold running water, peel and halve them, and cut each half (depending upon size) into three or four pieces. Put the turnips into the saucepan, cover with water to a depth of 2 inches (5 cm), add about 1 teaspoon salt, cover the saucepan, and set it over high heat. Bring the water to a boil, uncover the pan, and adjust heat so that the turnips simmer until slightly underdone (5 to 7 minutes). Test for doneness by inserting the tip of a knife into a turnip piece. The knife should meet some resistance. When the turnips are ready, drain them into the sieve and set aside until you want to finish the dish.

When you are ready to serve the turnips, set the sauté pan over medium high heat, add butter and sugar, bring them to a simmer and cook, stirring with the wooden spoon, for 1 minute. Add the turnips to the pan, season lightly with salt, reduce heat to medium, and sauté, stirring gently, until

the turnips are glacéed (covered with a light-brown glaze). This should take 4 to 5 minutes. Serve at once.

🌿 Snow Peas

These edible pod peas must be only half-cooked before reheating, so watch them very carefully lest you violate their appearance and flavor.

Yields 6 to 8 servings

2 pounds (900 g) snow peas
Salt
2 tablespoons (30 g) butter
Freshly ground white pepper

Recommended equipment

A 5-quart (5 L) saucepan with lid, colander, 12-inch (30 cm) sauté pan, wooden spatula.

Fill the saucepan with water, add about 1 tablespoon salt, and bring it to a boil, covered, over high heat.

While the water is coming to a boil, snap the blossom end off of each pea pod and pull off any "string" if it is mature enough to have one. Put the peas in the colander, wash well under running cold water, and set aside to drain.

When the water is boiling, add the peas all at once and return the water to a boil as quickly as possible. Then adjust heat so that the peas cook, uncovered, at a rapid simmer until tender but crisp. This will take 1 to 2 minutes depending upon the size of the pods and their age. Watch the peas very carefully and test a pod after 1 minute—fish it out of the pot, cool briefly under cold water, and bite into it. When done, remove saucepan from heat, put it under running cold water to stop the cooking process and refresh the peas. Remove the peas when they are cold and drain them in the colander.

When ready to serve the peas, set the sauté pan over medium low heat, add the butter, and, when it is melted, add the pepper, stir in the peas, and sauté them until they are hot (3 to 4 minutes). Serve at once, lest the peas turn gray and soft while waiting in the pan.

Creamed Spinach

The perfect companion for any fish, shellfish, poultry, game, beef, lamb, pork, or veal. Prepare the variation for a well-remembered treat.

Yields 6 servings

1 1/2 pounds (675 g) fresh spinach
Salt
1 cup (235 ml) milk
1 teaspoon butter
1 1/2 teaspoons flour
2 tablespoons (30 g) butter
Freshly ground white pepper
Freshly ground nutmeg
A pinch of Maggi
1/3 cup (80 ml) half-and-half

Recommended equipment

A 5-quart (5 L) saucepan with lid, colander, large chef's knife, blender or food processor, small saucepan for warming milk, 1 1/2-quart (1 1/2 L) saucepan, wire whisk, 2-quart (2 L) saucepan, wooden spatula, nutmeg grinder.

Fill the large saucepan with water, add about 1 tablespoon salt, and bring it to a boil, covered, over high heat.

While the water is coming to a boil, wash the spinach gently yet thoroughly in several changes of cold water. The easiest way to do this is to fill your sink with water, dump in the spinach, pump it up and down in the water, lift it out into the colander (leaving the sand and grit in the sink bottom), and then repeat the process twice. The last time you lift the spinach out of the water, pick it over and discard any damaged or withered leaves and remove any large stems. Set the spinach aside to drain in the colander.

When the water is boiling, add the spinach all at once, pushing it down under the water, and return the water to a boil as quickly as possible. Then adjust heat so that the spinach cooks, uncovered, at a rapid simmer for 2 minutes (1 minute will be enough for very young spinach). Remove saucepan from heat, put it under running cold water, and refresh the spinach until it is cold. Then lift spinach into the colander to drain. Rid the spinach of excess water by squeezing it in small handfuls. Put the squeezed spinach on your chopping surface and roughly chop the spinach. Purée the spinach in small batches in the blender or food processor until smooth. Reserve the purée while you start the cream sauce.

Put the milk in the small saucepan to warm over low heat. Set the 1 1/2-quart saucepan over low heat, add the teaspoon of butter and the flour, stirring together for 1 minute before whisking in the warm milk. Raise heat to medium and stir continuously with the whisk until the sauce is smooth, then adjust heat so that the sauce simmers gently for 5 minutes.

When the sauce is ready, set the 2-quart saucepan over medium heat, add the 2 tablespoons butter, and stir with the wooden spatula until the butter has melted and turned light brown. Then stir in the reserved spinach purée and the cream sauce, season to taste with salt, pepper, nutmeg, and Maggi, and bring to a simmer. Stir in enough half-and-half for a creamy consistency, adjust seasoning if needed, and serve the spinach very hot.

The spinach may wait for a short while, dotted with bits of butter and drops of cream, in the top of a double boiler.

Variation

Epinards Etouffés
Spinach à l'étuvée

Etouffée (from étouffer, to smother) refers to cooking something tightly sealed, with little moisture. This method, excellent for other tender greens such as young Swiss chard, kale, mustard, beet, or turnip, results in a garden-fresh color and a taste that is a little less rich and more immediate than the suave purée.

Follow the instructions for washing and cleaning the spinach, then place it in a saucepan or sauté pan just large enough to hold it, and cook it, tightly covered, over medium high heat for 2 or 3 minutes. Lift the cover just enough to peek and see whether the spinach has wilted. If it has, remove the cover and rapidly work in about 4 tablespoons (60 g) of softened butter, stirring continuously. When the liquid is completely absorbed, remove the pan from the heat, season with salt, freshly ground white pepper, and a grind of nutmeg (or the tiniest bit of finely minced garlic for the stronger greens) and serve immediately.

Squash

Acorn Squash Baked with Honey

A simple and very tasty fall and winter vegetable to be enjoyed with any grilled meat or fowl.

Yields 4 servings

2 medium acorn squash

FOR EACH SQUASH HALF
1 teaspoon butter
1 teaspoon honey
A pinch of ground ginger
A pinch of ground cinnamon
A dash of salt

Recommended equipment

A slicing knife, a teaspoon, baking pan.

Preheat oven to 325F (163C).

Rinse the squash under cold running water, pat dry, and set on your work surface. Remove a 1/4-inch (2/3 cm) thick slice from the blossom end of each squash to facilitate slicing them in half. Stand the squash on this level base and slice it evenly in half from the stem to the blossom end. Then cut a 1/8-inch (1/3 cm) thick slice from the bottom of each half so the squash will sit evenly in the baking pan (and on your plate). Scoop out the seeds and stringy insides with the teaspoon, set the squash halves into the baking pan, and put the butter, honey, ginger, cinnamon, and salt into each cavity.

Put the baking pan into the middle level of the oven and bake for 40 to 50 minutes or until the squash halves are soft and mushy and a knife point meets no resistance when thrust into the thickest part of the squash. Serve while very hot.

Ratatouille of Zucchini

Ratatouille, a Provençal word, means a stew of vegetables—this "stew" goes nicely with Rognonnade de Veau and Pollo alla Cacciatora. Prepare the variation with eggplant and black olives for a taste of Provence on your plate.

Yields 4 to 6 servings

1 1/2 pounds (675 g) zucchini
1/2 medium green bell pepper
1/2 medium onion
1 recipe Stewed Tomatoes *(see page 476)*
1/3 cup (80 ml) olive oil
A pinch of chopped fresh thyme
1/3 medium bay leaf
1 small garlic clove
Salt
Freshly ground black pepper
1/2 cup (118 ml) grated Parmesan cheese

Recommended equipment

A paring knife, slicing knife, medium mixing bowl, garlic press, box grater, baking dish 11 x 7 x 2 inches (27 1/2 x 17 1/2 x 5 cm), aluminum foil.

Preheat oven to 350F (177C).

Rinse the zucchini under running cold water, trim off the ends, and, with the slicing knife, cut the squash crosswise into 1/8-inch (1/3 cm) thick slices, and reserve. Rinse the bell pepper half, remove the seeds and pithy white, slice into 1/8-inch thick slices, and reserve. Peel the onion half and slice it very thinly. In the mixing bowl, combine the stewed tomatoes, zucchini, green pepper, and onion, and mix together with the olive oil, thyme, and bay leaf. Peel the garlic clove and press it into the mixture. Season lightly with salt and pepper to taste, blend thoroughly, and pour the mixture into the baking dish.

Grate the Parmesan cheese on the finest side of the box grater and sprinkle the cheese over the zucchini mixture. Cover the baking dish loosely with aluminum foil and set it into the middle level of the oven to bake for 45 minutes. Then remove the foil, bake 15 minutes, remove dish from oven, and dip out any excess oil before serving.

Variation: Use only 12 ounces (340 g) zucchini and add a medium eggplant. Prepare the eggplant by rinsing, peeling, and slicing it into 1/2-inch (1 1/4 cm) thick round slices. Quarter each slice and set the wedges on a lightly oiled baking sheet (use olive oil). Season the eggplant lightly with salt and freshly ground black pepper and sprinkle with olive oil. Cover the eggplant loosely with foil and set it into the middle of a preheated 350F oven to bake for 10 minutes. Remove from oven and mix the eggplant with the zucchini and tomatoes in the bowl before pouring them into the baking dish. If you wish, add some sliced pitted black or oil-cured olives to the dish before baking.

Sautéed Zucchini Oregano

The oregano draws out the zucchini flavor in this quick and simple preparation. Cook this at the last minute when everything else is ready to be served.

Yields 4 to 6 servings

1 1/2 pounds (675 g) zucchini
3 tablespoons olive oil
Salt
Freshly ground white pepper
1 small garlic clove
A pinch of oregano
1 tablespoon (15 g) butter
2 tablespoons water

Recommended equipment

A paring knife, swivel-bladed vegetable peeler, 12-inch (30 cm) sauté pan, wooden spatula, garlic press.

Rinse the zucchini under running cold water. Trim off the ends. Using the vegetable peeler, peel off two strips of skin lengthwise on opposite sides of each zucchini and discard the strips. Cut each squash lengthwise into pencil-width pieces and reserve.

Set the sauté pan over medium high heat, add the olive oil, and, when it is hot, stir in the zucchini. Season lightly with salt and pepper, mix thoroughly, and when the zucchini is sizzling, adjust the heat so that the squash sautés gently. Peel the garlic clove, press it into the sauté pan, and stir it into the squash. Add the oregano and sauté the zucchini, stirring, for 30 seconds. Add the butter and water and sauté for 5 minutes, stirring occasionally. The zucchini should not be mushy—young, tender squash will take less time to cook, so watch it carefully. Serve at once when done.

The addition of water (which evaporates) prevents browning.

Zucchini alla Genovese

Barely 125 kilometers from the French border, Genoa makes a "stew" of vegetables (not unlike a ratatouille) using oregano rather than thyme and garlic (the French favorites).

Yields 4 to 6 servings

1 1/2 pounds (675 g) small to medium zucchini
1/2 medium green bell pepper
1 medium red bell pepper
1/3 cup (80 ml) olive oil
1 recipe Stewed Tomatoes (see page 476)
A pinch of chopped fresh oregano
Salt
Freshly ground white pepper
Olive oil for the baking dish

Recommended equipment

A paring knife, 2-quart (2 L) bowl, wooden spoon, baking dish 11 x 7 x 2 inches (27 1/2 x 17 1/2 x 5 cm), aluminum foil.

Preheat oven to 350F (177C).

Rinse the zucchini under running cold water, trim off the ends with the paring knife, halve the squash, cut into matchstick-size strips, and put them into the bowl. Rinse the bell peppers, halve and seed them, remove the white pith, cut into slices 1/8 inch (1/3 cm) thick, and add them to the bowl. Stir in the olive oil and stewed tomatoes, mixing thoroughly, and then season with oregano, salt, and pepper to taste. Spread the mixture in the lightly oiled baking dish, cover with foil, and set into the oven to bake for 1 hour.

Before serving, dip out any excess oil.

Tomatoes

Fassifern Tomatoes

In the early 1900s, guests of the Homestead would travel on horseback or in buggies to the Fassifern Tavern in Warm Springs to enjoy a luncheon menu that included southern fried chicken, corn pudding or spoon bread, and this tomato dish.

Yields 10 servings

1 28-ounce (790 g) can whole tomatoes
1/2 cup (100 g) sugar
Salt
Freshly ground black pepper
1 tablespoon cornstarch
1/4 cup (60 ml) cold water
2 cups (475 ml) toasted bread cubes
1/3 cup (80 ml) melted butter

Recommended equipment

A 3-quart (3 L) saucepan, wooden spoon, small bowl, baking dish 8 x 8 x 2 inches (20 x 20 x 5 cm), baking sheet, small saucepan for melting butter.

Put the tomatoes with their juice into the saucepan, add the sugar, salt, and pepper, and bring to a boil over medium high heat. While the tomatoes are coming to a boil, mix the cornstarch with the cold water in the small bowl and set aside. When the tomatoes are boiling, remove the saucepan from heat and slowly pour the cornstarch mixture into the tomatoes, stirring constantly with the wooden spoon. When well blended, set the saucepan back over medium heat and bring the tomatoes to a simmer. Adjust heat so that the tomatoes will cook gently for 10 minutes. Stir them occasionally.

Preheat oven to 300F (149C).

While the tomatoes are simmering, cut the bread into 1/2-inch (1 1/4 cm) cubes, set them on the baking sheet, and put them into the oven for 5 to 10 minutes or until lightly browned. When done, remove from oven and reserve.

Put the butter in the small saucepan and set it over low heat.

When the tomatoes have finished simmering, pour them into the baking dish, arrange the toasted bread cubes over the top, drizzle on the melted butter, and put the baking dish into the middle level of the oven to bake for 20 minutes.

The tomatoes can be simmered several hours ahead of time and wait in the baking dish for their final cooking. Top with bread cubes and butter just before baking.

Stewed Tomatoes

Whenever vine-ripened tomatoes are available, prepare the recipe using fresh tomatoes and enjoy it in Zucchini alla Genovese, Ratatouille of Zucchini, or Baked Eggplant Niçoise. Off season, prepare the variation using canned tomatoes of good quality (such as Hunts Natural Whole Tomatoes) and you won't be disappointed.

Yields about 3 cups

6 medium, ripe tomatoes (blanched, peeled, and seeded; see page 568)
2 tablespoons chopped fresh shallots
1 small garlic clove
1 tablespoon (15 g) butter
1 tablespoon olive oil
1/4 teaspoon sugar
Salt
Freshly ground white pepper

Recommended equipment

A large chef's knife, paring knife, 12-inch (30 cm) sauté pan, garlic press, wooden spatula.

Prepare the tomatoes and chop into pieces about 3/4 to 1 inch (2 to 2 1/2 cm) square. Chop the shallots and peel the garlic clove. Set the sauté pan over low heat, add butter and olive oil, and, when warm, add the shallots and press in the garlic. Sauté for 30 seconds, stirring with the spatula, without browning and then add the tomatoes. Season with sugar and salt and pepper to taste. Raise heat to medium high and sauté the tomatoes briskly until most of the liquid has evaporated and the tomatoes are bound together by a smooth sauce. This should take 10 to 12 minutes but may take several minutes longer if there is a lot of juice.

When done, remove the tomatoes from heat and either serve them at once or use them in one of the suggested recipes.

Variation

Winter Stewed Tomatoes

Before dismissing the thought of canned tomatoes, you should know that Escoffier developed the preservation technique in 1895, when he was the chef at the London Savoy. Tomato purée had been readily available but only could be used for sauces. He wanted crushed (or chopped) tomatoes to use during the winter months and worked with manufacturers in the Rhône Valley and département of the Vaucluse to provide him with a reliable source. An immediate success, the product caught on first in Italy and then in the United States.

1 28-ounce (800 g) can whole tomatoes
2 teaspoons cornstarch
1 1/2 tablespoons water

Drain the canned tomatoes in a colander and catch the juice in a bowl. Squeeze the tomatoes gently with your hands to extract the juice and reserve it. Put the tomatoes on your work surface, cut into pieces 1/2 to 3/4 inch (1 1/4 to 2 cm) square, and then return them to the juice in the bowl.

Follow the instructions for fresh stewed tomatoes, adding the canned tomatoes with their juice to the sauté pan and seasoning carefully. (Some canned tomatoes already have salt.) When you raise the heat, bring the tomatoes to a boil and then adjust heat so that the tomatoes simmer steadily for

❧ Tomatoes

❧ Fassifern Tomatoes

In the early 1900s, guests of the Homestead would travel on horseback or in buggies to the Fassifern Tavern in Warm Springs

to enjoy a luncheon menu that included southern fried chicken, corn pudding or spoon bread, and this tomato dish.

Yields 10 servings

1 28-ounce (790 g) can whole tomatoes
1/2 cup (100 g) sugar
Salt
Freshly ground black pepper
1 tablespoon cornstarch
1/4 cup (60 ml) cold water
2 cups (475 ml) toasted bread cubes
1/3 cup (80 ml) melted butter

Recommended equipment

A 3-quart (3 L) saucepan, wooden spoon, small bowl, baking dish 8 x 8 x 2 inches (20 x 20 x 5 cm), baking sheet, small saucepan for melting butter.

Put the tomatoes with their juice into the saucepan, add the sugar, salt, and pepper, and bring to a boil over medium high heat. While the tomatoes are coming to a boil, mix the cornstarch with the cold water in the small bowl and set aside. When the tomatoes are boiling, remove the saucepan from heat and slowly pour the cornstarch mixture into the tomatoes, stirring constantly with the wooden spoon. When well blended, set the saucepan back over medium heat and bring the tomatoes to a simmer. Adjust heat so that the tomatoes will cook gently for 10 minutes. Stir them occasionally.

Preheat oven to 300F (149C).

While the tomatoes are simmering, cut the bread into 1/2-inch (1 1/4 cm) cubes, set them on the baking sheet, and put them into the oven for 5 to 10 minutes or until lightly browned. When done, remove from oven and reserve.

Put the butter in the small saucepan and set it over low heat.

When the tomatoes have finished simmering, pour them into the baking dish, arrange the toasted bread cubes over the top, drizzle on the melted butter, and put the baking dish into the middle level of the oven to bake for 20 minutes.

❧

The tomatoes can be simmered several hours ahead of time and wait in the baking dish for their final cooking. Top with bread cubes and butter just before baking.

Stewed Tomatoes

Whenever vine-ripened tomatoes are available, prepare the recipe using fresh tomatoes and enjoy it in Zucchini alla Genovese, Ratatouille of Zucchini, or Baked Eggplant Niçoise. Off season, prepare the variation using canned tomatoes of good quality (such as Hunts Natural Whole Tomatoes) and you won't be disappointed.

Yields about 3 cups

6 medium, ripe tomatoes (blanched, peeled, and seeded; see page 568)
2 tablespoons chopped fresh shallots
1 small garlic clove
1 tablespoon (15 g) butter
1 tablespoon olive oil
1/4 teaspoon sugar
Salt
Freshly ground white pepper

Recommended equipment

A large chef's knife, paring knife, 12-inch (30 cm) sauté pan, garlic press, wooden spatula.

Prepare the tomatoes and chop into pieces about 3/4 to 1 inch (2 to 2 1/2 cm) square. Chop the shallots and peel the garlic clove. Set the sauté pan over low heat, add butter and olive oil, and, when warm, add the shallots and press in the garlic. Sauté for 30 seconds, stirring with the spatula, without browning and then add the tomatoes. Season with sugar and salt and pepper to taste. Raise heat to medium high and sauté the tomatoes briskly until most of the liquid has evaporated and the tomatoes are bound together by a smooth sauce. This should take 10 to 12 minutes but may take several minutes longer if there is a lot of juice.

When done, remove the tomatoes from heat and either serve them at once or use them in one of the suggested recipes.

Variation

Winter Stewed Tomatoes

Before dismissing the thought of canned tomatoes, you should know that Escoffier developed the preservation technique in 1895, when he was the chef at the London Savoy. Tomato purée had been readily available but only could be used for sauces. He wanted crushed (or chopped) tomatoes to use during the winter months and worked with manufacturers in the Rhône Valley and département of the Vaucluse to provide him with a reliable source. An immediate success, the product caught on first in Italy and then in the United States.

1 28-ounce (800 g) can whole tomatoes
2 teaspoons cornstarch
1 1/2 tablespoons water

Drain the canned tomatoes in a colander and catch the juice in a bowl. Squeeze the tomatoes gently with your hands to extract the juice and reserve it. Put the tomatoes on your work surface, cut into pieces 1/2 to 3/4 inch (1 1/4 to 2 cm) square, and then return them to the juice in the bowl.

Follow the instructions for fresh stewed tomatoes, adding the canned tomatoes with their juice to the sauté pan and seasoning carefully. (Some canned tomatoes already have salt.) When you raise the heat, bring the tomatoes to a boil and then adjust heat so that the tomatoes simmer steadily for

Tomatoes Provençale

This classic presentation of garden-ripe tomatoes is the perfect accompaniment for so many entrées that it is difficult to choose among them. For starters, try the tomatoes with Roast Saddle of Lamb with Green Peppercorns and Rosemary, Escalopes de Veau Cordon Bleu, Côtes de Veau Pojarski, or Sweetbreads Sautéed Souvaroff. Our tour of the Main Kitchen ends here, right where it began so many pages ago with Henri Le Huédé standing by the tomates farcies in his salamanders on the France. See you in the Bake Shop.

Yields 6 servings

3 medium, ripe tomatoes
Salt
Freshly ground white pepper
1/2 cup (118 ml) fine white bread crumbs
4 sprigs parsley
1 medium garlic clove
6 tablespoons olive oil

Recommended equipment

A paring knife, small chef's knife, small bowl, broiler pan large enough to hold tomatoes in a single layer.

Rinse the tomatoes under running cold water, cut out the stem ends and cores with the paring knife, and halve each tomato. Gently squeeze out the seeds and excess juice, season each tomato half lightly with salt and pepper, and set them aside while you prepare the stuffing.

Measure the bread crumbs and put them in the small bowl. Rinse the parsley, spin or pat dry, mince with the chef's knife, and add to the bread crumbs. Peel the garlic clove, mince, and combine with the bread crumbs and parsley. Stir well to mix. Stuff each tomato half and thoroughly moisten the top with about a tablespoon of olive oil for each half. Lightly oil the broiler pan and set the tomato halves into it in a single layer. (They can sit comfortably for an hour at room temperature.)

Preheat oven to 350F (177C).

To finish the tomatoes, set them into the middle level of the oven for 4 to 5 minutes or until soft. Remove the tomatoes and set the broiler on high heat, moving the rack so the tomato tops will be about 5 inches (12 1/2 cm) from the heat. To brown the stuffing, grill the tomatoes until lightly brown. Serve them at once while hot. If they sit they will become soggy and unappealing.

---

8 minutes. Mix the cornstarch with the water in a small bowl until it has formed a smooth, loose paste. Remove sauté pan from heat, stir the cornstarch vigorously into the tomatoes until thoroughly blended, return pan to heat, and stir continuously until the mixture simmers. Simmer for 1 minute. Then reduce heat to low, simmer 3 more minutes, stirring occasionally, and then either serve at once or use in one of the suggested recipes.

Breads from the Bake Shop

Breads

Aboard the S.S. *France* at 3:30 o'clock in the morning, there were men at work only on the bridge, in the engine room and in the *pâtisserie*. Outside, in the cool September air, the ocean was calm but black under a moonless sky. In the pastry shop, however, the lights were bright as M. Marcel Gousse and his helpers placed dozens of trays of fresh-cut croissants on every conceivable resting place in the room.

Finally, when the filled trays began to nudge even into the small work space kept open for M. Gousse, the morning's quota was pronounced filled. Two apprentices, meanwhile, were moving past the uncovered trays to brush each croissant with the first of the two egg-and-milk coatings they would get during the hour's rising time.

Four hours later, when M. Gousse and his men at last were in their bunks, the first of 2,000 warm, tender and flaky croissants were carried to the first arrivals in the dining rooms.

—Bernard Clayton, Jr.

The analogy of an ocean liner for this hotel once again is apt. Like a captain on a ship, the executive chef at a resort such as the Homestead should be familiar with every aspect of the operation. Having been here since 1962, I believed that I knew pretty well how things worked. Well, in the course of preparing this cookbook we discovered how the Bake Shop really works. Let us lead you on a nighttime tour which begins long after retiring guests have left completed breakfast orders hanging on their doorknobs, and you will see what you can learn only if you decide to stay awake all night.

At 3:00 A.M., the night staff has been in charge at the reception desk in the Great Hall for several hours. Beyond the glow of the wide verandah and the porte cochère, the velvet depth of a mountain night is limned by starlight. The cool silence outdoors is undisturbed. Down in the village, Sam Snead's Tavern has closed for the evening, leaving only the glimmer of light in the Power House windows to signal that the night watch is tending the boilers which generate steam for the Kitchen.

In the hotel, two floors below the Main Kitchen level, the lights are burning brightly in the Bake Shop. Having arrived at

2:00 A.M., Thomas Woodzell, head baker since 1977 (and with the Homestead since 1960), began mixing dough for sourdough rye, whole wheat, pumpernickel, and French bread, and now is mixing dough for his croissants. At 11:00 P.M. the night bakers and their helpers had arrived and had begun their evening ritual. First, they fired the two main ovens to prepare them for the baking ahead. Then they began to mix, scale, and pan seven gallons of Pullman dough; mix and scale English muffin dough and form the muffins; and mix, scale, and form enough sweet dough for about 450 pieces of sweet rolls, cinnamon and pecan buns, and snowflake rolls. These are the routine items for the early morning hours.

Meanwhile, forced-air gas torch blowers have ever so gradually brought the ovens to their required 475°F temperature. In continuous service since the nineteenth century, these firebrick-lined ovens have a brick hearth and a low rise domed interior which provides ample air circulation space around the risen bread. In addition to possessing the ideal ceramic interior so much prized by bakers, they are also spacious, measuring approximately twelve by thirteen feet each, for a baking surface equal to more than one hundred fifty large home ovens. But, as you will see, every bit of it is needed.

Because the ovens are fired only once a day, the baking schedule is arranged according to heat and steam requirements for the various doughs. Cinnamon and pecan rolls lead off, followed by Pullman, sourdough rye, whole wheat, and pumpernickel loaves, and the remaining sweet rolls. In the meantime, corn bread and biscuits are mixed and readied for the oven along with the croissants and Danish pastries. By this time the oven temperatures have lowered sufficiently to bake French bread and as many as three batches of dinner rolls (approximately fifteen hundred), both of which require steam injection into the ovens at thirty pounds of pressure to ensure a crackly brown crust.

A complicated baking schedule is unavoidable in providing our guests with a wide variety of fresh baked goods for every meal. At breakfast there is a choice among croissants (or brioches on alternate days), English muffins, Danish pastry, sweet rolls and buns, toasted slices of Pullman loaf, *and* freshly made doughnuts. By lunchtime, depending upon where you choose to eat, you will encounter baking powder or buttermilk biscuits, petits pains, hamburger buns (baked for Sam Snead's Tavern), and French, rye, or pumpernickel bread. At 4:00 P.M. there is no hope for it but to succumb to temptation, as tea service begins in the Great Hall, featuring such special items as banana nut bread or sour cream raisin tea loaf. And the dinner hour is approaching with its choice among plain, poppy seed, or sesame seed rolls. All of these items are prepared on a daily basis, and Thomas Woodzell derives the quantities from the handwritten yellow sheets I post outside my office. But then there are the special requests which I send down almost daily—a luncheon here, a private function there—that may require several hundred more rolls or many dozens of extra loaves of bread. It is all in a day's work for the bakers, but before the "day" is over and the long-handled wooden peels are set to rest in their ceiling racks, this group will have produced more individual items than any other kitchen department.

By now, you have read our preachments elsewhere about freshly prepared foods. Nowhere is this more true than for baking. Unless you have a good *boulangerie* in your town, you are left with "store-bought" bread, and, these days, that is increasingly a mysterious chemical compound and less and less a product of the tradition we observe every day at the Homestead. Here, each bakery item is made from fresh ingredients. Most of the twenty-four hundred pounds of all-purpose flour and the forty-eight pounds of yeast on B. G. McElwee's Shopping List is used in the Bake Shop, not to mention vast quantities of butter, eggs, and milk. In addition, skill, experience, and teamwork are obligatory in order for bakers to bake such prodigious quantities consistently well and on schedule. The saucier is not alone in dealing with chemistry, for baking requires a thorough understanding of the complex interaction among flour, moisture, yeast, and heat. For example, our Bake Shop, located about two thousand feet above sea level, is hot and moist in summer and cool, dry, and drafty in winter. Only care and experience enable the daily adjustment for these conditions, but the bakers' diligence and labor are well rewarded when the tantalizing aroma of baking bread fills the air with the promise of good things to come.

The bakers follow traditions developed during centuries of man's quest for his daily bread. More than any other food, bread is symbolic of life, physical and spiritual, and the nourishment derived from it has sustained mankind throughout history. The beginnings of bread can be traced to the Egyptians, who are credited with the discovery of leavening, the building of the dome-shaped brick oven, and the cultivation of wheat that was much prized for the bread that could be made from it. This wheat from Alexandria is believed to be the ancestor of the European grain which eventually reached North America, where it flourishes today.

The weight of history is not a burden because bakers today have the advantage of all the practical and scientific knowledge gleaned from those who have gone before. The flour available today is milled under controlled conditions so you will have no argument with the miller over the quality or quantity. If you can find it, buy flour that has "stone milled" on the package, and you can be assured that it was ground much as it was in the old days when wind- and water-powered mills covered the countryside. More important than the milling process is the flour itself. Only wheat produces gluten that can trap gas produced by yeast; other cereals yield flat breads, which is why rye flour must be mixed with white flour for a loaf of rye bread. Buy all-purpose flour, a blend of flours milled from hard and soft wheat, because it will yield an elastic and plastic dough for breadmaking. Buy only unbleached flour. Bleaching became popular when a uniform whiteness was fashionable, but it is an unnecessary chemical process which in some countries—France, for example—is prohibited by law. Now that you have a bag of stone-milled, all-purpose, unbleached flour, you are ready to buy your leavening.

Leavening can be done with yeast, either fresh or dried, or with baking powder (used in biscuits) or baking soda (often used in fruit breads, such as banana). The latter are straightforward and produce the so-called quick breads which have their own section in this chapter. Yeast is a more complicated story. You can buy a cake of fresh, compressed yeast that is sold by the ounce and will keep in the refrigerator for ten to fourteen days (or it can be wrapped carefully and frozen). Active dry yeast is sold in packets of about one tablespoon. Yeast comes to life with water and warmth—the compressed yeast is dissolved in liquid no warmer than 95°F and the active dry yeast in liquid with a temperature of 100 to 115°F. These limits are important because too much heat kills yeast. Use an instant-read thermometer for accuracy when heating liquids. A dried, vacuum-packed granular yeast, available in Europe for many years, is showing up with increasing frequency in this country. This convenient yeast does not need to be proofed—it is mixed directly with the dry ingredients before any liquid is added. (This yeast is kept on your pantry shelf until opened and will stay fresh for weeks if sealed in a moisture-tight bag and kept refrigerated.) A comparison among these yeasts is helpful: 1/2-ounce cake of compressed yeast = 1 envelope active dry yeast (or 1 scant tablespoon active dry yeast) = 1 1/2 teaspoons granular yeast.

You can decide which yeast you like to work with. Each kind is reliable, thanks to Louis Pasteur, who discovered that yeast is a living plant that breaks down starch and sugar and releases carbon dioxide. Before yeasts were understood, the spontaneous leaven system was used (and still is for sourdough bread), much as it was in biblical times. A leaven was made by mixing flour and warm water and letting it ferment. Then more flour was added to make the dough, after saving a portion to be the leaven for the next batch. Flemish and English bakers used ale barm or beer yeast and when compressed grain yeast was introduced from Hungary it was a milestone for bakers. Today, baking bread with commercial yeast is simple by comparison with the guesswork required in ages past.

So, now you have your flour and yeast. A few guidelines will help before you prepare your chosen recipe. The work required of the home baker can be divided into three steps: mixing and kneading the dough, shaping it, and baking it (the dough does the work of rising). Mix the dough according to the recipe, proofing your yeast as directed and measuring the flour by scooping the cup into the bag. We would recommend using spring water and kosher salt. Unsalted butter is the best fat for bread, providing a good crust, crumb, and flavor to the loaf. To knead the dough, lightly flour your work surface and your hands and turn the dough out of the bowl. The idea is to knead it until the dough is smooth, elastic, and no longer sticky. Using one or both hands, push, fold, and turn the dough continuously. For a sticky dough, a pastry scraper is a useful tool. The kneading can take from five to ten minutes. Handle the dough firmly and with authority—it loves being pushed around. To be sure that the dough has been kneaded enough, poke it with two fingers, and if the indentations stay the dough is ready. Form the dough into a ball, set it into a buttered bowl, turn the dough over so the buttered surface is on top, cover the bowl with a damp kitchen towel, and set it into a warm, draft-free place until the dough has doubled in size (one to two hours). A room temperature of 70°F is fine and 80°F is not too hot. Doughs that are enriched with butter, milk, or eggs need a warmer rather than a cooler place. During the winter months, a snug place for dough can be made by turning a cold oven on for a minute, turning it off, setting the bowl onto the oven rack, and closing the door. The time required for the dough to double in size depends upon several variables—the warmth and humidity of the room, the yeast and the flour, and the thoroughness of the kneading. You will notice a lovely "yeasty" aroma in the air when you check on the dough after an hour or two. Do not attempt your first loaf of bread on a thundery, humid, hot summer day—you will struggle to make the dough behave and be disappointed with the result.

When the dough has doubled in size, turn it out of the bowl, punch it down, knead it again (push, fold, turn) for several minutes, and let it rest under the damp towel for five minutes. This rest period relaxes the gluten so the loaf will be easier to form. An easy way to form a loaf is to pat the dough into a rough rectangle, roll it up jelly-roll fashion and set the loaf seam side down in the pan. (Tuck the ends under and fold them toward the seam if the loaf is too long for the pan.) The pan size can be chosen after you have shaped the loaf. Keep in mind that the dough will double in size again during the next rise and will get a final push from the heat when it is put into the oven. (When the oven heat penetrates to the center of the loaf and raises its internal temperature to 130°F, the yeast dies and the dough will stop rising.) The dough should fill the pan by two-thirds for a nicely rounded loaf and by one-half for a flatter loaf. Cover the dough with the damp towel and set the pan aside in a warm, draft-free place until the dough has doubled in size.

When the dough has risen, set it into the middle of the pre-heated oven to bake. If you have several pans, arrange them so that the air can freely circulate around them. Most ovens heat unevenly and you may need to move the pans around from front to back part way through the baking period. When you believe the bread is done, rap the top of the loaf with your knuckles—it should give a hollow sound. Just to be sure, slip the loaf out of the pan and test the bottom in the same way. If the loaf needs a few more minutes, set it on the rack without the pan and it will emerge with a lovely crust (or return it to the oven in the pan for a softer crust).

When the bread is done, remove it from the oven and let it cool on a rack (without the pan) in a draft-free place. Let it cool completely before slicing. A serrated knife, reserved solely for bread, is the best knife to use. Bread with a good crust can be sliced more easily from the side than from the top. Any bread will stay fresh if frozen as soon as it has cooled completely. Wrap it airtight, label it, and when you need it, let it thaw, unwrapped (or wrapped in a kitchen towel), at room temperature. Otherwise, for immediate use, keep bread at room temperature loosely wrapped in a towel or brown paper bag. The loaf must breathe. If you find yourself with stale slices of bread, turn them into crumbs by whirring small batches in a blender or food processor (or cut them into croutons). The crumbs will keep well in an airtight container in a cool place.

A few *conseils* about breadmaking: try it soon, and often, and your experience will be your best guide. You are in control of the dough: a rise can be slowed or stopped by putting the dough into the refrigerator (for several hours or overnight), or speeded up if necessary by using more yeast in the beginning or a warmer rising place. Above all, after you have made a few loaves, you will realize the joy and satisfaction of participating in one of the ancient mysteries of life.

❧ Yeast Breads

"Leavening" means fermenting to promote action. The term is ancient and can be found, for example, in the Gospel of Matthew (13.33). In English, according to the *Oxford English Dictionary*, "leavened bread" first appeared in print in John Baret's *An alvearie or triple dictionarie* (1573). The breads which follow are leavened with yeast, which, unlike baking powder, requires several hours to do its work. Needless to say, these breads are not "kneadless"; in fact, working with the dough as it is transformed provides the sense of accomplishment which every seasoned baker feels. As the potter molds clay, so does the baker mold dough, each producing something intensely personal and at the same time deeply rewarding for those fortunate enough to enjoy the result. So, set aside some time, flour the counter, get out the rolling pin, and you may find yourself having more fun than you have had in years—not to mention being able to have better bread than is available in most stores.

🌾 White Bread

William Harlan Hale relates that "bakers and millers were licensed and were considered so essential to the economy as a whole that at one point Louis IX, the sainted king of thirteenth century France, ordered that they be relieved of the military watch duties expected of his other subjects in Paris, in order not to interrupt their work."

Yields 4 loaves

1 1/2 envelopes active dry yeast
1/2 cup (118 ml) lukewarm water
2 cups (475 ml) boiling water
2 cups (475 ml) scalded milk
4 tablespoons (60 g) butter
1/4 cup (50 g) sugar
1/4 cup (60 ml) salt
12 cups (1520 g) flour
Butter for the bowl and pans

Recommended equipment

A small bowl, thermometer, two 1 1/2-quart (1 1/2 L) saucepans, large mixing bowl, blending fork, wooden spoon, pastry scraper, kitchen towel, 4 bread pans 9 1/2 x 5 1/4 x 2 3/4 inches (23 3/4 x 13 1/3 x 7 cm), two wire cooling racks.

Stir the yeast into the lukewarm water (110 to 115F or 44 to 46C) in the small bowl and set aside to proof.

Heat the water to boiling in one saucepan and the milk to scalding (180F or 82C) in the other. Put the butter, sugar, and salt in the mixing bowl, pour in the boiling water and scalded milk, and stir together with the fork until the butter is melted and the sugar and salt have dissolved. Cool mixture to lukewarm.

When the mixture is cool, stir in the yeast and about 3 1/2 cups (420 g) of flour. Beat with the wooden spoon until smooth. Then add more flour, 1 cup (120 g) at a time, until the dough is stiff and cannot be worked with the spoon. You may need an additional 9 cups (1080 g) of flour. Turn the dough out onto a lightly floured work surface and knead until it is smooth and elastic. Let the dough rest while you rinse out the mixing bowl and butter it. Form the dough into a ball, set it into the bowl, turn the dough over so the buttered side is up, and cover the bowl with a damp kitchen towel. Set the bowl in a warm, draft-free spot and let the dough rise until doubled in bulk (1 1/2 to 2 hours).

When doubled in bulk, punch the dough down, turn it out onto your work surface, knead for several minutes, then let it rest, covered with the damp towel, while you butter the bread pans. Divide the dough into four equal pieces, shape into loaves, set into the pans, cover with a damp towel, and let rise in a warm place until almost double in size.

Preheat oven to 400F (204C).

Remove the towel and set the pans into the middle level of the oven to bake for about 30 minutes or until done. When done, remove pans from oven, remove the bread from the pans, and let it cool on the racks in a draft-free place before slicing.

🌾

For a detailed description of making bread, see pages 483–84.

French Bread

The home baker can make a loaf whose shape and crust are reminiscent of true French bread. The shape is easier to come by than the crust. When the French adopted the Vienna baking system in the 1870s, their bread evolved into what today is usually called French bread. The Viennese oven had a sloping floor and steam injectors. The steam and the softer flour from French wheat are responsible for the crust. You can approximate the effect by using all-purpose flour and brushing the loaves with water just before they go into the oven (or by using a spray bottle). As far as pans are concerned, your local kitchen store will have either the now familiar black steel baguette *pans or the ceramic baking stone, which, when preheated in the oven, becomes a type of "floor" on which you set the dough to bake. The baking sheet called for here will produce a satisfactory result, but bread from the other two will be more likely to have the crunchy brown crust "à la française."*

Yields 2 loaves

1 envelope active dry yeast
1 tablespoon sugar
1 1/2 cups (355 ml) lukewarm water
4 1/2 cups (540 g) flour
2 teaspoons salt
1 lightly beaten egg white
Butter for the bowl
Cornmeal for the pan

Recommended equipment

A small bowl, thermometer, large mixing bowl, wooden spoon, pastry scraper, kitchen towel, baking sheet, sharp paring knife or razor blade, pastry brush or spray bottle, wire cooling rack.

Stir the yeast and sugar into the lukewarm water (110 to 115F or 44 to 46C) in the small bowl and set aside to proof.

Put 4 cups (480 g) of flour in the large mixing bowl, sprinkle the salt over the flour, stir it in, add the yeast mixture all at once, stir together, and scrape it out of the bowl onto a lightly floured work surface. Knead the dough until it is smooth and elastic, adding more flour as needed. Let the dough rest while you rinse out the mixing bowl and butter it. Form the dough into a ball, set it into the bowl, turn the dough over so the buttered side is up, and cover the bowl with a damp kitchen towel. Set the bowl in a warm, draft-free spot and let the dough rise for 1 hour, or until doubled in bulk.

When doubled in bulk, punch the dough down (it will be stiff and sticky), stir in the lightly beaten egg white, mix with the wooden spoon for 1 minute, cover with the towel, and let rise again for 1 hour or until doubled in bulk.

When doubled in bulk, punch the dough down, turn it out onto your lightly floured work surface, divide in half, cover with the towel, and let rest for 5 minutes. While the dough rests, prepare your baking sheet by sprinkling it evenly with cornmeal. When the dough has rested, remove one-half from under the towel and shape it into the long, narrow loaf called a *baguette*. Pat the dough out into a rectangle about 8 x 10 inches (20 x 25 cm) and, beginning with the long side, roll it up, pinch the edge together, and pinch the ends of the roll together. Shape the dough into an 18-inch (45 cm) long loaf by rolling the dough gently underneath your hands. Set the *baguette* onto the pan seamside down, cover with the towel, and shape the remaining dough into another loaf. Set the second loaf on the pan 4 inches away from the first one, cover them both with the towel, and let them rise for an hour or until doubled in bulk.

When the dough has risen, preheat the oven to 400F (204C). When the oven is hot, remove the towel from the *baguettes*, slash the top of each loaf three or four times with shallow, diagonal cuts along the length of the loaf, brush (or spray) the tops with cold water, and set the baking sheet into the middle level of the oven. Bake for 10 minutes, reduce oven heat to 325F (163C), and brush loaves with cold water again. Bake *baguettes* for 35 to 40 minutes or until they are golden brown.

When done, remove *baguettes* from the oven and set them on the wire rack to cool.

❦

The only cornmeal we have found so far that will not burn under high heat is Quaker brand. For a detailed description of making bread, see pages 483–84.

❦ *Pullman Loaf*

In 1865, George Mortimer Pullman built his first railway sleeping car, the Pioneer, *which was a modest forerunner of the luxurious Pullman rolling palaces, sleepers, and diners which came to dominate American railroads until the late 1950s. His designs also inspired the European wagons-lit and ultimately the rolling stock of the* Orient Express, *which made its inaugural run in 1883. Originally a cabinet maker, Pullman designed in meticulous detail, used space efficiently, and provided first-class service—especially in the dining car, where he insisted that everything be prepared on board. Menus of the 1870s boasted thirty-seven meat entrées, fifteen fish and seafood preparations, and countless types of game. And, as these transcontinental "hotel cars" full of sleeping*

passengers sped through the night, the bakers were at work, using lidded tins to bake loaves in the coal-fired ovens for toast and sandwiches which would grace the passengers' tables the following day. For habitués of the Twentieth Century Limited, Southern Crescent, California Zephyr, Santa Fe Chief, *and other legendary overnight trains, this bread will bring back fond memories. The rest of you have a new treat in store.*

In the United States the bread is known as Pullman loaf because of the four-square tin with the sliding top in which it is baked. In France it is known as pain de mie *because of its excellent texture (*mie *means crumb) and as* pain anglais *after the British travelers who first acquainted the French with it. Now the French have been converted and appreciate the bread for canapés, sandwiches, croutons, and crumbs.*

Yields 1 loaf

1/2 envelope active dry yeast
1 teaspoon sugar
1/4 cup (60 ml) lukewarm water
1 cup (235 ml) milk
4 tablespoons (60 g) butter
3 1/2 cups (420 g) flour
2 teaspoons salt
Butter for the bowl and pan

Recommended equipment

A small bowl, small saucepan, thermometer, two medium mixing bowls, blending fork, pastry scraper, kitchen towel, loaf pan with sliding lid 8 1/2 x 4 1/2 x 2 1/2 inches (21 1/4 x 11 1/4 x 6 1/4 cm), wire cooling rack.

Stir the yeast and sugar into the lukewarm water (110 to 115F or 44 to 46C) in the small bowl and set aside to proof.

Put the milk in the saucepan and heat until it is warm (110F). While the milk is heating, butter one of the mixing bowls for the dough to rise in and break up the 4 tablespoons of butter into small pieces in the other bowl. When the milk is warm, pour it over the butter and stir together to melt the butter. Stir 1 1/2 cups (180 g) flour and the salt into the milk mixture, mix with the fork, add the yeast all at once, stir it in, add the remaining flour, mix well, and turn the dough out onto a lightly floured work surface.

Knead the dough vigorously for 5 to 7 minutes or until it is smooth and elastic. Form the dough in a ball, set it into the buttered bowl, turn the dough over so the buttered side is up, and cover the bowl with a damp kitchen towel. Set the bowl in a warm, draft-free place and let the dough rise until doubled in bulk (about 1 1/2 to 2 hours).

When the dough has risen, punch it down, turn it out of the bowl onto your lightly floured work surface, cover with the towel, and let it rest. While the dough rests, butter the pan and the inside of the sliding lid. When the dough has rested, shape it into a loaf, set it into the pan, and let it rise in a warm place, covered with the towel, until it is within about 1 inch (2 1/2 cm) of the edge of the pan.

Preheat the oven to 400F (204C).

When the oven is hot, slide the lid on the pan and set the pan on the rack in the middle of the oven to bake for about 40 minutes or until the top is lightly browned. After 35 minutes you may remove the lid and, if the loaf is brown, remove it from the pan and set it back into the oven directly on the rack for 2 to 3 minutes to brown the crust. When the loaf is done, set it on the rack to cool.

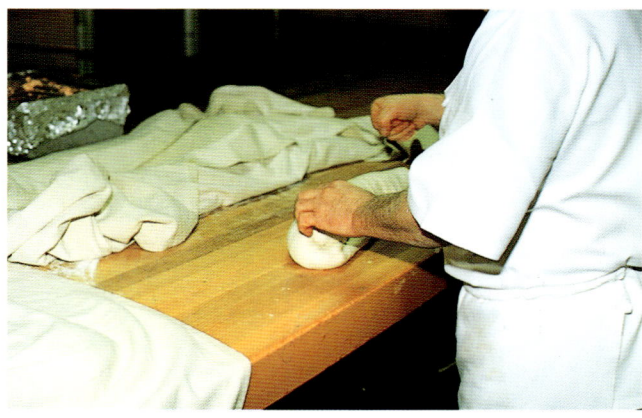

You may improvise a lid for any loaf pan by wrapping a board with aluminum foil and holding the board down on top of the pan with a 4- to 5-pound (2 to 2 1/2 kg) weight. For a detailed description of making bread, see pages 483–84.

Brioche Bread

Elizabeth David's comprehensive volume English Bread and Yeast Cookery *gives the following account of a recipe from 1655: "La Varenne's second recipe is for a fine and delicate version of* pain bénist . . . *and seems to be approaching what we know today as brioche dough. The basis is a leaven prepared from 2 lb of fine flour. When this is ready it is kneaded into a dough made from another 4 lb of flour, warm milk, 1 lb of butter, and 1/2 lb of soft fresh white cream cheese—this would have been the equivalent of thick ripe cream, rather than cheese—plus, if you wished, three or four eggs beaten with a little milk."*

Now that is a recipe with proportions that the bakers at the Homestead would understand. For the home cook, however, follow the brioche dough recipe and bake it any way you wish—as large or small loaves, braids (made from three equal pieces), or tall cylinders baked in a coffee tin. The greatest pleasure derived from bread is that it is malleable, and, no matter how you shape the dough, when you bake it you will have bread to enjoy.

Yields 2 loaves

1 recipe Brioches *(see page 493)*
Butter for the pans

Recommended equipment

Two bread pans 9 1/2 x 5 1/4 x 2 3/4 inches (23 3/4 x 13 1/3 x 7 cm), kitchen towel, cake tester.

Prepare the brioche dough up to the final rise.

Butter the bread pans and set aside.

Divide the prepared dough in half before the last rise, shape each half into a loaf, and set the loaves into the pans. Cover the pans with a damp kitchen towel and set them to rise in a warm place, at least 72F (22C), until they have doubled in size. This may take 2 to 3 hours, depending upon how cold the dough was to begin with.

When the dough has risen, preheat the oven to 350F (177C). When the oven is hot, remove the towel from the pans and set them on the rack in the middle of the oven to bake for 45 minutes or until the bread is a lovely golden brown. The brioche loaf is fragile while hot, so use a cake tester to check for doneness rather than thumping the loaf with your hand, which could dent the loaf and ruin its appearance.

When done, remove pans from oven and unmold bread to cool on a rack. Do not slice the loaves until they are completely cool.

For a detailed description of making bread, see pages 483–84.

Rye Bread

Rye is the most important European grain after wheat and makes a soft, flavorful bread with a tantalizing aroma. You must begin the sour a day before you want to enjoy the bread, and when you work with the dough use a pastry scraper—the dough will be very sticky.

Yields 4 loaves

FOR THE SOUR
1/2 cup (72 g) rye flour
3/8 cup (90 ml) water
1 tablespoon caraway seeds
A small onion
1 envelope active dry yeast

FOR THE DOUGH
2 envelopes active dry yeast
4 cups (950 ml) lukewarm water
1/2 cup (100 g) sugar
5 teaspoons salt
4 tablespoons (60 g) butter, melted
1/4 cup (60 ml) molasses
4 cups (575 g) rye flour
7 to 8 cups (840 to 960 g) flour

Cornmeal for the pans

Recommended equipment

A small glass bowl, wooden spoon, paring knife, plastic wrap, thermometer, large mixing bowl, small saucepan for melting butter, kitchen towel, pastry scraper, two baking sheets, sharp paring knife or razor blade, wire cooling rack.

Prepare the sour by combining the rye flour, water, and caraway seeds in the glass bowl. Quarter the onion and stir it into the mixture along with the yeast. Cover the bowl tightly with plastic wrap and set aside in a warm place for 24 hours.

The next day, remove the onion pieces from the sour and discard. Combine the yeast with the lukewarm water (110 to 115F or 44 to 46C) in the mixing bowl and stir in the sugar, salt, melted butter, and molasses. Add half of the rye flour and half of the flour to the bowl and beat with the wooden spoon until smooth. Stir in the remaining flours and the reserved sour mixture and mix completely (about 3 minutes). Then cover the bowl with a damp kitchen towel and let the dough rise in a warm, draft-free place for 1 hour, or until it has doubled in bulk.

When the dough has risen, punch it down and turn it out onto your lightly floured work surface. Divide the dough into four parts and make each one into a round loaf, using the pastry scraper and adding flour lightly as needed. Sprinkle the baking sheets with cornmeal, set two loaves on each one, cover with a damp towel, and set in a warm, draft-free place until doubled in bulk (1 1/2 to 2 hours).

When the dough has risen, preheat the oven to 375F (190C). When the oven is hot, slash the tops of the loaves slightly with a sharp knife (or razor blade) and set the pans in the oven to bake for 50 minutes. When the loaves are done, remove them from the oven and let them cool completely on the wire rack before slicing.

For a detailed description of making bread, see pages 483–84.

Dinner Rolls

On your kitchen tour you may be fortunate enough to see the heavy, square wooden boxes piled high with hundreds of dinner rolls on their way to the waiters' stations. In the Main Dining Room, when the rolls are served at your table on a tray, you can choose plain, poppy seed, or sesame seed rolls. Even if you have one of each (a likely event), you will still not know which is your favorite. After all these years, even we cannot decide. Of course, when you make these at home you can indulge yourself by making some of each in one batch.

Yields about 1 dozen

2 tablespoons (30 g) butter
  (or shortening)
1 tablespoon salt
1 cup (235 ml) milk
1 envelope active dry yeast
3 1/2 cups (420 g) flour
Butter for the bowl
Cornmeal for the baking sheet
Poppy seeds and/or sesame seeds

Recommended equipment

A wooden spoon, medium mixing bowl, small saucepan for warming milk, thermometer, pastry scraper, large mixing bowl, kitchen towel, sharp paring knife or razor blade, pastry brush, baking sheet, wire cooling rack.

Cream the butter and salt together in the medium bowl with the wooden spoon and set aside. Set the saucepan over low heat, add the milk, and heat until lukewarm (110 to 115F or 44 to 46C). When the milk is warm, remove from heat, stir in the yeast, and let it proof for 3 to 4 minutes. Then add the milk all at once to the creamed butter, stir together, and add the flour while mixing with the spoon. Turn the dough out of the bowl onto a lightly floured work surface and knead until smooth and elastic (about 5 to 7 minutes). Butter the large bowl. Shape the dough into a ball, set it into the bowl, turn the dough over so the buttered side is up, and cover the bowl with a damp kitchen towel. Set the bowl in a warm draft-free place until the dough has doubled in bulk (1 1/2 to 2 hours).

When the dough has doubled in bulk, punch it down and turn it out onto your lightly floured work surface. Divide the dough into twelve even pieces, shape each piece into a roll, and cut an "X" on the top of each one. Sprinkle cornmeal evenly over the baking sheet, set the rolls on the sheet, cover with the damp towel, and let rise until doubled in size (about 1 hour).

When the rolls have doubled in size, preheat the oven to 400F (204C). When the oven is hot, brush the rolls lightly with water, sprinkle the tops with either poppy or sesame seeds (or leave them plain), and set them into the middle level of the oven to bake for 12 to 15 minutes or until golden brown.

When the rolls are done, remove them from the oven and set them on a rack in a draft-free place to cool.

Make a double batch of rolls and freeze some for another time. Thaw the frozen rolls in a 325F (163C) oven for 10 to 12 minutes or at room temperature. For a detailed discussion of making bread, see pages 483–84.

Overnight Sweet Rolls

These rolls satisfy that "in-between" craving for something sweet at breakfast time—you know, the occasions when your conscience tells you that you should simply have cereal but you really want an assortment of Danish pastry, doughnuts, and a piece or two of Cinnamon Pecan Ring, after your eggs and bacon. Here is a tasty compromise—a roll that is lightly sweet and unglazed. To dress it up a bit, work some raisins into the dough as you are kneading it. Because the dough contains a fair amount of butter, you can serve the rolls fresh from the oven as is. The bacon and eggs are between you and your conscience.

Yields about 22 rolls

2 envelopes active dry yeast
1/2 cup (118 ml) lukewarm water
1 cup (235 ml) boiling water
2 teaspoons salt
3/4 cup (145 g) sugar
12 tablespoons (175 g) butter
1 cup (235 ml) cold water
3 eggs
8 cups (960 g) flour
Butter for the bowl and the
  baking sheet

Recommended equipment

A small bowl, thermometer, small saucepan, large mixing bowl, wooden spoon, medium mixing bowl, wire whisk, pastry scraper, kitchen towel, baking sheet.

In the small bowl, stir the yeast into the lukewarm water (110 to 115F or 44 to 46C) and set aside to proof. Bring the 1 cup of water to a boil, pour it into the large bowl, and add the salt, sugar, and butter, stirring until the butter melts. Add the cold water to the bowl and stir it in. Whisk the eggs together in the medium bowl until lightly beaten and then add them, the yeast, and half of the flour to the bowl. Beat all together well with the wooden spoon. Stir in the remaining flour, scrape dough out of the bowl onto a lightly floured work surface, and knead until the dough is smooth and elastic. It will be a soft dough.

Let the dough rest while you rinse out the bowl and butter it. Shape the dough into a ball, set it into the bowl, cover with a damp kitchen towel, and refrigerate overnight.

The next day, remove dough from refrigerator, punch it down, scrape it out onto your lightly floured work surface, divide into roughly 4-ounce pieces, and shape each one into a roll. Butter the baking sheet, set the rolls on it 2 inches (5 cm) apart, cover with a damp kitchen towel, and let rise until doubled in size (2 hours or more).

When the dough has risen, preheat the oven to 375F (190C). When the oven is hot, remove the towel and set the baking sheet in the middle level of the oven to bake for 15 to 20 minutes or until the rolls are browned. When the rolls are done, remove them from the oven and set them on a rack in a draft-free place to cool.

To make these rolls look as if they just came up fresh from our Bake Shop, dust them lightly with rye flour before baking. For a detailed discussion of making bread, see pages 483–84.

Brioches

The buffet breakfast served in the Grille features an assortment of sweet rolls, muffins, toast, biscuits, doughnuts, Danish pastry, and croissants or brioches. Steaming coffee, fresh fruit, and brioches, their browned topknots hiding the perfect place for sweet butter and jam, make an ideal beginning for a day in Hot Springs—or in your own home.

Yields about 2 dozen brioches

8 tablespoons (115 g) butter
1/3 cup (65 g) sugar
1/3 cup (80 ml) milk
1 teaspoon salt
1 envelope active dry yeast
1/4 cup (60 ml) lukewarm water
3 eggs
3 1/2 cups (420 g) flour
1 egg yolk
1 tablespoon milk
Butter for the muffin tins

Recommended equipment

A large mixing bowl, hand mixer, small saucepan, thermometer, wooden spoon, plastic wrap, kitchen towel, pastry scraper, muffin tins or brioche molds, pastry brush.

In the mixing bowl, cream the butter, add the sugar, and beat with the hand mixer until the mixture is light in color, fluffy, and the sugar is no longer granular. When done, set aside.

Heat the milk in the saucepan to 180F (82C), stir in the salt, remove from heat, and let cool to lukewarm (110 to 115F or 44 to 46C). Dissolve yeast in the lukewarm water and when the milk has cooled add the yeast to it, pour mixture into bowl with the creamed butter, stir together, add the eggs and flour, and beat with the mixer at medium speed for 2 minutes. Cover the bowl with a damp towel and set the dough into a warm (80F or 31C), draft-free place until it has doubled in bulk. This may take 2 1/2 to 3 hours.

When the dough has risen, punch it down, turn it out onto a lightly floured work surface, and knead for 2 minutes. Shape the dough into a ball, return it to the bowl, cover the dough with a piece of plastic wrap pressed directly onto its surface, cover the bowl with the damp towel, and set the dough into the refrigerator overnight.

The next day, punch the dough down, scrape it out of the bowl onto your lightly floured work surface, pat it out into a rough rectangle, and cut one-quarter of the dough away. Let the dough pieces rest under the towel while you butter the tins. Cut the small piece of dough into 24 even pieces and form them into small balls (these will become the topknots). Cut the large piece of dough into 24 even pieces, shape them into balls, and set them one by one into the muffin tins. Make a deep indentation (so you can see the tin bottom) in the center of each ball, dampening the hole lightly with cold water, and press a small ball down into the hole. Cover the dough with a damp kitchen towel and set it to rise in a warm place (80F or 31C) until the dough has doubled in bulk. This will take 1 to 2 hours.

When the dough has risen, preheat the oven to 375F (190C). Combine the egg yolk with the milk and brush some over the top of each small ball and around the top of the large one. Try not to let the wash run down and around the base of the small ball because this will prevent the brioche from rising properly in the oven. Set the muffin tins into the middle level of the oven to bake for 15 to 20 minutes or until the brioches have a rich brown crust.

When the brioches are done, remove the tins from the oven, turn out the brioches, and serve at once while piping hot.

Although muffin tins are readily available and give excellent results, the authentic appearance of a brioche, with its fluted and slanted sides, can only be had by using brioche molds (usually tin and imported from France). For baking, set them on a baking sheet and set the sheet into the oven.

This recipe yields about 4 pounds (1800 g) of brioche dough—more than twice the amount needed for the Coulibiac de Saumon à la Russe.

Croissants

In 1686, when the Turks were tunneling underground to get into Budapest, the city was alerted to the invasion by the bakers who were working their usual all-night shift. They heard noises from the digging and sounded the alarm for a successful defense of their city. In celebration of the victory the bakers were given the authority to create a commemorative pastry and the crescent roll, reminiscent of the sickle-shape on the Ottoman flag, was born. In the early 1900s a Parisian baker made the popular crescent roll with puff pastry and it was an instant success. Today, the luxurious layers of flaky pastry are within reach of the home cook and can be found on your own breakfast table.

Yields about 48 croissants

1 cup (235 ml) milk
1 envelope active dry yeast
1/2 cup (118 ml) lukewarm water
4 cups (480 g) flour
2 teaspoons salt
2 1/2 tablespoons sugar
1 cup (225 g) butter
Butter for the bowl

FOR THE GLAZE
1 egg
1 tablespoon milk

Recommended equipment

A small saucepan for warming milk, thermometer, small dish, medium mixing bowl, blending fork, plastic wrap, kitchen towel, pastry scraper, hardwood rolling pin, sharp paring knife or croissant cutter, two baking sheets, pastry brush, wire cooling racks.

Head Baker Thomas Woodzell

Put the milk in the saucepan, set it over medium heat, and heat until the milk is lukewarm (110 to 115F or 44 to 46C). While the milk is heating, stir the yeast into the lukewarm water in the small dish and set aside to proof. Combine the flour, salt, and sugar in the mixing bowl and stir together with the fork. When the milk is warm stir it into the flour mixture, add the proofed yeast, and mix to make a soft dough. Scrape the dough out of the bowl onto a lightly floured work surface and knead gently for 3 to 5 minutes or until the dough is smooth and elastic. Let the dough rest while you rinse out the bowl and butter it. Form the dough into a ball, set it into the bowl, turn so that the buttered side is up, cover the bowl with a damp kitchen towel, and set it in a warm, draft-free place for about 1 1/2 hours or until the dough has doubled in bulk.

When the dough has risen, punch it down, turn it out on a lightly floured work surface, and cover it with the towel while you prepare the butter. Knead the butter with the pastry scraper on an unfloured work surface to soften it and make it malleable. The butter must be plastic enough to stretch with the dough when it is rolled out but not so soft that it will ooze through the dough.

When the butter is ready, roll out the dough into a rectangle about 12 x 24 inches (30 x 60 cm). Using the pastry scraper, smear the butter over two-thirds of the dough rectangle, beginning at one end and coming to within 1 inch (2 1/2 cm) of the dough edges. Fold the remaining one-third of plain dough over the buttered dough and then fold the remaining buttered dough over the first fold, as if you were folding a business letter. (This is the first "turn.") Turn the dough so the end is toward you and roll out into a rectangle about 12 x 24 inches. Fold in thirds again, cover the dough with a damp kitchen towel, and let it rest for about 10 minutes. If at any time the butter seems too soft, set the dough into the refrigerator for 12 to 15 minutes to firm it up. After the dough has rested, you are ready to complete turns three through six. Roll out the dough just as you did before, fold in thirds, and continue rolling and folding until you have completed a total of six turns. Then wrap the dough in plastic and a damp towel and set it into the refrigerator for 1 1/2 hours or overnight.

When the dough has been chilled, set it on your lightly floured work surface, tap it gently with the rolling pin to deflate the dough, cut it in half, and reserve one-half in the refrigerator while you work with the other. Roll out one-half into a rectangular shape to a thickness of 1/8 to 1/4 inch (1/3 to 2/3 cm). Now you will cut out the triangles of dough that will become croissants (*see illustrations*). This can be done with a croissant cutter that is designed to cut triangles as it rolls over the dough, or with a sharp paring knife or pastry scraper. For the knife or pastry scraper, cut the dough into 4- or 5-inch (10 or 12 1/2 cm) squares and then cut each square on the diagonal into two triangles.

Roll the triangles up from the base toward the point and, as you set them onto a lightly buttered baking sheet, pull the ends toward each other into a crescent shape, with the point at the center pointing down between the ends. Roll out and shape the remaining dough. Set the baking sheets aside to let the croissants rise, covered lightly with plastic wrap, at room temperature until they have nearly doubled in size. If the butter becomes too soft, set the croissants into the refrigerator at intervals.

When the croissants have risen, preheat the oven to 375F (190C). Make the glaze for them by lightly mixing the egg with the milk. When baking croissants in batches, glaze them just before baking, and if the room is warm, let the second batch wait in the refrigerator. Brush some of the glaze over each croissant and set them into the middle level of the oven to bake for about 25 minutes or until they are golden brown. When done, remove them from the oven and let them cool slightly on a wire rack before serving.

Croissants freeze well. Cool them completely, wrap airtight, and freeze. When you want to serve them, take them straight from the freezer and heat in a 400F (204C) oven for 12 to 15 minutes.

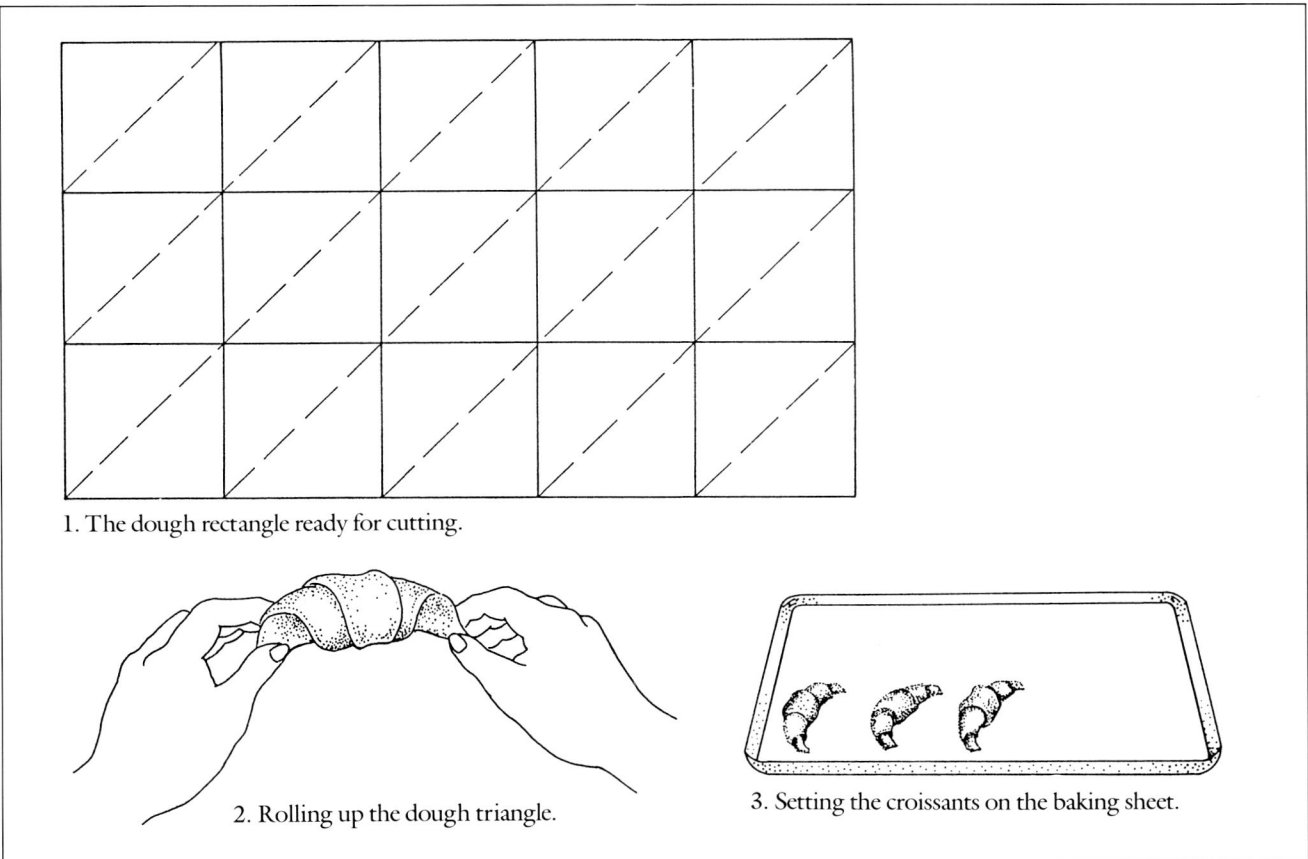

1. The dough rectangle ready for cutting.
2. Rolling up the dough triangle.
3. Setting the croissants on the baking sheet.

≋ Cinnamon Pecan Ring

You have read about the influence of Catherine de' Medici throughout this book, but in English Bread and Yeast Cookery Elizabeth David reminds us that "it must not be forgotten how much European cookery owes to the Arab influence (the Arabs were skilled pastrycooks long before the Italians took over) and to the peoples of the Near East and Asia Minor; it was they who originated so many of the dough-making and baking traditions which have descended to us, they who first supplied the fruit, the spices, the sugar and the flavourings we now regard as our own."

Yields 8 servings

1 cup (235 ml) milk
1/4 cup (50 g) sugar
1 teaspoon salt
4 tablespoons (60 g) butter
1 envelope active dry yeast
1 egg
3 3/4 cups (300 g) sifted flour
4 tablespoons melted butter
3/4 cup (145 g) sugar
1 teaspoon cinnamon
2 tablespoons honey
1/4 cup (48 g) dark brown sugar
1 cup (235 ml) pecans
Butter for the bowl

Recommended equipment

A small saucepan, thermometer, medium mixing bowl, blending fork, pastry scraper, kitchen towel, small saucepan for melting butter, small dish, 9-inch (22 1/2 cm) tube pan.

Put the milk in the saucepan, set it over medium heat, and heat until it is lukewarm (110 to 115F or 44 to 46C). When the milk is warm, pour it into the mixing bowl and add the 1/4 cup sugar, salt, butter, and yeast. Stir with the blending fork until the sugar is dissolved and the butter melted. Mix in the egg and then add the flour a cup at a time until the dough forms a mass that can be handled. Scrape the dough out of the bowl onto your lightly floured work surface and knead until smooth and elastic. Let the dough rest while you rinse out the bowl and butter it. Form the dough into a ball, set it into the bowl, turn the dough over so the buttered side is up, cover the bowl with a damp kitchen towel and set it in a warm, draft-free place to double in bulk (about 2 hours).

When the dough has risen, punch it down, knead briefly, and return it to the bowl to rise for 45 minutes. Melt the butter in the small saucepan and set aside. Combine the 3/4 cup sugar and the cinnamon in the small dish. Spread the honey around the bottom of the tube pan and sprinkle the dark brown sugar over the honey. Punch the dough down, scrape it out of the bowl onto your lightly floured work surface, and shape the dough into small round balls the size of a walnut. One at a time, dip the dough balls into the melted butter and then roll them in the cinnamon and sugar mixture. Place them into the tube pan in two layers, sprinkling each layer with pecans. Cover the pan with the damp towel and let the dough rise in a warm, draft-free place for 45 minutes.

When the dough has risen, preheat the oven to 350F (177C) and when the oven is hot set the pan into the middle level to bake for 35 to 40 minutes. When the pecan ring is done, remove the pan from the oven, remove the bread from the pan, and serve it while still warm.

For a detailed discussion of making bread, see pages 483–84.

Danish Pastry

The favorite sweet bread served with coffee in Denmark is called Wienerbrød, *or Viennese bread, in honor of its lineage. The Danes were smitten by the yeast puff pastries from Vienna and carried them home and then to America, where they have become known as Danish pastry. If what is usually passed off as a "Danish" holds no interest for you, this buttery, rich pastry will change your mind.*

Yields 2 dozen

1/2 cup (118 ml) milk
1/4 cup (50 g) sugar
4 tablespoons (60 g) butter
1/2 teaspoon salt
3 eggs
1/2 cup (118 ml) warm water
2 envelopes active dry yeast
1/2 teaspoon vanilla
1/2 teaspoon mace
3 1/2 cups (420 g) flour
8 tablespoons (115 g) butter

FOR THE FILLING
4 tablespoons (60 g) butter, melted
Sugar
Cinnamon

Butter for the bowl and the baking sheets

Recommended equipment

A small saucepan, thermometer, hand mixer, medium mixing bowl, blending fork, pastry scraper, kitchen towel, hardwood rolling pin, small saucepan for melting butter, pastry brush, two baking sheets, wire cooling racks.

Put the milk in the saucepan and set it over medium heat until it is lukewarm (110 to 115F or 44 to 46C). While the milk is warming, cream the sugar, butter, and salt in the mixing bowl with the hand mixer. Then add the eggs one at a time, mixing well after each addition. When the milk is lukewarm, remove from heat. Stir the yeast into the lukewarm water and let it proof for several minutes. Add the vanilla and mace to the mixing bowl, stir them in with the fork, and mix in the milk and yeast. Gradually add the flour and mix to make a soft dough. Scrape the dough out of the bowl onto your lightly floured work surface and knead the dough for 2 minutes. Let it rest while you rinse out the bowl, dry, and butter it. Shape the dough into a ball, set it into the bowl, turn it so the greased side is up, cover the bowl with a damp kitchen towel, and set it in a warm, draft-free place until the dough has doubled in bulk (1 to 1 1/2 hours).

When the dough has risen, punch it down, scrape it out onto your floured work surface, and let it rest while you prepare the butter. Knead the butter with the pastry scraper on an unfloured work surface until it is soft and pliable. It must be plastic enough to move with the dough when it is rolled out but not so soft that it will ooze. If at any point the butter becomes too soft, set it in the refrigerator for several minutes until it firms up. When the butter is ready, set it aside while you roll out the dough.

Roll out the dough into a rectangle about 9 x 12 inches (22 1/2 x 30 cm). Using the pastry scraper, smear the butter over two-thirds of the dough rectangle, beginning at one end and coming to within 1 inch (2 1/2 cm) of the dough edges. Fold the remaining one-third of plain dough over the buttered dough and then fold the remaining buttered dough over the first fold, as if you were folding a business letter. (This is the first "turn.") Turn the dough so the end is toward you and roll out into another 9- x 12-inch rectangle, fold in thirds as before, and continue rolling and folding until you have completed a total of six turns. If the dough becomes difficult to handle at any point, set it into the refrigerator for 20 to 30 minutes, wrapped airtight, and then proceed.

After the sixth and final turn, chill the dough, well wrapped, for 30 minutes. While the dough is chilling, butter the baking sheets and set aside. When the dough is chilled, remove it from the refrigerator and roll it out on your lightly floured work surface into a rectangle that is about 12 x 16 inches (30 x 40 cm). Melt the butter for the filling and brush it over the dough. Sprinkle sugar and cinnamon over the surface and roll up the dough, beginning at the shorter side, like a jelly roll. Cut the roll into 1/2-inch (1 1/4 cm) wide pieces and lay them about 2 inches (5 cm) apart, cut side down, on the baking sheets. Set the sheets in a warm, draft-free place until the dough has doubled in size.

When the dough has risen, preheat the oven to 350F (177C) and set the baking sheets into the middle level of the oven to bake for 20 minutes. When the Danish pastries are golden brown, remove them from the oven and set them individually on the racks to cool briefly before serving.

These Danish pastries may be successfully frozen and thawed in a 400F (204C) oven for 10 to 12 minutes. For a prune or apricot (or any other fruit) filling, make up 1 cup (235 ml) of puréed fruit, season it with orange or lemon rind, and spread it after the melted butter in a band along the short side of the rectangle before rolling the dough like a jelly roll. Then slice, bake as directed, and spread a sugar glaze over the cool pastry.

Quick Breads

Just as the name implies, this group of recipes is perfect for those spur of the moment situations which call for a little baked item on the side. Hungry friends dropping in unexpectedly on a winter afternoon, fresh market blueberries just waiting to jump into a muffin, fried chicken or ham looking for partners on a plate, and family members haunting the kitchen in late afternoon in quest of a side dish for dinner—all of these life dilemmas can be readily and tastily resolved by the following collection. And, if you have budding apprentice bakers coming up in the younger generation, don't hesitate to put them in charge of making any of these breads; they offer an excellent way to acquire the technique and confidence necessary for graduating to breads leavened with yeast.

Banana Nut Bread

Whenever you have bananas on hand that are too ripe to slice, mash them instead and turn them into bread. Sliced thinly and spread with soft butter, this loaf is an ideal snack and is also delicious when lightly toasted.

Yields 1 loaf

8 tablespoons (115 g) butter (or shortening)
1 cup (195 g) sugar
2 eggs
1 teaspoon soda
3 tablespoons hot water
2 cups (240 g) flour
1/4 teaspoon salt
3 ripe bananas
1 teaspoon vanilla
1/2 cup (118 ml) chopped walnuts
Butter for the pan

Recommended equipment

An electric mixer with mixing bowl, wire whisk, 1-quart (1 L) bowl, rubber spatula, small bowl, wooden spoon, large fine-mesh sieve, 6-cup (1425 ml) loaf pan, wire cooling rack.

Preheat oven to 375F (190C).

In the bowl of the electric mixer, combine the butter (or shortening) with the sugar and beat on medium speed until the mixture is light and fluffy and the sugar has dissolved (about 3 minutes). Meanwhile, whip the eggs with the whisk in the other bowl until well beaten and then add them to the mixing bowl and blend completely with the butter and sugar. Dissolve the soda in the hot water in the small bowl, add it to the mixing bowl, and blend. Add 1 cup (120 g) flour and the salt to the mixture and beat well.

Using the wooden spoon, force the bananas through the sieve one by one (you should have about 1 cup or 235 ml mashed bananas) and add them to the mixing bowl. Add the remaining flour and vanilla, mix until smooth, and stir in the nuts. Butter the loaf pan generously, pour the batter into the pan, and set it into the middle level of the oven to bake for 45 minutes or until the edges of the loaf have pulled slightly away from the pan. When done, turn the loaf out onto the rack to cool before slicing.

Sour Cream Raisin Tea Loaf

After an active day outdoors, come to the Great Hall (yours or ours), rest awhile, and enjoy this favorite Homestead bread with your tea.

Yields 1 loaf

12 tablespoons (170 g) butter
3/4 cup (145 g) sugar
1/2 cup (118 ml) sour cream
1 teaspoon vanilla
3 eggs
1 cup (235 ml) milk
2 cups (240 g) flour
2 tablespoons baking powder
2/3 teaspoon salt
1 cup (235 ml) raisins
Butter for the pan

Recommended equipment

An electric mixer with mixing bowl, sifter, 2-quart (2 L) bowl, rubber spatula, 6-cup (1425 ml) loaf pan, wire cooling rack.

Preheat oven to 325F (163C).

In the bowl of the electric mixer, combine the butter with the sugar and beat on medium speed until the mixture is light and fluffy and the sugar has dissolved (about 3 minutes). Scrape down the bowl, add the sour cream, vanilla, and eggs and beat for 1 minute. Add half of the milk and mix well.

Sift the flour, baking powder, and salt together, add to the mixing bowl, combine well, add the remaining milk, mix, and stir in the raisins. Butter the pan generously, pour the batter into the pan, and set it into the middle level of the oven to bake for 50 to 60 minutes or until the loaf has pulled away from the edge of the pan and the top is lightly browned. When done, set the pan on a rack for 5 minutes and then turn the loaf out onto the rack to cool before slicing.

Variation: When the loaf is cool, dust the top with powdered sugar before slicing.

Blueberry Muffins

Farms often have "pick-your-own" days when you can brave the noonday sun and fill buckets and baskets with enough fruits or vegetables to keep you busier than you had anticipated. If you can pick your own blueberries, do so. You will always remember the still, perfumed air among the bushes, and, if you live in an area of acid, sandy soil, you will want to plant a blueberry hedge for the lovely white flowers in the spring, the crimson leaves in the fall, and—of course—your own private supply of berries.

Yields 16 to 18 muffins

8 tablespoons (115 g) butter
1/2 cup (100 g) sugar
3 eggs
2 cups (240 g) flour
2 teaspoons baking powder
1/2 teaspoon salt
1 cup (235 ml) milk
3/4 cup (180 ml) blueberries
Butter for the muffin tins
Powdered sugar in a shaker

Recommended equipment

An electric mixer with mixing bowl, sifter, 2-quart (2 L) bowl, rubber spatula, large spoon, muffin tins, serving plate.

Preheat oven to 400F (204C).

Generously butter the muffin tins and set aside.

In the bowl of the electric mixer, combine the butter and sugar and beat on medium speed until the mixture is light and fluffy and the sugar has dissolved (about 3 minutes). Add the eggs and beat until well mixed.

Sift the flour with the baking powder and salt and add to the bowl alternately with the milk. Mix completely before folding in the blueberries with the rubber spatula. Spoon the batter into the muffin tins and set them into the middle level of the oven to bake for about 20 minutes or until the muffins have pulled away slightly from the edges of the pan. When done, turn the muffins out onto your serving plate, dust the tops with powdered sugar, and serve while hot.

When you return from the fields with buckets filled to overflowing with blueberries, lay in a supply for cold weather muffins that will top any you can buy at the store. Set the berries in a single layer on baking sheets and freeze them. Then pour them into plastic bags, where they will keep until baking time. When you want to make muffins, take the quantity needed from the freezer before starting the other preparations and fold them in as above. Baking may require a minute or two longer because the berries will chill the dough, but keep a close eye on them so they do not overcook.

Baking Powder Biscuits

Not more than two generations ago, famished families feasted on hot biscuits every day as part of breakfast, lunch, or dinner. Truly a quick bread, these biscuits can be on your table in twenty minutes, which is a tangible advantage when compared with the patience demanded for yeast-leavened doughs. In the 1860s, ready-mixed baking powders, or chemical raising agents, became available for home baking of biscuits, scones, and cakes. Baking powders are a mixture of an alkali (bicarbonate of soda) and an acid (either cream of tartar or tartaric acid, derived principally from grapes), which combine to form a gas (carbonic acid gas) when milk or water is added. This gas works immediately on the dough, so as soon as you have combined your liquid and dry ingredients you must work quickly to get the biscuits into the oven lest the gas escape. The product called double-acting baking powder contains both tartaric acid and cream of tartar, the former for an initial push of the dough and the latter for a sustained rise in the oven. The baking powders include a starch—either rice, corn, or potato flour or arrowroot—to prevent a reaction between the acid and alkali until you add the liquid. So, keep your powder dry and mix your dough deftly with a light touch and you can enjoy hot biscuits whenever you please.

Yields about fourteen 2-inch (5 cm) biscuits

2 cups (160 g) sifted flour
4 teaspoons baking powder
1 teaspoon salt
1 teaspoon sugar
4 tablespoons (60 g) butter (or shortening)
1 cup (235 ml) milk

Recommended equipment

Two 1-quart (1 L) bowls, sifter, blending fork, pastry scraper, rolling pin, 2-inch (5 cm) biscuit cutter, baking sheet, napkin-lined basket.

Preheat oven to 450F (232C).

Sift the flour, baking powder, salt, and sugar into a mixing bowl. Working quickly, crumble the butter (or shortening) into the dry ingredients so that it is in pea-sized pieces. Make a well in the center of the flour mixture, pour in the milk, and stir together with the blending fork. When the mixture has come together and formed a mass in the bowl, scrape it out onto a lightly floured work surface. Pat the dough out, lift and scrape it into a ball with the pastry scraper, and roll (or pat) out again to a thickness of 1/2 to 3/4 inch (1 1/4 to 2 cm). Cut with the biscuit cutter, set biscuits close to each other (but not touching) on the baking sheet, and set them into the middle level of the oven to bake for about 12 minutes or until the tops are lightly brown. When done, remove from oven and serve in the basket while very hot.

❧ Buttermilk Biscuits

Formerly, buttermilk was known as "churn milk" and was what remained in the churn after making butter. Nowadays, commercial buttermilk is cultured from skim milk for twelve to fourteen hours in a slow fermentation process to develop the flavor. Bakers have been partial to the tangy taste of buttermilk in cakes and breads, and these biscuits are no exception. They rely on the lactic acid action of the buttermilk on the bicarbonate of soda to lighten the dough and impart texture and flavor to the baked biscuit.

Yields about fourteen 2-inch (5 cm) biscuits

- 5 1/3 tablespoons (80 g) butter (or shortening)
- 1 tablespoon sugar
- 2 cups (160 g) sifted flour
- 1 1/2 teaspoons salt
- 2 teaspoons baking powder
- 1/4 teaspoon cream of tartar
- 1 cup (235 ml) buttermilk
- 1/2 teaspoon soda

Recommended equipment

Two 1-quart (1 L) bowls, wooden spoon, sifter, wire whisk, blending fork, pastry scraper, rolling pin, 2-inch (5 cm) biscuit cutter, baking sheet, napkin-lined basket.

Preheat oven to 475F (246C).

Cream the butter (or shortening) together with the sugar in one of the bowls, working with the wooden spoon. Sift the flour, salt, baking powder, and cream of tartar together in the other bowl. Working quickly, crumble the butter mixture into the dry ingredients so that it is in pea-sized pieces. Combine the buttermilk and soda, make a well in the center of the flour mixture, and add the buttermilk all at once. Stir together with the blending fork. When the mixture has come together and formed a mass in the bowl, scrape it out onto a lightly floured work surface. Roll (or pat) the dough out to a thickness of 1/2 to 3/4 inch (1 1/4 to 2 cm). Cut with the biscuit cutter, set biscuits close to each other (but not touching) on the baking sheet, and set them into the middle level of the oven to bake for about 10 minutes or until the tops are lightly browned. When done, remove them from the oven and serve in the basket while very hot.

Corn Bread

Several crewmen who sailed with Christopher Columbus returned home to the Basque country in southwestern France, bringing corn with them. It replaced millet in the peasant's diet and assumed such importance that its spirit is portrayed in annual festivals. The Basques would enjoy this bread as much as you will.

Yields 4 servings

- 3 tablespoons sugar
- 1/2 teaspoon salt
- 3 tablespoons (45 g) butter (or shortening)
- 2 eggs
- 3/4 cup (90 g) flour
- 1/2 cup (118 ml) cornmeal
- 1 tablespoon baking powder
- 1 cup (235 ml) milk
- Butter for the baking dish

Recommended equipment

Two 1-quart (1 L) bowls, wooden spoon, baking dish 8 x 8 x 2 inches (20 x 20 x 5 cm).

Preheat oven to 350F (177C).

Cream the sugar, salt, and butter (or shortening) together in one of the bowls with the wooden spoon. Add the eggs and mix until smooth. Stir the flour, cornmeal, and baking powder together in the remaining bowl and then add all at once to the creamed mixture. Pour in the milk and beat with the spoon until all the lumps have dissolved.

Butter the baking dish, pour in the mixture, and set the dish into the middle level of the oven to bake for 30 minutes or until the corn bread is lightly browned and has pulled away from the sides of the pan. When done, remove from oven, cut into squares, and serve while piping hot.

Executive Pastry Chef Michel Finel

Pastry and Desserts

> Pierrette . . . lived to the ripe age of ninety-nine years and ten months. One day as she was dining in bed, she suddenly shouted to the family servant, "Quick, bring the dessert! I feel that I am going to give up the ghost! . . . The servant ran, but too late; her mistress, leaving the dessert, had departed to take her coffee in the other world."
> —Samuel Chamberlain

When Brillat-Savarin's sister Pierrette departed this earthly life, the dessert she left behind may have been a refreshing ice cream or water ice, custard, some marzipan, a pastry, or possibly a sampler of all five. What it was matters less than how she viewed it—clearly, her last wish was for dessert, however it was defined that evening in her household.

Sweets have tempted mankind ever since honey was gathered in Egypt and India around 4000 B.C. Honey was the first sweetener, and the cuisine and culture of Greece and Rome depended upon it for flavoring breads, cakes, and sauces. Honey wine, or "mead" (from the Sanskrit word for honey), was produced by the Assyrians and became a favorite in Central Europe and Scandinavia. Germany and Slavic countries were major producers of honey, and, in China, a restaurant in Hangchow in the thirteenth century sold only honey fritters. The dominance of honey as a sweetener persisted until around 1500, when easily stored cane sugar became available.

The word "sugar" comes from the Arabic name *sukkar* derived from the Sanskrit *sárkarā*. In European languages sugar came to be known variously as *azucar*, *sucre*, *zucchero*, and *Zucker*.

The Persians, who brought so many vegetables along the ancient trade routes, also carried sugar cane (and the method for extracting sugar) from India westward. When the Arabs conquered Persia around 640 they introduced sugar cane to northern Africa, Syria, and Spain. By the twelfth century, Venice was the center for sugar trade to the west, and the year 1319 marked the first large shipment of sugar to England.

This remarkable substance was first used widely as a medicine and as a way of obscuring medicinal tastes in confections put together by druggists—indeed, the Latin *conficere*, to prepare or put together, is the root word for the word confection. The mystical qualities of sweeteners—honey and sugar—are bound up in our innate love of sweet tastes (bitter flavors repel us), and the magical, medicinal, and purifying powers attributed to sweeteners have their beginnings in Mesopotamian folklore. Even today, we are likely to feel better after enjoying something sweet—whether fresh, natural fruit or a manmade confection.

The earliest record of a confection is found in Bartolommeo de Sacchi's *De Honesta Voluptate*, written in 1475, where he describes an almond-sugar paste similar to marzipan. In Elizabethan England, "marchpane" was a fad. The pounded almonds and pistachio nuts were mixed with sugar and flour and flavored with vanilla—a treat which survives as the marzipan of today. By 1825, sugar's popularity had become so great that, according to Brillat-Savarin, it "has become a staple food of the first necessity; there is a not a woman, especially if she be well-to-do, who does not spend more for her sugar than she does for her bread." At present, in many affluent countries, the per capita consumption of sugar exceeds one hundred pounds a year. Where does all this sugar go? The confectionery art commands enormous quantities of sugar—whether for preparing cakes, custards, ices, and sweet pastry, or sweetening chocolate, which is inherently bitter. To satisfy the world's demand for sugar, it is necessary to extract it from sugar cane, sugar beets, the sugar maple, and corn—four quite different plant sources of the same organic compound.

As for the term pâtissier, or more to the point, the domain of the pâtissier, it has not always been confection. In the Middle Ages, pastry cooks made *oublie*, little wafers cooked in hot irons, and came to be known as *oubleyeurs*. As time passed, separate guilds of bakers, pastry cooks, and pork butchers arose, and increasingly were seen to be poaching on each other's territory. Bakers started making cakes, and pastry cooks baked hams in a crust, provoking a howl of protest from the pork butchers, who claimed (rightly as the courts ruled) that the ham in a crust was not a pie (which pastry cooks were allowed to bake) because the crust did not adhere to the ham. So it went until the nineteenth century, when Carême started to define the role of the pâtissier as one whose specialty was working with sugar, sweetened pastry, and cake confections.

The pâtissier, or executive pastry chef, at the Homestead is Michel Finel (a native of Normandy). He is responsible for the desserts, chocolates, and sweets served daily at the hotel. (He also makes paillettes and other savory baked goods, but we won't tell Carême.) I have the deepest respect for our Pastry Department, which is staffed by artists and perfectionists who share a particular responsibility with the saucier. If the soup or sauce is badly prepared, it will color the perception of the rest of the meal. If the dessert is poor, that is the last thought a guest will take away from the table, which would be an unfortunate memory—especially after such hard work by all the other kitchen departments. So Michel and his staff must see to it that everything is carefully prepared and consistently excellent. As with the saucier, their success comes from years of experience and dedication to an exacting task that demands a knowledge of the physical and chemical interactions of ingredients as they are blended, cooked, or chilled. Pâtissiers must measure very carefully, and often their department (and the bakers') is the only one with weighing scales in a prominent and convenient location. If you visit the Pastry Shop early in the morning, you will see the scales in constant use.

Following the tradition of Carême and *la grande cuisine*, Michel is also responsible for preparing the great *pièces montées* which grace banquet and buffet tables for the visual enjoyment of our guests. Carême, who studied architecture, once said: "The fine arts are five, as follows: painting, poetry, music, sculpture, and architecture—which has for its principal branch *la pâtisserie*." And here is where sauces and confections are at once alike and different. They are alike in being constructed from basic stages, each of which rests on another—remember our house of sauces. They differ in that confection exists in a discernible spatial dimension and is therefore architectural, whereas, save for a chaud-froid or thick gravy, sauces are two dimensional. Carême's sketchbooks for *pièces montées* are reminiscent of Leonardo, so thorough and yet fanciful are they, replete with minarets, pagodas, and Roman towers made from spun sugar and pastry. Here in Hot Springs you will find their confectionery offspring as we celebrate the holidays with stunning cornucopiae, gingerbread houses, Easter eggs, and entire villages, according to the season. But you will have to come to the Homestead to enjoy them because they are simply not possible at home and must be left in Michel's competent hands.

But that is a historical digression. The desserts included here *are* well within reach of the home cook, and just as with sauces, if you have not made pastry before, begin at the beginning. The section on pastry basics is just that—the place where you will pick up the tools of the pâtissier's trade and build your own repertoire. Mastering the basics of pastry making is every bit as important as becoming the saucier's apprentice before earning the title of saucier. With practice here you can go on and fill your pastry with apples or pumpkin purée, prepare a tart "foundation" for plums or other fruits, and turn a sugar crust into dozens of irresistible cookies. Pâte Feuilletée makes several delights possible: Vol-au-Vents, Paillettes, and Palmiers, each one of which will help to establish your reputation forever as a superb and generous pâtissier. The custards, thin for sauce and thick for filling, are indispensable. The butter cream frosting will turn your cakes into a disappearing act. Wine-based Sauce Sabayon will surround many a dessert or stand well alone, chilled, in a tall glass. You can choose the liqueur-flavored syrup to enhance the flavor of your cakes and the Succés will bring you exactly what its name says: success. This crunchy meringue is layered with génoise in the two tortes, either one of which will bring you accolades around the table. Dessert crêpes are included under basics because they are one the simplest of all to make. If you can make pancakes, you can make these.

Start with the basics and you will be well on your way to earning the *toque blanche* of the pâtissier. The ending of any meal should complement the beginning, whether it is a simple plate of fruit and cookies for a light luncheon or a sumptuous cake for an elegant dinner. Michelin three-star chef Louis Outhier said it best—"One must never neglect the exit. It must be in grand style." Pierrette would have agreed.

Pastry Basics

We mentioned in the introduction that confectionery uses vast quantities of sugar. It also requires substantial amounts of other basic ingredients which must be of first-class quality for the recipe to succeed. From B. G. McElwee's Shopping List, for example, the Pastry Department would make the following daily requisition: 900 eggs, 100 pounds of sugar, 12 gallons of milk, 50 pounds of butter, 6 gallons of half-and-half, 5 gallons of heavy cream, 60 pounds of flour, and miscellaneous amounts of fruit and chocolate. Because ingredients are so important, we are going to start you off with a few *conseils* drawn from our own kitchen.

The following recipes are based on all-purpose flour which is measured by scooping a dry measuring cup into the flour and then leveling the cup with a straight edge. You may also weigh the flour if you prefer, and metric equivalents are given for this purpose. Unsalted butter is called for as a shortening, but you may substitute a good, solid vegetable shortening if necessary for dietary purposes. Eggs are graded "large," and should always be fresh—pastry is one culinary area in which "thousand-year-

old" eggs (i.e., two to three weeks old) will jeopardize the results.

When working with pastry, mix the dough quickly, handle it very little, and refrigerate it for several hours or overnight before rolling it out. This rest allows the flour starch to absorb moisture and mellows the dough—a cold dough absorbs less flour, making it easier to roll out. A heavy hardwood rolling pin is essential and a pastry scraper is an excellent aid for working quickly and keeping your warm hands away from the pastry.

There is only one more bit of advice: if at first you do not succeed and the result is not the pastry of your dreams, do not despair—try again. Michel has told us that anyone who makes pastry every day for a week will have it down pat and not need to look at the recipe again.

Pie Pastry

As Julia Child has said, "Il faut mettre la main à la pâte!" So, get your hands in the pastry—often—and your fingers will learn when the flour is ready to accept the water and when the pastry needs to rest. Practice makes perfect pastry and every pie possible.

Yields 22 ounces (625 g)

2 cups (240 g) flour
1/2 teaspoon salt
16 tablespoons (225 g) butter
1/2 cup (118 ml) cold water

Recommended equipment

A medium mixing bowl, pastry blender or blending fork, waxed paper or plastic wrap.

Combine the flour, salt, and butter in the mixing bowl, working with both hands, until the texture resembles coarse meal and the mixture will not stick to your fingers. Sprinkle the cold water by tablespoons over the flour mixture, adding it gradually and stirring gently with the blending fork until mixture pulls together and away from the sides of the bowl. You may not need all the water. Do not overmix.

Shape dough into a ball, sprinkle lightly with flour, and wrap airtight in waxed paper or plastic wrap. Refrigerate overnight (or for several hours) before using. This will keep about a week refrigerated.

 ## Pâte à Foncer
Foundation Pastry

The addition of butter and egg turns simple pie pastry into nonsweet short pastry, the perfect foundation for a tart. The French word foncer *means "to put a bottom under," so logic will dictate the position of this pastry in the pan.*

Yields 34 ounces (960 g)

4 cups (480 g) flour
1 tablespoon plus 2 teaspoons (30 g) sugar
1/2 teaspoon salt
14 tablespoons (205 g) butter
1/3 cup (80 ml) shortening
1/4 cup (60 ml) cold water
1 egg

Recommended equipment

A medium mixing bowl, blending fork, waxed paper or plastic wrap.

Combine the flour, sugar, and salt in the mixing bowl. Cut the butter and shortening into small pieces and combine them with the flour mixture in the bowl, working with both hands, until the texture resembles coarse meal and the mixture will not stick to your fingers. Make a well in the center of the flour, pour in the cold water all at once, and add the egg. Working from the center toward the edge of the bowl, stir gently with the blending fork until the mixture pulls together and away from the sides of the bowl. Do not overmix.

Shape dough into a ball, sprinkle lightly with flour, wrap airtight with waxed paper or plastic wrap, and refrigerate overnight (or for several hours) before using.

This recipe makes sufficient pastry for two 10-inch (25 cm) tarts.

 ## Pâte Sucrée
Sugar Pastry

The proportion of butter, sugar, and eggs to the flour creates a sweet short pastry that is called for in the Strawberry Tart and the Honey Cookies, two of our most popular desserts at the Casino buffet.

Yields about 5 pounds (2250 g)

2 cups (455 g) butter
2 cups (390 g) sugar
7 eggs
7 3/4 cups (930 g) flour
A pinch of salt

Recommended equipment

A kitchen scale, heavy duty electric mixer with 5-quart (5 L) bowl, rubber spatula, large mixing bowl, blending fork, pastry scraper, waxed paper or plastic wrap.

Cut the butter into chunks and cream it with the sugar in the bowl of the electric mixer, scraping down the bowl from time to time, until the mixture is light yellow in color, fluffy, and the sugar is no longer granular (about 5 to 8 minutes). Add the eggs one at a time, mixing well after each addition. Remove bowl from the mixer stand.

Stir the flour and salt together in the other bowl and then add that mixture all at once to the butter mixture. Combine them with the blending fork until the ingredients come together and pull away from the side of the bowl. Do not overmix the dough; it will be very soft. Scrape the dough out of the bowl onto your lightly floured work surface. Working quickly, shape the dough into a ball or rectangle (whichever is easier to handle) by pushing it together with a pastry scraper and your lightly floured hands. Handle the dough as little as possible. Dust the dough all over with flour, wrap airtight with waxed paper or plastic wrap, and refrigerate overnight (or for several hours) before using.

The recipe yields enough pastry for two sheet pans of Honey Cookies, one Strawberry Tart, and a half-dozen or so sugar cookies. You can successfully freeze the dough or halve this recipe if 5 pounds of pastry is more than you can use.

Pâte Feuilletée
Puff Pastry

The elegance associated with puff pastry presentations need not be intimidating—the technique is simpler than it appears—as you will discover when you prepare Vol-au-Vents, Paillettes, and Palmiers. Something this good has been around in one form or another for a very long time. Light, flaky pastry was known in ancient Greece as well as during the Middle Ages, and the Bishop of Amiens specifically mentioned flaky pastry cakes in a charter drawn up in 1311. The seventeenth-century painter Claude Gelée, known as Claude Lorrain, served also as a pastry cook's apprentice, and is sometimes credited with the creation of this delicious pastry. History does record that he helped it regain popularity during his lifetime and you, too, can perform a similar service.

Yields about 3 pounds (1350 g)

4 cups (480 g) flour
1/2 teaspoon salt
1 1/3 cups (315 ml) cold water
2 cups (455 g) butter, chilled

Recommended equipment

A small mixing bowl, blending fork, paper towels, waxed paper, rolling pin, plastic wrap.

Combine the flour and salt in the mixing bowl, make a well in the center, and pour in the cold water while stirring with the blending fork. Turn out onto your lightly floured work surface, mix gently with your hands until soft but not sticky, shape the dough into a ball, dust with flour, wrap in plastic wrap, and let rest for 15 minutes in the refrigerator.

While the dough is resting, sprinkle your hands with cold water and knead the butter with the heels of your hands on your work surface until soft and pliable. Pat butter dry with paper towels if necessary.

Sprinkle your work surface with flour and roll the dough into a 10-inch (25 cm) square. Shape the butter into a 7-inch (17 1/2 cm) square on waxed paper, place the butter square diagonally on top of the pastry square (waxed paper on top), remove the waxed paper, and fold up the corners of the pastry so that they meet in the center of the butter. Pinch the pastry edges together, forming a seal, and let stand 5 minutes.

Turns 1 and 2. With the rolling pin, gently roll the dough, keeping an even thickness throughout, into a rectangle 7 by 18 inches (17 1/2 x 45 cm) and about 1/2 inch (1 1/4 cm) thick. As needed, dust the rolling pin with flour. Fold dough in thirds (as you would a business letter) and seal the ends with the rolling pin. Turn dough so that the open edge of the fold is facing to your right as if it were a book about to be opened. Roll out again to a 7- by 18-inch (17 1/2 x 45 cm) rectangle, fold into three layers, poke dough twice with your finger (indicating two complete turns), wrap airtight, and refrigerate for 15 to 20 minutes.

Turns 3 through 6. Repeat the folding and rolling process four more times, letting the dough rest for 10 minutes after each turn (remember to poke the dough to mark the number of times it has been turned). When turns are completed, wrap dough airtight and chill overnight. The dough will keep for one week under refrigeration or can be frozen for several months.

Vol-au-Vents
Patty Shells

If you have been served frozen imitations of patty shells, filled with creamed chicken and peas, take heart! The real patty shell is as close as your kitchen. Once you have Pâte Feuilletée in your repertoire and in your freezer, the joys of light, flaky pastry can satisfy your quest for the perfect vol-au-vent.

Yields 6 vol-au-vents

16 ounces (455 g) Pâte Feuilletée *(see page 513)*
1 egg

Recommended equipment

A rolling pin, 3-inch (7 1/2 cm) vol-au-vent cutter, baking sheet, small bowl, wire whisk, pastry brush, wire cooling rack, paring knife.

Prepare the pâte feuilletée and let it chill overnight.

When the dough is ready, roll it out to a thickness of 1/2 inch (1 1/4 cm) and, using the vol-au-vent cutter, cut out 3-inch (7 1/2 cm) circles. Lightly dampen the baking sheet, set the pastry rounds on it, and set it into the refrigerator to chill the vol-au-vents for at least 30 minutes before baking.

When the dough is chilled, preheat the oven to 430F (221C). When the oven is hot, remove the vol-au-vents from the refrigerator. Whisk the egg in the small bowl to mix it thoroughly and brush a little all over the top edge of each patty shell, being sure that the egg wash does not drip down the side (which would prevent the dough from puffing up when it is baked).

Set the pan into the middle level of the oven and bake the vol-au-vents until they have puffed up and are golden brown. This should take about 20 minutes. When the vol-au-vents are done, remove them from the oven, set them on the rack to cool, and cut out the center circles with the paring knife and remove them. The vol-au-vents will be soggy if the center is left in place. These pieces may be used as lids after the shells are filled.

If you do not have a vol-au-vent cutter, you can use a 3- and a 2-inch (7 1/2 and 5 cm) biscuit cutter. Cut out twelve 3-inch circles and set six of them on the dampened baking sheet. Using the 2-inch cutter, cut a circle out of the center of the remaining rounds of pastry, leaving a ring. Brush some water all around the outside circumference of each pastry circle on the baking sheet and carefully lay a pastry ring on top where it is moistened. Then chill the pastry according to the recipe, brush with egg wash, and bake as directed.

If your vol-au-vents rise unevenly or threaten to topple over, the next time you prepare them try this to ensure an even rise: Brush some shortening on a sheet of parchment paper and lay the sheet with the shortening side down on top of the vol-au-vents. Bake as directed.

Paillettes
Cheese Straws

At the Homestead, these crisp, flaky sticks are passed on a silver plate to accompany the classic English Beef Tea for a first course. You will find that this "new twist" on the southern cheese straw (offered throughout the South for generations) makes a superior hors d'oeuvre. One conseil: *make far more than you think you can possibly use because your party guests will have no shame when it comes to picking the serving tray clean.*

Yields 8 servings (32 pieces)

5 ounces (145 g) Pâte Feuilletée (see page 513)
1 1/2 ounces (45 g) Parmesan cheese, grated
1/2 teaspoon Hungarian paprika
1 egg

Recommended equipment

A box grater, two small bowls, wire whisk, rolling pin, pastry brush, pastry scraper or knife, baking sheet, wire cooling rack.

The day before you plan to make the paillettes, prepare the pâte feuilletée and reserve the rest for another use (such as Vol-au-Vents, Palmiers, or a tart shell).

To make the paillettes, grate the Parmesan cheese on the finest side of the box grater and combine it in one of the bowls with the paprika. Whisk the egg together thoroughly in the other bowl.

Preheat oven to 375F (190C).

Using the rolling pin, roll out the puff pastry to a thickness of 1 inch (2 1/2 cm). Brush the top with the egg wash and pat all the grated cheese onto it. Continue rolling out the pastry until it is 1/4 inch (2/3 cm) thick and about 12 inches (30 cm) long and 3 inches (7 1/2 cm) wide. Using the pastry scraper or knife, cut the pastry into 3/8-inch (1 cm) wide strips (you should have about eight strips). Dampen the baking sheet with cold water. Working with one strip at a time, lay it lengthwise in front of you on your work surface, place a hand on each end of the strip, and, keeping light pressure on each end, move your hands in opposite directions—one away from you and one toward you—to twist the strip. Place the strips 1 inch apart on the baking sheet.

Set the baking sheet in the middle level of the oven and bake the paillettes until they are crisp and golden brown (about 15 to 20 minutes). As soon as they are done, remove the baking sheet from the oven, cut each paillette into 3-inch (7 1/2 cm) long pieces, and set them on the wire rack to cool.

When cool, store them in a tightly covered tin. Do not refrigerate. Before serving, they may be crisped in a slow oven (250F or 121C) for 5 to 10 minutes.

For a paillette reminiscent of southern cheese straws, add cayenne pepper to your taste to the grated cheese and paprika before spreading it on the dough.

Crème Anglaise
Custard Cream

A sweet, light custard sauce, also known as vanilla sauce, this is the perfect companion for Soufflé au Chocolat, Double Apple Sauce Cake, and Rice Pudding. The basic vanilla goodness can be flavored with hazelnut paste, melted chocolate, or various liqueurs as the occasion may require.

Yields about 8 cups (1900 ml)

4 cups (950 ml) milk
10 egg yolks
1/2 cup (100 g) sugar plus 2 tablespoons
2 teaspoons vanilla extract

Recommended equipment

A 3-quart (3 L) saucepan, wooden spoon, electric mixer with mixing bowl, rubber spatula, wire whisk, wooden spatula, fine-mesh sieve, small mixing bowl.

Put the milk into the saucepan and set over medium heat, stirring from time to time to prevent scorching, until it reaches the boiling point.

While the milk is heating, set the egg yolks, sugar, and vanilla extract to mix at medium speed in the bowl of the electric mixer. Beat, scraping down the sides of the bowl from time to time, until the sugar is dissolved and the mixture is light in color (about 3 minutes).

When the milk is boiling, remove from heat and pour about 1/2 cup (118 ml) into the egg mixture, stirring with the wire whisk to mix well. (This will warm the eggs before the next step.) Pour the egg mixture into the saucepan with the remaining milk and set over very low heat, stirring constantly with the wooden spatula for 1 to 2 minutes or until the mixture has thickened just enough to coat the spatula. When done, remove immediately from heat and pour through the fine-mesh sieve into a clean bowl. Let cool at room temperature in a cool place and then set it into the refrigerator, covered with plastic wrap, where it will keep well for three or four days.

Crème Pâtissière
Pastry Cream

For those of us who fondly remember the desserts of our childhood, a proffered bowl filled with this thick, flavored custard would be accepted instantly. For an adult memory, prepare the Coconut Cream Cake, Strawberry Tart, or Crêpes Parisienne or Noisette, each of which includes pastry cream.

Yields about 6 cups (1425 ml)

5 eggs
1/2 cup (100 g) sugar plus 2 tablespoons
1/4 cup (60 ml) plus 1 tablespoon cornstarch
2 cups (475 ml) milk
2 cups (475 ml) half-and-half
2 teaspoons vanilla extract
10X powdered sugar in a shaker

Recommended equipment

An electric mixer with mixing bowl, rubber spatula, 3-quart (3 L) saucepan, wooden spoon, wire whisk, fine-mesh sieve, small mixing bowl.

In the bowl of the electric mixer, beat three of the eggs and the sugar at medium speed until the sugar is dissolved. Scrape down the sides of the bowl with the rubber spatula, add the cornstarch, beat at medium speed for 2 minutes, scrape down the bowl, add the remaining two eggs, and beat for 1 minute.

Combine the milk and half-and-half in the saucepan, set over medium heat, and bring to a boil, stirring from time to time with the wooden spoon to prevent scorching. When the milk is boiling, pour about 1/2 cup (118 ml) into the egg mixture, stirring with the wire whisk, then pour it back into the saucepan with the remaining milk stirring constantly, and bring to a boil. Let boil for about 2 minutes, stirring to prevent sticking and scorching. Remove from heat, pour through the sieve into mixing bowl, stir in the vanilla extract, and let cool. Sprinkle top with some powdered sugar to prevent a crust from forming. When the custard is cool, cover it with plastic wrap and set it into the refrigerator, where it will keep for two days.

Butter Cream

Whenever our guests request a special cake for an anniversary or a birthday, the frosting will be some variation on the butter cream theme. Having enjoyed this once, you will be twice as eager to plan an occasion worthy of the Gâteau Princess Marie or the Rum or Swiss Kirsch Torte.

Yields about 3 cups (710 ml), enough for one 10-inch cake

5 egg whites
3/4 cup (145 g) sugar
1 teaspoon vanilla extract
1 cup (225 g) butter, at room temperature

Recommended equipment

A double boiler, wire whisk, rubber spatula, electric mixer with mixing bowl.

Combine the egg whites, sugar, and vanilla in the top of the double boiler. Bring the water in the bottom of the double boiler to a steady simmer, set the top part over it, and stir egg mixture with the whisk until the mixture is very hot to the touch (130F or 56C) and the sugar is dissolved. Scrape the mixture into the bowl of the electric mixer and beat at medium speed until thick (about 5 minutes). Then add the butter, one piece at a time, scraping the sides and bottom of the bowl from time to time with the rubber spatula. Mix well until smooth and fluffy (this may take 15 to 20 minutes). Store in the refrigerator, well covered, until ready to use. Will keep well for one week.

Sauce Sabayon

This lovely sauce stands alone when served by itself in a chilled Champagne glass or as a refined accompaniment for the Mousse au Chocolat Glacé. Another gift from Catherine de' Medici to the French, this frothy wine sauce comes from Italy, where the wine used is Marsala and the name is zabaglione.

Yields 3 to 4 servings

3 egg yolks
3 tablespoons sugar
1/2 cup (118 ml) dry white wine
Zest of one orange

Recommended equipment

A hand mixer or wire whisk, double boiler, box grater.

Combine the egg yolks, sugar, and wine in the top part of the double boiler and mix thoroughly with the hand mixer or the wire whisk. Bring the water in the bottom of the double boiler to a steady simmer, set the top part over it, and continue to beat the mixture constantly until it is hot to the touch or has doubled in volume and forms soft mounds. Remove from heat and continue stirring to help the mixture cool.

Using the fine side of the box grater, remove the zest from the orange, being careful to leave all bitter white behind. Stir zest into the sauce before it cools completely. When cool, pour into chilled dessert dishes to serve right away or refrigerate, covered, until ready to serve as an accompanying sauce for another dessert.

You may add other flavors in place of the orange zest. Before the mixture is completely cool, whisk in a tablespoon (or more) of Triple Sec, kirsch, eau de framboise, or Grand Marnier. Delicious!

Sugar Syrup

This basic syrup can be mixed with a tablespoon or two of framboise, kirsch, Triple Sec, or other liqueur and brushed onto a cake for a delicious flavor.

Yields slightly less than 2 cups (475 ml)

2 cups (390 g) sugar
1 cup (235 ml) water
1 1/2 teaspoons white corn syrup

Recommended equipment

A 1 1/2-quart (1 1/2 L) saucepan, wooden spoon, candy thermometer.

Combine the sugar, water, and corn syrup in the saucepan and set over medium heat. Stir with the wooden spoon until the sugar is dissolved, then raise heat and let boil undisturbed for 5 to 10 minutes or until the candy thermometer registers about 220F (104C).

When done, pour into a storage container (the syrup will continue cooking if left in the pan) and let cool uncovered. This syrup may be used immediately, plain or flavored with liqueur (stirred in as the syrup cools), or it will keep for about two weeks if stored covered in the refrigerator.

Succès

"Success," said Fernand Point, "is the sum of a lot of small things correctly done." In this instance, the "small things" are génoise, sugar syrup, butter cream, and this crunchy succès meringue which form the Rum Torte and Swiss Kirsch Torte. The cooked meringue is made of egg whites, sugar, and ground almonds. The name "succès" apparently comes from using the cooked meringue disk, called a *fond, for foundation or layer in a cake called Le Succès. The meringues are sometimes called* succès japonais *after the British custom of calling a meringue and nut layer cake* gâteau japonais.

By whatever name, you will enjoy success after preparing the meringue and serving it as one of the "small things" in a torte.

Yields two 10-inch (25 cm) rounds

1/3 cup (65 g) sugar
1 cup (235 ml) finely ground blanched almonds
1 1/2 teaspoons flour
4 egg whites, at room temperature
1/2 cup (100 g) sugar

Recommended equipment

A sifter, small mixing bowl, electric mixer with mixing bowl, rubber spatula, two baking sheets, aluminum foil, pastry bag with plain number 4 tube, two wire cooling racks.

Sift together the 1/3 cup sugar, ground almonds, and flour into the small mixing bowl. Set aside.

Preheat oven to 325F (163C).

In the bowl of the electric mixer, beat the egg whites on low until they are frothy, then turn mixer to medium speed and beat until soft peaks have formed. (If egg whites are cold when you begin—and it is easier to separate an egg without breaking the yolk when it is chilled—warm the bottom of the mixing bowl by setting it into hot water before you begin beating the whites. Egg whites at room temperature mount more rapidly and completely than cold ones.) Then gradually sprinkle on the 1/2 cup sugar, little by little, and beat until the sugar has dissolved and the whites are stiff, smooth, and glossy. Remove bowl from mixer and, using the rubber spatula, delicately fold in the sifted almond mixture.

Cover each baking sheet with aluminum foil and mark out a 10-inch (25 cm) circle (use a pencil) on each one. Insert the plain tube into the pastry bag and fill the bag about two-thirds full with the meringue. (If you do not have a pastry bag, divide the meringue between the baking sheets and spread it evenly with the rubber spatula to a depth of 1/4 inch or 2/3 cm.) Fold over the top of the bag and, beginning at the center of a circle, fill it in solidly. When both circles are complete, smooth the top lightly with the spatula, set the baking sheets onto racks into the lower middle and upper middle positions of the oven, and bake for 45 minutes to an hour. When done, the meringues will be a pale brown and should lift easily from the foil. To remove the meringue from the foil, lift the foil (the edges cool quickly) off the baking sheet and turn it upside down over a wire rack so that the meringue is on the rack. Peel the foil from the back of the meringue and let it cool on the rack before storing in an airtight container, where it will keep for about a week. The meringues are pliable while still warm and they will break easily when cool. If one cracks, do not despair; fit it back together when you layer the meringues in the cake. The pieces will be held together by the butter cream.

❧

To grind blanched almonds, put them through a nut grinder or whir by small batches in an electric blender (be careful not to blend so long that the almonds become oily and sticky).

Crêpes Sucrées
Dessert Crêpes

For those of you who must begin your day with griddle or buckwheat cakes, try ending your day with dessert crêpes. These very thin pancakes are versatile and satisfying—any fruit or cream filling pairs well with the lightly sweetened cake. Cook the crêpes ahead of time, have the filling ready, and you will be prepared for dessert at a moment's notice. If you have a cast aluminum omelette pan, you will find it to be perfect for cooking crêpes.

Yields about 16 crêpes

8 tablespoons (115 g) butter, melted
1 cup (120 g) flour
2 tablespoons sugar
A pinch of salt
2 eggs
1 cup (235 ml) milk
1 teaspoon vanilla extract
Peanut oil

Recommended equipment

A small saucepan for melting butter, two 1-quart (1 L) bowls, wire whisk, large fine-mesh sieve, 6-inch (15 cm) sauté pan or omelette pan, flat turning spatula, waxed paper.

Set the butter to melt in the saucepan over low heat.

Combine the flour, sugar, and salt in one mixing bowl. Gradually stir in the eggs, mixing with the whisk, and then stir in the milk, adding it slowly, and whisking continuously. Pass the mixture through the sieve into the other bowl and whisk in the melted butter and the vanilla extract. Set the bowl into the refrigerator to chill the mixture for at least 30 minutes before using (it can wait as long as 2 hours).

When ready to make the crêpes, set the sauté pan over medium high heat, pour in about 1 tablespoon oil, and, as the pan heats, swirl the oil around to completely cover the bottom. If there is any excess oil, pour it out before adding the batter. When the pan is very hot and the oil sizzling, pour about 1/4 cup (60 ml) batter into the pan, and tilt it in every direction to spread the batter evenly and completely over the bottom. (Pour any excess batter back into the bowl.) In about 1 minute the first side of the crêpe should be nicely browned and you can turn the crêpe over to cook the second side for about 30 seconds. The first crêpe is really a test for the thickness of the batter and the heat of the pan. If the batter did not run easily around the pan, add a teaspoon of water, and cook another crêpe. The crêpe should be very thin. The first side is always the more nicely browned and therefore should be the "public" side. Continue making crêpes until the batter is gone, and, as they are done, stack them on a plate. When cool, cover them with waxed paper (or a damp towel) and let them wait at room temperature (or in the refrigerator if you have made them well in advance).

❧

Omit the sugar to make crêpes for nonsweet dishes, such as Coulibiac de Saumon à la Russe. If you refrigerate the crêpes, bring them back to room temperature before separating them.

Crêpes Parisienne

The simplicity of this preparation belies the sophistication of its presentation, which is worthy of the appellation "Parisienne."

Yields 1 serving

FOR EACH SERVING
1 Crêpe Sucrée *(see page 520)*
1 tablespoon Crème Pâtissière *(see page 516)*
1 teaspoon Grand Marnier
2 to 3 strawberries
1/2 teaspoon butter
1/2 teaspoon sugar
Butter for the baking dish

FOR THE GARNISH
1 strawberry
10X powdered sugar in a shaker

Recommended equipment

A 1-quart (1 L) bowl, wire whisk, paring knife, baking dish large enough to hold crêpes in a single layer.

Prepare the crêpes sucrées and crème pâtissière and reserve.

Preheat oven to 350F (177C).

In the mixing bowl, combine the crème pâtissière and the Grand Marnier to taste. Rinse and hull the strawberries and slice them lengthwise. Spread each crêpe with crème pâtissière, arrange the sliced strawberries on top, roll up the crêpes jelly-roll fashion, and set them in the buttered baking dish. Dot the crêpes with butter, sprinkle with sugar, and bake for 5 to 10 minutes until heated through.

When hot, garnish each crêpe with a whole strawberry, dust with powdered sugar, and serve at once.

Crêpes Noisette

Hazelnuts are as ubiquitous in European cuisine as the bushes they grow on are throughout the countryside. Cultivated hazelnuts come from a variety of the common hazel tree known as a filbert tree because the nuts ripen around 22 August, which is Saint Philbert's day. When shopping for noisettes, buy hazelnuts or filberts. Here, their subtle flavor suffuses the filling and the sauce for a delectable chilled dessert.

Yields 1 serving

FOR EACH SERVING
1 Crêpe Sucrée *(see page 520)*
1 tablespoon Crème Pâtissière *(see page 516)*
1/2 teaspoon hazelnut paste
2 tablespoons Hazelnut Sauce *(see below)*

FOR HAZELNUT SAUCE
2 cups (475 ml) Crème Anglaise *(see page 516)*
1 teaspoon hazelnut paste

Recommended equipment

A 1-quart (1 L) bowl, wire whisk.

Prepare the crêpes sucrées and reserve.

Prepare the crème pâtissière and combine it with the hazelnut paste to taste. Mix well with the whisk, spread the cream mixture evenly on the crêpes, roll them up jelly-roll fashion, and set them into the refrigerator while you prepare the hazelnut sauce.

To make the sauce, combine the crème anglaise and the hazelnut paste in a bowl and mix well with a whisk. Keep the sauce chilled until serving time.

When ready to serve, set the crêpes on a serving plate, pour some sauce over them, and pass any leftover sauce separately.

Cakes

Marie Antoinette notwithstanding, a lovely cake is everyone's favorite dessert. Having first mastered génoise, you will have a basic up your sleeve for preparing a simple cake at a moment's notice, or, with advance planning, the foundation for the more elaborate cakes flavored with chocolate, coconut, raspberry, or chestnut purée which come later in the section.

A trio of picnic and bake sale favorites follows, led by the Homestead Pound Cake, whose elegant simplicity can stand alone or be enhanced by homemade ice cream, fresh fruit, or a sweet sauce. Next comes a fruit and nut cake based on apple sauce, and last is a dark composition redolent with complex spices and covered with a piquant frosting. Moving down the pastry table, the focus narrows a bit as we enter the chocolate lover's realm. Easing us into this category is a milk chocolate version of the New York standby, cheesecake, followed by a Swiss rolled confection which combines the light texture of chocolate sponge cake with whipped cream and a hazelnut-flavored sauce. Dark chocolate lovers have their day as well with a Homestead version of an American specialty featuring a dark chocolate with coconut and pecan frosting, followed by a traditional Black Forest cherry and chocolate preparation second in fame only to the cuckoo clocks of the same region.

Six preparations, each based on mastering one or more of the basic techniques, lead you to the end of the cake collection and your postgraduate degree. First, génoise goes exotic when it encounters coconut and then acquires a southern accent under a delectable blanket of Bourbon, pecans, and raisins. And now the final four. Since I am Swiss, you know which one I am partial to, but each of these deserves first place. France is seeded number one and two, with a stunning raspberry fantasy, followed by a chestnut and chocolate creation which is truly fit for royalty. Number three, flavored with rum, would make a sailor in Her Majesty's Navy smile, and I will say, in all immodesty, that the best, a torte flavored with Swiss kirsch, is last.

 ## *Génoise à la Vanille*
Whole-egg Cake

The repertoire of a successful pastry cook must include the fundamental génoise. Any child or adult would appreciate this cake served simply with a luscious Butter Cream frosting. But combine it with other ingredients for Gâteau Chambord, Schwarzwald Kuchen, or Gâteau Princess Marie, and you will serve a memorable finish for a special dinner.

Yields 16 servings

4 eggs, at room temperature
1/2 cup (100 g) sugar
1/2 teaspoon vanilla extract
4 tablespoons (60 g) butter, melted
1 1/4 cups (175 g) flour
Butter and flour for the pan

Recommended equipment

A 10-inch (25 cm) cake pan, electric mixer with mixing bowl, small saucepan, sifter, rubber spatula, wire cooling rack.

Preheat oven to 400F (204C).

Butter and flour the cake pan.

In the bowl of the electric mixer, combine the eggs, sugar, and vanilla and beat at medium speed until the mixture triples in volume (about 10 minutes).

In the meantime, melt the butter over low heat and set aside until needed (it must be warm, not hot). Measure and then sift the flour. When the egg and sugar mixture has tripled in volume, alternately fold in the flour and tepid melted butter. Begin with the flour and sprinkle a handful of it over the batter, gently fold it in, add 2 tablespoons butter, fold it in, sprinkle on more flour, and fold the ingredients together. Continue until the flour and butter are folded in. Then pour batter into the prepared pan and bake for about 20 minutes in the middle level of the oven. When done, the cake will pull away from the sides of the pan and spring back when lightly touched. Turn it out of the pan onto the wire rack to cool.

Variation

Génoise au Chocolat
Chocolate Cake

Follow the same technique as described above, but use 1 cup (120 g) of flour sifted with 2 tablespoons of cocoa powder.

Pound Cake

This moist, rich cake is perfect when paired with a scoop of ice cream or sorbet, or served with a fresh fruit sauce. A simple cake, it continues to be one of our most requested desserts and is always waiting to be discovered in our picnic boxes by a hungry guest returning home after a visit to the Homestead. Some of our regular visitors have even been known to ask a sympathetic waiter to supplement their pound cake with a serving of that evening's Homestead-made ice cream—thus getting two *desserts at one time!*

Yields 8 to 10 servings

12 tablespoons (170 g) butter, softened at room temperature
1 cup (195 g) sugar
5 eggs, at room temperature
1/2 teaspoon vanilla extract
Grated rind from 1/2 lemon
1 1/2 cups (180 g) flour
1/2 teaspoon baking powder
Butter and flour for the pan

Recommended equipment

A 3-cup (3/4 L) loaf pan, electric mixer with mixing bowl, rubber spatula, box grater, sifter, wire cooling rack.

Butter and flour the loaf pan.

Preheat oven to 350F (177C).

In the bowl of the electric mixer, cream the butter and sugar thoroughly until the mixture is light in color and the sugar has dissolved. Scrape down the sides of the bowl with the spatula and add the eggs gradually, one by one, beating completely and scraping the sides and bottom of the bowl after each addition.

Add the vanilla and then the lemon rind which

can be grated directly into the bowl, using the box grater (be careful to leave the bitter white behind). Mix a moment on low speed. Sift the flour and baking powder together and add gradually to the mixing bowl, mixing on low speed for about 1 minute or until well mixed. Pour into the loaf pan and bake in the middle level of the oven for 50 to 60 minutes or until a cake tester put into the center of the cake comes out clean and the top has browned. When done, turn out of the pan onto the rack to cool. This cake, wrapped airtight, will keep for two to three days under refrigeration.

❧ Double Apple Sauce Cake

A moist cake, best when warmed slightly and deserving of a pool of Crème Anglaise or a generous scoop of Vanilla Ice Cream.

Yields 16 servings

8 tablespoons (115 g) butter
1 cup (195 g) sugar
1 teaspoon vanilla extract
1 egg
2 cups (240 g) plus 2 tablespoons flour
3/4 teaspoon baking soda
1/4 teaspoon allspice
1/2 teaspoon cinnamon
1/4 teaspoon freshly ground nutmeg
1 1/3 cups (315 ml) raisins
1 cup (235 ml) chopped walnuts
1/2 cup (118 ml) crushed pineapple
3/4 cup (180 ml) chopped glacéed cherries
1 cup (235 ml) apple sauce
Butter and flour for the pan

Recommended equipment

A 10-inch (25 cm) cake pan, electric mixer with mixing bowl, rubber spatula, sifter, 1-quart (1 L) bowl, wire cooling rack.

Butter and flour the cake pan and set aside.
 Preheat oven to 350F (177C).
 In the bowl of the electric mixer, cream the butter until light and fluffy, add the sugar gradually, and beat until the sugar is dissolved and the mixture is light in color. Scrape down the sides of the bowl with the spatula, add the vanilla, and blend well. Scrape down the bowl again, add the egg, and mix on medium speed until completely combined. Sift the flour together with the baking soda, allspice, cinnamon, and nutmeg, and stir the mixture into the batter. Add the raisins, walnuts, pineapple, cherries, and apple sauce. Stir the mixture until well blended, pour it into the pan, and set the pan on a rack in the middle level of the oven to bake. Bake the cake for about 45 minutes or until it has pulled slightly away from the sides of the pan and a cake tester comes out clean when put into the center of the cake.
 When done, remove cake from oven and turn it out of the pan onto a rack to cool.

Old-fashioned Spice Cake

Sometimes savoring the aroma of a baking cake is almost as satisfying as eating it. This one is a good case in point, especially during the winter months when the kitchen windows are snugly shut against the chill and the promising smells of cooking fruit and spices will simply not leave a hungry body alone. To really keep the cold winds from blowing around the cabin door, you might think about offering hot mulled cider or hot buttered rum as we do at Sam Snead's Tavern.

Yields 16 servings

FOR THE CAKE

7/8 cup (105 g) flour
1/3 teaspoon baking powder
1/4 teaspoon baking soda
1/4 teaspoon ground cinnamon
1/8 teaspoon ground ginger
1/8 teaspoon ground clove
A pinch of freshly ground nutmeg
A pinch of salt
4 tablespoons (60 g) butter
1/2 cup (100 g) dark brown sugar
1/3 cup (65 g) sugar
1 egg yolk
2 eggs
1/4 cup (60 ml) plus 1 tablespoon buttermilk
2 2/3 tablespoons chopped raisins
2 1/2 teaspoons chopped orange peel
Butter and flour for the pans

FOR THE FROSTING

11 tablespoons (165 g) butter
3 cups (340 g) 10X powdered sugar
1/4 cup (50 g) sugar
1/3 cup (80 ml) milk
1/3 cup (80 ml) orange peel
1 cup (235 ml) raisins

Recommended equipment

Two 10-inch (25 cm) cake pans, sifter, 1-quart (1 L) bowl, electric mixer with mixing bowl, rubber spatula, small chef's knife, 2-quart (2 L) bowl, two wire cooling racks, small saucepan, icing spatula.

Butter and flour the cake pans and set aside.

Preheat oven to 350F (177C).

Sift the flour with the baking powder, soda, cinnamon, ginger, clove, nutmeg, and salt into the 1-quart bowl and reserve.

In the bowl of the electric mixer, cream the butter until light and fluffy, add the brown sugar and sugar, and beat until the sugar is dissolved and the mixture is fluffy. Scrape down the sides of the bowl with the spatula, add the egg yolk and eggs, and mix thoroughly. Scrape down the bowl again, add the reserved flour mixture, and blend well. Scrape down the bowl, add 2 tablespoons buttermilk, mix well, and reserve.

Chop the raisins and orange peel separately with the chef's knife. Add them to the mixture and blend. Add the remaining buttermilk, mix to combine thoroughly, and then divide the batter evenly between the two pans.

Set the pans into the lower middle and upper middle levels of the oven to bake for about 20 minutes or until the cake springs back when touched lightly in the center. When done, remove pans from oven and turn the cakes out of the pans onto the racks to cool.

While the cakes are cooling, prepare the frosting. In the bowl of the electric mixer, cream the butter until light and fluffy. Add the powdered sugar and sugar gradually and mix until well blended. Heat the milk in the small saucepan until it feels warm to your finger. While the milk is heating, mince the orange peel and reserve. When the milk is ready, add it little by little to the butter and sugar while mixing on low speed, and, when the frosting is perfectly smooth, add the raisins and orange peel, blend thoroughly, and reserve until the cake layers are cool.

When the cake layers are cool, set one on a serving plate, cover with one-half of the frosting, top with the second layer, and spread the remaining frosting evenly over the top and sides of the cake. Refrigerate for at least an hour and keep chilled until half an hour before serving.

When baking two pans at one time, set them on the racks on the diagonal (i.e., not one directly above the other) to ensure even baking.

Milk Chocolate Cheesecake

For some of us, dessert does not count unless it is chocolate, and here is a choice cheesecake which is delectable for milk chocolate devotees. If you want a more intense chocolate flavor, use bittersweet chocolate, but above all, use the best baking chocolate you can afford, preferably Swiss or French.

Yields 18 servings

5 tablespoons (75 g) butter
2 cups (475 ml) graham cracker crumbs
30 ounces (840 g) milk chocolate
8 tablespoons (115 g) butter
2 pounds (900 g) cream cheese, softened at room temperature
1/2 cup (60 g) 10X powdered sugar
6 eggs
1 cup (235 ml) sour cream
1/2 cup (118 ml) coffee mint liqueur
Butter for the pan

Recommended equipment

A 10-inch (25 cm) springform pan, 1-quart (1 L) mixing bowl, double boiler, small pan for melting butter, electric mixer with mixing bowl, rubber spatula, small mixing bowl, wire whisk or hand mixer, cooling rack.

Butter the springform pan.

Melt the 5 tablespoons of butter in the small saucepan. Prepare the graham cracker crumbs. (An easy way to do this is to put the crackers into a plastic bag, fold the top over tightly, place bag on your work surface, and roll over it firmly and slowly with a rolling pin.) Put the crumbs in the 1-quart mixing bowl and stir in the melted butter so that it binds the crumbs without soaking them. Press the crumb mixture in a layer onto the bottom of the pan and smooth it out so it has an even thickness.

Preheat oven to 350F (177C).

Break the chocolate into pieces, put them into the top half of the double boiler, and set it over simmering water to melt the chocolate. When melted, remove from heat and reserve.

Melt the 8 tablespoons of butter in the small saucepan.

In the bowl of the electric mixer combine the cream cheese and powdered sugar and mix at medium speed until the sugar is dissolved. Then add the eggs one at a time, mixing well after each addition and scraping the sides and bottom of the bowl with the rubber spatula. The mixture must be very smooth and free of lumps. When done, set aside.

Stirring with the wire whisk, combine the sour cream and the mint coffee liqueur in the small mixing bowl. (If you need the hand mixer, begin with that.) Add the melted butter, mixing thoroughly and scraping down the bowl with the rubber spatula. Next, pour in the melted chocolate and mix until very smooth.

When it is smooth and free of lumps, combine

the chocolate mixture with the cream cheese in the bowl of the electric mixer. Beat at medium speed until light and perfectly smooth.

Pour into the prepared pan and bake for 45 minutes to 1 hour in the middle level of the preheated oven. The top of the cake should have a light caramel color when done. Let cool in the pan on a rack, then remove from pan and place on a serving plate. Chill for several hours before serving. This will keep for two to three days under refrigeration.

Swiss Chocolate Roulade

In 1875, Daniel Peter produced the first milk chocolate in Switzerland, and four years later another canny Swiss had put into production a method for mixing and kneading chocolate called "conching" (after the shell-shaped machine first used). With this beginning the Swiss have always been a step ahead—today, they are the champion chocolate eaters, annually consuming twenty-two pounds per person. If you cannot beat us, join us, by preparing the chocolate roulade soon and enjoying it often.

Yields 8 to 10 servings

FOR THE CAKE
4 egg whites, at room temperature
1/2 cup (100 g) sugar
3 ounces (85 g) sweet chocolate
1/3 cup (40 g) flour

1 recipe Hazelnut Sauce (see page 521)

FOR SERVING
Sugar for unmolding
1 cup (235 ml) whipping cream
1 cup (235 ml) raspberry jam

Recommended equipment

An electric mixer with mixing bowl, small saucepan for melting chocolate, rubber spatula, sheet pan 15 x 10 x 3/4 inches (37 1/2 x 25 x 2 cm), parchment or waxed paper, pastry bag with plain number 5 tube, wire cooling rack, 1-quart (1 L) bowl, wire whisk.

In the bowl of the electric mixer, beat the egg whites on low until they are frothy, then turn mixer to medium speed and beat until soft peaks have formed. (If egg whites are cold when you begin—and it is easier to separate an egg without breaking the yolk when it is chilled—warm the bottom of the mixing bowl by setting it into hot water before you begin beating the whites. Egg whites at room temperature mount more rapidly and completely than cold ones.) Then, gradually sprinkle on the sugar, little by little, and beat until the sugar has dissolved and the whites are stiff, smooth, and glossy.

Meanwhile, break the chocolate into pieces, set them in the small saucepan over low heat, and let them melt. Watch the chocolate carefully and remove it from heat as soon as it is completely melted and smooth.

Preheat oven to 400F (204C).

When the egg whites are stiff, sprinkle on the flour, add the melted chocolate, and, using the rubber spatula, fold them both into the egg whites.

Line the sheet pan with parchment or waxed paper.

Fit the pastry bag with the plain tube and scoop the egg white mixture into it, using the rubber spatula. Pipe the mixture onto the sheet pan going down the length of the pan and filling it from side to side. (You may also spread the mixture evenly and gently in the pan using a rubber spatula.) When the pan is full, set it into the middle level of the oven to bake for about 5 minutes. Watch it carefully. The top should be crusted over and the mixture should pull slightly away from the sides of the pan.

When done, remove pan from oven and set it on the rack to cool. When cooled to room temperature, cover the cake with plastic wrap, and set the sheet pan into the refrigerator to chill the cake.

While the cake is chilling, prepare the hazelnut sauce and chill.

When ready to finish the cake, remove pan from the refrigerator. Spread a piece of waxed paper, as long as the pan, on your work surface and sprinkle sugar in a thin layer all over it (this will prevent the cake from sticking to the paper). Unmold the cake onto the waxed paper. Discard the baking paper.

With the electric mixer, beat the whipping cream in the bowl until stiff.

Spread a thin coat of raspberry jam over the cake and then a coating of whipped cream. Roll the cake up, jelly-roll fashion, beginning at the long side, and using the paper as a guide. Cover the cake with plastic wrap and set it into the refrigerator to chill until serving time. When ready to serve the cake, cut it into slices, set them on a plate, and spoon some hazelnut sauce around each one.

❧ German Chocolate Cake

In 1780, Dr. James Baker founded the first chocolate factory in the United States, and, in 1851, one S. German developed a process for producing a dark chocolate that was richer and sweeter than that previously available. For quite some time now the General Foods Corporation has made Baker's German's Sweet Chocolate, and included among the recipes inside the wrapper is one for German Sweet Chocolate Cake with Coconut Pecan Frosting. But our recipe has another history. When former Homestead President Thomas J. Lennon came from Washington in 1952, he brought a particular fondness for this cake, which he remembered from the Restaurant Paul Young, located across from the Mayflower Hotel. The recipe belongs to Paul Young's mother, who was kind enough to share it with Resident Manager Clifford Nelson so that we could introduce it when the Grille opened in 1965. It has been a favorite ever since. Where the recipe originated is uncertain, but references prior to the 1940s are hard to locate—as they say, its beginnings are shrouded by the swirling mists of history.

Yields 16 servings

FOR THE CAKE
5 ounces (145 g) bitter chocolate
1 cup (235 ml) warm water
2 cups (240 g) plus 1 tablespoon flour
1 teaspoon baking soda
1/6 teaspoon salt
1 cup (225 g) butter, softened at room temperature
2 cups (390 g) sugar
4 egg yolks
1 cup (235 ml) buttermilk
4 egg whites, at room temperature
A few drops red food coloring
Butter and flour for the cake pans

FOR THE FROSTING
2 1/2 cups (390 g) sugar
2 1/4 cups (535 ml) evaporated milk
4 egg yolks
2 3/4 cups (620 g) butter, at room temperature
1 tablespoon vanilla extract
3 cups (710 ml) pecan pieces
3 cups (710 ml) shredded coconut

Recommended equipment

Two 10-inch (25 cm) cake pans, double boiler, sifter, medium mixing bowl, electric mixer with mixing bowl, rubber spatula, small mixing bowl, hand mixer, two wire cooling racks, 2-quart (2 L) saucepan, wire whisk, blender or nut grinder, rectangular cake pan.

Butter and flour the cake pans and set aside.

Break the chocolate into chunks and put them into the top part of the double boiler with the warm water. Set the double boiler over medium heat, bring the water in the bottom to a gentle simmer, and let the chocolate melt.

Sift the flour, baking soda, and salt together twice and then set aside.

Preheat oven to 350F (177C).

Cut the butter into chunks, put them into the bowl of the electric mixer, and beat until the butter is pale yellow in color and creamy. Add the sugar

1/2 cup (118 ml) at a time to the butter, mixing thoroughly after each addition and scraping down the sides of the bowl with the rubber spatula. Then cream the butter and sugar together until the sugar has dissolved and the mixture is smooth. Scrape the sides of the bowl down and add the egg yolks one at a time, mixing completely and scraping the sides and bottom of the bowl after each addition. Add the melted chocolate while mixing at a low speed and scraping the sides and bottom of the bowl. Continue mixing at low speed while you add the flour mixture and blend it in thoroughly. Slowly add the buttermilk while mixing at a low speed and scrape down the sides and bottom of the bowl. When mixed, turn off mixer and set the bowl aside.

Whip the egg whites in the small mixing bowl with the hand mixer until stiff. Fold in a few drops of red food coloring until the whites are light pink in color and then fold the whites into the chocolate mixture until they are thoroughly mixed. Divide the batter between the cake pans and set them on a rack in the middle of the oven. Bake for 35 minutes or until the cake has pulled away slightly from the edge of the pan and springs back when touched lightly in the center. When done, let the cake cool in the pans on a rack for 5 minutes, then remove from the pans and leave the cake on the racks until completely cool.

While the cake is baking, prepare the frosting. Put the sugar, evaporated milk, and egg yolks into the saucepan over medium high heat and stir constantly while bringing the mixture to a boil. Cook for 2 to 3 minutes and then remove saucepan from heat. Break the butter into small pieces, add it to the saucepan while mixing with the whisk, and then whisk in the vanilla. Grind the pecans in a blender or nut grinder so that they are the consistency of cornmeal and stir them into the frosting with the rubber spatula. Add the shredded coconut and mix until well blended. Then pour the mixture into the rectangular pan, spread it out with the spatula, and refrigerate it for about 2 hours or until the frosting can be easily spread over the cake.

When the cake is cool and the frosting ready, set one layer of the cake on a serving plate, spread some frosting on top, add the other layer, and frost the top and sides of the cake. Keep refrigerated until half an hour before serving.

Schwarzwald Kuchen
Black Forest Cake

*Along the Black Forest Crest Road (*Hochstrasse*) between the small, dark lake called Mummelsee and the village of Ruhestein, you can follow a route that circles the upper reaches of the Seebach Valley. From this vantage point, when the cherry trees are blooming, the valley is especially lovely. An area of dark and mysterious spruce forests where cherry trees thrive, the region is home to such culinary specialties as ham (*Schwarzwaldschinken*) and the cherry liqueur, kirsch. Often served very cold in small glasses at the end of a meal (like aquavit), kirsch also has a particular ability to enhance the flavor of fresh fruit as well an extraordinary way with chocolate, both of which are celebrated in this luscious cake.*

Yields 16 servings

1 recipe Génoise au Chocolat *(see page 524)*
1 recipe Génoise à la Vanille *(see page 523)*
1 can dark sweet cherries, weighing 1 1/2 pounds (675 g)
1/2 cup (100 g) sugar
1/2 cup (118 ml) cornstarch
1/2 cup (118 ml) kirsch
1 cup (235 ml) Sugar Syrup *(see page 518)*
4 cups (950 ml) whipping cream
1/2 cup (60 g) 10X powdered sugar
2 teaspoons vanilla extract
6 ounces (170 g) sweet dark chocolate
Grated chocolate

Recommended equipment

A large sieve, medium mixing bowl, 1 1/2-quart (1 1/2 L) saucepan, wooden spatula, small bowl, serrated slicing knife, 1-quart (1 L) bowl, pastry brush, electric mixer with mixing bowl, small saucepan for melting chocolate, wire whisk, rubber spatula, box grater.

Prepare the génoise au chocolat and génoise à la vanille and let cool completely.

Drain the cherries, using the sieve set over the mixing bowl. Reserve 1/2 cup (118 ml) of the cherry juice and put 2 cups (475 ml) into the saucepan with the sugar, set over medium heat, and bring to a boil, stirring from time to time to prevent scorching. Meanwhile, mix the reserved juice in the small bowl with the cornstarch and stir until completely dissolved. When the juice and sugar have come to the boil, add the cornstarch, boil for 1 minute, and remove from heat. Add the cherries and 2 teaspoons of kirsch, stirring gently with the wooden spatula to keep the cherries whole, and set aside.

Slice the chocolate génoise into two slices, one about 1/2 inch (1 1/4 cm) and the other 1/4 inch (2/3 cm) thick. Slice the vanilla génoise so that you have two slices 1/4 inch (2/3 cm) thick.

Prepare the sugar syrup.

Using the 1-quart bowl, combine the syrup and the remaining kirsch. Set the 1/2-inch thick chocolate génoise layer on a serving plate and sprinkle with some of the syrup. Spread the cherry mixture evenly over the bottom layer and place the second chocolate layer on the cherries. Brush this layer thoroughly with the syrup, letting it soak in.

Beat the cream with the powdered sugar and vanilla on medium speed until stiff. Spread about one-quarter of the whipped cream evenly onto the second chocolate layer, add one of the white layers, and brush thoroughly with the syrup.

Melt the chocolate in the small saucepan over low heat and, when melted, stir it together with about one-quarter of the whipped cream. Mix thoroughly, first with the whisk and then the rubber spatula. Spread the chocolate whipped cream evenly over the white cake layer, add the last white layer, and brush the remaining syrup thoroughly over it.

Cover the whole cake with the remaining whipped cream and sprinkle with grated chocolate. Refrigerate 2 to 3 hours before serving.

Coconut Cream Cake

It is tempting to label this recipe "for residents of tropical shores only" because fresh coconut really is the flavor secret. Even though coconuts are now available in many markets, it may have been a long time since they saw the tree, and you should inquire before making a purchase. Having mastered the recipes for Crème Pâtissière and Génoise à la Vanille, you are now ready to combine them with the meringue blanket which insulates the cake layers while the coconut flakes are toasting.

Yields 16 servings

1 recipe Génoise à la Vanille (see page 523)
1 recipe Crème Pâtissière (see page 516)
6 cups (1425 ml) shredded coconut
12 egg whites, at room temperature
2 cups (390 g) sugar

Recommended equipment

A serrated slicing knife, heatproof serving plate, small mixing bowl, wooden spatula, icing spatula, wire whisk, hand mixer, rubber spatula.

Prepare the génoise and crème pâtissière.

Using the serrated knife, cut the génoise into three even layers and put the bottom one on the heatproof serving plate.

In the mixing bowl, combine the crème pâtissière and 3 cups (710 ml) of shredded coconut, stirring thoroughly with the wooden spatula. Spread half of this mixture on the bottom génoise layer, evening it out with the icing spatula. Add the second génoise layer and spread evenly with the remaining coconut cream. Top with the third génoise layer, pressing gently for a secure fit.

Put water in the bottom of the double boiler, set over medium high heat, and bring to a steady simmer. In the top of the double boiler, combine the egg whites and sugar. Mix from time to time with the whisk while the mixture is heating. When the mixture feels very hot to the touch, remove the top of the double boiler and, using the hand mixer, whip the hot egg whites until they form a stiff, glossy, satin-white meringue.

Preheat oven to 350F (177C).

Using the rubber spatula, mask the whole cake with the meringue. Then cover the cake generously, top and sides, with the remaining shredded coconut. Set the cake into the middle level of the oven until lightly browned (about 5 to 10 minutes). Remove from oven and reserve in the refrigerator until one-half hour before serving time.

To obtain shredded fresh coconut, cut it into chunks and grate it by 1/2 cup (118 ml) lots in a blender or food processor.

Bourbon Pecan Cake

A real treat which combines two southern favorites, pecans and Bourbon, this is one instance in which you will be glad to have the doctor make a house call—as long as his name is Jack. For the best flavor, soak the pecans and raisins overnight before you prepare the cake (no sampling allowed—well, maybe one or two raisins). And it never hurts to garnish each slice with a scoop of homemade Vanilla Ice Cream.

Yields 16 servings

FOR THE CAKE
1 1/2 cups (180 g) flour
3/4 cup (180 ml) ground hazelnuts
1/4 teaspoon cinnamon
5 eggs, at room temperature
1 cup (195 g) sugar
1/8 teaspoon salt
1/2 teaspoon vanilla extract
Butter and flour for the pan

FOR THE FROSTING
3/4 cup (180 ml) Bourbon
2/3 cup (160 ml) raisins
2/3 cup (160 ml) pecan pieces
1 cup (225 g) butter
2 cups (225 g) 10X powdered sugar
1/4 cup (60 ml) milk

Recommended equipment

A 10-inch (25 cm) cake pan, 1-quart (1 L) mixing bowl, sifter, small mixing bowl, electric mixer with mixing bowl, rubber spatula, cooling rack, small saucepan, serrated slicing knife, icing spatula.

Butter and flour the cake pan. Start soaking the pecans and raisins for the frosting now if you have not done so overnight. Combine the Bourbon, raisins, and pecan pieces in the 1-quart mixing bowl, cover, and let macerate.

Sift together the flour, hazelnuts, and cinnamon into the small mixing bowl.

Preheat oven to 375F (190C).

In the bowl of the electric mixer combine the eggs, sugar, salt, and vanilla. Beat at medium speed until the eggs triple in volume (about 10 minutes). Then, using the rubber spatula, gently fold the flour mixture into the beaten eggs.

Pour the batter into the prepared pan and bake for 20 minutes in the middle level of the oven or until the cake springs back when lightly touched (begin checking after 15 minutes). Cool in the pan for 2 minutes, then turn out onto the rack to cool completely.

While the cake is cooling, prepare the frosting. In the bowl of the electric mixer, whip the butter until light in color and then add the powdered sugar 1/4 cup (30 g) at a time, mixing well after each addition and scraping down the sides of the bowl. Beat on medium speed until butter is light and fluffy. Warm the milk in the small saucepan and add little by little to the butter and powdered sugar while mixing on low speed. Then add the Bourbon, pecan, and raisin mixture and mix on low speed for a few seconds. Remove bowl from mixer and finish blending with a rubber spatula.

Using the serrated knife, cut the cooled cake into three even layers. Set the bottom layer on a serving plate and spread one-third of the frosting evenly over the cake. Add the second layer, spread with another third of the frosting, top with the last cake layer, and spread the remaining frosting over the top and around the sides. Refrigerate for 2 hours before serving.

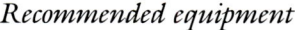 Gâteau Chambord

Construction of the 440-room Château Chambord spanned three monarchies, beginning with François I and ending with Louis XIV. Second in grandeur only to Versailles, this sprawling "country house" has lent its name to many imposing culinary preparations, as it does here. The cake makes a stunning statement in a symphony of red and pink and is an elegant choice for a special occasion or when fresh red raspberries are available. To augment the fruit flavor, brush the cut surfaces of the génoise with framboise as soon as you slice the cake in two.

Yields 16 servings

1 recipe Génoise à la Vanille (see page 523)
2 cups (475 ml) raspberry purée
1 cup (195 g) sugar
Juice of 1/2 lemon
2 cups (475 ml) whipping cream
2 teaspoons vanilla extract
1 2/3 tablespoons unflavored gelatin
1/2 cup (118 ml) unsweetened framboise
1 cup (235 ml) raspberry jelly, melted
2 1/2 ounces (70 g) sliced almonds

Recommended equipment

A 10-inch (25 cm) cake pan, waxed paper, serrated slicing knife, large fine-mesh sieve, electric blender, small mixing bowl, wire whisk, electric mixer with mixing bowl, small saucepan, rubber spatula, baking sheet, pastry brush.

Prepare the génoise and let it cool completely.

Line the cake pan on the bottom and sides with waxed paper, letting the paper on the sides stand up 1 inch (2 1/2 cm) above the pan edge. (Use dots of soft butter or dabs of peanut oil under the paper to help hold the paper in place.) Using the serrated knife, slice the génoise cake in two as evenly as possible. (Brush both halves on the cut sides with additional framboise to add flavor and help maintain moistness.) Set one half into the cake pan, cut side up, and reserve the other, wrapped airtight, in the refrigerator.

Prepare the raspberry purée. If you are using fresh berries, whir them in the blender and then strain out the seeds. If you are using frozen berries, you will need two 10-ounce (285 g) packages. Let them thaw completely, drain off the sugar syrup, and then proceed as with the fresh berries.

Using the small mixing bowl, combine the raspberry purée, sugar, and lemon juice. Mix well with the whisk until the sugar is dissolved and reserve.

Beat the heavy cream and the vanilla with the electric mixer until stiff and refrigerate.

With the whisk, stir the gelatin into the framboise, let it soften, then heat in the small saucepan until the gelatin is dissolved. When completely dissolved, pour the mixture into the raspberry purée. Mix well with the whisk, and then, using the rubber spatula, fold in the whipped cream, reserving about 3/4 cup (180 ml) to mask the sides of the cake. Pour the mixture onto the cake in the pan and chill until firm (about 1/2 hour). When firm, set the other cake half on top and return to the refrigerator until completely firm (about 3 hours).

While the cake is chilling, preheat oven to 325F (163C), spread the almonds in a single layer on a baking sheet, and roast in the middle level of the oven until lightly browned (about 5 minutes). Keep a sharp eye on them because they can burn quickly. Reserve.

When filling is solid, remove cake from the pan and set on a serving plate. Melt the raspberry jelly over low heat and brush it over the top of the cake. Mask the sides with the reserved whipped cream and sprinkle with roasted almonds. The cake may wait for 2 hours, refrigerated, before serving.

Gâteau Princess Marie

The Mediterranean area has been the point of departure for countless culinary delights, including the single, large nut known as a "marron," or chestnut, which grows abundantly on Corsica and was a favorite of Napoleon I. The pleasures of this versatile nut, which can be dried and ground for flour, boiled, braised, or puréed, have spread far and wide. Chestnuts are served as a garnish, vegetable, part of a stuffing, or sweetened and served as a dessert. Here the joys of chocolate combine with those of chestnuts to produce a cake which will make your family and guests smile every time it appears.

Yields 16 servings

1 recipe Sugar Syrup
  (see page 518)
Dark rum
1 recipe Butter Cream
  (see page 517)
5 ounces (145 g) chestnut
  spread
1 recipe Génoise au Chocolat
  (see page 524)
8 ounces (225 g) sweet
  chocolate
1 cup (235 ml) half-and-half

Recommended equipment

A serrated slicing knife, pastry brush, small saucepan, 1-quart (1 L) bowl, hand mixer, icing spatula.

Prepare the sugar syrup, add dark rum to taste, mix well, and set aside.

Prepare the butter cream, combine with the chestnut spread, blend completely, cover, and keep under refrigeration until needed.

Prepare the génoise au chocolat and let it cool thoroughly. When the cake is cool, slice it into three layers. Set one layer on your serving dish and brush it all over with some of the flavored syrup. Spread the cake layer with one-half of the butter cream, set another layer on top of the butter cream, brush the cake with syrup, and spread with the remaining butter cream. Top with the last cake layer and brush it with the remaining sugar syrup.

Break the chocolate into small pieces and set it to melt over low heat. When melted and perfectly smooth, pour it into the bowl and immediately pour in the half-and-half while mixing with the hand mixer. When completely combined, spread the frosting evenly over the top and sides of the cake and set it into the refrigerator to chill for 2 hours before serving.

Chestnut spread (usually imported from France) is a sweetened purée made for desserts and usually can be found in the specialty department of your food market.

Rum Torte

Rum is inextricably tied to American history. Originally a product of water from the West Indies and sugar cane possibly carried there by Columbus from the Azores on his second voyage, it was first recorded in Barbados in 1600. By 1775 it was clearly the beverage of choice—more than twelve million gallons per year were being consumed by the thirsty colonists. And coming closer to home, Alexis Lichine records the following in his Encyclopedia of Wines & Spirits: *"George Washington, at any rate, was launched on rum. He was elected to the Virginia House of Burgesses in 1758 not by campaigning but by distributing among the voters 75 gallons of rum; and it was the Virginia House of Burgesses which later sent him to the Continental Congress." What better setting could there be for such a prominent New World spirit than this torte, which is a glorious combination of a light génoise, crunchy meringue, and smooth butter cream.*

Yields 16 servings

1 recipe Génoise à la Vanille *(see page 523)*
1 recipe Succès *(see page 519)*
2 recipes Butter Cream *(see page 517)*
1 cup (235 ml) Sugar Syrup *(see page 518)*
1 1/2 cups (355 ml) sliced almonds
1/2 cup (118 ml) dark rum
10X powdered sugar in a shaker

Recommended equipment

A baking sheet, electric mixer with mixing bowl, wire whisk, serving plate, icing spatula, pastry brush.

Prepare the génoise, succès, butter cream, and sugar syrup.

Preheat oven to 325F (163C), spread the almonds on the baking sheet, and set the sheet into the middle level of the oven. Bake until the almonds are lightly browned (about 5 minutes), remove from oven, and let cool.

Whip the butter cream with the electric mixer until light and fluffy. Combine the sugar syrup and the dark rum, mixing well with the whisk. Set one of the meringues on a serving plate and cover evenly with 1 1/2 to 2 cups (355 to 475 ml) of the butter cream, using the flexible icing spatula. Place the génoise on the butter cream, pressing down lightly. Brush the syrup and rum mixture all over the top of the cake, letting it soak in thoroughly. Spread 1 1/2 to 2 cups of the butter cream evenly over the génoise, using the icing spatula. Place the second meringue on the butter cream, pressing down lightly to secure it.

Spread the remaining butter cream around the sides of the cake and sprinkle with the roasted almonds. Refrigerate the torte for at least 2 hours, and, just before serving, shake a thin layer of powdered sugar over the meringue top.

Swiss Kirsch Torte

Pâtisserie is a Swiss specialty and, along with chocolate, kirsch is another of Switzerland's important culinary exports. In fact, when it comes to first-class kirsch, Switzerland and Germany are it, period. To understand why, all you have to do is to take a leisurely (and meandering) drive from Lucerne along the shore of Lake Lucerne (Vierwaldstätter See), passing through Küssnacht (near where William Tell purportedly waited to settle matters with Gessler) and Weggis, surrounded by a countryside richly planted with orchards and walnut trees, and then along the steep shore on an outcrop that seems to be a continuous quai, to Brunnen, where kirsch distilleries are to be found. Leaving Brunnen via Arth and the east side of the Zuger See, whose shoreline orchards and gardens bound the wooded foothills of the Zugerberg, you arrive at the ancient town of Zug, also a major location for kirsch production. We are indeed fortunate that the black mountain cherry grows so well in this area because sixty pounds are required to yield eleven bottles of kirsch. So, this many-layered torte receives a generous kirsch kiss in honor of the Swiss as well as their pastry tradition, and, if you want to be truly regional, you could replace the almonds in the Succès with walnuts.

Yields 16 servings

1 recipe Génoise à la Vanille (*see page 523*)
1 recipe Succès (*see page 519*)
2 recipes Butter Cream (*see page 517*)
1 cup (235 ml) Sugar Syrup (*see page 518*)
1 1/2 cups (355 ml) sliced almonds
A few drops of red food coloring
1/2 cup (118 ml) imported Swiss kirsch
10X powdered sugar in a shaker

Recommended equipment

A baking sheet, electric mixer with mixing bowl, wire whisk, serving plate, icing spatula, pastry brush.

Prepare the génoise, succès, butter cream, and sugar syrup.

Preheat oven to 325F (163C), spread the almonds on the baking sheet, and set the sheet into the middle level of the oven. Bake until the almonds are lightly browned (about 5 minutes), remove from oven, and let cool.

Whip the butter cream with the electric mixer until light and fluffy, adding a few drops of red food coloring for a light pink color. Combine the sugar syrup and the kirsch, mixing well with the whisk. Set one of the meringues on a serving plate and cover evenly with 1 1/2 to 2 cups (355 to 475 ml) of the butter cream, using the flexible icing spatula. Place the génoise on the butter cream, pressing down lightly. Brush the syrup and kirsch mixture all over the top of the cake, letting it soak in thoroughly. Spread 1 1/2 to 2 cups of the butter cream evenly over the génoise using the icing spatula. Place the second meringue on the butter cream, pressing down lightly to secure it.

Spread the remaining butter cream around the sides and top of the cake and sprinkle with the roasted almonds. Refrigerate the torte for at least 2 hours and, just before serving, shake a thin layer of powdered sugar over the top.

Pies, Tarts, and Cookies

This is the section where you get to show off, now that you have your *pâte* down pat and can whip up a fresh fruit pie or tart whenever you choose. The possibilities are unlimited—whatever is in season will make a lovely presentation and a sweet mouthful. Even the few fruits available during the colder months can be the basis for reliable and delicious desserts. By the way, the tart is one of the few culinary items Switzerland can claim as its own. It seems that carbon-dated samples from Early Stone Age excavations near Twann am Bielersee have revealed remnants of a mold for fruit-filled pastry dated between 3600 to 3500 B.C.

Excellent as the base for a tart, sugar pastry combined with three of cuisine's oldest and most-loved treats—honey, fruit, and nuts—yields a delight for which our Pastry Department is justly

famous (as will be your pastry corner). The puff pastry cookies shaped like palm trees and made sticky with caramelized sugar are deceptively simple. Once the pastry is in your refrigerator (or freezer), these can be rolled out, baked, and on your serving plate in less than half an hour. The perennial favorite, macaroons, are well worth having on hand to accompany ice cream, sorbet, or fruit for a complete dessert. Whatever you choose for the last course of your meal, whether simple or complex, be sure to tailor it to the rest of your menu, so you leave the table mindful that the conclusion of one meal brings the promise of another—dining is an eternal beginning.

Apple Pie

At the very moment when the waning heat of summer turns suddenly and inexplicably into the first cool breath of autumn, get out your rolling pin and take advantage of that first dry day by baking an apple pie. Discover what natives of the Vallée d'Auge and Shenandoah Valley have known for centuries—apples say autumn better than anything else. A classic, this pie is especially welcome when served warm with a scoop of Vanilla Ice Cream.

Yields 8 servings

1 recipe Pie Pastry *(see page 511)*
8 apples, preferably Granny Smith or Winesap, weighing about 3 1/2 pounds (1575g)
6 tablespoons (90 g) butter
1/2 cup (100 g) sugar
1/2 teaspoon ground cinnamon
1/3 cup (80 ml) raisins
Butter for the pan

Recommended equipment

A swivel-bladed vegetable peeler, paring knife, 12-inch (30 cm) sauté pan, wooden spatula, rolling pin, pastry scraper, 10-inch (25 cm) pie pan, wire cooling rack.

Prepare the pie pastry and chill it for several hours or overnight.

Peel and core the apples and cut them into 1/4-inch (2/3 cm) thick slices. Put the butter in the sauté pan, set the pan over medium heat, and, when it is hot, add the apple slices. Stir them about with the wooden spatula and when they begin to cook add the sugar, cinnamon, and raisins, and cook until the apple slices are tender. When done, remove pan from heat and set aside to cool.

When the apples are cool, preheat the oven to 375F (190C) and lightly butter the pie pan. Divide the pastry into two pieces, one slightly larger than the other, and roll out the larger one on a lightly floured work surface, rolling the pastry from the center to the outside edges and lifting with the pastry scraper as necessary to sprinkle small amounts of flour on the work surface. Roll out a circle 1/8-inch (1/3 cm) thick and when done, lift it with the rolling pin into the pie pan and gently fit the pastry into the pan. Spoon the apples evenly into the pastry shell. Roll out the remaining pastry into a 1/8-inch thick circle. Moisten the edge of the bottom crust with water, place the second pastry circle over the filling, trim the edges neatly, crimp together to make a tight seal, and cut a small hole in the center of the top crust to allow steam to escape.

Set the pie on a rack in the middle of the oven and bake for about an hour or until the crust is golden brown. When done, remove pie from oven and set the pan on the cooling rack to cool before serving.

If you measure ingredients on a scale as often as we do, you need to know that 12 ounces (340 g) of dough are required for the bottom crust and 10 ounces (285 g) for the top crust.

Apple Pumpkin Pie

When winter holidays are just around the corner and you want a new approach to a traditional theme, add apples—the only possible improvement—to your pumpkin pie. But be prepared: once you have served it, the requests will keep coming until spring—long after the ham, turkey, and goose have become distant memories.

Yields 8 servings

12 ounces (340 g) Pie Pastry (see page 511)
2 apples, preferably Granny Smith or Winesap, weighing about 12 ounces (340 g)
2 tablespoons (30 g) butter
5 eggs
1/4 cup (50 g) sugar
1/2 teaspoon ground cinnamon
1/2 teaspoon ground ginger
1/2 cup (118 ml) maple syrup
1/2 teaspoon melted butter
2 cups (475 ml) pumpkin purée
1/2 teaspoon salt
2 1/2 cups (590 ml) milk
1 1/2 tablespoons flour

Recommended equipment

A rolling pin, pastry scraper, 10-inch (25 cm) pie pan, swivel-bladed vegetable peeler, paring knife, 10-inch (25 cm) sauté pan, wooden spatula, waxed paper, dried beans, wire cooling rack, electric mixer with mixing bowl, rubber spatula.

Prepare the pie pastry and chill it for several hours or overnight. When chilled, remove it from the refrigerator, roll it out, line the pie pan with it, and set the pan into the refrigerator to chill the dough for at least 30 minutes. After chilling, the dough is ready to be prebaked.

Preheat oven to 350F (177C).

When the oven is hot, remove the pie pan from the refrigerator, prick the crust all over with a fork, place a piece of waxed paper over the pastry, and fill it with about 1 pound (450 g) dried beans (or raw rice), pushing them evenly up to the pastry edge to prevent it from collapsing. Set the pan onto the rack in the middle position of the oven and bake for 10 minutes. Then remove pan from oven, lift out the waxed paper with the beans inside, and return the pan to the oven to bake the crust about 5 minutes or until the dough is no longer raw. When done, remove pan from oven and set it on a rack while you prepare the filling.

Peel and core the apples and cut them into 1/4-inch (2/3 cm) thick slices. Put the 2 tablespoons butter in the sauté pan, set the pan over medium heat, and, when it is hot, add the apple slices. Stir them about with the wooden spatula and sauté them until they are tender. When done, remove pan from heat and reserve.

In the bowl of the electric mixer, beat the eggs together until well mixed. Add the sugar, cinnamon, ginger, maple syrup, and melted butter and blend well with the eggs. Mix in the pumpkin purée, salt, milk, and flour and beat on a low speed until well mixed.

Spread the reserved apples in the bottom of the prebaked pastry crust and then spread the pumpkin mixture evenly over the apples, smoothing the top with the rubber spatula.

Set the pie pan into the middle level of the oven to bake for about 45 minutes or until a knife inserted into the center comes out clean (this may take an hour). When done, set the pie on the rack to cool before serving.

🌿 Strawberry Tart

A Mediterranean native known before the birth of Christ, the strawberry was being cultivated in Spain for export to French markets by the year 1200. During the reign of Louis XIV, a rich pastry such as the one called for here had come into use, paving the way for all sorts of fresh fruit tarts—long before Billy Boy had to answer the fateful question concerning cherry pie. If you have a local farmers' market, be sure to get early spring sun-ripened strawberries, for their extraordinary perfume will permeate every mouthful of this tart. And, as blueberries, blackberries, and raspberries come into season, you can adapt the recipe as needed. As far as accompaniments are concerned, heed the words Thomas Venner, "Doctor of Physic," penned in 1660: "Verily, with strawberries and sugar, Creame is, for them for whom it is convenient, a very delicate and wholesome dish. And whosoever he be that delighteth to eat a dish of Creame, let him not be parsimonious of sugar." To update the doctor, we would recommend lightly sweetened whipped cream or a dollop of Crème Fraîche.

Yields 12 servings

18 ounces (510 g) Pâte Sucrée (see page 512)
4 cups (950 ml) Crème Pâtissière (see page 516)
2 pounds (900 g) strawberries
5 ounces (145 g) red currant jelly
Butter for the mold
Flour

Recommended equipment

A 10-inch (25 cm) tart mold (1 1/2 inches or 3 3/4 cm deep), rolling pin, pastry scraper, aluminum foil, dried beans, wire cooling rack, paring knife or strawberry huller, rubber spatula, small saucepan, pastry brush.

Prepare the pâte sucrée and chill it for several hours or overnight.

When chilled, lightly butter the tart mold and set aside. Sprinkle flour on your work surface, set the ball of pastry in the center, and roll it out to a thickness of 1/8 inch (1/3 cm), working from the center of the circle to the outside edges and turning and lifting the pastry with the scraper. As necessary, sprinkle small amounts of flour on the work surface. When done, lift the pastry with the rolling pin into the tart mold and gently fit the pastry into the pan. Form a rounded ridge of pastry around the inside of the mold folding any extra pastry to make an even edge and press it together. Set the tart mold into the refrigerator for at least 30 minutes before prebaking the crust. While the pastry is chilling, prepare the crème pâtissière, and, when it has cooled, reserve it in the refrigerator until needed.

After the pastry shell has been chilled thoroughly in the pan, preheat the oven to 375F (190C). When the oven is hot, remove the pan from the refrigerator, prick the crust all over with a fork, place a sheet of aluminum foil (or waxed paper) over the pastry, and fill it with about 1 pound (450 g) of dried beans or raw rice, pushing them evenly up to the pastry edge to prevent it from collapsing. Then set the pan into the middle level of the oven to bake for about 6 minutes or until the dough is set. Remove from oven, gently lift the foil with the beans or rice out of the pan, and return the crust to the oven to bake for 8 to 10 minutes or until it is lightly browned and has pulled away from the sides of the pan. When done, remove pan from oven and set on a rack to cool the pastry.

While the pastry is cooling, rinse the strawberries gently in cold water and remove their stems with the paring knife or strawberry huller. Set them aside to drain while you prepare the glaze by slowly melting and stirring the red currant jelly in a small saucepan. Keep the glaze warm over very low heat while you unmold the tart.

Unmold the tart pastry, spread a 3/4-inch (2 cm) thick layer of crème pâtissière in the pastry shell, and fill it with strawberries by standing them closely together, stem end down. Brush the strawberries with the warm jelly glaze and set the tart into the refrigerator until ready to serve.

The beans (or rice) may be kept in a tin or jar and used over and over again.

Variation: Prepare one recipe of Génoise à la Vanille *(see page 523)*, and after it has cooled completely, slice a 1/4-inch (2/3 cm) thick layer off the top with a serrated knife (reserving the rest for another use). Set this layer on top of the crème pâtissière, arrange and glaze the strawberries, and chill the tart until serving time. If you wish, you may brush some Sugar Syrup *(see page 518)* flavored with kirsch over the génoise before adding the strawberries.

Plum Tart

Although plum trees flourish throughout the world, the major sources are California and southwestern France, especially the area comprising the Lot and Garonne valleys. The Agen plum, named for the town which lies between Toulouse and Bordeaux on the vast central Garonne region, is the source of an annual prune production exceeding 10,000 tons. Were you to be in the Agenais region for dinner, you most likely would find a clafoutis *made with plums and short pastry. Here is our version, which you should bake as soon as fresh plums come to market. Greengage plums (known in France as* Reine-Claude, *after the first wife of François I) are considered the choicest, but mirabelle is a good alternative, and the richest visual treat is in store for those who choose the damson. Whichever you choose, if they are ripe, they will be sweet enough to suit your purpose. To point up the flavor a bit, add just a touch of eau-de-vie mirabelle to the Crème Pâtissière before turning it into the shell.*

Yields 10 to 12 servings

4 cups (950 ml) water
2 1/3 cups (455 g) sugar
1 lemon slice
1 2-inch (5 cm) piece cinnamon stick
2 1/2 to 3 pounds (1125 to 1350 g) plums
10 ounces (285 g) Pâte à Foncer *(see page 512)*
2/3 cup (160 ml) Crème Pâtissière *(see page 516)*
5 ounces (145 g) red currant jelly
Butter for the mold
Flour

Recommended equipment

3-quart (3L) saucepan, paper towels, paring knife, a 10-inch (25 cm) tart mold (1 1/2 inches or 3 3/4 cm deep), rolling pin, pastry scraper, aluminum foil, dried beans, wire cooling rack, rubber spatula, small saucepan, pastry brush.

Early in the day poach the plums. Bring the water and sugar to boil in the saucepan over high heat. Rinse the plums, add them with the lemon and cinnamon to the syrup in the saucepan, and adjust heat so that they simmer for 5 to 6 minutes or until tender. When done, remove from heat and set aside so the plums can cool to room temperature in the syrup. When cool, drain the plums on paper towels (or on a rack) and then halve, pit, and peel them. Reserve until needed.

Prepare the pâte à foncer and let it chill for several hours or overnight.

When chilled, lightly butter the tart mold and set aside. Sprinkle flour on your work surface, set the ball of pastry in the center and roll it out to a thickness of 1/8 inch (1/3 cm), working from the center of the circle to the outside edges and turning and lifting the pastry with the scraper. As necessary, sprinkle small amounts of flour on the work surface. When done, lift the pastry with the rolling pin into the tart mold and gently fit the pastry into the pan. Form a rounded ridge of pastry around the inside of the mold folding any extra pastry to make an even edge and press it together. Set the tart mold into the refrigerator for at least 30 minutes before prebaking the crust.

While the pastry is chilling, prepare the crème pâtissière, and when it has cooled, reserve it in the refrigerator until needed.

After the pastry shell has been chilled thoroughly in the pan, preheat the oven to 375F (190C). When the oven is hot, remove the pan from the refrigerator, prick the crust all over with a fork, place a sheet of aluminum foil (or waxed paper) over the pastry, and fill it with about 1 pound (450 g) of dried beans or raw rice, pushing them evenly up to the pastry edge to prevent it from collapsing. Then set the pan into the middle level of the oven to bake for about 6 minutes or until the dough is set. Remove from oven, gently lift the foil with the beans or rice out of the pan, and return the crust to the oven to bake for 8 to 10 minutes or until it is lightly browned and has pulled away from the sides of the pan. When done, remove pan from oven and set on a rack to cool the pastry.

While the pastry is cooling, prepare the glaze. Melt the red currant jelly over low heat, stirring until it is free of lumps and perfectly smooth. Keep the glaze warm over very low heat while you unmold the tart shell.

Unmold the tart shell, spread a 3/4-inch (2 cm) thick layer of crème pâtissière in it, and fill with the plums by setting the halves closely together, cut side down. Brush the plums with the warm jelly glaze and set the tart into the refrigerator until ready to serve.

Other fruits such as peeled and seeded grapes; poached or canned peaches, pears, or apricots; or sliced bananas can also be used, according to the season.

Homestead chocolates, honey cookies (in the center), and chocolate chip cookies

Honey Cookies

A variation on the theme of the Swiss honey cookie Basler leckerli, *these sinful little morsels have been known to make our guests wait in line to buy them at Café Albert after having sampled them at the Casino luncheon buffet. I defy you to eat just one! They keep well in an airtight tin and freeze beautifully (if there are enough left in the tin to freeze).*

Yields eighty 1 x 2 inch (2 1/2 x 5 cm) cookies

1 recipe Pâte Sucrée (see page 512)
1 1/2 cups (275 g) sugar
1 1/2 cups (340 g) butter
1 cup (235 ml) honey
3/4 cup (180 ml) whipping cream
1 1/2 cups (355 ml) glacéed cherries
4 cups (950 ml) sliced almonds
3/4 cup (180 ml) raisins

Recommended equipment

A rolling pin, pastry scraper, sheet pan 15 x 10 x 3/4 inches (37 1/2 x 25 x 2 cm), aluminum foil, dried beans, 3-quart (3 L) saucepan, candy thermometer, small chef's knife, wooden spatula, wire cooling rack, waxed paper, serrated knife.

Prepare the pâte sucrée and let it chill for several hours or overnight. When chilled, remove the pastry from the refrigerator, divide it in half, return one half to the refrigerator to reserve for another purpose, and set the other half on your lightly floured work surface. The pastry is fragile and you must work quickly while it is still cold. Roll out the pastry to a thickness of 1/4 inch (2/3 cm), fit it into the sheet pan, trim the edges so the pastry lies flat in the pan, and set it into the refrigerator to chill for at least an hour. If you are making two sheet pans of cookies (an excellent idea), roll out the reserved pastry, fit it into another pan, chill, and prepare a double batch of the topping.

When the pastry is thoroughly chilled, preheat the oven to 350F (177C) and, when it is hot, remove the sheet pan from the refrigerator, prick the pastry all over with a fork, cover it with aluminum foil, spread the dried beans over the foil, and set the pan on a rack in the middle of the oven to bake for 30 minutes or until the pastry is barely beginning to color. When done, remove pan from oven, remove the foil and beans, and leave the oven turned on.

Make the topping for the pastry. In the saucepan, stir together the sugar, butter, honey, and whipping cream. Set the saucepan over high heat, bring the mixture to a hard boil, and cook, without stirring, until the candy thermometer registers 260F (127C). While the mixture cooks, lightly chop the cherries and reserve. When the mixture is done, remove pan from heat and add the cherries, almonds, and raisins, stirring with a wooden spatula to mix completely. Spread the mixture evenly over the prebaked pastry and set the pan into the oven for 15 to 20 minutes or until the top is golden brown.

When done, remove pan from oven and set it on a rack to cool completely. When cool, let sit overnight at room temperature, covered loosely with waxed paper, and the next day slice into 1 x 2 inch (2 1/2 x 5 cm) pieces with a serrated knife. The pastry and topping must rest before cutting. Store the cookies in an airtight tin and do not refrigerate because they will become soggy.

If the topping is within 1/4 inch (2/3 cm) of the edge of the sheet pan it may boil over; in this case, set an extra pan underneath the sheet pan on the lower rack in the oven to catch any overflow.

Palmiers
Palm Tree Cookies

When the Casino opens for luncheon, those who are regular guests have been known to pick up their dessert first—especially if they have a fondness for these sweet flaky cookies. A Parisian specialty, palmiers made small are just the thing for a mignardise, *that little* quelque chose *you want with Cognac and coffee to ruminate over a memorable feast. Made larger, they are a dessert unto themselves. Preparing them can be mastered on the first attempt, and you will soon discover that they are about the tastiest way to use up any extra pâte feuilletée from other recipes. One* conseil, *do not bake any more than you think you will need because their freshness fades quickly.*

Yields about 18 palmiers

16 ounces (455 g) Pâte Feuilletée *(see page 513)*
Sugar
Butter for the baking sheets

Recommended equipment

A rolling pin, pastry scraper or paring knife, two baking sheets, two turning spatulas, wire cooling rack.

Prepare the pâte feuilletée and chill it, wrapped airtight, for several hours or overnight.

When chilled, butter the baking sheets.

Sprinkle your work surface with sugar, center the pâte feuilletée on it, and roll it out to a depth of 1/4 inch (2/3 cm) in a rectangular shape about 10 inches long and 6 inches wide (25 x 15 cm). Sprinkle the pastry surface with sugar and fold the long sides toward the center of the pastry strip so they meet edge to edge in the center (the rectangle is now about 3 x 10 inches or 7 1/2 x 25 cm). Sprinkle the pastry surface with sugar and roll lightly with the rolling pin to press the sugar into the pastry. Fold the long sides toward the center again so you have a pastry strip about 1 1/2 inches wide and 1/2 inch thick (3 3/4 x 1 1/4 cm). Cut crosswise into strips 1/4 inch wide with the edge of a pastry scraper or knife.

Arrange the shapes cut side down on the baking sheets, separate the ends slightly to form a shape similar to the Greek letter omega, and leave 2 inches (5 cm) of space around each cookie. (They will more than double in size as they bake.) Set the cookie sheets into the refrigerator to chill for 30 minutes before baking and chill any dough that must wait for a second batch.

When the dough is chilled, preheat oven to 450F (232C) and bake the palmiers one pan at a time, in the middle level of the oven until they are golden brown on the bottom and then turn over quickly (two spatulas are helpful) to brown the other side. This may take about 8 to 10 minutes on the first side and 3 to 5 minutes on the second. When done, remove pan from oven and remove palmiers to a rack to cool. When cool, store the palmiers airtight in a tin and enjoy them as soon as possible. Do not refrigerate.

Macarons à la Vanille
Vanilla Macaroons

Almonds are mentioned as early as the third century A.D. *in* The Deipnosophists *by Athenaeus and have been at the heart of sweets and confections in many forms as well as flavorings and decorations. Medieval crusaders encountered ground almond paste in the Middle East in the form of marzipan, which was to take Europe by storm. So popular was it as holiday fare that Queen Elizabeth I received New Year's gifts of models of Saint Paul's Cathedral and Saint George constructed entirely from marzipan. Almond paste is also the basis for macaroons, which were first known in Italy, came to France with Catherine de' Medici, and from thence spread throughout the civilized world—wherever cookie jars are to be found.*

Yields about 2 dozen

- 1 cup (235 ml) almond paste
- 1/2 cup (60 g) 10X powdered sugar
- 2 egg whites
- 1/2 teaspoon vanilla extract

Recommended equipment

An electric mixer with mixing bowl; rubber spatula; pastry bag with plain, round tube; baking sheet; aluminum foil, parchment paper, or brown paper bag.

Preheat oven to 375F (190C).

Put the almond paste and powdered sugar in the mixing bowl and combine at low speed until the mixture is a smooth paste. Add egg whites one at a time, scraping sides and bottom of the bowl after each addition. Add the vanilla and continue mixing until the almond paste is smooth and free of lumps.

Prepare the baking sheet by lining it with perfectly smooth aluminum foil, parchment paper, or a brown bag (which can be flattened with an iron if necessary).

Fit a plain, round tube into the pastry bag and fill the bag with the almond mixture. Squeeze the mixture onto the baking sheet in 1-inch (2 1/2 cm) mounds spaced 2 inches (5 cm) apart. Set the baking sheet onto a rack in the middle of the oven and bake for about 20 minutes or until the macaroons are a light golden brown. When done, remove the pan from the oven and let the macaroons cool before removing them from the paper. Store them in an airtight tin, separating the layers with waxed paper.

If you use brown paper on the baking sheet and the macaroons stick, dampen a kitchen towel, lay it on your work surface, lift the paper from the baking sheet onto the towel, and as the dampness soaks into the paper you will be able to work the macaroons loose.

Variation

❧ *Macarons au Chocolat*
Chocolate Macaroons

Follow the instructions for Macarons à la Vanille and add 2 teaspoons melted sweet chocolate to the mixture when you add the vanilla.

❧ *Mousses, Soufflés, and a Pudding*

"What, me make a mousse or soufflé?" some of you may ask. Well, let me tell you, these desserts, like the wizard in Oz, are undeservedly intimidating. So, following Toto's lead, we will pull the curtain away and show you how simple they are. Proper whipping of cream, egg yolks, and egg whites is the secret for success here. The raspberry mousse relies upon the cream and a small amount of gelatin for firmness. Accordingly, buy cream with the highest percentage of butterfat (sometimes called heavy cream) that you can find, chill your bowl, and beat on medium speed until the cream is stiff. Fold the cream into the fruit purée, chill until firm, and serve. The frozen mousse takes a step toward greater richness with an egg yolk and milk custard in combination with the cream and chocolate. When we ask you to beat egg yolk and sugar together it is to dissolve the sugar and also incidentally incorporate some air for lightness. Then the custard is cooled and folded with the whipped cream (a warm mixture would melt the whipped cream). Having mastered the mousses with cream and egg yolks, you are ready to whip the whites and come up with a dessert soufflé.

The three hot soufflés have a flavored thick base (vanilla, chocolate, or orange liqueur) that is combined with beaten egg whites to leaven the mixture as it bakes. When you separate the eggs be absolutely certain that not a speck of yolk gets in the whites because it might reduce their volume by as much as two-thirds. Your bowl must be metal or glass (plastic bowls inevitably retain a slightly oily film) and completely clean. The beaters must be greaseless too. If the whites are chilled, let them warm up to room temperature or set the bowl briefly into some hot water to remove the chill. They will whip up more rapidly if they are not cold. Beat the whites on low speed until foamy, increase speed to medium, and beat until stiff but not dry. The whites should hold a peak when the beater is turned off and removed. Fold the whites into your reserved soufflé base, bake, and prepare to savor a scrumptious treat.

One *conseil:* do not omit soufflés from an elaborate menu because you are concerned about timing. The base can be prepared as much as an hour in advance of baking and it will wait patiently for you to serve your entrée. Let the base sit uncovered in a warm (not hot) place or rewarm the mixture to tepid over low heat before folding in the whites. The egg whites must be beaten and folded in *just before* baking. Now that you have learned this lesson, choose your flavor and practice on your family tonight. They will love it.

Sometimes the best surprise is no surprise, and here is a pudding to fill the bill—a tasty dish of rice seasoned with cinnamon, vanilla, and raisins, similar to what you were most likely served as a child. You may well wonder why a common rice pudding is keeping company with soufflés. Well, now that we are all adults we can rediscover some of the simpler joys of our youth and, besides, it is too good to be forgotten in the mists of those formative years. So, return home to Auntie Em in Kansas and fix this pudding.

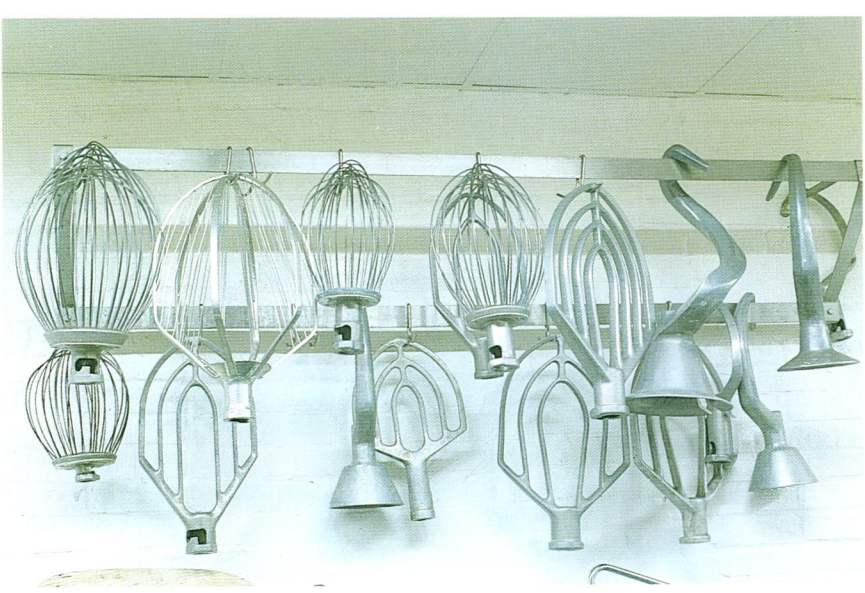

Mousse à la Framboise
Raspberry Mousse

When the hot, humid days of summer produce a bumper crop of red raspberries, make up a purée, mix it with whipped cream, chill, and you will please the most fastidious berry devotee.

Yields 16 servings

4 cups (950 ml) fresh raspberries
1/3 cup (65 g) sugar
Juice of 1/2 lemon
3 tablespoons framboise (raspberry liqueur)
1/4 cup (60 ml) water
1 1/3 tablespoons unflavored gelatin
2 cups (475 ml) whipping cream

Recommended equipment

A blender or food processor, large fine-mesh sieve, rubber spatula, 2-quart (2 L) bowl, wire whisk, small dish, 1-quart (1 L) bowl, small saucepan, hand mixer, 2-quart (2 L) soufflé dish.

Purée the raspberries in the blender or food processor, force the purée through the sieve (discard the seeds) with the spatula into the large bowl, and, mixing with the whisk, stir in the sugar, lemon juice, and the framboise. Taste the purée and adjust the flavor if necessary, depending upon the sweetness of the berries. Set the bowl aside.

Put 1/4 cup (60 ml) cold water in the small dish, sprinkle on the gelatin, and let it soften.

Pour the cream in the 1-quart bowl, and, using the hand mixer, whip until stiff.

Heat the gelatin mixture in the small saucepan until it is dissolved. Then stir the gelatin into the raspberry purée, fold in the whipped cream, pour the mixture into the soufflé dish, and chill for at least 4 hours in the refrigerator before serving.

Four cups of fresh raspberries should yield about 2 cups (475 ml) of purée.

Mousse au Chocolat Glacé
Chocolate Mousse

For those of us addicted to chocolate, another chocolate dessert will not be one too many. Besides, every pastry chef has to have a "little chocolate mousse" up the sleeve. Because it is frozen, this one is especially welcome during warm weather when advance meal preparation is de rigueur. To dress it up at serving time, spoon some slightly sweetened whipped cream or Sauce Sabayon over each portion and dust with a couple of grinds of bittersweet chocolate.

Yields 16 servings

5 egg yolks
1/2 cup (100 g) sugar
2 1/2 tablespoons cocoa powder
1/4 cup (60 ml) water
1 1/3 tablespoons unflavored gelatin
2 cups (475 ml) milk
2 cups (475 ml) whipping cream
2 tablespoons 10X powdered sugar

Recommended equipment

An electric mixer with mixing bowl, rubber spatula, small bowl, 3-quart (3 L) saucepan, wire whisk, large sieve, small mixing bowl, large mixing bowl containing iced water, 2-quart (2 L) serving dish.

Combine the egg yolks and 1/2 cup sugar in the bowl of the mixer and beat at medium speed until the sugar is dissolved (about 3 minutes). Add the cocoa powder, mix for 2 minutes, scrape down the bowl with the rubber spatula, mix for 30 seconds, and then set aside.

Put 1/4 cup (60 ml) water in the small bowl, sprinkle the gelatin over the water, and let it soften.

Bring the milk to a boil in the saucepan over medium heat, stirring from time to time to prevent scorching. When boiling, remove from heat and pour a little of the hot milk into the cocoa mixture, beat for 30 seconds, then pour the cocoa mixture into the hot milk in the saucepan. Mix well with the whisk. Stir in the gelatin and mix until completely dissolved. Then pass the mixture through the sieve into the small mixing bowl.

Set this bowl over the iced water in the larger bowl and stir the mixture from time to time until it has cooled and thickened slightly. While the mixture is cooling, whip the cream with the powdered sugar at medium speed. When the mixture is cool and thickened, fold in the whipped cream using the rubber spatula and then pour the mousse into the serving dish and freeze for 4 to 5 hours before serving.

The amount of cocoa powder called for here is on the conservative side. If you prefer a more intense flavor, increase the cocoa, tasting the mixture for sweetness and adding sugar as needed. Using Crème de Cacao to soften the gelatin will give the mousse a soupçon of flavor that is likely to produce a stampede of empty dessert plates looking for encores.

Soufflé à la Vanille
Vanilla Soufflé

Dessert was always eagerly awaited at dinner time on the North Atlantic, and passengers on the great Cunard liners Queen Mary *and* Queen Elizabeth *were offered individual soufflés in several flavors every evening. Some agonized over the choice, and others unconcerned with their waistlines could (and would) order two if they wished, knowing that repentance was possible after the ship docked. This preparation and the two which follow may surprise you because they are in the sturdy soufflé tradition rather than the light and airy category, so do not be alarmed when they first rise and then sink some as they are cooking.*

Yields 6 to 8 servings

FOR THE SOUFFLÉ
1/4 cup (50 g) plus 1 teaspoon sugar
1/2 cup (60 g) flour
10 tablespoons (145 g) plus 2 teaspoons butter, softened at room temperature
1 teaspoon vanilla extract
2 cups (475 ml) milk
1 2-inch (5 cm) piece vanilla bean
5 egg yolks
5 egg whites
1/3 cup (65 g) plus 2 teaspoons sugar
Butter and sugar for the dish

FOR THE SAUCE
1 recipe Crème Anglaise *(see page 516)*
2 to 3 ounces (60 to 85 g) semisweet chocolate

Recommended equipment

A 2-quart (2 L) soufflé dish, electric mixer with mixing bowl, rubber spatula, 2-quart (2 L) saucepan, wire whisk, 2-quart (2 L) bowl, hand mixer, 1-quart (1 L) bowl.

Butter the soufflé dish, coat the bottom and sides of the dish with sugar, and set aside.

Preheat oven to 375F (190C).

In the bowl of the electric mixer, combine the sugar, flour, butter, and vanilla extract into a smooth paste and reserve.

Put the milk and vanilla bean in the saucepan, set over medium heat, and bring the milk to a boil. Remove pan from heat, remove vanilla bean, and, using the whisk, combine the reserved sugar and butter mixture with the milk in the saucepan. Stir well and set the saucepan back over medium heat for 2 minutes or until the mixture is well blended and quite thick. Remove mixture from heat and add the egg yolks one by one, mixing well after each addition with the whisk. Scrape the mixture into the larger bowl and set aside.

Using the hand mixer and the smaller bowl, beat the egg whites until they form soft peaks and then sprinkle on the 1/3 cup plus 2 teaspoons of sugar little by little, while beating on low speed. When the sugar is completely incorporated, increase speed to medium and beat the whites until stiff but not dry. Using the rubber spatula, fold the egg whites into the soufflé base and pour the mixture into the prepared dish. The dish should be three-quarters full.

Set the dish into the middle level of the oven to bake the soufflé for about 45 minutes or until it is puffed up and lightly browned.

While the soufflé is cooking, prepare the chocolate sauce. Break the chocolate into pieces and add it to the boiling milk, mixing well with a whisk, before pouring the milk into the egg mixture in the crème anglaise. Then continue with the recipe for the crème anglaise. Let the sauce cool at room temperature and then refrigerate until ready to serve.

When the soufflé is done, remove it from the oven, spoon it onto plates and serve at once, surrounded by chocolate sauce.

When the soufflé is baking, look through the oven window during the first part of the cooking period to see whether it is rising evenly. If one side is rising faster than the other, turn the dish so the soufflé will cook evenly. Some ovens may be hotter toward the back and this uneven heat may make parts of the soufflé rise at different rates.

Soufflé au Chocolat
Chocolate Soufflé

A chocolate soufflé would as surely follow a vanilla one as night follows day—most everyone can choose a favorite between these two.

Yields 6 to 8 servings

FOR THE SOUFFLÉ
4 ounces (115 g) semisweet chocolate
1 recipe Soufflé à la Vanille (see page 551)

FOR THE SAUCE
1 recipe Crème Anglaise (see page 516)

Recommended equipment

A small saucepan for melting the chocolate, 2-quart (2 L) soufflé dish, electric mixer with mixing bowl, rubber spatula, 2-quart (2 L) saucepan, wire whisk, 2-quart (2 L) bowl, hand mixer, 1-quart (1 L) bowl.

Break the chocolate into pieces, put them in the small saucepan over low heat, and let them melt. When melted, take off heat and set aside.

Proceed with the soufflé à la vanille recipe, omitting the vanilla extract and vanilla bean. Mix the melted chocolate into the soufflé base after the egg yolks have been incorporated, and follow the rest of the instructions.

While the soufflé is baking, prepare the crème anglaise. When the soufflé is done, spoon it onto dishes and serve at once, surrounded with the sauce.

Souffé au Grand Marnier
Grand Marnier Soufflé

The original orange-flavored liqueur was made by the Dutch from skins of oranges that grew on Curaçao, an island off the coast of Venezuela. The brandy-based liqueur became so popular that similar ones were made under proprietary names such as Cointreau and Grand Marnier, and they each have their loyal following.

Yields 6 to 8 servings

FOR THE SOUFFLÉ
1 recipe Soufflé à la Vanille *(see page 551)*
1 tablespoon orange marmalade
1/4 cup (60 ml) Grand Marnier (orange liqueur)

FOR THE SAUCE
1 recipe Crème Anglaise *(see page 516)*
2 to 3 tablespoons Grand Marnier

Recommended equipment

A 2-quart (2 L) soufflé dish, electric mixer with mixing bowl, rubber spatula, 2-quart (2 L) saucepan, wire whisk, 2-quart (2 L) bowl, hand mixer, 1-quart (1 L) bowl.

Proceed with the soufflé à la vanille recipe, omitting the vanilla extract and vanilla bean. Mix the marmalade and Grand Marnier in a small bowl and then add to the soufflé base after the egg yolks have been incorporated, blending completely, and follow the rest of the instructions.

While the soufflé is baking, prepare the crème anglaise and stir in the Grand Marnier to taste before chilling the sauce. When the soufflé is done, spoon it onto dishes and serve at once, surrounded with the sauce.

Variation

 ## Homestead Bourbon Soufflé

Even though this is a simple variation on the Grand Marnier preparation, it has gotten enough attention over the years to be reprinted in Gourmet, so to save you the trouble of writing for the recipe, here is the French classic with a Tennessee accent, which we are only too happy to claim as our own.

1 recipe Soufflé au Grand Marnier *(see above)*

Replace the marmalade with eighteen crouton-sized cubes of day-old génoise soaked in Jack Daniel's Black Label and replace the Grand Marnier with Jack Daniel's Black Label. Make a similar substitution in the sauce, tasting (but not too much!) for additional sugar, if needed.

❧ Rice Pudding

Happily, rice can be served almost any way you want—plain, savory, or sweet as in this nourishing, traditional dessert. Spoon Crème Anglaise around each serving or use individual ramekins, put a dollop of whipped cream on the top of each, and run them briefly under the broiler until lightly toasted.

Yields 8 servings

4 cups (950 ml) milk
1/2 cup (118 ml) raw long grain rice
1/2 cup (100 g) sugar
3 egg yolks
1/2 teaspoon cinnamon
2 teaspoons vanilla extract
1/2 cup (118 ml) raisins

Recommended equipment

A 1 1/2-quart (1 1/2 L) saucepan, wooden spatula, small bowl, wire whisk, 1 1/2-quart (1 1/2 L) serving dish or eight individual ramekins.

Bring the milk to a boil in the saucepan, add the rice, then reduce heat immediately and simmer slowly on low heat. Stir from time to time with the wooden spatula to prevent scorching. Cook the rice until tender, about 15 or 20 minutes, then add the sugar and cook slowly 5 more minutes. Remove pan from heat and reserve.

Put the egg yolks in the small bowl and, mixing with the whisk, pour on 1 cup (235 ml) of the rice and milk mixture. Then pour this back into the large saucepan, mix well, add the cinnamon and vanilla, and continue mixing over very low heat until well blended. Remove pan from heat and let the mixture cool in the saucepan for 15 to 20 minutes, stirring occasionally.

Butter the serving dish or ramekins, put the raisins into the bottom, and pour in the pudding. Let cool before serving.

❧ Ice Creams and Sorbets

The Arabs and Chinese knew the art of making ice sweets, especially water ices, and this knowledge followed the trade routes, eventually reaching Italy. So when Catherine de' Medici was married to Henri II in 1533, her Florentine cooks prepared a different flavor of iced cream for each day of the wedding festivities, and voilà—France had a new treat. It should come as no surprise that a Sicilian, Francisco Procopio, is credited with making ice cream and ices generally available in Paris when he opened a shop in 1660 on the rue de l'Ancienne Comèdie on the Left Bank. The Parisians clamored for the novelty and sixteen years later more than two hundred and fifty people were selling ices. By 1750, ices were made and sold year-round, and during the period of the First Empire, egg yolk and syrup were used as the basic mixture by the many Italian ice cream manufacturers working in Paris.

Closer to home, the American ice cream industry received a boost when Nancy Johnson invented the hand-cranked ice cream freezer in 1846. The mechanical action kept the mix moving for even freezing with no large ice crystals, making the process reliable if not easier (and enlarging millions of American biceps). By 1851, the first large-scale manufacturer of ice cream went into business in Baltimore when a milk dealer, Jacob Fussell, decided to freeze his excess milk into ice cream. Other ice cream concoctions such as sodas (called "phosphates") and sundaes soon followed. The cream used in sodas was replaced with ice cream around 1874, creating a perennially popular sweet dessert, which also led in a curious way to the creation of the sundae. Some midwestern states banned the sale of ice cream sodas on Sundays, so the sodaless dish of ice cream became the legal "sundae" treat. And we all know what happened after that—a sundae is as original and limitless as your imagination. The birth of the ice cream cone is even more specifically documented. At the 1904 St. Louis World Exposition, an ice cream vendor ran out of dishes and borrowed waffles from his neighbor, Ernest Hamwi, to wrap around his ice cream. The rest is history.

When making ice cream at home, you will get the best results with an electric ice cream freezer that will rapidly cool the mixture while keeping it moving continuously. This will guarantee a creamy texture rather than one that is coarse and icy. Texture is particularly critical for sorbets, where the fruit- or spirit-based mixture must be smooth as silk when it is frozen, and this is best achieved by the addition of a simple syrup, followed by rapid freezing, requiring about twenty-five minutes. The memory of an excellent fruit sorbet will be with you for years, especially if the fruit is fresh and its flavor is intensified by the appropriate liqueur. We are not talking about artificially flavored inexpensive sweet brandies, we are referring to the clear eaux-de-vie from Alsace, Germany, or Switzerland. They are expensive because vast quantities of fresh fruit go into the distillation process, producing a spirited essence whose aroma is equivalent to being inside the fruit.

Here at the Homestead we serve a sorbet during banquets to provide a refreshing moment among several courses, honoring the traditional French custom of offering a *trou de milieu* before the roast. In southwestern France this meant an assortment of liqueurs passed on a large silver tray by the youngest daughter of the house—in Normandy, the *trou Normande* meant a glass of Calvados. In Hot Springs, we offer a sorbet, usually based on Calvados, which surely will restore and refresh your appetite far better than a liqueur.

Before cranking up your machine, we should give you one *conseil*. Properly made ice cream is not low in calories, in fact a one-half cup serving of one of these recipes will contain about 350 to 400 calories, compared to about 125 for the sorbets. However, fresh ice cream should be a treat which is anticipated and savored, not a sweet substance full of fillers and artificial flavorings mindlessly scooped out of a cardboard carton. There are calories and there are calories. Make one of these ice creams and you will have fond thoughts of it for months—in between these occasions, enjoy the fresh taste and color of the sorbets.

Vanilla Ice Cream

Ah, vanilla ice cream—according to one source it is a three-to-one summer American back porch favorite over chocolate, thus outstripping the supply of the vanilla bean, which is hand pollinated and requires a period of exposure to strong sun and months of drying to develop its complex flavor. Needless to say, its expense (second only to saffron) leads most manufacturers to use artificial flavoring, but still, there is nothing which can match the genuine article. Catherine de' Medici may have had all those flavors made for her wedding to Henri II, but this egg yolk preparation is uniquely French. In fact, in Entertaining in the French Style, *Roger Vergé includes a similar recipe in a menu called* Un Dîner d'Amoureux. *Need we say more?*

Yields 8 servings

4 cups (950 ml) half-and-half
2 vanilla beans
10 egg yolks
1 cup (195 g) sugar
3/4 cup (180 ml) whipping cream

Recommended equipment

A 2-quart (2 L) saucepan, paring knife, wooden spatula, electric mixer with mixing bowl, rubber spatula, large fine-mesh sieve, ice cream machine.

Pour the half-and-half into the saucepan and set it over medium heat. Split the vanilla beans lengthwise with the paring knife and, holding them over the saucepan, scrape the inside of the beans with the point of the paring knife, letting bits of bean fall into the half-and-half. Cut the beans in several pieces, add them to the liquid and bring it to a boil, stirring from time to time with the wooden spatula and watching it carefully lest it scorch.

While the half-and-half is heating, combine the egg yolks and sugar in the mixing bowl and beat at medium speed for about 3 minutes or until the mixture is thick, light yellow, and the sugar has dissolved. While mixing, scrape down the sides of the bowl with the rubber spatula from time to time. When done, reserve the mixture in the bowl.

When the half-and-half comes to a boil, remove it from heat and *slowly* pour about 1 cup (235 ml) of the hot half-and-half into the egg yolk mixture, beating continuously on low speed. This will warm the yolks before the next step. Then add the yolk mixture to the saucepan with the half-and-half, set it over low heat, and cook, stirring constantly with the wooden spatula, for 1 to 2 minutes or until the mixture has thickened enough to coat the spatula. When done, remove from heat at once, pour the custard through the sieve into a bowl, and let cool at room temperature.

When the custard is cool, stir in the whipping cream and freeze the mixture in the ice cream machine according to the manufacturer's instructions.

Chocolate Ice Cream

In 1519, when Spanish explorer Hernando Cortés "visited" the Aztec emperor Montezuma II in Mexico and discovered chocolate, he probably would have enjoyed it more in an ice cream had it been available than in the bitter, red-pepper flavored drink he was offered. If you are familiar with mole de guajolote, you know that chocolate does have a curious way of taming chili peppers, but dessert lovers can be thankful that history has provided alternatives when you prepare this ice cream.

Yields 8 servings

1 recipe Vanilla Ice Cream *(see page 556)*
4 ounces (115 g) sweet chocolate

Recommended equipment

A 2-quart (2 L) saucepan, wooden spatula, electric mixer with mixing bowl, rubber spatula, large fine-mesh sieve, wire whisk, ice cream machine.

Follow the instructions for vanilla ice cream, omitting the vanilla beans.

While the half-and-half is heating, break or cut the chocolate into small pieces and reserve. After the hot custard is poured through the sieve into the bowl, add the chocolate pieces, stirring with the whisk until they are melted and the mixture is completely blended. Let cool at room temperature and continue with the rest of the instructions.

Coconut Ice Cream

To develop its full flavor the coconut mixture must steep for two hours before combining it with the other ingredients. For an attractive color contrast, sprinkle some lightly toasted shredded coconut on top of the ice cream when serving.

Yields 8 servings

4 cups (950 ml) half-and-half
8 ounces (225 g) shredded coconut
2 tablespoons coconut syrup
10 egg yolks
1 cup (195 g) sugar
3/4 cup (180 ml) whipping cream

Recommended equipment

A 2-quart (2 L) saucepan, wooden spatula, 2-quart (2 L) bowl, large fine-mesh sieve, 1-quart (1 L) glass measure, electric mixer with mixing bowl, rubber spatula, ice cream machine.

Pour the half-and-half into the saucepan, add the shredded coconut and the coconut syrup, set it over medium heat, and bring the liquid to a boil, stirring from time to time with the wooden spatula and watching it carefully lest it scorch. When the half-and-half is boiling, remove it from the heat and pour it into a bowl to steep for 2 hours. Wash out the saucepan and reserve.

After steeping, pour the mixture through the sieve into the glass measure. Add more half-and-half if necessary to make 1 quart. Discard the shredded coconut. Pour the half-and-half into the clean saucepan, set over medium heat, and bring to a boil, stirring from time to time and watching it carefully.

While the half-and-half is heating, combine the egg yolks and sugar in the mixing bowl and beat at medium speed for about 3 minutes or until the mixture is thick, light yellow, and the sugar has dissolved. While mixing, scrape down the sides of the bowl with the rubber spatula from time to time. When done, reserve the mixture in the bowl.

When the half-and-half comes to a boil, remove it from heat and *slowly* pour about 1 cup (235 ml) of the hot half-and-half into the egg yolk mixture, beating continuously on low speed. This will warm the yolks before the next step. Then add the yolk mixture to the saucepan with the half-and-half, set it over low heat, and cook, stirring constantly with the wooden spatula, for 1 to 2 minutes or until the mixture has thickened enough to coat the spatula. When done, remove from heat at once, pour the custard through the sieve into a bowl, and let cool at room temperature.

When the custard is cool, stir in the whipping cream and freeze the mixture in the ice cream machine according to the manufacturer's instructions.

❧ *Banana Ice Cream*

A ripe banana is one of nature's most balanced and complete foods. What better reason than that can I give you to enjoy bananas any way you can—fresh, baked, fried, or frozen as they are here. Perhaps because they come from similar climates, rum and bananas have an affinity for each other, so for an exotic flavor add Jamaican dark rum (but no more than one-quarter cup) just before you start to freeze the mixture.

Yields 8 servings

2 cups (475 ml) Crème Anglaise (see page 516)
4 to 5 medium, ripe bananas
Juice of 2 lemons
1/2 cup (100 g) sugar
1/2 cup (118 ml) whipping cream

Recommended equipment

A blender or food processor, rubber spatula, 2-quart (2 L) bowl, wire whisk, ice cream machine.

Prepare the crème anglaise.

Purée the bananas in the blender or food processor with the lemon juice. You should have about 2 cups. Scrape the purée into the bowl and add the crème anglaise, sugar, and whipping cream. Mix well with the whisk (adding the dark rum if you wish) and then freeze the mixture in the ice cream machine according to the manufacturer's instructions.

Rum Raisin Ice Cream

Wherever sugar cane is grown and pure water is available, rum is sure to be found. Compared to other spirits, its distillation process is relatively simple, which no doubt partially accounts for its early popularity in the New World. Its presence documented in the West Indies at the beginning of the seventeenth century, rum has been (and continues to be) rationed out daily to the personnel of the British Royal Navy since the eighteenth century. Here it combines forces with raisins, which provide both a texture and flavor contrast, to yield a real favorite from our Main Dining Room and Commonwealth Room menus.

Yields 8 servings

2/3 cup (160 ml) raisins
1/2 cup (118 ml) dark rum
4 cups (950 ml) half-and-half
10 egg yolks
1 1/4 cups (240 g) sugar
3/4 cup (180 ml) whipping cream

Recommended equipment

A small dish for soaking raisins, plastic wrap, 2-quart (2 L) saucepan, wooden spatula, electric mixer with mixing bowl, rubber spatula, large fine-mesh sieve, ice cream machine.

Combine the raisins and dark rum in the small dish, cover with plastic wrap, and let them macerate overnight.

The next day, pour the half-and-half into the saucepan, set it over medium heat, and bring the liquid to a boil, stirring from time to time with the wooden spatula and watching it carefully lest it scorch.

While the half-and-half is heating, combine the egg yolks and sugar in the mixing bowl and beat at medium speed for about 3 minutes or until the mixture is thick, light yellow, and the sugar has dissolved. While mixing, scrape down the sides of the bowl with the rubber spatula from time to time. When done, reserve the mixture in the bowl.

When the half-and-half comes to a boil, remove it from heat and *slowly* pour about 1 cup (235 ml) of the hot half-and-half into the egg yolk mixture, beating continuously on low speed. This will warm the yolks before the next step. Then add the yolk mixture to the saucepan with the half-and-half, set it over low heat, and cook, stirring constantly with the wooden spatula, for 1 to 2 minutes or until the mixture has thickened enough to coat the spatula. When done, remove from heat at once, pour the custard through the sieve into a bowl, stir in the reserved raisins and rum, and let cool at room temperature.

When the custard is cool, stir in the whipping cream and freeze the mixture in the ice cream machine according to the manufacturer's instructions.

Rose Ice Cream

Long before edible flowers became the rage, this was featured in the 1950s at many of the elegant ladies' luncheons served during my early years in New York. (To be historically correct, flowers were part of Sung dynasty cuisine, Carême used roses in a Bavarian cream, and more recently, the famous Toulouse violets, which you find candied as a confectionery garnish, were gracing salads in southwestern France before the turn of the century.) Nowadays you must be very careful and choose red or pink roses from a reliable grower who does not use poisonous sprays. The subtle perfume provides an aromatic treat that is perfect for luncheon but not dinner.

Sugar flower pièce montée by Michel Finel

Yields 8 servings

12 to 18 roses
1/2 cup (100 g) sugar
4 cups (950 ml) half-and-half
10 egg yolks
1/2 cup (100 g) sugar
3/4 cup (180 ml) whipping cream
A few drops of red food coloring

Recommended equipment

A blender, glass bowl, plastic wrap, 2-quart (2 L) saucepan, wooden spatula, electric mixer with mixing bowl, rubber spatula, large fine-mesh sieve, ice cream machine.

Remove the petals from the roses, put them in the blender jar with the sugar, and purée them. Scrape the mixture into the glass bowl, cover tightly with plastic wrap, and let the sugar absorb the perfume of the roses overnight.

The next day, pour the half-and-half into the saucepan, add the rose purée, stirring with the wooden spatula, and set the saucepan over medium heat. Bring the liquid to a boil, stirring from time to time with the spatula and watching it carefully lest it scorch.

While the half-and-half is heating, combine the

egg yolks and sugar in the mixing bowl and beat at medium speed for about 3 minutes or until the mixture is thick, light yellow, and the sugar has dissolved. While mixing, scrape down the sides of the bowl with the rubber spatula from time to time. When done, reserve the mixture in the bowl.

When the half-and-half comes to a boil, remove it from heat and *slowly* pour about 1 cup (235 ml) of the hot half-and-half into the egg yolk mixture, beating continuously on low speed. This will warm the yolks before the next step. Then add the yolk mixture to the saucepan with the half-and-half, set it over low heat, and cook,stirring constantly with the wooden spatula, for 1 to 2 minutes or until the mixture has thickened enough to coat the spatula.

When done, remove from heat at once, pour the custard through the sieve into a bowl, and let cool at room temperature.

When the custard is cool, stir in the whipping cream and food coloring and freeze the mixture in the ice cream machine according to the manufacturer's instructions.

If fresh roses are unavailable, add rose water (imported from France) to taste to the custard when it is cool and before the whipping cream is added. For a festive presentation, stir fresh or crystallized rose petals into the mixture before freezing.

Caramel Ice Cream

Caramel is a conjurer of many memories. To the seasoned European traveler, it is the inevitable entry on the dessert trolley—a simple creation which, in the right hands, can provide a foretaste of confectionery heaven.

Apple tart lovers know it as tangible evidence of the apocryphal legend surrounding the famous dessert from the sisters Tatin of Lamotte-Beuvron. For children, it is the soft candy which comes in individual wrappers or the true Halloween treat, a chewy covering for a fresh fall apple on a stick. The lovely burnt-sugar flavor and color of caramel also make a superb ice cream year-round.

Yields 8 servings

1 cup (235 ml) whipping cream
1 cup (195 g) sugar
4 cups (950 ml) half-and-half
10 egg yolks
1/2 cup (100 g) sugar

Recommended equipment

A 1-quart (1 L) saucepan, wooden spatula, two 2-quart (2 L) saucepans, candy thermometer, electric mixer with mixing bowl, rubber spatula, large fine-mesh sieve, ice cream machine.

Put the whipping cream in the smaller saucepan, set it over medium heat, and bring the cream to a boil, stirring from time to time with the wooden spatula and watching it carefully lest it scorch. When the cream is boiling, remove it at once from heat and set the saucepan aside.

Put the sugar in one of the larger saucepans, stir in just enough water (about 1 tablespoon) to dissolve the sugar, set the saucepan over medium heat, and cook until the sugar is light golden brown and registers 302F (150C) on the candy thermometer. Remove from heat immediately and little by little pour in the reserved cream, stirring constantly and working carefully because the cream will foam up as it is added. When all the cream has been added, set the saucepan with the caramel aside.

Pour the half-and-half into the remaining saucepan, set it over medium heat, and bring the liquid to a boil, stirring from time to time with the wooden spatula to keep it from scorching.

While the half-and-half is heating, combine the egg yolks and sugar in the mixing bowl and beat at medium speed for about 3 minutes or until the mixture is thick, light yellow, and the sugar has dissolved. While mixing, scrape down the sides of the bowl with the rubber spatula from time to time. When done, reserve the mixture in the bowl.

When the half-and-half comes to a boil, remove it from heat and *slowly* pour about 1 cup (235 ml) of the hot half-and-half into the egg yolk mixture, beating continuously on low speed. This will warm the yolks before the next step. Then add the yolk mixture to the saucepan with the half-and-half, set it over low heat, and cook, stirring constantly with the wooden spatula, for 1 to 2 minutes or until the mixture has thickened enough to coat the spatula. When done, remove from heat at once, stir in the reserved caramel, pass the mixture through the sieve into a bowl, and let cool at room temperature.

When cool, freeze the mixture in the ice cream machine according to the manufacturer's instructions.

Simple Syrup

A sorbet should be silky smooth in texture without a trace of graininess. Even though sugar can be added directly to the fruit, one way to ensure smoothness is to dissolve the sugar in water by making a simple syrup. The name tells you how easy this is. Make a generous quantity of syrup whenever you have time, let it cool to room temperature, and store it in a covered jar in the refrigerator, where it will keep indefinitely and be ready when you are. One conseil: water quality is just as important here as it is in sauces—after all you are making a kind of chilled fresh fruit sauce. If your tap water has a strong chemical taste, be sure to get bottled spring water to make simple syrup.

Yields 4 cups (950 ml)

4 cups (950 ml) water
4 cups (780 g) sugar

Combine the water and sugar in a 2-quart (2 L) saucepan, set it over medium heat, and bring the liquid to a simmer to dissolve the sugar. Do not stir. Remove at once from heat and let cool before using.

Sorbet à la Framboise
Raspberry Sorbet

Fresh raspberries! If you grew up with them in picking reach, you know the extraordinary sensation of the perfume of the berry just plucked from the vine. In fact, you know the flavor of the first handful or two of berries, which never make it into the container you are using to gather them. Some of us have even been known to take cream, bowl, and spoon straight to the garden for a daybreak treat. Now that air transport has extended the raspberry patch to California and New Zealand, local markets have lengthened the season by making the berries available for much of the year—giving you just the excuse (if you need one) to make this sorbet. Generally speaking, framboise comes in three strengths, ranging from a dark, rather sweet, lower proof liqueur from Burgundy, to a lighter, less sweet liqueur and a dry, clear eau-de-vie, both of which come from Alsace. All are expensive—nearly sixty pounds of berries are used to produce one bottle of eau-de-vie—but worth every penny. To enliven your sorbet with the spirit of the Belle de Fontenay, increase the amount of framboise, but not to more than a total of one-quarter cup lest the mixture not freeze properly.

Yields 8 to 10 servings

6 cups (1425 ml) fresh raspberries
1 cup (235 ml) Simple Syrup (see page 562)
1/4 cup (60 ml) lemon juice
2 teaspoons framboise (eau-de-vie)

Recommended equipment

A blender or food processor, wooden spoon, large fine-mesh sieve, 2-quart (2 L) bowl, wire whisk, ice cream machine.

Purée the raspberries in the blender or food processor and pour the purée through the sieve into the bowl, stirring with the wooden spoon to get all the purée through. You should have about 3 cups (710 ml) of purée. Mixing with the whisk, stir in the simple syrup, lemon juice, and framboise (adding more framboise if you wish). Then freeze the mixture in the ice cream machine according to the manufacturer's instructions.

Sorbet à l'Ananas
Pineapple Sorbet

Anana, *the name Caribbean Indians had given the fruit Columbus brought back from his second voyage to the New World, persists throughout Europe as the name for pineapple. Oddly enough, unlike other fruits, it did not take readily to the benign Mediterranean climate, so we should be thankful that it seems to like Hawaii so much. This sorbet is a real showcase for the unique flavor of fresh pineapple, which you should make the effort to find. If it is unavailable, unsweetened canned fruit is an acceptable substitute.*

Yields 8 to 10 servings

1 ripe pineapple
1/2 cup (100 g) plus 2 tablespoons sugar
1/4 cup (60 ml) lemon juice

Recommended equipment

A serrated slicing knife, blender or food processor, rubber spatula, large fine-mesh sieve, 2-quart (2 L) bowl, wire whisk, ice cream machine.

Remove the rind and core from the pineapple, cut the fruit into chunks, and purée it in the blender or food processor. Scrape the purée into the sieve set over the bowl and reserve the juice. You should have about 2 cups (475 ml) fruit purée and 3/4 cup juice (if you have less, add canned juice, if you have more, pour off the excess and reserve).

Combine the purée, juice, sugar, and lemon juice in the bowl and mix well with the whisk to dissolve the sugar. Taste and adjust the flavor with lemon juice or sugar as needed. Freeze the mixture in the ice cream machine according to the manufacturer's instructions.

Sorbet au Calvados

If the Vallée d'Auge in Normandy is the French apple orchard, it follows that one might expect to find the best cider there as well. Indeed that is the case, for not only is the best cider made in the département of Calvados, but this name has become attached to a magnificent brandy made from the cider. Don't be talked into buying apple jack as a substitute because Calvados simply has no equal. This sorbet is included specifically for use as a palate-clearing stage in a formal dinner—as we use it for banquets. We will not deceive you, this calls for a great deal of Calvados, which is expensive. However, the yield is sufficient for a large number of guests because each portion should be about one-eighth of a cup.

Yields 2 cups

3 3/4 cups (890 ml) Calvados
6 tablespoons Simple Syrup *(see page 562)*

Recommended equipment

A small saucepan, wire whisk, ice cream machine.

Main Dining Room

Pour 3 1/2 cups (830 ml) Calvados into the saucepan and heat over medium heat. When it is hot, take it off heat, set it aflame (be sure to stand back), and let the alcohol burn off. This will take a little less than 10 minutes. Add the simple syrup and let the mixture cool to room temperature. When it is cool, add the remaining Calvados and adjust the flavor with sugar if needed. Freeze the mixture in the ice cream machine according to the manufacturer's instructions.

Sorbet au Pamplemousse
Grapefruit Sorbet

Unlike the orange, which is an ancient Southeast Asian native, the grapefruit is an eighteenth-century newcomer, albeit with a fascinating history. In 1696, Captain Shaddock of the East-India company called on the port of Barbados, leaving as part of his shipment seeds from the pummelo *tree (by some accounts native to China), which bears large pear-shaped fruit with a loose rind and rather dry pulp. The tree was named after him, and when it was crossed with an orange tree, the resulting hybrid fruit came to be known as a small Shaddock, small pompelmoose, or grapefruit. From* pompelmoose *it is a short sea voyage to* pompelmoes *(Dutch),* pompelmo *(Italian), or the French given here. To confuse matters further, some American produce markets will also display grapefruit as pomelos. Rest assured, however, that there is no confusion about this sorbet—it is delicious.*

Yields 8 servings

2 1/2 cups (590 ml) unsweetened frozen grapefruit juice concentrate
2 cups (475 ml) Simple Syrup (see page 562)
Juice of 2 lemons

Recommended equipment

A 1-quart (1 L) bowl, wire whisk, ice cream machine.

Combine the grapefruit juice, simple syrup, and lemon juice in the bowl, taste, add sugar or lemon juice if necessary, and then freeze the mixture in the ice cream machine according to the manufacturer's instructions.

For a subtle color variation, use pink grapefruit concentrate, and for an interesting flavor variation, substitute some honey for sugar when you make the simple syrup.

Sorbet à la Poire
Pear Sorbet

The texture and flavor of poached fresh pears marry perfectly in sorbet. Buy William pears, if you can, or else Bartlett, Comice, or Anjou, and allow enough time to poach and cool the pears before using. To point up the pear flavor, stir in as much as one-quarter cup Poire William (pear brandy) before freezing the purée.

Well, this recipe ends our kitchen story, and unlike Pierrette, I will make a quick exit to go and work on B. G. McElwee's Shopping List for next week. We've enjoyed showing you around and hope that what is in these pages will serve you well as you try to capture a bit of the Homestead at home.

Yields 8 servings

1 pound (450 g) William pears
2 cups (475 ml) Simple Syrup
 (see page 562)
Juice of 4 lemons

Recommended equipment

A swivel-bladed vegetable peeler, paring knife, saucepan large enough to hold pears in a single layer, slotted spoon, blender or food processor, rubber spatula, 2-quart (2 L) bowl, wire whisk, ice cream machine.

Peel and halve the pears and remove the stem, core, and seeds. Rub the pear halves with lemon juice to keep them from turning brown. Place the halves cut side down in a single layer in the saucepan. Cover them with a syrup made of 1 part sugar dissolved in 2 parts water (about 3/4 cup or 145 g sugar and 1 1/2 cups or 355 ml water), set the saucepan over medium heat, and bring the liquid to a boil. Then adjust heat so that the pears simmer gently for about 10 to 15 minutes or until pears can be lightly pierced with the point of a paring knife. Remove the pears with a slotted spoon and let cool at room temperature.

When the pears are cool, purée in the blender or food processor, scrape them into the bowl, and whisk in the simple syrup and lemon juice (and Poire William if you are using it). Adjust seasoning if necessary, and freeze in the ice cream machine according to the manufacturer's instructions.

❧

To lend an even more intense pear flavor to the sorbet, substitute the poaching liquid for an equal amount of simple syrup by adding another scant 3/4 cup of sugar and dissolving it in the warm liquid. Then you will need approximately 1/2 cup (118 ml) of simple syrup.

Notes on Ingredients and Techniques

Ingredients

Baking powder is of the double acting variety.

Bread crumbs are understood to be fine white bread crumbs from Pullman loaf or *pain de mie*. Do not use any bread which does not have a dense, firm crumb.

Butter is unsalted.

Caviar is called for in several instances and is meant to be refrigerated and packed in tins. Bottled vacuum-packed caviar may also be used if the fresh product is unavailable.

Eggs are 2 ounces (57 g), called "large" in the store.

Flour is unbleached all-purpose.

Gelatin typically comes in individual packets containing one-quarter ounce in granular form—enough to jell two cups of liquid. It is also available in sheet form and will require one-half ounce for the same amount of liquid.

Herbs are understood to be fresh, unless otherwise specified. If they are unavailable, used dried instead and reduce the quantity by one-half.

Oil for frying, sautéing or greasing pans is peanut oil. Because it is natural, it has the advantage of being tasteless. It also does not break down under high heat. If you substitute another oil, be sure it satisfies these criteria.

Saffron comes either in threads or powdered form and one-half teaspoon chopped is equivalent to one-third teaspoon powdered. If you are using threads, be sure to dissolve them in hot broth or water before using.

Salt is kosher-style flake salt with no additives.

Sugar is either plain granulated or 10X powdered.

Whipping cream should contain at least 30 percent milk fat. Heavy cream, which can contain 36 percent milk fat or more, may also be used.

Techniques

Deglazing is a process by which wine, vinegar, water, or stock is added to a pan to loosen the bits left behind from roasting or sautéing. These bits are thus dissolved and serve to add flavor and color to the sauce being prepared.

Blanched, peeled, and seeded tomatoes are prepared as follows: Core each tomato and make a crosswise ½ inch (1 cm) skin-deep incision at the stem end. Drop the tomatoes into a large pot of boiling water for about 15 seconds. Drain into a colander and put under running cold water until well cooled. With a sharp paring knife, peel tomatoes and cut them in half crosswise. Then gently squeeze out all seeds and pulp. For a yield of 2 cups (475 ml), you will need three large tomatoes. To skin a perfectly ripe garden tomato when you would rather not boil a pot of water for one or two tomatoes, do the following: rub the tomato skin all over with the flat back edge of a paring knife using gentle, even pressure. Then turn the knife to the cutting edge and peel away the loosened skin.

For last minute preparation or finishing of dishes ("à la minute" cooking), thickening can be done without using roux or flour. This binding method, popularized by Escoffier, calls for reducing stocks to one half or one third and adding heavy cream or crème fraîche to produce the desired consistency. Where cream does not lend itself to a specific recipe, reduce stock by two-thirds, remove from heat, and work in soft butter with a whisk a little at a time. Do not boil or reheat sauce after this addition or it will break down. Occasionally a sauce will need a last minute taste adjustment beyond the addition of salt and pepper. Two commercial preparations which are particularly useful in the professional kitchen are Maggi seasoning (liquid) and Aromat (dry). These are available in smaller quantities for domestic use. But, be careful please, they are very concentrated.

In cooking *en papillote*, parchment paper is preferable, although white or brown heavy butcher paper may be substituted. (Heavy foil should be used for outdoor cooking on a grill, but it will not puff up.) Fold an 18-by-14-inch (45 x 35 cm) piece of paper in half and cut it into the shape of half a heart. Open it up and, before adding any ingredients, brush the inside surface with clarified butter or olive oil. Arrange the ingredients (with their widest part toward the rounded top) on one half of the heart. Fold the paper over the ingredients and, beginning at the top, make tight overlapping small folds all along the edges to form a tight seal. When properly sealed, the paper will puff up for a most attractive presentation at the table.

To clarify butter put it in a saucepan over *low* heat until completely melted. (Butter should not boil.) Remove from heat and let sit for several minutes without stirring, allowing sediments to sink to bottom of pan. Skim foam from surface before using and omit the milky solids on the pan bottom.

To bone fresh or smoked salmon fillets, it is best to have a hemostat (easily purchased at a store selling medical supplies) or needle-nose pliers. With the fillet laying skin side down on a cutting board or counter, carefully run your fingers along the center of the fillet to find the embedded bones. Then, grasping them with the hemostat or pliers, carefully tug at them to remove them without tearing the fillet.

To truss a bird you will need a trussing needle and white kitchen string. Put the bird on its back on your work surface. At the vent end, push the needle from one side through the skin and cavity to the other side, looping the string back over the end of one leg. Push the needle through the tip of the breastbone and loop the string over the end of the other leg, coming out where you began. Cut the string and tie a secure knot, drawing the legs together over the vent opening. (If you are stuffing the bird, or cooking it on a spit, you should also sew up the vent with several stitches.) Continue on the other end with the bird on its back. Holding one wing close to the body, push the needle and string through the wing-tip joint into the body and through the same joint on the other side. Then turn the bird over and bring the string across, catching the skin flap under it, and tie a knot.

Notes on sautéing fish: A good quality peanut oil should be used for sautéing fish because it will not break down under the necessary high heat. (Clarified butter is less heat resistant and may burn, leaving a bitter taste.) When sautéing fish in several batches, pour out the old oil, wipe the pan with paper towels, and add fresh oil after the first two batches.

It is most important to start the sauté over high heat to form a good crust that protects the delicate fish meat from direct contact with the oil. The crust also prevents the fish from drying out. Once the crust is formed the heat should be reduced so the fish finishes cooking more gently. The secret of sautéing fish (and all fish cooking) is to cook the fish until just done and not a moment more. The thickness of the fish is one of the keys to success. For example, if the fillet is larger than 6 to 8 ounces and thicker than ¾ inch, brown well on both sides (2 minutes each) and then set pan into a preheated 325F (163C) oven for 3 to 8 minutes depending upon the size of the fillet. This method of brief oven cooking after sautéing is especially suited to thicker fillets like red snapper, salmon, halibut, or striped bass. For these allow 5 minutes in the oven for a fillet 1 inch thick and 8 minutes for one 2 inches thick.

For a variation on this technique, marinate the fish for 10 to 20 minutes before sautéing by seasoning the fillets lightly with salt and freshly ground white pepper, a few drops of Worcestershire sauce, and the juice from one-half a lemon. Cover the fillets, refrigerate, and turn them over halfway through the marinating interval.

When you are ready to cook, dip the fish into milk or half-and-half, let the excess drip off and dredge the fillets in flour, patting the flour on both sides. Shake lightly to remove excess flour, and cook as above.

To flambé with a liqueur either the pan or the liqueur must be warm. For a warm sauté pan, pour in the liqueur, ignite, and stir until the flame dies. For other situations, warm the liqueur separately in a small saucepan, pour over the food, ignite, and stir until the flame dies. The process burns off the alcohol and leaves the flavor of the liqueur or brandy.

Cheesecloth, when new, must be rinsed of its sizing lest it flavor the food.

To pulverize nuts put one-half cup in an electric blender and whir at full speed. Do not let the nuts get too hot or they will become oily.

Batterie de Cuisine

The following list contains all the items that you will need to prepare the recipes in this cookbook. When buying kitchen equipment look for solid, practical ware that will stand up during years of use, and remember that the cheapest is the dearest in the end. Any cooking utensil must be made of nonreactive material, and mixing bowls should be stainless steel or glass.

Saucepans

Small (for melting butter, warming liqueurs, etc.)
1 1/2 quart (1 1/2 L) with lid
2 quart (2 L) saucepan
3 quart (3 L) with lid
4 to 5 quart (4 to 5 L) with lid
Double boiler insert for one of the above saucepans

Stockpots

8 quart and 16 quart (8 and 15 L) with lids

Sauté pans

6, 8, 10, and 12 inch (15, 20, 25, and 30 cm) cast-iron, enameled cast-iron, stainless steel, or copper with nickel or stainless steel lining

Baking and roasting pans

Cake pans (3): 10 inches (25 cm)
Pie pans: 9 and 10 inches (22 1/2 and 25 cm)
Tart pan: 10 by 1 1/2 inches (25 × 3 3/4 cm)
Baking dishes (2): 11 × 7 × 2 inches (27 1/2 × 17 1/2 × 5 cm)
4 and 8 quart (4 and 8 L) enameled cast-iron or lined copper baking dishes or plats à sauter
Baking sheets (2): 11 × 15 inches (27 1/2 × 37 1/2 cm)
Baking dish: 1 quart (1 L)
Heatproof serving dish: 1 quart (1 L)
Glass or ceramic soufflé dish: 2 quarts (2 L)
Small ovenproof crocks or bowls
Tube pan: 9 or 10 inches (22 1/2 or 25 cm)
Muffin tins
Springform pan: 10 inches (25 cm)
Sheet pan: 15 × 10 × 3/4 inches (37 1/2 × 25 × 2 cm)
Loaf pans:
 8 1/2 × 4 1/2 × 2 1/2 inches (21 1/4 × 11 1/4 × 6 1/4 cm)
 9 1/4 × 5 1/4 × 2 3/4 inches (23 1/2 × 13 1/3 × 7 cm)
 12 × 5 × 3 inches (30 × 12 1/2 × 7 1/2 cm)
Dutch oven: 7 to 8 quarts (7 to 8 L)
Heavy roasting pan: about 11 × 15 inches (27 1/2 × 37 1/2 cm)
Broiler pan with rack

Knives

2-inch (5 cm) paring knife
5-inch (12 1/2 cm) flexible-bladed boning knife
9-inch (22 1/2 cm) slicing knife
12-inch (30 cm) slicing or carving knife
8-inch (20 cm) chef's knife (called "small" in the text)
10-inch (25 cm) chef's knife (called "large" in the text)
Fileting knife

Oyster knife
Serrated knife
Heavy cleaver: about 1 pound (450 g)
Butcher's steel for sharpening knives

Small wares

Fine-mesh sieves (3): 3 1/2, 6, and 8 inches (8 3/4, 15, and 20 cm) in diameter
Metal colander or strainer—about 12 inches (30 cm) in diameter with a solid base, not tipsy legs
Coarse-mesh sieve
Fine-mesh skimmer
Piano wire whisk: about 10 to 12 inches (25 to 30 cm) in length
Wooden whisk
Potato ricer
Swivel-bladed vegetable peeler
Garlic press
Wooden spoons (2)
Metal slotted spoon
Oven thermometer
Instant-read meat thermometer
Candy thermometer
Frying thermometer
Poultry shears
Stainless steel box grater
Pepper grinders (2)
Nutmeg grinder
Flexible icing spatula: 6 inches (15 cm)
Large rubber spatula: about 12 inches (30 cm) in length
Flat turning spatula

Wooden spatulas (2)
Long-handled fork
Metal tongs
Apple corer
Flour sifter
Metal shaker for powdered sugar
Biscuit cutters (3): 1, 2 1/4, and 3 inches (2 1/2, 5 2/3, and 7 1/2 cm) in diameter
Cookie cutters
Vol-au-vent cutter: 3 inches (7 1/2 cm) in diameter
Pastry brush with natural bristles
Pastry blender or blending fork
Pastry scraper
Wire cooling racks (2)
Stiff natural bristle brush
Large basting spoon
Large serving spoons (2)
Ladle with 10-inch (25 cm) long handle
Fork with 10-inch (25 cm) long handle
Hardwood rolling pin
Marble mortar and pestle
Large pastry bag with tubes
Shrimp deveiner
Funnel
Timer
Trussing needle
Bulb baster (preferably metal)
Glass measure: 4 cups

Mixing bowls

1 quart (1 L)
2 quart (2 L)
3 quart (3 L) (called "small" in the text)
4 quart (4 L) (called "medium" in the text)
5 quart (5 L) (called "large" in the text)
For marinating: 3-quart glass or china bowl

Supplies

White kitchen string
Waxed paper
Aluminum foil
Plastic wrap
Cheesecloth
Hardwood charcoal

Special equipment

Electric deep fryer with thermostat
Stainless steel or tin-lined fish poacher

Appliances

Blender
Food mill
Meat grinder
Hand mixer
Stationary mixer with processing attachments or food processor
Charcoal grill
Accurate kitchen scale

Photography Credits

James and Eleanor Ferguson: 14 bottom left, 16 top, 20, 21, 27 first, second, and fourth from top, 30, 32 top, 33 first and second from top, 34, 35, 36, 37, 39 first, second, fourth, and fifth from top, 40, 41 second and third from top, 42 on right and top and bottom on left, 43 second, third, and fifth from top, 44 second, third, fourth, fifth, and sixth from top, 45, 46 first, third, fourth, and fifth from top, 47 bottom right, 48, 60, 64, 67, 69, 77, 79, 81, 85, 89, 94, 96, 100, 102, 117, 118, 122, 131, 133, 137, 143, 147, 151, 153, 162, 165, 166, 175, 177, 179, 199, 207, 218, 221, 226, 230, 243, 247, 248, 250, 253, 264, 271, 281, 286, 313, 314, 321, 331, 341, 345, 347, 349, 353, 357, 366, 368, 370, 392, 395, 402, 407, 408, 410, 416, 420, 422, 427, 436, 439, 441, 455, 459, 463, 466, 467, 471, 477, 485, 486, 487, 488, 489, 491, 492, 499, 503, 505, 511, 513, 514, 517, 519, 530 lower left, 537, 539, 542, 549, 554, 557, 565

Werner Gattinger: iv, xxiii, 14 top right, 15, 22 top three, 24, 25 top, 27 third from top, 32 bottom, 39 third from top, 41 top, 43 fourth from top, 46 second from top, 106, 127, 145, 172, 186, 189, 211, 239, 266, 275, 283, 291, 294, 300, 303, 310, 339, 377, 379, 424, 437, 457, 469, 472, 475, 524, 526, 530 top right, 532, 559

Kris Kable: 22 bottom, 387, 453

Romulo Yanes: 8, 9, 10, 11, 16 bottom, 18, 19, 23, 25 bottom, 33, 42 second from top at left, 43 top, 44 top, 47 top left, 72, 104, 110, 116, 124, 130, 135, 155, 158, 169, 182, 185, 190, 201, 204, 215, 223, 233, 236, 256, 258, 277, 288, 296, 307, 318, 324, 334, 337, 360, 374, 381, 390, 401, 413, 418, 431, 434, 444, 462, 473, 478, 495, 501, 506, 522, 535, 544, 547, 560, 563, 564, 567

Charts by Heidi Perry, pages 29, 38, 55, 56, and 57. Illustrations by Tina Re, pages 265, 347, 394, and 497.

The Keith H. Knost shop graciously allowed the following items to be used: page 155, English Beef Tea, crystal bowls and candlesticks by Zwiesel; page 307, Roast Pheasant, platter by Porta. Two photographs were taken at the shop. On page 318, the French Venison Stew: china, Quimper; flatware, Kirk Stieff "Old Annapolis"; napkins, Chicago Weaving Company; water goblet, Royal Copenhagen "Holmegaard." On page 381, the Carré d'Agneau Persillé: china and cachepot, Herend "Chinese Bouquet Green"; centerpiece, bowl of artichokes by Oggetti; silver-plate flatware, Georg Jensen "Bernadotte"; silver-plate carving set by Towle; stemware, Leerdam "Airtwist"; silver-plate candlesticks, by Michael Feinberg; service plates and silver-plate cobalt salt by Landes; linens, Jabara "Shell" design, made in Madeira.

Bibliography

Allen, Geoffrey Freeman. *Luxury Trains of the World*. New York: Everest House, 1979.

Beard, James. *Beard on Pasta*. New York: Alfred A. Knopf, 1983.

Blake, Anthony, and Crewe, Quentin. *Great Chefs of France*. New York: Harry N. Abrams, Inc., 1978.

Blanc, Georges. *The Natural Cuisine of Georges Blanc*. New York: Stewart, Tabori and Chang, Inc., 1987.

Chamberlain, Samuel. *Bouquet de France*. New York: Gourmet Distributing Corporation, 1957.

———. *Italian Bouquet*. New York: Gourmet Books, Inc., 1958.

Child, Julia. *From Julia Child's Kitchen*. New York: Alfred A. Knopf, 1975.

Claiborne, Craig, with Pierre Franey. *The New New York Times Cookbook*. New York: Times Books, 1979.

Clayton, Bernard, Jr. *The Breads of France*. Indianapolis: The Bobbs-Merrill Company, Inc., 1978.

David, Elizabeth. *An Omelette and a Glass of Wine*. New York: Viking Penguin Inc., 1984.

———. *English Bread and Yeast Cookery*. New York: Viking Press, 1980.

de Groot, Roy Andries. *Revolutionizing French Cooking*. New York: McGraw-Hill Book Company, 1976.

Escoffier, Georges Auguste. *Le Guide Culinaire*. Paris: 1902.

Given, Meta. *Meta Given's Modern Encyclopedia of Cooking*. Chicago: J. G. Ferguson Publishing Company, 1969.

Grigson, Jane. *Jane Grigson's Vegetable Book*. New York: Atheneum, 1979.

Hale, William Harlan. *The Horizon Cookbook*. New York: American Heritage Publishing Co., Inc., 1968.

Hazen, Marcella. *The Classic Italian Cookbook*. New York: Alfred A. Knopf, 1983.

Herbodeau, Eugène, and Thalamas, Paul. *Georges Auguste Escoffier*. London: Practical Press Ltd., 1955.

Lamb, Charles. *A Dissertation upon Roast Pig*. London: Sampson Low, Marston, & Company, n.d.

La Reynière, Grimod de (Alexandre-Balthazar-Laurent). *Almanach des Gourmands*. Paris: Maradan, 1803–12.

Le Huédé, Henri. *Dining on the France*. New York: The Vendome Press, 1981.

Lichine, Alexis. *Alexis Lichine's Encyclopedia of Wines & Spirits*. New York: Alfred A. Knopf, 1973.

McClane, A. J. *The Encyclopedia of Fish Cookery*. New York: Holt, Rinehart and Winston, 1977.

McGee, Harold. *On Food and Cooking*. New York: Charles Scribner's Sons, 1984.

Montagné, Prosper. *The New Larousse Gastronomique*. New York: Crown Publishers, 1977.

Neal, William F. *Bill Neal's Southern Cooking*. Chapel Hill: University of North Carolina Press, 1985.

Offrey, Charles. *Normandie, Queen of the Seas*. New York: The Vendome Press, 1985.

Oliver, Raymond. *La Cuisine*. New York: Tudor Publishing Company, 1969.

Point, Fernand. *Ma Gastronomie*. Paris: Flammarion et Cie., 1969.

Reboul, J. B. *La Cuisinière Provençale*. 22d ed. Marseille: Tacussel, n.d.

Tropp, Barbara. *The Modern Art of Chinese Cooking*. New York: William Morrow and Company, Inc., 1982.

Vergé, Roger. *Roger Vergé's Entertaining in the French Style*. New York: Stewart, Tabori and Chang, Inc., 1986.

Wolfert, Paula. *The Cooking of South-West France*. New York: The Dial Press, 1983.

Index

References to recipes are in italics

Aegean sea, 198, 257
Agen, France, 542
Al dente: cooking defined, 412
Alexander I (Czar of Russia), 136, 194, 372
Alexandria, Egypt, 198, 257, 481
Allegheny Mountains (Va.), 15, 17, 194, 198
Almonds: history of, 547; sliced, how to toast, 199
Alps, the, 325, 326, 355, 357
Alsace (France), 79, 191, 555, 562
Apicius, 20, 406, 464; *De Re Coquinaria*, 387, 406; on sauces, 50, 53; on soups, 387
Architects: Mies van der Rohe, Ludwig, 326; Mizner, Addison, 16; Schultze, Leonard, 16; Warren and Wetmore, 14; Wright, Frank Lloyd, 16
Arezzo, Italy, 412
Argenteuil, France, 447
Asparagus: *Asparagus* (trimmed and blanched), 453–54; in *Asparagus Butter Sauce*, 89; *Asparagus Parmesan* (blanched and gratinéed with butter and Parmesan), 454; in *Asparagus Vichyssoise*, 123; in *Cream of Asparagus Soup*, 141; history of, 447
Aspic, 5; how to serve, 124
Auvergne (France), 206
Avocado: in *Avocado Southampton*, 176

Bacon, Sir Francis, 402; quoted, 361
Bake Shop (at the Homestead), 479–81; baking schedule for, 480; ovens described, 480
Ballottine: defined, 222
Barbecue: beef, 363–64; pork, 400
Barcelona, Spain, 197, 254
Barley: history of, 387
Basel, Switzerland, 114, 134
Bath County, Va., 318
Beans: dried, 448; *Flageolets Bretonne* (white beans simmered with aromatic vegetables, garlic, and bacon, in a tomato sauce), 456–57; green, history of, 447–48; *String Beans* (blanched, lightly sautéed, garnished with butter), 455; *String Beans Country Style* (cooked with bacon and onion in an aromatic broth), 456

Beard, James: quoted, 412
Béarn (French province), 93
Beef, discussed, 361, 362, 401; Charolais, 362, 368; Fillet of Beef Prince Albert (or Prince of Wales), 379; Limousin, 368; roast tenderloin, 364–65; steak, 364; stews, 364; tenderloin, 364; types of, 363, 365. *See also* Beef marrow; Beef short ribs; Beef sirloin; Beef spareribs; Beef stews; Beef tenderloin, roast; Beef tenderloin, sautéed
Beef marrow: in *Risotto*, 428; in *Sauce Bordelaise*, 79
Beef short ribs: *Barbecued Short Ribs of Beef Homestead* (marinated with ginger, garlic, mustard, brown sugar, and sherry, baked, and glazed with honey), 366–67; *Teriyaki Marinated Short Ribs of Beef Homestead* (marinated with teriyaki sauce, soy sauce, brown sugar, garlic, and ginger and baked), 365
Beef sirloin: *Marinated Steaks* (with bell peppers, shallots, and garlic, sauced with wine deglaze), 370–72
Beef spareribs: marinade for, 366
Beef stews: *Boeuf à la Bourguignonne* (marinated in red wine with aromatic vegetables, served with pearl onions, croutons, and mushrooms with a demi-glace sauce), 368–70; *Sauerbraten* (boneless chuck roast marinated with wine, vinegar, and aromatic vegetables, served with a wine deglaze), 367–68
Beef tenderloin, roast: *Roast Black Pepper Tenderloin of Beef with Armagnac Sauce, Green Peppercorns, and Raisins* (marinated with black pepper and sauced with Armagnac, green peppercorns, and golden raisins), 377–78; *Roast Tenderloin of Beef London House with Truffle Sauce* (filled with foie gras and served with Madeira and truffle sauce), 378–79; *Roast Three-Pepper Tenderloin of Beef with Armagnac Sauce* (marinated with white, green, and black pepper, sauced with shallots, demi-glace, and Armagnac), 376–77
Beef tenderloin, sautéed: *Sauté de Mi-*

gnonettes de Boeuf à la Printanière (filets mignons seasoned with garlic and pepper, served with onion, bell peppers, carrots, mushrooms, Chinese cabbage, and red wine deglaze), 374–76; *Tenderloin of Beef Café Martin* (with shallots and garlic, sauced with demi-glace, tomatoes, onion, mixed peppers, and mushrooms), 373–74; *Tenderloin of Beef Stroganoff* (sauced with tomato-flavored stock, herbs, mushrooms, and sour cream), 372–73
Beets: in *Beet Salad*, 183–84; in *Borscht à la Russe*, 136
Bell pepper: soup cup made from, 116
Belshazzar (king of Mesopotamia), 139
B. G. McElwee's Shopping List. *See* McElwee, B. G.: shopping list
Black Forest (Germany), 530
Blake, Anthony: quoted, 11–12
Booke of Cookerie, A (anon.), 6
Bordeaux, France, 262, 270, 378
Bouquet de France (by Samuel Chamberlain), 313
Bourbonnais (France), 318
Bourg de Batz, France, 12
Bourgogne (France), 318. *See also* Burgundy (France)
Bread making: flour discussed, 481–82; leaven discussed, 482–83, 485, 503; technique discussed, 483–84; Vienna baking system, 487; yeast discussed, 482
Breads, discussed: banana nut bread, 480; biscuits, 480; corn bread, 480; croissants, 480, history of, 494; Danish pastry, 480; dinner rolls, 480; doughnuts, 480; English muffins, 480; French bread, 480; history of, 494; Pullman loaf, 174, 480; rye bread, 480; sour cream raisin tea loaf, 480
Breads, quick: *Baking Powder Biscuits*, 503; *Banana Nut Bread* (with walnuts), 500–501; *Blueberry Muffins*, 502; *Buttermilk Biscuits*, 504; *Corn Bread*, 504–5; *Sour Cream Raisin Tea Loaf* (enriched with butter, sour cream, and eggs and flavored with vanilla and raisins), 501

Breads, yeast: *Brioche Bread* (enriched with butter, eggs, and milk), 490; *Brioches* (sweet rolls enriched with butter, eggs, and milk), 493–94; *Cinnamon Pecan Ring* (enriched with milk, butter, egg, and flavored with honey, dark brown sugar, cinnamon, and pecans), 497–98; *Croissants* (crescent rolls enriched with milk and butter), 494–96; *Danish Pastry* (sweet rolls enriched with milk, butter, eggs, and flavored with vanilla, mace, and cinnamon), 498–500; *Dinner Rolls*, 491–92; *French Bread*, 487–88; *Overnight Sweet Rolls* (enriched with butter and eggs), 492–93; *Pullman Loaf* (fine-textured bread for toast and sandwiches), 488–89; *Rye Bread*, 490–91; *White Bread*, 486

Bresse, France, 15, 260, 298, 368, 445

Brillat-Savarin, Anthelme, 4, 311, 382; *La Physiologie du Goût*, 3; quoted, 303, 306, 508; sister Pierrette, 507, 565

Brittany (France), 12, 71

Brussels sprouts: *Brussels Sprouts* (blanched, lightly sautéed, garnished with butter), 457–58; history of, 448

Brussels, Belgium, 466

Bullitt, Thomas, 14, 361

Burgundy (France), 27, 206, 291, 306, 327, 351, 364, 368, 562. *See also* Bourgogne (France)

Cabbage: *Braised Red Cabbage* (marinated with clove, bay leaf, cinnamon, juniper berries, and red wine, braised with onion and apple slices), 458–59; history of, 448

Caen, France, 266

Café Albert (at the Homestead), 31, 303, 545

Cake frosting: *Butter Cream*, 517

Cakes: *Bourbon Pecan Cake* (made with ground hazelnuts, frosted with butter cream flavored with Bourbon, raisins, and pecans), 533; *Coconut Cream Cake* (vanilla génoise layered with crème pâtissière and coconut, frosted with coconut meringue), 532; *Double Apple Sauce Cake* (flavored with allspice, cinnamon, nutmeg, raisins, walnuts, apple sauce, crushed pineapple, and glacéed cherries), 525; *Gâteau Chambord* (vanilla génoise layered with raspberry purée), 534; *Gâteau Princess Marie* (chocolate génoise layered with chocolate chestnut cream and frosted with chocolate cream), 536; *Génoise à la Vanille* (vanilla whole-egg cake), 523–24; *Génoise au Chocolat* (chocolate whole-egg cake), 524; *German Chocolate Cake* (chocolate buttermilk cake with butter cream frosting flavored with pecans and coconut), 529–30; *Milk Chocolate Cheesecake*, 527–28; *Old-fashioned Spice Cake* (flavored with cinnamon, ginger, clove, nutmeg, raisins, and orange peel, with butter sugar frosting), 526–27; *Pound Cake*, 524–25; *Rum Torte* (vanilla génoise layered with meringue and butter cream), 537; *Schwarzwald Kuchen* (Black Forest cake made with chocolate and vanilla génoise layered with cherry compote and flavored with kirsch), 530–31; *Swiss Chocolate Roulade* (chocolate sponge cake rolled with raspberry jam and whipped cream), 528–29; *Swiss Kirsch Torte* (vanilla génoise layered with meringue and butter cream and flavored with kirsch), 537–38

Cakes, discussed, 522–23; Pound Cake, 523

Calf's liver. *See* Veal, calf's liver

Calvados (France), 564

Camargue, the (France), 423

Canapé: defined, 174; Morgon, 174–75

Capon: in *Galantine of Capon*, 179–81; in *Galantine of Capon Jardinière*, 181–82

Cap Vert (Senegal), 119

Carême, Marie-Antoine, 6, 7–9, 194, 296, 453, 508, 560; *L'Art de la Cuisine Française*, 8; career of, 8–9; catalog of sauces, 8, 11; father of, 8; quoted, 509; in Saint Petersburg, Russia, 136, 364, 372; sauce system of, 52, 56

Carrots: *Carottes Glacées* (simmered and glazed with butter and sugar), 459; *Carottes Vichy* (simmered with Vichy water and glazed with butter and sugar), 460; in *Carrot Vichyssoise*, 122–23; history of, 448; *Purée of Carrots* (simmered, puréed, seasoned), 460

Cascades Club Restaurant (Healing Springs, Va.), 22

Cascades Inn (Healing Springs, Va.), 15, 17, 22, 25

Casino, the Homestead, 8, 13, 22, 25, 119, 121; luncheon buffet, 161, 179, 314, 462, 512, 545, 546

Catering Department (at the Homestead): function of, 25–26

Celeriac (celery knob), 448–49, 461–62

Celery: in *Celery Broth*, 153; in *Cream of Celery Soup*, 142; *Hearts of Celery Parmesan* (cooked *blanc à légume* and gratinéed with butter and Parmesan), 460–61; history of, 448; *Purée of Celery* (simmered with celeriac, puréed with potatoes, seasoned with butter and cream), 461–62

Central America, 447, 449

C.G.T. *See* French Line

Chamberlain, Samuel, 313; *Bouquet de France*, 313; quoted, 445, 507

Chanterelles. *See* Mushrooms: chanterelles

Charles V (king of France), 448

Charles IX (king of France), 192

Charolles, France, 363, 368

Châteaux, 16, 204, 318; Azay-le-Rideau, 4; Beauregard, 4; Chambord, 4, 13, 16, 534; Chaumont, 4; Chenonceau, 4; Montmorency, 216; Versailles, 7

Chaud-froid preparation: history of, 216

Cheese, Roquefort: history of, 343

Chefs, French *Michelin* three-star, 260, 349, 362, 397, 510; Barrier, Charles, 20; Bise, François, 20; Blanc, Georges, 397; Bocuse, Paul, 20–21; Chapel, Alain, 20–21; Guérard, Michel, 20, quoted, 349; Haeberlin, Paul, 79; Meneau, Marc, 159; Outhier, Louis, 20, 234, quoted, 510; Pic, Jacques, 13, 20; Thuilier, Raymond, 20. *See also* Haeberlin brothers; Haeberlin family; Point, Fernand; Troisgros, Jean; Troisgros brothers; Vergé, Roger

Chefs, maritime: Bainbridge, John, 22, quoted, 23; Grangier, Clement, 98, 289; Grangier, Raymond, 289. *See also* Le Huédé, Henri

Chefs, profession of, 7, 8, 10

Chef's Department (at the Homestead), 26

Chefs-patron, 7, 12, 13, 20

Cherbourg, France, 234

Chestnuts: in *Gâteau Princess Marie*, 536; how to peel fresh, 323; in stuffing for *Roast Stuffed Tenderloin of Venison with Cream Mustard Sauce*, 321–23

Chicken: baked with barbecue sauce, 403; Breast of Chicken Cordon Bleu, 268; breasts, 261–62; Chicken Kiev, 261; côtelette defined, 264; how to buy, 260–61; marinade for, 366–67; roast, 263; suprême defined, 264. *See also* Capon

Chicken, braised: *Arroz con Pollo* (with smoked ham, Italian sausage, tomatoes, black olives, and rice), 288–89;

Chicken in the Pot Homestead (with vegetables and noodles), 294–95; *Coq au Vin Mode de Bourgogne* (with red wine marinade, smoked bacon, demi-glace, pearl onions, and mushrooms), 291–93; *Pollo alla Cacciatora* (with mushrooms, red wine, tomatoes, and demi-glace), 287–88; *Poulet Mode de Meurice* (with lemon, white wine, and two-cream sauce), 289–91
Chicken, roast: *Poulet Rôti à l'Estragon* (with tarragon, white wine, and crème fraîche), 295–96; *Roast Boned Chicken with Wild Rice and Hazelnut (or Chestnut) Stuffing*, 296–97
Chicken breasts, baked: *Baked Breast of Chicken Ambassador* (with foie gras and truffle stuffing, sauced with sherry, lemon, and crème fraîche), 283–85; *Baked Breast of Chicken with Anisette Sauce*, 279; *Baked Breast of Chicken with Caraway Sauce*, 277–79; *Baked Breast of Chicken Florentine* (with spinach and ricotta stuffing, sauced with tomato and Mornay), 285–87; *Baked Breast of Chicken Kaunaoa* (with mango, coconut, and tropical garnish), 281–82; *Baked Breast of Chicken Maharajah* (with raisins, banana, pineapple, coconut, chutney, and curry sauce), 279–80; *Baked Breast of Chicken with Tarragon Stuffing* (sauced with white wine, vermouth, crème fraîche, and glace de viande), 282–83; *Baked Breast of Chicken Virginia* (with white wine, mushrooms, Virginia ham, sauced with cream and stock), 276–77
Chicken breasts, deep fried: *Suprêmes de Volaille Kiev* (filled with chilled butter and breaded), 264–66
Chicken breasts, grilled: *Papillons de Poulet avec Sauce Framboise* (butterfly chicken breasts with Raspberry Vinegar Butter Sauce), 269–70
Chicken breasts, sautéed: *Breast of Chicken Homestead with Essence of Wild Mushroom Sauce* (marinated with black pepper and sauced with cèpes, morels, Port and crème fraîche), 270–72; *Fillets of Chicken Breast Hungarian* (with paprika, sour cream, and white wine), 272–73; *Homestead Sweet and Sour Lemon Chicken* (with oriental vegetables and sauced with pineapple juice, brown sugar, pomegranate juice, and lemon), 274–75; *"Some Like It Not So Hot" Chicken Breast Fillets* (with ginger, mixed vegetables, and curry), 273–74; *Suprêmes de Volaille Cordon Bleu* (with smoked ham and Emmentaler cheese), 268–69; *Suprêmes de Volaille Normande* (with apples, Calvados, and crème fraîche), 266–67
Chicken liver: *Foies de Volaille Sautés Chasseur* (with parsley, garlic, lemon, and Sauce Chasseur), 298
Child, Julia, 112, 382, 389–90; *From Julia Child's Kitchen*, 389; *Julia Child and Company*, 362; quoted, 389, 511
China, 300, 414. See also Cuisine: Chinese
Chocolate: discovery of, 557; production of, 528, 529
Chocolate desserts: *Chocolate Ice Cream*, 557; *Gâteau Princess Marie* (chocolate génoise layered with chocolate chestnut cream and frosted with chocolate cream), 536; *Génoise au Chocolat* (chocolate whole-egg cake), 524; *German Chocolate Cake* (chocolate buttermilk cake with butter cream frosting flavored with pecans and coconut), 529–30; *Macarons au Chocolat* (chocolate macaroons), 548; *Milk Chocolate Cheesecake*, 527–28; *Mousse au Chocolat Glacé* (frozen chocolate mousse), 550–51; *Schwarzwald Kuchen* (Black Forest cake made with chocolate and vanilla génoise layered with cherry compote and flavored with kirsch), 530–31; *Soufflé au Chocolat* (chocolate soufflé), 552–53; *Swiss Chocolate Roulade* (chocolate sponge cake rolled with raspberry jam and whipped cream), 528–29
Claiborne, Craig, 120; quoted, 362
Clams: *Clams Casino* (broiled on the half shell with pimientos and bacon), 166–67
Classic Italian Cookbook, The (by Marcella Hazen), 186; quoted, 330
Clayton, Bernard, Jr.: quoted, 479
Colmar, France, 191
Commonwealth Room (at the Homestead), 400, 559
Compagnie Générale Transatlantique. See French Line
Cookbooks, authors of early: Audiger, *La Maison Réglée*, 6; Marin, *Les Dons de Comus*, 6; Massialot, *Le Cuisinier Roial et Bourgeois*, 6; Menon, *La Cuisinière Bourgeoise*, 6; Taillevent, *Le Viandier*, 6, 448. See also Apicius; Platina
Cookies: *Honey Cookies* (pâte sucrée layered with glacéed cherries, almonds, raisins, and honey cream), 545; *Macarons à la Vanille* (vanilla macaroons), 547; *Macarons au Chocolat* (chocolate macaroons), 548; *Palmiers* (pâte feuilletée rolled with sugar and cut into palm tree shapes), 546
Cooking techniques: barding defined, 377; beating egg whites, 548–49; *blanc à légumes*, 449, 450; étouffée for greens, 471; larding defined, 377; poaching fish and lobster, 60; poaching shellfish, 60; sautéing fish, 569; stir-fry, 273–75; using papillotes for fish, 201, 230–31; using papillotes for scallops, 248–49
Cordon bleu (Royal Order of Saint Esprit), 7, 327; history of, 268
Corn: *Gnocchi alla Romana* (grits baked with or mixed with cheese, shaped, and sautéed), 464–65; history of, 449; *Homestead Corn Pudding*, 462–63; *Polenta alla Milanese* (cornmeal simmered with bouillon and seasoned with cheese and butter), 463–64; *Spoon Bread* (cornmeal, buttermilk, and eggs baked in a soufflé dish), 464
Côte d'Atlantique (France), 114, 147
Côte d'Azur (France), 197
Couvet, Switzerland, 207
Covington, Va., 401
Crabmeat: in *Baked Oysters with Crabmeat Gratinée Homestead*, 169–70; *Crabmeat Ravigote* (with Sauce Ravigote, served on avocado halves), 176; *Crabmeat Remick* (baked with Homestead Seafood Sauce), 170; in *Fisherman's Salad*, 187; *Gratinéed Lump Crabmeat Homestead* (with shallots, minced mixed bell peppers, mustard, white wine, and cream), 239; *Homestead Crab Cakes* (with shallots, mustard, minced red and green peppers, breaded and fried, served with Sauce Tartare), 171–72
Crabs, soft-shelled: 196; *Breaded Fried Soft-shelled Crabs with Fried Parsley*, 237–38; *Sautéed Soft-shelled Crabs with Lemon Butter*, 236–37
Crewe, Quentin: quoted, 11–12, 31
Croutons: how to make, 126, 135
Cucumbers: in *Cucumber Soup* (with sour cream, yogurt, and dill), 118–19; in *Pressed Cucumber Salad* (marinated with parsley, chives, and dill), 183; in *Sauce Doria* (with tarragon, white wine, and cream), 226–27
Cuisine: American, 20, 411; American southwestern, 240; Arabian, 497, 554; Austrian, 277–79; Austro-Hungarian, 464; Cajun, 273; California, 3; Chinese, 273, 274, 402, 411, 422, 426, 452, 554, 560; classic, 3, 4, 5, 11 (sauces in), 21, 54, 114, 115, 168; Creole, 3, 273; English, 4, 6, 111;

575

Cuisine (*continued*)
European, 192, 325; fads in, 11–12, 13, 362; flowers in, 560; German, 327, 464; Greek, 162, 507; history of, 3–12; at the Homestead, 3, 15, 20, 193; hotel, 13; Hungarian, 272–73, 437; Italian, 5, 287, 330, 341, 353, 411, 412, 423, 463, 464; Japanese, 422; maritime, 9–11, 21–22; middle-class, 6; Middle Eastern, 383–85; *minceur*, 3, 327, 349; à la minute, 193, 336; natural, 3; nouvelle, 3, 11–12, 20, 54; Persian, 162; railroad, 488; Roman, 507; royal, 7; Russian, 114, 135, 136, 157, 159, 194, 212, 264–66, 327, 340, 346, 372; Spanish, 262, 288–89, 296; Swiss, 435, 436–37, 537, 538; Szechuan, 149; Turkish, 162, 494; Viennese, 498. *See also* Cuisine, French; Cuisine, haute; Cuisine, la; Cuisine, la grande
Cuisine, French, 14, 133, 262, 263, 287, 325, 327, 349, 430, 435–36, 452, 560; bourgeois, 6, 10, 291, 351, 364, 380; classical, 20; provençal, 430; regional, 27; southwestern, 298. *See also* France: cuisine in
Cuisine, haute, 10, 245, 327, 380, 382. *See also* Cuisine, la; Cuisine, la grande
Cuisine, la, 194, 195, 283. *See also* Cuisine, haute; Cuisine, la grande
Cuisine, la grande, 5, 8, 10, 54, 509. *See also* Cuisine, haute; Cuisine, la
Cunard Line, 17, 551
Curnonsky (pseud. for Maurice Sailland), 71
Curry, 114, 382; in *Baked Breast of Chicken Maharajah*, 279–80; in *Basic Curry Sauce*, 80–81; in *Curry Mayonnaise*, 95; in *Orange Cream Curry Sauce*, 86; in *Senegalese Soup*, 119–20, 144
Custards: *Crème Anglaise* (custard cream), 516; *Crème Pâtissière* (pastry cream), 516–17

Dauphiné (France), 203, 440
David, Elizabeth, 113, 120; *English Bread and Yeast Cookery* quoted, 490, 497; quoted, 111, 380, 424
de Groot, Roy Andries: quoted, 4–5
De Honesta Voluptate (by Platina), 5, 508
de' Medici, Catherine, 7, 192, 195, 262, 287, 311, 325, 355, 357, 497, 518, 547, 554, 556; marriage of, 4–5; and sauces, 51
de' Medici, Lorenzo, 4
de' Medici, Marie, 5, 7

De Re Coquinaria (by Apicius), 387, 406
de Sacchi, Bartolommeo. *See* Platina
Dessert crêpes: *Crêpes Noisette* (with crème pâtissière and hazelnuts), 521–22; *Crêpes Parisienne* (with crème pâtissière and strawberries), 521; *Crêpes Sucrées* (thin sweet pancakes), 520
Dessert mousses: *Mousse à la Framboise* (chilled raspberry mousse), 550; *Mousse au Chocolat Glacé* (frozen chocolate mousse), 550–51
Desserts. *See* Cakes; Chocolate desserts; Cookies; Dessert crêpes; Dessert mousses; Ice cream; Pies; Sorbets; Soufflés; Tarts
Diat, Louis, 111, 113, 120
Dijon, France, 368
Dordogne (France), 361
Drake, Sir Francis, 302
Du Barry, Madame, 262; and *cordon bleu*, 7, 268, 327
Duck: *Canard Rôti à la Framboise* (roast duckling with raspberry sauce), 298–300; *Canard Rôti à l'Orange* (roast duckling with orange sauce), 300–301; *Roast Duckling with Walnut and Pomegranate Sauce*, 301–2
Duck, discussed, 260, 261, 263, 298, 308; frozen, how to thaw, 300; popularity of at Homestead, 298; produced in France and North Carolina, 298
Duckling. *See* Duck

Eggplant: *Baked Eggplant Niçoise* (with tomatoes and olive oil), 466; history of, 450; how to buy, 450
Egg whites: how to beat, 548–49
Egyptians, 302, 309, 447; and bread baking, 481
Elizabeth I (queen of England), 302, 547
Encyclopedia of Fish Cookery, The (by A. J. McClane), 193, 195
Encyclopedia of Wines & Spirits (by Alexis Lichine), 536
Endive, Belgian: *Belgian Endive* (cooked *blanc à légume*, gratinéed with butter and Parmesan), 466–67; history of, 466
England, 314, 414, 430, 452; cuisine in, 4, 6, 111
English Bread and Yeast Cookery (by Elizabeth David), 490, 497
Entertaining in the French Style (by Roger Vergé), 556
Escoffier, Georges Auguste, 4, 6, 7, 9–11, 13, 30, 47, 51, 54, 71, 100, 128, 192, 194, 196, 198, 209, 221, 230, 362, 380, 382, 476; career of, 9–11; collaboration with César Ritz, 9–10; culinary philosophy of, 1–2, 3, 11–12; legacy of, 11; *Le Guide Culinaire*, 11, 230; quoted, 191; sauce system of, 52
Evian-les-bains, France, 206
Explorers, 452; Columbus, Christopher, 449, 536, 563; Cortés, Hernando, 557; da Gama, Vasco, 300; Portuguese, 447; Spanish, 411, 430, 447. *See also* Traders

Farmers' markets, 114, 282, 450; in America, 446; Les Halles (Paris), 114, 133, 445; in Lucerne, 445–46
Fat: discussed, 54–55, 261, 326, 401; poultry, 261
Fennel: *Hearts of Fennel Parmesan* (cooked *blanc à légume*, gratinéed with butter and Parmesan), 467–68
Fiesole, Italy, 412
Finel, Michel, 31, 194, 383, 508–9, 511
Fish. *See* Flounder; Halibut; Pompano; Red snapper; Salmon; Sea bass; Shad; Sole: Dover; Swordfish; Trout; Turbot
Fish, discussed, 362; freshwater, 194; paella, 197; as religious symbol, 192, 246; smoked in salad, 187
Florence, Italy, 4, 5, 195, 262, 357, 383
Flounder, 195; *Baked Fillets of Flounder Homestead* (with crabmeat, Homestead Seafood Sauce, and Sauce Nantua), 225–26
Foie gras, 262, 296, 298, 328, 365; in *Baked Breast of Chicken Ambassador*, 283–85; production in Egypt, 302; production in France, 302, 378; production in United States, 378; in *Roast Tenderloin of Beef London House with Truffle Sauce*, 378; in *Sautéed Sweetbreads Souvaroff*, 358; sautéed, 312
Fraisse, Pierre, 71
France, 5, 314, 411, 414, 450, 547; cuisine in, 4, 5, 6, 7, 9. *See also* Cuisine, French
François I (king of France), 4, 93, 534
French Line, 15, 17, 289
From Julia Child's Kitchen (by Julia Child), 389
Fruit: apricots, history of, 406; blueberries, 54; cantaloupe, in *Homestead Cantaloupe Soup*, 117; grapefruit, history of, 565; in *Islander Salad*, 188–89; mangoes, in *Homestead Mango Soup*, 118; oranges, in *Cum-*

berland Sauce, 100, history of, 300, Valencia, 296; passion fruit, in *Homestead Passion Fruit Sauce*, 101–2; pears, in *Pear Brandy Sauce*, 102–3; plums, production of, 542; pomegranates, in *Roast Duckling with Walnut and Pomegranate Sauce*, 301–2; raspberries, 54, production of, 562; rhubarb, in *Rhubarb Sauce*, 101; strawberries, history of, 541; in *Winter Salad of Fresh and Dried Fruits*, 189
Fulton Fish Market (New York), 234
Fumet, 52; Escoffier revises classical sauces with, 52

Galantine: defined, 221
Game, 263. *See also* Pheasant; Quail; Rabbit; Venison
Garnishes: ambassadrice, 283; *à la bouquetière*, 391, 397, 447, 469; *Brunoise*, 153; *Celestine*, 153; *Chasseur*, 153; *Julienne*, 153; à la printanière defined, 374; *Vermicelli*, 153
Garonne region (France), 542
Gascogne (France), 378
Gautier, Théophile, 329
Gelée, Claude (pseud. Claude Lorrain), 513
Geneva, Switzerland, 206
George II (king of England), 100
Germany, 364, 411, 414, 555; cuisine in, 4, 327, 464
Gogh, Vincent van, 253
Good Hous-wives Treasurie, The (anon.), 6
Goose, 261, 263, 298, 308; *Oie Rôtie au Jus Lié* (roast goose with brown sauce), 302–3
Gorgonzola, Italy, 343; cheese from, 343
Gourmet (magazine), 20
Great Depression, the, 16
Greece, 257, 301, 411, 414; cuisine in, 162, 507
Greeks, 448, 451
Gremolada, 298, 404; with *Ossobuco alla Milanese*, 353; with *Sautéed Sea Scallops Gremolada with Tomato Butter Sauce*, 247–48
Grigson, Jane, 226; quoted, 118
Grille, the Homestead, 13, 22, 59, 159, 164, 250, 383, 391, 397, 529
Grissini (bread sticks), 415, 416
Guide Michelin, 12; rating system, 12, 13, 16, 20, 21. *See also* Chefs, French *Michelin* three-star

Haeberlin brothers, 20
Haeberlin family, 191
Hale, William Harlan: quoted, 331, 421, 486

Halibut, 195; in *Fisherman's Salad*, 187; in *Paella*, 254–55; *Suprêmes of Halibut with Sauce Doria* (with tarragon, Sauce Vin Blanc, and cucumber), 226–27
Ham, baked: glazes for, 409. *See also* Pork: Baked Virginia Smithfield Ham
Ham, cured: *jambon de Bayonne*, 276; prosciutto, 276; *Schwarzwaldschinken*, 276; Virginia, 276
Hamburg-Amerika Lines, 9–10, 191
Hamwi, Ernest, 555
Hapsburg family, 326, 331
Haut Dauphiné (France), 306
Hawaii, 262, 279, 281, 563
Hazelnuts: history of, 521; in *Roast Boned Chicken with Wild Rice and Hazelnut (or Chestnut) Stuffing*, 296–97
Hazen, Marcella, 186; *Classic Italian Cookbook, The*, quoted, 330
Healing Springs, Va., 15
Henri IV (king of France), 5, 93, 294
Henry the Navigator (prince of Portugal), 119
Henri II (king of France), 4, 93, 325, 554, 556; marriage of, 5
Hettich, Eddie, 104, 233, 326, 329
Holidays, 8, 16, 22, 24, 303; Christmas, 8; Easter, 8; Thanksgiving, 8, 263, 303
Homestead, the: afternoon tea at, 18, 20; cuisine of, 3, 15, 20, 193; defined, 13; description of, 17–18; early history of, 14–15; farming operations at, 446; food service, 24–27; food service daily operation, 32–47; food service locations, 22; holidays at, 8, 16, 22, 24, 509; local produce for, 27; ownership of, 3; prix fixe menu, 30; produce for, 446; room service at, 32
Homestead personnel: Bock, Harold P., 185; Bogan, Charlie, 192, 446; Bryan, Arthur, 32; Carpenter, Steve, 47; Fisson, Chef Armand, 20, 23; Huebner, Hans, 25; Lennon, Thomas J., 20, 25, 529; Marian, Paul, 23, 32; May, Walker, 263; Nelson, Clifford H., 20, 25, 26, 529; Rhett, Walter, 308; Schelch, Josef, 23, 277; Williams, Vince, 103; Wolfe, Jim, 159, 164, 383, 397; Woodzell, Thomas, 31, 480, 481. *See also* Finel, Michel; McElwee, B. G.; Puhle, Brian; Schnarwyler, Albert
Honey: history of, 507–8
Hors d'oeuvres, cold: *Avocado Southampton* (with chilled Gazpacho), 176; *Canapé Morgon* (with tomato, shrimp, smoked salmon, and caviar), 174–75;

Crabmeat Ravigote (with avocado and Sauce Ravigote), 176; *Galantine of Capon* (with aromatic stuffing of veal, pork, and pistachios, lined with strips of ham, smoked tongue, and truffle), 179–82; *Galantine of Capon Jardinière* (with aromatic stuffing of veal, pork, and pistachios, lined with strips of fresh vegetables and truffle), 179–82; *Gravlax with Dill and Mustard Sauce* (dill marinated salmon), 177; *Hummus* (chick-pea spread with garlic, sesame oil, and lemon juice), 172–73; *Marinated Mushrooms* (with onion, olive oil, lemon juice, garlic, and red wine vinegar), 173; *Marinated Shrimp* (with Bermuda onion, olive oil, white wine vinegar, Dijon mustard, and fresh red and green pepper), 174; *Pâté Maison* (liver, veal, and pork with aromatic spices, juniper, and truffles), 178–79
Hors d'oeuvres, discussed, 157; cold, 159–60; hot, 159
Hors d'oeuvres, hot: *Baked Oysters with Crabmeat Gratinée Homestead*, 169–70; *Broiled Persian Chicken Kebabs* (marinated with onion, lemon, and saffron and broiled on skewers), 162–63; *Clams Casino* (broiled on the half shell with pimientos and bacon), 166–67; *Coquilles Saint-Jacques au Beurre Blanc et Essence de Citron* (scallops in lemon, white wine, and butter sauce), 168–69; *Crabmeat Remick* (baked with Homestead Seafood Sauce and Parmesan), 170; *Homestead Crab Cakes* (with English mustard, onion, red and green peppers, and spices), 171–72; *Mélange de Champignons au Vol-au-Vents* (mixed creamed mushrooms in a patty shell), 165–66; *Mussels Provençale* (with white wine, shallots, garlic, olive oil, and parsley), 167–68; *Pirojskis* (Russian meat pies with beef, cabbage, onion, parsley, and Sauce Béchamel), 163–64; *Shiitake Mushrooms with Mustard Sauce* (sautéed with shallots), 164–65
Hotels: Ambassador (New York), 98, 163, 185, 221, 264, 288, 289; Carlton (London), 9; Carlton (Washington), 20; Grand Hotel (Monte Carlo), 9; Hershey (Hershey), 16; Hotel du Luxembourg (Nice), 9; Mayflower (Washington), 529; Meurice (Paris), 289; National (Lucerne), 221; Palace (Lucerne), 221; Ritz (Paris), 9; Ritz-Carlton (New York), 111, 113, 120; Savoy (London), 9,

577

Hotels (*continued*)
476; Schweizerhof (Lucerne), 221; Sheraton East Ambassador (New York), 20, 185; Sheraton (Tel Aviv), 383
Hotels, discussed, 12; chains, 12–13, 17; convention, 16; resort, 13, 15–16, 27
Hot Springs, Va., 3, 14, 15, 27, 47, 127, 240, 361, 362, 363, 509, 556

Ice cream: *Banana Ice Cream*, 558; *Caramel Ice Cream*, 561–62; *Chocolate Ice Cream*, 557; *Coconut Ice Cream*, 557–58; history of, 554–55; *Rose Ice Cream*, 560–61; *Rum Raisin Ice Cream*, 559; *Vanilla Ice Cream*, 556–57. See also Sorbets
Illhaeusern, France, 191, 193
Indians: Caribbean, 438, 563; Incas, 411, 430; native American, 202, 449, 452; Winepesaukees, 202
Italy, 414, 450, 518, 547. See also Cuisine: Italian

James, Saint, 246
Jefferson, Thomas, 448
Johnson, Nancy, 555
Julia Child and Company (by Julia Child), 362

Kiev, Russia, 261, 262, 264
Kitchen, professional, 9, 10, 11; teamwork in, 21, 22, 23, 32; training in, 23
Kona coast (Hawaii), 281

Lac Léman (Lake Geneva, Switzerland), 206
La Cuisine (by Raymond Oliver), 4
La Cuisinière Bourgeoise (by Menon), 6
Lafayette, Marquis de, 202
Lake of the Four Cantons (Switzerland), 221
La Maison Réglée (by Audiger), 6
Lamb, 361, 362, 401; curry of Madras, 56; how to buy, 380, 381; Scotch stew, 56
Lamb, braised: *Curry of Lamb Madras* (seasoned with curry, clove, white wine, and coconut milk), 385–86; *Irish Lamb Stew* (with potatoes and onions, garnished with peas, onions, turnip, and carrot), 388–89; *Scotch Lamb Stew* (with barley and aromatic vegetables), 387–88
Lamb, broiled: *Broiled Marinated Tenderloin of Lamb with Fresh Mint Cream Sauce* (marinated with fresh ginger and garlic, sauced with white wine, lamb stock, fresh mint, and cream), 394–95
Lamb, Charles: quoted, 400
Lamb, grilled: *Shaslik Caucasian* (cubes marinated with lemon, onion, oil, and black pepper, grilled on skewers), 384–85; *Shish Kebab* (cubes marinated with lemon, onion, oil, and pepper, grilled on skewers with bell peppers, onions, and mushrooms), 385
Lamb, roast: *Carré d'Agneau Diable* (rack of lamb with mustard and parsley crust, sauced with white wine and brown lamb stock), 393; *Carré d'Agneau Persillé* (rack of lamb with parsley, shallot, rosemary, and bread crumb crust, sauced with white wine and brown lamb stock deglaze), 391–93; *Roast Leg of Lamb au Jus* (with fresh rosemary and garlic, sauced with demi-glace), 389–90; *Roast Saddle of Lamb with Green Peppercorns and Rosemary* (with fresh rosemary and an aromatic stuffing of lamb, veal, and green peppercorns, sauced with white wine and demi-glace), 395–97; *Tenderloin of Lamb en Croûte à l'Estragon* (with a tarragon, parsley, and bread crumb stuffing and wrapped in pâte feuilletée), 399; *Tenderloin of Lamb en Croûte Florentine* (with a spinach, bread crumb, walnut, cream, and cheese stuffing and wrapped in pâte feuilletée), 397–99
Lamb, sautéed: *Muslin Kababs* (ground patty seasoned with lemon juice, yogurt, sour cream, and parsley), 383–84
Lamotte-Beuvron, France, 561
La Physiologie du Goût (by Anthelme Brillat-Savarin), 3
Larousse Gastronomique, 218, 242, 255, 388
L'Art de la Cuisine Française au 19ième siècle (by Marie-Antoine Carême), 8
La Varenne, François Pierre de, 5, 6, 453, 490
Le Cuisinier Français (by François Pierre de La Varenne), 5
Le Cuisinier Roial et Bourgeois (by Massialot), 6
Leeks: *Gratin of Leeks* (served with Sauce Mornay), 468–69; in *Leek Butter Sauce*, 88
Le Guide Culinaire (by Georges Auguste Escoffier), 11, 230
Le Havre, France, 234, 363
Le Huédé, Henri, 10, 12, 15, 22, 23, 24, 32, 47, 112, 151, 363, 391, 477; quoted, 21, 22

Les Dons de Comus (by Marin), 6
Lettuce, 139; Boston, 187, 188; chicory, 188; *mâche*, 183; red leaf, 188; Romaine, 188
Le Viandier (by Taillevent), 6, 448
Lichine, Alexis: *Encyclopedia of Wines & Spirits* quoted, 536
Liguria (Italy), 330
Liqueurs. See Spirits
Lisbon, Spain, 300
Lobster: *Baked Lobster Thermidor* (with shallots and mushrooms and gratinéed with Mornay, white wine, mustard, and tarragon), 242–43; *Broiled Maine Lobster* (dressed with cracker crumbs, minced peppers, and shallots), 243–44; *Mousse d'Homard Américaine* (served chilled with sauces Américaine and Chantilly), 245
Lobster, discussed, 196; as base for *Lobster Butter and Cream Sauce*, 69; as base for *Sauce Américaine*, 71; in *Fettuccine Fruits de Mer*, 250–51; how to grill over charcoal, 244; how to handle live, 73; Maine, 243; in *Mixed Seafood Newburg*, 241–42; in *Paella*, 254–55; poaching in court bouillon, 60
Lombardy (Italy), 343, 449
Lorrain, Claude (pseud. for Claude Gelée), 513
Louhans, France, 445
Louis XV (king of France), 7, 262, 268
Louis XIV (king of France), 4, 6, 160, 447, 534, 541
Louis IX (king of France), 486
Louis XVI (king of France), 6, 7
Louis XIII (king of France), 5
Lower Cascades Club (Healing Springs, Va.), 22
Lucerne, Switzerland, 195, 221, 314, 445, 537
Lyon, France, 373

McClane, A. J., 193, 195; *The Encyclopedia of Fish Cookery* quoted, 193, 228
McElwee, B. G., 26, 32, 192, 260; and produce suppliers, 446; shopping list, 26, 28–29, 161, 193, 361, 446, 481, 510, 565
Maggi, Michael Johannes Julius, 128
Main Dining Room (at the Homestead), 559
Málaga, Spain, 197
Marie Antoinette, 430
Marquis d'Uxelles, 6
Marsala, Italy, 335
Marsala wine: history of, 335
Marseilles, France, 167, 197, 255, 429
Marzipan, 508, 547

Medici family, 285, 383. *See also* de' Medici, Catherine; de' Medici, Lorenzo; de' Medici, Marie
Mediterranean: region, 450, 536; sea, 197, 198, 253, 255; seaboard, 448
Messiaen, Olivier, 283
Mexico, 447, 452
Middle Ages, 450, 508, 513
Mignonette: defined, 374
Milan, Italy, 113, 328, 353, 429
Mobil Travel Guide: banquet at Homestead, 115; rating system, 16, 20
Modena, Italy, 137
Montreux, Switzerland, 206
Mont-Saint-Michel, France, 266
Moscow, Russia, 327, 346
Mosul, Iraq, 383
Mourier, Léopold, 242
Mushrooms, 262, 327; cèpes, 165, 270–71; chanterelles, 80, 165, 173, 270, 320; in *Cream of Mushroom Soup*, 143; dried, 165, 166; marinated, 173; in *Mélange de Champignons au Vol-au-Vents*, 165–66; morels, 165, 270–71, 320, 327; morels in *Escalopes de Veau aux Morilles*, 341; in *Rahmschnitzel*, 338–39; shiitake, 159, 164, 165, 173, 320; wild, 270
Mussels, 197; in *Billi Bi*, 147–48; in *Fisherman's Salad*, 187; in *Mussels Provençale*, 167–68; in *Paella*, 254–55; *Pilaff of Mussels à la Marinière* (with rice, white wine, and shallots), 253

Napoleon Bonaparte, 7, 10, 296, 536
Narbonne, France, 197
New Orleans, La., 196, 230
New World, 448, 449, 452, 536, 559, 563
New York, N.Y., 20, 27, 79, 98, 149, 163, 185, 196, 221, 234, 264, 288, 289, 321, 363, 373, 560
Nice, France, 9, 71
Nivernais (France), 318
Normandy (France), 266, 327, 340, 508, 556, 564
North Africa, 451
North America, 447, 449
North Atlantic (ocean), 151

Ocean liner: compared to Homestead, 16–18
Ocean liners, 234; *Amerika*, 10; *Flandre*, 289; *France*, 10, 12, 15, 17, 21, 22, 32, 47, 112, 151, 363, 391, 477, 479; *Ile de France*, 289; *Imperator*, 10, 191, 209; *Kaiserin Auguste Victoria*, 10; *Liberté*, 289; *Normandie*, 17, 18; *QE2*, 17, 22, 23; *Queen Elizabeth*, 17, 18, 551; *Queen Elizabeth II* (*QE2*), 151; *Queen Mary*, 17, 551
Oliver, Raymond, 4; *La Cuisine*, 4
Olives: in *Roast Double Breast of Turkey with Olive Stuffing*, 305–6
Olives, picholine (French green): in *Roast Young Pheasant with Green Olives and Raspberry Vinegar Sauce*, 313–14
Oxford English Dictionary, 485
Oysters: in *Baked Oysters with Crabmeat Gratinée Homestead*, 169–70; in *Fisherman's Salad*, 187

Palladin, Jean Louis, 378
Palm Beach, Fla., 233, 326, 329
Panade: for quenelles, 218, 220
Paris, France, 7, 8, 9, 21, 189, 306, 445, 554; "City of Light," 195
Parma, Italy, 412
Parmentier, Antoine, 430
Parsley: fried, 238
Pasta: *Fettuccine Alfredo* (with cream and grated Parmesan), 415; *Fettuccine Carbonara* (with mushrooms, zucchini, bell pepper, and prosciutto in cream sauce with grated Parmesan), 417–18; in *Fettuccine Fruits de Mer*, 250–51; in *Fettuccine Orientale with Shrimp and Scallops*, 251–52; *Fettuccine Primavera* (with mixed spring vegetables in cream sauce with grated Parmesan), 416–17; *Homestead Noodle Pudding* (custard baked with raisins and mandarin orange sections), 420; *Pesto* (sauce with garlic, olive oil, parsley, basil, and pine nuts), 418; *Spätzle* (tiny free-form egg dumplings), 419; *Spinach Spätzle* (spinach flavored tiny free-form egg dumplings), 420; in *Tortellini Salad*, 186
Pasta, discussed, 197; fettuccine, 197, 412; fettuccine Alfredo, 412; fettuccine carbonara, 414; fettuccine primavera, 414; history of, 411, 412, 414; how to cook, 412–14; noodle pudding, 414; pesto, 414; spätzle, 414
Pastries: *Paillettes* (cheese straws), 515–16; *Vol-au-Vents* (patty shells), 514–15
Pastry: *Pâte Feuilletée* (puff pastry), 513–14; *Pâte à Foncer* (foundation pastry for tarts), 512; *Pâte Sucrée* (sugar pastry), 512–13; *Pie Pastry*, 511–12
Pastry, discussed, 5; basics, 509, 510–11; Paillettes, 510; Palmiers, 510; Pâte Feuilletée, 509–10; Succés, 510; Vol-au-Vents, 510
Pastry Department (at the Homestead), 508–9, 510, 538

Patty shell: in *Mélange de Champignons au Vol-au-Vents*, 165–66
Pays d'Auge (France), 266
Peanuts: in *Cream of Chicken Soup Virginia*, 145
Pea soup. *See* Soups, hot: Potage St. Germain
Pepper: in dry marinade for *Roast Three-Pepper Tenderloin of Beef with Armagnac Sauce* and *Roast Black Pepper Tenderloin of Beef with Armagnac Sauce, Green Peppercorns, and Raisins*, 376–77; in *Sauce Mignonette*, 103
Périgord (France), 262, 302, 306, 378
Persia, 285, 451; cuisine in, 162
Pheasant, 308; *Roast Young Pheasant with Green Olives and Raspberry Vinegar Sauce*, 313–14; *Suprêmes de Faisan au Bordelaise* (breast of pheasant with red wine, shallot, and black pepper sauce), 312–13; *Suprêmes de Faisan au Madère* (breast of pheasant with Sauce Madère), 311–12; *Suprêmes de Faisan au Périgueux* (breast of pheasant with Sauce Périgueux), 312; *Suprêmes de Faisan avec Sauce Vinaigre de Vin et Poivre Vert* (breast of pheasant with red wine, wine vinegar, and green peppercorn sauce), 312
Pièce montée, 4, 509; invention of, 8
Piedmont (Italy), 330
Pies: *Apple Pie*, 539–40; *Apple Pumpkin Pie*, 540–41. *See also* Tarts
Platina (Bartolommeo de Sacchi), 5, 508; *De Honesta Voluptate*, 5, 508
Point, Fernand, 12, 32, 47, 51, 54, 210; M. and Mme, 27; quoted, 49, 59, 519; students of, 20
Point, Madame, 21
Poitou-Charentes (France), 147
Pompano, 195–96; *Baked Fillets of Pompano with Balsamic Vinegar Butter Sauce*, 228–29; cooking in papillotes, 230–31; *Pompano en Papillote* (with wild rice, mushrooms, shallots, and Sauce Vin Blanc), 230–31; *Sautéed Fillets of Pompano Moderne* (with blanched almonds, pineapple, banana, and kiwi fruit), 229–30
Po River valley (Italy), 423
Pork, 56, 361, 362, 401; *Baked Virginia Smithfield Ham with Homestead Southern Fruit Dressing* (brown sugar sherry glaze with dressing of peaches, pears, pineapple, apricots, raisins, and walnuts), 407–9; barbecue, 400; *Chinese Barbecued Spareribs* (sweet and sour marinade with pomegranate syrup, pineapple juice, sherry, brown sugar, vinegar, and fresh ginger),

579

Pork (*continued*)
402–3; *Noisettes de Porc en Sanglier* (tenderloin marinated with juniper berries and aromatic vegetables, sliced, sautéed, and sauced with demi-glace, marinade, and cream), 405–6; *Piccata of Pork* (sliced tenderloin dipped in egg and sage batter, sautéed, and served with Sauce Chasseur), 404; *Roast Loin of Pork Stuffed with Apricots* (filled with apricots, rubbed with fresh rosemary and lemon, and served with mustard cream sauce), 406–7; *Roast Loin of Pork Stuffed with Prunes in the Style of Sweden* (filled with prunes, rubbed with fresh sage and lemon, and sauced with white wine, cream, and demi-glace), 407

Potatoes: in *Ambassador Potato Salad*, 185; *Baked Stuffed Potatoes* (crisp potato skins filled with mashed potatoes), 434; in *Homestead Potato Salad*, 184; *Hungarian Potatoes* (bite-size cubes simmered with stock, tomato paste, paprika, and onions), 437; *Pommes de Terre Boulangère* (sliced and baked with stock and onions), 435–36; *Pommes de Terre Dauphine* (enriched with pâte à choux, chilled, shaped, and deep fried), 440–41; *Pommes de Terre Duchesse* (mashed, enriched with egg and butter, piped onto baking sheet, and browned), 437–38; *Pommes de Terre Macaire* (mashed, seasoned with ham, onion, chives, and parsley, shaped into cakes, and sautéed), 439; *Pommes de Terre Noisette Rissolées* (oval shape, sautéed in clarified butter, rolled in parsley), 443; *Pommes de Terre Parisienne Rissolées* (round shape, sautéed in clarified butter, rolled in parsley), 442; *Potato Croquettes* (mashed, enriched with egg and butter, cooled, shaped, lightly breaded, and deep fried), 440; *Potato Croquettes with Almonds* (mashed, enriched with egg and butter, cooled, shaped, rolled in crushed almonds, and deep fried), 440; *Roesti* (baked, chilled, grated, sautéed in butter and bacon fat), 435; *Sweet Potatoes Duchesse* (baked, puréed, seasoned with ginger and cinnamon, enriched with egg, piped onto baking sheet, and baked), 438–39; *Swiss Stewed Potatoes* (bite-size cubes simmered with stock and seasonings), 436–37; *Whipped Potatoes* (mashed with cream and butter), 433

Potatoes, discussed: baking, 432; boiling, 432; croquettes, 432; dauphine, 432; duchesse, 432; history of, 411, 430, 432; how to buy, 432; Idaho, 432; Macaire, 432; Maine Russet, 432; Parisienne rissolées, 432–33; Roesti, 432; sweet, 438–39; yams, 438

Potato soup. *See* Soups, cold: Vichyssoise; Soups, hot: Potage Parisienne

Poultry. *See* Capon; Chicken; Chicken, braised; Chicken, roast; Chicken breasts: baked; deep fried; grilled; sautéed; Chicken liver; Duck; Goose; Turkey

Poultry, discussed, 362; how to buy, 260–61

Prosperity, W.Va., 401

Provence (France), 196, 197, 234, 253, 255, 313, 450, 452, 466

Pudding: *Rice Pudding* (with cinnamon, vanilla, raisins), 554

Puhle, Brian, 30, 32, 51, 59, 69, 102

Pullman, George Mortimer, 488

Pyrenees mountains, 197

Quail, 308; in *Essence de Caille Royale*, 150–51; *Roast Stuffed Quail Virginia* (filled with wild rice, apple, quail livers, cream, and cranberry, sauced with red wine, raspberry vinegar, and demi-glace), 309–10

Rabbit: *Hasenpfeffer* (marinated with vegetables, juniper berries, wine, and red wine vinegar and braised with bacon and demi-glace), 314–16; *Southern Fried Rabbit*, 316–17

Red snapper, 196; *Broiled Fillets of Red Snapper Maître d'hôtel*, 232; in *Paella*, 254–55

Restaurants: Alfredo all'Augusteo (Rome), 415; L'Arbre Vert (Illhaeusern), 191; L'Auberge de l'Ill (Illhaeusern), 79, 191; beginnings of, 6–7; La Cabro d'Or (Les Baux), 313; Café de la Paix (Paris), 223; Café de Paris (Paris), 242; Chez Hansi (Paris), 20; Le Chien qui Fume (Paris), 133; Delmonico's (New York), 196, 241; Doney (Florence), 357; Embassy Club (of Ambassador Hotel, New York), 98, 163, 264; L'Esperance (Saint-Père-sous-Vézelay), 159; Everglades Club (Palm Beach), 233, 326, 329; Fassifern Tavern (Warm Springs), 453, 475; Fish House (Andalusia, Pa.), 202; Lutèce (New York), 20, 24, 25, 79, 159; Martin's (New York), 373; Mère Poulard (Mont-Saint-Michel), 266; Morateur (Lyon), 373; Moulin de Mougins (Mougins), 159, 316; in Paris, 6, 7; Le Père Tranquille (Paris), 133; Peter's (Paris), 71; Le Petit Moulin Rouge (Paris), 9; Le Pied de Cochon (Paris), 133; La Regalido (Fontvielle), 313; Restaurant de la Pyramide (Vienne), 12, 21; Le Restaurant Français (Nice), 9; Restaurant of the Republic—Palace of Equality (Paris), 7; Restaurant Paul Young (Washington), 529; Restaurant Pic (Valence), 13; Restaurant Troisgros (Roanne), 159; Ritz-Carlton (Hamburg-Amerika Lines), 10; Sabatini (Florence), 357; Salle Chambord (on the *France*), 12, 21, 391; Salle Versailles (on the *France*), 12, 21; Scandia (Los Angeles), 96; Tour d'Argent (Paris), 21; La Truite (Illhaeusern), 191

Revolution of 1789 (French), 7, 10, 52

Rhineland (Germany), 367

Rice: *Exotic Fried Rice* (with sautéed shrimp, ham, bell pepper, garlic, scallions, Chinese cabbage, water chestnuts, and fresh ginger), 426–27; in *Paella*, 254–55; *Rice Creole* (boiled and then baked with butter), 426; *Rice Pilaff* (sautéed in butter and cooked in stock), 424–25; *Rice Pudding* (with cinnamon, vanilla, and raisins), 554; *Risotto* (sautéed in butter, baked with stock, mixed with grated Parmesan), 428; *Risotto alla Milanese* (sautéed with mushrooms in butter, baked with stock and saffron, mixed with grated Parmesan), 429; *Risotto con Pomodori* (sautéed with tomato paste and butter, baked with stock, mixed with diced, cooked tomatoes), 429; *Riz Valencienne* (pilaff mixed with peas and pimientos), 425; *Saffron Rice* (cooked in saffron-flavored stock), 424; *Steamed Rice*, 423–24; *Turkish Rice* (saffron-flavored pilaff mixed with raisins, chutney, and pimiento), 426

Rice, discussed, 197; cultivation of, 421, 423; history of, 411, 421–22, 423; paella, 197; risotto, 423; types of, 421–22; wild, 422

Ritz, César, 9, 221; collaboration with Escoffier, 9–10

Rivers, European, 192–93; Isère, 203; Loire, 204, 318; Rhône, 203

Rivers, in United States, 193; Delaware, 202

Roanne, France, 6, 182

Roanoke, Va., 23, 27

Romans, 448, 450, 451
Rome, Italy, 4
Roquefort-sur-Soulzon, France, 343
Rouen, France, 266
Royal Order of Saint Esprit (*cordon bleu*), 7, 327; history of, 268
Rum: history of, 536; production of, 536, 558, 559; in *Rum Raisin Ice Cream*, 559; in *Rum Torte*, 536–37
Russia, 282. *See also* Cuisine: Russian; Soups, Russian

Sacchi, Bartolommeo de (Platina), 5, 508
Saffron: cultivation of, 424; in rice, 422–23; in *Risotto alla Milanese*, 429
Sailland, Maurice (pseud. Curnonsky), 71
Saint-Père-sous-Vézelay, France, 159
Saint Petersburg, Russia, 136, 194, 346, 364, 372
Salad dressings, 59, 161; *Buttermilk Dressing*, 108; *Cocktail Sauce*, 108; *Fine Herbs Dressing*, 107; *Homestead Cocktail Sauce*, 108; *Homestead French Dressing*, 106–7; *Homestead Grille Hot Bacon Dressing*, 105; *Homestead Sauce Vinaigrette*, 105–6; *Olive Oil and Lemon Juice Dressing*, 104–5; *Raspberry Vinegar and Poppy Seed Dressing*, 104; *Roquefort Dressing*, 107; *Sauce Ravigote*, 106
Salads: *Ambassador Potato Salad* (with Beef Bouillon, vinaigrette, chives, and tarragon), 185; *Beet Salad* (with horseradish, onion, and caraway seeds), 183–84; *Fisherman's Salad* (with shrimp, mussels, oysters, scallops, smoked salmon, marinated herring, and lump crabmeat simmered with aromatic vegetable broth, served with potatoes, tomatoes, and green beans), 187–88; *Homestead Potato Salad* (with mayonnaise, onion, and mustard), 184; *Islander Salad* (with pineapple, mango, water chestnuts, bean sprouts, and snow peas), 188–89; *Pressed Cucumber Salad* (with parsley, chives, and dill), 183; *Salade Tiède d'Epinards* (warm spinach with hot bacon dressing), 182; *Tortellini Salad* (with olives, mixed peppers, pine nuts, Genoa salami, and artichoke hearts), 186; *Winter Salad of Fresh and Dried Fruits* (with dried apricots, dates, prunes, raisins, walnuts, and fresh fruit), 189
Salads, discussed, 160; fruit, 161; medieval, 157; position of during meal, 157–58; potato, 161; salade composée, 160–61; salade simple, 160–61

Salmon, 194–95; *Chaud-Froid Mousse de Sole et Saumon "Tricolor"* (with layers of salmon, sole, and cream, and spinach, basil, and watercress, served with "Another" Cold Fish Sauce), 216–17; *Coulibiac de Saumon à la Russe* (with filling of salmon, rice pilaff, diced vegetables, crêpes, baked in brioche dough and sauced with Mousseline), 212–14; *Escalopes de Saumon Homestead* (sautéed salmon scallops with Raspberry Vinegar Butter Sauce), 204–5; *Escalopes de Saumon Lac Léman* (sautéed salmon scallops, sauced with tomato, shallot, white wine, and crème fraîche), 206–7; in *Fisherman's Salad*, 187; in *Gravlax with Dill and Mustard Sauce*, 177; *Quenelles de Saumon* (fillets puréed with crème fraîche and poached), 211–12; *Saumon Poché* (poached in court bouillon and served hot or cold), 214–15; *Soufflé de Saumon en Croûte* (puréed with smoked salmon and cream and baked in pâte feuilletée), 210–11; *Suprêmes de Saumon Amoureuse* (lightly poached fillets sauced with essence of lobster, tarragon, Pernod, white wine, and cream), 207–8; *Suprêmes de Saumon avec son Caviar et Sauce Champagne* (lightly poached fillets sauced with lemon, Champagne, cream, and saffron, garnished with fresh salmon caviar), 209–10
Sam Snead's Tavern (Hot Springs, Va.), 25, 169, 400, 479, 480, 526
Santiago de Compostela, Spain, 246
Sauces, cold butter: *Beurre Café de Paris* (garlic, shallots, English mustard, curry, anchovy paste, tarragon, Cognac), 82–83; *Beurre Maître d'hôtel* (shallots, lemon, parsley, chives, and Worcestershire), 81–82
Sauces, discussed, 5, 6; Allemande, 53, 55; Américaine, 55, 71; Béarnaise, 51, 58, 93; béchamel, 55; beurre blanc (hot butter), 58; Bordelaise, 56; butter and egg yolk, 57, 58; buttermilk, 59; café de Paris (cold butter), 57; Carême's catalog of, 8, 11, 52, 56; chemistry of, 49–50, 51; cold butter, 57; construction of, 53, 55–57; Cumberland (fruit), 58; curry, 56; dark, 53; demi-glace, 53; Demi-glace Brun I, 56; Demi-glace Brun II, 56; Duxelles, 6; fish, 55; flavored vinegar, 59; French dressing, 59; French system of, 53; fruited, 58; Gremolada, 57; hollandaise, 51, 58 (group), 91; Homestead Cocktail, 59; hot butter, 57–58; light, 53; Lobster Butter and Cream, 55; Madère, 55, 56; maître d'hôtel (cold butter), 57; Marchand de Vins, 56; mayonnaise, 57, 58, 94 (history); Mornay, 55; Nantua, 55; olive oil and lemon juice, 59; passion fruit, 58; pear brandy, 59; Périgueux, 56; poppyseed and raspberry, 59; Ravigote, 160; rhubarb, 58; roquefort, 59; seafood, 59; Suprême, 53, 54, 67; velouté de poulet, 55; velouté de veau, 55; vinaigrette, 59; Vin Blanc, 55
Sauces, egg yolk: *Mayonnaise* (with lemon juice, vinegar, Dijon and English mustards, and oil), 94; *Sauce Béarnaise* (Hollandaise I with shallots, tarragon-flavored wine vinegar, tarragon, shallots, and glace de viande), 93–94; *Sauce Hollandaise I* (with clarified butter, white wine vinegar, white pepper, and lemon), 91–92; *Sauce Hollandaise II* (Hollandaise I with shallots), 92; *Sauce Maltaise* (Hollandaise I with orange juice and rind), 93; *Sauce Mousseline* (Hollandaise II with whipped cream), 92
Sauces, flavored vinegar: *Homestead Raspberry Vinegar* (with Cognac, raspberries, and vinegar), 103–4; *Mignonette* (with black pepper and shallots), 103
Sauces, hot butter: *Asparagus Butter Sauce* (with puréed asparagus), 89; *Basil Butter Sauce* (with basil, shallots, lemon, white wine), 87; *Beurre Blanc* (with white pepper, white wine vinegar, white wine, and shallots), 84–85; *Beurre au Citron* (foamed over high heat and lemon added), 83; *Beurre Noir* (Beurre Noisette with capers), 84; *Beurre Noisette* (browned over high heat and lemon added), 84, 199; *Green Herb Butter Sauce* (with parsley, spinach, watercress, basil, tarragon, shallots, and white wine), 87–88; *Gremolada* (Beurre au Citron with garlic and parsley), 83; *Leek Butter Sauce* (with puréed leeks), 88; *Lobster Butter and Cream Sauce* (with tomato, Cognac, stock, and white wine), 69–70; *Orange Cream Curry Sauce* (with orange juice, lemon juice, shallots, curry, whipping cream, and butter), 86; *Raspberry Vinegar Butter Sauce* (with Homestead Raspberry Vinegar, crème fraîche, and Melba Sauce), 85–86; *Red Pepper Butter Sauce*, 90; *Tomato Butter Sauce*, 89–90

Sauces, mustard: in *Shiitake Mushrooms with Mustard Sauce*, 164–65; simple, in *Shish Kebab*, 385

Sauces, sweet: *Sauce Sabayon* (chilled wine sauce), 518; *Sugar Syrup*, 518

Sauces based on brown stock: *Armagnac Sauce with Green Peppercorns and Grapes*, 77–78; *Demi-glace Brun I* (veal bones simmered with onion, celery, tomato paste, white wine, and brown stock), 75–76; *Demi-glace Brun II* (demi-glace with browned or roasted flour), 76; *Sauce Bordelaise* (Sauce Marchand de Vins with poached beef marrow), 79; *Sauce Chasseur* (red wine reduction with mushrooms, tomatoes, shallots, garlic, and demi-glace), 80; *Sauce Duxelles* (Sauce Chasseur with tomatoes omitted), 80; *Sauce Madère* (shallots, black pepper, Madeira, and demi-glace), 76; *Sauce Marchand de Vins* (lemon, shallots, black pepper, bay leaf, red wine and demi-glace reduction), 78; *Sauce Marsala* (Sauce Madère with dry Marsala replacing Madeira), 77; *Sauce Périgueux* (Sauce Madère with black truffles and their juice), 77; *Sauce Vinaigre de Vin Alsacienne* (Sauce Marchand de Vins with a mixture of red wine vinegar and red wine), 79

Sauces based on fruit: *Cumberland Sauce* (orange, lemon, Port, red currant jelly, mustard, and ginger), 100; *Homestead Passion Fruit Sauce* (with red wine, stock, black pepper, and orange juice), 101–2; *Pear Brandy Sauce* (with pears, pear brandy, white wine, and green peppercorns), 102–3; *Rhubarb Sauce* (with red currant jelly, green peppercorns, and brandy), 101

Sauces based on mayonnaise: *"Another" Cold Fish Sauce* (with red bell pepper, sun-dried tomatoes, Dijon mustard, curry, lemon juice, and ketchup), 98–99; *Curry Mayonnaise* (with curry, chutney, and sour cream), 95; *Green Herb Mayonnaise* (with parsley, spinach, watercress, tarragon, basil, dill, shallots, white wine, Dijon mustard, and lemon juice), 99; *Homestead Seafood Sauce* (with ketchup, cocktail sauce, chutney, Cognac, vodka, lemon juice, vinegar, chives, and tarragon), 98; *Mustard Sauce* (with Dijon and English mustards), 95; *Quick Green Sauce* (with tarragon vinegar, Dijon mustard, garlic, parsley, watercress, spinach, dill, and basil), 96; *Sauce Chantilly* (with whipped cream), 95; *Sauce Remoulade* (Sauce Tartare with anchovy, paprika, minced shallots, and Tabasco sauce), 97; *Sauce Tartare* (with chopped hard-boiled eggs, sour pickles, parsley, onion, Dijon mustard, capers, and chives), 97; *South of the Border Mayonnaise* (with tomatoes, shallots, garlic, scallion, jalapeño, red and green bell peppers, chili, and Tabasco sauce), 97–98; *Swedish Mustard Sauce* (with egg yolk, brown sugar, Dijon and English mustards, and dill), 96

Sauces based on roux: *Sauce Béchamel* (butter, flour, milk, nutmeg, and white pepper), 66–67; *Sauce Mornay* (Sauce Béchamel, Parmesan, Gruyère, and cream), 67

Sauces based on roux and stock: *Basic Curry Sauce* (with velouté, onions, celery, apple, and chutney), 80–81; *Sauce Allemande* (Velouté de Veau and cream), 75; *Sauce Américaine* (lobster, aromatic vegetables, tarragon, Cognac, tomatoes, and white wine), 71–73; *Sauce Doria* (Velouté de Poisson, shallots, white wine, tarragon vinegar, tarragon, parsley, cucumber, and cream), 226–27; *Sauce Nantua* (shrimp, shallots, tomato paste, white wine, cream, and Cognac), 70–71; *Sauce Suprême* (Velouté de Poulet, shallots, white wine, and cream), 74; *Sauce Velouté de Poisson* (fish stock, roux, and lemon peel), 68; *Sauce Velouté de Poulet* (chicken stock, roux, and lemon peel), 73; *Sauce Velouté de Veau* (veal stock, roux, and lemon peel), 74–75; *Sauce Vin Blanc de Poisson* (Velouté de Poisson, shallots, white wine, and cream), 68–69

Scallops: in *Coquilles Saint-Jacques au Beurre et Essence de Citron*, 168–69; in *Coquilles Saint-Jacques en Papillote au Printemps* (with Beurre Maître d'hôtel, Pommes de Terre Parisienne, zucchini, red and yellow peppers, snow peas, scallions, ginger, lemon, and basil), 248–50; discussed, 197; in *Fettuccine Fruits de Mer*, 250–51; in *Fettuccine Orientale with Shrimp and Scallops*, 251–52; in *Fisherman's Salad*, 187; *Marinated Bay Scallops* (with lime juice, garlic, olive oil, red, green, and jalapeño peppers, oregano, and tomato), 246–47; in *Mixed Seafood Newburg*, 241–42; *Sautéed Sea Scallops Gremolada with Tomato Butter Sauce*, 247–48

Schnarwyler, Albert, 15, 25, 26; culinary philosophy of, 13–14, 21, 27, 30–31, 47, 361–62, 481; menu planning by, 26–27, 30, 31; à la minute cuisine, 22–23, 193; quoted, 21; teamwork by, 23–24

Sea bass, 196; *Suprêmes de Loup de Mer à l'Orange et Poivre Vert* (fillets of sea bass with green peppercorn and orange sauce), 234–35

Seafood, mixed: *Fettuccine Fruits de Mer* (with shrimp, scallops, lobster, fresh vegetables, and pesto), 250–51; *Fettuccine Orientale with Shrimp and Scallops* (with fresh vegetables, curry, and cream), 251–52; *Mixed Seafood Newburg* (with lobster, scallops, paprika, cream, shallots, sherry, and mustard), 241–42; *Paella* (mussels, shrimp, lobster, snapper, and cod with smoked ham, chicken, fresh vegetables, aromatic broth, and rice), 254–55

Seviche, 197; pickling technique, 246

Seville, Spain, 452

Shad, 194; *Baked Shad and Roe in Phyllo Pastry* (with lemon, bacon, shallots, and white wine), 202–3; feasts, 202; *Sautéed Shad and Roe Grenobloise* (with lemon, butter, and capers), 203–4

Shellfish. *See* Crabmeat; Crabs, soft-shelled; Lobster; Mussels; Oysters; Scallops; Shrimp

Shiitake mushrooms, 159, 165, 173, 320; in *Shiitake Mushrooms with Mustard Sauce*, 164

Shrimp, 196; in *Bisque of Shrimp*, 146; in *Canapé Morgon*, 175; in *Fettuccine Orientale with Shrimp and Scallops*, 251–52; in *Marinated Shrimp*, 174; in *Mixed Seafood Newburg*, 241–42; in *Paella*, 254–55; in *Sauce Nantua*, 70–71; *Shrimp Bahía* (with mixed bell and jalapeño peppers, tomatoes, Tabasco, lemon, and capers), 240

Ski Lodge (at the Homestead), 22–25

Smithfield, England, 407

Smithfield, Va., 407

Snow Peas (blanched and lightly sautéed with butter), 470

Sole: Dover, 195, 218; fillets "en goujons," 249–50; *Fillets of Sole Amanda* (with pesto, leek, zucchini, red bell pepper, tomatoes, shallots, white wine, lemon, and saffron), 218–19; in *Fisherman's Salad*, 187; *Paupiettes de Sole Tout-Paris* (with Sauce Nantua, Sauce Vin Blanc, truffles, and shrimp), 223–25; *Paupiettes of Sole Florentine with Tomato Butter Sauce* (with mousse of sole, spinach, shallots, and cream), 222–23; *Quenelles de Sole*, 219–20; *Soufflé de Sole Lucernoise* (fillets poached in white wine, with sole mousse, mushrooms, and Sauce Vin Blanc), 221–22

Soltner, André, 23, 31, 79, 378; quoted, 20–21

Sorbets: discussed, 555–56, 562; *Simple Syrup* for, 562; *Sorbet à la Framboise* (raspberry sorbet), 562–63; *Sorbet à l'Ananas* (pineapple sorbet), 563; *Sorbet à la Poire* (pear sorbet), 565–66; *Sorbet au Calvados*, 564; *Sorbet au Pamplemousse* (grapefruit sorbet), 565. *See also* Ice cream

Sorrel: in *Potage Germiny*, 140

Soufflés: *Homestead Bourbon Soufflé*, 553; *Soufflé à la Vanille* (vanilla soufflé), 551–52; *Soufflé au Chocolat* (chocolate soufflé), 552–53; *Soufflé au Grand Marnier* (Grand Marnier soufflé), 553

Soups, bouillon: *Beef Bouillon* (beef stock with aromatic vegetables), 151–52; *Cantonese Egg Drop Soup* (Chicken Bouillon with chicken, onion, celery, leek, and scallion garnish), 149; *Chicken Bouillon* (with stock, chicken, onion, leeks, and celery leaves), 148; *Essence de Caille Royale* (Chicken Bouillon with quail, aromatic vegetables, and white wine), 150–51

Soups, cold: *Asparagus Vichyssoise* (Chicken Bouillon with onion, leek, potato, and half-and-half), 123; *Aspic* (Consommé Double with gelatin), 124–25; *Carrot Vichyssoise* (Chicken Bouillon with onion, leek, potato, and half-and-half), 122–23; *Celery Vichyssoise* (Chicken Bouillon with onion, leek, potato, and half-and-half), 123; *Cucumber Soup* (with half-and-half, sour cream, yogurt, and dill), 118–19; *Gazpacho* (finely diced cucumber, celery, green bell pepper, scallions, and tomato with tomato juices, chives, and parsley), 116–17; *Homestead Cantaloupe Soup* (with orange juice, apple juice, white wine, and tapioca), 117; *Homestead Mango Soup* (with white wine, pineapple juice, apple juice, tapioca, and lemon), 118; *Homestead Watercress Vichyssoise* (chicken stock with leek, onion, potato, and half-and-half), 121–22; *Jellied Madrilene* (Consommé Madrilene with gelatin), 125; *Obroschka* (Beef Bouillon with cucumber, apple, smoked ham, dill, watercress, and sour cream), 123–24; *Persian Yogurt Soup* (with raisins, half-and-half, cucumber, walnuts, parsley, and dill), 119; *Senegalese Soup* (with diced onions, celery, apples, chicken stock, curry, cream, and chutney), 119–20; *Vichyssoise* (chicken stock with leeks, onion, potato, half-and-half, and chives), 120–21

Soups, consommé: *Celery Broth* (Beef Bouillon simmered with celery and celery leaves), 153; *Consommé Double* (Beef Bouillon simmered with beef and aromatic vegetables), 152–53; *Consommé Madrilene* (Consommé Double simmered with tomato, celery, and green bell pepper and garnished with tomato and chives), 154; *English Beef Tea* (Beef Bouillon simmered slowly with lean beef), 154–56

Soups, discussed: asparagus, 123; beet, 136–37; Billi Bi, 114; Bisque of Vegetables Rosa, 112; bouillon, 114, 115; celery, 123; consommés, 113, 114, 115; English Beef Tea, 112, 115; garnishes for Consommé Double, 153; garnishes for Royal Essence of Quail, 150–51; Gazpacho, 113; hot cream, 114; lentil, 112, 127; Minestrone Milanese, 112; Navy Bean, 128; onion, 113–14, 133–35; Potage Garbûre, 131; Potage Germiny, 114; potato, 113; vegetable, 113, 114; vichyssoise, 111, 113

Soups, hot: *Basler Mehlsuppe* (Beef Bouillon with onions, browned flour, white wine, nutmeg, gratinéed with Emmentaler), 134; *Bisque of Vegetables Rosa* (chicken stock with bacon, aromatic vegetables, broccoli, potato, cabbage, lima beans, marjoram, and tomatoes), 131–32; *Borscht à la Russe* (Beef Bouillon with duck, bacon, beets, aromatic vegetables, cabbage, beef brisket, and sour cream), 136–37; *Lentil Soup with Frankfurters* (chicken stock with aromatic vegetables, potato, ham or bacon, and cream), 127; *Minestrone alla Milanese* (Beef Bouillon or chicken stock with bacon, aromatic vegetables, cabbage, potato, tomatoes, spaghetti, zucchini, lima and navy beans, fresh peas, spinach, and pesto), 130–31; *Old-fashioned Navy Bean Soup* (Lentil Soup with navy beans replacing lentils and frankfurters omitted), 128; *Potage Crécy* (Carrot Vichyssoise served hot), 123; *Potage Cressonière* (Homestead Watercress Vichyssoise served hot), 122; *Potage Parisienne* (Vichyssoise served hot), 121; *Potage St. Germain* (chicken stock with aromatic vegetables, potato, split and green peas, ham or bacon, and cream), 125–26; *Rossolnik* (chicken stock with barley, chicken, aromatic vegetables, dill pickle, cream, and chives) 129–30; *Russian Onion Soup* (with Beef Bouillon, caraway, browned flour, white wine, green peppercorns, and sour cream), 135; *Soup à l'Oignon Gratinée* (Beef Bouillon with onions, white wine, gratinéed with Parmesan and Gruyère), 133–34; *Swiss Barley Soup* (chicken stock with bacon, ham, aromatic vegetables, and half-and-half), 128–29

Soups, hot cream (with stock): *Billi Bi* (with mussels, white wine, shallots, white pepper, and chives), 147; *Bisque of Shrimp* (with aromatic vegetables, tomatoes, Cognac, blond roux, herbs, and black pepper), 146; *Cream of Asparagus Soup* (with aromatic vegetables and blond roux, garnished with asparagus tips), 141; *Cream of Celery Soup* (with aromatic vegetables and blond roux, garnished with celery), 142; *Cream of Chicken Soup Virginia* (with aromatic vegetables, peanuts, and blond roux), 145; *Cream of Mushroom Soup* (with aromatic vegetables, blond roux, and chives, garnished with mushroom caps), 143; *Cream of Watercress Soup* (with aromatic vegetables and blond roux), 139; *Mulligatawney* (with aromatic vegetables, curry, chutney, tomato paste, and blond roux, garnished with apple), 144; *Potage Germiny* (with sorrel, aromatic vegetables, and blond roux, with egg and cream liaison and sorrel garnish), 140; *Zuppa alla Modenese* (with spinach, aromatic vegetables, and blond roux, garnished with nutmeg, spinach, and Parmesan), 137–39

Soups, Russian. *See* Soups, cold: Obroschka; Soups, hot: Borscht à la Russe, Rossolnik, Russian Onion Soup

South America, 449

Southampton, England, 234, 363

Southampton County, Va., 407

Spain, 303, 450. *See also* Cuisine: Spanish

Spice trade, 119, 144, 162, 382; routes, 114, 262, 279. *See also* Trade routes

Spinach, 5, 187, 195; with *Baked Breast of Chicken Florentine*, 285–87; with *Braised Sweetbreads Catherine de' Me-*

Spinach (*continued*)
dici, 357; Creamed Spinach, 470–71; *Epinards Etouffés* (smothered and seasoned with butter and nutmeg), 471; history of, 285; in *Salade Tiède d'Epinards*, 182; in *Zuppa alla Modenese*, 137–38

Spirits: absinthe, 207; Calvados, 564; Framboise production, 562; kirsch production, 530, 537; Pernod invented, 207. *See also* Rum

Squash: Acorn Squash Baked with Honey, 47; *Ratatouille of Zucchini* (baked with bell pepper, onion, tomatoes, thyme, garlic, and Parmesan), 473; *Sautéed Zucchini Oregano*, 474; summer, 452; winter, 452; zucchini, 452; *Zucchini alla Genovese* (baked with bell peppers, tomatoes, and oregano), 474

Stews: beef, 364, 368–70; lamb, 382, 387–89; venison, 318–20. *See also* Stews, fish

Stews, fish, 191, 197–98; *Aegean Fisherman's Stew* (Velouté de Poisson with aromatic vegetables, potato, bacon, garlic, fish, herbs, and fresh peas), 257; *Bouillabaisse* (mixed fish with leek, onion, tomato, fennel, garlic, saffron, herbs, stock, and white wine), 255–56

Stocks: *Brown Chicken Stock*, 62; *Brown Stock*, 63–64; *Court Bouillon*, 60; *Fish Stock*, 60–61; *White Chicken Stock*, 61; *White Veal Stock*, 63

Stocks, discussed, 50; beef, 112; brown, 56; chicken, 112; defined, 52; duck, 62; fish, 52, 55; game, 52, 64; how to freeze, 52; lamb, 64; meat, 52; pheasant, 62; for poaching fish (Court Bouillon), 60; poultry, 52; white veal, 61

Strasbourg, France, 191

Succès (cooked meringue disk), 519–20

Sugar: history of, 507–8

Swabia (Germany), 419

Sweetbreads, 328. *See also* Veal sweetbreads

Sweet potatoes. *See* Potatoes: Sweet Potatoes Duchesse

Switzerland, 555. *See also* Cuisine: Swiss

Swordfish, 196; *Grilled Swordfish Steak Everglades* (with Beurre Maître d'hôtel), 233–34

Table service: *à la Française*, 9; *à la Russe*, 9

Taillevent (Guillaume Tirel): *Le Viandier*, 6, 448

T'ai Tsung (T'ang emperor), 285

Tarragon: history of, 282; with roast chicken, 295–96

Tarts: *Plum Tart*, 542–43; *Strawberry Tart*, 541–42. *See also* Pies

Tatin sisters, 561

Thickening agents: *Beurre Manié*, 64–65; *Blond Roux*, 65; *Browned or Roasted Flour*, 64; *Brown Roux*, 65; *Crème Fraîche*, 66; *Egg Yolk and Cream Liaison*, 65–66; *Glace de Viande*, 65; *Roux*, 65; *White Roux*, 65

Thickening agents, discussed: arrowroot, 53, 64; blond roux, 53; cornstarch, 53, 64; crème fraîche, 53–54, 55; egg yolk and cream liaison, 53; glace de viande, 53, 64; roux, 54, 55, 64; white roux, 53

Thurgau (Swiss canton), 128

Tirel, Guillaume. *See* Taillevent

Tomatoes: in *Consommé Madrilene*, 154; *Fassifern Tomatoes* (simmered, topped with croutons, and baked), 475; in *Jellied Madrilene*, 125; *Stewed Tomatoes* (seasoned with shallots and garlic), 476; *Tomatoes Provençale* (halved, stuffed with bread crumbs, garlic, and parsley, and broiled), 477; *Winter Stewed Tomatoes*, 476–77

Toulon, France, 167, 255

Toulouse, France, 302, 560

Trade routes, 257, 422–23, 507, 554, 565. *See also* Spice trade

Traders, 565; Arabs, 282, 450, 451, 507; Moors, 448; Persians, 507

Trains: *California Zephyr*, 488; *Crescent*, 488; *Orient Express*, 391, 488; Pullman cars, 488; *Santa Fe Chief*, 488; *TGV*, 195; *Train Bleu*, 195; *Twentieth Century Limited*, 488

Troisgros, Jean, 182, 326, 327; quoted, 6, 325

Troisgros brothers, 20–21, 27, 31, 204; quoted, 24

Trout, 194; how to cook in papillotes, 201

Trout, mountain: *Baked Mountain Trout with Tarragon Stuffing*, 199–200; *Charcoal Grilled Mountain Trout*, 200–201; *Sautéed Mountain Trout Homestead* (with lemon butter, parsley, almonds, and grapes), 198–99

Trout, rainbow: poaching in court bouillon (truite au bleu), 60

Truffles, 5, 262, 296, 311, 328, 355; in *Baked Breast of Chicken Ambassador*, 283–85; cultivation in France, 378; in *Galantine of Capon*, 179; in *Galantine of Capon Jardinière*, 181; in *Pâté Maison*, 178; with *Paupiettes de Sole Tout-Paris*, 224–25; in *Sauce Périgueux*, 77; in *Sautéed Sweetbreads Souvaroff*, 358

Turbot, 195; *Suprêmes of English Turbot with Beurre Blanc and Red Pepper Butter Sauce*, 227–28

Turkey (country), 253, 257; cuisine in, 162, 494

Turkey (poultry), 260, 261, 263; history of, 303; *Roast Double Breast of Turkey with Ham, Apricot, and Pecan Stuffing*, 303–5; *Roast Double Breast of Turkey with Olive Stuffing*, 305–6; wild, 308

Turnips: *Navets Glacés* (simmered, glazed with butter and sugar), 469

Tuscany (Italy), 412

United States, 430, 449; inns in, 13; rivers in, 193

U.S.S.R. (Union of Soviet Socialist Republics), 384. *See also* Russia

Valence, France, 13

Valencia, Spain, 197, 254, 296, 423, 425

Vallée d'Auge (France), 262, 340, 539, 564

Vanilla bean: production of, 556

Vatel, Henri, 218

Vaucluse (France), 476

Veal, braised: *Blanquette de Veau à l'ancienne* (cubes simmered with aromatic vegetables and sauced with white wine, mushrooms, onions, and cream), 349–51; *Côtes de Veau Bourguignonne* (chops simmered in red wine and demi-glace, served with pearl onions, mushrooms, lardons, and croutons), 351–52; *Ossobuco alla Milanese* (shank in aromatic vegetable broth, garnished with gremolada), 353–54

Veal, calf's liver, 328; *Foies de Veau Suisse* (with shallots, green peppercorns, and wine vinegar sauce), 354–55; *Sauté de Foies de Veau au Madère* (with demi-glace and Madeira sauce), 355

Veal, discussed, 56, 361; history of, 325–26; how to cut scaloppine, 326; ossobuco, 327–28

Veal, roast: *Roast Loin of Veal with Tarragon Cream Sauce*, 347–48; *Rognonnade de Veau* (loin of veal with veal and kidney stuffing), 348–49

Veal, sautéed: *Côtes de Veau Pojarski* (ground, shaped into cutlets, and served with lemon butter), 346; *Escalopes de Veau à la Russe* (with grilled tomatoes, caviar, and cream sauce), 340; *Escalopes de Veau au Calvados* (with baked apple rings and Calvados cream sauce), 340; *Escalopes de Veau aux Morilles* (with morel cream sauce), 341; *Escalopes de Veau Cordon Bleu* (with smoked ham and Emmentaler filling), 344–45; *Medallions of Veal Picante* (with fresh ginger, curry cream sauce, garnished with sautéed banana, pickle, and watercress), 329–30; *Piccata di Vitello Veronese* (scaloppina with tomato, zucchini, and a Marsala sauce), 336–38; *Rahmschnitzel* (with mushrooms and cream sauce), 338–39; *Rollatini di Vitello* (with a sausage, prosciutto, and sage filling, and a Marsala sauce), 341–42; *Roulades de Veau au Roquefort* (rolled and filled with Roquefort, cream cheese, and prosciutto, served with a cream sauce), 343–44; *Saltimbocca alla Romana* (with prosciutto, fresh sage, and a Marsala sauce), 333–35; *Scaloppine di Vitello al Limone* (with lemon sauce), 330–31; *Scaloppine di Vitello al Marsala* (with Marsala sauce), 335–36; *Scaloppine di Vitello Milanese* (breaded, flavored with Parmesan, and served with fried fresh sage), 333; *Wienerschnitzel* (breaded and garnished with anchovies and capers), 331–33

Veal sweetbreads: *Braised Sweetbreads Catherine de' Medici* (braised with aromatic vegetables, served with spinach, mushrooms, and a Madeira sauce), 357; *Braised Sweetbreads with Sherry Favorite* (with aromatic vegetables, served with julienne of ham, celery, mushroom, and leek and a sherry cream sauce), 355–57; *Sautéed Sweetbreads Cordon Bleu* (filled with smoked ham and Emmentaler, breaded, and served with lemon butter sauce), 359; *Sautéed Sweetbreads Gismonda* (breaded with Parmesan crumbs and served with sherry and caper sauce), 359; *Sautéed Sweetbreads Souvaroff* (filled with foie gras and truffles, breaded, and served with lemon butter sauce), 358–59

Vegetables. *See* Asparagus; Beans; Brussels sprouts; Cabbage; Carrots; Celery; Corn; Eggplant; Endive, Belgian; Fennel; Leeks; Snow Peas; Spinach; Squash; Tomatoes; Turnips

Vegetables, discussed, 5; Baked Eggplant Niçoise, 450; Belgian endive, 450, history of, 466; *à la bouquetière*, 391, 397, 447, 469; Braised Red Cabbage, 448; corn-on-the-cob, 449; cornmeal, 449, 450; Creamed Spinach, 452; endive, history of, 450; fennel (finocchio), 450; Flageolets Bretonne, 448; Gnocchi alla Romana, 449; grits, 449–50; Hearts of Fennel Parmesan, 450; Homestead Corn Pudding, 449; hominy, 449; how to cook, 446; Leek Butter Sauce, 451; leeks, history of, 450–51; in menu planning, 447; Navets Glacés, 451; peas, history of, 451; Polenta alla Milanese, 449; Purée of Celery, 449; semolina, 449; snow peas, 451; spinach, history of, 451–52; Spoon Bread, 449; Stewed Tomatoes, 453; tomatoes, history of, 452–53; Tomatoes Provençale, 453; turnips, history of, 451

Venetia (Italy), 449
Veneto Euganea (Italy), 336
Venice, Italy, 4, 5, 411, 507
Venison, 308; *French Venison Stew* (marinated with red wine, red wine vinegar, aromatic vegetables, and juniper, braised with bacon, tomato paste, and demi-glace, served with pearl onions, mushrooms, and croutons), 318–20; medallions of, 56; *Medallions of Venison with Juniper Cream Sauce*, 320–21; popularity of at Homestead, 308; *Roast Stuffed Tenderloin of Venison with Cream Mustard Sauce* (stuffed with chestnuts, wild rice, walnuts, and fruit), 321–23

Vergé, Roger, 20, 125, 159, 234, 377, 556; *Entertaining in the French Style*, 556; his Aunt Celestine, 259–60, 261, 283; quoted, 316, 430
Verona, Italy, 336
Vichy, France, 113, 120, 459
Vienne, France, 21
Villeneuve-Loubet, France, 9
Vinegars, flavored: *Homestead Raspberry Vinegar*, 103; *Sauce Mignonette* (for clams and oysters), 103
Virginia Hot Springs, Inc., 15, 17, 20
Vonnas, France, 397
Voralps (Switzerland), 221

Walnuts: with roast duckling, 301–2
Warm Springs, Va., 15, 475
Warm Springs Mountain (Va.), 308, 400
Warm Springs Valley (Va.), 15, 27, 361, 368
Washington, D.C., 20, 27, 529
Washington, George, 202, 234
Water, spring, 52, 112, 115, 562
Watercress, 187; in *Homestead Watercress Vichyssoise*, 121–22; in *Cream of Watercress Soup*, 139
Wechsberg, Joseph: quoted, 10, 12, 21–22, 363
Wenberg, Ben, 241
West Indies, 536, 559
Wilhelm II (kaiser of Germany), 191, 209
William Augustus, Duke of Cumberland, 100
World War I, 448
World War II, 16, 120, 266, 423